Contents

Series Foreword

Addiction represents one of the most significant challenges to modern society. Addition to cigarettes is currently estimated to cause some 3 million deaths in the world per year, and this figure is set to rise to 10 million in the next decade. Alcohol dependence is believed to account for more than a million premature deaths each year while dependence on opiates and illicit stimulants, with its associated crime, is a scourge which affects the lives of all of us directly or indirectly, and the problem is not receding – if anything it is growing.

Our knowledge and understanding of what addiction is and what can be done to mitigate the problems has also increased in leaps and bounds in the past 50 years and important new findings are emerging all the time. Addiction Press encompasses the Society for the Study of Addiction's journal *Addiction* and a new book series, launched with this volume. Addiction Press was set up with the express purpose of communicating current ideas and evidence in this expanding field, not only to researchers and practising health professionals but also to policy makers, students and interested non-specialists.

The study of addiction involves many academic disciplines including psychology, psychiatry, public health, epidemiology, pharmacology, physiology, genetics, sociology, history, and so on. Therefore this series is, of necessity, multidisciplinary in scope and style. No artificial constraints have been imposed on the type of book that will be included – if the idea is fresh and there is a need for a volume of a particular type, it will be considered to form part of the series.

The series is intimately linked with Blackwell Publishing's major journal in the field, *Addiction*, and it is hoped that my involvement in the editorial staff of the latter will help with developing ideas for topics and authors for the former.

Finally, it is my fervent hope that the series will do more than communicate ideas in this important field; it will be part of the process for generating and stimulating though and debate and so play some role in taking the field forward.

Robert West
Series Editor

St George's Hospital Medical School
London, UK

Preface

Addictions: Bringing Voices Together

The interviews and commentaries published in this book speak of the vast quantity, high quality and broad variety of human endeavour in the addictions field over recent decades. The individual interviews matter greatly, but the whole is greater than the parts, and one may suspect that when looking through the contents pages readers will share a sense of amazement – so much done by so many people, and the scope of the enterprise revealed.

As the book's title suggests, the theme which gives it coherence is that of evolution. The voices in this book come together to tell us how addiction, as a multi-substance, international, multidisciplinary field to which scientists, practitioners, activists and policy makers all contribute, is moving towards self-definition and self-image. What characterises every single contributor to this book is their belief that the field matters, that much has been achieved, but also that, undoubtedly, much still needs to be done. This is not a book about triumphalism.

The interviews were originally published in the journal *Addiction* between the years 1990 and 2001, and follow an earlier volume of interviews published in 1991.[1] Why does *Addiction* foster its interview series? The editorial team believes that the journal should not only be interested in science, but also in how addiction science develops and how addiction policies are made. Within that perspective we suggest that interviews with key figures in the field constitute invaluable source material. They tell us about individual endeavour in ever-changing historical, political and cultural contexts. We are immensely grateful to the people who both granted and conducted the interviews.

This book is, however, more than just a collection of published interviews. It is enriched by the addition of specialist commentary, authored respectively by Wayne Hall, Jerome H. Jaffe, Ulrich John, Mark Kleiman, Alan Ogborne, Robin Room, Gerry Stimson, Jessica Warner and Robert West. As they have come across my desk, I have read them with great pleasure. Thomas Babor provides an end piece which brilliantly brings individual and diverse lifetime experiences together to capture exactly the sense of the field as it develops. To all these authors goes much gratitude.

The other day I was enjoying the pleasant company of an American friend. We fell to playing the game of whom from the past we would have most liked to interview. I had no hesitation in naming Thomas Trotter[2], to lead him into talking about the Edinburgh university of his time, to ask whether he ever met up with that young American postgraduate, Benjamin Rush, or if he heard David Hume lecture. Tell me about your poetry, Dr Trotter. Was it misty at the Battle of the Dogger Bank, and did the French shot fall close? Do you think your 1804 *Essay on Drunkenness* read better in the original Latin? Do you really believe in spontaneous combustion? Interviews, life and times, the unique voices talking across space and time.

Griffith Edwards

References

1. EDWARDS, G. (ed.) (1991) *Addictions. Personal Influences and Scientific Movements.* New Brunswick: Transaction Publishers.
2. TROTTER, T. (1804) *An Essay on Drunkeness and its Effects on the Human Body.* London: Hurst, Rees and Ovine.

Acknowledgements

The demanding tasks inherent in the making of this book were handled with skill and generous patience by Patricia Davis. I am grateful to Dr Jon Walmsley of Blackwell Science for his editorial support. The Society for the Study of Addiction (SSA) has kindly agreed to the reproduction of copyright text, and has given financial support towards the book's production. The staff of the library at the Athenaeum Club, London, assisted with biographical searches.

Statement on interests

The editor of this book is not aware of any significant potential conflict of interest which might bear on his editorial responsibilities, but declarations of interest by himself and senior members of *Addiction*'s staff are to be found at www.blackwell-science.com.

Part I
Addiction Scientists from the USA

Vincent Dole

Vincent Paul Dole was born in Chicago in 1913. He graduated from Stanford in 1934 and was awarded his MD from Harvard in 1939. He interned at Massachussetts General Hospital and was a member of staff at Rockefeller Hospital, New York, from 1941 to the present, becoming a professor in 1951. He trained and practised in internal medicine before pioneering the methadone maintenance treatment of heroin dependence.

Addiction as definitely a medical issue

Addiction: *There are many people who would be interested in knowing how you got started in your famous studies of narcotic addicts.*
Vincent Dole: Sometime in the early 60s I began to feel that I was working in an oasis in Manhattan (at Rockefeller University) but commuting to it from the suburbs through an epidemic of drugs and poverty in the inner city. It seemed to me that this was a problem that should be considered by the medical community. And, particularly, since I was associated with an institute of medical research, it was mandatory that I try to understand the epidemic that surrounded us. So, I began to look into it. In the course of time my interests grew to the point that I decided to devote the full efforts of my laboratory to further investigation.

A: *Did you see any addicts at 125th Street?*
VD: Yes. I would come in from the suburbs and often times get off the commuter train at the 125th Street station and then take the Third Avenue elevated to the 68th Street station, which was near Rockefeller University. In the course of walking between stations on 125th Street, I encountered many derelicts. Bars were open at nine in the morning; there were people on the Street who were obviously on drugs, and many buildings were abandoned and empty. As I rode the Third Avenue elevated, I would be given a moving view through the windows of the tenements that lined Third Avenue. I could see the barren insides of these homes and idle people who should have been working or in school. Alcoholism and drug addiction obviously were contributing factors.

A: *In terms of seeing this from a medical point of view, how did you come to treat the first addict patients that you were involved with?*
VD: I realized that I didn't know anything about addiction in any medical sense. There was no training on the subject at Harvard Medical School, nor was there any experience in my internship which prepared me to understand the problem. So having acquired an interest in the problem, I decided to learn more by consulting experts and visiting treatment facilities. In the course of this research, I visited Lexington [the US Public Health Service Hospital in Lexington, Kentucky] among other places and talked with everyone who had a reputation of being an expert in the field.

I talked to Lewis Thomas who had been a colleague and friend at Rockefeller Hospital and, at the time, was head of the working group on narcotics for the Health Research Council in New York. Hearing of my interest, he said, 'Why don't you take over the chairmanship of this group as I will be going on a year's sabbatical and leaving New York?' So I said 'I accept. I'll learn more that way.' In the course of a year of looking into what was known and what was being done, I decided to undertake the research myself – to study addict subjects in the hospital at Rockefeller, where as a member of the institution I had the right to admit patients for research studies.

I discussed procedures with Detlev Bronk, President of Rockefeller. I said that there was a real need for a study of addiction from a medical perspective. This condition had struck me as being a neurochemical disease needing medical treatment. Moreover, I said, because of legal constraints and institutional prejudices, there is no other hospital or research institution in the country, outside the prison hospital in Kentucky, that feels safe to deal with addicts. He asked me if I thought it could be handled here (at Rockefeller). I said, yes, I believe that we can. He said, then it is our job and we will begin immediately.

I said that there was a real need for a study of addiction from a medical perspective. This condition had struck me as being a neurochemical disease needing medical treatment

---

The birth of methadone maintenance

With that support, which never wavered in the course of our work, I was able to set up a clinical research program in the center of Manhattan. Fortunately, in the course of meeting many people in the field, I had discovered Marie Nyswander and persuaded her to join me in this endeavor.

A: So you set up a clinical research program?
VD: Initially, we set up a ward at Rockefeller Hospital with elaborate security precautions because that was the arrangement everybody assumed you must have to study addict patients. In the course of time, this advice proved to be false. The normalizing effect of methadone was discovered. What originally was a locked ward became an open suite of rooms. The doors to the corridor were taken off because they impeded passage back and forth. And, then subsequently, since we used only part of the patients' time in studies of narcotic effects and measurements of tolerance, we permitted them to leave the hospital each day and work in part-time jobs. The patients

developed pride in our program, no longer thinking of themselves as addicts. I recall an occasion when one of the patients reproached a nurse for her carelessness in leaving needles and syringes lying around. He said you never can tell when addicts might come into the area.

A: You learned on the job?
VD: This, of course, happened only after we had found the beneficial effects of stabilization on methadone. Originally, when we admitted these addict patients, they were very much the same as addicts are everywhere else – namely, always thinking about where they could get their next shot of drugs. When, in the initial studies,[1] they had been given controlled doses of various narcotic drugs, such as morphine and heroin and other short-acting narcotics, they would be content for only two to four hours and then begin to get restless and demand another injection. It wasn't until we got to the stage of the study in which we were testing methadone that the beneficial effects of a medical treatment became evident.

Getting services into a general hospital

A: What year was this?
VD: The studies were started in 1963, and extended into 1964. At the end of 1964 and going into 1965, I realized that we had *potentially* a medical treatment for heroin addiction[2] – one that could normalize the function of otherwise hopeless addicts and get them back into the mainstream of life. But it wasn't clear how this treatment could be generalized. The studies were being conducted by people who were experienced, and within the limits of a research institution. The question was whether the treatment would be feasible in the setting of a general hospital.

A: So what did you do?
VD: I pulled our data together, made an appointment to see Dr Ray Trussell, Commissioner of Hospitals for the City of New York, and showed him what we had done. I asked him whether it would be possible to attempt a replication of this

work in the context of a general hospital. He looked at my papers, smiled in an enigmatic way and said, 'Well I can assure you that you wouldn't get to first base if you went to any of our city hospitals. But I will send you to Beth Israel where you will have suitable space to give this a try.' He also said, 'I think this may be what I've been waiting to see.'

A: *Next stop?*
VD: At his suggestion, I took a cab to Beth Israel Hospital. In the meantime, Trussell had telephoned the director. When I arrived, I was received hospitably by him and told that the Commissioner had requested that he provide facilities that would be paid for by the City. What did we want? I said that we would like to have a ward in the general hospital and the privilege of selecting our support staff. I told him that we would like to choose this staff in order to escape established prejudice. We were given an empty ward, as requested.

A: *And you moved in?*
VD: At the beginning, Marie Nyswander and I helped the patients clean the ward and make their beds. Gradually, Marie chose staff. They were an exceptionally fine and dedicated group. Together we built up a unit. There was a great deal of pride in it and in its accomplishments. It became a showplace that physicians and administrators from all over the country came to see.

A: *You and the patients were working on the same site?*
VD: The patients developed into a loyal and supportive group, many of whom today are old friends that I can call on anytime to give help when needed. And, in fact, some years later (jumping about seven years ahead in the story), the chance came for me to go into prisons and set up treatment for the addicts being taken into detention. All I had to do was ask a half dozen of these older patients and I had an experienced team that was ready, in a course of one weekend, to take over the medical treatment of hundreds of addicts in the detention jails.

A: *So that's the story of the first five years?*
VD: The first five years of the methadone program were an extraordinary period. There was no governmental bureaucracy; we established the rules, which were both conservative and flexible. We were fortunate to have this opportunity to work under optimal conditions and thus discover the potential of good treatment. Having seen this, one cannot be content with anything less successful.

Bitter opposition from the FBN

A: *You mentioned the individuals who supported you in the early years. What were some of the problems you encountered?*
VD: One problem was the bitter opposition from the Federal Bureau of Narcotics, which was absolutely opposed to the idea of doctors having authority to prescribe narcotics for addicts. Addiction was their turf. The condition in their view was not a disease, but criminal behavior. Any doctor who prescribed a narcotic was subject to prosecution by them, and, indeed, a number of physicians had been prosecuted.

One problem was the bitter opposition from the Federal Bureau of Narcotics, which was absolutely opposed to the idea of doctors having authority to prescribe narcotics for addicts. Addiction was their turf

---

Early in our work, I realized that we would fall foul of this attitude on the part of the Bureau. They were professional enforcers who had become unemployed by the repeal of laws prohibiting the manufacture and sale of alcoholic beverages, so they moved into narcotic enforcement. I asked the counsel for the Rockefeller Institute to advise me on relevant law. He provided a thorough legal brief outlining the significant statutes and precedents. The brief made it plain that the purported authority of the Federal Bureau of Narcotics at that time was based upon a self-determined interpretation of law which gave them more powers than could be justified by a strict legal interpretation. The courts had consistently held that physicians are not to be indicted for treatment 'in the course of medical practice'. So the issue turned on the criteria of legitimate medical practice.

A: *So you had established a secure portion?*
VD: Yes. Since the research we were doing had been initiated by the Health Research Council of the City of New York and was funded by it, and since I had consulted medical leaders (all of whom endorsed the idea of legitimate medical research), I didn't feel insecure. Also, I had solid backing from the President of Rockefeller University, Detlev Bronk, and advice from the university counsel. One day a grim-looking fellow, wearing a detective-style trench coat, entered my office, put his hands on my desk and said, 'You're breaking the law. If you don't stop we'll put you in jail.' I suggested that perhaps we differed in our interpretation of the law. Since my understanding differed from that of the Bureau, then the option for them was to sue me and let the issue be decided in court. At that point, his face dropped and he said, 'I'll talk to you later.' He stood up abruptly and left. About a month later, he came back and said the Bureau had discussed my situation and they were willing to allow a limited amount of research, but that I must outline the studies ahead of time and report the results to them. I said that we again have a difference of opinion, because it is not the way I can do research. He left.

A: *Well done!*
VD: The Federal Bureau then circulated the rumor to the effect that we were operating under their jurisdiction and with their permission. This fiction didn't survive long, but they did what they could to keep the posture of control. Meanwhile, they appeared to be the source of rumors about what we were doing, such as denying our reports of success in treatment. On one occasion they attempted to seize our clinical records. Some ten to fifteen years later, when the Freedom of Information Act enabled people to examine the contents of Federal records, a lawyer with our group offered to apply for disclosure of reports in Bureau files. After a long delay, we did get some photo-copies but with so much of the text blocked out that about 80% was deleted.

The program goes forward

A: *And despite all this you kept going?*
VD: Despite opposition from the Federal Bureau of Narcotics, and subsequently from the State Narcotic Control Commission, the program went forward because it was producing results. Physicians and legislators who came to visit us were favorably impressed. Programs were established around the country. By 1968 we were able to convene the first National Methadone Conference. Methadone maintenance quickly became a recognized, legitimate treatment. Paradoxically, new laws were passed to limit the treatment. With the collapse of the authority of the old Bureau of Narcotics, responsibility for supervising maintenance treatment passed to the Food and Drug Administration (another federal agency). By asserting that maintenance treatment was experimental and not adequately tested (although by then thousands of people were in treatment and the results had been carefully documented), the FDA was able to limit treatment to programs that were licensed by it. Ultimately it became necessary to rectify this anomalous situation. Laws were passed to replace the investigational permits with a set of restrictive and punitive regulations, euphemistically called 'guidelines.'

I was excluded from the formulation of these regulations which established a much more intrusive control over methadone treatment than the Federal Bureau of Narcotics had pretended to have. They encouraged a punitive, controlling attitude on the programs. These [FDA] regulations would have destroyed the treatment except that methadone, even under the worst conditions, is a limited success. Addicts were so desperate to get help that they kept applying and hanging in even though many of the programs were functioning at a sub-optimal level with prescription of inadequate doses of methadone, punitive rules and pressure on patients to terminate treatment. Abstinence, not rehabilitation, was the goal of treatment.

A: *Was the medical profession itself involved in any way in these new FDA regulations?*

VD: No. Practically all the input for the FDA regulations came from non-medical sources. Of course the regulators always could recruit a selected number of people with MD degrees to support punitive restrictions, but on the whole, the medical profession was simply absent from this problem. And to a large extent, it still is.[3]

A: *So you're saying that the role the medical profession has played in the development and advancement of methadone maintenance treatment in the United States has been one of benign neglect, or how would you describe it?*

VD: I would say neglect.

Methadone maintenance: the need to ensure adequate dosage and long-term prescribing

A: *You mentioned the role of the federal government over the years and the role of the medical profession. Thinking about the present time, why has it proved so difficult to get methadone maintenance treatment programs to prescribe adequate doses for patients?*

VD: The pharmacological rationale has never been effectively conveyed to the medical profession. From a medical perspective, a medication is prescribed to enable the patient with a chronic disease to be as functional as possible, to live as effectively as he can, for as long as he can, with whatever pharmacological support optimizes his functional state. Now, addiction has never really been accepted in these terms by the medical profession, despite our efforts to identify addictions as chronic, relapsing diseases in every publication[4] and speech for the last 25 years.

The philosophy that has prevailed is that addiction is a disorder of behavior, that somehow or other drug seeking behavior is evidence of a psychological defect or weakness, and that the only acceptable goal of treatment is total abstinence. This approach puts the emphasis upon the chemical and not upon the person. I hope that someday it will be possible to bring to addiction the same perspective that applies to the medical problems of chronic heart disease, diabetes, gout, arthritis, and the like.

A: *The central purpose of treatment?*

VD: Treatment should aim to normalize function, and its value should be measured by results. Lack of recognition of this objective has been a serious block to understanding maintenance treatment. Many times in the past 25 years we have presented data showing cessation of heroin use and normalization of function under maintenance treatment, patients returning to school, getting jobs, taking care of their families and so on, and yet the question that almost always comes from the audience is, yes, that's all right, but 'when are you going to get them off methadone?'

There is an obsession with the chemical and not a concern for the human being – that's why it's difficult. Data that show normal function and constructive behavior on the part of people who used to be addicts[5] do not persuade critics who still keep asking the question – yes, but when are they going to stop using methadone?

I hope that someday it will be possible to bring to addiction the same perspective that applies to the medical problems of chronic heart disease, diabetes, gout, arthritis, and the like

A: *I think your answer helps explain this emphasis on methadone dosage on the part of the public – an emphasis which is not common in medicine with other medications.*

VD: A wrong belief exists in the general public and in the medical profession, and even, I'm sorry to say, in many methadone programs around the world. This is the illusion that by giving a very low dose you facilitate the evolution of this treatment into complete abstinence. The opposite really is the truth.

Unless patients can become well stabilized physiologically, and live a normal life both physiologically and socially while in treatment, there is little chance of successful abstinence after withdrawal of methadone. Even under the best conditions, I think that people who have been habitual addicts, damaging their nervous system with the ups and downs of high-dose heroin, may never recover normal nervous function. Only under conditions of being stabilized by a long-acting medicine such as methadone do they return to normal function. Withdraw the stabilizing medication, and they once more relapse to the unstable neurological condition that leads them to use illicit narcotics.

A: *Many methadone programs are utilizing non-therapeutic dosages which are too low. Is this because they just are not getting the correct information? What is the reason that we are finding it so difficult to get this knowledge implemented at the program level?*
VD: I regret to say that dosage decisions are frequently made by people who do not understand the pharmacology of methadone. They're made on behavioral, sociological and ideological bases by uninformed people who see the medication as an instrument of reward and punishment. The adverse behavioral effects of low dosages, including use of illicit drugs, are rarely interpreted as being due to inadequate doses. Unfortunately in the practice of medicine, if a patient fails to respond to the therapist, the patient is likely to be blamed rather than the treatment.

In past years some politicians who have been on record as opposing methadone treatment have also quietly arranged that their addicted relatives were admitted to methadone programs

---

A: *You've said that addiction is a chronic disease. Why has it proved so difficult to convince both the public and professionals about the need for long-term treatment for heroin addicts?*
VD: Understanding of addiction has not advanced much beyond what it was 50 years ago. Addictive behavior is attributed to weakness of character. The argument is a logical circle: If the treatment fails, the addict is responsible and the failure is taken as evidence showing his weakness of character.

What your question is asking is: 'How is it possible for the medical profession to learn nothing from fifty years of failure?' The answer is that it is easier to blame patients rather than wonder whether a treatment is at fault.

A: *You mentioned the FDA regulations and how methadone maintenance treatment started here at Rockefeller Institute. Looking over the last 25 years, what would you say have been some of the other turning points, or key events, in the development of methadone maintenance treatment?*
VD: Rather than dramatic turning points, I see a slow evolution of understanding. Despite mistakes at all levels of administration, there nonetheless has emerged a body of experience and wonderful, caring clinicians, counselors, nurses, and brave patients.[6] Today there is a moderate-sized community of people who know what to do and how to do it. What gives me the greatest feeling of pride is the quality of people who have emerged under conditions of discrimination and opposition.

Politically the climate has changed with the emergence of AIDS as a frightening threat. Curiously enough, this change in attitude has revealed the inner thinking of some people who previously have been opposed to methadone. Many people who in the past have been ideologically opposed to methadone maintenance treatment now are advocating, albeit in a begrudging way, support of methadone programs as a public health measure because it is the only treatment with demonstrated large-scale efficacy in controlling intravenous narcotic use. This is no great surprise. In past years some politicians who have been on record as opposing methadone treatment have also quietly arranged that their addicted relatives were admitted to methadone programs.

The AIDS epidemic and political necessity have revealed a recognition underneath some of the anti-methadone propaganda that methadone maintenance is an effective treatment.

A: *I thought what you just said was crucial: that over the years what has happened with regard to methadone maintenance treatment is that we built a body of knowledge and an experienced cadre that provides a nucleus for addressing a lot of the problems that we now face in the USA about drug abuse problems.*

VD: No doubt. There is no question that with really good-hearted, honest support at social and political levels, one could increase the amount of services being provided in this area. But the problem is huge, and even under the best of circumstances, it is doubtful that within a reasonable time that we could expand treatment to reach everyone who could benefit. Nonetheless, there is no question that within, say, a three or four year period, it would be possible to treat four times as many people as are now receiving methadone. What's more, with a rational allocation of resources, to see to it that a coordinated public health campaign reached out to these persons most in need of help – namely, those on the streets, in shelters, and jails. The return to society would be well worth the expense of the effort. It is really a matter of political will.

Importance of research

A: *How important has research been in the development of methadone maintenance treatment?*

VD: At the beginning, it was important to be sure that this treatment was normalizing people and not simply stupefying them or creating other medical problems. So our research on the functional effects of maintenance was intensive during the early years. We were especially concerned about the alertness and coordination of patients given large doses of a narcotic over long periods of time. Could they safely drive a motor car or work in a factory? All of this has been thoroughly examined by now. The results of many tests show that methadone has a normalizing effect – the patient is not impaired in intellectual or motor function. He does not feel narcotized. He is functionally normal.[7]

We then looked at health problems. As an example, women who typically become amenorrheic while using heroin return to normal rhythms and fertility. That concerned us in the early days of the program. What would happen to babies conceived by mothers receiving methadone? Fortunately it turned out that the pregnancies and the babies were quite normal. Some of the children have been followed for two decades. It is now well established[8] that both mother and newborn under a methadone program are in far better shape than they would be if she were not in treatment.

Furthermore, ongoing studies show that some disabilities that have been attributed to methadone (e.g., low birth weight) are actually due to such other causes as smoking (a practice common to most drug users) or concomitant usc of other drugs. Follow-up studies of the early patients in treatment show that they have lived longer than their untreated peers.[9–11]

A: *What should the United States do now, today, with regard to methadone maintenance treatment, or drug abuse treatment in general?*

VD: That really is too big a question to answer, One must be careful not to lose perspective. Methadone is a specific treatment for one kind of drug addiction (namely to narcotic drugs) and not necessarily for all people addicted to narcotics. It's for people who want the treatment. It should never be compulsory. It's for people who have advanced to a hopeless stage of addiction where it is clear that maintenance is a better option for them than attempted abstinence. What to do about the so-called 'drug problem' in the USA, when the question is asked in that way, can't be answered because there are several different drug problems to be considered and different treatments are indicated. It would almost be like asking the question, what does one do about 'the infectious disease problem'?

The need to expand the treatment base

A: *But what about methadone maintenance, what needs to be done there?*

VD: The number of people who could benefit

The number of people who could benefit from methadone maintenance, properly conducted, . . . is somewhere between five and ten times the number of people now in treatment

---

from methadone maintenance, properly conducted, . . . is somewhere between five and ten times the number of people now in treatment. That is a very rough estimate, but the practical question is what is feasible?

One limiting factor is the lack of qualified personnel. There is no sense in multiplying programs that are administered by people who do not understand the pharmacology of methadone, or who lack a feeling of compassion and a grasp of what it is to be an addict. You need competent people to staff good programs; even today only a limited number of programs are adequately staffed. I don't see that there are enough qualified personnel available for a rapid, massive expansion of methadone programs, and enough administrators capable of directing programs of large size.

A second major impediment is the attitude of the public. Communities refuse to have treatment programs in their neighborhoods even when there is a demonstrated local need. It has been impossible for the last 15 years to open a new methadone clinic anywhere in the city of New York.

I was reading in the paper the other day that a community in New York rose in opposition to having a residential facility set up for orphan babies. If they consider the babies a threat, how would they react to a clinic that treats addicts? In public health terms we have reached a stage in the drug problem at which society is getting what it asks for. It is not just a question of funding for treatment. The limiting issue is political will to confront the problem and put to work what we know about it.

A: *Are you optimistic or pessimistic about the years ahead in this regard?*
VD: In this business, one cannot afford to be anything but an optimist.

References

1. KREEK, M. J. (1992) The addict as a patient, in: LOWINSSON, J. H., RUIZ, P & MILLMAN, R. B. (Eds) *Substance Abuse – a Comprehensive Textbook*, pp. 997–1009 (Baltimore, Williams & Wilkins).

2. DOLE, V. P. & NYSWANDER, M. E. (1965) A medical treatment for diacetylmorphine (heroin) addiction, *Journal of American Medical Association*, **193**, 80–84.

3. DOLE, V. P. (1992) Hazards of process regulations – the example of methadone maintenance, *Journal of American Medical Association*, **267**, 2234–2235.

4. DOLE, V. P., NYSWANDER, M. E., WARNER, A. (1968) Successful treatment of 750 criminal addicts, *Journal of American Medical Association*, **206**, 2708–2714.

5. DOLE, V. P., NYSWANDER, M. E. & KREEK, M. J. (1966) Narcotic blockade, *Archives of Internal Medicine*, **118**, 304–309.

6. LOWINSON, J. H. (1992) Methadone maintenance, in: LOWINSON, J. H., RUIZ, P. & MILLMAN, R. B. (Eds) *Substance Abuse – a Comprehensive Textbook*, pp. 550–561 (Baltimore, Williams & Wilkins).

7. DOLE, V. P. & NYSWANDER, M. E. (1976) Methadone maintenance treatment – a ten-year perspective, *Journal of American Medical Association*, **235**, 2117–2119.

8. FINNEGAN, L. P. & KANDALL, S. R. (1992) Maternal and neonatal effects of alcohol and drugs, in: LOWINSON, J. H., RUIZ, P. & MILLMAN, R. B. (Eds) *Substance Abuse – A Comprehensive Textbook*, pp. 628–656 (Baltimore, William & Wilkins).

9. METHADONE MAINTENANCE EVALUATION COMMITTEE (1968) Progress report of evaluation of methadone maintenance treatment program as of March 31, 1968, *Journal of American Medical Association*, **206**, 2712–2714.

10. DOLE, V. P. (1971) Methadone maintenance treatment for 25 000 heroin addicts, *Journal of American Medical Association*, **215**, 1131–1134.

11. DOLE, V. P. & JOSEPH, H. (1978) Long-term outcome of patients treated with methadone maintenance, *Annals of the New York Academy of Sciences*, **311**, 181–189.

Charles S. Lieber

Charles Lieber was born in 1931 in Antwerp, Belgium. He was a refugee in Switzerland during the Second World War. He qualified in medicine from Antwerp in 1955. Most of his professional life has been spent in the USA with senior research appointments at the Thorndike Memoral Laboratory (Harvard Medical School), 1958–63; Bellvue Hospital, Cornell Medical College, 1963–68; Bronx VA Medical Center, Mt Sinai Medical School, 1968 to the present. His work has centred on biological aspects of alcohol abuse, and among the awards he has won have been the Distinguished Achievement Award of the American Gastroenterological Society (1973), the E.M. Jellinek Award (1976), Scientific Excellence Award of the Research Society on Alcoholism (1980), the Kone Award of the Association of Clinical Biochemists, UK (1994), the Mark Keller Award from NIH/NIAAA (1996), and Master of the American College of Physicians (1999).

A wartime childhood

Addiction: *You have such an enormous input into the alcohol field and I would like to start off by asking you about some of the preliminary experiences before you started in this field.*
Charles Lieber: My interest in GI-liver was prompted by my experiences during World War II. In 1940, at the age of 9, I fled Belgium with my parents to escape the invading German forces but we got stuck in France, in Dunkirk where we tried to survive the bombardments of the British fleet (covering the retreat of their troops), and the bombarding German planes attacking the retreating forces. There was also a French cavalry division in town which could not be accommodated on the British ships and surrendered the next morning to the incoming Germans. That morning after the British retreat, we crawled out of our cellar where we had survived the bombardments. I will never forget the bloody street scene: many dead horses

---

That morning after the British retreat, we crawled out of our cellar where we had survived the bombardments. I will never forget the bloody street scene

---

intermingled with some dead soldiers lying on the pavement. We returned to Brussels and, in the following two years, suffered untold chicaneries from the occupying forces and their local Nazi collaborators. When they became unbearable and when hiding became too dangerous, my mother and I fled from Belgium in 1942. After nightly marches and daylight hidings in the woods, we finally reached unoccupied France. There, however, the Vichy government was very hostile and sent refugees back to the Germans. After a difficult period of hiding in Lyon, we went out of hiding and made a daring escape into Switzerland where we were put in refugee camps. Although I was only 11 years old, I was separated from my mother because of gender and spent the better part of the year by myself in a refugee camp under most adverse conditions. I was finally sheltered by a childless Swiss family where I spent the next four years in German-speaking Winterthur, not far from the German border. The family was very kind to me and were concerned about my education, since I did not speak German. However, after a few months in grade school, I acquired proficiency in the language and they decided to send me to the Gymnasium, the local elite school, despite the high tuition fees for foreigners. After one year of junior high, I was at the head of the class and the school administration decided I should skip the second year, to recoup the time I had lost in the woods and in the camps. However, when I returned to Brussels after the war in 1946, I was told that I could not get a high school diploma because of the skipped year. Therefore, I dropped out of high school, studied the curriculum by myself and passed a governmental high school equivalency exam that allowed me to enter Pre-Medical School at the University of Brussels at the age of 17, 1 year ahead of schedule. There, however, I faced another problem. Ever since I had been in the camps, I had suffered from recurrent, severe epigastric pain and vomiting, finally diagnosed when I was a pre-med student as a gastroduodenal ulcer, considered to be related to the wartime stress. Eventually, three massive bleeding episodes developed, requiring 10 units of blood each, and the surgeons convinced me that the only way to survive was to undergo a subtotal gastrectomy, performed at the age of 18.

Prompted by my personal GI bleedings, I decided to study factors that might precipitate such bleedings

A: *And your decision to take up medicine?*

CL: The war experience had an impact by letting me see under difficult circumstances, especially in the internment camps, how much people can suffer from lack of medical care, and how important it is to be able to give them some relief, and I hoped that becoming a physician would enable me to do that.

Studies on gastric acid secretion, gastric urease (Helicobacter pylori) and hepatic encephalopathy (1950–58)

A: *Tell us about that early work.*

CL: During my entire medical school and the two subsequent years, I worked as a research assistant in the Department of Pharmacology under Professor J. La Barre and his associate, Professor J.J. Reuse. I conducted studies on gastric effects of drugs, first in experimental animals, and eventually in man,[1] for which I received a prize from the Belgian government. I also was awarded a fellow-

ship from the Belgian Council for Scientific Research (1956–58). Prompted by my personal GI bleedings, I decided to study factors that might precipitate such bleedings, and A. Lefevre, a medical student, joined me in that endeavour. Fortuitously, as part of my duties as a GI fellow, I became aware of the fact that of 23 patients suffering from acute anuria and submitted to haemodialysis in our hospital over the preceding years, nine had gastroduodenal ulcerations with severe upper GI bleeding, lethal in six.[2] We formulated several possible explanations.

A: *At that time were there any reports on the presence of organisms in the gastric mucosa?*

CL: Spirochete-like organisms had been described on the human gastric mucosa.[3] We wondered whether they might provide the urease responsible for the splitting of urea into ammonia and consequently, whether the antibiotics given routinely to the hemodialysed patients might have prevented this ammonia production, thereby exacerbating the effect of hemodialysis. The nephrologists agreed to have this hypothesis mentioned in the account of these bleedings and they included my name and that of my coworker Andre Lefevre on that paper,[2] but they did not allow us to test this hypothesis directly in their hemodialysis patients. Accordingly, we searched for a substitute approach: consequently, we gave normal and uremic volunteers oxytetracycline, and indeed, we observed a striking decrease by this antibiotic of the capacity of the gastric juice to convert urea into ammonia, documenting thereby the probable infectious nature of this urease activity.[4]

A: *That sounds like a pretty important piece of work.*

CL: These results were presented at the first World Congress of Gastroenterology in Washington in 1958[5] together with data showing the increased ammonia production from urea in uremics, thereby explaining the neutralization of the gastric juice and the hypoacidity in uremia. However, the medical community did not believe our bacterial explanation because the dogma was that bacteria could not survive in an acid milieu.

Urease activity had been found in the stomach already in 1924 by Luck and Seth,[6] but they believed it to be an enzyme intrinsic to the mucosal cells. The most common argument used against our bacterial thesis was the alternate hypothesis that the oxytetracycline may not have been acting as an antibiotic but rather in some direct chemical way. Our further results strongly supported the bacterial hypothesis and, after I got to Boston, I submitted these observations for publication to the *Journal of Clinical Investigations* in March 1959, and the paper was accepted the same month.[7] After I moved subsequently to the Mount Sinai School of Medicine in New York, we repeated the same experiment but used ampicillin (administered orally or intramuscularly), or oral neomycin in normal as well as azotemic subjects and found results similar to those observed before with oxytetracycline or erythromycin.[8] Thus, the fact that four structurally different antibiotics had similar effects on gastric urease activity supported the original hypothesis that this effect was of an antibacterial nature.

A: *And next?*
CL: Next we studied patients with liver disease, to test the hypothesis that ammonia produced in the stomach could also play an important role as a precipitant factor of hepatic encephalopathy. Accordingly, antibiotics were given to patients with cirrhosis and we observed that the disappearance of the ammonia from the stomach was indeed paralleled by a clinical improvement of their encephalopathy.[9] Forty years later, I returned to my original interest in gastric ammonia: we confirmed our initial studies using two different antibiotics (ampicillin or neomycin), documented the disappearance of the Helicobacter and quantified the effect on encephalopathy with a Number Connection Test.[10]

A: *Did it prove difficult to culture bacteria from the stomach?*
CL: When we carried out our original studies in 1955–58, I had no doubt that there were bacteria in the stomach: they could be seen under the microscope and chemically they were characterized by their high urease activity which we suc-

ceeded in measuring. The problem was that we could not culture the bacteria with our limited bacteriology skills. After I came to the United States, I tried to get bacteriologists interested but I failed because nobody believed our claim that a significant number of bacteria could survive in an acid environment. I was considered a dreamer at the time despite the fact that my 'dreams' were based on evidence painstakingly gathered in tedious studies carried out in a total of 68 patients.[4,7,8] Twenty-six years passed before Marshall eventually convinced the medical public that there were indeed bacteria in the stomach when he successfully cultured *H. pylori*.

The Thorndike Memorial Laboratory (Harvard Medical School), 1958–1963: an awakening interest in alcoholic liver disease

A: *So what was the next step in your career?*
CL: In 1958, I received an award from the Belgian-American Educational Foundation enabling me to spend a fellowship at any academic institution in the United States. I selected the Thorndike Memorial Laboratory (Boston City Hospital, Harvard Medical School) where the chairman was Dr W.B. Castle, to work under the auspices of C.S. Davidson (Chief of the Section of Liver Disease and Nutrition).

The dogma prevailing at that time in the United States was that the liver disease caused by alcohol was due to malnutrition and not to any toxicity of the alcohol

A: *They felt that the study of alcohol was ripe for new research because of the large number of patients affected and little work carried out in that field. Is that what started your major work in the alcohol field?*
CL: Correct, I was persuaded that it would be more profitable to pursue my interest in the role of alcohol in liver disease. Accordingly, I did not follow up immediately on gastric ammonia and

encephalopathy at the Thorndike but I came back to it later in my career. What intrigued me more was the pathogenesis of alcoholic liver disease which I felt had no satisfactory explanation. Actually, the dogma prevailing at that time in the United States was that the liver disease caused by alcohol was due to malnutrition and not to any toxicity of the alcohol. This puzzled me since many of my cirrhotic patients in Belgium had a rather good diet and did not appear to suffer from malnutrition. I wondered whether alcohol itself was toxic to the liver and it seemed to me that a direct approach to test this hypothesis of alcohol's hepatotoxicity was simply to add alcohol *in vitro* to liver slices and to determine whether alcohol had any effect on fat accumulation, the earliest stage of alcoholic liver injury.

A: And your approach?

CL: Well, to that end, I used various radioactive precursors and their products, mainly $C^{14}O_2$ and C^{14}-lipids, were counted at New England Nuclear which, at that time, had the only scintillation counter in town. I was extremely fortunate that Dr Davidson assigned to me Miss Lee DeCarli, one of his technicians, a superb person with great technical skills. This was the start of a most productive and enjoyable collaboration lasting up to this date. I was also privileged to have the valuable input of Dr Rudi Schmid who was supervising Dr Davidson's fellows at the time. Because of his world fame in bilirubin metabolism, he was attracting outstanding research fellows and I established a life-time friendship with one of them, Dr S. Schenker. The results of our *in vitro* experiments quickly exceeded our expectations and showed clearly that alcohol had a direct effect on both the oxidation of fat and on lipogenesis and that these effects could be related to the metabolism of ethanol, which is associated with the conversion of NAD to NADH. The experiments were completed, working late the day before Christmas, 1958. My first paper generated in the United States appeared that year[12] and additional studies followed.[13] In addition to the productive research environment, social life at the Thorndike was also very pleasant: fellows working late often had the stimulating company of Dr W.B.

Castle at dinner in the cafeteria, and Dr C.S. Davidson took us regularly to the Boston Symphony Orchestra.

A: How did you find the research academic medicine environment in the United States? Was it different to that in Belgium?

CL: There was a tremendous difference. At Harvard, young people were encouraged to do research, to pursue their own ideas and they were given proper credit for their work whereas in Europe, the professors routinely took most of the credit and, with few exceptions, wanted fellows to do their own research and did not accept suggestions from younger people.

A: But after the initial experience at the Thorndike you still decided to go back to Belgium for a try. What were the reasons?

CL: It was a mixture of motivations. My mother was still there and she had difficulties in emigrating to the United States. Thus, I wanted to go back for her sake. Another reason was that Professor P. Govaerts, my original chairman in Brussels, was more supportive than other European professors. For instance, since only members could present papers at the French Society of Biology, he presented our data in Paris on 4 May, 1957,[4] without claiming co-authorship. Actually, his attitude was very much influenced by a sabbatical he had spent at Columbia University in New York.

Return to Belgium and faculty position at Harvard (1960–63)

A: And how did things go in Belgium?

CL: When, at the end of my fellowship, I was offered a position at Harvard, I decided first to test the waters back home in Belgium. There, however, the conditions had become disastrous. Because of the Congolese uprising, the funds of the foundation that had supported my small laboratory had dried up. More importantly, Professor P. Govaerts, the Chairman of my department, had died. His successor was interested exclusively in the kidney and he told me unequivocally '*ce sera le rein, ou rien*' [it will be the kidney or nothing].

My response was *'ce sera le foie, aux USA'* [it will be the liver in the States]. Consequently, I returned to Harvard as a junior faculty member. By that time, Schmid had left for Chicago and I succeeded him as the supervisor of the Liver Disease and Nutrition research fellows at the Thorndike where I also resumed my own research.

A: *On what did you then focus?*
CL: First, our discovery of the direct hepatotoxicity of ethanol led to a search for a biochemical mechanism. Since the oxidation of ethanol via its main pathway, namely alcohol dehydrogenase (ADH), causes a striking redox change associated with the conversion of NAD to NADH, I had postulated that the latter may be responsible because the effect was mimicked by another NADH generating system, such as sorbitol.[12] This was then corroborated by the observation that the ethanol-induced stimulation of lipogenesis and the decrease in fatty acid oxidation was prevented by a hydrogen acceptor, such as methylene blue.[13] Next, we addressed two leading questions: one, the possibility that other metabolic effects of alcohol might also be related to NADH generated by its metabolism and, two, that the toxicity of alcohol, shown *in vitro* in liver slices, could also be reproduced *in vivo* in experimental animals, resulting in hepatic lipid accumulation. This approach and my interest in lipids was fostered by my membership in the Committee on Fats, Food and Nutrition Board, National Academy of Science–National Research Council (1961–67). I believe I was its youngest member at the time. In any event, additional changes of lipids were also studied such as the effects of alcohol on circulating free fatty acids[14] and other blood lipids,[15] together with M. Losowsky, a fellow from England who later became chairman of the Department of Medicine in Leeds.

A: *Other work at that time?*
CL: In addition, we observed that a number of other hepatic and metabolic effects of ethanol, such as hyperuricemia,[16] could also be attributed to this redox change. Indeed, alcoholic hyperuricemia was described and its mechanism elucidated on the basis of the conversion of pyruvate

to lactate under the influence of NADH and the impairment of renal uric acid excretion by the lactate.[15] These studies aroused great interest in other departments, including Psychiatry, where Dr Jack Mendelson (from the Massachusetts General Hospital) studied the effects of chronic alcohol administration and its withdrawal in long-term studies in volunteers. He provided us with some of their blood samples which allowed us to expand the studies of the effects of alcohol on lipid and uric acid metabolism in man.[17] This also started a long-lasting friendship with Jack and his coworker, Dr Nancy Mello.

Charles Best had claimed that alcohol was not more toxic than sugar water

A: *One of your major endeavors when you came back to Boston was to study the concept that nutrition is not the key to the development of alcoholic liver disease and, as I remember, Charles Best had claimed that alcohol was not more toxic than sugar water.*
CL: Yes, the dogma on the lack of hepatotoxicity of alcohol had been enunciated by Charles Best.[18] This dogma was based on the fact that when Best gave rats alcohol in drinking water, the liver remained unchanged unless the diet was deficient. It was a concept that was universally accepted at the time. The only problem was that it did not fit my own experience in Belgium where, as I mentioned, the nutrition of our subjects was generally good yet many of my Belgian patients developed cirrhosis. Thus, we first repeated Best's experiments and confirmed his results but we went one step further: we measured blood alcohol and found it to be negligible. Indeed, although there are many similarities between rats and humans, especially behaviorally, in terms of appetite for alcohol, there is a great difference: rats have a severe aversion to it. Obviously, Best's model, because of its negligible blood alcohol, was not reproducing the human condition. The naivety of my young age (I was 28 years old) helped me to challenge the dogma of the non-hepatotoxicity of alcohol, enunciated by Best,[18] the codiscoverer of insulin, and thus a giant in medicine. Our task was

to find an experimental model with adequate alcohol intake and a blood level similar to that present in humans when they drink. This aversion of the rat for alcohol was finally overcome by incorporating the alcohol into totally liquid diets. All that the rats were given was that liquid diet and, therefore, in order to eat or to drink, they had no choice but to take the alcohol with whatever diet we selected. Under these conditions, the blood levels achieved were comparable to those of humans and, in addition, striking liver changes were produced, including fatty liver, despite a nutritionally adequate diet.[17] This procedure has now evolved into a technique used worldwide for the feeding of alcohol to rats,[19] assuring not only an adequate alcohol intake, but also enabling the investigator to modify at will any element of the diet and to facilitate pair-feeding with controls. After the successful experiments in rats, the hepatotoxicity of alcohol was next also shown in man, even in the presence of adequate diet.[20] Thus, the years at the Thorndike were both productive and exhilarating, but clouds were appearing on the horizon.

Bellevue Hospital – Cornell Medical College (1963–68)

A: *Clouds of what kind?*
CL: Rumors appeared that the days of Harvard at the Boston City Hospital were limited. Accordingly, I became receptive to an attractive offer in 1963 from Cornell University Medical College, offering me my own laboratory with realistic initial support and a tenured associate professorship at the Cornell Medical College, with the position of chief of the clinical Section of Liver Disease and Nutrition at Bellevue Hospital. I also became codirector, with Tom Almy, of a GI-Liver Training Program.

A: *Did you have clinical responsibilities at the same time or was this primarily a research and teaching position.*
CL: My position at Cornell was a mixed one: as head of the Section of Liver Disease and Nutrition, I supervised the liver fellows rendering liver

consults and I also made regular ward rounds. The time we had to spend on the wards was, however, limited and I had the opportunity to continue the clinical studies on the hepatotoxicity of alcohol which I had started at the Thorndike, with a new pathologist, E. Rubin, of the Mt Sinai Medical Center. We confirmed the hepatotoxicity of alcohol in non-alcoholic volunteers.[21] We also demonstrated the role of dietary, adipose and endogenously synthesized fatty acids in the pathogenesis of the alcoholic fatty liver,[22] including the importance of the amount and fatty acid chain length of dietary fat[23] as well as the role of dietary proteins.[24] Corresponding ultrastructural changes were also described.[25] J. Crouse, then a medical student at NYU, showed that acetate produced from the ethanol was responsible for the blockage in the free fatty acid release from adipose tissue.[26]

A: *When you came to Cornell I think that your scope of research extended considerably beyond the liver and actually went on to studies on the intestinal tract.*
CL: We had productive interactions not only with the other Cornell sections, such as the Metabolism section (Dr N. Spritz, chief) or the GI section (Dr M. Lipkin, chief) but also with faculty members of the Columbia Division, including the late J. Lindenbaum, with whom we described the hematological effects of alcohol in man in the absence of nutritional deciencies[27] and the alcohol-induced malabsorption of vitamin B12.[28] We also discovered that alcoholism depresses intestinal lactase activity,[29] resulting in symptomatic lactase deficiency in some individuals, particularly blacks who frequently have low lactase baseline levels. Before this study, we were routinely giving milk-rich diets to alcoholics after their hospitalization, both to replenish them nutritionally and to alleviate some gastritis-associated symptoms. We soon noted that these patients commonly develop diarrhoea but when we became aware of the low intestinal lactase caused by alcohol, we stopped the practice of high milk diets in these subjects and the diarrhoea also ceased. While at Bellevue, I became acquainted with the NYU faculty, including Dr J. Moor-Jankowski, who was also the

director of the Laboratory for Experimental Medicine and Surgery in Primates (LEMSIP) center in Sterling Forrest (upstate New York). When he made us aware that a baboon trailer had become available and that a group of baboons was for sale we started our baboon colony which, in the intervening years, has allowed us to make much progress in a primate model relevant to humans, including the production, for the first time, of alcoholic cirrhosis despite an adequate diet.[30]

Enter the baboons

A: *How did your baboon work get started?*
CL: The baboon colony offered a unique opportunity but it was also a major problem in terms of the costs involved and therefore we applied for a large NIH grant to start this colony. Accordingly, we had a site visit, and one of the members of the site visiting team was an old friend of mine, a very distinguished biochemist, who took me to the side and told me: 'Charles, I am going to save you from a tremendous mistake and waste of time. You have done marvellous work up till now because you focused on solvable problems, but chances are that this baboon project will be a non-productive diversion. Your time could be better spent on more direct biochemical projects and I am going to do you a favor and vote against this grant.' I pleaded for the privilege to make some mistakes, he reluctantly consented and our baboon venture started.

Studies at Bronx VA Medical Center – Mt Sinai Medical School (1968–present)

A: *And the next move?*
CL: Our activities at Bellevue came to a halt when what we had feared at Harvard happened also at Bellevue. To solve the ensuing crisis, we took advantage of the fact that the Mt Sinai Hospital was starting a new medical school with Dr Saul Berson, of radioimmunoassay fame, as its first chairman. He and Drs Hans Popper, Chairman of Pathology and H. Janowitz, chief of the GI division, made a concerted effort to have me come

to Mt Sinai. In view of the space shortage at Sinai, Dr S. Berson convinced us to go to the VA in 1968 where he also had his own laboratory, run by Dr R. Yalow (who subsequently won a Nobel prize for their radioimmunoassay work). In addition to a professorship at Sinai, I became the chief of a newly created Liver section and Director of the GI-Liver Program at the VA and Co-Director, with Dr H. Janowitz, of a combined Mt SinaiVA GI-Liver Fellowship Program.

A: *And how did your research program then develop?*
CL: Our clinical and experimental research with alcohol was extended beyond the liver and GI tract to most organs of the body, and this required an interdisciplinary approach. Accordingly, we applied for, and were awarded in 1977, funding for one of the first alcohol research centers in the country. The Alcohol Research Center Program is one of the very successful initiatives of the National Institute of Alcohol Abuse and Alcoholism (NIAAA).

I pleaded for the privilege to make some mistakes, he reluctantly consented and our baboon venture started

The importance of NIAAA

A: *You have also made major contributions in many areas besides research – the National Institute of Alcohol and Alcoholism (NIAAA), the Research Society and you are the founding father of the journal* Alcoholism: Clinical Experimental Research. *Something on those activities?*
CL: NIAAA was created to address a major issue that has plagued the alcoholism research community for decades, namely the lack of recognition of alcohol research as a legitimate science, coupled with a lack of funding. This was caused, in part, by the prevailing, pervasive and truly pernicious perception, both among the public and the health professionals, that there was not much that could be done about the alcoholism issue. In the 1960s, the small amount of federal funding available for

alcohol research was provided by a division of ADAMHA (Alcohol, Drug and Mental Health Administration), a governmental institution separate from the NIH. ADAMHA had a broad mission, research being only one of its mandates. Within ADAMHA, there was internal competition for funding between alcohol and other drugs. Although in terms of cost to society the effects of alcohol exceeded those of all the other drugs combined, alcohol research funding was much less and, even today, after years of improvement, it is still less than half that for other drugs: 293 versus 687 million dollars for fiscal year 2000 (NIH Budget Office). In the 1960s, it was felt that the situation would be improved if the alcohol field had its own institute. Accordingly, a campaign was launched to have such an institute and, due to the efforts of many, including those of the National Council on Alcoholism (NCA), NIAAA was finally created in the early 1970s. NIAAA provided the alcohol researcher with respectability in the research community and with a home in Washington to approach for help and advice. The Institute made long-term planning possible and long-range research feasible and it also allowed an interdisciplinary approach to the problem of alcoholism.

A: *The focus for your own center?*
CL: We established our own center with a truly integrated medical and basic science approach to address alcoholism problems in a comprehensive manner on a regional basis. In addition to our metabolically oriented unit at the Bronx VA, and one with biochemical emphasis at Mt Sinai (A. Cederbaum and G. Cohen), the Center comprised a unit at North Shore Hospital (S. Fisher) with emphasis on the fetal alcohol syndrome and one at New Jersey Medical Center (A. Garro) with focus on alcohol and cancer. The latter was the site of several studies, many carried out with H. Seitz, one of our fellows from Germany.[31,32] For the subsequent 20 years, this Alcohol Research Center allowed us to carry out a broad based approach, both clinical and experimental. In keeping with my GI interest, I was also very active in the New York Gastroenterological Association and I became its president (1974–5).

A: *You also had a hand in setting up RSA?*
CL: Yes, to achieve a forum focused on alcohol research at a national level I founded, with a small group of like-minded friends, the Research Society on Alcoholism (RSA). RSA was created to fill an important need, namely to provide the researchers in alcoholism with an organization where they could meet and exchange ideas and plan for joint experiments. What was particularly needed was a society where clinical investigators (mainly MDs) and basic scientists (mostly PhDs) could interact. The only society of relevance at the time was an outgrowth of the New York Society on Alcoholism, namely the American Medical Society on Alcoholism (AMSA, presently ASAM: American Society on Addictive Medicine). I had helped to launch AMSA and subsequently I became its president (1974–77). However, AMSA accepted only MDs in its ranks. Some members of AMSA felt strongly that PhDs and other professionals active in the field had much to offer and should be included in the organization. This proposal was defeated by AMSA's board in 1976. Although I was president of AMSA at the time, I ended up on the losing side. However, with a handful of like-minded members of AMSA and other interested scientists, as well as NCA's blessing, I formed a task force on the creation of the Research Society on Alcoholism in 1976 and, in 1977, RSA was founded as a society open to all investigators in the field. In 1976, those of us who started this society could fit around one table, whereas at the 2000 RSA banquet, there were 92 tables and RSA has now grown to over 1400 members. As RSA's first president, I am very proud of this rapid growth.

A: *You also established a new journal?*
CL: In terms of the journal, we also felt that it was important for alcohol researchers to have an outlet to publish their research without the handicap of the then common prejudice against such investigations. At the time, I was the President of AMSA and I was also on the board of NCA and I convinced my colleagues on the boards of these two organization to found such a journal. I signed the contract with the publisher using my personal credit because RSA was not as yet incorporated.

Thus, the journal *Alcoholism: Clinical and Experimental Research* (ACER) was created in 1977 by AMSA and RSA under the sponsorship of NCA (as a joint publication). As President of AMSA (1974–77), and also as the first President of RSA (1977–79), I was in a good position to foster the journal's early development. I organized the selection of the first editor, Frank Seixas, who was very instrumental in getting the journal off the ground. ACER is unquestionably by now the most prestigious journal in the field and its accomplishments give me great pleasure and pride.

A: *Going back to your personal research contributions, a very major discovery that you have made was the discovery of the microsomal ethanol oxidizing system (MEOS). This not only affected the area of alcohol metabolism but also spread to the areas of oxidative stress and eventually to other drugs. Would you comment?*

CL: One of the highlights of our research at the Bronx VA–Mt Sinai included this discovery of a new pathway of ethanol metabolism. We had observed, both in animals and also in man, a striking proliferation of the endoplasmic reticulum (also called microsomal fraction when obtained by ultracentrifugation).[25] This proliferation of the membranes of the hepatic endoplasmic reticulum was very similar, if not identical, to what was described at about the same time after other drugs by several investigators (Dr Conney and coworkers in the United States, Dr Remmer and others in Europe). There seemed to be an adaptive system which helps us survive in modern society because it is relatively non-specific and detoxifies foreign compounds even when the body has never been exposed to them before. When we observed a similar morphological response after alcohol, I postulated that alcohol may therefore also be a substrate for this system. This hypothesis led to the discovery of the microsomal ethanol oxidizing system (MEOS) as a new pathway of ethanol metabolism.[33,34] Our proposal that this new pathway involves a cytochrome P-450 and plays a significant role in ethanol metabolism initiated a decade of lively debate: some invoked ADH contaminating the liver microsomes,[35] others believed in a hydrogen peroxide-dependent reaction pro-

moted by contaminating catalase,[36] but eventually MEOS was separated from ADH and catalase,[37] characterized[38,39] and reconstituted with a semi-purified preparation of cytochrome P-450.[40] The role of the microsomes in ethanol metabolism and its increase after chronic ethanol consumption was demonstrated in a variety of species, including rats[41] and non-human primates.[42] An ethanol-inducible form of cytochrome P-450 was discovered[43] which contributes to the metabolic tolerance that these various species develop with chronic ethanol consumption. A catalytically active preparation of the alcohol-inducible cytochrome P-450 (now called CYP2E1) was puried by various groups in the livers of different species, including rats[43] and humans.[44] It was shown that CYP2E1 predominates in the perivenular hepatocytes and that the induction resulting from feeding ethanol to rats prevails in that zone,[45] where maximal liver injury also occurs.

One of the highlights of our research at the Bronx VA–Mt Sinai included this discovery of a new pathway of ethanol metabolism

A: *In human beings?*

CL: Application of similar techniques to human biopsy sections obtained from recently drinking alcoholics also showed the induction and perivenular localization of CYP2E1. Immunoblot analysis of human liver microsomes disclosed that the hepatic microsomal CYP2E1 content in recently drinking alcoholics was at least four times higher than that found in non-drinkers.[45] CYP2E1 induction was demonstrated with normal and low-fat diets.[46] It was shown in hepatocytes as well as in non-parenchymal cells of the liver[47] and also in extrahepatic tissues.[48,49] MEOS induction by ethanol was found to 'spill over' to other microsomal enzymes,[50] to enhance the degradation of other drugs[51] and to accelerate the clearance of drugs, including psychoactive agents, both in rats and in man.[52] In addition, the induction was found to have an impact on sex hormones in normal men[53] and to enhance fatty acid v-oxidation, with an associated gender difference.[54,55]

A: *What is the present concept of the molecular biology of the induction of the microsomal ethanol oxidizing system?*

CL: It is an important physiological enzyme which is not simply induced in response to xenobiotics but which also plays an important role in diabetes because it helps to convert ketones into glucose, and it is also important in obesity because this enzyme can metabolize fatty acids and thus helps us get rid of excess fat. These natural substrates are also good inducers of the enzyme and, therefore, ketones for instance can be used as excellent inducers instead of alcohol. This brings up the interesting issue of so-called NASH: nonalcoholic steato-hepatitis which is seen predominantly in diabetes and in obesity. In obese overfed rats, we found an induction of CYP2E1.[56] Since an induction of the enzyme has also been shown later in men with NASH, CYP2E1 may explain many of the similarities of the pathology in alcoholic and non-alcoholic steatohepatitis which had been very puzzling before.

When consumed in large amounts, alcohol calories were found not to 'fully count'

A: *How much alcohol is metabolized by the MEOS, as compared, for example, to alcohol dehydrogenase (ADH)?*

CL: MEOS is an inducible system whereas alcohol dehydrogenase is not and, therefore, in chronic drinkers, MEOS (because of its induction) acquires much greater significance. CYP2E1 can also affect the metabolism of other drugs that are substrates for this system. They include tranquilizers, sedatives, hypoglycemic agents, anticoagulants, analgesics and other commonly used medications, the dosage of which must be increased in heavy drinkers, as reviewed recently.[57] Contrasting with chronic ethanol consumption, which results in microsomal induction with tolerance to a number of substrates, the presence of ethanol was shown to slow down drug disposition, in part through competition for a partially common microsomal degradation process, thereby enhancing the pharmacological effects of the corresponding drugs. This was shown for meprobamate,[58] acetaminophen,[59] a commonly used over-the-counter analgesic (called paracetamol in Europe) as well as methadone,[60] both in man and experimental animals.

A: *Other implications?*

CL: In addition, one of the most important consequences of the discovery of this new microsomal pathway of ethanol metabolism was the realization that the ethanol-inducible CYP2E1 does not only catalyze the oxidation of ethanol to its product acetaldehyde, but that it can also activate various other compounds to highly toxic metabolites. This pertains to anesthetics,[61] hepatotoxins,[62] industrial solvents,[63] carcinogens (e.g. nitrosodimethylamine: NDMA)[31] as well as analgesics, such as acetaminophen.[64] This explained an important observation, namely that heavy drinkers (or even some social drinkers) are very vulnerable to the toxicity of acetaminophen. Contrasting with the enhancing effect on acetaminophen toxicity by chronic alcohol consumption due to MEOS induction,[64] it was found that acute alcohol intake decreases the toxicity, because of competition of ethanol with the acetaminophen[65] for a common enzyme. The inducibility of MEOS is of course also important in view of the increased production of the toxic metabolite acetaldehyde which, coupled with decreased acetaldehyde disposition due to mitochondrial injury,[66] results in higher levels of acetaldehyde in the alcoholic than in non-alcoholic subjects.[67] Although we focused on MEOS, we did not neglect ADH. Gender differences were defined[68] as well as the contribution of the stomach ADH to the first-pass metabolism of ethanol,[69,70] the cloning of the gene of a new ADH isozyme, namely Sigma ADH,[71] its localization to chromosome 4, as well as the increased blood alcohol levels through inhibition of the gastric first-pass metabolism[69,70] or the acceleration of gastric emptying[72] by commonly used H_2 blockers.[69-73]

Experimental and clinical nutrition

A: *You have also had a great interest in the area of alcohol and nutrition.*

CL: Yes. The induction of MEOS contributes to the understanding of the energy cost associated with the abuse of alcohol[74] and possibly other drugs.[75] When consumed in large amounts, alcohol calories were found not to 'fully count'.[76] In addition, an alteration in the energy utilization derived from fat may play a major role. We found that chronic alcohol consumption causes striking alterations of the mitochondria[25] and their electron transport chain,[77] including uncoupling of oxidation with phosphorylation in the mitochondria damaged by chronic ethanol consumption. That system is, of course, important to recover the energy from fat. Accordingly, when we consume substantial amounts of alcohol and a diet with a significant amount of fat, we do not recover fully the energy of that fat and this is why this loss of energy caused by alcohol is most evident when alcohol is associated with a high-fat diet. The consequences are striking: even under metabolic ward conditions, an increase of total calories from 2500 to 4500 per day failed to produce weight change after one month.[73]

A: *Do the polyunsaturated fats, when taken in with alcohol, potentiate the effects of alcohol on liver damage?*
CL: Yes. Polyunsaturated fatty acids, particularly linoleic acid, are preferential targets for lipid peroxidation caused by free radicals. In the metabolism of alcohol via MEOS (and its CYP2E1) there is release of free radicals. These then selectively attack the unsaturated fatty acids and cause the peroxidation of these lipids which may result in membranes destruction since these fatty acids are part of the backbone of the membrane. Therefore, linoleic acid (or triglycerides containing such unsaturated fatty acids) will exacerbate liver damage. By contrast, when the same fatty acids are given as phospholipids, we actually observed an opposite effect, namely a protection against oxidative stress.[78] We have not proven the mechanisms of this paradoxal protection, but we have a plausible hypothesis.[79,80]

A: *Dr Leo has made quite important contributions to your team's research on nutrition?*
CL: A major expansion of our nutritional studies occurred when Dr Leo joined us from France in 1974. She was originally from Italy but received her training in hepatology with Professor Caroli in

Paris, with whom I had enjoyed a long-standing friendship, fostered by several visiting professorships at his St Antoine hospital in Paris, and who advised Dr Leo to join us in New York. Dr Leo's studies included the discovery that liver microsomes harbor previously unrecognized pathways for retinol metabolism[81,82] which were shown to play a role in the homeostatic control of hepatic vitamin A levels.[83] Using puried cytochrome P-450 isozymes, including the human CYP2C8, retinol[84] and retinoic acid[85] metabolizing systems were reconstituted; chronic ethanol or drug administration was shown to result in increased microsomal degradation of retinoic acid[86] and retinal,[87] a possible mechanism for the striking hepatic vitamin A depletion which was discovered to result from chronic ethanol consumption in rats,[88] non-human primates[88] and men.[89] This hepatic vitamin A depletion was found to be associated with striking lysosomal lesions.[90] Potentiation of the deleterious effects of vitamin A depletion by ethanol was also observed in other tissues, including a profound loss of the ciliated epithelium in the lining of the respiratory tract and the exacerbation of squamous metaplasia, a precancerous lesion.[91] Hepatic depletion of vitamin A was also demonstrated after administration of other drugs;[92] the combination of ethanol with drugs or food additives (such as butylated hydroxytoluene) resulted in a striking potentiation of the depletion, with almost all of the vitamin A disappearing from the liver,[93] even in animals given vitamin A-enriched diets.

A: *And the practical bearing on nutritional advice?*
CL: Vitamin A requirements had to be revised for the large segment of our population that chronically abuses ethanol and/or other drugs. The practical limits of vitamin A supplementation, however, were delineated by the demonstration that vitamin A toxicity can be markedly exacerbated by chronic ethanol consumption, with development of mitochondrial injury,[94] necrosis and fibrosis.[95] Indeed, amounts of ethanol and vitamin A which, by themselves, do not produce fibrosis, when combined resulted in necrosis and fibrosis in the liver,[95] with development of severe mitochondrial injury.[94] Furthermore, it was discovered in

non-human primates that alcohol interferes with the clearance of β-carotene, possibly by impairing its conversion to vitamin A, resulting in its enhanced hepatic and blood levels in baboons[96] and also in man,[97] with associated potentiation of hepatotoxicity,[96] exacerbated by the beadlets used as carriers for the β-carotene.[98] In addition, carotenoids were discovered to undergo significant biliary excretion in man,[99] a process affected by liver pathology. In aggregate, this work has led to the recognition of a narrowed therapeutic window for vitamin A and β-carotene in moderate and heavy drinkers which, in turn, has prompted a redefinition of the optimal conditions for their therapeutic use, in order to avoid adverse interactions with ethanol not only in terms of hepatotoxicity, but possibly also carcinogenicity, as recently reviewed.[100] Because of these and other nutritional endeavors and interests, I was very active in the American Society of Clinical Nutrition and I assumed at one point its presidency (1975–76).

A: *In the course of these last 40 years of doing very significant research in alcohol and other areas you have been very richly rewarded with a large number of major awards, including in 1976 the Jellinek Award. When I glanced at your CV I noted the undoubtedly still provisional total of 15 major national and international awards.*
CL: Yes, let's hope so.

The satisfaction I get from the training of fellows is in some way like the satisfaction I derive from my biological children

---

The satisfaction in training

A: *You have trained many people, not only in the United States but also all over the world, and this must be a source of enormous satisfaction for you.*
CL: Yes. The satisfaction I get from the training of fellows is in some way like the satisfaction I derive from my biological children. The well-being

of my five children and four grandchildren is very important to me. I cherish this sizeable family. I always regretted having been an only child, and I have only faint but nostalgic memories of the large family gatherings with my many cousins, aunts and uncles before 1942 in Antwerp, all of whom perished subsequently during World War II. In a way, I extended the family concept to my fellows whom I considered as intellectual offsprings.

The family base

A: *It is surprising to me that since there are only 24 hours in a day, you have nevertheless been able to do so many different things and in addition maintained a happy family, many of whom I have known. What has been your interaction with your family members, have they been supportive of all this?*
CL: My family members have been extremely supportive and I am sure that without them, I could not have had the intellectual serenity to carry out and to focus on my many endeavors. They always gave me warm support, even though the other members of the family are also very busy. Dr Leo has continued until this day the valuable research she started with us in 1974, despite her clinical duties and her family responsibilities with me and our three children. I also have two children from my first marriage.

Unresolved issues in alcoholic liver disease

A: *Let us finally go back to science again. There are still many unresolved issues in the field of alcoholic liver disease and alcoholism in general. Tell me what you think are the priorities and the areas most likely to be solved.*
CL: I believe that in the alcohol field we are at a stage where we can foresee significant progress because we have reached a point where we begin to understand the pathogenesis of many of the lesions that are produced by alcohol. We should be able to come up with significant progress in prevention as well as in therapy.

Hippocrates pointed out that the liver is the site of the soul

A: *Inevitably people must sometimes ask you whether you are ready for retirement?*

CL: These multiple remaining and important tasks are the main reason why I am not ready for retirement; I feel compelled to complete this journey which I started half a century ago trying to unravel the effects of alcohol on the liver, including the interactions between liver and brain. Hippocrates pointed out that the liver is the site of the soul, a relationship which still is not fully understood. We have finally reached the point where sufficient elucidation of pathogenesis allows us to contemplate effective prevention and treatment of alcohol-induced liver failure, still a major cause of disease and death.

References

1. LIEBER, C. S. (1956) Comparison on the inhibitory effects of atropine and two synthetic parasympatholytic agents on the postinsulin and basal gastric secretion in man, *Acta Gastroenterologica Belgica*, **19**, 819–832.
2. VERBANCK, M., TOUSSAINT, C., LIEBER, C. S. & LEFEVRE, A. (1957) Gastroduodenal bleeding complicating acute anuria during treatment by articial kidney, *Acta Gastroenterologica Belgica*, **20**, 798–809.
3. DOENGES, J. L. (1939) Spirochetes in the gastric glands of *Macacus rhesus* and of man without related disease, *Archives of Pathololology and Laboratory Medicine*, **27**, 469–477.
4. LIEBER, C. S. & LEFEVRE, A. (1957) Effect of oxytetracycline on acidity, ammonia and urea in gastric juice in normal and uremic subjects, *Comptes Rendus des Séances de la Société de Biologie (Paris)*, **151**, 1038–1042.
5. LIEBER, C. S. & LEFEVRE, A. (1959) Effects of antibiotics on gastric juice in normal and uremic subjects: ammonia as source of hypoacidity in uremic patients, in: *Proceedings of the World Congress on Gastroenterology*, **1**, 117–118 (Baltimore, Williams and Wilkins Publishing Company).
6. LUCK, J. M. & SETH, T. N. (1924) Gastric urease, *Biochemistry Journal*, **18**, 1227–1231.
7. LIEBER, C. S. & LEFEVRE, A. (1959) Ammonia as source of gastric hypoacidity in patients with uremia, *Journal of Clinical Investigation*, **38**, 1271–1277.
8. MEYERS, S. & LIEBER, C. S. (1976) Reduction of gastric ammonia by ampicillin in normal and azotemic subjects, *Gastroenterology*, **70**, 244–247.
9. LIEBER, C. S. & LEFEVRE, A. (1958) Ammonia and intermediary metabolism in hepatic coma: value of the determination of blood ammonia in the diagnosis and management of cirrhosis, *Acta Clinica Belgica*, **13**, 328–357.
10. DASANI, B. M., SIGAL, S. H. & LIEBER, C. S. (1998) Analysis of the risk factors for chronic hepatic encephalopathy: the role of *Helicobacter pylori* infection, *American Journal of Gastroenterology*, **93**, 726–731.
11. MARSHALL, B. J. (1983) Unidentified curved bacilli on gastric epithelium in active chronic gastritis, *Lancet*, **I**, 1273–1275.
12. LIEBER, C. S., DeCarli, L. M. & SCHMID, R. (1959) Effects of ethanol on fatty acid metabolism in liver slices, *Biochemical and Biophysical Research Communications*, **1**, 302–306.
13. LIEBER, C. S. & SCHMID, R. (1961) The effect of ethanol on fatty acid metabolism: stimulation of hepatic fatty acid synthesis *in vitro*, *Journal of Clinical Investigation*, **40**, 394–399.
14. LIEBER, C. S., LEVY, C. M., STEIN, S. W., GEORGE, W. S., CHERRICK, G. R., ABELMANN, W. H. & DAVIDSON, C. S. (1962) Effect of ethanol on plasma free fatty acids in man, *Journal of Laboratory and Clinical Medicine*, **59**, 826–832.
15. LOSOWSKY, M. S., JONES, D. P., DAVIDSON, C. S. & LIEBER, C. S. (1963) Studies of

alcoholic hyperlipemia and its mechanism, *American Journal of Medicine*, **35**, 794–803.

16. LIEBER, C. S., JONES, D. P., LOSOWSKY, M. S. & DAVIDSON, C. S. (1962) Interrelation of uric acid and ethanol metabolism in man, *Journal of Clinical Investigation*, **41**, 1863–1870.

17. LIEBER, C. S., JONES, D. P., MENDELSON, J. & DECARLI, L. M. (1963) Fatty liver, hyperlipemia and hyperuricemia produced by prolonged alcohol consumption, despite adequate dietary intake, *Transactions of the Association of American Physicians*, **76**, 289–300.

18. BEST, C. H., HARTROFT, W. S., LUCAS, C. C. & RIDOUT, J. H. (1949) Liver damage produced by feeding alcohol or sugar and its prevention by choline, *British Medical Journal*, **2**, 1001–1006.

19. LIEBER, C. S. & DECARLI, L. M. (1994) Animal models of chronic ethanol toxicity, in: Packer, L. (Ed.) *Methods in Enzymology: oxygen radical in biological systems*, Part C, 233, pp. 585–594 (Orlando, FL, Academic Press, Inc.).

20. LIEBER, C. S., JONES, D. P. & DECARLI, L. M. (1965) Effects of prolonged ethanol intake: production of fatty liver despite adequate diets, *Journal of Clinical Investigation*, **44**, 1009–1021.

21. RUBIN, E. & LIEBER, C. S. (1968) Alcohol induced hepatic injury in non-alcoholic volunteers, *New England Journal of Medicine*, **278**, 869–876.

22. LIEBER, C. S., SPRITZ, N. & DECARLI, L. M. (1966) Role of dietary, adipose and endogenously synthesized fatty acids in the pathogenesis of the alcoholic fatty liver, *Journal of Clinical Investigation*, **45**, 51–62.

23. LIEBER, C. S., LEFEVRE, A., SPRITZ, N., FEINMAN, L. & DECARLI, L. M. (1967) Difference in hepatic metabolism of long and medium-chain fatty acids: the role of fatty acid chain length in the production of the alcoholic fatty liver, *Journal of Clinical Investigation*, **46**, 1451–1460.

24. LIEBER, C. S. & RUBIN, E. (1968) Alcoholic fatty liver in man on a high protein and low fat diet, *American Journal of Medicine*, **44**, 200–206.

25. LANE, B. P. & LIEBER, C. S. (1966) Ultrastructural alterations in human hepatocytes following ingestion of ethanol with adequate diets, *American Journal of Pathology*, **49**, 593–603.

26. CROUSE, J. R., GERSON, C. D., DECARLI, L. M. & LIEBER, C. S. (1968) Role of acetate in the reduction of plasma free fatty acids produced by ethanol in man, *Journal of Lipid Research*, **9**, 509–512.

27. LINDENBAUM, J. & LIEBER, C. S. (1969) Hematologic effects of alcohol in man in the absence of nutritional deficiency, *New England Journal of Medicine*, **281**, 333–338.

28. LINDENBAUM, J. & LIEBER, C. S. (1969) Alcohol-induced malabsorption of vitamin B_{12} in man, *Nature*, **224**, 806.

29. PERLOW, W., BARAONA, E. & LIEBER, C. S. (1977) Symptomatic intestinal disaccharidase deficiency in alcoholics, *Gastroenterology*, **72**, 680–684.

30. LIEBER, C. S. & DECARLI, L. M. (1974) An experimental model of alcohol feeding and liver injury in the baboon, *Journal of Medical Primatology*, **3**, 153–163.

31. GARRO, A. J., SEITZ, H. K. & LIEBER, C. S. (1981) Enhancement of dimethylnitrosamine metabolism and activation to a mutagen following chronic ethanol consumption, *Cancer Research*, **41**, 120–124.

32. SEITZ, H. K., GARRO, A. J. & LIEBER, C. S. (1981) Enhanced pulmonary and intestinal activation of procarcinogens and mutagens after chronic ethanol consumption in the rat, *European Journal of Clinical Investigation*, **11**, 33–38.

33. LIEBER, C. S. & DECARLI, L. M. (1968) Ethanol oxidation by hepatic microsomes: adaptive increase after ethanol feeding, *Science*, **162**, 917–918.

34. LIEBER, C. S. & DECARLI, L. M. (1970) Hepatic microsomal ethanol oxidizing

system: *in vitro* characteristics and adaptive properties *in vivo*, *Journal of Biological Chemistry*, **245**, 2505–2512.

35. ISSELBACHER, K. J. & CARTER, E. A. (1970) Ethanol oxidation by liver microsomes: evidence against a separate and distinct enzyme system, *Biochemical and Biophysical Research Communications*, **39**, 530–537.

36. ZIEGLER, D. M. (1972) Discussion on microsomes and drug oxidation, in: ESTABROOK, R. W., GILLETTE, R. J. & LIEBMAN, K. C. (Eds) *Microsomes and Drug Oxidations*, pp. 458–460 (Baltimore, MD, Williams & Wilkins).

37. TESCHKE, R., HASUMURA, Y. & LIEBER, C. S. (1974) Hepatic microsomal ethanol oxidizing system: solubilization, isolation and characterization, *Archives of Biochemistry and Biophysics*, **163**, 404–415.

38. TESCHKE, R., HASUMURA, Y. & LIEBER, C. S. (1975) Hepatic microsomal alcohol oxidizing system: affinity for methanol, ethanol, propanol and butanol, *Journal of Biological Chemistry*, **250**, 7397–7404.

39. TESCHKE, R., HASUMURA, Y. & LIEBER, C. S. (1975) Hepatic microsomal alcohol oxidizing system in normal and acatalasemic mice: its dissociation from the peroxidatic activity of catalase-H_2O_2, *Molecular Pharmacology*, **11**, 841–849.

40. OHNISHI, K. & LIEBER, C. S. (1977) Reconstitution of the microsomal ethanol oxidizing system (MEOS): qualitative and quantitative changes of cytochrome P-450 after chronic ethanol consumption, *Journal of Biological Chemistry*, **252**, 7124–7131.

41. LIEBER, C. & DECARLI, L. M. (1972) The role of the hepatic microsomal ethanol oxidizing system (MEOS) for ethanol metabolism *in vivo*, *Journal of Pharmacology and Experimental Therapeutics*, **181**, 279–287.

42. NOMURA, F., PIKKARAINEN, P. H., JAUHONEN, P., ARAI, M., GORDON, E. R., BARAONA, E. & LIEBER, C. S. (1983) The effect of ethanol administration on the metabolism of ethanol in baboons, *Journal of Pharmacology and Experimental Therapeutics*, **227**, 78–83.

43. RYAN, D. E., IIDA, S., WOOD, A. W., THOMAS, P. E., LIEBER, C. S. & LEVIN, W. (1984) Characterization of three highly purified cytochromes P-450 from hepatic microsomes of adult male rats, *Journal of Biological Chemistry*, **259**, 1239–1250.

44. LASKER, J. M., RAUCY, J., KUBOTA, S., BLOSWICK, B. P., BLACK, M. & LIEBER, C. S. (1987) Purification and characterization of human liver cytochrome P-450-ALC, *Biochemical and Biophysical Research Communications*, **148**, 232–238.

45. TSUTSUMI, M., LASKER, J. M., SHIMIZU, M., ROSMAN, A. S. & LIEBER, C. S. (1989) The intralobular distribution of ethanol-inducible P-450IIE1 in rat and human liver, *Hepatology*, **10**, 437–446.

46. LIEBER, C. S., LASKER, J. M., DECARLI, L. M., SAELI, J. & WOJTOWICZ, T. (1988) Role of acetone, dietary fat and total energy intake in induction of hepatic microsomal ethanol oxidizing system, *Journal of Pharmacology and Experimental Therapeutics*, **247**, 791–795.

47. KOIVISTO, T., MISHIN, V., MAK, K. M., COHEN, A. & LIEBER, C. S. (1996) Induction of cytochrome P-4502E1 by ethanol in rat Kupffer cells, *Alcohol: Clinical and Experimental Research*, **20**, 207–212.

48. SHIMIZU, M., LASKER, J. M., TSUTSUMI, M. & LIEBER, C. S. (1990) Immunohistochemical localization of ethanol-inducible P-450IIE1 in the rat alimentary tract, *Gastroenterology*, **99**, 1044–1053.

49. KESSOVA, I. G., DECARLI, L. M. & LIEBER, C. S. (1998) Inducibility of cytochromes P-4502E1 and P-4501A1 in rat pancreas, *Alcohol: Clinical and Experimental Research*, **22**, 501–548.

50. SALMELA, K. S., KESSOVA, I. G., TSYRLOV, I. B. & LIEBER, C. S. (1998) Respective roles of human cytochrome P-4502E1, 1A2, and 3A4 in the hepatic microsomal ethanol oxidizing system, *Alcohol: Clinical and Experimental Research*, **22**, 2125–2132.

51. JOLY, J.-G., ISHII, H., TESCHKE, R., HASUMURA, Y. & LIEBER, C. S. (1973) Effect of chronic ethanol feeding on the activities and submicrosomal distribution of reduced nicotinamide adenine dinucleotide phosphate (NADPH)-cytochrome P-450 reductase and the demethylases for amino-pyrine and ethylmorphine, *Biochemical Pharmacology*, **22**, 1532–1535.

52. MISRA, P. S., LEFEVRE, A., ISHII, H., RUBIN, E. & LIEBER, C. S. (1971) Increase of ethanol, meprobamate and phenobarbital metabolism after chronic ethanol administration in man and in rats, *American Journal of Medicine*, **51**, 346–351.

53. GORDON, G. G., ALTMAN, K., SOUTHREN, A. L., RUBIN, E. & LIEBER, C. S. (1976) The effect of alcohol (ethanol) administration on sex hormone metabolism in normal men, *New England Journal of Medicine*, **295**, 793–797.

54. MA, X., BARAONA, E. & LIEBER, C. S. (1993) Alcohol consumption enhances fatty acid oxidation, with a greater increase in males than in females, *Hepatology*, **18**, 1247–1253.

55. MA, X., BARAONA, E., GOOZNER, B. G. & LIEBER, C. S. (1999) Gender differences in medium chain dicarboxylic aciduria in alcoholics, *American Journal of Medicine*, **106**, 70–75.

56. RAUCY, J. L., LASKER, J. M., KRAMER, J. C., SALAZAR, D. E., LIEBER, C. S. & CORCORAN, G. B. (1991) Induction of P-450IIE1 in the obese rat, *Molecular Pharmacology*, **39**, 275–280.

57. LIEBER, C. S. & ABITTAN, C. (1999) Pharmacology and metabolism of alcohol, including its metabolic effects and interaction with other drugs, *Clinical Dermatology*, **17**, 365–379.

58. RUBIN, E., GANG, H., MISRA, P. S. & LIEBER, C. S. (1970) Inhibition of drug metabolism by acute ethanol intoxication: a hepatic microsomal mechanism, *American Journal of Medicine*, **49**, 801–806.

59. ALTOMARE, E., LEO, M. A., SATO, C., VENDEMIALE, G. & LIEBER, C. S. (1984) Interaction of ethanol with acetaminophen metabolism in the baboon, *Biochemical Pharmacology*, **33**, 2207–2212.

60. BOROWSKY, S. A. & LIEBER, C. S. (1978) Interaction of methadone and ethanol metabolism, *Journal of Pharmacology and Experimental Therapeutics*, **207**, 123–129.

61. TSUTSUMI, R., LEO, M. A., KIM, C., TSUTSUMI, M., LASKER, J., LOWE, N. & LIEBER, C. S. (1990) Interaction of ethanol with enflurane metabolism and toxicity: role of P-450IIE1, *Alcohol: Clinical and Experimental Research*, **14**, 174–179.

62. MA, X., BARAONA, E., LASKER, J. M. & LIEBER, C. S. (1991) Effects of ethanol consumption on bioactivation and hepatotoxicity of N-nitrosodimethylamine in rats, *Biochemical Pharmacology*, **42**, 585–591.

63. HASUMURA, Y., TESCHKE, R. & LIEBER, C. S. (1974) Increased carbon tetrachloride hepatotoxicity, and its mechanism, after chronic ethanol consumption, *Gastroenterology*, **66**, 415–422.

64. SATO, C., MATSUDA, Y. & LIEBER, C. S. (1981) Increased hepatotoxicity of acetaminophen after chronic ethanol consumption in the rat, *Gastroenterology*, **80**, 140–148.

65. ALTOMARE, E., LEO, M. A. & LIEBER, C. S. (1984) Interaction of acute ethanol administration with acetaminophen metabolism and toxicity in rats fed alcohol chronically, *Alcohol: Clinical and Experimental Research*, **8**, 405–408.

66. HASUMURA, Y., TESCHKE, R. & LIEBER, C. S. (1975) Acetaldehyde oxidation by hepatic mitochondria: its decrease after chronic ethanol consumption, *Science*, **189**, 727–729.

67. KORSTEN, M. A., MATSUZAKI, S., FEINMAN, L. & LIEBER, C. S. (1975) High blood acetaldehyde levels after ethanol administration: differences between alcoholic and non-alcoholic subjects, *New England Journal of Medicine*, **292**, 386–389.

68. FREZZA, M., DI PADOVA, C., POZZATO, G., TERPIN, M., BARAONA, E. & LIEBER, C. S. (1990) High blood alcohol levels in women: role of decreased gastric alcohol dehydrogenase activity and first-pass metabolism, *New England Journal of Medicine*, **322**, 95–99.

69. GUPTA, A. M., BARAONA, E. & LIEBER, C. S. (1995) Significant increase of blood alcohol by cimetidine after repetitive drinking of small alcohol doses, *Alcohol: Clinical and Experimental Research*, **19**, 1083–1087.

70. DI PADOVA, C., ROINE, R., FREZZA, M., GENTRY, R. T., BARAONA, E. & LIEBER, C. S. (1992) Effects of ranitidine on blood alcohol levels after ethanol ingestion: comparison with other H_2-receptor antagonists, *Journal of the American Medical Association*, **267**, 83–86.

71. YOKOYAMA, H., BARAONA, E. & LIEBER, C. S. (1996) Molecular cloning and chromosomal localization of ADH7 gene encoding human class IV ADH, *Genomics*, **31**, 243–245.

72. AMIR, I., ANWAR, N., BARAONA, E. & LIEBER, C. S. (1996) Ranitidine increases the bioavailability of imbibed alcohol by accelerating gastric emptying, *Life Sciences*, **58**, 511–518.

73. ARORA, S., BARAONA, E. & LIEBER, C. S. (2000) Blood alcohol levels are increased in social drinkers receiving ranitidine, *American Journal of Gastroenterology*, **95**, 208–213.

74. PIROLA, R. C. & LIEBER, C. S. (1972) The energy cost of the metabolism of drugs, including ethanol, *Pharmacology*, **7**, 185–196.

75. PIROLA, R. C. & LIEBER, C. S. (1976) Energy wastage in alcoholism and drug abuse: possible role of hepatic microsomal enzymes, *American Journal of Clinical Nutrition*, **29**, 90–93.

76. LIEBER, C. S. (1991) Perspectives: do alcohol calories count? *American Journal of Clinical Nutrition*, **54**, 976–982.

77. ARAI, M., GORDON, E. R. & LIEBER, C. S. (1984) Decreased cytochrome oxidase activity in hepatic mitochondria after chronic ethanol consumption and the possible role of decreased cytochrome aa3 content and changes in phospholipids, *Biochimica et Biophysica Acta*, **797**, 320–327.

78. LIEBER, C. S., LEO, M. A., ALEYNIK, S. I., ALEYNIK, M. K. & DECARLI, L. M. (1997) Polyenylphosphatidylcholine decreases alcohol-induced oxidative stress in the baboon, *Alcohol: Clinical and Experimental Research*, **21**, 375–379.

79. NAVDER, K., BARAONA, E. & LIEBER, C. S. (1997) Polyenylphosphatidylcholine attenuates alcohol-induced fatty liver and hyperlipemia in rats, *Journal of Nutrition*, **127**, 1800–1806.

80. LIEBER, C. S., ROBINS, S. J. & LEO, M. A. (1994) Hepatic phosphatidylethanolamine methyltransferase activity is decreased by ethanol and increased by phosphatidylcholine, *Alcohol: Clinical and Experimental Research*, **18**, 592–595.

81. LEO, M. A. & LIEBER, C. S. (1985) New pathway for retinol metabolism in liver microsomes, *Journal of Biological Chemistry*, **260**, 5228–5231.

82. LEO, M. A., KIM, C. & LIEBER, C. S. (1987) NAD+-dependent retinol dehydrogenase in liver microsomes, *Archives of Biochemistry and Biophysics*, **259**, 241–249.

83. LEO, M. A., KIM, C. I. & LIEBER, C. S. (1989) Role of vitamin A degradation for the control of hepatic levels in the rat, *Journal of Nutrition*, **119**, 993–1000.

84. LEO, M. A., LASKER, J. M., RAUCY, J. L., KIM, C., BLACK, M. & LIEBER, C. S. (1989) Metabolism of retinol and retinoic acid by human liver cytochrome P-450IIC8, *Archives of Biochemistry and Biophysics*, **269**, 305–312.

85. LEO, M. A., IIDA, S. & LIEBER, C. S. (1984) Retinoic acid metabolism by a system reconstituted with cytochrome P-450, *Archives of Biochemistry and Biophysics*, **234**, 305–312.

86. SATO, M. & LIEBER, C. S. (1982) Increased metabolism of retinoic acid after chronic ethanol consumption in rat liver microsomes, *Archives of Biochemistry and Biophysics*, **213**, 557–564.

87. LEO, M. A., LOWE, N. & LIEBER, C. S. (1986) Interaction of drugs and retinol, *Biochemical Pharmacology*, **35**, 3949–3953.

88. SATO, M. & LIEBER, C. S. (1981) Hepatic vitamin A depletion after chronic ethanol consumption in baboons and rats, *Journal of Nutrition*, **111**, 2015–2023.

89. LEO, M. A. & LIEBER, C. S. (1982) Hepatic vitamin A depletion in alcoholic liver injury, *New England Journal of Medicine*, **307**, 597–601.

90. LEO, M. A., SATO, M. & LIEBER, C. S. (1983) Effect of hepatic vitamin A depletion on the liver in humans and rats, *Gastroenterology*, **84**, 562–572.

91. MAK, K. M., LEO, M. A. & LIEBER, C. S. (1987) Potentiation by ethanol consumption of tracheal squamous metaplasia caused by vitamin A deficiency in rats, *Journal of the National Cancer Institute*, **79**, 1001–1010.

92. LEO, M. A., LOWE, N. & LIEBER, C. S. (1984) Decreased hepatic vitamin A after drug administration in men and in rats, *American Journal of Clinical Nutrition*, **40**, 1131–1136.

93. LEO, M. A., LOWE, N. & LIEBER, C. S. (1987) Potentiation of ethanol-induced hepatic vitamin A depletion by pheno-barbital and butylated hydroxytoluene, *Journal of Nutrition*, **117**, 70–76.

94. LEO, M. A., ARAI, M., SATO, M. & LIEBER, C. S. (1982) Hepatotoxicity of vitamin A and ethanol in the rat, *Gastroenterology*, **82**, 194–205.

95. LEO, M. A. & LIEBER, C. S. (1983) Hepatic fibrosis after long-term administration of ethanol and moderate vitamin A supplementation in the rat, *Hepatology*, **3**, 1–11.

96. LEO, M. A., KIM, C. I., LOWE, N. & LIEBER, C. S. (1992) Interaction of ethanol with β-carotene: delayed blood clearance and enhanced hepatotoxicity, *Hepatology*, **15**, 883–891.

97. AHMED, S., LEO, M. A. & LIEBER, C. S. (1994) Interactions between alcohol and beta-carotene in patients with alcoholic liver diseases, *American Journal of Clinical Nutrition*, **60**, 430–436.

98. LEO, M. A., ALEYNIK, S., ALEYNIK, M. & LIEBER, C. S. (1997) β-carotene beadlets potentiate hepatotoxicity of alcohol, *American Journal of Clinical Nutrition*, **66**, 1461–1469.

99. LEO, M. A., AHMED, S., ALEYNIK, S., SIEGAL, J. H., KASMIN, F. & LIEBER, C. S. (1995) Carotenoids and tocopherols in various hepatobiliary conditions, *Journal of Hepatology*, **23**, 550–556.

100. LEO, M. A. & LIEBER, C. S. (1999) Alcohol, vitamin A, and beta-carotene: adverse interactions, including hepatotoxicity and carcinogenicity, *American Journal of Clinical Nutrition*, **69**, 1071–1085.

John Ball

John Ball MA PhD is an authority on the social epidemiology of drug abuse, and particularly the association of criminal behaviour with illicit drug use. He was President, of the American Society of Criminology from 1972–73 and is a Fellow of the American Society of Sociology. His publications include four books: Social Deviancy and Adolescent Personality, University of Kentucky Press, 1962; Narcotic Addiction (with John A. O'Donnell), Harper and Row, 1966; The Epidemiology of Opiate Addiction in the United States (with Carl D. Chambers), Charles C. Thomas Publishers, 1970; The Effectiveness of Methadone Maintenance Treatment (with Alan Ross), Springer-Verlag, 1991. This latter volume won the 1992 Addiction Book Prize.

Early career

Addiction: *You were born in New York City and received your early education there. How did you become interested in criminology and drug abuse research?*

John Ball: Although I had several encounters with youthful gangs while growing up in Manhattan, my real interest in criminology occurred during my graduate studies at Vanderbilt University in Tennessee. The Sociology Department was expanding there and I received the offer of an attractive fellowship.

A: *How did your interest in criminology develop at Vanderbilt?*

JB: Certainly a big influence in fostering my commitment to criminology was the fact that my dissertation involved interviewing hundreds of juvenile delinquents in a local reformatory and this first-hand experience was challenging in many ways. In particular, the task of testing or investigating theoretical concepts in the real world of criminal behavior was both difficult and stimulating. In addition, my major professor, Dr Albert J. Reiss Jr, was a criminologist, so this was a concomitant influence.

A: *What led you to move to the University of Kentucky, in Lexington?*

JB: When I finished my PhD in 1955, I looked around for professorships (or assistant professorships, as the case was at that time), and the offer at the University of Kentucky was the most attractive, so I went there to teach. I didn't know it when I went to Lexington, but the Federal Narcotics Hospital was located there. And in 1962, they established a social science section in the well-known Addiction Research Center which was located at this US Public Health Service Hospital. Dr Harris Isbell was the director of the ARC at the time.

Lexington

A: *Tell us a bit about that hospital.*

JB: The Federal Narcotics Hospital at Lexington was a combined hospital and prison with a thousand beds for narcotic, that's to say opiate, addicts. Half of the patients were prisoners and half were voluntary patients; they came from throughout the US. The Addiction Research Center was a separate entity within the hospital which was devoted to scientific research.

Dr Harris Isbell and Jack O'Donnell invited me to join them at ARC and establish a social science section. Jack and I planned a course of research studies that would give us an idea of the scope of the drug abuse problem in the United States with particular reference to opiate abuse. These studies focused on the demographic characteristics of the patients, their criminality, drug abuse history, etiology, treatment experiences and other aspects of their lives. So that was how we got started in Lexington. It was an extraordinary research opportunity. We didn't have any direction from Washington whatsoever, nor from Harris Isbell. We were given a completely free hand to develop a whole social science research program from the ground up, as it were. Harris Isbell merely said, 'Develop your own program'. And that's what we did.

So we amassed a database on some hundred thousand patients that proved to be tremendously efficacious

A: *Can you give us some idea of the scope and content of this research?*

JB: We focused on a number of topics. First, we sought to delineate the general characteristics of opiate addicts in the United States at the time – 1962. There were some 2300 admissions per year coming into the hospital, so we had ample opportunity to collect data from thousands of addict patients. We also had adequate staff and related resources, cooperation from the hospital and access to the records of all patients. Actually I decided to compile and computerize data on all patients who had been admitted to the hospital since it opened in 1935. Later, comparable data from the other Federal Narcotics Hospital at Fort Worth, Texas was added. So we amassed a database on some hundred thousand patients that proved to be tremendously efficacious in delineating the demographic characteristics of the patients at these two hospitals, their drug abuse history, criminal behavior, life history, treatment experiences, and so on.

A: *How did these studies work out?*

JB: This plan of initial studies worked out, I think, even more successfully than we had thought likely at first. We were able to collect a tremendous amount of information about the drug abuse

problem throughout the United States. In addition, we undertook special studies on the etiology of opiate addiction and related topics. For example, we pioneered follow-up field studies of patients after they left the hospital. Jack O'Donnell directed one such field study, which is a classic, of cohorts of Kentucky patients who were discharged from the beginning of the hospital until 1960.[1]

A: *You wrote a paper, which some workers in the field consider a classic, on two patterns of narcotic addiction.*

JB: Yes, we noted that there were different types of drugs being abused in various regions of the United States. In the two-patterns paper,[2] I identified two major types of opiate use in the United States, one which included concomitant marijuana use and heroin use and one which involved other prescription opiates without marijuana use. In another study of our addict population, we traced the life histories of a sample from the 900 Chinese-American patients who had been admitted to the Lexington Hospital. This project was undertaken with Dr M. P. Lau who was a visiting research fellow. These patients were found to be rather unique in that most had steady employment and a primary reason for their coming to Lexington was to obtain medical services. They also established a little Chinatown community within the hospital.[3]

A: *In retrospect what for you personally was the importance of the Lexington experience?*

JB: The Hospital and ARC were quite adequately staffed in terms of psychiatry, general medical coverage and related support. So this Lexington experience was my initiation into the field of drug abuse research. One of the most important aspects of this experience was that it involved first-hand interviews and informal conversations with hundreds of patients over a period of six years. This set the stage for later research, in two ways. One was the importance of direct contact with addict patients. Thereafter, I never lost sight of patients and always wanted to collect information directly from the patients or from whomever we were studying.

A second major outcome from my time at Lexington was the development of new methodology to employ in the study of drug abuse. In addition to the database that I described, we developed procedures for follow-up field studies. For instance: how to locate and interview former addict patients, how to collect urine samples from addicts in the community, how to assess the reliability and validity of interview data collection from patients and similar issues.

Our studies, of course, built upon the prior research experience amassed at Lexington. For, by this time, the ARC had established itself as a leader in biomedical and pharmacological research. And Michael Pescor's studies of thousands of addict patients admitted during the early years (1936–40) were especially valuable in planning our social science research program.[4,5]

A: *Did you know Michael Pescor?*
JB: No, I never met Michael Pescor. But I should mention some of the other staff who were at Lexington. In addition to Dr Isbell there was Abraham Wikler, Frank Fraser, William Martin and, later, Don Jasinski and Chuck Gorodetsky. We also had medical residents coming through on 2-year military service, some of whom turned out to be leaders in the field – Jerome Jaffe, Herb Kleber, George Valliant and others. During this period, Lexington was a center for most of the drug abuse research going on – not all of it certainly, but a great deal of it. We had a critical mass of scientists, so it was a special place at which to develop a social science section because we had not only extensive laboratory support but also continual interaction with senior scientists.

A: *Did Harris Isbell later get interested in the sociology of drug abuse?*
JB: He was interested from the beginning.

A: *But you said he gave you little direction?*
JB: He was interested from the beginning in studying the drug abuse problem from a social science viewpoint. And he had a strong commitment to scientific methods. In this regard, he said: 'My job is to support you and keep Washington off your back and let you go ahead and do your research'. Once when we said that we had a new

staff person who seemed promising because he was empirically orientated and doesn't get off into ideology and politics, I recall Harris saying: 'Isn't that true of all sociologists?' And we said: 'No, Harris, it isn't. It's difficult to get social scientists who will be researchers and be objective and stick with the task at hand'.

So Lexington, I think, was a formative period in terms of my career. Everything that happened after those six years seemed to build on this foundation of first-hand research involving patients, site visits and looking at the problem in depth.

Once when we said that we had a new staff person who seemed promising because he was empirically orientated and doesn't get off into ideology and politics, I recall Harris saying: 'Isn't that true of all sociologists?' And we said: 'No, Harris, it isn't'

The move to Temple University

A: *What were the factors that led you to leave the ARC as a full time researcher and go on to Temple University, in Philadelphia?*
JB: There were two factors that led to my leaving Lexington. One was government censorship of scientific publications. The federal government is usually not a congenial place for social scientists because what social scientists report is often at variance with government policy, and that causes problems. So we were having problems with delay and censorship of scientific publications, and that was one reason I left. Another reason was that I had better opportunities elsewhere.

A: *When you talk about the censorship, how many levels of the bureaucracy had to read your materials before you were actually free to publish it?*
JB: As far as I know, the delay and censorship was just at ARC.

A: *Are you saying that some people at the ARC felt they had to read everything that you produced before you could submit it for publication?*
JB: That's correct.

A: *And that slowed things down in the late 1960s to the point that you felt that you had to move on?*
JB: Yes, and some things could not be published. They were just prohibited.

A: *Were there findings that seemed controversial then, that seem less controversial now? I wonder if you could mention a couple of papers that the government seemed reluctant to release at that time?*
JB: It wasn't on that level. It was on the level of biomedical scientists believing that social science is not scientific enough. Thus, when you talk about peer group involvement and the beginning of drug abuse, even though it's data collected directly from patients or through observation, it's not regarded as scientific enough from a bench scientific viewpoint. So if the people over you are bench scientists, they may be reluctant to support what you are doing, or they may fundamentally not understand. This was not true of Dr Isbell.

A: *Well, then, in 1968 you began to look around for another position.*
JB: Yes, there were lots of opportunities at that time.

A: *The Narcotic Addict Rehabilitation Act was being implemented and the Federal Hospital at Lexington was turned into a research demonstration facility at that time. Did that impact upon your decision to stay in any way?*
JB: No, I left before that happened. Shortly after I left, the social science section was closed, never to be resurrected in the federal government. The federal government has had problems with the social sciences. Many social scientists are difficult people to work with; there's a political aspect.

A: *Did Jack O'Donnell leave about the same time?*
JB: No, Jack O'Donnell stayed on and he completed a number of significant studies.[6,7]

A: *And you went on to Temple?*
JB: I went to Temple University, in Philadelphia, to the Department of Psychiatry, where I was able to analyze and publish additional drug abuse research findings collected at Lexington.[8,9] In this regard leaving Lexington had the advantage of affording me a new perspective on our research findings. I was less occupied with such topics as hospital policies, but focused more upon broader epidemiological and life history issues.

A: *What do you think were some of your key achievements at Temple?*
JB: During my 17 years in the Department of Psychiatry at Temple University, I continued to study the criminality and life career of heroin addicts and other drug abusers.[10–12] Another series of studies carried out at Temple focused on site visits to and study of various drug treatment programs.[13] One of the most significant of these was a statewide survey of all drug abuse programs in Pennsylvania. This involved site visits to 77 programs with 5578 patients. This early statewide on-site study was important as it provided the first overview of the various types of drug treatment programs which were operating in Pennsylvania.[14]

Looking at treatment programs

A: *Isn't it true that this Pennsylvania study was one of the very early examples of attempting to look at across-program data?*
JB: Yes, we certainly were struck by the tremendous variations among the drug abuse treatment programs we visited with respect to treatment objectives, staff, services provided and patients admitted. Indeed, at this early period (1971) it was often quite difficult to ascertain the number and location of the programs within the state.

A: *How did it happen that there were so many programs and so little knowledge about what was being developed at various levels within the state?*
JB: Well, what happened in the United States in the 1960s was that numerous drug treatment programs sprang up with or without public funding or approval. These programs were private pro-

grams, religiously orientated programs, city, state or federal programs. At the beginning, these diverse programs were not coordinated in any way, so no one knew the number of treatment, counselling or rehabilitation programs that existed. It was for this reason that the State of Pennsylvania funded our state wide survey.

A: *Coming from the Lexington environment, what was your feeling about methadone programs? The people at Lexington were somewhat skeptical about methadone. Did you share that skepticism when you first came to Pennsylvania?*

JB: I wasn't thinking of methadone programs in particular at the time of our Pennsylvania survey. As to skepticism, I suppose one could say that I had equal skepticism about all drug abuse treatment programs (with regard to outcome). In this regard, I tried to keep our site-visiting team orientated toward objectivity as we visited and studied the programs. With regard to their skepticism and bias, this was only evident with regard to religious programs like Teen Challenge. That is, there was a definite bias against these programs at that time among professionals and, unfortunately, it has continued up to the present time, even though on an objective basis some of the religiously orientated programs are as effective as others.

A: *Didn't you also have some national experience in studying drug abuse treatment with Ray Glasscote?*

JB: Yes. I'd been part of a team of psychiatrists and social scientists who conducted a national on-site survey of drug treatment programs for the American Psychiatric Association. The five of us (Raymond M. Glasscote, James N. Sussex, Jerome H. Jaffe, Leon Brill and myself) visited nine drug treatment programs in five states. During our site visit (and afterwards) we collected descriptive data about the history, staffing, policy, operation and patients at these drug treatment programs.[15]

A: *Did your interest in surveys of drug abuse treatment programs continue at Temple?*

JB: Yes, while at Temple, I also became interested in the international aspects of drug abuse epidemiology and treatment. This interest led to studies in England, Sweden and other countries as well as to an international survey of drug abuse treatment in 25 nations.[16–18]

A: *How did this international study come about? Were you selected or funded for this activity?*

JB: No. This is an interesting question that you raise. In my career, I've been fortunate in being able to conduct research that I believe in personally. There has been little or no requirement that I conduct research or prepare reports that I don't believe in. Almost none. In the case of the drug abuse survey of 25 nations, I decided that I was going to do this with or without funding, I just did it.

What I'm going to do, I'm going to do. If I have funding, I can do it larger or faster; but I'm going to do it if I think it's important in advancing our knowledge of drug abuse

A: *That seems surprising. In the United States, most people believe they need grant support to undertake the smallest investigation. What made you so confident that you'd find the support to undertake such a world-wide study?*

JB: Well, everything again goes back to Lexington. Jack O'Donnell's follow-up life history study of Kentucky addicts was done with little additional funding other than the ongoing support from the hospital. Today, it would cost at least 10 times more, even controlled for inflation. In the Kentucky follow-up study, the cost of data collection was $40 000. The other part of the Lexington experience was that it was not money orientated. We had 6 years during which we were part of the federal annual budget, so we didn't have to go seeking funds. We could concentrate on the research. I guess that experience always held me in good stead as time went on. What I'm going to do, I'm going to do. If I have funding, I can do it larger or faster; but I'm going to do it if I think it's important in advancing our knowledge of drug abuse.

A: *So the study in 25 nations was largely your own personal investigation of what was happening in 25 nations? You didn't hire research assistants?*

JB: That's correct. But of course, I always had some assistants or secretaries wherever I was.

A: *You didn't need to get a grant that would then tie you to the specifics, but you could pursue that which you felt was important at the time.*

JB: Yes, but it's not one or the other. Of course you need support from outside sources in most projects. The state survey was supported by the State of Pennsylvania, for example. But I want to emphasize that if you feel you want to do something and you're committed to do it, then you find whatever resources you can or you get by and you just go ahead and do it. I think in the history of science there's quite a bit of this. Nowadays I think we're missing the boat when we believe that we have to have tremendous funding to do anything.

A: *Who were some of your important colleagues during that period in Philadelphia?*

JB: I worked with Dr David Nurco, Dr Carl Chambers, Dr A. Thomas McLellan, Dr Jerome Jaffe, Dr Vincent Dole and others. It was also while I was at Temple that I worked at the Special Action Office for Drug Abuse Prevention, in the Executive Office of the President, Washington, DC. I spent a year at this office. Dr Jerome Jaffe at first was the Director, and for the second half of my stay there, in 1973, Dr Robert Dupont was the Director.

The Special Action Office

A: *Was that year at the Special Action Office interesting?*

JB: This was an exceedingly challenging year for me. It was almost the exact opposite of the Lexington experience, because here I was at the top policy level, not directly involved with patients, but now involved with the media, with the White House, and with planning and developing national programs. My work involved developing research and evaluation programs. I did not do research myself in the sense that I've been describing previously, but this was research direction – assisting others in planning and conducting research throughout the United States. It was during this period that the Special Action Office supported studies about the Vietnam veterans coming back, the national household survey, the national survey of high school students, career training programs for physicians, and treatment strategies for states in drug abuse treatment and prevention. There was, at the same time, a tremendous expansion of methadone maintenance treatment in the United States.

So this year in Washington was quite important in helping me understand how the drug abuse problem is addressed at the highest government levels. The Special Action Office was involved in establishing the structure for the National Institute of Drug Abuse.

This, then, was an exceptional experience in which I learned about the political and bureaucratic complexities of national drug abuse policies and the role of research in Washington. I came to understand why in Washington, 'inside the beltway' is the name of the game; that is, most of the players in the Special Action Office and in Washington were interested in what's going on in the capital because that's where their future lies. There are advantages and disadvantages to this beltway orientation. I also came to understand the role (or roles) of research in the government and the difficulty of articulating national policies and the allocation of resources with research findings.

Before I went to the Special Action Office I was naïve in assuming that research funding was allocated on the basis of research priorities. But I found that research is allocated on the basis of pressure from States, federal bureaucracies and powerful politicians, as well as other considerations. I also learned about the pervasive role of the media in addressing the drug abuse problem in the United States. The media was of paramount importance in terms of the allocation of resources because it is a major part of the political arena. So, in some ways, the Special Action Office was a world in which tomorrow's *New York Times* and *Washington Post* became exceedingly important.

It wasn't just at this office either, but wherever I went in the government I came to realize that there's a tremendous gap between research findings and policy.

The difficulty of articulating policy with research funding exists because in Washington, and throughout the country, people have their own agenda and interests. Thus, they want more money for particular agencies or cities or states, and they're not as interested in research results which are based on scientific criteria.

A: *Can you give me some concrete examples to help appreciate your experience?*
JB: Yes. I recall the administrative officer coming to see me one day and he said: 'Do we have anything – any projects – out on polydrug abuse, because Congress is very interested about polydrug abuse, and the media is interested, and this new term is a buzzword'. I said: 'Ralph, we're lucky on this one. We happen to have two projects out on polydrug abuse; one is at Harvard and one is at Chicago'.

This and similar experiences led me to formulate three reasons for funding research at this government level. One was a political payoff; that is, a mayor might come from New York or another city and say: 'I'm not getting my share of money'. Well, one way of giving him money is to give him research and development money, which is just a gift and nothing is expected of this. That's one reason for putting out money for research. Another is to cover the bases, and this is what Ralph was talking about. The media and Congress are happy if we have anticipated the problem and we have studies already under way. If these are at Harvard and Chicago, nobody can fault us – we're intelligent and have anticipated the problem. So this is covering your bases. And of course the third reason is you might actually want to find out something.

A: *After the Special Action Office, you returned to Temple.*
JB: After I returned to Temple, I got quite involved in studying methadone maintenance treatment and evaluating methadone maintenance as a modality of treatment.

Evaluating methadone programs

A: *How did you come to develop so specialized an interest in this?*
JB: Well, I was awarded a considerable NIDA grant, partly through happenstance. Dr David Nurco was instrumental in this regard. He invited me down to Washington. NIDA was interested in looking in depth at specific modalities of treatment. The idea was to look at the effectiveness of methadone maintenance treatment in numerous programs. I was asked to outline how I thought it should be done. Then, quite unexpectedly, someone said: 'Well, why don't you do it?' So, I was trapped. That was, I guess, good fortune.

So then I planned a systematic evaluation of methadone maintenance treatment programs in New York, Pennsylvania and Maryland. The National Institute on Drug Abuse supported this large scale project. Again the same principle applied in terms of site visits. We went ourselves to the programs many times. I interviewed all of the doctors and directors; others (Dr Eric Corty, Henrietta Bond and Anthony Tommasello) interviewed the rest of the staff and collected the program data. There was a tremendous amount of fieldwork involved in collecting data at the programs and 'on the street'. I believe that we collected more information about the programs than has ever been collected before as we went to the programs repeatedly over a 3-year period. So that was the beginning.

Then I moved from Temple (while we were still in the midst of this project, actually) to the University of Maryland at Baltimore, in the Department of Epidemiology at the medical school. From there I had an opportunity, as the 3-year grant was finishing, to go back to the Addiction Research Center (which meanwhile had moved to Baltimore) in order to continue the analysis of the data on this large scale project. I thought it was important to publish these findings in a volume[19] as well as special papers.[20-22] I spent the next 6 years at the Addiction Research Center focusing primarily on methadone maintenance treatment.

As I got more and more involved with methadone maintenance treatment, I discovered that there was a definite constituency associated with this modality of treatment. This constituency of providers, researchers, administrators, patients and others were not only interested in my evaluation project but provided significant advice and support. Thus, Dr Vincent Dole provided advice and encouragement from the start and program directors were especially helpful over the years. Mark Parrino and the American Methadone Association assisted by promoting the published evaluation results.

A: *Were the results of your evaluation of methadone programs different from your original expectations?*
JB: What happened was, quite to my surprise, that we found that the programs were much more effective than we had originally thought.

We were quite surprised to find the magnitude of the effectiveness of the methadone programs; a tremendous reduction in patients' intravenous drug use occurred

---

A: *That suggests, does it not, that even though you had studied methadone programs with the APA survey and in Pennsylvania, you had remained somewhat skeptical of their effectiveness?*
JB: It wasn't a question of skepticism. The surveys looked at the programs in a general descriptive sense. But what we did in the three-state study was collect detailed information on programs, patients, services and outcome. In a technical sense, we determined how effective the programs were. So these two were quite different types of studies. The first (e.g. APA and PA) were one-shot surveys of programs and their patients while the 3-year study of programs in New York, Pennsylvania and Maryland were comprehensive evaluations of patient and program outcomes which were replicated at the programs a year later to ascertain the stability of the findings.

Methadone is effective, but with great variation between programs

A: *Could you elaborate a little on what influence you think your study of methadone may have had?*
JB: As I mentioned, we were quite surprised to find the magnitude of the effectiveness of the methadone programs; a tremendous reduction in patients' intravenous drug use occurred; over 80% gave up needle use after a year in treatment. Concomitantly there was a 79% reduction in crime. Indeed, I came to see that methadone maintenance programs were a way of impacting the drug abuse and crime problem in the United States in a substantial manner. So that if one were to ask me today how one might reduce the drug abuse problem in the United States, I could say there's one way that we absolutely know is effective.

A: *So, you consider expansion of drug abuse treatment as a high priority for the United States?*
JB: I think that the expansion of methadone maintenance programs would certainly impact the crime problem, but it is important to note that some programs are markedly more effective than others. So, improvement of the programs is equally as important.

Beyond this point, it's important to emphasize that drug abuse treatment alone is not a solution for the drug abuse problem. Effective treatment is a way of mitigating the problems associated with drug abuse; it is a way of reducing drug abuse, crime and HIV infection among the 500 000 active heroin addicts in the United States. It's a way of containing this social problem until such time as prevention or other measures are brought to bear.

A: *Does this suggest that before you personally evaluated methadone maintenance programs that you were somewhat unconvinced about the efficacy of these programs, and that you became more convinced only after you yourself had collected the data?*
JB: No question about that. That's absolutely true. I'm a hardnose researcher. So it was only after I personally had conducted this comprehen-

sive treatment evaluation in three states that I felt comfortable explaining in detail about the effectiveness of methadone maintenance treatment. Indeed, some of our findings had not been reported before, such as the tremendous difference in effectiveness of specific methadone maintenance programs. We found some programs to be twice or three times as effective as others, and these results had not been reported before.

A: *So would it be fair to say that the major thrust of the book was to point out the variability among treatment programs in a way that led people to focus on how to improve the quality of treatment, as well as on how effective they can be?*

JB: Two further points seem worthy of note. First, we found a general insufficiency of treatment and rehabilitation services at almost all programs. The level of staffing and funding was such that medical services were often inadequate or unavailable; vocational services were virtually nonexistent. So, the findings of considerable (but partial) effectiveness must be viewed with regard to the services provided. From a research perspective, we cannot say what effectiveness we might obtain if maximum and comprehensive services were provided.

Secondly, our repeated visits to scores of drug treatment programs – but especially the in-depth study of programs, in New York, Pennsylvania and Maryland – led to a realization that drug abuse treatment *programs* have been neglected as a focus of study. We came to see the programs as social entities. Each of these can have a positive collective treatment and rehabilitation ethos or a mere bureaucratic dispensing orientation. In any case, the importance of studying programs seems paramount.

Difficulties in the science – policy connection

A: *Does your experience lead you be optimistic or pessimistic about the future role of research in influencing government policy? Why is this so difficult?*

JB: I would mention several reasons why, in my view, we have had only limited success up to the present. First, there's no one academic or scientific discipline that provides direction and credibility in this field. So our understanding of the drug abuse problem is disjointed and segregated. I frequently speak with scientists who find it remarkable when I say that the etiology of drug abuse in the United States (and in most of the world) is a peer group recreational endeavour among adolescents and young people. The biomedical and social science knowledge is not integrated. There's no one lead discipline that is committed to the drug abuse problem comprehensively.

The same is true within the federal government. There is no lead agency to effectively direct and coordinate research and programs. Thus, we have the National Institute on Drug Abuse, but it's reduced in status from the Special Action Office in the federal bureaucracy. But neither this nor any other agency has effective control over the other agencies that also are involved in drug abuse treatment, evaluation and research. So it's not becoming a higher priority; it's becoming a lower priority.

There's no one lead discipline that is committed to the drug abuse problem comprehensively

All of this is related to the fact, as I referred to before, that the politicians and the media have their own interests. Their interests are survival, maintaining the bureaucracy, and developing news stories. There's a lack of any commitment of one discipline, or political group, or the media to addressing the drug abuse problem consistently and systematically. So that's where we are today. We drift along in this way. The research has been successful, but the political aspects of it – or putting research into practice – has been less successful.

References

1. O'DONNELL, J. A. (1969) *Narcotic Addicts in Kentucky,* Public Health Publication No. 1991 (Washington, DC, US Government Printing Office).

2. BALL, J. C. (1965) Two patterns of narcotic drug addiction in the United States, *Journal of Criminal Law, Criminology and Police Science*, **56**, 203–211.

3. BALL, J. C. & LAU, M. P. (1966) The Chinese narcotic addict in the United States, *Social Forces*, **45**, 68–72.

4. PESCOR, M. J. (1943) A statistical analysis of the clinical records of hospitalized drug addicts, *Public Health Reports* (suppl. 143), 1–30.

5. PESCOR, M. J. (1943) Follow-up study of treated narcotic drug ddicts, *Public Health Reports* (suppl. 170), 1–18.

6. O'DONNELL J. A. (1968) Social factors and follow-up studies in opioid addiction, in: WIKLER, A. (Ed.) *The Addictive States*, ch. 26, pp. 333–346 (Baltimore, William & Wilkins).

7. O'DONNELL, J. A. & CLAYTON, R. R. (1982) The stepping-stone hypothesis – marijuana, heroin, and causality, *Chemical Dependencies: Behavioral and Biomedical Issues*, **4**, 229–241.

8. BALL, J. C. & CHAMBERS, C. D. (1970) *The Epidemiology of Opiate Addiction in the United States*, pp. 1–337 (Springfield, Illinois, Charles C. Thomas).

9. BALL, J. C. & URBAITIS, J. C. (1970) Absence of major medical complications among chronic opiate addicts, *British Journal of Addiction*, **65**, 109–112.

10. BALL, J. C. (1976) Sex differences in criminality among drug abuse patients in the United States, in: GIBBINS, R. J. *et al.* (Eds) *Alcohol*, ch. 10, pp. 457–469 (New York, Wiley).

11. BALL, I. C., ROSEN, L., FLUECK, J. A. & NURCO, D. N. (1981) The criminality of heroin addicts when addicted and when off opiates, in: INCIARDI, J. (Ed.) *The Drugs–Crime Connection*, ch. 2, pp. 39–65 (Beverly Hills, Sage).

12. BALL, I. C., SHAFFER, J. W. & NURCO, D. N. (1983) Day-to-day criminality of heroin addicts in Baltimore – a study in the continuity of offense rates, *Drug & Alcohol Dependence*, **12**, 119–143.

13. BALL, J. C., GRAFF, H. & SHEEHAN, J. J. (1974) The heroin addicts' view of methadone maintenance, *British Journal of Addiction*, **69**, 89–95.

14. BALL, J. C. & GRAFF, H. (1975) Drug treatment programs in Pennsylvania – a statewide evaluation, *American Journal of Public Health*, **65**, 592–598.

15. GLASSCOTE, R., SUSSEX, J. N., JAFFE, J. H., BALL, J. C. & BRILL, L. (1972) *The Treatment of Drug Abuse: Programs, Problems, Prospects* (Washington, DC, American Psychiatric Association).

16. GLASER, F. B. & BALL, J. C. (1971) The British narcotic 'register' in 1970 – a factual review, *Journal of the American Medical Association*, **216**, 1177–1182.

17. BALL, J. C. & BEJEROT, N. (1975) A Swedish heroin addict, *Addictive Diseases*, **1**, 391–393.

18. BALL, J. C. (1977) Issue Editor. Drug Abuse and its treatment as seen from 25 nations, *Addictive Diseases*, **3**, 1–140.

19. BALL, J. C. & ROSS, A. (1991) *The Effectiveness of Methadone Maintenance Treatment* (New York, Springer-Verlag).

20. BALL, J. C. & CORTY, E. (1988) Basic issues pertaining to the effectiveness of methadone maintenance treatment, in: LEUKENFELD, C. G. & TIMS, F. T. (Eds) *Compulsory Treatment of Drug Abuse: Research and Clinical Practices*, NIDA Research Monograph 86, pp. 178–191 (Washington, DC, Department of Health and Human Services).

21. BALL, J. C., LANGE, W. R., MYERS, C. P. & FRIEDMAN, S. R. (1988) Reducing the risk of AIDS through methadone maintenance treatment, *Journal of Health and Social Behavior*, **28**, 214–226.

22. BALL, J. C. (1991) The similarity of crime rates among male heroin addicts in New York City, Philadelphia and Baltimore, *Journal of Drug Issues*, **21**, 413–427.

LeClair Bissell

LeClair Bissell BA, MA, MD is a founder of the Smithers Center, Roosevelt Hospital, and was its Director from 1968–82. She was President of the American Society of Addiction Medicine (ASAM), and won the Elizabeth Blackwell Award from the American Medical Women's Association in 1998, and the ASAM Award in 1999. Books include Alcoholism in the Professions (with Paul Haberman), Oxford University Press, 1984, and Ethics for Addiction Professionals (with James Royce), Hazelden Press, 1987, revised 1994.

Addiction: *LeClair, you were one of the early members of the American Medical Society on Alcoholism. You also started – created, in fact – the Smithers Center in 1968 which was one of the first rehabilitation units in the USA to be part of a major medical center, Roosevelt Hospital, and the first in the USA to be part of a university hospital, Columbia. You have also done a great deal of work, research and teaching about impaired health professionals. You did a first longitudinal follow-up study of impaired physicians, as well as impaired nurses, lawyers, dentists, social workers and psychologists.[1, 2] In addition to all that, you have been a tireless lecturer, educator and advocate for the cause of the alcoholic and addicted person. Which of these various things has been most rewarding to you?*

LeClair Bissell: That depends upon how you interpret rewarding. I don't think there is anything more gratifying than having an individual patient get well. In terms of what might have been most significant about a lifetime of work and what might have created change in the field, I suppose working with impaired professionals would have to be the most rewarding.

A: *In 1968 when you started Smithers Center you had just completed a fellowship in endocrinology.*

LeCB: Yes, although I had never been particularly interested in endocrinology. It was part of a bargain with Dr Nicholas Christy, my then chief of medicine and an endocrinologist himself.

We agreed that if I worked with him in endocrinology for two years, at the end of that time he would give me attending privileges at the hospital where we both worked and permit me to do an alcoholism service there if I could find the funding.

I don't think there is anything more gratifying than having an individual patient get well

---

A: *During your residency in internal medicine (1964–68) what were the attitudes towards alcoholics who were patients and towards you as an alcoholic physician?*

LeCB: The attitude toward the patients who were alcoholic was basically that their alcoholism was not something that was of concern to a physician. This was something that should be dealt with – if addressed at all – by the social workers. It was not a medical responsibility. Physicians did scold and threaten. They were very good at warning people that continued drinking was going to irreparably damage their livers or result in repeated bouts with pancreatitis but there were no indications that they were trying to tell the patient how not to drink or where to obtain help. They didn't even do as simple a thing as refer the patient to AA. In fact, to me, one of the saddest things and one of the real failures in all of the years that

I worked at Roosevelt was that it never became fully understood that an alcoholic patient admitted to the hospital should have an alcoholism consultation and be offered treatment if indicated at the, to my mind, very excellent alcoholism service that existed right under the hospital roof.

Setting up an alcoholism treatment unit in New York

A: *How was the alcoholism service funded?*
LeCB: I had to be able to fund myself completely, which meant that I had to find a way to pay my own salary and that of any help. Brinkley Smithers had evidently heard good things about me and liked what he'd heard. He was also trying to find a place where alcoholic patients could be hospitalized within New York City other than at a drying-out facility.

The attitude toward the patients who were alcoholic was basically that their alcoholism was not something that was of concern to a physician

---

A: *Was everything at that time limited to alcoholism? Obviously, there are a lot of alcoholics who have used other drugs. Did you treat other substance abusers?*
LeCB: No, not initially. From the very beginning, we had patients who were in trouble with benzodiazepines which were introduced in the early 1960s – it was already 1968 when we got started and although there was not much literature about benzodiazepine addiction, there were certainly a lot of people who were addicted. As a matter of fact, one of our major problems was the tendency of colleagues to substitute one sedative addiction for another. Soon we had Valium addicts created largely by our colleagues. On the other hand, there was relatively little smoking of marijuana and cocaine had really not made its debut to any significant degree.

A: *And heroin was doubtless in another system entirely.*
LeCB: Initially, no. Things tended to divide not so much by drug, even then, as by social class.

A: *How did the residential rehabilitation unit get started in 1974 and how did patients get referred?*
LeCB: It came about, again, through the generosity of Brinkley Smithers who, quite to my astonishment, asked me to lunch at the Plaza Hotel one fine day and announced that he was prepared to give several million dollars for the establishment of a first-class alcoholism center for both treatment and training at the Roosevelt Hospital. When the Rehab opened it had 44 beds. There was absolutely no competition for alcoholic patients. Nobody wanted them, you see. And prior to Senator Hughes' Bill in 1970, hospitals were allowed to – and in fact did – reject alcoholic and addicted patients just because of their diagnosis.

A: *When you were setting up the rehabilitation unit was it a state-of-the-art of alcoholism treatment at that time? How did you know what to do? What kind of models were available?*
LeCB: What I did was try to visit those places whose models appeared to be successful. Now this was not a great research study but I was very familiar with AA (Alcoholics Anonymous) in New York and for a variety of reasons had access to many people who had been through treatment. I heard constantly what they had to say about their treatment, what they found effective and what they hadn't. It became very clear to me that at least in an AA population there was an enormous amount of recovery coming from places like Hazelden in Minnesota, Caron Foundation in Pennsylvania and for older sedative addicted women, at Little Hill Alina Lodge in New Jersey.

A: *How did you get involved with the studies of the healthcare professionals?*
LeCB: Well, actually that began with a kind of internal temper tantrum on my part. I was

a second-year student in a psychiatry class at Psychiatric Institute at Columbia and I had been waiting eagerly for the lecture on alcoholism that was going to tell me more about the disease that I had experienced. What I was told was that all alcoholics had passive dependent personalities and latent homosexual problems and that they were extremely difficult to treat. Not only were they not amenable to treatment but, among other things, they would never find AA acceptable except perhaps for a small group of unsophisticated alcoholics who were likely to accept a rather evangelical, fundamentalist religion.

A: *That negative experience inspired you?*
LeCB: Well, I was mad! I was particularly angry in that I was just back from a meeting of a group called International Doctors in AA where I had had a delightful weekend with some 70 other physicians in Toronto. Many of them were considerably brighter and more competent than the psychologist who was giving us the lecture. So I decided that some day when I had the time and money, I was going to do a paper which was going to be up-front propaganda. I was going to locate and interview face-to-face, nose-to-nose and breath-to-breath, at least 100 alcoholics who were in recovery who were physicians and who were themselves members of AA. I wasn't going to include anyone who had been sober for less than one calendar year at the time of interview. Since all were going to be AA members, I could show that physicians did find AA acceptable and that the program worked because I wasn't going to talk to anyone who was still drinking. It didn't much matter what I found out about them. My point would be made by the existence of the sample. Now, you have to realize that I had never done any research so when I announced that I was going to do this, and some dentists started asking me why they weren't included, I said I would include them. It was the same story with the nurses. Then some social workers said they wished to be included. Someone else said the idea was interesting but these would all be healthcare people and, since I couldn't have a control group, I could at least have a comparison group of people of equal education who were not medical. I

decided on 50 attorneys and 50 college women and by the time we got through talking we had agreed to interview 500 people. Then, to make it even worse, there were other folks saying that we should do a 5-year follow-up study because that would be better science. We didn't know you couldn't do this kind of thing using volunteer people to do the bulk of the interviewing. Even though one used volunteers it would still be much too costly unless one had an enormous federal grant. So, since we didn't know it wasn't possible, we did it but it did not get done in five years. The interviewing took too long initially and then it took longer than five years to follow up on everybody.

What I was told was that all alcoholics had passive dependent personalities and latent homosexual problems

A: *This is a huge study. How many people did you have in it and what percentage of those did you follow up on after five years?*
LeCB: We had slightly over 500 people all together and we followed up on over 95% where we were able to get good information. In some cases they had died and we found out very quickly that the next of kin was an extremely bad source of information because they frequently were still into denial that the alcoholism had ever existed. But the AA sponsor, the next-door neighbor and other friends and acquaintances vigorously tried to help us learn what had occurred so we did get the information, and in the process we learned that it is entirely possible to follow up on alcoholics if one only puts the time and energy into it, particularly if the sample one starts with are people who have a year or more of recovery initially.

A: *If you had to say, what do you think was the most important finding of your study?*
LeCB: It would be its propaganda value.

A: *Besides the propaganda what would it be?*
LeCB: I would say that probably one of the most important things was that there had been such an

enormous variety of treatment experiences. Every-one in the study was, in a sense, a success because they had been sober a minimum of one year and in most cases several years. A number of them – just under 20% – of that original study and sub-sequent studies managed to get sober and stay that way using Alcoholics Anonymous alone. Then, for those who did have treatment, frequently the treatment didn't occur until after sobriety and was used to deal with problems and difficulties not directly alcohol related. Other people had been to as many as 30 or 40 different hospitals. I think another thing that was extremely significant was that there were many, many admissions and contacts with the treatment professions, with indi-viduals who were not delivering alcohol-specific treatment. As soon as people were being treated for alcoholism *per se*, and that was acknowledged up front, then a variety of treatments appeared to be able to work.

As soon as people were being treated for alcoholism *per se*, and that was acknowledged up front, then a variety of treatments appeared to be able to work

A: *What portion of the people who were one year sober at the beginning of the study was sober at the 5-year interval?*
LeCB: Almost all. It was close to 90%. But anyway, when you are starting with a group that has been sober, in many cases, two or three years, the chances of their being sober another 5 years – or another 10 years – are much greater than if they are fresh from an initial treatment.

Are addicted professionals special?

A: *Having done this large study on health pro-fessions – is there any justification to the claim, particularly about doctors, that they are sicker than other people, that they are more vulnerable to addiction due to the stress of medicine? Based on your treatment experience as well as your study, what are your thoughts about that?*

LeCB: Well, based on my treatment experience, I think they are less sick and much easier to treat than many other groups. I think one reason for that is that in order to become a physician or a dentist or a veterinarian or a pharmacist, one has to have jumped over a great many hurdles. One must pass the exams, survive the screening tests and the interviews, be able to organize oneself well enough to do examinations and so on, and be observed by a good many colleagues along the way. Therefore I think the more grossly psychotic, or sicker, are frequently screened out along the way. The ones we get in treatment are usually people who are less brain-damaged, are still quite capable of learning, are reasonably bright. Not only that, but they are quite well motivated in most cases to hang on to their license, the threat of the loss of which is frequently what puts them in treatment in the first place. So are they hard to treat? No! Are they easy patients? Yes! Are they more likely to be addicted than other groups? We don't know. I could make a case that perhaps they are, since they may believe the widespread myth that information about other drugs and alcohol equals prevention. People think that once you teach high school students a lot of facts about drugs and what they do, then they won't become addicts. Well, if that were the case you would never have an alcoholic pharmacist. But I think the alcoholic doctors buy into it and think they know too much to become alcoholic.

A: *Physicians are people who believe in drugs?*
LeCB: Yes, I think we physicians have a faith in drugs. We prescribe them all the time. They do good things for our patients. We see them working miracles for other people. It's very tempt-ing to try to create the same miracles for ourselves. There certainly is the issue of availability as well. If we choose to use, the drugs are handy and we know how to lay hands on them. How im-portant that is I don't know, and I don't think anyone else knows either, but I do believe that availability very, very clearly influences the choice of drug. For instance, when I was interviewing attorneys and comparing them to physicians, there were almost equal numbers of them who, in addition to alcohol, were using barbiturates, tran-

quilizers and amphetamines. Where one saw the difference was not in the fact of being addicted to a drug other than alcohol. Very similar numbers reported themselves as addicted, but when you asked what the drug was, that was quite different. Each profession used what was easily available. Veterinarians used ketamine, dentists used nitrous oxide, nurses used Demerol, but the simple fact of addiction to a drug other than alcohol did not differ across the professions within or outside health care.

A: *All this is in your book,* Alcoholism in the Professions,[2] *and other papers.[3,4] Switching now to your work with the American Medical Society on Alcoholism. Now, as the American Society of Addiction Medicine, it has more than 3000 members. How many were there when you were in it in the beginning?*
LeCB: I can't tell you how many there were, but I can tell you that we fitted very easily into Ruth Fox's living room.

A: *In your years in the field, there have been a number of enduring controversial topics. None of them has really gone away. The first one, of course, is the very old topic of controlled drinking. Could you tell me your feelings about it.*
LeCB: My own feeling is very straight forward, and very rigid and very absolute. I do not believe that an alcoholic should ever attempt to go back to controlled or social drinking.

A: *Why?*
LeCB: Simply because experience shows that relatively few people are able to do this successfully and that those who fail at it pay a terrible price. Now, that does not mean that this never happens. I'm very aware of the fact that people exist who definitely were alcoholics – no question about it, most of whom remained abstinent for quite a prolonged period of time, made major changes in their lives and then subsequently went back to fairly light-weight drinking. But just because you do have exceptions to a general rule, I don't think that ever justifies setting up a patient to make the attempt, particularly since we are quite incapable of saying which person is going to be able to do it

successfully and who will pay with his life for the attempt. I simply don't think that being able to drink is something of such extremely marvellous value that we should encourage people to do it. It would be like saying of former heavy smokers that a certain number of them will be able to go back to light-weight smoking and not have any problems with their hearts and lungs. We don't encourage abstinent heroin addicts once they have become 'main liners' to return to weekend skin popping, nor would we even if heroin were legal. Alcohol is society's favourite drug and one we don't even like to call a drug.

I do not believe that an alcoholic should ever attempt to go back to controlled or social drinking

Understanding alcoholics anonymous

A: *Another issue is the role of Alcoholics Anonymous and other self-help groups in the process of treating patients and the extent to which these groups are religious organizations, subjecting many to a kind of brainwashing which some claim goes on there. What are your thoughts about that?*
LeCB: My thoughts on that are pretty complicated but to start out with, *AA does not claim to be doing treatment.* Other people call it treatment. AA doesn't use the word. It's a mutual support group of men and women in a fellowship trying to keep each other sober. Now, I don't see AA and other treatment as mutually exclusive at all. I would think that AA provides something for many people that most treatment systems do not and cannot. One is availability – 24 hours a day in many cities, at virtually no expense to the members, a life-long support group should they feel that they need and want it. Very different from offering one appointment on Thursday at 3:00! AA for a time was hypercritical of treatment and frequently interfered with medications prescribed by doctors for alcoholic patients and I think in many cases rightfully so, because there was a great deal of foolish pre-

scribing going on. However, some AA members tried to interfere beyond their level of competence and expertise with other medications and caused harm.

A: *What about the religious part?*
LeCB: This is very different depending on which AA meeting you attend. AA was founded initially by white male Christians who thought it was a fine idea to have a Christian prayer at the end of AA meetings, something still done at most of them – the Lord's Prayer. Some groups begin with another prayer or sometimes readings from the big book of Alcoholics Anonymous and sometimes from other readings. There's as much liturgy in these groups as there is at many churches and a great many AA members when asked about their churchgoing behavior, according to some of our research, made it very clear that they didn't go to church anymore but they did go to AA and found it filled the same need. It is also true that, at least in one case, a judge found that AA could be classified as a religion. He sided with an atheist who objected to being forced to go to AA meetings. There is in certain parts of the country an enormous amount of religiosity in some AA groups but each group is autonomous and it is quite possible for groups to decide that they are not going to do that.

A: *AA as substitute dependence?*
LeCB: The notion of substitute dependence, using AA as a crutch, frankly doesn't much bother me. You know the old truism that if you have a broken leg, a crutch isn't such a bad idea. Ruth Fox used to say one of her jobs in treating alcoholics was to get rid of their dependence on drugs and alcohol and substitute a dependence on people. I don't find that too objectionable. I certainly find it not as objectionable as being dependent on a Fundamentalist church and an individual pastor who may or may not be a particularly healthy person. Does it result in an over-dependence on the program? For some individuals, I think yes. I have known some people who attend AA on a daily basis even after some years of being members. The vast majority, though, decrease meetings over time. In our orig-

inal study many of the participants who had been sober for 20 or 30 years were going to one or two meetings a year, if that, and then usually just to take a newcomer to the meeting. Also, I know many atheist and agnostics who are quite comfortable in AA as are many Jewish alcoholics, some of whom supplement AA with additional meetings designed for Jews.

A: *There have been a number of charges also leveled against the notion that AA is for everyone. Do you think there are people who cannot use AA?*
LeCB: Yes. But I say that with less conviction now than I used to. I used to say that people who were very schizoid and very withdrawn, and very unattractive, who stood too close to you, had bad breath, sprayed saliva in your face, were almost certainly not going to be asked to go for coffee by the other members of the AA group. They could not use AA. Now that we are in the days of the computer, with the on-line chat rooms and the vastness of AA offerings available on the Internet in any language, at any time of day, a great many of those lost and homeless souls are finding their own way into AA. I would hope that AA and the treatment community might outgrow the posture of competition and learn to complement one another. There are quite enough alcoholics and addicts to go around and we haven't the time or the money to contend with one another.

References

1. BISSELL, L. & JONES, R. W. (1976) The alcoholic physician: a survey, *American Journal of Psychiatry*, **133**, 1142–1146.
2. BISSELL, L. & HABERMAN, P. W. (1984) *Alcoholism in the Professions* (New York, Oxford University Press).
3. BISSELL, L. & SKORINA, J. K. (1987) One hundred alcoholic women in medicine: an interview study, *Journal of the American Medical Association*, **257**, 2939–2944.
4. BISSELL, L., HABERMAN, P. W. & WILLIAMS, R. L. (1989) Pharmacists recovering from alcohol and other drug addictions: an interview study, *American Pharmacy*, NS29, 391–402.

Avram Goldstein

Avram Goldstein was born in 1919 in New York, USA. He is a pharmacologist and neuroscientist whose career has been devoted mainly to research on addictive drugs. He gained an MD from Harvard in 1943 and for 34 years until 1989 was at Stanford University (for 15 years Chairman) as Professor of Pharmacology. He established the first methadone program in California, and was also founder and director of the Addiction Research Foundation at Palo Alto. He is a recipient of the Franklin Medal and the Nathan B. Eddy and Torald Sollmann Awards, a member of the National Academy of Science and Honorary Professor of Beijing University. Books include Biostatistics: an Introductory Text (1964), Principles of Drug Action (1968, revised 1974) and Addiction: From Biology to Drug Policy (1994).

Addiction: *Avram, can you tell us something about how your early interests and career developed?*
Avram Goldstein: I didn't really know what I was going to do before I entered Harvard. Once I was there, I knew I was going to be some sort of a scientist because I knew that was what interested me in life, but I didn't know much about it. In my sophomore year I took a course in organic chemistry and I was fascinated by it, and I thought, 'I'm going to be an organic chemist.' But in those days there was a lot of antisemitism and I was a bit concerned about that. So I went to see my organic chemistry professor, Louis Fieser, who was a great organic chemist, to get some advice from him. I told him I wanted to be a chemist, and I expressed my concern about the issue of a Jew making a career in chemistry. And he said, 'You're right; it's a tough field. Why don't you go to medical school so you have some options in case you can't make it in chemistry?' So I took his advice. The curious thing was that medical schools had quotas [limiting the number of Jewish students], but I did get into Harvard Medical School. I had a good record in college, and I had gotten involved in my first research in my senior year there. Harvard had a really wonderful honors program in biochemical sciences and I was in that program. You were assigned to a tutor and then often you could get a chance to do research in the tutor's lab. My tutor was Friedrich Klemperer, a biochemist in Baird

Hasting's department of biochemistry at Harvard Medical School. Klemperer had his lab at the medical school, so at the beginning of my senior year I got involved in a research project there. That was the first that I saw of the medical school and my experiences there were so good that I then later applied to Harvard Medical School and managed to get in. I think I probably got in on the basis of this research project that I did with Klemperer, which – in some ways – was a very funny research project.

I knew I was going to be some sort of a scientist because I knew that was what interested me in life

---

A: *What did that research involve?*
AG: There were some elements of it that were prescient about my future career because the project involved the question of chirality in the compound allantoin. Certain dogs excrete allantoin instead of uric acid as an end product of nitrogen metabolism; uric acid is not chiral, but allantoin has one chiral center, so there are two forms of allantoin – an L and a D form. The question was, is there chirality or not? So, we had a dog, and I had to go around collecting this dog's urine. It was an absurdity, because I would take the dog out into the little courtyard at the medical school, and I was holding a pan and running after

the dog, and as soon as the dog began to squat I was there with the pan to collect the urine. This went on day after day, week after week, getting enough urine to isolate the allantoin and then to put it in a polarimeter. Anyway the long and short of it was that the allantoin was in fact of one kind, it was not racemic. It was optical rotatory allantoin. That in turn implied that it must be formed by an enzymic process, otherwise you would get racemic allantoin. That sounds dumb, nowadays; of course it would be formed by enzymes. But this was a long time ago – 1940. Now, I said that this was prescient in a way of my future interest in chirality and receptors and in a lot of the stuff that came later.

A: *You were clearly interested in pharmacology before you developed an interest in substance abuse. What led you eventually to substance abuse research?*

AG: I had no interest in substance abuse at all for at least half my career in pharmacology. I was interested in various aspects of pharmacology. My main interest was in mechanisms of action, and that started while I was still in medical school and embarking on my research career. I was interested in mechanisms of enzyme action. I published papers that were at that time seminal papers on the mechanism of enzyme substrate inhibitor interactions and inhibition. The enzyme I was interested in then was cholinesterase and I published a lot on the cholinesterase enzyme. Later on I became interested in other aspects of pharmacology and drug action. Early in the days of molecular biology that seemed to be the really exciting thing to get into. You may remember that the turning point in molecular biology was 1953. That was the date of the Watson/Crick paper, but there was a lot of exciting molecular biology going on even before the structure of DNA was understood. I got involved in antibiotics and how antibiotics worked on bacteria.

A: *What was the first thing that pointed you towards drug abuse?*

AG: I guess the first thing that pointed toward drug abuse, in a way, was my interest in drug resistance. Looking back on it, that was when I was a second-year medical student taking phar-

macology and I went to Professor Otto Krayer and said, 'I want to work in your department.' I was precipitated to do that by a particular experience in the student teaching lab. That was the application of epinephrine to a little piece of smooth muscle in a tissue bath. You add this tiny bit of epinephrine – much too little to measure by any chemical means – and this piece of smooth muscle contracted. Because I was interested in mechanisms I said to my lab instructor (Rafael Mendez, who's now a professor in Mexico) 'What's going on? Why did it do that?' He said, 'I don't know.' I said, 'What do you mean you don't know?' And he said, 'Well nobody knows. That's what happens.' I said, 'Well, that's interesting that you don't know something as obvious as that. You put a compound on a piece of muscle, it contracts, and they don't know why – that sounds like a field for research.' So I went to Krayer and said how do I get to do research in his department? And he said to me somewhere along the way in my first few months working in his department, 'Why don't you write down what you would be interested in if you were doing a career in pharmacology?' And I typed out a naive paragraph or two saying that the issue of adaptation to drugs – adaptation in terms of tolerance and dependence – was certainly the most fascinating thing that we had learned about in the lectures in pharmacology. I found out that nobody knew anything about that either, and I thought that some day I would study that.

A: *And you subsequently made major contributions in this area of research?*

AG: Well, I had it in the back of my mind for many years after that, but I never got around to it until the bacterial work. In the bacterial work one was dealing, on the surface, with a similar situation, in that you have an antibiotic and it looks like the bacteria somehow adapt to living with the antibiotic, and what are the changes that take place? Well, it turned out that was completely wrong. Even in streptomycin dependence, where you would think it must be an adaptive process because the bacteria come to require streptomycin in order to live, it all turns out to be a matter of selection on pre-existing mutations and not an adaptation at all. So in a way that was kind of a blind alley. I participated in a very modest way in demonstrating the pre-existing mutations in streptomycin dependence while I was an instructor at Harvard and had my lab there.[1] The fact that it was not an adaptation had something to do with pointing me off bacteria and on to real life, real animals and real people.

A meeting that had consequences

A: *Was there any other impetus that led you in that direction?*

AG: Yes, but it happened only around 1969 by a convergence of interesting events on the social scene, on the socio-economic scene, and in science. Vincent Dole, who had with Marie Nyswander just invented methadone treatment in New York a few years before that, came to Stanford to lecture. I didn't know anything about his work before he came and when I heard about it I thought it was absolutely fascinating. But my lab was doing bacterial genetics and things like that, and I think nothing would have come of that first personal meeting with Dole if not for the cultural changes of the 1960s. There was tremendous feeling that science wasn't serving the people, if I can put it in what at that time were Maoist terms. Students were radicalized, and a lot of things were going on. So I thought very deliberately after Dole's talk. I reexamined what we were doing, and in the light of this upheaval I thought, what am I really doing? What we're doing in the lab has very little to do with real problems that need to be solved and here is this guy in New York who's actually doing something.

A: *What did you think of Dole's position at that time?*

AG: He's a scientist – a good scientist. (Of course Dole was a lipid biochemist before Marie dragged him into real life.) But, I thought here's something real going on and it sounds like there's a lot of research to be done there to understand the realities of heroin addiction and the people who are ruining their lives with it, and to understand methadone that somehow works. And I thought about what Dole had to say and, from discussions that I had with him, about what he really

knew about how methadone works mechanically – mechanistically. Certainly he had evidence that seemed persuasive that it did work, although I must say I thought his evidence was pretty anecdotal. He didn't conduct any kind of rigorous experimentation on methadone itself and when it came down to how this had worked there really wasn't any clear concept. Obviously it was substituting in some way for the morphine or heroin that the addicts were using. But exactly how it was doing that wasn't clear. Dole attributed it partly to tolerance – to developing a tolerance for heroin and partly to better pharmacokinetics. But I must say the thing was kind of fuzzy.

I thought, what am I really doing? What we're doing in the lab has very little to do with real problems that need to be solved and here is this guy in New York who's actually doing something

A: *How did you react to this situation?*

AG: After some soul searching about what we were doing, I called my lab group together (I had a small group then of six or eight students and post-docs) and I said, 'We're going to switch all the research we're doing, quit the microbial stuff, wind up what we're doing on the existing grants and apply for new grants to work on opiates. And there's no way we're going to find out anything about opiate addiction or opiate tolerance or opiate dependence unless we know where the opiate receptors are. That's the way it is. If you're going to find out something, you've got to know what receptor you're dealing with. So we're going to start searching for the opiate receptor and see if we can pin it down.' We made that transition over a few months and started work looking for the opiate receptor.

A theory of dependence

A: *Is it possible that your interest in this area of research actually developed somewhat independently of your meeting Vincent Dole? You made a wonderful presentation on a theory of enzyme expansion in terms of the nature of physical dependence at the 1967 meeting of the Association for Research on Nervous and Mental Diseases. In 1968, when Abe Wikler pulled together the state of knowledge at the time, your paper was published in a volume called The Addictive States, the Proceedings of that symposium.[2]*

AG: Right.

A: *Were you looking at receptors in 1967 when you presented those data at that conference?*

AG: The data were microbial.

A: *It appears that you were interested in the issue of tolerance and even physical dependence even before you met Vincent Dole until 1969. Meeting him must have stimulated you to shift your focus a little bit.*

AG: Yes, that's right.

A: *Can you say something about your work on caffeine? In 1969 you published one of the great pioneering studies of caffeine withdrawal.[3]*

AG: You're absolutely right. The caffeine study was a flat-out classic study of addiction. It's still the best study in the literature on caffeine withdrawal, although there's an interesting aspect to that. Most studies have their own lifetime. They're forgotten eventually and people reinvent them. And that's what happened with the caffeine work. An amazing number of people studying caffeine now don't cite that study and apparently don't read it. I think one of the reasons is that MEDLINE only begins in 1966.

A: *A number of older researchers have noted that people are repeating experiments because of the limits of computer searches.*

AG: Yes, it's true. Well, now that you mentioned it, let me say a word about this enzyme expansion theory. This is something that was developed jointly with my wife [Dora B. Goldstein], and she deserves full credit with me. I don't know which of us had the idea first. It was just an idea, and was published in only two places. There's a preliminary abstract somewhere – just a short abstract/presentation called 'Enzyme expansion

theory of drug tolerance' or something like that, and it was just an application of what we had learned in molecular biology with respect to microbial systems. And we said, 'Hey, this could be an explanation of tolerance and dependence.' Then that was expanded in the 1968 paper that you're talking about, which was published in the *Journal of Research on Nervous and Mental Disease* (it was a symposium presentation).

A: *You've studied a number of drugs over the years, caffeine – a classic study – and opioids, for example, but not alcohol. Did you stay away from alcohol research in deference to your wife, Dody, who is a distinguished alcoholism researcher?*

AG: Absolutely. And that opens a whole interesting discussion about women and feminism and so on. Dody was stuck in the situation of being my wife and making the huge mistake of taking my name when we married (a mistake for scientific purposes) and publishing under that name. For a long, long time it was just assumed that she was my lab assistant or something like that whenever we published jointly. We realized that and decided we were not going to work together or publish together any more. And I didn't say it to her, but I said to myself, 'You're going to stay away from alcohol.'

A: *So it was deliberate.*

AG: It was very deliberate.

Setting up a methadone clinic

A: *You mentioned that when Vincent Dole came to Stanford and talked about switching from lipid metabolism to clinical studies, you were inspired to take a similar step. Although you were pursuing research on the opioid receptor, you established a methadone clinic in San José. In doing so, you became one of the few basic scientists who developed a treatment program in order to learn more about addicts. Was your clinic the first methadone clinic in California, and how did you go about establishing it? Also, given your productivity as a basic pharmacologist, why were you willing to sacrifice so much to set up a clinic?*

AG: Well, my problem was that I was jumping into the field of opiates and I didn't know anything about heroin addiction, and I felt that I had to. And since I was trained as an MD and had a little bit of clinical experience in the Army, I felt competent to do clinical research. I've always had a great respect for clinical research and I think that many of my basic science colleagues don't have a clue about how difficult clinical research is to do, so they have this arrogant attitude that clinicians really don't know what they're doing and they're not scientists. The fact is that lab research is easy, easy, easy compared with doing good, rigorous clinical research. I've always had that attitude, so I felt that I ought to be able to do controlled, rigorous clinical research and I could use the occasion to learn about heroin addicts.

Now there was no way to learn about heroin addicts, because they were hidden out there, except to set up a treatment program. And since Dole had inspired me I thought I'd look around California to see where they were doing it. There was one tiny little methadone program that had gotten started out in the Central Valley. So our program was the first major program. It was difficult to establish because the attitudes were entirely negative toward heroin addicts, as Dole had found in New York. The law enforcement folks had taken complete control of the issue of heroin addiction. That had happened all over the country following the Harrison Act in 1914, so to establish the idea that this was a disease that you were going to try to treat was very difficult to do. It had to begin with a few people.

A: *So how did you get started with your clinic?*
AG: San José was the big city nearest to us. I had a lot of help from Bob Campos who was involved with treating heroin addicts in San Francisco on the hospital wards there. He'd never been a drug user or an addict himself but he had a lot of friends who were. He came from Albuquerque, New Mexico, and he was of Chicano (Mexican American) background. He knew one or two physicians in San José who were on the right side of the issue and had a humane interest in heroin addicts, and so with them we began to organize a citizens' advisory committee. Then we had to go

to the County Board of Supervisors to get them on our side. Then it was a matter of going to the police and getting police cooperation. So it all finally worked out, and we then went to the mental health system where we decided to establish the clinic and we got to the director there, a man named Meinhardt, who was very supportive and interested.

A: *Your clinic was specifically designed as a research base?*
AG: Yes. This was in contrast to what Vincent Dole had done initially. We were going to study some issues and to try to settle them in controlled experiments. One that I thought was important to begin with was the issue of dosage. Of course, Dole was not the only one in the world doing methadone at that time. There was Jerome Jaffe in Chicago, who probably set up the second program in the country (I don't know the exact history.) So people were starting to do it in different places and the Chicago program did have some research protocols in place, I think, from the beginning.

The fact is that lab research is easy, easy, easy compared with doing good, rigorous clinical research

A: *Why did you focus on dosage?*
AG: We decided to study the issue of dosage because a lot of people were beginning to say that these methadone patients are 'zonked out' on too much methadone, and the Dole program seemed to have no limits on dosage. So we started to do blind dosage studies, and we found out what was an adequate average dosage and what was not, and we published all those findings. It turned out that this work was misunderstood a little bit. I did establish that, for most of our patients at any rate, a dosage of 50 mg/day was an adequate dosage, but there were certainly people who needed more. I don't think there were many who needed less. And what we understand now is that 60 to 80 mg is the correct dosage range, so I think that we were on the right track about that. We did some interesting studies in which we did blind escalation of dosage for people who were complaining that their

methadone 'wasn't holding them' and their urines were showing that they were still using heroin, and those results were very clear that, for those people at any rate, escalating dosage was no use at all. Whatever the reasons were that they were not being satisfied, higher dosage up to 120, 150 mg, didn't make any difference at all. We also established an absolutely rigorous system of urine monitoring, urine collection. We had random systems of urine collection, and that business of urine assays led to other interesting developments.

We couldn't keep people on naltrexone any more than others could, except for a very selected few professionals who did do well on naltrexone

A: *Were there other ways your clinic differed from Dole and Nyswander's clinic at Rockefeller?*
AG: Yes. There was something else that we did that was quite different from Dole's approach and leads to a general issue about how you treat patients. There is a tendency – it's still out there – among people working with heroin addicts to get sentimentally overattached to them as people and they can't imagine that a heroin addict would lie, or claim that they weren't using heroin when they were. I just thought that was ludicrous and I still do. I guess I use a sort of 'tough love' approach in helping them – you can't help anybody unless you know what the facts are, and you can't know what the facts are about their drug use unless you measure it in the urine; there's nothing else that substitutes for that. Of course that applies to everything about treatment and treatment success.

A: *After starting this research clinic, you decided to create an entire institute which had a built-in treatment program. Did you do that because you became fascinated with clinical research, or did you think you had to learn even more about heroin addiction?*
AG: No, it wasn't to learn more about heroin addiction. As I got more and more interested both in the basic research and in the clinical research on opiates, I had the dream of establishing an institute for addiction research. At that time the only such institute in the world, as far as I know, was the Addiction Research Foundation in Toronto, and I thought that the only way to make real progress in this fascinating problem that was such a mix of basic science and clinical science was to study the whole thing in one place through an integrated interdisciplinary approach to the problem. So in one place you would have basic lab research going on, and you would have human volunteer subject research going on, and you would have clinical treatment research going on. And I tried to establish that at Stanford. I got support from the Drug Abuse Council, which was active in those days, which was a consortium of foundations interested in drug abuse. Tom Bryant who ran the Council was very supportive and they gave me a lump sum that was enough to build a small institute near the Stanford campus. So I established what we called the Addiction Research Foundation of Palo Alto right next door to the medical school. I wanted to do something new. I didn't want to replicate all this methadone stuff but LAAM was the hot thing as I saw it. So we set up specifically a LAAM clinic, and we never used methadone at the Foundation. We eventually treated about 150 patients on LAAM and established some new policies for its use and collected a lot of toxicology data on it that eventually went to the FDA [Food and Drug Administration]. Eventually, I guess, it was part of a submission that a million years later led to the New Drug Application that was eventually approved.

A: *I guess you were disappointed that it took 23 years for the federal government to get around to approving LAAM for clinical use.*
AG: It was outrageous, ridiculous. Even now LAAM is approved by the federal government and still not approved by various states. The whole system is insane, of having 50 State by State approvals of essentially the same medical procedure. It just doesn't make any sense.

A: *Did you also use naltrexone at the clinic?*

AG: Yes we did. We did some studies of naltrexone after LAAM withdrawal to see whether we could have any more luck with naltrexone than anybody else had had. And the brief answer to that was – no. We couldn't keep people on naltrexone any more than others could, except for a very selected few professionals who did do well on naltrexone.

The most interesting study that we published on LAAM has not been picked up and used. The concept was that since LAAM is so persistent in its effect and you only have to give it three times a week, might it be possible to get off LAAM by abruptly terminating it and letting it self-detoxify? We did an elaborate experiment in which we did exactly that. It was a placebo controlled kind of thing; one group was tapering, and the other group was holding steady and then abruptly dropping. Then we measured withdrawal effects and our general conclusion from the data was that you could just as well stop LAAM abruptly. Of course you got withdrawal symptoms, but when you did it gradually you also got withdrawal symptoms and they lasted for a longer time, and our impression was that people were worse off that way than if they just went through an abrupt termination.

A: Regarding getting people off, at one time you advocated a controversial approach – at least it was controversial in the US – of getting people to make contact with treatment by providing intravenous heroin, then moving them to methadone, then to LAAM, and eventually withdrawing opioids and giving them naltrexone. Looking back on it, what do you think of that approach?
AG: That's the famous 'steps' approach. Nobody ever tried it because it's too difficult and complicated to try it. I think that's the problem with it. You could give people heroin, but at least in this country the issues of liability and litigation prospects have to be taken into account. You're going to have addicts in an outpatient environment, you're going to give them heroin, you're going to send them out, they're going to go out under the influence of an acute dose of heroin – it's just terribly complicated from a practical point of view, and I suspect that it really isn't practical.

But I still think it's a good idea as a way of reaching out and getting people; you sort of get them where they are. I think that getting methadone to people out where they are is more worth thinking about, such as mobile methadone delivery vans as they're doing in Baltimore and a few other places. I saw it done in Amsterdam, where you have a methadone van that goes around and it looked like a hell of a good idea.

A: Have you done a follow-up study of the Albuquerque clinic in which you were involved?
AG: We completed a 22-year follow-up. After I retired at Stanford I had a little time, and I wondered what happened in Albuquerque – what happened to all those people from 20 years ago, and so I mounted a study to look at that. I wanted to do it myself. That idea of doing something myself has always been prominent in my scientific career. I want to do hands-on work. I was able to get some private foundations funding. The happiest day of my life was the day I applied for my last research grant from NIDA [National Institute on Drug Abuse]. That whole grant process – you live with it all your life, you get fed up with it – so I was not going to apply for any research grants from NIDA to do this thing.

It was a lot of searching and a lot of interviewing, using a structured interview. The study was published in 1996 in *Drug and Alcohol Dependence*.[4] The results were both very interesting and very depressing because the group had an average age of 26 at the time they entered treatment and 22 years later 30% of them were dead. That's an extraordinary death rate. We did a Kaplan/Myers survivorship plot and the standard mortality ratio is five times the comparable population group in New Mexico. The causes of death were almost all drug overdose, sequelae of alcoholism and violence. There were very few natural deaths. These people of course are on and off methadone throughout that 22 years; and they're in and out of prison – the criminality story is not very good either. Some people argue that if treatment were only available all the problems of heroin addiction would be solved. Here you had treatment available from the beginning and all the way through, and it's not true – at least in that group.

Very bad prognosis. The second thing it shows is what a lethal chronic disease heroin addiction is. That's an extraordinary death rate. As for criminality – again the kinds of crimes don't really change: property crimes, violent crimes, burglary continue.

A: *In your Palo Alto clinic, didn't you find that you saw some improvement while people were actually in treatment?*
AG: Yes, absolutely. And we saw the same thing in Albuquerque if you look at the people who are actually in methadone treatment. We did that two ways. We did it first concurrently – the ones that are now in methadone treatment (some of them have been in long term treatment, and some of them have been on and off), are doing a lot better than the others with respect to all of these measures. But the other thing that was interesting – we did a retrospective interview asking people to reconstruct their lives over that whole 20-year period. Now that's subject to all the pitfalls of subjective recall and all of that, but what's interesting about it is that all of these people had periods in which they were on methadone and periods in which they were not on methadone and so they could relate how they were doing in both of those times. So you're looking at within-subject comparison of time on methadone/time off methadone, as recalled subjectively, and there methadone comes out way ahead.

> I have to say honestly that when you look at it in the harsh light of reality, I missed the boat on two major discoveries – I mean really major discoveries

A: *It argues, does it not, for efforts to make it easier to stay in treatment and for more effort to reach out and get people into treatment?*
AG: Absolutely. Our conclusion also agrees with Nurco's, where he showed very clearly in Baltimore that people on methadone engage in less criminality.

A: *And also, perhaps, one should argue for some significant restructuring of the regulations that make it difficult to stay in treatment?*

AG: That's a very important point. About regulations, I don't know; I think that's a tricky issue. Yes, you want to make it easier to stay in treatment, but if you don't have any kind of discipline in the treatment you're not teaching people what they need to know to run their lives. There's got to be a certain amount of regulation.

The great race to find the opiate receptor

A: *Let's talk about your work on receptors. With all of the important studies on treatment, you still managed to be active in basic science research and to be on the forefront of opiate receptor studies and endogenous ligand studies. Do you think that in the great race to find the opiate receptor your seminal contributions (which come from your allantoin studies, if you will), have been under-appreciated?*
AG: I have to say honestly that when you look at it in the harsh light of reality, I missed the boat on two major discoveries – I mean really major discoveries. One was this opiate receptor characterization, and the other was the discovery of endogenous opioids – the characterization of endogenous opioids. With respect to the first, you asked the question, 'How could you do all of these things?' I have always believed that we had everything we needed to crack that opiate receptor problem. We were doing it right.

A: *That was your 1971 paper?*
AG: Yes, that was in 1971.[5] What I mean is, we actually had it. All we needed was a very high-specificity radioactive ligand. What you don't know (and what I have not talked about before) is that we had that high-specificity radioactive ligand in the safe. And I think the reason that we didn't push on and crack that problem had a lot to do with these other things that were going on and distracting me. I really think if I had been in my lab all the time that we would have done it differently and we would have cracked it. As it was, we didn't and, yes, the 1971 report was a seminal paper; it was how to do it, and the three guys who did it two years later followed that exact methodology. But that's a little like sour grapes. The fact

is that their 1973 papers really put the opiate receptor on the map and our paper did not, even though we clearly showed the stereospecific binding, but you had to do some handwaving to show it – it was based on a lot of statistical analyses of differences between D and L. It was a missed boat.

A: *Even though you showed others the slipway?*
AG: I think so.

A: *You said you missed the boat on the endogenous ligand, yet there are those who would say you didn't, that others missed some of it and you were the one who showed that extra family.*
AG: That's right. The extra family I'm very proud of. That was the kind of accomplishment that puts one on the map, and that's fine. Yes, others didn't believe it. I believed it; I pushed it. I remember very well (this was before the Hughes and Kosterlitz paper in early 1975), that when I was saying we have something here that is different from what Kosterlitz seems to have, nobody knew what it was. And then when they actually demonstrated the sequence, I said we have something that is really different. And I remember Roger Guilleman saying, at some meeting or other, 'I'll believe you when you tell me the sequence.' Well, he was right. And when we eventually showed him the sequence – that was 4 years later – that was it.[6]

But I say we missed the boat because we were both, Kosterlitz and I, privy to the same information at the same time. We had the same ideas; that was in 1972. When Huda Akil in John Leibeskind's lab showed that naloxone blocked stimulation-produced analgesia, it made it crystal clear that there was an endogenous opioid system controlling nociceptive inputs. Kosterlitz had more experience with smooth muscle than I did. In fact, I went to Kosterlitz's lab – it must have been in 1972 when we were in Aberdeen for the INRC [International Narcotics Research Club] meeting. I knew Kosterlitz well, we were old friends; we had founded the INRC together. I went to his lab to have him show me how to do the little longitudinal muscle preparations. I brought the technique back to my lab and we set it up immediately.

So there was a real competition, and we were in a good position to compete. Brian Cox was working with me. He was in charge of my lab, and started right away looking for the endogenous opioid. We knew exactly how to do it, which was of course the same way that Kosterlitz was doing it. We were looking for inhibition of the electrically stimulated contraction of that little bit of muscle, an inhibition that would be blocked by naloxone. We decided to use as starting material pituitary powder that was available in large quantity at Armour because of the cleverness of a biochemist there named Fisher. He had been setting aside all the stuff they didn't need in producing endocrine materials and he had a huge amount of pituitary powder, so we could get a kilogram of porcine pituitary powder, and that looked like a good source of material. Now, Kosterlitz and Hughes had decided to use pig brain, so they used very large numbers of pig brains, and that was the source of their material. If you look at pituitary powder you find dynorphin; if you look at brain you're more likely to find enkephalins and beta-endorphin.

So, by March of 1975 we had the first hit. We found what we were looking for – material that was naloxone reversed, and we reported that in 1975 at the INRC meeting that I was the organizer of at Airlie House in Virginia.[7] That was where Kosterlitz and Hughes reported their progress, too. They still didn't know what they had, but they had something and we had something and they looked different. So later that year they had enough material to purify to get them a sequence, and it took us another four years to purify enough material to get a sequence, but we were dealing with much less material than they were. I wouldn't say we were stupid or anything like that; we were doing the right thing, but it just happens they got there first.

A: *The readers who are not in biological science may not fully understand the issue of being first. You were the first to discover dynorphin – a totally separate group of endogenous ligands. Are you saying that that doesn't count as much as finding the enkephalins, which are a different group of endogenous ligands?*

AG: I can say two things about that. One is that we know now that there are three genes that code for the endogenous opioids. The endogenous opioids were a novel family of related peptides, so therefore the first endogenous opioid to be characterized carries more weight in the world of science than the third one to be discovered. But certainly dynorphin was an important discovery. The second thing is that in relation to addiction, so far, at least, it looks as though the enkephalins and beta-endorphin and their receptors are more intimately involved in the process of opiate addiction than the dynorphins and their receptors; although more and more evidence keeps turning up of an interaction between them, with kappa agonists opposing the effects of mu agonists. We know that the mu receptor is the primary receptor that mediates the discriminative cue of morphine and that mediates most of the morphine effects and opiate addiction. And the endogenous mu-receptor agonists are the enkephalins and endorphins, primarily beta-endorphin.

I guess when you put old things together in a new way you have an invention

Inventing a methodology for drug testing

A: *Let's turn back to another area of invention where you made an important contribution. You actually invented the methodology for accurate, rapid, inexpensive assessment of drug use by urine testing. Most clinicians fully appreciate the importance of being able to monitor the drug consuming behavior of patients if you're going to interact and help them. Given the revolutionary effect of that invention for clinical practice, measuring treatment outcome, work place testing, and in the political history of the field, what aspects of the invention of immunoassay for drugs give you satisfaction or even cause for regret?*
AG: First of all, let's not exaggerate. Urine testing was going on before the invention of radioimmunoassays. It just took a long time to get the answer. It was being done by TLC methods, mass spectrometry methods, all kinds of ways, so

the concept of finding something in urine was a pretty old, long-established, concept. What was new was the idea that you could do it immediately and have immediate feedback rather than feedback a week later, and that has therapeutic implications that are very important. So, yes, the invention of that method was something I feel very good about. But again, science depends on a lot of things happening simultaneously. When I did that, it was Harden McConnell's free radicals that allowed it to be done – that set me thinking. Immunoassay was old stuff. Rosalyn Yalow was the person who invented it years before. (I forget the date of that invention of immunoassay.) Anyway, immunoassay was there. Now these stable free radicals – that was something new. With a stable free radical you could have an immediate readout as to whether it was immobilized by an antibody or whether it was freely tumbling in solution. So all I did there was to take something that was new, the free radical, and something that was known, which was the immunoassay, and conceptualize that if you put those together you could have a system in which you got an immediate readout in an ESR spectrometer. I guess when you put old things together in a new way you have an invention.[8]

That was improved on very quickly by the invention of EMIT, because this ESR spectrometer was a hopelessly expensive machine and really wasn't practical for clinics. But that same approach was modified by a chemist at SYVA Company, Ed Rubenstein, who saw that you could couple an enzyme to the morphine and then, depending on whether it was tied up in the antibody or not, the enzyme would be inactive or active and the enzyme then could do anything. If you get a color reaction, that becomes very simple. So once the principle of homogeneous immunoassay was established, the enzyme modification, which is really what matters and what everybody uses, was developed. The effect of this was to push the SYVA Company into drug abuse testing. This invention pushed SYVA immediately into the drug abuse testing field and so they got a commanding position in that field and then expanded into the whole area of clinical drug testing, and that's what the company is all about today.

But from a personal point of view it didn't work out very well because that coincided with setting up my Addiction Research Foundation, and I perceived that if I was going to run this foundation and do research that would involve drug testing, then I saw conflict of interest between my having a position in the SYVA Company and my running this Foundation. So I told them that and resigned my consultancy.

A: *Were you gratified when this methodology actually helped to change the way US servicemen in Vietnam who were addicted were handled, and that the success of that program helped change national policy?*

AG: During a chance meeting with Jerome Jaffe (who later became the first 'drug czar'), I told him about the new method, and I know that he used that knowledge in setting up the screening and treatment in Vietnam. Clearly this was of great importance in Vietnam, because you didn't want to send home addicted people before they were detoxified, so you wanted to have a detection and detoxification point before they got on the airplane. You had to have an immediate system, so the ESR machines were placed there and got the system going. I knew that the devices were of great importance, but only recently did Jaffe tell me that he believed that without the invention there would have been no way to suggest an effective solution to the heroin problem among US troops in Vietnam and, consequently, the Nixon administration might not have been inclined to sharply increase funding for treatment and research.

In my opinion, Jaffe has never received the credit he deserves for being the first person to pour federal money into addiction treatment on a really big scale. When you talk to treatment people in the field now, they don't know anything about that – where it all came from.

Teaching and the culture of science

A: *Can you say something about what motivates you to dedicate so much of your time to teaching?*

AG: It's a bad time to ask me that question, because by the time I retired at Stanford I was fed up with teaching medical students. It was just too much; but it is true that I loved teaching. The best teaching is one-on-one graduate student teaching, of course. But I have a kind of a built-in quality: if I know anything I have to teach it to somebody. I don't know why – some kind of disease – I can't keep it to myself. And that found its expression in relation to flying, which was an addiction of mine for 25 or 30 years. It wasn't enough to learn how to fly and to get all the advanced certificates in flying; but I had to teach, which I did, and I had to write books teaching about flying. I can't explain it all, but I get great satisfaction from teaching and being able to communicate not only information, but ways of looking at things and ways of doing things, to other people, particularly the graduate students. It's enormously important.

> It wasn't enough to learn how to fly and to get all the advanced certificates in flying; but I had to teach, which I did, and I had to write books teaching about flying

There's no written manual about how to be a scientist. What there is is a collection of history and culture and the lives of great scientists. But there are principles about being a scientist, and sometimes, and by some people, these are not understood. I'm very concerned about the issue of citation, for example. The fundamental ethic in science on which the whole of science depends is that there be honest and correct citation of previous work, because otherwise everything is chaotic. Science builds on previous work. It may be positive or negative. It may refute the earlier work, but if somebody worked on something before, it has to be cited. There are scientists who think that by not citing their competitors' work they somehow advance their own standing and careers. That's an enormous mistake. Graduate students have to learn that. The generosity of citation is terribly important. Nobody does things in a vacuum. They're building on what someone else did and that person has to be acknowledged by citation. You're building on a historical record that's important. That's one issue.

A: *And what other issues do you see as important to the culture of science?*

AG: Another issue that concerns me is authorship. Some people regard authorship as a kind of a prize or commodity that you barter, that if you contribute a little bit of something to somebody's work, then you get to be a coauthor, and it distorts science. It's important to know who really did what because it's not only the reputation of the scientist that's built by that scientist's work but it's also the validity of the work, of the data. I mean, obviously, there are frauds and that's not what I'm talking about. I'm just talking about the validity in the sense of, you know that if you read work in certain journals you'll get work that's more solid and more to be believed than reading in other journals, and that's because of the peer review system of the journal. And the same thing is true of some scientists. There are some scientists that if you see their name you take the paper very seriously and others for whom maybe that's not the case. That's an important issue.

I have strong feelings that the field of addictions was in a curious way set back by the tremendous concentration on tolerance and dependence that came out of the Lexington group and Nathan Eddy's work, and Martin's work, and so on. The reason I say that, is that in practical terms tolerance and dependence are not really problems in addiction, because we know how to deal with withdrawal, no matter what the drug is; it's medically manageable in a very easy way.

You go to CPDD meetings . . . you thumb through all the abstracts, you can see that there are very few people doing really fundamental, imaginative things. It's a kind of a crisis in the drug abuse field

---

Research horizons

A: *On what would you like to see science concentrating?*

AG: It seems to me that the fundamental problem in addiction is the problem of relapse – relapse after withdrawal and after abstinence. One way to rationalize what that's all about is to talk about protracted abstinence. I don't believe that's a valid concept; I don't think it's ever been demonstrated.

A: *Any other important research in the drugs area that you would wish to identify?*

AG: Another issue is the question of genetic predisposition. It's terribly important. There may be people who because of their genetic predisposition in fact are self-medicating when they use the drug that they use. And in that case, when they stop using it, their disease is back again. It's not really a relapse if you can show that kind of predisposition. In animals we know there's genetic predisposition. In humans, the evidence is there for alcohol. We know that you can attach numbers. We can say 50% inheritability for vulnerability to alcoholism. For the other drugs we don't know anything about it. So I think it's a very important issue that needs more attention.

In terms of funding, NIDA ought to be proactive and bring more people into studying the major questions. Another issue is fetal damage through drug use in pregnancy – a terribly important issue but all you hear is media hysteria about crack babies. Nobody knows if there's such a thing as a crack baby. This is a very complicated issue because of concomitant drug use and no prenatal care and all that. It needs a lot more attention and the surprising thing is that in animals it's easy to do the studies that haven't been done, and those studies have to include time of administration of drugs because we know from teratology that even a single exposure to a teratogenic agent at a particular time in the development of the fetus can profoundly affect development.

A: *And the general state of drug abuse research?*

AG: You go to CPDD meetings [College on Problems of Drug Dependence], you thumb through all the abstracts, you can see that there are very few people doing really fundamental, imaginative things. It's a kind of a crisis in the drug abuse field.

A: *Why do you think there is this sort of disparity between the need to focus on relapse, for example, and the tendency to do more specific, predictable, easy to study phenomena?*

AG: I really don't know. It doesn't make any sense to me. In animal studies, the number of studies on relapse in animals – relapse to self-administration behavior – is minuscule. Abe Wikler studied it. But you know, you mention Wikler and people say, 'Who?' He said it all – about conditioning and conditioned relapse. Now, a few people, like Chuck O'Brien, are doing it. Of course the other important work that is going on is the molecular neurobiology – trying to understand what each of these drugs does in its own right – and that's important work. We need more molecular neurobiologists to come into the field. The field itself doesn't have a great reputation and has lagged behind in attracting the new young scientists who go into some aspect of neurobiology.

A: *You've had a deep interest in drug policy and you wrote a book that dealt with policy. Would you like to comment on the essence of that book?*

AG: The book is intended to influence policy-makers, but it's a broad book that tries to explain to the intelligent lay person what addiction is all about.[9] It does it from molecular biology on through describing the syndromes associated with each drug, and then goes on to talk about policy and make policy recommendations. I guess it would be no surprise that my fundamental view about policy is what has been the British view of addiction all along, that this is some kind of disease and that what's needed is a public health approach to it, some kind of harm reduction approach, and the question is how best to do that.[10] There's a group that I call the 'libertarian legalizers' the 'LLs' and it's an increasing group and there's an increasing amount of noise coming from the LLs in this country. I think they're on the wrong track because I think it is necessary to regulate these drugs. But each drug requires its own degree of regulation depending on a complex of things – on the biology of the drug, behavioral effects of the drug, addiction potential of the drug, danger of the drug to the individual and society, and so on. So a good national policy would be crafted to fit each drug and our present national policy is totally off base from that point of view, and I think that that needs gradual changing. There are drugs that ought to be more strictly regulated, like alcohol and tobacco, and there are drugs that ought to be less strictly regulated, like cannabis; and there are drugs that probably shouldn't be changed in the degree of their regulation, although I don't see any purpose served by incarcerating people for possession for personal use of any drug. There's no sense at all in it. I've never seen an argument in its favor except it fills up the jails and prisons; it's expensive. You just come to the conclusion that politicians who make policy are not really interested in the facts; it's all based on emotions or vindictiveness. How do you change that? I don't know how to change it. It needs to be changed. Libertarian legalizers would cause a lot of harm if they really took all the regulations off all the drugs. They don't admit they want to do that. They've changed their tune in the last couple of years. Some of them are distinguished people, like my colleagues at the Hoover Institutions, where Milton Friedman works, with that kind of thinking, and people like Ethan Nadelmann in New York. I'm chairing a task force that we set up in CPDD to try to formulate a policy statement about national drug policy.

Of course, number one is to be a workaholic. I mean, that's a scientist's life

A: *Well, I think most of us will find it pretty remarkable that one man has done so much. Let us into the secret.*

AG: Of course, number one is to be a workaholic. I mean, that's a scientist's life. I never played golf; I never played bridge; can't stand the TV. I mean, time is really the problem. Maybe to some extent I have been able to do more than one would expect; but those who don't waste their time accomplish more. That's pretty obvious. Look at how people spend their lives. They waste a lot of time.

I think my father taught me. When I was a kid, I had to work by a schedule. Every day I had a lot of cards that he made for me with the times so I would know what to do every hour. I knew when I was going to practise the violin, when I could have a half hour to myself. Maybe he had some-thing to do with it, but I've always been very dis-ciplined about the use of time. And the second thing, I guess, is you should only do what you like to do. I have an enormous fascination with every-thing that I've done, and I like the breadth and diversity.

And I guess the other thing is having good people to actually do the work, because when you come down to it, I stopped handling test tubes in the lab certainly by half way through my career. In the past 25 years, if I came into the lab every-body would scream, 'Hey, watch out! Put away what you're doing,' cause he'll screw it up.' So I had very good people in the lab, and I was lucky in that; and I had very good people to run the clinic for me. One person in particular, Barbara Judson, was mainly responsible for running the clinic and for being on the same wave length about how the clinic ought to run. I guess that has a lot to do with it; you can delegate a lot of things. You can also have some bad experiences.

I don't know how to explain it. It never struck me as that remarkable. Every person does a lot of different things; it's a choice of what different things you do. There are people who travel a lot. I haven't traveled a lot except on sabbatical. We happened to have lived abroad for a number of years, but that was in association with work. Many people play sports, like tennis. I've never done that. Only recently I've actually worked out every day because I believe it's a good idea, so I still regard it as a waste of time but at least while I'm riding the exercise bike I'm listening to National Public Radio at the same time so I learn something. So, I don't know, maybe I'm a freak of some kind.

References

1. GOLDSTEIN, A. (1954) The origin of strepto-mycin-dependent variants of *Escherichia coli*, *Journal of Pharmacology and Experi-mental Therapeutics*, **112**, 326–340.
2. GOLDSTEIN, A. & GOLDSTEIN, D. B. (1968) Enzyme expansion theory of drug tolerance and physical dependence, *Proceedings of the Association on Research in Nervous and Mental Disease*, **46**, 265–267.
3. GOLDSTEIN, A., KAISER, S. & WHITBY, O. (1969) Psychotropic effects of caffeine in man. IV: Quantitative and qualitative differ-ences associated with habituation to coffee, *Clinical Pharmacology and Therapeutics*, **10**, 489–497.
4. GOLDSTEIN, A. & HERRERA, J. (1995) Heroin addicts and methadone treatment in Albuquerque: a 22-year follow-up, *Drug and Alcohol Dependence*, **40**, 139–150.
5. GOLDSTEIN, A., LOWNEY, L. I. & PAL, B. K. (1971) Stereospecific and nonspecific inter-actions of the morphine congener levor-phanol in subcellular fractions of mouse brain, *Proceedings of the National Academy of Science, USA*, **68**, 1742–1747.
6. GOLDSTEIN, A., TACHIBANA, S., LOWNEY, L. I., HUNKAPILLER, M. & HOOD, L. (1979) Dynorphin-(1–13), an extraordinarily potent opioid peptide, *Proceedings of the National Academy of Science, USA*, **76**, 6666–6670.
7. COX, B. M., OPHEIM, K. E., TESCHEMACHER, H. & GOLDSTEIN, A. (1975) A peptide-like substance from pituitary that acts like morphine. 2: Purification and properties, *Life Science*, **16**, 1777–1782.
8. LEUTE, R. K., ULLMAN, E. F., GOLDSTEIN, A. & HERZENBERG, L. A. (1972) Spin immunoassay technique for determination of morphine, *Nature New Biology (London)*, **236**, 93–94.
9. GOLDSTEIN, A. (1994) *Addiction: from biology to drug policy* (New York, W. H. Freeman).
10. GOLDSTEIN, A. (1976) Heroin addiction: sequential treatment employing pharmaco-logic supports, *Archives of General Psychia-try*, **33**, 353–358.

Howard T. Blane

Howard T. Blane MA PhD was an Associate Psychologist at the Massachusetts General Hospital, and Assistant Clinical Professor at Harvard Medical School from 1956–1970. He was Professor of Education and Psychology at the University of Pittsburgh from 1970–1986; Director of the Research Institute on Addictions (RIA), 1986–96; Consultant at the National Institute of Health (NIH) from 1970–99; Associate Editor of the Journal of Studies on Alcohol, *1992–1998; and Research Professor at the State University of New York at Buffalo, where he is now Director emeritus, and Professor emeritus. He has been Editor of the* Substance Abuse Series, *Guilford Press, since 1980 and Vice-President of the Health Education Foundation and a member of its board of directors, both since 1976. His research on treatment relations formed the basis for the development of motivational interviewing techniques. Interests include adolescent and young adult drinking and the prevention and control of alcohol problems. Books include The Personality of the Alcoholic (1968), Frontiers of Alcoholism (1970), Youth, Alcohol, and Social Policy (1978) and Psychological Theories of Drinking and Alcoholism (1987, second edition 1999).*

Drinking seen in developmental terms

Addiction: *Tell us something about your personal background.*

Howard I. Blane: I did my undergraduate work at Harvard and then went on to do graduate work at Clark University. Received my PhD in 1957. Harvard had a great influence on me. At the time a new department – social relations – had just been formed, on the assumption that there was a common language linking cultural anthropology, social psychology, sociology and clinical psychology. It had started right after World War II, and there were some very impressive people on the faculty, including Talcott Parsons, Clyde Kluckhohn, Jerome Bruner, David McClelland and others. My majoring in social relations had a permanent impact on my thinking because, unlike many psychologists, I tend to think of individuals in broad socio-cultural terms. Also at Harvard I was much taken with child psychology, and I have continued to maintain developmental interests throughout my career. Robert Sears was there at that time and I had the good fortune of doing my undergraduate honors thesis in his laboratory and under his direction. I was fortunate, too, to take

courses with Thelma Alper, who went on to a distinguished career at Clark University and Wellesley College. This developmental interest was furthered during my graduate training in clinical psychology. Clark University was not in the mainstream of American psychology in those days. The chairman, Heinz Werner, was a developmental psychologist from Germany who had been much influenced by the Gestalt School. European developmentalists such as Werner and Piaget were not in vogue, or even much known, at that time in American graduate psychology programs. At Clark I gained a developmental perspective that has stayed with me through the years and has influenced the ways I think about drinking.

A: *In what way?*

HTB: I have always been interested in looking at young people. Early on I became extremely interested in delinquency and how alcohol related to serious delinquency in early adolescence. In the 1960s I led a project which was, I think, one of the earliest attempts at secondary intervention with delinquent youngsters. It involved alternatives to drinking and working with parents. Later, during the 1970s, I conducted a review of the literature on drinking patterns in youth for the National Institute on Alcohol Abuse and Alcoholism (NIAAA). For years after it had the good fortune to become a standard reference on the topic. I view the roots of serious drinking, heavy drinking and alcoholism in developmental terms as well as in terms of more immediate environmental, social and internal phenomena. These are all developmentally conditioned from my point of view.

It may be hard to imagine today how tiny the alcohol field, research and clinical, was during the 1950s

---

Getting into the alcohol field

A: *How did you become interested in alcoholism, generally, and alcoholism treatment more specifically?*

HTB: During the latter days of my predoctoral program I worked as a research assistant at Massachusetts General Hospital (MGH) in Boston. When I got the doctorate, I joined the MGH psychology department, which was located within the MGH psychiatry program. I had no particular interest in alcohol at that time, although I did have a history of alcoholism on both sides of my extended family. If I thought of alcoholism at all in those days, I thought of it as one of the impulse disorders within a psychoanalytic framework. I knew the director, Morris Chafetz, of the alcohol clinic at MGH, primarily through the often heated, but always interesting, conversations held by members of the psychiatry group during lunch in the hospital cafeteria. It turned out that a friend of mine, Irving Wolf, was the psychologist working with Chafetz on the alcohol unit and they had submitted a grant application to the National Institute of Mental Health (NIMH) to test a technique for motivating alcoholics who came through the MGH emergency service to enter and continue outpatient treatment in the alcohol clinic. About the time the grant was funded, Irv was offered a position at Boston

University. He had been slated to be the project director for the grant. Irv asked if I would be interested in the project director position and that is basically how I got into the alcohol field.

A: *What did the alcohol research and treatment world look like in those days?*

HTB: It may be hard to imagine today how tiny the alcohol field, research and clinical, was during the 1950s. The MGH alcohol clinic was supported by the state public health department, an unusual arrangement then. Virtually none of the states supported alcohol treatment or research programs, other than poorly funded voluntary associations such as the National Council on Alcoholism. There were private drying-out facilities and a few psychoanalytically-oriented hospitals such as Austin Riggs Sanatarium in western Massachusetts, the McLean Hospital in Boston, or the Menninger Clinic in Kansas. Many alcoholics were in state mental hospitals. Other than that, there was very little. Research was minimally supported. NIMH had only a very small program on alcohol research. However, the lack of resources did not mean there was a lack of demand. Once you were identified as an alcoholism specialist, demands for your services and expertise grew tremendously and the longer you stayed in the field, the more you became enmeshed in the beginnings of its organization. At the same time one became less marketable in other areas, partly because of time constraints, but also because of the pejorative views a majority of other professionals held about alcohologists. Later in my career I became active in broader arenas of mental health and clinical psychology, but I was always drawn back into the alcohol field. I have always said I did not stay in the field because of the fairly extensive alcoholic history in my family, but as I get older I think it could not but have helped to play its part.

A: *How did that innovative work on establishing treatment relations with alcoholics[1-3] develop and evolve?*

HTB: It developed from some observations that Morris Chafetz and Jack Mendelson, who was also at MGH then, made in the emergency ward.

They observed that the alcoholics who came through the service were mostly skid row drinkers, with no social resources. If they had social resources at one time, they had lost them. They were admitted with a variety of physical complications, or brought by the police after passing out in the street. They tended to be regular emergency ward customers, who were patched up and sent out and that was it. There was virtually nothing in their care orientated towards alcoholism treatment or rehabilitation. On the basis of those observations, Chafetz and Mendelson conducted a study of emergency room records, discovering that few alcoholics admitted to the emergency room were referred to the alcohol clinic, but even if they were they rarely appeared at the clinic. The consequences of emergency ward admission were overutilization of medical resources and poor clinical care of the alcoholic patient. Further, there was evidence that the alcoholics shopped around at other hospitals when they felt they were becoming unwelcome at MGH. The results of this survey formed the empirical basis for submitting a grant proposal.

A: *The rationale for the proposed new treatment approach?*
HTB: The rationale was very simple: if alcoholics were treated with respect and dignity, if their needs in the broader sense were met, they would respond to recommendations to enter treatment. I refer here not only to their immediate physical, medical needs, but to a variety of other needs that destitute, essentially homeless people present with, such as the need for a pair of eyeglasses, to have dental work done, to be assured that if they were admitted to the hospital their pet would be taken care of, and the need for decent clothing and decent food. An intervention team of a psychiatric resident and a social worker met with patients admitted to the emergency service. The attempt was to select randomly 100 experimental cases and 100 cases that were simply logged in, received routine treatment, and were followed. The social worker and the psychiatrist met with the individual patient. The psychiatric residents rotated so they were on call 24 hours a day throughout the week. All experimental cases were referred to the outpatient alcohol clinic, and appointments were made for the patient before discharge from the emergency ward.

A: *And what were the outcomes?*
HTB: We had two criteria of success – one initial visit and five or more total visits. The bottom line is that this approach turned out to be successful. Two-thirds of the experimental cases and 5% of the control cases made initial visits to the clinic. Over 40% established treatment relationships, based on a criterion of five or more visits, compared to 1% of the controls. A smaller study with less socially isolated patients showed similar, actually slightly better, results. There were other things – patients stopped shopping around and centralized their care at MGH, which was encouraged. There were fewer serious ailments, and medical services were not used as much, either at our hospital or other hospitals. Some patients worked more, instead of being completely unemployed. They worked part-time, or full-time for a few weeks at a time. While these may seem like less than modest improvements, these changes are really dramatic given their previous histories. The fact that they came back five or more times is stunning even today. These are the people who are automatically excluded from any clinical trial today on grounds of severity, medical status, or other contingencies.

Research on patient–staff interactions

A: *And that led on to further research?*
HTB: This project led to a number of other studies, but it is the original research that gives me greatest pride. It was accomplished before there was anything like an NIAAA. Instead there was a small center buried deep within the NIMH bureaucracy run by Carl Anderson, who is no longer with us. Carl had a staff of two or three people and a small amount of money administered through the standard grant route.

Related studies involved investigating the effect of follow-up letters and telephone calls to patients on maintenance of treatment involvement. Each of these techniques had a positive effect. Even in those days the treatment interventions were costly, especially because they used the time of psychiatrists and social workers. Today, of course, such interventions by professionals would be impossibly costly. However, with training and proper supervision, such services could be provided by non-professional staff. It is ironic in these days of the popularity of brief treatment that we were psychodynamically-oriented and our idea was to form a treatment relationship that included once- or twice-weekly treatments for a year, two years, or more. We thought of alcoholism in quite different terms from the way it is conceived of today. We viewed alcoholic drinking as symptomatic of an underlying emotional disorder and if the underlying disorder were treated the alcoholism would take care of itself. This is not to say that we did not ask for abstinence, but we did not use the confrontational techniques which later came into vogue. We simply pointed out to patients that we could not do our job if they came to sessions after they had been drinking, and further that drinking between sessions complicated the work that we had to do.

We viewed alcoholic drinking as symptomatic of an underlying emotional disorder and if the underlying disorder were treated the alcoholism would take care of itself

---

A: *I think you also did some research looking at the perceptions staff had of alcoholics.*
HTB: We also conducted other studies in the emergency ward on the way medical and surgical residents dealt with and perceived alcoholic patients. We found that residents diagnosed skid row alcoholics, the down-and-outers, as alcoholic, but when a middle-class or upper-middle-class alcoholic came to the emergency ward they were more often than not admitted to a medical or surgical ward with a medical or surgical diagnosis. The alcoholism was either not mentioned or it was treated as very subsidiary.

We also performed a study where we taped the perceptions of the residents about alcoholic

patients, as elicited in an interview. The tone of voice of the resident was analyzed by means of a system that had been developed by Bob Rosenthal at Harvard. We then correlated the tone of voice with the success these residents had in referring patients to the alcohol clinic. Interestingly, an anxious tone of voice was correlated with a positive return; we thought this might reflect a tentativeness and uncertainty that was interpreted by the patients as not being pushy. An angry tone of voice was, as expected, indicative of low success rates. An edited book[4] emerged from these studies that Chafetz, I, and the rest of our group had conducted.

A: *Are you struck today by the recent enthusiasm for motivational interventions?*
HTB: Yes, I certainly am. I think it is extraordinarily important. I believe that some of the advances that have been made in recent years can be seen as refinements of our early work. For example, the work of DiClemente on assessing stages of change orients the motivational interview according to the readiness level of the client. It also helps to guide the clinician in useful and efficient ways. We did things by the seat of our pants, and of course in our studies we dealt with a very homogeneous group of patients. These were people who for the most part had drifted into a life-style that they might not have loved, but it was what they knew. They were not necessarily comfortable with it, but they were not about to change it, and I think they taught us that it is best to treat them gingerly – going easy, not pushing. The last thing in the world you wanted to do was to confront. We never told anyone they were an alcoholic. We would say, after listening to them, that it seems you have some problems with drinking and then we would go from there. Other patients would come in and say, 'I don't know why I'm here, I've got a broken leg'. We developed a technique – I do not know how effective it might have been from a research point of view, but it seemed to be clinically useful – whereby we would say, 'You say you drink. How do you manage to keep away from problems with drinking?' In the heyday of the confrontation approach, it was felt that you had to force patients into believing they had a problem. To me, that

does not necessarily signify intrinsic motivation but factors like level of suggestibility, the extent to which one can be hypnotized, relationship with authority, and a host of other things that really may confuse and complicate a relationship. There is no question that the confrontational method works with many patients, but for many it does not. There are just as many topics of study today as there were 30 or 40 years ago.

Working with Morris Chafetz

A: *You worked in collaboration at that time, and later as well, with Morris Chafetz. Tell us about that relationship.*

HTB: Morris and I worked closely together in Boston for about 12 years. It was an extraordinarily productive period for both of us. Although I was a newcomer to the field, Morris was already something of an old timer in it. He was bright, articulate and ambitious, with an infectious sense of humor. He knew everyone who had anything to do with alcoholism and it was this network of relationships, along with his native abilities, that propelled him to the top of the field. He has always been a man of principle with regard to his views about alcohol; for him there is as much, perhaps more, good to alcohol than evil. This led to positions that ultimately made him the *bête noire* of the field. His creation and advocacy of responsible drinking programs during his tenure as the first director of the National Institute on Alcohol Abuse and Alcoholism (NIAAA), and his earlier recommendation that children be taught to learn how to drink within the family, are instances in point. At the same time there is no question that Morris, again in his role as NIAAA chief, was the primary force in the nation-wide development of treatment programs for alcoholics, employment assistance programs and the initiation of uniform standards of care for alcoholics.

A: *So after Boston, what was your next career move?*

HTB: In 1970 I joined the University of Pittsburgh, after a year at the University of Hawaii's Social Science Research Institute. This institute sponsored a cross-national program focused on Asia. When I was there the program included Korean, Japanese, Filipino and Chinese participants as well as several Americans. It was a fascinating and exciting group of people. I conducted a project on delinquency and its relationship to alcohol among Hawaiian high school students, and a corollary project with Kazuo Yamamoto, a psychologist on leave from the Japanese NIMH. We examined alcohol use in students of Japanese-American descent in Hawaii, Japanese-Americans in mainland United States and Japanese students in Japan. These data formed the basis for a cross-national study, the results appearing in the *Journal of Cross-Cultural Psychology*.[5] During the year after returning to MGH, I was recruited by the University of Pittsburgh to become Director of Research for a rehabilitation research center there. That was something that spun off my earlier experience in rehabilitation psychology.

About the time I went to Pittsburgh, Morris went to Washington. As I recall it, NIAAA came into being a few months after Morris arrived. Its predecessor was still part of the National Institute on Mental Health. However, the Hughes Bill, authorizing and establishing NIAAA, was on President Nixon's desk on 31 December and, as the story, perhaps apocryphal, goes, he signed it just before midnight – otherwise it would have expired and there would have been no NIAAA – at least in 1970.

During this period Morris and I kept in touch, and I did a fair amount of consulting for the new institute. He hoped I would join his staff as Director of Research, a post I seriously considered but ultimately turned down. As it happened, my decision was the right one. I went on to have a stimulating and productive career at the University of Pittsburgh and it turned out not to be in rehabilitation psychology, but in alcoholism.

Within a year from the time Morris stepped down from the NIAAA directorship in 1975, he established the Health Education Foundation, a non-profit organization devoted to promulgating health advice. I have served as vice-president of the foundation since its inception. Morris and I are the closest of friends, and I think as we age and see things change and to some extent pass us by, we feel closer than ever. He is a marvelous man and he has not lost a bit of his drive. I learned a great deal from him, actually. My directorship of the Research Institute on Addictions was informed positively and also in a cautionary way by experiences I had with Morris over the years at Massachusetts General Hospital, at NIAAA, and later. He has tremendous political know-how, an excellent sense of timing and a knack for stimulating excitement, curiosity and controversy in others.

At that time, oral fixations and latent homosexuality were very prominent in the way psychoanalysts thought about alcoholism

---

Dependence as a psychological construct

A: *Also during that period you wrote* The Personality of the Alcoholic.[6] *Tell us about that volume and what is your current thinking on that topic?*
HTB: Well, it is odd how that started. The small NIMH center on alcohol used to develop regional symposia around the country. In the mid-1960s I was asked to present at one of these symposia on the personality of the alcoholic, a topic which I had begun to think seriously about in connection with bringing my clinical work within researchable grasp. At that time, oral fixations and latent homosexuality were very prominent in the way psychoanalysts thought about alcoholism. While I felt these were clinically useful, as a researcher I despaired of studying them. Instead of focusing directly on unconscious motivations, I began to think of the behavioral consequences of these kinds of motivation. This led me to develop the idea of overtly dependent alcoholics, independent alcoholics and alcoholics who were a mixture between the two. Although there was a fair amount of dissension about the term 'the personality of the alcoholic', it was then much in vogue.

A: *That paper won some attention?*
HTB: The paper was quite positively received, and was published as a chapter in the symposium's proceedings. I decided to expand the chapter into a book-length treatment. The book was intended as a broad clinical guide, and here I believe it served its purpose. What I termed the openly dependent alcoholic is the kind of person you have to be cautious of. In the early stages of the first interview they take pride of ownership of a terrible alcohol problem, a problem they do not know what to do about, they have tried all sorts of things, and they are putting themselves in your hands for you to take care of it for them. The lack of responsibility for one's own actions is dangerous because clinicians, especially relative beginners, are often impressed with a client's honesty and knowledge of his or her condition and flattered by what they see as the patient's obvious faith in the doctor. It is only later that one wonders why these patients do not change. The independent alcoholic is often off-putting and would be thought of as the person in deep denial or in terms of stages of change the least motivated, whereas the openly dependent alcoholic would probably be seen as the most motivated and the least in denial, which may illustrate the difficulties of thinking solely in terms of levels of changes or degree of denial as you plan your treatment and make your prognosis. I always found the mixed dependent–independent group the most interesting, and I think it probably includes most alcoholics. This is the person who, depending upon the context, the situation and other factors, will deny completely that they have a problem and will refuse to look at themselves, and in another situation will be open and amenable to change.

A: *For you at that time dependence was psychological dependence?*
HTB: Having been trained as a psychologist, and clinically in the psycho-dynamic tradition, I rather naively thought of dependence only as a psychological variable. One of the first papers I published on alcoholism dealt with behavioral dependence and length of stay in treatment,[7] and I found that people who were more in conflict about behavioral dependency stayed in treatment longer. Anyhow, I

sent the paper to the *Quarterly Journal of Studies on Alcohol*, and Mark Keller, then the editor, a wonderful person, wrote back saying he loved it, he thought it was excellent, but asked, what about this dependency you are talking about, and what about physical dependence? I was so immersed in the psychological side that I did not know that when you spoke of dependence in alcoholism, you were talking about physical dependence on the substance. In any event, we have come a long way since then in thinking about dependence, physical or psychological.

Slipping toward prevention

A: *You said earlier that you joined the faculty at the University of Pittsburgh in 1970. It appears that this move coincided with some movement away from clinical research and into survey research with a slant toward primary and secondary prevention.*
HTB: Yes, I would say that is an accurate perception, although it was not just a move away from clinical research – it was more a growing disenchantment with how little an individual could do in changing a serious public health problem simply by treating individuals. Another element in my move was my desire to deal more with general populations rather than the diseased portions of those populations. This was more easily achievable in a university than in a teaching hospital setting.

The need was to study drinking, seeking to reduce drinking behavior that was hazardous. Strange as it seems now, that was big news in 1968

A: *And survey research?*
HTB: With regard to survey research I viewed, and still view, survey methods as one set of tools in the research investigator's kit-bag. I have conducted many surveys, but they were usually in the service of testing an idea or assessing change rather than simply counting heads. Also, in moving more toward a population-orientated preventive

approach in my thinking, I did not give up clinical research entirely. Herbert Barry and I published a series of papers on birth order in alcoholics shortly after I arrived at the University of Pittsburgh. This extended a collaboration I had begun with Herb's father at the MGH.

A: *But you were slipping toward an interest in prevention?*
HTB: The move to Pittsburgh was not a sharp demarcation between clinical and prevention research, but a mark that the balance between the two had shifted to prevention. Before I left Boston, I had presented a paper at a meeting in Washington on the importance and relevance of prevention in comparison to treatment. This paper influenced the thinking of clinicians and researchers alike with respect to prevention at a time when the focus of the field was almost exclusively upon the treatment of alcoholics. The thesis was simple: treating alcoholics was important, but essentially a delaying, ameliorative strategy; the focus needed to be on drinking behavior in general, because drinking precedes alcohol problems and alcoholism. The need was to study drinking, seeking to reduce drinking behavior that was hazardous. Strange as it seems now, that was big news in 1968. I attended some of NIAAA's early planning sessions and argued for the inclusion of a strong prevention effort in its program. While he could not fully commit to this because the power and momentum was heavily towards treatment and rehabilitation, Morris did go on to develop an impressive public awareness program that had preventive overtones, notably his call for responsible drinking, a notion he had developed long before coming to Washington. Again, this was not a complex idea, but one derived in large part from observation of other cultures, and reflecting a humanist tradition. He claimed that we live in a society where most people drink, there are responsible ways to drink, and there are rules for responsible drinking, which he outlined. Of course, the notion that drinking could be responsible infuriated the alcoholism movement which at that time believed that any drinking could trigger the disease and offended the Calvinistic strain in the general public. Morris became a pariah in a

field whose expansion and power he initially led and shaped.

A: *So in what directions was your own work then moving?*

HTB: I became more involved in prevention. An important initial aspect was to record and systematize what was known about drinking in adolescence and young adulthood. The term 'underage drinking' was not known at the time and it was generally accepted that underage drinking was statistically normative and viewed either as a necessary evil or an indication that the informal social control structure and formal legal sanctions were unbalanced. With the advent of the virtually universal 21-year-old age limit, this imbalance only increased. In any event, my review of the literature attempted to catalog what was known about youthful drinking behavior. More than anything, however, its purpose was to inform planning for prevention research. Simultaneously, I was also completing a survey of generational change in Italian-American and Irish-American drinking practices that I had begun in Boston.[8] The general findings showed that the cultural norms of Italians against harmful drinking eroded slightly with successive generations in the United States, but that the pattern of drinking with meals and seeing alcohol as a food rather than an alcoholic beverage remained largely intact, with the exception that beer seemed to replace wine. The Irish, on the other hand, showed much higher rates of heavy episodic drinking, suggesting that the cultural restraints that helped to limit such drinking in Ireland were no longer operative in the United States. This study served to reinforce thoughts about the power of national, cultural and ethnic forces in shaping drinking behavior. In these days, thoughts such as these are a much-needed antidote against neuroscientific and genetic reductionistic excesses.

A: *You also at that time conducted some prevention research in a high school setting?*

HTB: The prevention research I planned and then conducted on the basis of my review of youth compared a target high school with several similar non-target schools. The findings, alas, showed that while short-term gains in information and attitudes were achievable, behavioral change proved to be the chimera it has since proved to be for most school-based prevention efforts (despite anecdotes right-thinking impressionists regale us with).

A: *Were you ever actually a federal employee?*

HTB: My one stint with the federal government occurred through my work in prevention. I spent a year as associate director in charge of a special NIAAA prevention effort. While this turned out to be frustrating from a professional standpoint, I learned a great deal about the symbiotic relationship between contractors and government agencies, the cautious deliberation with which government initiatives are adopted (or not adopted), and bureaucratic rediscovery of the wheel. These negative learning experiences I was unexpectedly able to put to what were better uses when I later assumed directorship of a state-supported research institute. As an extension of this leave-of-absence from the University of Pittsburgh, I spent an additional half-year at the Health Education Foundation. This was another productive interlude, its most outstanding aspect being the planning and negotiation of a pact between the Republic of Ireland and an Irish brewers association to help the government and industry come to terms with what would be acceptable to both around the use of alcohol – beer, in particular – in Ireland. This was an extraordinarily valuable experience, during which I learned that government and industry can indeed work toward an agreement that satisfies both and does not ruffle the public.

A: *One of your focuses was the delineation of frequent heavy drinking as a major problem, a problem distinct from the traditional view of alcoholism but nevertheless a problem with significant social costs.*

HTB: A majority of young people, mostly but not exclusively men, in their late teens and early 20s drink heavily and in the aggregate contribute disproportionately to social consequences of alcohol misuse, such as marital disruption, disorderly conduct, vandalism, sex offenses and other criminal behaviors. Also, while they contribute less to such direct consequences of heavy drinking as liver cirrhosis mortality or health care episodes, youthful drinkers contribute more to drunk driving mortality, DWI offenses and liquor law violations. This general argument and the findings about age differences with respect to direct and indirect consequences of abusive drinking served the foundation for the prevention strategy I attempted to implement during my brief tenure with the federal government. Some of Robin Room's work on disaggregation of problems, as it was then termed, from a sociological perspective antedated my work, and Bob Zucker and I were independently working from very similar perspectives, although his approach reflected a stronger developmental foundation. While much of this is now in the past, it continues to inform issues on the heterogeneity of alcoholic disorders.

A: *Did your ideas translate into research?*
HTB: The thinking behind this paper led to the development of a research project on young men's drinking that I conducted with Ken Leonard. We collected information from a national sample of young men about their drinking behavior and its consequences on aspects of their behavior. We focused on what we termed heavy frequent drinkers, those individuals who had five or more drinks at a sitting, once a week or more often. This is somewhat like the definition used in the current vogue on 'binge' drinking. In my mind, the term 'binge' distorts the nature and quality of drinking among young people, recalling images of the lost weekends and serious memory losses that characterize severe alcoholics who have gone on a 2–3-day bout of around-the-clock heavy drinking. Most youthful drinking, on the other hand, is time-limited, lasting a few hours or at most a day, and most youthful drinkers give up this pattern of drinking by their mid-to-late 20s. In any event, a number of papers resulted from this project, most in coauthorship with Ken Leonard.

Where do prevention strategies need to go?

A: *What is your opinion on prevention work today, and where does it need to go?*

HTB: That is a tough one. Despite the many reports about the promise of school-based education, I believe careful analysis shows that the tremendous resources required are not worth the rather meager results. Changes in information level or attitudes toward alcohol and other substances do not appear to bear much relation to the bottom line of behavioral change, and it is behavioral change that shows the weakest, most equivocal results. Apologias about refining programs, making them more intensive, more theoretically grounded, introducing booster sessions, involving the community, sharpening the timing and nature of measurement, ensuring higher follow-up rates and so on, have still made little difference in outcomes over the 20–25 years such programs have been conducted and evaluated.

Despite the many reports about the promise of school-based education, I believe careful analysis shows that the tremendous resources required are not worth the rather meager results

A: *So where does that leave prevention?*
HTB: The approach most in vogue now in the United States and some other countries is to change public policy regarding substances, notably with respect to alcohol and tobacco. Most of these policies focus on reducing the availability of alcohol. The key example of this policy shift in the States is found in legislation which raises the minimum drinking age to 21 years. Advocates of this change point to its positive outcomes, particularly with respect to reduction in drinking-driving fatalities, injuries and accidents in the under-21 age group. With respect to drinking behavior itself the evidence is more equivocal. But even the decreases in drinking-driving-related accidents have occurred in the context of a reduction across the age range generally, both for accidents that are alcohol involved as well as those that are not. Similarly, alcohol consumption has shown declines over the past decade or so. In conducting outcome analyses, investigators have

failed to take into account improved safety of vehicles and highways. More ominously, but more difficult to quantify, is the effect of proscribing behavior in an age group, behavior that traditionally was seen as a positive rite of passage somewhere between the ages of 16 and 18 and which is still recognized in the drinking regulations of virtually every western nation. The fact that drinking behavior in the affected ages has not changed that much under the new law suggests that informal social controls will supersede formal social controls when there is a significant disparity between the two. In the States, we thought Prohibition had taught us this lesson.

I liked to move around from one thing to another, more of a butterfly than a bee, I suppose

A: *And other approaches to availability reduction?*
HTB: Other examples of availability reduction methods include increasing taxes on alcoholic beverages and banning advertising of alcohol. While neither of these have been tried in the United States as public health measures, taxation has been used in several other countries. The evidence for taxation is mixed – higher taxes generally reduce consumption but have less or nil effects on consumption by heavy drinkers, presumably those most at risk for problems. To my knowledge, there is no reliable evidence that advertising affects overall consumption, although it may influence the market share of different brands. In countries such as Russia, which has a severe and increasing alcohol problem, advertising is a minor factor, whereas in the United States alcohol beverage use has been decreasing during the past 15 years with advertising budgets increasing. Again, I am very cautious about the advisability of major policy changes and governmental control when it comes to alcohol. They often run afoul of public sentiment, have unintended, frequently deleterious consequences, and are often more costly to administer than anticipated. Government control of private behaviors, even when they have effects on the commonweal, is a messy business.

Much of the often tragic difficulty young people suffer from over-drinking comes about as a result of inexperience, complicated by drinking in under-controlled situations. I believe that many of these negative experiences would not have happened if these young people had had an opportunity to learn experientially about the effects of alcohol in a controlled environment, such as within the family or classes designed for such purposes. The notion of youngsters being exposed early to alcoholic beverages within the context of family life and special occasions is, as a preventive measure, of course anathema to most people, but I sincerely believe it is a means worth exploring scientifically.

A: *You also collaborated in the editing of a well-received volume pulling together in one place the varied theories of alcohol use disorders.[9] Tell us about the development of that text.*
HTB: The genesis of the idea for the book came out of a graduate seminar on alcoholism that I taught in which we covered theories of drinking and alcoholism. One semester I was not at the University and Ken Leonard, then an advanced post-doctoral fellow, stood in for me. In discussing his experiences with the course, I became more and more interested in providing a single reading resource for students, rather than the scattered papers and chapters that I had been using. Around that time, a mini-explosion of psychological models took place, mainly spun off from aspects of social learning theory, self awareness theory and so on. So the idea just developed. We have now produced a second edition.

Directorship of a research institute

A: *You left the University of Pittsburgh in 1986 to become Director of the Research Institute on Alcoholism (now the Research Institute on Addictions). Why did you take on this position?*
HTB: I had been on the faculty at the University of Pittsburgh for 15 years and the challenges it once presented were no longer there. Some people begin to work on an area and they work on it and they begin to understand it in such depth that it is

illuminating not only for them, but also for their field. I am not like that. I liked to move around from one thing to another, more of a butterfly than a bee, I suppose. So when I learned about the position, I saw both challenges and opportunities. It turned out to be the finest career decision I ever made, and I am absolutely delighted that I made it late in my career. Oddly enough, much of the job involved research administration, but I had never been an administrator and had actually avoided such work. Yet it turned out that I took to the Institute. Of course, I had a marvelous, talented staff to work with, who showed great forbearance as I stumbled through the bureaucratic morass. I was not a particularly good administrator, nor manager, but I was able to provide a mission and a focus to the Institute that it had previously lacked. The first five or six years were the most exciting in my career – to see something grow, begin to mature and to become top notch – was eminently gratifying, not only to me but to the scientists who conducted the work and the staff that supported them.

A: *Like other research institutes, RIA has scientists representing a variety of disciplines. How has that interdisciplinary mix worked out?*
HTB: Because I was known as a social researcher, I was more of a magnet for recruiting scientists from psychological, social and behavioral research than from clinical and preclinical biomedical research. None the less, our relative weakness in the biological area did not mean that there was not an interdisciplinary mix associated with the Institute. Our relationship with universities and hospitals helped to expand our interdisciplinary portfolio.

A: *One of your primary initiatives at RIA was the establishment of a clinical research center. What was the background to that, and how did you go about setting it up?*
HTB: When I came to the Institute, I was absolutely amazed that there was no clinical capability in which to conduct clinical research. The then-Director of the New York State Division of Alcoholism and Alcohol Abuse saw this exactly in the same way, and we formed a partnership to work with the state legislature to get the resources to establish a viable clinical research service within the Institute. We were fortunate enough to obtain those resources, and with the help of two of our senior clinical psychologists particularly interested in treatment research, Gerard Connors and Bob Rychtarik, who took the lead in planning the center, it became a reality in 1990. The result was a state-of-the-art inpatient unit and a modest outpatient unit.

Blueprint for the good functioning of a research centre

A: *Did you have a specific plan for RIA, or was it more a case of judiciously taking advantage of opportunities as they arose?*
HTB: No, I had a definite plan in mind. I had the luxury of having a number of positions that I could fill and I wanted to fill them with young, up-and-coming, top-drawer researchers who had already demonstrated a record of conducting and reporting research and acquiring external funding. I was extremely fortunate in being able to fulfill that objective fairly quickly. I also felt, prior to my coming, that there had been too high a premium placed on the mere submission of grant applications, whatever their outcomes might be. Many of these submissions did not result in funding and I was determined to change this situation. My goal was to submit fewer applications for external funding, but to have a high percentage funded. Consequently, I instituted a prior review policy, whereby scientists were provided ample time to prepare a first draft for pre-review by senior investigators in the field, particularly those investigators who had recently served on review committees. The investment to implement this policy was modest and resulted in handsome returns. I had also observed that the criteria for promoting scientists within the state scientist series lacked specificity, so in consultation with the staff a set of criteria was established that would need to be satisfactorily met before promotion was recommended. These included, for example, publication record, recognition on regional, national and international levels, acquisition of external funds

and plans for continuing programs of research. These criteria were also useful in providing staff with an explicit set of standards by which performance could be judged.

A: *How do you protect staff from too heavy an administrative presence?*
HTB: A final part of my plan was to establish an atmosphere at administrative levels in which the overriding purpose of the Institute would be viewed as the conduct of research and that all operations of the Institute were to be seen as subservient to that goal. A subsidiary notion was that administrative functions and other such operations were 'noise' for conducting science, and that scientists did not need to be aware of those activities. I wanted to make the infrastructure of the Institute as transparent as possible. This is not to say that there were not interested scientists who wished to serve on committees that looked at various functions within the Institute. They were certainly welcomed and encouraged to serve, but at the same time I did not want to burden the scientists with unnecessary rules and regulations. We were quite successful in attaining this goal. I think that at most levels within the Institute the perception was that administrative and other vital functions were not to disturb the scientists. I might add that I tried to accomplish my plan by asking for input from all levels of staff, by sharing ideas and plans and by keeping an open-door policy.

A: *Subsidiary aims?*
HTB: I had subsidiary aims as well, to be considered after the first year or two. One was the development of a clinical research center, as we discussed earlier. Another was to create a career development program for junior scientists and postdoctoral fellows. In general that program has proved to be quite successful. Another goal, or perhaps I should say hope, was the establishment of a national alcohol research center, and towards the end of my tenure this hope became a reality under the direction of Marcia Russell, in conjunction with scientists at the State University of New York at Buffalo, with the funding of an epidemiology center to study the medical and clinical aspects of alcohol.

A: *What advice do you have for budding researchers in the addictions field?*
HTB: To learn the field, to align oneself with one or more mentors in your area or areas of interest, to identify the critical unanswered questions, and to increase your own record by publishing as much as you can on work that you did in your predoctoral years. As you develop your research, begin pilot studies that can support applications outlining more comprehensive projects, and learn as much as you can about writing and preparing grant submissions. Given the fact that positions in research institutes like ours tend to be funded with soft money, the most important grant route these days is to apply for a research development award which provides a salary and modest research support for 5 years, with the proviso that during that time you develop your research well enough to apply for more substantial support in your area of inquiry. These goals can be achieved within 3 to 4 years after the doctorate. You need to be on guard in working with a mentor or mentors that you do not get so involved in their research that you neglect your own. It is important to join your mentor in research areas that are very closely related to your own, so that you can benefit from those and use them as a springboard to further develop your own area ideas.

A: *You have been a researcher for over 40 years. What are the most significant changes in the field from your perspective?*
HTB: I think the bottom line is that we know little more about alcoholism today than we did 40 years ago. I think what we know is in detail, in technique. I think one change is that we are much more sympathetic to the importance of the cumulative nature of science and that we are less influenced by fads. The accumulation of findings leads to a canon of knowledge that can be assumed by people coming into the field. With that kind of bedrock foundation, one can begin to look at areas that have not been attacked, rather than areas that seem to be interesting because somebody else in another field has talked about them. I think the science is more integrated, and I think in that sense that research on alcoholism is more mature than it was 35 years ago. But in terms of 'answers', I do not think there has been a great deal of change.

There remains a tremendous void between what is known from clinical research and what is practiced in the field. The discoveries with respect to genetics and neurochemical action have begun to fill out general conceptions that existed even before I entered the field. The danger, of course, is falling into the same kind of determinism and reductionism that characterized the field in my early days – this time it is biology, then it was psychoanalysis.

A: *You formally retired in 1996, but still are seen around the Institute. What are you doing now?*
HTB: I just can't keep away from the place! I cannot imagine that I will ever stop being in the field.

References

1.   CHAFETZ, M. E., BLANE, H. T. & ABRAM, H. S. *et al.* (1962) Establishing treatment relations with alcoholics, *Journal of Nervous and Mental Disease*, **134**, 395–409.
2.   CHAFETZ, M. E. & BLANE, H. T. (1963) Alcohol-crisis treatment approach and establishment of treatment relations with alcoholics, *Psychological Reports*, **12**, 862.
3.   BLANE, H. T. & MEYERS, W. R. (1964) Social class and establishment of treatment relations with alcoholics, *Journal of Clinical Psychology*, **20**, 287–290.
4.   CHAFETZ, M. E., BLANE, H. T. & HILL, M. J. (1970) *Frontiers of Alcoholism* (New York, Science House).
5.   BLANE, H. T. & YAMAMOTO, K. (1970) Sexual role identity among Japanese and Japanese-American high school students, *Journal of Cross-Cultural Psychology*, **1**, 345–354.
6.   BLANE, H. T. (1968) *The Personality of the Alcoholic* (New York, Harper & Row).
7.   BLANE, H. T. & MEYERS, W. R. (1963) Behavioral dependence and length of stay in psychotherapy among alcoholics, *Quarterly Journal of Studies on Alcohol*, **24**, 503–510.
8.   BLANE, H. T. (1977) Acculturation and drinking in an Italian-American community, *Journal of Studies on Alcohol*, **38**, 1324–1346.
9.   BLANE, H. T. (1987) (Ed) *Psychological Theories of Drinking and Alcoholism* (New York, Guilford).

Murray Jarvik

Murray Jarvik was born in New York in 1923. He obtained his MD from the University of California (San Francisco) in 1951 and a psychology PhD from Berkeley in 1952. He has held academic positions in universities across America, with a professorship at UC Los Angeles since 1972. He has broad interests in psychopharmacology and has made outstanding contributions to understanding of nicotine dependence. He has been elected to fellowships of several major professional societies, both in the USA and elsewhere.

Getting interested in science

Addiction: *Murray, you have had a long, varied, and fascinating career in psychopharmacology research. Can you tell us what led you into this career?*
Murray Jarvik: I think I first got interested in what could be called 'science' at George Washington High School, in New York City. I was lucky to have had a biology teacher named Carl Brandwein, a PhD and refugee from Germany who was extremely inspiring. He could have led a motivational seminar. He allowed me to culture a giant amoeba. Chaos-chaos, I remember it even today. He encouraged me to enter the Westinghouse Science Fair and with another classmate, Ernest Schwartz, I built a wooden working model of an iron lung. We wrote to the scientist who had invented the real iron lung, Philip Drinker, I think it was, and got some plans from him. The model won first prize at the fair at the American Museum of Natural History and was exhibited there. This must have been around 1940.

A: *The first prize in the Westinghouse Science competition? That's quite an achievement.*
MJ: Yes, but there was kind of an ironic twist to this. The iron lung was a very highly publicized treatment for bulbar poliomyelitis in the 1930s. Many years later in 1951, when I was 28 years old, I got bulbar polio myself. I was lucky, though. While it did impair my swallowing and my voice, it didn't paralyze my breathing.

But it was a strange and rather unpleasant coincidence.

A: *Is it something you've reflected back on?*
MJ: No, I never have until right now. Not until this interview.

A: *Did this success encourage you to go further on into science?*
MJ: Yes, it did, and I knew at that point that I wanted to go on to college, even though we were very poor. My father died when I was 11 years old, which was pretty bad, and a year later I developed rheumatic fever, which was also pretty bad. I had all the characteristic problems, including severe aortic insufficiency. We were extremely poor and had to go on 'relief', the term then for what is 'welfare' now. So when the time came there really wasn't enough money for me to go to college full time, even though I was going to the 'free' City College of New York, so I also had to work. In my sophomore year at City College, I switched to night school so I could work during the day. I looked for a job on Wall Street, and the first question every Wall Street firm asked me was, 'What is your religion? I tried to be evasive. In 1944 anti-Semitism was acceptable on Wall Street, and the fact is I couldn't get even the lowest level job there. Instead, I got a job working for a chemical company – they didn't ask me if I was Jewish – which later was taken over by Fisher Scientific Company. I worked in their complaints department but I quit after a couple of weeks, because

the complaints bothered me. Then I thought I might try the famous Rockefeller Institute, just to see what would happen. This was in 1943–44, the middle of World War II, and the rheumatic heart disease actually helped me here because it had kept me out of the Army. Rockefeller Institute had a need for research assistants because there was a severe manpower shortage, and I got a job as a technician in the Department of Physical Chemistry. The Rockefeller Institute was just an incredible, amazing place. It was full of older, world famous scientists, like Wendell Stanley who discovered filterable viruses and got the Nobel Prize, and Leonor Michaelis who developed the Michaelis–Menten equation, Lorente de No, Karl Landsteiner, Peyton Rous, Oswald Avery and many others.

A: *What kind of work did you do at the Rockefeller Institute?*
MJ: I worked for Alexander Rothen, a Swiss physical chemist who was working on a strange project. My job was to prepare monomolecular films of stearic acid so that Rothen could produce antigen–antibody reactions through the film. This was to prove that biological actions could occur at a distance. He succeeded in getting reactions through several layers of film and was convinced that there were some long range forces, magnetic forces, or something mysterious at work. Unfortunately, Irving Langmuir, a scientist working somewhere else, discovered that what Rothen was seeing was the reactions of antibodies going through holes in the film – because the film had holes in it – and it wasn't action at a distance. That was a great disappointment for poor Dr Rothen. Despite this setback, I enjoyed the work making those one molecule thick films. I still remember exactly how I did it.

A: *Any other responsibilities at that time?*
MJ: Another part of my job was to run a new gadget called an ultracentrifuge, which was built in Sweden by The Svedberg. The Rockefeller Institute had one of only three of these in the world at the time. The ultracentrifuge filled up a whole room. It was run by compressed air at tremendous speeds, and just before I was hired, there had been

a terrific explosion. Nobody was hurt, but the rotor was melted down and they had saved it. It looked like a meteorite. So I had to be very careful with what I was doing. One other part of my job was with another new gadget called electrophoresis. This was invented, in fact, by one of the people in the Rockefeller Physical Chemistry Department, Dr Longsworth. I had to run the electrophoresis apparatus as well. Little did I realize what electrophoresis would turn into later on – a prime tool in the era of molecular biology. Just on a personal note, I used to frequent the library there, and one of the books I came across was May Wilson's big tome on rheumatic fever.[1] I looked through the various cases for which she had compiled statistics on life expectancy according to cardiac lesions. I found to my horror that according to my lesion – and I was then 20 years old – was going to live only another 13 years.

I found to my horror that according to my lesion – and I was then 20 years old – was going to live only another 13 years

A: *That must have had some influence on you.*
MJ: That was a little discouraging, yes, I must say. I can say that now, when I'm 77 years old. But that was the prognosis for people with severe aortic insufficiency, and indeed I had it. Somehow, I seem to have survived. What was unknown then was that there would be surgery for valvular disease, but it took a long time until I had my surgery. In any case, I did enjoy my Rockefeller experience.

A: *It's hard to imagine that you also had time to study while you were working as a research assistant at Rockefeller Institute, but you did complete your degree at City College of New York. What was your major field of interest during your undergraduate years there?*
MJ: At first I majored in chemistry. Then I became much more interested in psychology. Any connection between chemistry and psychology was interesting to me, and I switched to psychology as a major. I remember some of my

professors. I took my introductory psychology course from Isidore Chein, who later wrote *The Road to H*.[2] Most of his course was about psychoanalysis, which somehow never took root with me. Another of my teachers was Leopold Bellak who wrote the book *Dementia Praecox*.[3] He asked me if I would like to help him to rewrite the next edition of the book, but I didn't think that I was quite ready for it at that time. In my last year I worked as an assistant to several faculty members there. One of them was Dr Kenneth Clark, whose experiment with black and white dolls helped the Supreme Court decide the *Brown* v. *Board of Education* landmark desegregation case.

A: *It appears you had a very rich undergraduate experience at City College of New York. It must have been hard to decide where to go from there.*
MJ: When I graduated from City College, I wanted to go the idyllic sounding state of California for graduate work, so I wrote to the head of the Psychology Department at the University of California at Los Angeles, Dr Roy Dorcus, asking if he had a position open. Dr Dorcus was fairly well known at that time and had written a textbook of abnormal psychology.[4] To my surprise and pleasure, he had a teaching assistantship available. So soon I took the train to the sunny state of California – to a different world. In those days, City College was still a nest of left wing politics (I never got involved with that though), whereas UCLA seemed to be full of fraternities and sororities and students going to the beach. I spent most of my time working in the Psychology Department. That's where I was first introduced to the use of rats as a laboratory animals and first became interested in experimental psychology.

A: *And is that where you first met Gordon Tomkins?*
MJ: Yes. Gordon was a brilliant fellow who became a good friend of mine and who had a big influence on me. He was actually a student of mine in a course where I was a teaching assistant, only he was about 3 standard deviations above the mean. He was so smart! Gordon was 18 years old; I was 21. His family befriended me and I used to have dinner at their home often. His father was

a general practitioner and his mother was a musician. Gordon was a musician, too, in addition to being a genius. He eventually became a very famous molecular biologist and went off to NIH (the National Institutes of Health) and set up the first molecular biology laboratory there. He counseled various people, including Marshall Nierenberg, who got the Nobel Prize after Gordon had spoken to him about chaining together uridine molecules to make something called poly-U, which was one of the first experiments in molecular biology.

A: *So you went to California.*
MJ: Gordon said he was going up to Berkeley [the University of California, Berkeley] to study biochemistry when he graduated from UCLA, and he asked, 'Why don't you switch? They have a much better psychology department at Berkeley than they do at UCLA.' I agreed. So I went to Berkeley that year. I studied under Edward C. Tolman. That was in the late 'forties, and there was a big controversy going on between Tolman and Hull about learning theory, which I thought was really interesting. I decided to focus on learning and memory. My major professor and thesis advisor was Egon Brunswik, who was interested in induction, or probability learning. My PhD thesis was a study of the psychology of probability learning – basically gambling.[5]

A: *When you went to Berkeley, then, you were still pursuing studies in psychology?*
MJ: Yes. I earned a master's degree in the one year at UCLA. At Berkeley I was in the PhD program, but for only two years. I took all the required courses but I didn't finish my thesis until later. That was the time, 1947, when I found out I could get into the University of California medical school. So for the next four years I was in medical school, and summer times I would work on my thesis.

A: *What brought you into medicine? Had you been interested in going to medical school for some time?*
MJ: My brother, who was 10 years older, was working for a degree in physiology at Columbia University, so I got some kind of taste for it then. But I never dreamed that I would go to medical

school because it was just too expensive. I thought that instead of becoming a doctor I'd become a clinical psychologist, but I never really pursued that course. When I studied psychology at UCLA, from 1944 to 1945, it was experimental psychology that interested me. Believe it or not, it was rheumatic fever, once more, that brought me into medicine. Not because I was reading books about rheumatic fever, which I certainly did even when I was in college, but because after I had been in California for about two or three years, I discovered that there was a Department of Rehabilitation for people with handicaps. And, lo and behold, I had a handicap. One of the things they were supposed to do, back in the forties, was help handicapped people go to school. I met a very helpful social worker (I've forgotten her name, but I'm very grateful to her), who said 'We can help you out. Is there any kind of school you'd like to go to?' And I said, yes, I'd like to go to medical school. To my surprise, she was able to provide the tuition to medical school, which I must admit was very low at the University of California. So my rheumatic fever did some good things for me.

A: *You were one of the great pioneers in understanding the actions of LSD. Can you tell us a little about that work?*
MJ: Actually, the LSD influenced an important segment of my life. It was polio that threw me into the LSD phase.

Starting on primate work and stricken by polio

A: *That's a curious association. Would you elaborate on that?*
MJ: Well, when I graduated from medical school in San Francisco, I was going to go back East for further training. I was very interested in memory and learning at that point. I wanted to find out about the biological basis of learning, and I jumped at the chance to work with the most pre-eminent physiological psychologist at that time, Karl Lashley. He was a professor at Harvard, but he spent most of his time at the Yerkes Laboratory, a primate laboratory, an ape colony

in Orange Park, Florida. I applied there, and indeed he had a job for an assistant, so I went there in 1951. I think the salary was $3000 a year. Lashley had a contract from the Navy and he said if I would work on the Navy project he would pay me $3500 a year. I said OK. The Navy project involved seeing what effect putting marbles into the heads of monkeys would have on their ability to learn. I thought this was a good opportunity to learn some neurosurgery. Interestingly enough, Lashley never used any sterile technique whatsoever. This was Florida, and it was hot as hell and humid, and I can still see Karl Lashley operating on this poor monkey's head with the sweat dripping off his nose into the brain of the monkey. But the monkeys always seemed to recover regardless of the lack of sterile technique. I decided after a few months of that, maybe I didn't like neurosurgery particularly.

A: *What did you turn to?*
MJ: So I then started to work with the chimpanzees – there was a big chimpanzee colony – looking at one-trial learning. I really didn't like the Orange Park area and I wasn't going to stay there, but I did stay a year and a half or so. By the way, when I was there, there was a big female chimpanzee named Alpha – I'll never forget it. Every morning the keepers would come around to feed the chimpanzees. The keepers all had cigarettes, always, and Lashley always had a cigarette in his mouth. For Alpha, the keepers would take out a cigarette, light it, and give it to her, and she would smoke it like any human being would. She'd really inhale with obvious great pleasure and blow out big billets of smoke. I was impressed by this, but I didn't do anything about it at that time because I didn't know I was interested in smoking.

A: *You got to like the chimpanzees?*
MJ: I sometimes found the chimpanzees more interesting than the people. There was a couple at Orange Park, Keith and Kathy Hayes, who were raising a chimp in their home like a child and tried to teach it to talk. Unfortunately, it never learned to talk. It was definitely aphasic. They didn't realize at that point that chimps probably could learn language, but not speech. Subsequently other

investigators have shown they can learn sign language.

A: *Where did you go when you left the primate lab in Florida?*
MJ: I became a Fellow in psychiatry at Mt Sinai Hospital in New York City.

I gave them LSD and various psychological tests I had worked out. The money to support this research was supposedly coming as a gift from a very wealthy physician . . . It turned out, of course, that it was the government that was supporting this research

---

A: *How did that come about?*
MJ: That was because I developed polio. While I was living in Florida, I thought I would invest in some land that was for sale near the laboratory – 12 acres of land that I was able to buy for $27. And I thought, I'll not only buy this land, I'll live on it. So I bought a trailer [a caravan] and put it on the land, and I dug myself a well. I think that was my undoing. One day I was so sick I couldn't come to the lab. Luckily I was running a 7-days-a-week experiment with monkeys at that point, and two of my colleagues, Ruth and Jack Ohrbach, noticed that I didn't come in to run my experiment. They came out to my trailer and found me there lying in bed unable to move. They realized that something was seriously wrong with me, so they carted me off to the hospital. It turned out that I had polio. Evidently the water I was drinking was contaminated. This was in 1952, one year before the Salk vaccine became available. As I said before, I was lucky in a sense, because I had bulbar polio but it only paralyzed my vocal cords and my swallowing muscles.

LSD – amazing!

A: *You left Florida for Mount Sinai Hospital in New York?*

MJ: At that point my brother, who by then was a physician practicing in Connecticut, said, 'Maybe it's time to leave Florida.' So I went to New York and looked for a job in the psychiatry department at Mt Sinai Hospital. I got a fellowship, and part of the job was to look at a new substance that nobody had ever heard of, LSD. It had been discovered 10 years before in Switzerland by Albert Hofmann, and it sounded interesting to me. I put notices in the *Village Voice* newspaper asking for volunteers, and hippies would volunteer to be subjects. I gave them LSD and various psychological tests I had worked out. The money to support this research was supposedly coming as a gift from a very wealthy physician named Dr Geschichter, who had set up the Geschichter Foundation to support this research. There was even a meeting with Dr Geschichter at one of the hotels downtown and he described how he gave this largesse from his personal fortune to support Mt Sinai Hospital. It turned out, of course, that it was the government that was supporting this research.

A: *Was Dr Geschichter a real doctor, or was he a government fiction?*
MJ: He was a real doctor in Washington, DC, and somehow or other he was involved in this 'plot'. I didn't know. I honestly believed that's where the grant was coming from for the research.

A: *Did you realize that you were at the beginning of the psychopharmacology revolution?*
MJ: Well, I preceded it, actually, because the psychopharmacology revolution started in 1955 with reserpine and chlorpromazine. But the fact that I had been working with LSD helped me to get into pharmacology. It was in 1955 that I worked with Dr Harold Abramson, who was very smart but somewhat peculiar. He was a physical chemist, a psychiatrist, and an allergist, all rolled up into one. I remember that he had interesting connections. Margaret Mead used to visit him. He would invite us to his rather palatial house out in Huntington, Long Island. I spent one summer at Cold Spring Harbor Laboratories looking at the effects of LSD on snails and fish and other things.[6]

One other fellow who worked with me on LSD was Dr Conan Kornetsky.[7] He was in the Public Health Service then, in uniform. [Public Health Service officers wore military uniform] I didn't think about it at the time, but it was strange that someone from the Public Health Service was assigned to work with us at Mt Sinai Hospital.

A: *Amazing.*

MJ: One really good thing happened to me at Mt Sinai Hospital. I met my future wife, Lissy, who was an intern there. Actually, she got lost and came into my lab once by accident. That's how we met the first time. And then I met her some more in the lunchroom. One thing led to another, and it was a good thing, and we got married. Lissy was really adamant that I had to get away from Dr Abramson and the LSD work, and get a real academic job with tenure. There's an interesting sidelight to the LSD story. One of my friends was a psychologist named Frank Barron, who was a fellow graduate student in psychology at Berkeley. He was interested in personality. When I told him I was working with this fascinating new drug, he said he wanted to learn more about it and suggested that we write an article about it together for *Scientific American*, which we did.[8] Interestingly enough, he had another friend whom I didn't know well at the time, named Timothy Leary. So, I introduced Frank to LSD, and Frank introduced Timothy Leary to LSD, and the rest is history.

Staying in research was unusual in 1955

A: *At this point in your career you seem to have been fully engaged in research. Did you ever consider taking further clinical training – a residency in psychiatry, for example – or were you certain that you would make a career in research?*

MJ: I thought about doing a residency, but I never did it. I figured, I'm just going to stay in research, which is exactly what happened to me.

A: *Was that an unusual choice to make at the time?*

MJ: Yes. I'm the only one in my medical school class that I know of who made that choice.

But maybe it's not such an unusual choice any more.

A: *Was there much support at that time for the kind of research you were doing, such as government grants?*

MJ: NIH [the National Institutes of Health] was just beginning to support research. It was a lucky circumstance for me, because a new medical school was starting right around then, the Albert Einstein College of Medicine. I wondered if my training with LSD might be of use there, so I wrote to the new chairman of pharmacology, Alfred Gilman, and he invited me to meet him. He realized there was a new field of 'psychopharmacology' developing – this was in 1955 – and he thought I might be a good person to have in his department. I already had a sizeable list of publications. So he gave me a position in the department of pharmacology as an assistant professor. In addition to drugs and behavior I found myself lecturing on antimalarials and all sorts of other things. I was at Albert Einstein for 17 years. One of the people I worked with there was Dr Alan Rothballer, a neurosurgeon. We injected drugs into the carotid arteries of cats to see their unilateral effects.[9] We even have a movie about it.

I figured, I'm just going to stay in research, which is exactly what happened to me

A: *Who funded your laboratory?*

MJ: Shortly after I went to Einstein, Dr Gilman suggested that I might like to set up a laboratory. The best way to do it was to get a grant from NIH, which was just beginning to give out grants. Luckily, Gilman happened to be on the study section, or whatever they had at that time, and he said I should prepare a grant application. I did, and lo and behold, it was awarded. I got $15 000 a year, which was a magnificent sum in 1955. I was able to hire assistants of various kinds, as well as set up a monkey laboratory and buy monkeys. Monkeys then cost $5 each; inflation really has been extraordinary. I had some very good people working for me. Post-docs from Europe and from other parts of the world.

A: *Some time early in your work at Einstein you began using the step-down memory test that you developed. Was that some of your work with drugs and memory?*

MJ: That's just what it dealt with. When I started at Einstein I did strictly animal research. That was before I got interested in smoking. I had a mouse lab and the monkey lab, and for both of those I was interested in memory. The mouse lab was where I did the work with the one-trial learning procedures – the step-down and step-through procedures – looking at consolidation of memory.[10] In one type of experiment, the mouse is placed on a small raised platform. When the platform is lowered the mouse steps off and receives a shock. The trial is then repeated. An increase in latency to stepping off is a measure of retention of the consequence of stepping off. One trial is usually sufficient for learning to occur in this situation. Drugs can be given before or immediately after the trial to see how they alter retention. Similar one-trial procedures can be used with other species. Seth Sharpless worked with me on retrograde amnesia and so did Steve Chorover.[11] I published a paper in *Science*[12] with a post-doctoral fellow from Germany named Rudolf Kopp, who was a very assiduous worker. We got a very nice gradient of memory using electroconvulsive shock. We also worked with a drug called Indoklon (flurothyl), which is a convulsant anaesthetic that produced a similar gradient of memory. Anne Geller, Stanley Glick, Larry Squire, and Elliot Gardner also worked with me on memory at Einstein. We did a lot of things like that, looking at gradients of memory.

A: *The one-trial learning procedure was a useful tool?*

MJ: I also used the one-trial learning procedures I had developed in work I did some years later with Sam Barondes. My old friend Gordon Tomkins suggested that I work with Sam, a bright young physician working in his lab at NIH. (I actually had met Sam in 1956 when he was an extremely bright undergraduate in a course in physiological psychology that I was teaching at Columbia University.) Gordon said to me, 'You're interested in memory. Why don't you use some of our inhibitors of protein synthesis and nucleic acid synthesis' (puromycin was one of these) – 'and work with Sam, because he's interested in psychology.' So Sam and I did some interesting experiments. We injected mice with either puromycin or actinomycin, and indeed we were able to impair their performance on this one-trial memory test.[13] Sam and others actually followed up on it. (Sam later became chairman of the Psychiatry Department at UC San Francisco and has written books about the relationship of psychiatry and molecular biology.) In the monkey lab at Einstein, I was also interested in memory. I had developed a one-trial procedure with monkeys and apes when I was at the Yerkes laboratory in Florida and I used that. But I was also interested in the new-fangled gadgetry that was coming out of Skinner's laboratory, so I set up a Skinner-box situation for monkeys, with delayed response. We looked at a variety of drugs in this situation.

A: *You also did some research focusing on pain in the early 1960s, didn't you?*

MJ: Yes, that was with Bert Wolff at New York University. There's an interesting sidelight to that. When I was a first year medical student in Berkeley, one of the instructors, Dr Burt Feinstein, was doing an experiment on pain. I was a subject. He injected my trapezius muscle with saturated saline solution and it was painful. When I worked with Bert Wolff 10 or 15 years later, we also injected people with solutions of saturated saline.[14] This was a side line for me, the pain business. My central interest at the time was memory – consolidation of memory. But I was interested in drug effects, of course, since I had become a pharmacologist. During the smoking phase of my career, which is the last part of my career, I've continued to be interested in drugs and less in memory *per se*, although a lot of people are interested in the possibility that nicotine might influence memory. I've done some experiments with nicotine and memory.

The 1960s and development of an interest in smoking research

A: *When did you first became interested in smoking research?*

MJ: I don't remember being interested in smoking before the Surgeon General's report of 1964. There was some interest in smoking before the Surgeon General's report came out – people who contributed to that report were doing research. I worked on other cholinergic drugs but I don't remember if we used nicotine when I did the carotid experiments with Rothballer. We should have. It would have made a lot of sense. I really started the work on nicotine in earnest after Dr Sam Hall from the American Cancer Society visited me around 1968 and encouraged me to apply for a grant. I applied and of course I got the grant. And then I had the monkeys smoking.[15,16]

A: *Smoking monkeys?*
MJ: That was not such a terrific success because I couldn't get monkeys to smoke like humans, but I did something with it. We built a smoking machine that let monkeys puff lit cigarettes through a mouthpiece connected to the front of their cage. Then we administered hexamethonium, mecamylamine, and other drugs to see whether that would affect their smoking behavior.[17]

A: *Did you publish any work on nicotine improving memory?*
MJ: My own memory isn't working too well on those specifics. Maybe that's because I don't smoke.

A: *How did you move from a focus on learning to your interest in smoking?*
MJ: First of all, I married a smoker. Lissy was a heavy smoker, and during the first five years of our marriage, I tried to get her to stop smoking. She ultimately did stop, but it wasn't easy. I realized then that it was an addiction, and I said so in an article I published in 1970.[18] I think the fact that Lissy was a smoker had a big influence on me. My brother also was a smoker and he died from the effects of smoking. He had a heart attack.

A: *How did your smoking research get going?*
MJ: At Einstein one of the first human experiments I did with cigarettes was to study the role of nicotine in smoking. There was a Mr Torigian who marketed Bravo cigarettes, which were made out of lettuce. I added nicotine to the lettuce cigarettes. The taste of the burning lettuce was so awful that most of the subjects complained bitterly. They smoked them because I paid them to, but they said lettuce cigarettes were no substitute for tobacco cigarettes. Also, one of the superb post-docs who came to my lab at Einstein during the 1960s was Ian Stolerman. Before that time, Ian worked in England on other aspects of pharmacology, not on smoking. Ian brought his own techniques and was able to study the effects of nicotine on rats in a very quantitative manner[19,20] and of course has continued to do so to this very day. He and Ron Siegel were with me at Einstein and came with me to UCLA. By the time I came to UCLA smoking was my total focus. Though interestingly enough, it was LSD that got me the job at UCLA. Jolly West (Louis Jolyon West) had also been working on LSD and had met me back in my Mt Sinai days. He remembered me when he was just setting up a new psychiatry department at UCLA around 1970. He offered me a job, I took it, and I am happy for the good move.

There was a Mr Torigian who marketed bravo cigarettes, which were made out of lettuce. I added nicotine to the lettuce cigarettes

A: *Do you recall when you began the titration experiments to explore the role of nicotine in smoking behavior?*
MJ: I think I began that work in the late 1960s, with Toni Goldfarb at Einstein, and I continued it with Ellen Gritz, at UCLA, in the early 1970s.

A: *When the National Institute on Drug Abuse decided to develop a new initiative on smoking as an addiction, they turned to you to launch it. How did that come about?*
MJ: It's interesting, because there was a time when NIH wouldn't touch smoking. They never supported any research on smoking. There was evidence that there was some influence, perhaps from the tobacco industry or the tobacco states' senators and representatives who didn't want people saying bad things about tobacco, so not

only was tobacco exempted from control by the FDA, but it was exempted from research by NIH. But then that changed at some point, and I don't remember how or why. I certainly got a grant from NIH to study smoking.

A: *Sounds like your career has had two main sections?*
MJ: There were two main parts to my career. The first one was studying memory and, hopefully, getting at some biological basis for memory. I worked on that up until the time I came to UCLA, or just a little bit before and then there was the study of cigarette smoking, which was a subvariety of addiction. That started at Einstein not so long before I left in the late 'sixties, and it has been the focus of the rest of my career – cigarette smoking, tobacco, and nicotine addiction.

They thought that there was not going to be a market for this nicotine gum, so they discontinued the project.... It's not going to work, and good-bye

---

The 1970s and research on the treatment of smoking.

A: *When you went to UCLA did you set up a laboratory specifically to study smoking?*
MJ: I don't remember the exact chronology, but what I wanted to do was to look at an animal model of human smoking. Actually, I had started this at Einstein, where I had smoking monkeys. When I moved to UCLA, one of the first things I did was to try to duplicate that. I had a monkey laboratory. In fact, I transported my monkeys from Einstein to UCLA. In the early 1970s, I was also interested in ways to treat smoking. I first learned about nicotine gum when I was at Einstein, actually indirectly from my pharmacology department colleague, Murdoch Ritchie. He was visited by Dr von Euler from Sweden who told me that they were using nicotine gum in Sweden to help cigarette smokers stop smoking.

A: *So the pharmaceutical industry became interested?*
MJ: Yes, I got a grant from a drug company to do some clinical studies with nicotine chewing gum. I got my early supplies of gum from Ove Fernö, whom I had met with at my apartment in New York in the early 1970s. The Swedish company that produced the nicotine gum was Leo Pharmaceuticals. They made an arrangement with an American company which launched nicotine chewing gum in this country. Nina Schneider was working with me at that time. She was a bright graduate student at UCLA, whom I had hired to work on a project investigating if nicotine gum given to human smokers would reduce their smoking. We recruited smokers. Half of them, we gave nicotine gum, and half of them we gave placebo gum, and looked at the results. Nina and I thought the results were encouraging, but the drug company didn't. They thought that there was not going to be a market for this nicotine gum, so they discontinued the project. They just said nobody's going to be interested in this, it's not going to work, and good-bye. That was a big mistake that they made.

A: *Did you publish that study?*
MJ: I think it was just reports at that time. Ultimately we did go on to publish, because the American company broke off their relationship with Leo Pharmaceuticals, and Leo found another American company, Merrill Dow, which was willing to take a chance on nicotine gum. We did some work for them and they also supplied us with some money to do clinical trials. Those trials were a success and Merrill Dow went on to market the gum. I don't know when it came out, but it had to have been some time in the 1980s.[21] Then, during the 1980s, Jed Rose came to work for me at UCLA, and I got him interested in studying tobacco. I was interested in the conditioned responses that went along with smoking, as they do with all addictions to all kinds of drugs, so Jed studied that. He did some very good work looking at the non-nicotine components of the smoking habit.

A: *Then you got interested in nicotine patches?*

MJ: Around that time, we also looked at the possibility of delivering nicotine through a nicotine skin patch. At first it appeared that it wouldn't be a useful way of giving nicotine, but Jed pursued it with great tenacity. The net result was that it worked out very well for us.[22] We were subsequently able to get a patent based on our research, which we turned over to the University of California. We started work on the patch about 1984 and worked all through the 'eighties. During that time we tried to convince the intellectual property department at the University of California to help us to patent it. There were a lot of problems and it wasn't until 1990 that we finally got the patent. We turned over the licensing to the University, and they in turn found a company, Ciba-Geigy, that was willing to market it.

A: Did that patent work out well?
MJ: In 1988, when I was a Fellow at the Center for Advanced Study in the Behavioral Sciences at Stanford University, Avram Goldstein heard that I was working on a nicotine patch. We had long since established priority and had published on it already. Avram said there's a company called Alza that's interested and we should go over and talk to them. So I went to Alza and had lunch with the founder of the company, Dr Zaffaroni, who was a specialist in transdermal patches. They asked me to give a talk about the nicotine patch and to give my opinion on whether or not they should try to make one. So I did, and I said I think it's a great idea. I don't know whether I was doing the right thing because, as it turns out, I was creating a competitor – not to me, but to Ciba-Geigy who was subsequently licensed by the University of California to produce our patch. In any case, Alza didn't do anything right away. It took them a couple of years. When they decided to make a patch, they teamed up with Merrill Dow to produce it. That led to a big series of lawsuits. Millions of dollars were spent on litigation, with four drug companies fighting each other. But it's a good thing that the University of California was our partner, because they have deep pockets and a corps of excellent lawyers. If we had tried to go it alone, we never would have gotten to first base. The University has done very well

with this, and I must say that we have not done too badly, either.

Nicotine: unresolved questions

A: Were you convinced that nicotine was the entire story to addiction to cigarette smoking?
MJ: I was never convinced, and I still like the experiment that I did with Toni Goldfarb. I think I can say without any doubt that Toni was my very best assistant. It was really a piece of luck having her work for me. We did an experiment in which we varied the tar and the nicotine levels of cigarettes. We found that when we lowered the tar, keeping the nicotine levels constant, smokers said that the cigarettes became harsher, subjectively harsher. Subjects actually preferred the cigarettes with higher tar, which indicated to us that maybe the tar has something to do with modulating the effects of the nicotine.[23] I don't think a nicotine-free cigarette would stay on the market for very long, although there have been a lot of attempts to market both low nicotine cigarettes and tobacco-free cigarettes. People buy them for a while and then they stop.

Although these nicotine substitution products seem to be better than placebo, their success is not that outstanding

A: What do you think are still the unresolved questions after the patch and the gum and the nicotine effect?
MJ: The major unresolved question is that although these nicotine substitution products seem to be better than placebo, their success is not that outstanding. With placebo, you may get 10 per cent of people who stay free of smoking and do not relapse for a year. With a nicotine product, it may go up to 20 per cent, but 80 per cent will have relapsed regardless. So that's a major unresolved problem. What do you do with these tremendous relapse rates? I think it's probably a common problem with all addictions that relapse is so high, even with successful treatment. It would obviously

be better if we could figure out something that worked 100 per cent of the time. Of course, we've all known people who successfully stopped smoking. We don't know what to do with the unsuccessful ones, except to keep trying.

A: *You are now working on smoking among the mentally ill.*
MJ: What I've worked on in the last year is the problem of smoking among the mentally ill, why it is that people with mental disorders, especially schizophrenics, have such a high tendency to smoke. Our hypothesis is that there's some disturbance in the dopamine systems. We thought maybe we should look at some of the drugs that influence dopamine. We know that nicotine influences dopamine – that it releases dopamine. But we also know that schizophrenics are treated with drugs that block dopamine – neuroleptics. So we decided to look at the effect of neuroleptic drugs on normal smokers to see if it influenced the rate of smoking. The results strongly suggested that giving a drug like haloperidol increased the smoking rate in non-psychotic smokers. We thought it might be interesting to look at the other side of the same coin – what would happen if we gave a drug that increased dopaminergic activity rather than blocked it. So we examined bromocriptine. We looked at it independently and then we did a crossover study in which we gave haloperidol and bromocriptine double-blind, to see if smoking rates would be affected. It came out just the way we expected: when we gave bromocriptine to non-psychotic smokers, their smoking rate went down; when we gave haloperidol, it went up over their normal rates. So that seemed to me to implicate dopamine as a very important factor. And of course dopamine is the focus of addiction research anyway for other kinds of drugs, especially cocaine, so I'm looking at that link. For the past few years, I've been talking to people who might even image the brain, like Edythe London, Arthur Brody and Mark Cohen, all of whom are at UCLA.

A: *You recently were honored by a Festschrift at the Society for Research on Nicotine and Tobacco (SRNT), and you also received the Ochsner Award.*

MJ: The Ochsner Award was actually given to me in 1992 by the American College of Chest Physicians. They give the award every year to somebody who is studying smoking. It was very nice, an incredibly fancy procession with purple gowns and everything. But it highlighted a second big irony. About half a year before the Ochsner Award I had a surgery for lung cancer despite the fact that I was a life-long non-smoker. Luckily it seems not to have recurred. The SRNT was entirely different. They called it a Festschrift, but that's a misnomer, because Festschrift means a book. It was a wonderfully kind tribute organized by Ellen Gritz and Ian Stolerman. It was ironic, because while they were planning it, they didn't realize that I was becoming tremendously ill and it seemed like I was going to die. At the end of 1997, in fact, my artificial heart valve broke. I had surgery followed by severe life-threatening complications. It was touch and go whether I was going to make it. I had a very stormy course but I came through. They wanted me to come to the SRNT meeting in March of 1998, but I was in no shape to go, so we decided to make a videotape, which was all I could manage. But it was nice that I was still alive! I was really very touched by the whole thing.

A: *What do you think about the explosion of interest in research on smoking in recent years?*
MJ: It's amazing, and the fact that there's actually a society devoted to this – the SRNT. But of course, as addictions go, it's deserving of attention. I don't know how many millions of smokers there are in the world – most of them are in China – but all of a sudden there's been a lot of interest in the health consequences and how much money it costs. Now that the US states have been able to bring suits against tobacco companies, they've been looking for the billions of dollars they can get, and even the Federal government wants to get some of that largesse. Its obviously very important. Of course, addictions generally are important. I don't know how the prevalence or incidence of smoking compares with alcohol. In the United States smoking prevalence is about 25 per cent now, but it used to be closer to 50 per cent. It's a big big problem.

A: *How do you view the future of research on smoking?*

MJ: I remember that at one point, the Surgeon General said that he was looking forward to the millennium, that in the year 2000 the US should be a smoke free nation. Well, the year 2000 is over and we're not smoke free yet. These habits have a remarkable tenacity. I do worry about the diseases that smoking causes. If it were possible to allow people to enjoy the effects of nicotine without causing heart or lung disease, I would be in favor of it. It's theoretically possible, just as it's possible to enjoy the pleasant effects of alcohol and caffeine without getting sick. But it's a dangerous road to follow, because it's easy to go from well regulated use of a drug to dangerous use, like cigarette smoking. Alcoholism is an example of escalating from limited controlled use to addiction. Of course, government regulations can play a role. I imagine that there are political and legislative measures that could be taken to reduce the incidence of smoking-related disease. Right now, for example, it's illegal to sell cigarettes to minors (children less than 18 years of age). Whether that helps or not I don't know. During the past 20 years, we've also seen increased restriction on smoking in public places – restaurants, even bars in California – and it does help. But the taxes collected on tobacco have gone down, and people who benefit from the taxes or penalties like the Tobacco Related Disease Research Program in California are going to lose out. It's like dentists trying to cure cavities. The more they succeed the less business they have. But this is a small cost for the public compared to the improved health from reducing tobacco consumption.

Pure science can save lives

A: *You care about improving health and seem to want to influence life outside the laboratory.*

MJ: Yes, I have had a very satisfying life in pure scientific research and am happy I could also make a practical contribution to smoking cessation that might have saved a large number of lives.

References

1. WILSON, M. (1962) *Advances in Rheumatic Fever, 1940–1961* (New York, Hoeber Medical Division, Harper & Row).
2. CHEIN, I. (1964) *Narcotics, Delinquency, and Social Policy: The Road to H* (London, Tavistock Publications).
3. BELLAK, L. (1948) *Dementia Praecox, the past decade's work and present status: a review and evaluation* (New York, Grune & Stratton).
4. DORCUS, R. & SHAFFER, G. W. (1935) *Textbook of Abnormal Psychology* (Baltimore, Williams & Wilkins).
5. JARVIK, M. E. (1955) Probability estimates and gambling, in: *Mathematical Models of Human Behavior*, pp. 75–82 (Stamford, Dunlap and Associates).
6. JARVIK, M. E. (1957) Effect of LSD-25 on snails, in: ABRAMSON, A. H. (Ed.) *Neuropharmacology: Third Conference on Neuropharmacology*, pp. 29–38.
7. ABRAMSON, H. A., JARVIK, M. E., KAUFMAN, M. R., KORNETSKY, C., LEVINE, A. & WAGNER, M. (1955) Lysergic acid diethylamide (LSD-25): I. Physiological and perceptual responses, *Journal of Psychology*, **39**, 3–60.
8. BARRON, F., JARVIK, M. E. & BUNNELL, S., Jr. (1964) The hallucinogenic drugs, *Scientific American*, **210**, 3–11.
9. ROTHBALLER, A. B., JARVIK, M. E. & JACOBS, G. B. (1961) Effects of intracarotid and intravertebral amobarbital and physostigmine in conscious, intact cats, in: *Regional Neurochemistry*, pp. 442–455, Pergamon Press.
10. JARVIK, M. E. & ESSMAN, W. B. (1960) A simple one-trial learning situation for mice, *Psychological Reports*, **6**, 290.
11. JARVIK, M. E. & CHOROVER, S. (1961) An apparatus for self-adjustment of the interval in delayed alternation by monkeys, *American Journal of Psychology*, **74**, 298–300.
12. KOPP, R., BOHDANECKY, Z. & JARVIK, M. E. (1966) Long temporal gradient and retrograde amnesia for a well-discriminated stimulus, *Science*, **3**, 1547–1549.

13. BARONDES, S. H. & JARVIK, M. E. (1964) The influence of actinomycin-D on brain RNA synthesis and on memory, *Journal of Neurochemistry*, **11**, 187–195.

14. JARVIK, M. E. & WOLFF, B. B. (1962) Differences between deep pain responses to hypertonic and hypotonic saline solutions, *Journal of Applied Physiology*, **17**, 841–843.

15. JARVIK, M. E. (1967) Tobacco smoking in monkeys, *Annals of the New York Academy of Science*, **142**, 280–294.

16. PYBUS, R., GOLDFARB, T. & JARVIK, M. E. (1969) A device for measuring cigarette smoking in monkeys, *Journal of Experimental Analysis of Behavior*, **12**, 88–90.

17. JARVIK, M. E., GLICK, S. D. & NAKAMURA, R. (1970) Inhibition of cigarette smoking by orally administered nicotine, *Clinical Pharmacology & Therapeutics*, **11**, 574–576.

18. JARVIK, M. E. (1970) The role of nicotine in the smoking habit, in: HUNT, W. A. (ed.), *Learning Mechanisms in Smoking*, pp. 155–190 (Chicago, Aldine Publishing Co.).

19. STOLERMAN, I. P., GOLDFARB, T., FINK, R. & JARVIK, M. E. (1973) Influencing cigarette smoking with nicotine antagonists, *Psychopharmacologia*, **28**, 247–259.

20. STOLERMAN, I. P., FINK, R. & JARVIK, M. E. (1973) Acute and chronic tolerance to nicotine measured by activity in rats, *Psychopharmacologia (Berlin)*, **30**, 329–342.

21. SCHNEIDER, N. G., POPEK, P., JARVIK, M. E. & GRITZ, E. R. (1977) The use of nicotine gum during cessation of smoking (Brief communication), *American Journal of Psychiatry*, **34**, 43–44.

22. ROSE, J. E., HERSKOVIC, J. E., TRILLING, Y. & JARVIK, M. E. (1985) Transdermal nicotine reduces cigarette craving and nicotine preference, *Clinical Pharmacology & Therapeutics*, **38**, 450–456.

23. GOLDFARB, T., GRITZ, E. R., JARVIK, M. E. & STOLERMAN, I. P. (1976) Reactions to cigarettes as a function of nicotine and 'tar', *Clinical Pharmacology & Therapeutics*, **19**, 767–772.

Frederick B. Glaser

Frederick B. Glaser was born in 1935 in Rochester, New York. He gained a BS in Psychology from the University of Wisconsin in 1955 and his MD from Harvard University Medical School in 1959. He has held various posts: Professor of Psychiatry, Faculty of Medicine, University of Toronto; Consultant in Psychiatry, Clarke Institute of Psychiatry; Head of Psychiatry, Addiction Research Foundation Clinical Institute, Toronto, 1975–89; Director, Study of Treatment and Rehabilitation Services for Alcohol Abuse and Alcoholism, Institute of Medicine, National Academy of Sciences, Washington, DC, 1987–89; Director, University of Michigan Substance Abuse Center, 1989–94; Medical Director, Center for Alcohol and Drug Abuse Studies, 1997–present. He was awarded a Nancy C. A. Roeske MD Certificate of Recognition of the American Psychiatric Association for Excellence in Medical Student Education, and is a Life Fellow of the American Psychiatric Association. His principal interest has been in the area of alcohol and drug problems, with a particular focus upon the improvement of delivery of treatment services.

A liberal education

Addiction: *Fred, you've had a lengthy career in the field of alcohol and drug problems. One thing that has struck me is your ability to consider layers upon layers of thought. You seem to be interested in making things clear that are often incredibly contradictory. I'd like to understand that.*

Frederick Glaser: I think that started early. I was one of a group of 30 or 40 Ford Foundation scholars who attended the University of Wisconsin; I was 15 years old when I entered college. I enrolled in the Integrated Liberal Studies program on the advice of my adviser, Dr Herbert Howe, and I think that ILS was the single most important formative influence on my development. We learned about things that I never would have studied on my own, because I didn't know what they were. The principal example was the course in Classics. We had a solid year of Classics with two of the most remarkable teachers, Professor Walter Agard and Professor Paul McKendrick. We also had courses in anthropology, literature, earth science, and many other subjects. We had courses in philosophy during each of the four semesters of the program. I think ILS provided a humanistic perspective that was invaluable and has influenced me all my life.

A: *The original concept for the Wisconsin Experimental College that preceded the Integrated Liberal Studies program, was that there would be a deep study of the classics and also a connection between classic thought and contemporary society. Was that still the philosophy?*

FG: Absolutely, and not just in ILS. For example, Professor McKendrick taught a course in the classical origins of contemporary literature. We met twice a week. In the first session, he would lecture about the classical source, and in the second session about a related contemporary example. For example, the first lecture of the week might be on Homer's *Odyssey* and the second on Joyce's *Ulysses*. The course well illustrated the relevance of earlier thought to contemporary life. It was the greatest imaginable treat. One reason I went into psychiatry was a wish to be involved in something in which multiple aspects of knowledge were relevant.

A: *Then to medical school.*

FG: After Wisconsin, I went to medical school. It had been fully ordained that I would do so; my father was a physician, and I never seriously considered anything else. But when I got my medical degree I had no idea what I wanted to do. I had wanted to be a psychiatrist since I was about eleven and I picked Karl Menninger's *The Human Mind* out of my aunt's library and read it.

A: *When you were eleven?*
FG: When I was eleven. I thought, 'Gee, this is fascinating – this is what I want to do.' But when I got to medical school one of the first psychiatry lectures we had was by a well-known psychoanalyst. She was very striking; she had silver hair which was pulled back very severely into a bun, she had a marked Viennese accent, and she smoked like a chimney.

A: *Even during the lectures?*
FG: Yes, she strode onto the stage, cigarette in hand. 'Chentlemen!' she said. 'Dere is nutting to life but sex und aggression, und the sooner you recognize that, the better.' Everybody looked at each other and said, 'What on earth is this?' Such was my introduction to psychiatry.

'Chentlemen! Dere is nutting to life but sex und aggression, und the sooner you recognize that, the better.' Such was my introduction to psychiatry

A: *Did this turn you off psychiatry?*
FG: Yes, it made me think I had been mistaken. As time wore on, however, we had very good experiences in psychiatry at the Massachusetts Mental Health Center and elsewhere. By the time I graduated, I was thinking about it again. But I continued to worry about psychiatry as a career because I had had some unsettling experiences with the children of psychiatrists, and I wondered about potential adverse effects on my future family. Fortunately I met a young staff psychiatrist at Massachusetts Mental Health who invited me to his home and I met his children. They were normal and I thought well, maybe I don't have to worry about that.

A: *Did you think it had something more to do with the quality of the parents?*
FG: I think so. Some of them didn't relinquish their professional role when dealing with family members.

Psychiatric training

A: *What next?*
FG: After medical school I took a two-year rotating internship, and had a significant amount of time in five different fields (surgery, ob-gyn, pediatrics, medicine and psychiatry). It gave me a chance to decide what I wanted to do based on actual experience. I received my greetings from the President of the US when I was an intern. I didn't want to go into the army. I knew that the life of a general medical officer in the army was not terrific. They could send you anywhere and ask you to do anything, and I would be far better off going in after I completed my specialist training. But the second thing was that I did not want to go to Vietnam. Had I not been successful in joining the Public Health Service, I think I would have gone to Canada earlier than I eventually did, because I was determined I was not going to participate in that war.

A: *How did you end up in the Public Health Service?*
FG: I learned that the Public Health Service offered a residency deferment program. The PHS was also not overtly militaristic. There wouldn't be things like drill and how to use weapons. We had to wear uniforms, but we didn't have to wear ties. And, we were not armed.

A: *So you applied to the US Public Health at the point that the government came calling and then the service was deferred to after that?*
FG: Exactly right. I then had my internship rotation in psychiatry, and took my four-month elective in psychiatry as well, so I had eight months of psychiatry and I really liked it. I decided that was what I wanted to do.

A: *What did you do in psychiatry?*
FG: Oh, it was fascinating; we had a variety of experiences. Most of my elective rotation was in the emergency department. We had a separate suite that consisted of a very large seclusion room and a couple of offices. We literally got to see everything. We frequently got police cases,

0

acutely psychotic people and all other kinds of things.

A: *Was there a supervisor right there in the beginning or did they just throw you in?*
FG: There was a chief resident who was responsible for emergency psychiatry, but it was understood that we wouldn't call him unless we really were in trouble. Occasionally, you couldn't get hold of him. It sort of aggravated me, and when that happened, I would call the professor and chairman of the department, Dr John Romano, 'The Professor' to all of us. He was one of the most remarkable people I ever met in my life. He was always extremely helpful. He never got angry at me for calling. His knowledge was truly amazing. I remember my colleague Howard Axelrod summing it up admirably: 'The Professor is BIG'.

A: *What made him so big?*
FG: He was a real gentlemen. He was kind to everybody. He was vitally interested in the residents. We met with him every week as a group. He did rounds on every one of the floors. He had a marvelous perspective on things. Psychoanalysis was a good example. At that time, psychoanalysis was the dominant body of thought in psychiatry.

A: *This was in the early 1960s?*
FG: Yes, I was a resident from 1961 to 1964. Everyone on the faculty was an analyst except for Dr Romano. Dr Romano said that he had been analyzed, but was not an analyst. He had a rule that residents were not to enter analytic training. He felt very strongly that they should be fully trained first. Then if they wanted to do it, fine, but not while they were residents, because he felt that we were too impressionable.

A: *Was his conceptualization primarily psychoanalytic?*
FG: No, I would say he was much more eclectic in his approach. It was at a time when medication was just coming in. The first two medications we ever used were reserpine and chlorpromazine, followed by chlordiazepoxide and imipramine, but we had nothing like the huge pharmacopoeia available today. We also made fairly significant use of ECT. The Professor was interested in all forms of psychotherapy, but he was not hostile to psychoanalysis. We had very distinguished psychoanalytic teachers. The principal analyst was a wonderful gentlemen by the name of Sandor Feldman. Dr Feldman had personally attended Freud's 'New Introductory Lectures on Psychoanalysis' while a young medical officer in the Austro-Hungarian army in World War I. A remarkable link to past history. He offered a seminar based on Freud's *Interpretation of Dreams*. Regrettably, only two of us attended it regularly in my year. We learned something about the interpretation of dreams, but we learned a lot more about Dr Feldman's life and his experiences and what Budapest was like when he was growing up.

A: *He was also teaching you about the human mind?*
FG: Yes. He'd written a book called *The Psychopathology of Everyday Life*, which was quite wonderful. Dr Feldman was also a very devout Jew and taking his class was a little bit like studying the Talmud. He would read a passage *from The Interpretation of Dreams*, and then he would associate to it, telling us about his experiences (usually in Budapest) and the patients he'd seen and some of the dreams he had interpreted. At about that time Erik Erickson published a paper suggesting that one of the major sources of psychoanalytic thought was the study of the Talmud. Many of us in the residency program were Jewish, but we had never studied the Talmud. So we engaged the services of a local conservative rabbi and studied the Talmud for a year. We concluded that Erickson was exactly right. By the time I finished my residency, my ambition was to become a psychoanalyst.

A: *Even though you hadn't been analyzed yet?*
FG: Yes; I had followed Dr Romano's advice, though not all of my colleagues did. I knew that the Public Health Service had an outpatient clinic in Washington, DC, and that if I were assigned there I could enter the Washington–Baltimore School of Analysis and begin my analytic training

while I was discharging my service obligation. But I then learned that the plan of the Public Health Service was not to send me to Washington. They were going to send me to Lexington.

The stereotype of addicts as 'horrible people'

A: *Kentucky.*
FG: Kentucky. And I thought, what have I gotten into? Who ever heard of Lexington, Kentucky? Plus, my big concern was I would ever after be typecast as a person who dealt with these horrible people – these addicts – and I didn't want that.

My big concern was I would ever after be typecast as a person who dealt with these horrible people – these addicts – and I didn't want that

---

A: *What were your experiences with alcoholics and addicts as a resident or intern?*
FG: Very few. We had admitted a number of women who had been prescribed sleeping pills and become dependent on barbiturates. It was also the era of the 'fat doctors', and we admitted a number of women who had become psychotic from using too many amphetamines. Everybody thought that if we put them in the hospital for 30 days they would revert to normal, but that was not what happened. Most of them had to be committed for long-term care because they continued to be psychotic. There was one case that was a real foretaste of Lexington, a man who had become dependent on meprobamate. When he came into our unit he was taking enormous quantities of meprobamate, as much as 14 grams a day.

A: *14 grams?*
FG: Just huge; the standard dose was 1.6 grams per day. I had no idea what to do. My attending said, 'Not to worry. We'll do what they do at Lexington.' I said, 'Oh – thank heavens – somebody knows something about this. What do they do at Lexington?' He said, 'Cold turkey; we

cold turkey him.' The poor man was completely psychotic for about two weeks.

A: *Did you think that was the right thing to do, to have him go cold turkey?*
FG: No, but I didn't know, and my attending was completely confident that this was the appropriate approach. When I got to Lexington, I found out that wasn't what they did at all. They withdrew people very gradually. For narcotics, they always used methadone. For barbiturates or any drugs that were cross-tolerant to them, including alcohol, they gave a pentobarbital challenge test. They would administer 200 milligrams of pentobarbital orally. If the patient became delirious, had a drop in blood pressure when they stood up suddenly, and so on, they didn't have to withdraw them because they had to have been on small doses. If they were not at all affected by the 200 mg dose, they did have to be gradually withdrawn. A loading dose would be calculated, administered, and then gradually reduced.

During my residency training we almost never saw people with alcohol problems in the department proper. They were sent to a special clinic which was run by one of the attendings who himself had had alcohol problems, and that was it; residents weren't assigned to that clinic. We never saw narcotic addicts either, and I developed the opinion there must not be any in the city. I found out at Lexington that I was wrong, because there were many patients there from Rochester. They were there all the time; we just didn't see them.

A: *How did you decide these alcohol and drug addicts were terrible people and that you didn't want to get branded as being the person who cared for them?*
FG: Well, I think it was sheer ignorance. Ignorance, and fear.

A: *Was there absence of contact or were there actively hostile and negative attitudes?*
FG: Both. As I said, we didn't see addicts or alcoholics during residency training. And there was a body of professional opinion in support of such an exclusion. For example, a very influential psychi-

atrist had written several articles in which he said that psychiatrists should not deal with people who took drugs or alcohol because it obscured the purity of the unconscious process. That influenced me. And, of course, there was my own experience. I'd worked on surgery and medicine, as well as in emergency psychiatry, and we saw a lot of people with alcohol problems. Many were drunk, sick, and difficult, and it was really not a good experience. I didn't want to have anything to do with them.

Lexington – remarkable place, intense experience

A: *Tell me about the transition. Here you were in Rochester where you hadn't seen many addicts, so you thought there weren't many of them. And you thought that they were people that psychiatry should have nothing to do with. And that to treat them you should deprive them or restrain them and let them tough it out. So this is the model you were trained in. And then you get to Lexington, and you became a staff physician?*
FG: Lexington was a remarkable place. The total census was about 1100; it was a big, big place.

A: *It was a hospital facility? Or a prison facility? Or some of each?*
FG: Both. There was a saying at that time that Lexington was more like a hospital than most prisons and more like a prison than most hospitals. It was a Federal prison.

A: *So everyone there was in jail?*
FG: Everyone there was in *a* jail, but some of them were there voluntarily. At that time, 1964 to 1966, Lexington and Fort Worth were the only two hospitals in the United States that would treat narcotic addicts. The majority of patients at Lexington were from New York City, a thousand miles away. They were also from every other big city. Lexington took men from east of the Mississippi river and all women from the country as a whole. Fort Worth took men from west of the Mississippi; it had no women's unit. Lexington accordingly had an incredibly polyglot population, and we were thrown right into it.

A: *What was your first reaction? Not happy?*
FG: No, I was filled with trepidation. I had tried to find articles in the literature about the treatment of narcotic addiction, and there was very little. I remember reading a section in the *American Journal of Medicine* that had been done by the staff at Lexington, but I started my tour with essentially no knowledge of narcotic addiction, and I was really very frightened. But I quickly found that Lexington had an excellent staff. Indeed, not only the professional staff, but the custodial staff were superb.

There was a saying at that time that Lexington was more like a hospital than most prisons and more like a prison than most hospitals

A: *When you say custodial, you don't mean people who are cleaning the floors?*
FG: No. These were security personnel, prison guards basically. Lexington was, in part, a prison. It looked like a prison. It had grilles everywhere, floor to ceiling iron gates. About three quarters of all patients were there as part of their prison sentence, almost always for violation of narcotics laws, but there were also volunteers. They could come and go as they pleased. Most of the admissions were volunteers, but most of the patient population were prisoners, since the volunteers often did not stay long.

A: *What was the treatment? Beyond the detox, what was the actual treatment?*
FG: There was a fairly well-structured course of treatment. It began with a very careful assessment. Patients were then staffed and a decision was made about treatment. The principal modality on offer, given the numbers, was group therapy. Staff were allowed to take a small number of patients into individual therapy, but group therapy was much more widely used. It was also felt that being confined was therapeutic and I think that was true. Lexington had very active medical, dental, and surgical services. I learned later that many volunteers came to Lexington purposely for these services because they couldn't get them elsewhere.

There was also an element of milieu therapy. It wasn't very well conceptualized, but all of us found ourselves working jointly with the security personnel to manage the patients. It was a particular pleasure to work with Mrs Redman, the wise and kindly security chief of the women's unit. There was a lot of debate about whether the treatment offered at Lexington was effective. A medical school classmate of mine, George Vaillant, was a member of the staff during the first year that I was there. His research suggested that if patients stayed at Lexington for a significant period of time, I believe nine months or longer, and if they had parole supervision in the community after leaving, they often did well.

To be even a modestly successful narcotic addict, you had to be very clever and very smart and you had to have your wits about you at all times

A: *Give me a feeling for what went on.*
FG: Let me tell you a medical story about Lexington. One of our principal duties was to be on sick call at night. When new medical staff came in, the lines for sick call went around the block. Everybody wanted to see what these new guys were made of. Their complaints were remarkably consistent. The men all said they had headaches, the women all said they had menstrual cramps, and everyone said they were allergic to aspirin. The hospital had provided elaborately for just this contingency. It had three unique medications, called Rubrasa, Flavasa, and Vertasa. They were (respectively) red, brown, and green aspirin. I fell into using them initially. But then I began to have second thoughts. Their complaints were of conditions that could not be objectively verified. In addition, perhaps because my father was an allergist, I began to worry that one of them might actually *be* allergic to aspirin. And I wondered whether using medications to which the patients attributed magical properties did not play into their basic problem with drugs. So I started saying to them, 'Look, here's the story. You're here because you have a problem with narcotics. One of the best things about this place is that it is relatively free

of narcotics. I don't think a lot of the people I see here are really having pain, but are looking for a drug. I think it would not be in your best interest for me to give you narcotics just because you say you're allergic to aspirin. If you're having pain and I should have given you medication, you have my apologies. I'm sorry, but the pain will pass and it's very important for you to learn that not every pain requires medication.'

A: *How many months had you been there?*
FG: A couple of months.

A: *Oh, so it didn't take you too long?*
FG: It didn't take me too long because I really was worried about the allergies. After I started this I noticed that, when I was on duty, few patients came to sick call. I thought, well, they probably all hate me. But one day a man to whom I had refused medication, provoking an angry outburst, tapped me gently on the shoulder and said, 'Atta boy, Doc.' From that time on, I had no qualms about what I was doing, because at least some of the patients recognized that I was really trying to act in their best interest. I found the patients absolutely fascinating.

A: *Because?*
FG: Because they were often highly self-aware, as the story shows. They were difficult. They were in many ways more like real or ordinary human beings than the patients that I had been used to. I had been used to chronically psychotic patients, who were enormously tractable. One of my first impressions of Lexington was that, although I had thought it was difficult dealing with the chronically psychotic patient, it was a piece of cake compared to these people. What became rapidly apparent was that to be even a modestly successful narcotic addict, you had to be very clever and very smart and you had to have your wits about you at all times. If you were seriously psychiatrically impaired, you very likely couldn't hack it. These patients had led eventful and often dramatic lives. They were a talented group of people. I well remember a young black woman, 16 years old, from New Orleans. She was one of the most difficult patients I ever had. She was not notably

intelligent. She was truculent. One day I asked her, 'What do you like to do?' 'Oh', she said, 'I like to sing. I'm a great singer'. I was very skeptical. There were several bands that played every day in the capacious central courtyard. There was a Latin band, a small jazz band, a large jazz band – all kinds of bands. We had a function on the women's unit and this woman got up to sing. I had never heard anything like her! It was just the most powerful . . . moving experience. I had listened to some good blues singers, but. . . .

A: *You seem very moved by this. It seems very deep in terms of how you reacted to these people.*
FG: What became clear to me is that these were good people. Oh yes, there were exceptions, but for the most part, these were good people who had enormously difficult lives, partly on their own initiative, partly not. They were despised and scorned and unable to get treatment, and they had to come a thousand miles to get any help at all, and they were very likeable and they were intelligent and they were fun. If they could only turn their intelligence and their charm and their ability to good effect, what a wonderful thing it would be.

A: *How did the Lexington experience influence your career plans?*
FG: The other important thing that happened to me at Lexington was on the professional side. It turned out to be possible to get analytical training while you were at there, but very difficult. I considered it but put it off. Then an article came out in the *American Journal of Psychiatry* by an analyst, Van Buren Hammett. He said (about being trained as an analyst) 'You probably think that the real roadblock is the money, but that isn't the real problem. The problem is time. If you go into analytic training, you will not have time for anything else. You have to devote yourself completely to being an analyst and that is all you can do.' And it wasn't a negative article.

A: *It was reality.*
FG: It was reality, and it was the first time I became aware of this aspect of analytic training. I had begun to read the literature on narcotic addiction. Lexington had a remarkable library, and was the home of the Addiction Research Center, which has evolved into the intramural program of the National Institute on Drug Abuse. There were excellent researchers at Lexington who had made seminal contributions to the field, such as Jack O'Donnell, John Ball, Bill Martin, Abraham Wickler and Harris Isbell, and I had begun to learn from them and from the library. After I had been there for a while I began to think, this is such an interesting field, I don't want to get out of it. I don't want to give it up to become an analyst.

A: *Other influences from that time?*
FG: There were additional turning points, sometimes stemming from the visitors who came to Lexington. At my very first staff meeting, Warren Jurgenson, the Deputy Medical Officer in Charge, said, 'We have a special visitor today'. We watched as a large chauffeured limousine came driving up. A very elegant lady with gloves, hat and a graceful manner emerged. This was our speaker for the day. Her message was: 'I am now very wealthy. I am the president of my own electronics firm. But I was a patient here at this institution, not once, not twice, but eight times. And what I want to tell you is, don't ever give up on anyone. Because it takes time.' Another visitor was David Deitch. David had been a heroin addict for 15 years, had gone through Synanon, and was then the Executive Director of Daytop Village in New York. This was my introduction to therapeutic communities. I had heard the term before in connection with Maxwell Jones. But what David was talking about was completely different.

Philadelphia years and a growing interest in treatment systems

A: *You moved to Philadelphia in 1966, and went back into general psychiatry then?*
FG: Yes. One of my teachers in residency, Al Gardner, was made head of the Community Mental Health Center at Temple. He recruited a number of people who had gone through the residency program. The idea of getting back together

and starting this new adventure was compelling. I was put in charge of the partial hospitalization program, about which I knew nothing.

A: *Another experience with doing things you knew nothing about.*

FG: Exactly, but why not? I continued to be interested in alcohol and drug problems. I began going up to New York to visit Daytop Village to see how it worked. I was very impressed with it and even set up the partial hospitalization program as a therapeutic community. Then there was a major political schism at Daytop. A lot of the staff and patients left, and we invited a group of them to come to Philadelphia. That was the beginning of Gaudenzia,[1] the therapeutic community.

A: *Where did the name come from?*

FG: In Siena, Italy, there was a famous horse race continuing from medieval times called the Palio della Contrede. One of its legends concerns a horse, Gaudenzia, who threw its rider, but who nevertheless finished first and was declared the winner. The idea was that the members of the community would succeed in spite of major difficulties. It was an apt name.

Although many of the people involved in treatment were excellent and did very good work, there was no overarching rhyme nor reason to what they were doing collectively

A: *What was your involvement?*

FG: I was a member of the board and Chair of the Research Committee. We did some research, principally directed at trying to figure out what the retention rate was and why some people stayed in and others did not. It turned out that the split rate was enormous, something like 95% in the first month. We developed data that suggested it was related to the season of the year. There were more splits in the summer than there were in the winter, and I thought that maybe it had something to do with temperature. Foolish me. It turned out that the drug market was far more

active in the summer. So that was no doubt the reason there were more splits in the summer. I came to like and respect the people I worked with and began to feel that the therapeutic community was a very significant innovation. I've been connected with it ever since, in the United States and in Canada.

A: *It seems to me that somewhere in these Philadelphia years your interest began to shift from the individual patient to systems of care. That's been a big focus for you since then.*

FG: A psychologist who had been on the faculty at Temple, Richard Horman, was appointed Director of the Governor's Office of Alcohol and Drug Problems. Rich asked me to be the principal treatment consultant to that office. I was able to bring in John Ball, who was an experienced epidemiologist. When we met with Rich, he said, 'I don't have any clear idea of what we're doing in treatment in this state. Help me to describe the treatment effort.' John came up with the simple but brilliant idea that the best way to do this would be to visit all the treatment programs to see what they were doing. We developed a uniform interview schedule, and visited all of the 80 or so programs. What became apparent was that there was no actual treatment system in terms of a planned, coherent effort. Treatment had just evolved, without any constraints or guidelines. Although many of the people involved in treatment were excellent and did very good work, there was no overarching rhyme nor reason to what they were doing collectively. For example, we found that there would be more than one program in the same building, and they wouldn't know of each other's existence.

A: *Literally?*

FG: Yes, absolutely, and when we would inform them, one of the programs would say 'Well, it doesn't matter.' We looked at whether there was any relationship between the prevalence of alcohol problems in a given county and the prevalence of treatment programs.[2] There was none. Most of the treatment programs were in or near large cities. There were areas where there were no large cities, in which there was an enormous problem and no treatment. It became apparent that there was no treatment system as such, and that evoked the notion that perhaps there should be. Perhaps there should be rational way of allocating treatment resources and of tying all of this together, and not simply leaving the provision of treatment to chance. The other observation was that there was no cross-referral. There were enormous animosities between certain types of programs, for example between methadone maintenance and drug-free programs. There were disparate philosophies of treatment and there was no idea that there are many paths to a good result, that the trick might be finding the right path for a particular individual. There was no mechanism whereby that could be done, other than trial and error. We began to think about developing a rational system of care that would try to deliver the most appropriate treatment to each individual. We surveyed the drug programs and then the alcohol programs and we found exactly the same situation in both instances. It was these experiences that led to the development of some things I did in the future.

The core-shell concept is created

A: *Was the core-shell concept part of what came out of that experience?*

FG: Yes.[3] In the very first book that was published, on the treatment of alcohol problems, the core-shell system was proposed, and we proposed it again in the second book on drug treatment programs. I think what also helped in my further thinking was that I spent a year as a Robert Wood Johnson Foundation Fellow in Washington, where I had a chance to look at the health system generally, as well as the system of treatment for people with alcohol and drug problems.

A: *What was your vision of the system?*

FG: We were in the midst of the first survey. For some reason, I was thinking about the physicist, Neils Bohr, and his conception of the atom. All of a sudden it occurred to me that maybe treatment should be modeled after that. There might be certain nuclear or basic therapeutic functions

that everybody needed and then, in terms of formal treatment, people probably needed different things. So I began to think of a core of universally applicable functions and, surrounding that, a shell of discrete treatment entities, which would be very different from one another, and which not everybody would use. No treatment would be universally applicable. In order to decide which of these treatments would be most appropriate for a given individual, they would first have to be carefully assessed. Thus, assessment was a core function.

A: *Did you have a sense that you were proposing something that could happen, or something you saw as an ideal?*

FG: Both, really. George Orwell had proposed the concept of doublethink, meaning that one could hold two things in mind that were contradictory and believe both of them. On the one hand, I believed that this was the way to go, and that given the appropriate leadership, it could be accomplished. On the other hand, I knew that it would be a very difficult thing, and indeed it's turned out to be extraordinarily difficult, and has not been accomplished. I believe that there is movement in that direction, but for very different reasons than I thought would ever be the case, largely the result of managed care. In a sense we are doing the right thing for the wrong reason, moving toward a systems approach not to provide better service but to save money. In the beginning I really had no conception of just how difficult it was going to be. It seems so logical and reasonable. Initially, I had the hope that we would do it in Pennsylvania. But it turned out to be politically infeasible and could not be done.

A: *What were your thoughts about the kinds of things that would have to occur before it could have happened?*

FG: I felt that if somebody in a position of sufficient authority said, 'This is what we're going to do,' it could be done. The problem was finding a venue in which that could happen. That *did* happen in Canada at the Addiction Research Foundation [ARF]. When I went there, however, I thought that all of this stuff about treatment systems was behind me. I was to be Head of Psychiatry. After I had been there for a few months, the Director of the Clinical Institute, Dr James Rankin, said in a staff meeting that he had some concerns about the overall thrust of our treatment effort and asked if anybody had any ideas about how we might improve it. I said, 'Well, as a matter of fact . . .'. And so he asked me to put some ideas on paper. I did just that, and the papers were well received. Jim gave me the go-ahead to put together a team and we implemented the core-shell system for a period of several years.

Toronto – radical treatment ideas and resistant clinicians

A: *What was it, specifically?*
FG: It was a little different from what I had envisioned in Philadelphia.[4,5,6] I had come to appreciate the concept of case management during my time in Washington. So one of the elements of the core became case management. We called it 'primary care' to differentiate it from treatment, because we felt it was more fundamental than treatment. Many of our patients were in survival mode. They lacked such fundamental things as food, clothing, shelter and gainful employment. They were often sick, both mentally and physically, and it was clear that before engaging in any sort of definitive treatment, these more pressing needs had to be met. I knew that treatment professionals were not well-equipped to do that, so we conceptualized having a cadre of primary care workers who would excel at this. We set up the system so that the initial contact was with the primary care worker, who had overall responsibility for the case. We also decided to make any treatment contingent upon an assessment. No assessment, no definitive treatment. If people didn't want to be assessed, that was their decision. They could continue with their primary care worker forever, but they would not have access to definitive treatment. The third element that we put into the core was follow-up. We felt there was an ethical obligation for us to know the outcome of every case we had treated, because if the treatment had not been effective for that particular individual, it seemed our responsibility to offer something else.

A: *This was done in a sufficient amount of time that a team could triage a person into another treatment?*
FG: Yes. We also felt that if we were going to assign people to treatments carefully, the treatments had to be clearly specified. We had to have written descriptions of all aspects of the treatment process. There had to be a delimited course of treatment, specified in terms of the number of sessions and the overall duration; a given treatment could not go on indefinitely. We felt that if after X amount of time there was no discernible effect, it was probably not the right treatment for this individual and we need reassessment and reassignment. Of all the things that we tried to do, getting therapists to specify treatment was by far the most difficult.

A: *You were using existing resources in the community for the treatments?*
FG: We largely used internal resources in the Foundation. We were able to identify some 21 discrete treatments within the Foundation that we could offer. In order to be eligible for any particular treatment, a person had to meet the specific selection criteria for that program: scoring such and such on a measure, subscribing to treatment goals which were consonant with what was done, and so forth. We also asked the patients what sort of treatment they thought was appropriate, and found that three-quarters of all patients said they wanted psychotherapy. But on further inquiry, virtually none of them had any idea of what psychotherapy was. Prospective patients know less about alternative treatment methods than we usually think.

A: *You said something which struck me as being reasonable but also probably being very radical – that if someone didn't do well in one of the treatments it was incumbent upon the treatment system to think about what else the person might need. Whereas the traditional view of treatment is the person was unmotivated, not ready, resistant, etc. Did you run into resistance to that concept?*

FG: Oh, absolutely. In fact, we ran into resistance to virtually everything we wanted to do. But especially to that concept, because it quickly became apparent that most of our therapists believed that their treatment method alone was effective, and that if a person didn't get a good result from them, it wasn't the therapy, it was the individual. We felt that was unreasonable.

A: *It seemed as though your experience in looking at so many different treatments and programs, and hearing so many clinicians with that passionate belief that their treatment was right, gave you the opportunity to have a perspective that was different to that of a person only working in one place.*

FG: The experience of going around and talking to different treatment programs was an utter revelation. We began to think that enthusiasm was an essential ingredient for therapeutic success. It followed that therapists would jump at the chance to deal exclusively with a carefully selected group of people who were very likely to benefit from what they did. That turned out not to be the case, because they 'knew' that whatever it was they did, it would benefit everybody. So yes, it was an eye-opening experience. We also learned that most therapists had no idea whom they were treating, in terms of their demographics as well as other characteristics.

A: *This was within ARF?*
FG: Yes, in ARF as well as elsewhere. Another basic notion of the core-shell was that it would be self-correcting. If we treated people and we looked at results, we would know whether they needed further treatment. If a treatment program was highly successful, that would be some evidence that the assignment criteria we used were accurate, but if success would be mixed or limited, then we would have to retool the criteria. We could learn whether there were segments in the larger population that were not coming to treatment. We could also find out what proportion of the treatment population was using program X, Y or Z. If the proportion was very small, then maybe that was not a program that we wanted to keep. Rather, we might want to develop a new program that would

be particularly appealing to a segment of the population that we weren't attracting, or to a segment we weren't doing well with despite our armamentarium of treatment alternatives.

A: *Over time, did the clinicians become more positive, or was it more like pulling teeth throughout?*
FG: It really was the latter. And it was not just the clinicians; the researchers objected, too. What the clinicians largely objected to was they did not get to pick the people with whom they did therapy. But the clinician's input was crucial in constructing the selection criteria. So we would say to them, 'No, you really are picking the people, because you told us the characteristics of those you thought would do well, and we used the information when we developed the assignment criteria.' But they could not see it. They wanted to pick people directly. They did not want to delegate control of that activity. Subsequent experience suggested that they wanted to use unspecified criteria of their own in selecting individuals to treat.

Most of our therapists believed that their treatment method alone was effective, and that if a person didn't get a good result from them, it wasn't the therapy, it was the individual

A: *And the objection from researchers?*
FG: Researchers had a different objection. We looked at the treatment system as a way of facilitating research, since every patient could be screened routinely for every ongoing research project. Previously all the recruiting had been done by each individual project. We showed that recruitment proceeded more effectively and efficiently if it was done centrally. It turned out researchers didn't like that. Why? They felt that since one research project was such an enormous part of their career, they had to have direct control over the personnel doing the assessment. Well, assessment workers worked for the system *per se,*

not for the researchers, and they didn't have that control. They didn't like that. Again, an issue of control. It turned out that they, too, wanted to use unspecified criteria, and would regularly violate their stated criteria to enrol larger numbers in their projects. The short and long of it was that although those of us who participated in it really thought highly of the treatment system, neither the researchers nor the clinicians participated enthusiastically, and it eventually went by the wayside.

Matching still matters

A: *Part of what you are talking about is patient–treatment matching, in an empirical, rational way, and it makes sense. Let's pause for a moment to talk about matching. We now have this big clinical trial in which, in a sense, matching didn't work. Do you still believe in the concept of the patient–treatment matching process?*
FG: Yes. I very much do.[7–10]

But, as one swallow doesn't make a summer, one study alone doesn't prove or disprove anything

A: *Why?*
FG: The people involved in Project MATCH did a tremendous job. But, as one swallow doesn't make a summer, one study alone doesn't prove or disprove anything. I think there were some fundamental design flaws in Project MATCH. I was concerned that its results would be a signal to the Federal funding apparatus to avoid this area completely in the future. That has not been the case. If anything, my impression is that the feeling about matching is much stronger now than it was, and data are increasingly coming out that suggest there is something to it. I think it will ultimately become clear that matching is extremely important. Is it the only thing? No. I think there are a lot of factors that make for successful treatment, but I continue to think matching of patients to treatment is one of them. Many interesting things were learned from Project MATCH. There were some matches

that seemed to hold up and some of them took a lot of time to become evident. Not all of its results were negative.

A: *You talked about matching prospectively, where you are saying, 'Here is this person with this set of characteristics and problems. How do those constellate – what are the most important sets of factors in terms of deciding on treatment?' As opposed to the Project MATCH model, which was retrospective matching, because they didn't change the treatment based on what the patients received.*
FG: No. They randomized the patients and did a mathematical analysis of what variables predicted outcome. Handling the data in this way treats each individual variable as if it existed in isolation. My guess is that the variables we use in matching are closely coupled to other variables. Each variable may well be a proxy for a host of related variables that are extremely important in determining outcome. Hence the effects of matching are more likely to become apparent if you actually match people to treatment programs, which did not happen in Project MATCH. A mathematical analysis simply won't cut it. You will not find the matches because the variables we use are only the tip of the iceberg. Human beings are enormously complicated, and the number of variables that are salient is probably almost infinite. Fortunately, we now have computers that can take a large proportion of those variables into account instantaneously. To me, the potential use of this technology to predict treatment outcome is a truly exciting prospect.

Broadening the base

A: *Let's go forward a little bit to* Broadening the Base of Treatment for Alcohol Problems. *I think people know the book, but the process to get to the book – how did it evolve? It seemed that it was enormously complex.*
FG: It was quite complex, but a wonderful experience. I had been a Robert Wood Johnson Foundation Fellow, which was a program administered by the Institute of Medicine. I had done some sub-

sequent work for the Institute and had become acquainted with Fred Solomon, a member of the staff. Congress had become concerned about what was going on in the treatment of alcohol problems in the United States, and as part of an omnibus bill, commissioned the Institute of Medicine to do a study of the treatment of alcohol problems in the United States. The National Institute of Alcohol Abuse and Alcoholism was instructed to fund this as part of their budget. When the Institute began looking for a study director, Fred Solomon thought of me. It seemed rather daunting, but I thought about it and decided, why not? The Institute's standard procedure for a study was to appoint a member of the Institute as the chairman of the steering committee for the study. In this instance they appointed Dr Robert Sparks. Bob was by far the best committee chair that I have ever worked with. He and I began recruiting other staff and committee members. I think we put together a committee that was superb. We had the good luck to hire Herman Diesenhaus as our Associate Study Director. Herman had a remarkable knowledge of the ephemeral literature of the field, materials that had not been formally published or widely circulated. This kind of material turned out to be crucial in developing the study.

A: *How did the project actually work?*
FG: The committee got together with no really preconceived idea; there were few precedents. We had a charge, indeed more than one charge, but the tradition of the Institute of Medicine has always been that the committees are completely independent. It was ultimately up to us to decide what we were going to do, and we did. The study process was a remarkably collegial interaction between the members of the committee, the staff, and a whole host of consultants. We were able to set up task forces which drew on people who weren't members of the steering committee and it all seemed to come together very well. There were of course differences of opinion, but Dr Sparks's leadership allowed us to deal with them creatively. Herman and I did all the drafting of the study, and it just evolved. When it came out, the report[11] was criticized by a number of people as

simply being 'the core-shell treatment system writ large'. Not so; many of the ideas from the core-shell were there, but they were only there because the entire committee endorsed them, and many of the ideas went well beyond the core-shell. We didn't do anything that was not unanimously agreed upon by the committee, and this was not necessarily easy. For example, I can remember Herman and I spending three hours on the telephone with a committee member who objected to a section of one of the chapters that we had written. What we learned from that experience was that it wasn't the content, it was the expression. We had used terms that were too stark; what this committee member wanted was to tone the rhetoric down. We worked with him and we were eventually able to come to an agreement about the wording.

A: *Were there any other major things that made it wonderful or difficult?*
FG: One of the things that made it so good was that we were all working together. It was a highly cooperative venture, much more so than I had experienced in most academic settings. It was a peak experience for me. But it was not an easy time for me and my family personally. Our daughter, Sarah, passed away during the course of the study. The study was dedicated to her, and to Mansell Pattison.

A: *Institute reports go through a review process?*
FG: The Institute has an agonizing review process. Nothing goes out over the Institute's name until an entirely separate committee looks at the report and determines that its recommendations are supported by the available data. Some reports had never come out because they hadn't gotten through review. So the review process was an unsettling one, if in retrospect a prudent one. Fortunately, we passed with flying colors. We also very much wanted to avoid a minority report, an option under Institute guidelines. We felt the impact of the report would be blunted if there was major unresolved dissent among the committee, and this had actually happened to another IOM report in the recent past. The issue that seemed likely to provoke a minority report was controlled

drinking, so we were very cautious about that. The thrust of the first RAND report had largely been missed because of the controversy over a small section on this subject. We did talk about controlled drinking in one section, where we construed some controversies in the field as resolvable if you used a matching perspective. We said, 'Maybe it is the case that controlled drinking is suitable for some people, especially those with mild to moderate alcohol problems, but not for others who have substantial or severe problems.' That was all we did, and the committee was worried about it.

We may have contributed to and or encouraged the ongoing evolution of the field, but I think we largely reflected the thinking of many people as to what the future might be

---

A: *Do you think the report changed anything?*
FG: I had hoped you would ask that. I don't know. My inclination is to think not. There are two ways of looking at the report. One is that it was a path-making, visionary, idealistic, perhaps even radical depiction of where the field ought to be. The other is to suppose that it captured the Zeitgeist, that it reflected what a lot of people were thinking about, and where the field was headed anyway. If that was the case, then I don't think it caused change as much as it was a reflection of changes that were already under way. I think that progress in this field, as in any other field, is largely incremental; so-called paradigm shifts are probably the end result of a multitude of incremental changes. We may have contributed to and or encouraged the ongoing evolution of the field, but I think we largely reflected the thinking of many people as to what the future might be. We gave expression to some of the aspirations in the field, but they already existed. I doubt that we caused anything to happen. We felt very good about the report. It has now been eleven years, and I continue to feel good about it. I do think that in some respects things are moving in the directions that

we endorsed, although, to be sure, there is a long way to go.

A: *I think, again, we are talking about a commitment to pluralism that is reflected in the report, in terms of: What is an alcohol problem? What is the treatment? What could be the nature of treatment and how do we allocate resources at different levels? It's a perspective that is accepted more in treatment now. Did the report make that happen? The report certainly has become a base from which people can draw.*
FG: I think – I hope – it's a touchstone. People who agree with it can draw upon it and say, honestly, this represents the opinions of a group of people who are knowledgeable about the field. As you know, our field is highly diverse, and there were some reactions to the report at fairly high governmental levels that were strongly negative.

A: *Can you give me examples, or are they unspeakable?*
FG: Our view of alcohol problems as a continuum, rather than an all-or-nothing phenomenon, wasn't acceptable to everyone. And many people felt that the only legitimate treatment for any kind of alcohol problem was to join AA and to stay with it, and those people were highly offended by the report. They need not have been, because we were very positive in the way that we dealt with AA and other self-help groups. The fact that we even talked about other self-help groups was seen as a slap in the face. We were also very clear that we didn't think that either AA or anything else was *the* answer, and that offended people. Others felt that the report was not sufficiently biological in orientation. But on the whole it was well received and was a good basis for discussion of where we might go in the future.

A: *What about the other end of the spectrum, which focused on problem drinkers and moderation and had more negative views of AA – were they critical because you didn't exclude the AA and disease end of the spectrum?*
FG: No, or if they were, we didn't hear about it. I think by that time most felt that controlled

drinking was not for everyone, and that there were certain people who were not suitable. Most of the people who had a cognitive–behavioral orientation were very favourable to the report. In essence, the report strongly underscored the validity of those approaches, particularly screening and brief intervention. You know, it's curious: you actually get very little feedback from anything you write. But we had a reunion of the committee that prompted me to look up how frequently the report had been cited, and we were really impressed with the number. It's hard to pick up a general paper in the field now that doesn't at least mention the report. I think we are far from realizing the vision embodied in the report. I don't think it's happened, but I think we are moving in that direction. For example, one of the things that I'm most happy about that happened since I came here to North Carolina was that we have established a Drink-Wise program here.

Rabbi Tarfon used to say, 'It is not your duty to finish the work, but neither are you at liberty to neglect it'

A: *One of the things that strikes me is your ability to be interested in and involved with things that are so disparate and typically contradictory. You have a whole series of papers over time about AA,[12,13] and now you're doing DrinkWise. On the surface of it, those are completely non-overlapping universes. How do you hold these in your mind or your values?*

FG: One of the insights for me that came, at least in part, from my experiences at Lexington, was the enormous diversity of the people who have these problems. They are as different as night and day. They may have certain things in common – they all use more alcohol and drugs than they should – but beyond that they're very different, and I think it follows that there have accordingly got to be a whole range of treatment approaches. All of them are valid in their own way, but not for everybody. Nothing works for everyone, but everyone can benefit from something.

A: *In a sense, you're completely nondoctrinaire in a typically doctrinaire field.*
FG: I try to be. I'm certain I have my prejudices.

Paris in a deserved summer

A: *Tell me about retirement. You've been in this field for 36 years. You retired in the Fall. What are you doing? Are you doing professional things or . . .?*
FG: Not really. I thought I would. I had the fantasy that retirement would at last give me the time to devote to studying the literature and keeping up with things. What I have found is that it is time for me to lay that burden down. Both in terms of my obligations to my family and to myself. I'm interested in a lot of things and I have had to put a lot of them aside in order to concentrate on things in the field. I don't regret what I did, but I remember from studying the Talmud that Rabbi Tarfon used to say, 'It is not your duty to finish the work, but neither are you at liberty to neglect it.' I have not neglected it, but I am not going to finish it. Others will have to do that and I, myself, will be able to spend time with my wife and my son, to read what I want, to listen to music, to travel, to play with my dog, and to do many of the things that I realize increasingly that I have missed very much. Others will take up the good fight. I have said what I needed to say. Others will decide whether they want to take it up or not. I intend to really retire. This summer my family and I will spend the whole summer in Paris. That is something I have wanted to do for a long time, and there will be other such things. My son has now become a Little League baseball player and, in eastern North Carolina, that's an enormous commitment, not only for the child but for the parents. To be at Adam's games and practices seems very important to me. I have worked all my life, and it is sufficient. I've done my share. It's time for me to turn my interest to other things.

References
1. GLASER, F. B. (1971) Gaudenzia, incorporated: historical and theoretical background

of a self-help addiction treatment program, *International Journal of the Addictions*, **6**, 615–626.

2. GLASER, F. B. & GREENBERG, W. (1975) Relationship between treatment facilities and prevalence of alcohol and drug abuse, *Journal of Studies on Alcohol*, **36**, 348–358.

3. GLASER, F. B. (1974) The treatment of drug abuse in the rural South: application of the core-shell treatment system model, *Southern Medical Journal*, **67**, 580–586.

4. GLASER, F. B. (1994) Slouching toward a systems approach to treatment, *Alcohol*, **11**, 467–470.

5. GLASER, F. B. (1986) Alcohol and drug problems: a challenge to consultation liaison psychiatry, *Canadian Journal of Psychiatry*, **33**, 259–263.

6. GLASER, F. B. (1995) A systems approach without a system design: a commentary on six papers on the Ontario experience, *Contemporary Drug Problems*, **22**, 137–150.

7. GLASER, F. B. (1977) The 'Average Pack of Help' vs. the matching hypothesis, *Journal of Studies on Alcohol*, **38**, 1819–1827.

8. GLASER, F. B. (1980) Anybody got a match? Treatment research and the matching by patients, in: EDWARDS, G. & GRANT, M. (Eds) *Alcoholism Treatment in Transition*, chapter 11, pp. 178–196 (London, Croom Helm).

9. GLASER, F. B. and SKINNER, H. A. (1981) Matching in the real world, in: GOTTHEIL, E., McLELLAN, A. T. & DRULEY, K. A. (Eds) *Matching Patient Needs and Treatment Methods in Alcoholism and Drug Abuse*, pp. 295–324 (Springfield, Charles C. Thomas).

10. GLASER, F. B. (1993) Matchless? Alcoholics Anonymous and the matching hypothesis, in: McCRADY, B. S. & MILLER, W. R. (Eds) *Research on Alcoholics Anonymous. Opportunities and Alternatives*, pp. 379–395 (New Brunswick and LI New Jersey, Rutgers Center of Alcohol Studies).

11. INSTITUTE OF MEDICINE (1990) *Broadening the Base of Treatment for Alcohol Problems* (Washington DC, National Academy Press).

12. OGBORNE, A. C. & GLASER, F. B. (1981) Characteristics of affiliates of Alcoholics Anonymous: a review of the literature, *Journal of Studies on Alcohol*, **42**, 661–675.

13. GLASER, F. B. & OGBORNE, A. C. (1982) Does AA really work?, *British Journal of Addiction*, **77**, 123–129.

Commentary
Addiction Science in the USA

Jerome H. Jaffe

The eight interviews in this chapter offer an unusual perspective from which to view what may be seen, in time, as the most scientifically important half century in the history of studies of addictive disorders. What accounts for the remarkable growth of research in this area? Undoubtedly, the availability of funding for research in the US played a role, especially following World War II when the economies of other developed nations were in disarray.

Yet, there were other elements in the American soil that would seem to make it unlikely to nurture such scientific growth. Probably the most important of them were residues from an earlier period when drug and alcohol problems were viewed from a decidedly moralistic perspective. The great American experiment with prohibition of alcohol had the effect of decreasing interest in alcoholism research. With the repeal of Prohibition in 1933, and a rise in alcohol-related problems, a new but quite small generation of researchers began to emerge. By 1941, enough studies on the treatment of alcohol addiction had been published for Bowman and Jellinek to write a review for the second volume of the *Quarterly Journal of Studies on Alcohol*. In 1942, the Yale School of Alcohol Studies was established. Alcoholics Anonymous (AA), an organization that was destined to profoundly influence both attitudes and treatment was founded in 1935. Apart from this, alcoholism research aroused little interest and was matched by an almost equal lack of concern for the alcoholic as patient until well into the 1960s. Influenced by popular dynamic psychoanalytic theories of the day, the predominating view of alcoholism saw it either as a manifestation of character defects or disordered affect. Alcoholics were rarely offered treatment for their behavioral disorder and sometimes were refused treatment for medical compli-

cations of their alcoholism, a lack of disinterest that certainly played a role in the growth of AA.

If a carryover of the moralism about drinking discouraged clinical and research interest in alcoholism, it had an even more profound effect on users of illicit drugs. Doctors were actively discouraged from treating opiate addicts, who were seen as criminals. It was not unusual for addicts to be refused admission to hospitals not just for the treatment of their addiction, but also for medical disorders unrelated to their drug use, an attitude and practice that continued well into the late 1960s. While it tolerated the exclusion of drug addicts from the mainstream of medicine, the US Congress nevertheless enacted a law in 1929 that established two federal hospitals specifically to confine and 'treat' those who had been arrested and also allowed non-prisoners seeking treatment to be admitted voluntarily. The same legislation provided funding for the establishment of a research center devoted to advancing knowledge about drug addiction. The federal hospitals, at Lexington, Kentucky and Fort Worth, Texas were opened in 1935 and 1938, respectively, and the Addiction Research Center became functional at Lexington toward the end of the decade.

Throughout the 1940s and 1950s, these two research centers at Yale and Lexington stood virtually alone as islands of scholarship in a sea of general indifference to questions about the nature and treatment of alcohol and drug problems. The few scholars who did become interested in these backwaters of science were either affiliated with those centers or dutifully made voyages to them, either physically or through a study of their publications. (Notably, there was no center where nicotine and tobacco problems were a focus of active research, and not until the mid-1970s would the scientific community begin to include tobacco dependence in the spectrum of addictive disorders.) Yet, over the next 20 years, a remarkable generation of researchers and clinicians emerged who devoted their considerable intellect and energy exclusively to alcohol and drug problems.

The American system in which these eight researchers worked erected and has maintained relatively strong boundaries between the study and treatment of alcoholism and that of addiction to opiates and other illicit drugs. Since the early 1970s, there have been separate government institutes devoted to alcohol problems (the National Institute on Alcoholism and Alcohol Abuse (NIAAA)), and to the other drugs (the National Institute on Drug Abuse (NIDA)). A few scholars have worked in more than one area. Some, like Fred Glaser, migrated from an interest in the treatment of drug dependence to research on the treatment of alcoholism. Largely, however, the peculiarly American separation between research on drug addiction and research on alcoholism and alcohol abuse is reflected in the professional affiliations and colleagues who are mentioned in these interviews and commentary.

In the early years, many of the researchers who worked primarily on opiate addiction, as exemplified by Vincent Dole, Avram Goldstein, John Ball, and at first Fred Glaser, were frequently in contact with each other. In his self-education process at the beginning of the 1960s, Vincent Dole, a professor at the prestigious Rockefeller Institute and a recognized authority on lipid chemistry, initially sought advice from the researchers at Lexington and eventually came to rely on the clinical judgement of Marie Nyswander, a psychiatrist whose early experiences treating addicts took place at the hospital there. (This clinical partnership was solidified when they married each other in the 1960s.) Avram Goldstein credits Vincent Dole for stimulating his switch from biochemistry and molecular pharmacology, where he was a recognized leader, to the pharmacotherapy and neurobiology of opiate addiction. Fred Glaser, trained in psychiatry, was assigned to Lexington during his period of compulsory military service in the US Public Health Service. John Ball's interest in the sociology of addiction was

a direct result of his work at Lexington with Jack O'Donnell and Harris Isbell. He later collaborated with Glaser on the evaluation of drug addiction treatment programs in Pennsylvania; still later, his work (with Alan Ross) on what was to become a landmark book on methadone treatment brought him into close contact with Vincent Dole.

The influence of Dole and Nyswander's work was far reaching. The early evaluation of methadone treatment involved both outside evaluation and objective measures of illicit drug use (urine tests). The methods and results of the studies showed both the safety and effectiveness of oral methadone, stimulating a demand not only for expanded access to that treatment, but also for applying similar rigorous evaluation to other treatment approaches. Dole lectured persuasively at universities across the US, mentored young investigators, and organized a series of conferences where investigators working on treatment could interact. For a brief period in the mid-1970s, the methadone conferences included clinicians and researchers working in all areas of drug addiction treatment.

The development of methadone maintenance as an effective treatment for opiate addiction helped to generate a sea change in the way the American political system looked at the problem of drug addiction. Along with the therapeutic community movement (see the interview with David Deitch in this volume), it was one of the major elements in creating public support for community-based treatment. The availability of practical treatments with demonstrable effects on drug use and crime led, indirectly, to the establishment of NIDA in 1973, and to support for the systematic study of the etiology of addiction, the efficacy of treatment, the training of clinicians, and the effort to develop new pharmacotherapies.

With the Nixon administration's declaration of a 'war on drugs' in 1971, political and monetary support for research on addiction expanded. But it is unlikely that the war would have been declared if many of the implements to pursue it had not already been developed (see the Jerome Jaffe interview in this volume). Equally important for the growth of addiction research was the example of distinguished scientists like Goldstein and Dole focusing on these problems, thereby bringing a respectability to this area of inquiry that it had not previously enjoyed. Current leaders in the field of both drug addiction and alcohol research, such as Mary Jean Kreek and Enoch Gordis, spent their early research years in Dole's laboratory at the Rockefeller Institute. Goldstein's work on the neurobiology of addiction and endorphins attracted other young neuroscientists into the expanding research on addiction. As an adviser to successive heads of relevant federal agencies for many years, Goldstein influenced the expansion of research support for neuroscience, and particularly for the neuroscience relating to drug addiction.

Thus, on the drug side of the drug–alcohol divide, the major drivers of the early scientific advances included the involvement of already established investigators whose motive was to solve a drug-crime problem that was at once social and scientific. The subsequent growth in funding that drove further scientific expansion was the belief of some researchers, who were able to convince policymakers that research and treatment could contribute to a reduction in the social problem. In turn, both the funding and the achievements of the early workers brought new scholars and clinicians into a once neglected field.

Although LeClair Bissell and Charles Lieber worked for much of their careers in New York, there is no mention in their interviews of the local ferment taking place there about opiate addiction. Along with Howard Blane, Bissell and Lieber were part of a different network – the world of alcohol treatment and research. Their interviews reveal the early beginnings of the growing interest of the medical profession in alcohol-related problems. Both Lieber and Bissell were important players in the founding of the American Medical Society on Alcoholism, which evolved into the American Society of Addiction Medicine (ASAM). But as late as the mid-1960s the number of physicians who were focusing on alcohol problems was quite small; small enough, as Bissell puts it, to 'fit into Ruth Fox's living room'. Many, but certainly not all, of these physicians were in recovery and

had benefited from membership of AA. Perspectives in AA on alcoholism as a disease had a strong influence on them, especially in the early years. In turn, their organization importantly influenced not only policy and research on alcoholism, but also the way alcoholism was defined. For many of the members of this group, the central issues were gaining recognition for alcoholism as a distinctly separate disorder (not a manifestation of an underlying disorder), and persuading the medical community to provide patients with alcoholism decent and humane care. Nevertheless, the practice of denying alcoholics hospital admission was prevalent until the Comprehensive Alcohol Abuse and Alcoholism Prevention, Treatment and Rehabilitation Act of 1970 (the 'Hughes Act') was passed by the Congress. Harold Hughes (interviewed in this volume), a US Senator from Iowa, was a recovered alcoholic who had experienced the discrimination that was the typical lot of alcoholics in the US. His was an articulate voice for change and his personal magnetism was such that he was able to mobilize support for both a major policy change in healthcare delivery and a substantial increase in funding for research.

With the formation of the Research Society on Alcoholism, in 1977, researchers working on alcohol problems established a forum to advance scientific understanding of alcohol related problems – a goal supported and encouraged by Lieber and others. The Committee on Problems of Drug Dependence of the National Academy of Sciences, begun in 1929 as the Committee on Drug Addiction, had provided such a forum for clinicians and basic scientists for nearly 30 years. Although research on alcohol dependence was within their area of interest, it was not their central focus. While the new society did much to facilitate scientific interchange in the field of alcohol research, it had the additional effect of reducing the interchange with researchers focusing on other drugs.

As was the case with the opiate researchers, in the early years of scientific inquiry the number of those working on alcohol-related problems was relatively small, and there was considerable personal interaction among them. For example, Howard Blane was hired by Morris Chafetz to work on a study of alcoholics and treatment seeking; Chafetz was working with Jack Mendelson on treatment issues; Mendelson was collaborating with Lieber on alcohol hepatotoxicity. In 1970, when the Hughes legislation established the National Institute on Alcoholism and Alcohol Abuse (NIAAA), Morris Chafetz was appointed its first director. Not surprisingly, given its origins in the Hughes Act, an early priority for NIAAA was the expansion of treatment, and the cost of providing treatment for so large a group soon made studies of treatment effectiveness a high priority as well.

It took a long time for nicotine and tobacco use to be recognized in the US as belonging to the spectrum of addictive disorders. This was partly due to the stigma attached to drug addicts and alcoholics. Tobacco use was a nearly normative behavior in the 1960s, so it was especially difficult for policymakers in government and academia to see themselves as 'addicts'. Further, the tobacco manufacturers and their advertising agencies had tried hard to convince the public and policymakers that nicotine dependence (if it existed), was more or less like a golf habit. In the early 1970s, even the Office of Smoking and Health, then part of the Department of Health, Education & Welfare, was reluctant to see smoking described as an addiction, lest users despair of being able to quit.

Murray Jarvik's interest in nicotine and tobacco began in the mid-1960s, at that time when neither academia nor government were particularly concerned about tobacco dependence and addiction. Nevertheless, his early work did receive support from the National Institute on Mental Health, as well as from the American Cancer Society, and he mentored many postdoctoral students who later became independent researchers. But it was 1976 before NIDA took an active role in stimulating interest in research on smoking as an addictive disorder, and William Pollin, head of the Division of Research, asked Murray Jarvik to organize the first NIDA supported conference on smoking behavior. This policy shift may have been influenced by the emergence of new behavioural techniques to aid smoking cessation and by the early work on nicotine gum, which perhaps conjured up the hope that, like methadone, newer technologies could alter the perception of the problem and stimulate new treatment approaches. As the interest in tobacco dependence and nicotine addiction grew and a critical mass of researchers evolved, the broad river of addiction studies split, once again, into another stream that appears to be inclined to run in its own channel. A separate society was organized, and the nicotine and tobacco addiction field now has its own specialized meetings and journals.

These three relatively distinct streams of scholarly work on the addictive disorders – alcohol, illicit drugs, tobacco – have been influenced by somewhat different social forces. The common themes they share are the impact that new ideas and technologies (methadone, treatment matching, brief interventions, nicotine gum) exerted on the interests of researchers and the attitudes of policymakers; the establishment of professional and scholarly forums where research and policy ideas could be communicated and debated; the emergence of role models and persuasive advocates for change in the scientific, professional, and political spheres. It was definitely not a handicap that the United States has held a longstanding conviction about the possibilities of science to improve the quality of life, and that the nation has enjoyed a prosperity since the early 1950s that has permitted a generosity of funding for research that is unprecedented in the entire history of science.

Part II
Canadian Addiction Scientists

Reginald G. Smart

Reginald G. Smart was born in 1936 in Canada. He gained a BA in Psychology from the University of Toronto in 1958, an MA in Psychology in 1959 and a PhD in Clinical and Social Psychology in 1963. He was a member of the Task Force on Alcohol, Drugs and Transportation, Transport Research Board, National Research Council (USA), 1982–84; Psychosocial Research Review Committee, National Institute on Alcohol Abuse and Alcoholism (USA) 1984–91; Pan American Health Organization, Working Group on the Epidemiology of Drug Abuse, 1989–92; Working Group on the Prevention of Drug Abuse, 1981–99; Behavioral and Social Advisory Council, ABMRF, 1992–98; and worked on various World Health Organization projects. He was Professor (Adjunct) at the Department of Preventive Medicine and Biostatistics, Faculty of Medicine, University of Toronto, 1990–99; Principal and Senior Scientist, Centre for Addictions and Mental Health, Toronto; 1990–2000. His principal interests are in the epidemiology of alcohol and drug abuse, prevention programs for all types of drug abuse, evaluation of prevention and treatment programs, and international variations in drug abuse.

Early days at the addiction research foundation

Addiction: *When and how did you decide to come into the field of alcohol and drug studies?*
Reginald Smart: That first happened in 1957. I was a student in psychology at the University of Toronto. I needed a summer job and I needed it to be in Toronto. I had been working in mental retardation hospitals outside of Toronto in the summers. There was a new girlfriend I had at that time who was going to work in Toronto and I didn't want to go outside of Toronto because I thought we would have a nice summer together. I looked around and one of the very few jobs I could find on short notice was with the Addiction Research Foundation. It was then called the Alcoholism Research Foundation. It was a very small place and had been around only for a few years. They were just starting to get the research area staffed and funded. However, they had been doing treatment and educational work for some time.

A: *Can you say what you liked about the field?*
RS: It was a lucky accident that I came into the field of alcohol study, but I found very quickly after I had been working with the Alcoholism Research Foundation that it was a very good field.

It was a multi-disciplinary field, a field where the skills of all sorts of different people seemed to be important. There were many interesting research areas. The whole field was just developing and as yet there were relatively few people in it. However, there were a number of very good research scientists already at the ARF that were willing to take on sort of a mentorship role for me. I thought that was very helpful. Having mentors was very helpful to me in deciding to be in the field and to stay in it as my interests developed. However, nothing much developed with the girlfriend.

The whole field was just developing and as yet there were relatively few people in it

A: *Who particularly helped you in your early days at the Foundation, or in the field generally?*
RS: One of the people who was most helpful was John Seeley. He was head of the new ARF research department when I first came. My first conversation with him was very striking because one could see how bright he was and how excited about the field. At that time he was looking into the rela-

tionships among alcohol consumption over time and various problems from heavy drinking. He was soon looking at the effect of the price of alcohol on alcohol consumption. It was that work that led eventually to the single distribution theory and all of the work that came after it. John Seeley's contributions to the field were very good but, unfortunately, short-lived. He wasn't with us a long time. He was one of the best research leaders in the field, and a thinker who impressed us with the quickness of his mind and his grasp of the interesting issues in research. He also established the tradition that researchers at ARF could follow their own interests guided by the field, theory and their previous research. In the early days we had no pressure to do research which was politically or socially acceptable or useful to practitioners. Of course that came later and we have heavy pressure now to be useful in our research.

Everyone knew everyone else and I remember too being pretty sure that I knew all of the research that was happening in the world, at least published in English

A: *I'm told that for his first paper on the correlations between the patterns of consumption, cirrhosis deaths and price, he got data from a newspaper article. Is that true?*

RS: Yes, that's tight. He got some of the data from Harold Greer, a reporter who was doing an article for the *Toronto Star*. The reporter just was doing, I think, a one-off piece and took relatively little interest in it over time. I don't think he had any idea what an interesting sort of finding it was that he had made. However, John Seeley and other people at the Addiction Research Foundation were able to make a career in following up the implications of a newspaper article.

A: *Were there other mentors as well?*

RS: Bob Popham was also here and he was the assistant director at that time. We had most of our contact with him. He was in anthropology and he was extremely helpful to me as well. Bob Gibbins

was also in Toronto. He'd just come from Kingston. He had done the first survey of alcoholics in the general population in the Kingston area. That was called the Frontenac study, where he'd tried to find out how many alcoholics there were according to his definition in the County of Frontenac in Eastern Ontario. He had just come to Toronto and was setting up a program in psychological studies. Seeley was interested in sociology and alcohol policy. Bob Popham was doing his studies of drinking in taverns. All those people made an interesting group to be with and it became an of exciting sort of experience. We had regular coffee sessions where work in the field was discussed. These would often last an hour or more if the discussion was interesting. I learned a great deal from Popham, Seeley and Gibbins and all helped immensely in my career.

A: *What do you remember of the early days in alcohol studies?*

RS: Well, one thing that I remember particularly was how small the field was. There were very few people in alcohol studies at that time and you could know just about everyone in the whole world. As a student I remember being at a meeting at the Alcoholism Research Foundation where almost all of the big experts in the field sat around a single table. Leonard Goldberg was there from Sweden, Seldon Bacon was there, Kettil Bruun, E. M. Jellinek, as well as Seeley, Popham and Gibbins and some others. David Archibald, the first Executive Director of ARF, was also there. It was exciting to think just everybody who knew anything about the alcohol studies field was in this one room. Of course, a few years later with the development of the ARF and with the development of the institutes in the United States and other countries, you would need a very very big room to have all of the experts. Now, probably, there's no room that would contain them all. However, in the early days it was quite a small field. Everyone knew everyone else and I remember too being pretty sure that I knew all of the research that was happening in the world, at least published in English. On a regular basis you could get that just by reading the *Quarterly Journal of Studies on Alcohol* and looking at the abstracts.

You really could know just about everything that was happening. Of course, these days one can't begin to know everything that is happening in the alcohol or drug studies field.

Founding figures

A: *Do you remember many of the early figures in the field?*
RS: I remember E. M. Jellinek quite well. Jellinek was spending time in Toronto at that time. Jellinek, as I remember him, was a short, sort of stooped-over, overweight man, with little hair left. Not at all a romantic figure, but he had married several times and he spoke often about his relationship with a Spanish ballet dancer, as well as his other romantic affairs. I remember him as a great rapporteur and teller of jokes.

He was older when I met him and he had a hearing aid. If a meeting became boring he would turn the hearing aid off and go to sleep. Several times I saw people awaken him and ask him to summarize the discussion. Usually these summaries were very good.

Jellinek was a man with a vast research experience. He spent his early days in the jungles of West Africa as a biometrician and during that time he told me that he noticed that many of his co-workers had alcohol problems. He later took an interest in alcohol problems in the United States and helped to found the Yale Center for Alcohol Studies. Jellinek was always easy to approach and easy to talk to. As a classicist and anthropologist by training he knew much esoteric literature that had to do with alcohol, as well as the literature from many countries. He was essentially a scientist and in the days that I knew him spent a lot of his time doing fairly small scientific studies. Then he wrote his famous book, *The Disease of Alcoholism*, and that shook up the field for years to come.

A: *Do you remember Sully Ledermann?*
RS: Yes, I met him several times briefly. He did visit Toronto once and I also met him in Europe. I remember him as a very keen researcher, a very clever fellow, somebody who had a large amount of interest in epidemiology, but he didn't have a great deal of interest in the alcohol field. He did do those famous French studies that everyone knows, but he didn't spend a long time in the field. He had no idea just how much impact his early studies had on the field or on theories of prevention. He also was a very heavy smoker, I remember. A few years after he completed his work he developed lung cancer and he died, so his career was not very long.

A: *What about Kettil Bruun?*
RS: When I met Kettil he had just finished his PhD and he had done a study of the effects of alcohol on group interactions. He was a nice person, easy to talk to, very bright and energetic. Kettil was keen to make a name for himself in the field and he certainly did. Kettil thought our research group was 'too Jellinek-centred' and we paid too much attention to his ideas. He was probably right. I also remember Leonard Goldberg, who was a sort of a gray eminence in the field. He had been a long-time member of the Nobel Prize committee and he was a large figure in Swedish academic science. He was easy to relate to if you could find out what he was doing. He was interested at that time in the effect of alcohol on positional nystagmus. He had also done very early studies of alcohol impairment and driving and he had been interested in the different effects of beer and brandy.

Questions asked

A: *The Addiction Research Foundation may be unique in the emphasis that it has given to research over the years and in combining research with policy, prevention and treatment. Can you comment on how that came about?*
RS: How it happened is interesting because back in the 1950s when I first came along, there was no other place in the world which was primed to do the kinds of things that were being done at the Alcoholism Research Foundation. The ARF did treatment, research, education and community development, as well as policy analysis. When I came there were only about 35 people working at the ARF and most of them worked in the treatment facility. We had an inpatient facility on

Bedford Street in downtown Toronto and an outpatient facility as well. There were a few people in research, perhaps half a dozen, and there were a few people in the library and a few people in administration, but the main focus was on treatment and research on treatment.

It was very perceptive of the first president, David Archibald, that he wanted to develop the Addiction Research Foundation to be an academic institute. Right from the beginning ARF had very strong connections to the university. We had people from the university on our board and it was encouraged that one should be either a university student, graduate student, undergraduate student or, if possible, that you would be teaching. Most treatment facilities up to that point in Canada, and in the United States, were very much dominated by the AA philosophy. It was very creative that Dave Archibald thought that alcohol studies could be divorced from AA concepts, that they could be part of general scientific thinking, and also that there could be research on treatment effectiveness. All of those things were relatively new and stood us in good stead over the years as the place developed. I don't mean to imply that we have any anti-AA philosophy at ARF. AA held meetings have always been held in our treatment facility. It's just that we didn't want all of the thinking on research or treatment dominated by the AA philosophy.

I came into the field when it was expanding rapidly and there always seemed to be more money for the kinds of things we wanted to do

A: *Do you see changes in the kinds of questions that we're asking now in research or have the questions remained relatively stable? Do we have answers?*
RS: We've come up with many answers. Most of the questions that I remember being asked when I first came into the field have been answered to some extent, but are still being asked in a differ-

ent form. Some of those questions were, 'what's the relationship between levels of alcohol consumption and levels of problems?' That's been largely answered when it comes to something like liver cirrhosis, but not for behavioural problems such as domestic violence, delinquency or crime. Another question that was very important was 'what is the effect of the price of alcoholic beverages on consumption and how does that show what government policy ought to be toward alcoholic beverages?'

There were other questions as well about alcohol availability, such as opening hours and numbers of outlets. Again, much early research shows that increases in price and availability relate to increased consumption and problems, but some more recent research shows that price and availability do not always determine levels of drinking and problems. There were questions asked, too, about drinking-driving and that was one of the first things that I got into. A friend of mine at that time, Wolfgang Schmidt, decided to make a study of alcoholics in our clinic. We tried to find out how many accidents alcoholic patients had, how many were due to alcohol, what kind of accidents they had and what sort of treatment experience they had. It was an interesting study that answered a few important questions. It was one of the first studies that indicated that single vehicle accidents were a big problem for people who had been drinking heavily. Of course, drinking-driving questions are still raised today, especially about the most effective types of intervention.

Personal contributions

A: *What sort of contribution do you think you've made to the field of alcohol and drug studies?*
RS: I like to think there are several contributions. I came into the field when it was expanding rapidly and there always seemed to be more money for the kinds of things we wanted to do. It was an affluent time, especially in the 1960s and 1970s and perhaps into the 1980s. We had many opportunities to expand that people don't have now. Those opportunities often increased year after year.

There was a time when our research budget was doubling every few years and we could add research staff each year. One thing that I'm happy about is the number of people I was able to attract to the field who later became important researchers in their own area. This includes people in treatment research and epidemiology, educational research and drinking-driving. These people have made their own careers, but I have some pride that I could find the right people for the right slot.

I also have some satisfaction in being able to establish our school drug use study. It started back in Toronto in the 1960s and it is the longest running school study. The primary purpose was to monitor and understand alcohol, and especially drug use in the youthful population in the 1970s, 1980s and 1990s. It's a large scale school study including students from all over Ontario. It's been a model for several of these kinds of studies in other provinces and countries. There has been a hundred or more papers produced on the results, so it has made a scientific contribution. It also has considerable practical significance to the understanding of youthful alcohol and drug use and methods of preventing them. In Ontario we have a very good picture of what's been happening with alcohol and drug use among young people over a long period of time. The study has produced a large number of important results of interest to teachers, parents and students as well. It tries to answer the types of questions many people ask of us, e.g. how many students use drugs? is the number increasing? and what can we do about it?

A: *And you worked quite a lot with WHO?*
RS: Yes I very much enjoyed and learned a lot from my work with the World Health Organization as a consultant. We helped to bring our technology and advice into developing countries, sometimes when they weren't quite ready for it. My work included developing methods and guidelines for doing research on epidemiology and rapid assessment, as well as giving advice to many researchers in other countries on how to set up research programs. I was also involved in the first WHO report on youthful drug abuse as well as reports on the health consequences of cannabis use, solvent and cocaine dependency and others. Our set of guidelines for epidemiological research on drug use first done in the 1980s is being redone now by the World Health Organization so it will have a longer life. There is also a general contribution to the field of epidemiology of alcohol and drug use. In my books I've tried to present a detailed picture of the nature of alcohol and drug use in Canada and to argue that it has an important contribution to the world understanding of the problem.

A: *Do you have any major disappointments in how your work has been accepted?*
RS: Most of what I've done has been middle of the road, non-controversial, epidemiological research, and has been well accepted. There are a few areas of research where I was surprised that the results weren't better accepted. I wouldn't call it a major disappointment, because the most controversial kinds of research often get more attention, even if negative. Some of the research that I did on the availability of alcohol, showing that the availability may not be as important as people thought, was not well accepted. There were our studies of advertising research. Colleagues and I did several studies of advertising bans in British Columbia and other places, as well as trying to look at the relationship between strictness of advertising rules and alcohol sales. We also did a number of experiments in which we gave people different levels of advertising and no advertising at all. We were unable to find much effect of advertising on people's desire to drink alcohol. This research was not very well accepted in many areas. There still are many public health people who believe that alcohol advertising is a potent influence but my understanding is that current research still shows it to be an insignificant factor for overall alcohol consumption. We had some trouble getting our research published in some journals, even though I thought it was pretty good and I still do. This advertising research is very much liked by people in the alcohol industry but not very much liked by people in public health.

A: *Any other research of yours that has had trouble winning recognition?*

RS: The other area with disappointing acceptance has been our recent work on what accounts
for the downward trends in Canadian and
American rates of alcohol consumption and
alcohol-related problems. We have a series of
research studies on the decline in alcohol-related
problems, such as liver cirrhosis, over the past 15
or 20 years and it shows that increases in levels of
treatment and increases in Alcoholics Anonymous
membership are important in those trends.
However, physical availability and the cost of
alcohol seems to be not much of a factor. Some of
the research shows that costs of alcohol have
almost remained the same as alcohol consumption
was stable and alcohol problems have declined but
sometimes on-premise sales for alcohol have
greatly increased. Availability may not be so
important as many people originally thought,
especially those people associated with the Single
Distribution theory. It remains to be seen what will
happen as more research is done, but it's slightly
disappointing that that work isn't being better
accepted. New ideas that challenge old ways of
thinking sometimes do not become accepted at
first.

A: *What do you consider your most important
achievements in research?*
RS: The most important research achievements
probably are in the area of looking at the factors
associated with the increases and decreases in
student drug use. We've monitored that well over
time and I think we have a better understanding
of that than in any other place in the world. The
other achievement is the research that has to deal
with the explanation for the decline in alcohol-
related problems. It makes an original and
controversial set of conclusions which calls into
question the Single Distribution theory of prevention. We have shown the need to consider variables such as increases in levels of prevention and
treatment, and increases in Alcoholics Anonymous
membership. Some of our research also shows that
you should take into account increased education
about alcohol-related problems and alcohol consumption in looking at reasons for the declines in
alcohol-related problems.

A: *The school study has been very significant in
your career at the Addiction Research Foundation
in the field of alcohol and drug problems. Could
you speculate on why we don't see more studies
of this type?*
RS: We often have data for adults in household
studies or telephone surveys. It's more difficult to
generate the same level of interest in those surveys
of adults and they are often not repeated surveys.
Traditionally in public health there's been a focus
on the importance of young people, particularly
when it comes to initiation of alcohol and drug
use. Both society and the research agencies tend to
focus more on youth. Good studies of youth are
often more likely to be funded than good studies
of more mature populations. There is, too, the fact
that some kinds of drug use and an early age of
initiation are important factors in later alcohol
and drug use. Age of initiation is a very important
factor in smoking, because we know that most
people that are ever going to be smoking are
smoking by about the age of 18. There are some
good reasons for having youth studies better supported than other kinds of studies. There is also a
large constituency for that kind of study itself.
Schools and school boards are very interested in
the outcome and they're in a position to influence
the kinds of alcohol and drug education students
will get. Parents are also very interested in our
school studies. We don't have the same focus with
adults. There's no large institution that is responsible for doing education with adults. It's very difficult to do family education except through the
school system.

A: *The school study is remarkable for the level
of cooperation you've been able to get among
the various schools and school boards across the
province.*
RS: We started the study because the school
board in Toronto wanted us to investigate drug use
among students in their schools. Hence we began
with a good level of cooperation and since that
time we've been able to enhance or maintain it
very well. The study was expanded from Toronto
to all of the areas in Ontario in the 1970s so we
tried to get the cooperation of all school boards

in the Province of Ontario. We were able to get almost complete cooperation from the school boards when we asked for it. Part of it has to do with the anonymity of the study. We never gave out information on drug use in particular schools, or particular school boards. We always had anonymity in the student's questionnaires. Nobody ever had to sign anything to participate. Students didn't have to participate if they didn't want to and very few ever refused to participate. We also had the policy of having our own people do the administration in the classroom. Teachers didn't get involved in the administration and didn't walk around to look at what the students were writing. That was an important set of procedures. We always made the reports available to all of the schools, teachers and school boards that participated. We traditionally made several kinds of reports available, a long technical report that not everybody wanted to read but also shorter summaries and press reports that were more interesting. We also made them available in French. There are also short video tapes telling about the methods used in the report and they're interesting. We tried to communicate our reports to the schools to show our appreciation for their cooperation.

The future of alcohol studies

A: *Where do you think the field of alcohol studies should go now? What direction should we be looking at?*
RS: It would be interesting if the field would take a long look at some neglected problems. The field should start studying biological markers of delinquency, alcohol related crime, alcohol related violence and the kinds of cognitive and learning problems that alcohol creates. Are there any biological markers for those sorts of things? Also it would be interesting to know what are the safe levels of alcohol consumption when it comes to things like delinquency, crime, violence, cognitive and other kinds of learning problems. We don't have safe levels established. We have safe levels established for things like drinking-driving and

perhaps for alcohol related problems such as dependency, but we've neglected a lot of new areas that should have safe levels established. We should be focusing always on problems of drinking, not on normal drinking.

I like the new emphasis that there is on patterns of drinking, looking at how modes of alcohol consumption relate to problems and to amounts of drinking, rather than just focusing on per capita consumption. I think also there should be more study made of the types of beverages people are consuming, studying how the type of beverage in relation to the pattern might tell us more about what problems people are going to have. The genetic aspects of alcohol consumption and problems are very important and they need to be pursued. When it comes to treatment, we need more long-term treatment evaluation studies, but we also need more studies of how self-help groups work and how effective they are. Some of our research shows that nearly as many people are doing self-help treatment as are getting treatment in the usual clinical settings. I also think we need to have more study of why alcohol-related problems are decreasing in some countries in the world. We've done some of that in Ontario and in Alberta, but many countries do have decreasing problems and we don't understand enough about why those problems are decreasing.

> I like the new emphasis that there is on patterns of drinking, looking at how modes of alcohol consumption relate to problems and to amounts of drinking, rather than just focusing on per capita consumption

A: *Do you see any trends in the field that you like or that you dislike?*
RS: I very much like to see the trend continue in which we are getting a lot of new people into the field. The people coming into the field now are much better trained than we were when we came into it. They're more sophisticated. They know more about multivariate analysis and the sophis-

ticated kinds of trend analyses that can be done. They're better trained and better able to take up the field. One trend that I don't especially like is that there probably are fewer generalists in the field than there used to be. Most people get into a very tiny area and stick in it. Another regrettable trend is that many places are having to give up hard money positions and develop grants or soft money positions. There's less freedom and more control in the granting system, than there is in the hard money system. Certainly at ARF we all have to try to get research grants. It's a system that ARF is not built on and it's going to be difficult to do. That kind of grant system means that the research institution has to do what the granting agencies would like to fund, rather than necessarily picking out the best or the most important problems and doing research on those. There are several places in the world where people are getting more and more pressure to apply for grants for alcohol studies. That's the trend I don't care for.

A: *Do you have any advice to new people coming into the field of alcohol studies?*
RS: Well, I'd encourage people to come into the alcohol and drug studies field. It's still a very good field. I still recommend people to try it. I think it's a field where you have to stay in it for quite a long time in order to make an important contribution. People coming into the field should try to pick a sub-area which is fairly new and has few people in it. It should be something that's important theoretically and also important in a practical sense.

Mentoring is important for young people to get if they possibly can. It helped me greatly. People should try to get an older person to take an interest in their career if they can. People coming into the alcohol and drug field should want to become famous in the field – famous for their research, that is. To do that they have to publish good papers in good places, but they also have to travel to give papers on their research. People new to the field should give as many papers as possible, in as many places as possible without ignoring their journal publications. In the alcohol and drug studies field you have to be seen in person to establish a good reputation. Going to conferences and seminars to report on research is the best way to do that sort of thing early in your career.

Martha Sanchez-Craig

Martha Sanchez-Craig BA PhD joined the Addiction Research Foundation, Toronto, as director of a halfway house for homeless alcoholics, where her main responsibility was the development of a rehabilitation program for this population which could be adopted throughout Ontario. In 1977 she moved to the Clinical Institute of the ARF as a Senior Scientist where her main line of research was in the area of secondary prevention developing brief interventions for alcohol and drug-related problems. She has been a Visiting Professor at Hjellestad Klinikken, Norway, at Escola Paulista de Medicina, Sao Paulo, and at Hospital Madre de Deus, Porto Alegre where she was involved in collaborative research on brief intervention. She has also been a Consultant for the Pan American Health Organization and the WHO Development Programme.

Early years in Mexico

Addiction: *Martha, you graduated in philosophy in Mexico, before coming to Canada, and you ended up in alcoholism research in Toronto. That's a big jump. Can you tell us something about your background in Mexico that might have led you to make such a move?*

Martha Sanchez-Craig Yes. I was born in Saltillo, in northeastern Mexico, and spent my first 10 years there. My mother had been a teacher, and her family were all professionals, with strong intellectual leanings. My father came from a family of business people, but he himself was an agronomical engineer, with post-graduate training at Texas A&M. When I was 10 years old, my father was offered a position in the Ministry of Agriculture. The new job meant that he had to travel a lot, and so I was put into a convent boarding school, and got my primary schooling and part of my secondary schooling there. The nuns were very strong on discipline, and so I was a very well-behaved girl.

A: *But you didn't finish school there?*

MS-C: No. I finished secondary school in Mexico City, where my family was then living. It was time for me to start thinking about a career. I had my heart set on two things. One was music, and my aspiration was to be a concert pianist. I had received piano lessons from the time I was 10 years old, and the nuns encouraged that in the convent. The other thing I wanted very much was to study chemistry. When I was a child, my favorite cousins, the ones that later on I admired and got my inspiration from, used to receive gifts such as chemistry sets and microscopes. We played a lot on my grandfather's ranch, swinging from tree branches, playing in the stream, catching frogs and lizards, and I was fascinated by looking at things.

We played a lot on my grandfather's ranch, swinging from tree branches, playing in the stream, catching frogs and lizards, and I was fascinated by looking at things

---

A: *Which of these two very different paths did you decide to follow?*

MS-C: I wanted to go to the university and study chemistry. My mother supported me strongly, but my father said 'No!' Even though he was a professional, he still had the traditional male viewpoint that women's role was to get married, have children and keep house.

A: *And that it was useless to waste education on them?*

MS-C: Exactly. And he held the purse-strings, so we had to do what he said. By this time he was no longer with the Ministry of Agriculture, but had set up his own company, importing glass and other objects from Italy. He decided that it would be good for me to get skills that would help him in his business. So I was sent to a school where I learned accounting, business administration, and so forth. But in exchange, I got part of my wish granted and I also enrolled in the School of Music. I went there for a year, but became convinced that I didn't have the talent to be a concert pianist, and I quit. As for the business school, I absolutely hated it.

A: *Where did that leave you?*
MS-C: At 22, I did what was expected of me, and got married to a lawyer whom I had met in the Music School. We had three children. But he was a very heavy drinker, and over time he became abusive and violent.

A: *Did that have any influence on your later choice of research field?*
MS-C: No, none at all. But after five years of this I was in very bad shape, extremely depressed, and on medical advice I took my children and went back to Saltillo, where my parents were again living. I moped around, and spent my time just listening to music, until one day my father ordered me to get out and start doing something. So I took up tennis with a vengeance. He had started a new business, importing selected poultry lines from the United States, and producing breeding stock to supply chicken farms all over Mexico. He put me in charge of this, gave me his best employees to help me, and figured that this would at least let me earn a good living. It did, but that took only a few hours a day, and I spent the rest of the time playing tennis.

A: *I understand you were a tennis champion in Mexico – is that right?*
MS-C: Well, I was a good tennis player, but I had to work at it. It didn't come easily. A year and a half later, my husband reappeared and told my father that he was now in a government position in which it was important for him to have a family, and he wanted us back. My father told me that it was my responsibility to go back to my husband,

and so off we went. But within a month he again became violent, and I quit for good. I packed the children into the car and drove for a thousand kilometers back to Saltillo, but just before getting there I had a terrible automobile accident and was badly injured.

Six months later, I was still on crutches when my father proposed that I should go back to the chick-breeding business, but this time I refused. I wanted to go back to school to study chemistry. He said that was a crazy idea because I had been out of school for over 15 years and he didn't think I would be able to cope. But after thinking it over for a couple of days, he decided that he would let me go back, provided it was to the private university, and not the public one. The private university was new, and had only four programs: philosophy, psychology, literature, and accounting! So I registered in psychology.

A: *Did you have any idea of what psychology was?*
MS-C: No. I had a smattering of it in my earlier schooling, but I really had no idea what to expect. The instructor had been trained in Germany and England, and also had degrees in physics and mathematics, but his psychology was heavily philosophical and humanistic in orientation. We had no laboratory work, our physiological psychology was limited to what we read in the books, and the behaviorist approach was almost ignored. There was great emphasis on the social aspects of psychology, normal and abnormal psychology, clinical testing methods and so forth.

A: *How did you react to this approach?*
MS-C: The professor in charge of the course had a tremendous impact on me. In his first lecture he said: 'Do not trust anyone who speaks to you in a dogmatic fashion. In science there are no dogmas. Theories arise and then they are abandoned. But the scientist never abandons his desire to keep looking and understanding.' I loved him. His lectures gave me real thrills, goose bumps. He would begin every topic with the ancient Greek philosophers, and then walk you through the whole history of the changing ideas until he brought you

to the current views of today. It was exciting, it was fun, it was an incomparable period of my life. In order to understand his approach better, I also enrolled in the philosophy program in the next semester. I think I really enjoyed the philosophy more than the psychology. And in psychology, what I enjoyed most was the neuroanatomy and neurophysiology. To be honest, I don't know that I have ever really been in love with psychology.

The move to Toronto

A: *Yet you came to Canada to continue further in psychology.*
MS-C: Yes, I came to Toronto in 1969 to do a PhD in clinical psychology, as an acceptable way of making a living. When I finished my PhD in 1972 I had to look after my three children, who were with me in Canada, and that meant finding a job in Canada or going back to Mexico. My children were very happy in the Canadian school system. So it would have been very difficult for me to tell them that we were going back to Mexico, and I would need to find a very good reason to give them. My strategy was to apply for jobs that would be too big for me, so that I would be turned down and we would have to go back. Two weeks after obtaining my PhD I began to look at the newspaper advertisements for positions open, and the first one I saw was from the Addiction Research Foundation. They were looking for a PhD in the social sciences, to conduct evaluation research on their halfway house. I didn't know anything about alcoholism, but my thesis was on treatment research. Next day I was hired. Later on, I learned from my supervisor that they had 54 applicants, that I was the last to apply, and that I was the only female applicant.

A: *What was the research question that you were supposed to tackle?*
MS-C: The halfway house for men had been in existence for six or seven years. It was run on the philosophy of Alcoholics Anonymous, and all the staff were recovering alcoholics. It was regarded as a home where residents had room and board, and informal support from staff. If they needed

treatment, medical services, or whatever, they were expected to find these in the community. The halfway house for women was just about to open next door, in early 1973. My mandate was to develop, and to evaluate scientifically, a model for the rehabilitation of homeless and unemployed alcoholics that could be adopted throughout Ontario. I was given three years to do it.

A: *But that stretched into . . . ?*
MS-C: Four years, at first. For extraneous reasons we had to look for new premises, and we decided to break with tradition and combine the men's and women's houses into one 'co-educational' house. What we learned from that experience became the basis for all of my work since then.

My strategy was to apply for jobs that would be too big for me, so that I would be turned down and we would have to go back

A: *The main finding?*
MS-C: The main finding was that the alcoholic who became successful acquired the characteristics of the socially stable problem drinker.[1] The criteria for deciding that an alcoholic was successful were a return to full-time employment, no evidence of having been on welfare, no arrests, no admissions to detox units or hospital emergency departments, and living outside the Skid Row area. About 15% of people like that said at follow-up that they had been abstinent for the past 6, 12 or 18 months. Another 8–10% told us that they had been drinking small amounts of alcohol without apparent problems, and were successfully holding a job, etc. I realized that some of these people, who were supposed to not be able to drink alcohol at all without losing control, were in fact able to do so for significant periods of time.

Moderate drinking as an international treatment goal

A: *These were the ones who had become like socially stable problem drinkers?*

MS-C: Yes. We concluded that if we offered moderate drinking as a possible goal for socially stable clients, it might improve the outcome of treatment. We also found something else very important in the halfway house study. When we put into the program the methods that I had developed in my thesis work with adolescents, the alcoholics were able to learn quite satisfactorily the specific skills we taught them for solving interpersonal problems: how to get along with others, how to set goals in various areas, how to cope with the drinking tendency, and so forth. But when we re-tested them a month later, most of them had forgotten the material they had learned successfully. We found that 46% of them had cognitive deficits of the kinds that interfered with the retention of what we were trying to teach them. But instead of abandoning these methods, we decided that we should tailor them to the limited abilities of the chronic alcoholic.

At ethical review I was told that it was unethical to do studies of controlled drinking. I had to convince the committee that it would be unethical *not* to do the research

---

I also realized that we would have to be able to apply these methods on an outpatient basis, for early problem drinkers who were still employed, still had families, but were drinking to the point of jeopardizing their ability to continue in that state. At about that time, in early 1976, the field underwent a major conceptual reformulation, when Griffith Edwards and Milton Gross began to talk of a continuum of dependence.[2] Before that, it was seen as all-or-none: either you were an alcoholic or you were not. But the idea of graded degrees of dependence legitimized the concept of graded degrees of response. Also, a review by Emrick showed that abstinence rates after treatment were not related to the intensity of the interventions.[3] The new concepts, plus the findings of the halfway house, led me to move into the area of secondary prevention. This would require us to

adapt the methods we had developed, and explicitly offer a goal of moderate drinking.

A: *But there must have been others who were thinking along those lines, too.*
MS-C: There were. William Miller's group, Vogler's group, and the Sobells in the United States, Heather and Robertson in the United Kingdom, and Lovibond *et al.* in Australia, were already evaluating controlled-drinking treatments. But research on controlled drinking was highly controversial and most alcoholism counsellors regarded controlled drinking as an impossible goal to achieve.

A: *There must have been many practical problems in trying to do that research?*
MS-C: At ethical review I was told that it was unethical to do studies of controlled drinking. I had to convince the committee that it would be unethical not to do the research. So I drew on the epidemiological and population studies by Cahalan, Room and others, showing that the largest incidence of problems related to drinking was in the 20–30-year-old group, whereas people in treatment were mostly 40–45 years old. I pointed out that the halfway house clients averaged about 17 years of heavy drinking, and asked, 'Do we have to wait all that time before we try to put something in place that is attractive to people with alcohol problems?'

A: *Did that argument win the day?*
MS-C: That argument convinced the committee, but they insisted that we modify the research design. Instead of random assignment to a goal of abstinence or controlled drinking within the same program, we had to agree that those assigned to a goal of controlled drinking could shift to a goal of abstinence, but not vice versa.

A: *Your follow-ups of the cases included other contacts who could verify the self-reports of drinking or abstinence?*
MS-C: Yes, and for validation we also used laboratory tests and neuropsychological tests that had been shown to be sensitive to the effects of

drinking. All these data confirmed that we could trust our clients' reports of their drinking. This study[4] yielded an immense amount of information, and had an important influence on my subsequent work. For example, it showed the importance of giving clients a choice of goal. Those in the abstinence condition did not abstain during treatment or the 2-year follow-up period – instead, they developed patterns of moderate drinking on their own, ultimately as successfully as those who were trained to drink in moderation, but it took them longer and required more help from their therapist. In subsequent studies we always allowed the clients to choose their goal.

A: *The success rate?*
MS-C: The rates of success were around 60–65%, comparable to those found for controlled drinking therapies with problem drinkers rather than alcoholics.

Treatment formats

A: *That leads us directly to the topic for which you are now best known, the evolution of a variety of interventions, including a so-called 'minimal intervention'.*
MS-C: Yes. Griffith Edwards really made the treatment community look much more critically at what it was doing in the name of 'treatment', when he emphasized two basic concepts: early intervention and brief, focused intervention. In the course of 22 years work at ARF our research program evolved into four formats of early intervention that vary in complexity and duration.

A: *And what are these formats? Can you describe them for us?*
MS-C: We refer to them as 'counselling', 'advice', 'education' and 'self-help'. All of them share the same core elements, and all of them include an initial motivational assessment and planned checkups. The counselling format is described in a manual for therapists.[5] In this manual I described the procedures we had used in the first study with problem drinkers. The counselling format demands the greatest level of therapist skill, and involves the greatest number of sessions – six has been the average. The clients come for help in specialized clinics. Most of them are already motivated to change, but believe that they need help to achieve their goals. The advice format came next. It was designed for use by primary care professionals who can't spend much time on each case.

A: *Such as family physicians?*
MS-C: Family physicians, nurses and others in primary care roles. This format came about when the clinical director of the Foundation asked me to train the medical interns to give such advice, which I laid out in a two-page pamphlet called *Guidelines for Sensible Drinking*. Advice typically involves a single session of about 15 minutes, given to patients at risk of alcohol problems who have been identified by health professionals during routine practice.

The WHO international study on primary care interventions suggested that such patients gain no benefit from the addition of a counselling component.[6]

In the course of 22 years work at ARF our research program evolved into four formats of early intervention that vary in complexity and duration

---

A: *Another format you mentioned is 'education' – how does that differ from the counselling and the advice formats?*
MS-C: Those who join the educational program are not looking for treatment – they want to be educated by a professional on the skills they need to avoid or eliminate alcohol problems. This format – that we call 'DrinkWise' – was developed at the request of the director of health promotion of a large psychiatric hospital in Guelph, Ontario.[7]

A: *And what about the fourth approach, 'Self-help'?*
MS-C: That one is for people who want to change their drinking habits on their own. Some

problem drinkers select this option because there are no counselling services in their community, but others just prefer to solve their problems by themselves. I wrote the first self-help manual in collaboration with a psychologist at the Foundation, Dr Gillian Leigh.

A: *And the evolution of these four approaches all resulted from your recognition of the heterogeneity of the client population in your earlier work?*
MS-C: Absolutely. But also, recognition of the heterogeneity of the care providers.

A: *Martha, I wonder if you would say a little more about self-help, because in some ways that's perhaps the most radical of the approaches you've outlined.*
MS-C: Yes. Let me tell you a little about how the self-help approach came about. Over the years I had many telephone calls from people who wanted advice about their drinking. The first call came from a man who heard about me through the *Toronto Globe and Mail*, which had done a major story on our first study with problem drinkers. He asked if he could come to see me, since there was no one in his community who could advise him on controlled drinking, and he was not prepared to go to AA. When I discovered he was calling from Calgary, I said 'I think that coming to Toronto for counselling would be very expensive for you, Sir'. In a very potent voice he replied, 'Money is not my problem'. 'Well', I said, 'if money is not your problem, why don't we spend 20 or 30 minutes on the phone, so I can tell you what is essential for you to know.' He agreed. First, I asked him to describe the situations where alcohol tended to cause him problems, and how much he drank then. Next, I tried to assess if he had a severe alcohol problem.

A: *Based on something like the Alcohol Dependence Scale?*
MS-C: No, just by checking if he had experienced the typical symptoms of severe alcohol dependence, which he had not. I then described the drinking patterns that the successful clients in the study had adopted, and asked him to pick, and

write down, the pattern he believed would fit best with his life-style. Finally, I said 'If you want to become a winner in controlled drinking, you ought to practice the following for several months. First, you must record every day how well you stick to the drinking pattern you just selected. I'm going to send you forms that can help you to keep accurate track of your drinking. Second, you must learn to pace your drinking – from now on, measure all your drinks so you know exactly how much you're drinking, dilute your drinks and drink them slowly, wait at least one hour before having the next drink, do not drink on an empty stomach. Third, the time that you would have spent in heavy drinking, you must fill with other enjoyable activities. Fourth, make a plan before going to social events where the pressures to drink are likely to be strong, or where you may experience strong temptation – don't improvise, decide ahead of time on the strategies you will use to avoid heavy drinking in those risky situations. Fifth, never use alcohol to cope with problems – if you do, it will come back to haunt you.'

A: *Martha, this approach seems to involve a very large degree of reliance on the truthfulness of the answers that the clients give. To what extent do you verify what they tell you?*
MS-C: In our research we always attempted to validate the clients' reports by using biochemical assays, neuropsychological tests, or reports from collaterals. Even in our last study,[8] which was designed to evaluate a telephone intervention based on the self-help manual, in which we obviously couldn't use the objective tests, we still managed to obtain corroboration of the subjects' reports from collaterals. But if clients believe that their reports will be kept confidential, and won't be used in ways they don't want, their reports tend to be quite reliable, particularly when they have been keeping track of their drinking.

A: *How have the outcomes in your studies compared with outcomes in conventional abstinence-based inpatient or outpatient programs?*
MS-C: This is difficult to say, because of the nature of the samples. Those entering conventional treatments are usually not screened for

problem severity. In contrast, in programs such as ours, clients with severe dependence or severe alcohol-related problems have been systematically excluded. Therefore, comparison of rates of success from traditional programs with those like ours would not be valid. In studies with problem drinkers, with characteristics similar to those in our studies, the rates of success have been similar – around 60%.

A: *With 'success' defined as what?*
MS-C: The criterion of success in moderate drinking has varied over the years, but has gradually become more stringent. The last we used, which we established empirically, was: for males, a maximum of four drinks on any day, and 12 drinks in any week; for females, a maximum of three drinks on any day, and nine drinks in any week. These are the levels we currently recommend as upper limits, to help clients set goals of moderation. We supplement these guidelines with strong recommendations to abstain in a number of situations where consumption of even one drink could be hazardous or harmful.

***

In Brazil, Adrian Wilkinson and I collaborated with the late Jandira Masur and her team, in a study in which our brief intervention (three counselling sessions) was compared with eight months of psychoanalytic psychotherapy, the typical treatment for alcoholism in Brazil

***

A: *Can you give us some examples of the range of societies or cultures in which it has been tested?*
MS-C: In our telephone study[8] the majority of clients were English-Canadian, but we had good representation of French-Canadians, Aboriginals and people of various European backgrounds. These four groups achieved similar reductions in the number of heavy drinking days, around 70% reduction from baseline, and all groups had similar proportions of clients who were rated as 'moderate drinkers' at the end of the study. Outside Canada, Moira Jacobs tested the Advice format in a general

hospital in India, and the results were very positive and validated by GGT levels. The counselling approach was tested in Spain by Bernardo Ruiz Victoria and his colleagues with excellent results, also validated by GGT. In Brazil, Adrian Wilkinson and I collaborated with the late Jandira Masur and her team, in a study in which our brief intervention (three counselling sessions) was compared with eight months of psychoanalytic psychotherapy, the typical treatment for alcoholism in Brazil. In Geneva, the International Labour Office got permission from The College of Family Physicians of Canada to use the patient workbook[9] that we had developed, in an international study in Poland, Sri Lanka, Egypt, Namibia and Mexico.

A: *Given the success rates that you have had, what economic and social impact would you expect if this approach were widely adopted internationally?*
MS-C: That's a tough question, and I'm not sure I can answer it. Let's suppose, for the sake of argument, that our approach and philosophy were adopted by all those providing services to people with alcohol problems. What would one expect to see? First, extensive treatments would become rare. This would be OK, since these treatments have not yielded better results than relatively brief ones, including one session of advice. We might also see that many problem drinkers who are afraid of seeking help in conventional programs could be attracted by approaches such as ours, if they knew that they would not labelled as 'alcoholic', that their privacy would be respected, that they could get help without putting their work or home responsibilities on hold, and that they would be given the opportunity to choose between quitting or cutting down. We know from our research that these are important needs of problem drinkers. If these assumptions were to materialize, no doubt there would be some savings to the health care system through use of briefer interventions. But the number of cases in the system would increase, although we don't know how big this increase might be. We don't know what proportion of the large population of 'at-risk' and 'problem drinkers' have any inclination to change their drinking, even if they are made aware of the

risks they are running, and the availability of tested strategies for cutting down. As we scientists always seem to say, 'more research is needed'.

Brief interventions and criteria for choosing the clients

A: *I understand that in Brazil, the brief intervention was applied independently of the severity of the drinking problems of those who entered the program. What are your thoughts now about the applicability of this approach to those who would be considered chronic alcoholics?*

MS-C: My view is that the level of alcohol dependence is not an obstacle for using a flexible approach such as ours. The real obstacles are the personal problems. For instance, you may have a person who looks like an ideal candidate for our intervention, in terms of being only moderately dependent, and with a drinking pattern that isn't too extreme. But if his life is in turmoil, because his marriage is falling apart, or he was just fired from his job, it will be difficult for him to achieve the goals of the program.

A: *Would it be fair to say that the AA philosophy, that an alcoholic is always an alcoholic, is really based on those that you would describe as severely dependent and with grave life problems?*

MS-C: I suppose so, but in my view, one cannot be dogmatic about what alcoholics can or cannot achieve. That slogan of AA, I believe, is used to instil in those who become members the conviction that drinking in moderation is impossible for anyone with alcohol problems. This is likely to be more true of those with severe dependence and severe life problems. In our clinic we always encouraged such persons to abstain. But there were some who refused adamantly to give up alcohol. In my experience, clients usually know best what they can or cannot achieve.

A: *The approach you have described has obvious and important implications for the meaning of dependence, and of problem drinking. How do you think it modifies the concept of dependence?*

MS-C: Our clients almost always endorse items

on 'impaired control' to indicate that they often drank more than they wanted, or that they continued to drink in spite of problems. But they typically do not endorse items reflecting severe alcohol dependence, such as withdrawal symptoms, or drinking to relieve them, or constant preoccupation with alcohol. In short, the notion of continuum of dependence provided the framework for our work, and the items describing the alcohol dependence syndrome have been useful in selecting clients for whom our approach is most appropriate.

A: *How long have you followed-up your earliest groups?*

MS-C: About eight years after the clients had been discharged from treatment. I got permission from the Ethics Committee to contact the 70 clients in the study, and a psychologist colleague began interviewing them. When she had interviewed about half of the sample, I saw that most of the clients still had the same status at eight years as they had had at the end of two years.

A: *You mean that those who had been successful at the end of two years were still successful after eight years?*

MS-C: And vice versa, with two exceptions. One client who was successful at two years had later deteriorated, and one who was unsuccessful at two years had become successful. At that point I decided to stop the follow-up, because my curiosity was satisfied. Adrian Wilkinson and I had published a chapter on brief intervention,[10] in which we argued that it would be foolish to pretend that brief psychological interventions are like radical surgery, and that their effects should be life-long.

A: *But on the other hand, if governments or treatment agencies are really going to be convinced that they should adopt widely the brief approach that you have outlined, they will quite properly want to be assured that the results they would get from the intervention would be for the maximum social good over the long haul.*

MS-C: I accept that. But the problem is not with the interventions. The real obstacles that prevent wide adoption of brief interventions in primary care settings are in the health care systems, where the emphasis is not on maintaining health, but on responding to crisis. Tom Babor and Peter Anderson have written extensively on this issue.[6]

A: *That could certainly be an important future development – to make the system not just short-term intervention to correct existing alcohol problems, but a way of maintaining an effective adjustment to prevent recurrence of the problems for the rest of the person's life.*

MS-C: I agree, but we are far from convincing most primary care providers that this should be part of their job. Let me give you an example. A few days ago, a friend of the family with a prominent job in the community was hospitalized for a respiratory problem. While in hospital he experienced withdrawal symptoms. His wife and children were very concerned, and asked the physician in charge to advise him about his drinking. The doctor refused, and told them that it was not her job to do that. I think that's a prevalent attitude.

While in hospital he experienced withdrawal symptoms. His wife and children were very concerned, and asked the physician in charge to advise him about his drinking. The doctor refused, and told them that it was not her job to do that

---

Personal motivations of a scientist

A: *We have talked at length about your work, but let's talk a little more about Martha Sanchez-Craig herself. Given all these strong passions that you've talked about, can you say what really drives you? What makes you tick?*

MS-C: The need to know, despite being fully conscious of the fact that you can't know everything. But discovery fascinates me, the kind of discovery that jumps out at you from the data. I spent countless hours with data print-outs, looking for patterns. I didn't want to rely on what the statis-

tical experts would come up with as a result of multivariate analyses and so forth. I wanted to see patterns with my own eyes.

A: *Would you say that that kind of discovery is what has given you the greatest satisfaction in your work?*

MS-C: That has certainly given me a great deal of satisfaction, but another thing that I enjoyed very much at the Foundation was talking, trading ideas, sharing thoughts, with colleagues in other disciplines.

A: *Do you think that would have been any different if you had been working in a university rather than in a dedicated research foundation?*

MS-C: Yes! I didn't have any experience working in a university myself, but when I went to conferences and talked with university-based people they told me I was very privileged, and I came to see that they were right. They had only limited research time, because of their teaching and administrative duties, and a lot of that precious research time had to be spent writing grant applications. There are compensations, of course. If you have bright students, they make you think, force you to be up to date with the literature, and so on. But I prefer to spend my time actually doing the research myself. In all the trials we did at the Foundation, I was involved as a clinician myself. And I think that is very important if you want to understand how to refine interventions.

A: *But no environment is perfect. Even in the Foundation, that had all those advantages you've just talked about, there must have been things that you disliked, that frustrated or annoyed you?*

MS-C: There were lots of internal politics in the Foundation, and although we were very well supported, many times the shifts in research directions seemed to be motivated by politics, either to satisfy the government or to benefit the careers of particular scientists. I didn't like that. The other problem was that the people in power, who would assess your performance, didn't have much idea of what it meant to do research on treatment. For example, one of the senior people, who was conducting experiments with small numbers of non-human subjects, said 'I don't have much regard for any scientist who doesn't publish at least six papers a year in peer-reviewed journals'. I was very worried about that. I met colleagues who would get depressed or seriously worried if they couldn't publish a paper every month. I began to think that there are a lot of people here who like to do science that looks good, and only a few who like to do good science.

A: *But in universities there is nobody who tells you what research you have to do. As long as you can get it funded, you can do pretty well whatever you like.*
MS-C: That used to be true of the Foundation as well, when I first started there . . . you could do whatever you were interested in, carry it as far as you wished, as long as it fitted with the objectives of the organization. But years later I came to the conclusion that many PhDs who should be doing their own research had been converted into reverent research assistants, doing what people at the top were saying they had to do. It changed from something very like a university to something resembling industry. One thing I enjoy very much is challenging authority. Whenever a dogmatic statement is made to me by somebody in power, especially if it is a male, I will find a way of trying to prove him wrong.

A: *Did that unwillingness to accept the 'voice of authority' get you into any difficulties?*
MS-C: If the 'top honcho' said something wrong, and said it with a voice of authority, I just couldn't let him get away with it.

A: *What would you say are your own greatest strengths as a researcher?*
MS-C: Persistence, and being directly involved in the work, knowing it from the inside and not trusting what the statistician or some one else tells me it means. And the ability to motivate others. I think that I have the capacity to look, to stay with things, to persist, if something really interests and excites me, regardless of what it is. When some-

thing really catches my fancy, I become like a one-track mind, I don't give up.

A: *What do you think your weaknesses are?*
MS-C: The inability to show moderation, to keep limits on myself. I get so deeply into the work that everything else loses out.

A: *If you had your whole career to do over again, but knowing what you do now in hindsight, would you change anything?*
MS-C: Yes, I wouldn't trust Presidents or other high-level bureaucrats! Otherwise, I don't think I'd change much in my work. I feel pretty happy about the way it turned out.

A: *One last question. Now that you have put down roots in Mexico again, and spend half the year there, where do you really feel most at home?*
MS-C: My life in Mexico now is not representative of Mexico. I live in a resort area where 99% of the residents are from the United States or Europe, so I live in an unreal world. It's beautiful, but it isn't a community. The only real Mexicans that I meet there are the gentle, polite Mayan people who work as servants, and are often abused, and I feel sad for them. No, the truth is that after 30 years I'm a Canadian, I love Canada, and this is my home.

References

1.   SANCHEZ-CRAIG, M. & WALKER, K. (1982) Teaching coping skills to chronic alcoholics: I. An outcome study of a coeducational halfway house, *British Journal of Addiction*, 77, 35–50.
2.   EDWARDS, G. & GROSS, M. M. (1976) Alcohol dependence. Provisional description of a clinical syndrome, *British Medical Journal*, 1, 1058–1061.
3.   EMRICK, C. (1975) A review of psychologically oriented treatment of alcoholism: II. Relative effectiveness of different treatment approaches and the effectiveness of treatment versus no treatment, *Journal of Studies on Alcohol*, 36, 88–108.

4. SANCHEZ-CRAIG, M., ANNIS, H. M., BORNET, A. R. & MACDONALD, K. R. (1984) Random assignment to abstinence or controlled drinking. Evaluation of a cognitive–behavioral program for problem drinkers, *Journal of Clinical and Consulting Psychology*, **52**, 390–403.

5. SANCHEZ-CRAIG, M. (1986) *A Therapist's Manual: secondary prevention of alcohol problems* (Toronto, Addiction Research Foundation).

6. BABOR, T. F. & GRANT, M. (Eds) (1992) *Project on identification and management of alcohol-related problems. Report on Phase II: a randomized clinical trial of brief interventions in primary health care* (Geneva, World Health Organization).

7. SANCHEZ-CRAIG, M. (1995) *DrinkWise: how to quit drinking or cut down – a self-help book* (Toronto, Addiction Research Foundation).

8. SANCHEZ-CRAIG, M., DAVILA, R. & COOPER, G. (1996) A self-help approach for high-risk drinking: effects of an initial assessment, *Journal of Consulting and Clinical Psychology*, **64**, 694–700.

9. SANCHEZ-CRAIG, M. (1993) *Low-Risk Drinking: patient workbook* (The College of Family Physicians of Canada, Mississauga, Ontario, Canada).

10. SANCHEZ-CRAIG, M. & WILKINSON, D. A. (1989) Brief treatments for alcohol and drug problems. Practical and methodological issues, in: LØBERG, T., MILLER, W. R., NATHAN, P. E. & MARLATT, G. A. (Eds) *Prevention and Early Intervention*, pp. 233–252 (Amsterdam, Swets & Zeitlinger).

Commentary
A Jewel in the Crown: the ARF, Toronto
Alan C Ogborne

Martha Sanchez-Craig and Reg Smart are two of the many distinguished scientists who worked at the Addiction Research Foundation of Ontario during its near half century as an independent agency (1949–1998). This remarkable organization was respected nationally and internationally for its research and, more locally, for its community development, education and treatment programs.[1,2,3] Success did, however, require constant attention to the alignment of operational process and objectives with the principal mandate and the expectations of different stakeholders.

Research at the Addiction Research Foundation

The Addiction Research Foundation was established at a time when many governments were increasingly looking to the social sciences to help solve social problems and to evaluate new programs. The hope was that research would bring reason to issues that were otherwise mired in emotion and politics. Initially the Foundation had very few research staff but provided grants to university-based researchers. Later researchers were hired and encouraged to make careers in the addiction field. The budget always included substantial funds for research and this ensured support for a wide range of projects. This hard funding for research was important in the early days when it was difficult to find people willing to undertake addiction research under a grant-in-aid system. There were few researchers with the necessary skills and addiction was not a popular subject of study.

Some of the Foundation's own researchers were, however, soon able to secure external research funds from both Canadian and US funding bodies. This was especially so for those involved in basic and biological research. Over time other researchers were first encouraged and later expected to seek external research funds. This move to grant-based research was driven by rising internal and external standards for research, external demands for independent review of the Foundation's research, and the increasing availability of research funds. The Foundation did, however, continue to provide seed funds for new projects and to support monitoring projects such as the school surveys described by Reg Smart.

Smart indicates that, in the early days of the Foundation, researchers were not especially pressured to do research of interest to policy makers and practitioners. Nonetheless, many researchers were interested in policy and practice issues and were encouraged to pursue these interests by respected mentors. Smart was an early champion of evaluation research and was for many years the head of the Foundation's Evaluation Studies department.

As the field matured, and priorities became clearer, researchers were hired by the Foundation for specific projects or lines of research. Martha Sanchez-Craig was initially hired to evaluate a halfway house for recovering alcoholics. This research was at the request of the Ontario Government and was associated with a number of new government initiatives concerning skid row alcoholics. Researchers did, however, have considerable freedom in a choice of projects and several, including Smart, made significant contributions to the literature on a wide range of issues. Sanchez-Craig went on to do ground-breaking research on self-help and therapist-led brief interventions.

Smart mentions some of the research lines pursued at the Addiction Research Foundation and some of the major findings and outcomes. These encompassed studies of basic biological, psychological and sociological processes as well as studies that monitored trends in substance use and related problems, and evaluated prevention and treatment policies and programs. Of particular note were studies that contributed to an increased awareness of the relationships between per capita alcohol consumption and alcohol-related problems. Many projects involved interdisciplinary teams of investigators and practitioners, and this capacity for interdisciplinary initiatives was one of the Foundation's greatest strengths.

Realizing the practical implications of research

From the start the Foundation invested considerable resources to promote research-based policies and programs. This included the development and dissemination of a wide range of materials for the general public, schools and professionals. The Foundation established community offices where staff promoted the Foundation's best advice to local policy makers and service providers. At its peak in the 1970s the Foundation had over 700 staff and offices in 38 Ontario communities. A 100-bed Clinical Institute with teaching hospital status was established in 1971 and a School for Addiction Studies was established shortly after. This school provided professional development opportunities to the Foundation's staff and other professionals.

During the 1980s the Foundation adopted an advocacy role with respect to a variety of alcohol- and drug-related issues. It became active in the development and promotion of its best advice on issues such as drinking and driving, alcohol monopolies and treatment.

Many individual researchers actively promoted their results and encouraged the development of research based policies and programs. This was particularly the case in the clinical area where researchers such as Martha Sanchez-Craig were very active in promoting their work, both in Canada and elsewhere. Some researchers, and especially Reg Smart, were active in promoting research and evaluation in developing countries.

Late in the Foundation's history as an independent agency, some researchers developed an interest in the dissemination of research knowledge and undertook studies to evaluate alternative dissemination strategies.[4]

The actual impact of the research conducted at the Addiction Research Foundation is difficult to assess. Certainly the impact on treatment was considerable locally, nationally and internationally. The local impact on policies at the community level was significant in some cases. The impact on provincial and national policies is uncertain. However, it seems clear that research has helped to inform the policy process and frame the issues. Foundation managers and staff always sought to ensure that research was considered at the policy table and that policy makers at least acknowledge what research has shown. At one time the Foundation was referred to as the 'jewel in the crown' by the Ontario Minister of Health – an accolade that clearly recognized the Foundation's success both in research and in the dissemination of research-based practices and advice. The Foundation's recognition as a centre of excellence by the World Health Organization is further testimony to its many strengths and accomplishments.

Fulfilling the vision

The Foundation was given a challenging mandate and there were frequent internal discussions about the ways in which this mandate might best be fulfilled. There were significant differences of opinion regarding the autonomy of regional offices, the appropriate balance between basic and applied research, research priorities and the relationships between researchers and practitioners. External stakeholders including the funding ministry (Health), service providers, educators and community developers all had views about the Foundation's priorities. Various stakeholder consultations had a significant impact on the research agenda.

Over time different organizational arrangements were developed to try to reconcile these differences of opinion and to create and encourage synergistic relationships between those with different primary interests. New departments came and went in the process and consultants variously encouraged such things as 'flat lining', 'vertical integration', 'matrix management' and 'de-siloing'.

After ARF

Since 1998 the work of the Addiction Research Foundation has continued under the umbrella of the Centre for Addiction and Mental Health. This new organization was formed from a merger of the Addiction Research Foundation, a major addiction treatment agency, a large psychiatric hospital and a major psychiatric research and treatment agency. The merger was ordered by a government-sponsored committee empowered to restructure Ontario's health system to better reflect community needs and fiscal realities. The committee's main rationale for merging addiction and mental health agencies was its view that there were high rates of comorbidity among people with primary mental heath or substance use disorders. However, the merger did not reflect the agendas of any of the four partners and came while ARF was implementing a new vision of itself as a knowledge-based provincial agency. This new vision reflected efforts to establish clear research priorities and to link research more closely with development and dissemination activities.[3]

Some researchers initially feared that prevention and policy research would become more difficult under a mental health umbrella but this is not clearly evident to date. Ongoing work has continued and new lines have opened up. There is increasing dialogue between those who have specialized in either mental health or addiction and some new projects have addressed comorbidity or other issues common to both mental health and addictions interests.

The main challenge to most researchers is now to obtain grants. Some are nostalgic for the days when most research was hard funded and the review process was more informal and collegial. However, external grants have substantially increased since the merger and thus the future of addiction research seems well assured. What is less clear is if the next generation of researchers will have time and energy left from playing the granting game to be as concerned about increasing the impact of their work as were Reg Smart, Martha Sanchez-Craig and many other researchers at the old ARF.

References

1. ARCHIBALD, H. D. (1990) *The Addiction Research Foundation: Voyage of Discovery* (Addiction Research Foundation, Toronto).
2. SMART, R. G. (1991) What made the ARF? in: EDWARDS, G. (Ed.) *Addictions: Personal Influences and Scientific Movements* (Transaction Publishers, New Brunswick and London).
3. ROOM, R. (1999) Farewell to a unique institution, *Addiction*, **94**, 1781–1783.
4. MARTIN, G. W., HERIE, M. A., TURNER, B. J. & CUNNINGHAM, J. A. (1998) A social marketing model for disseminating research-based treatments to addictions treatment providers, *Addiction*, **93**, 1703–1715.

Part III
Australia

Robert J. Hawke

Robert James Lee Hawke was born in 1929 in South Australia. He was Prime Minister of Australia from 1983–91. Since 1992 he has been Adjunct Professor, Research School of Pacific Studies and Social Sciences, Australian National University. Previously he has been a Research Officer and Advocate for the Australian Council of Trade Unions, 1958–69; President of the ACTU, 1970–80; MP (Lab) Wills, Melbourne, 1980–92; Australian Labour Party Member, National Executive, 1971–91; President, 1973–78; Leader, 1983–91; Leader of the Opposition, 1983; and Visiting Professor, University of Sydney 1992. He holds several honorary degrees. The Hawke Memoirs were published in 1994.

Addiction: *When you made a campaign speech in November 1984 in anticipation of the December Australian general election, you used the phrase 'National Campaign Against Drug Abuse'. The actual words used appeared to come right out of the blue, but they have continued to be used throughout following years.*
Robert J. Hawke: Well I don't think it is surprising. It seems to be a fairly accurate and precise use of words and picks up the point that anything in this area needed to be 'national'. So many of our problems in Australia are caused by the diffusion of power between the centre and the states and if you were going to be effective in dealing with this issue it had to be national. The word 'campaign' implies continuing education and action, and 'drug abuse' is self-explanatory. So it seems to me to be a fairly sensible use of words.

A: *The Americans used the word 'war'. Australia avoided that, but was there the hint of a war in the use of the term 'campaign'?*
RJH: It didn't get as semantic as that. No, that's chasing a rather shadowy rabbit down a non-existent burrow I think, that one.

A: *There had been the publication on 26 October of the Costigan Royal Commission which suggested that there were links between organized crime and illicit drugs. Was that in any way influential in the announcement at that time?*

RJH: It is very hard in hindsight when you are trying to give weight to various factors that were involved, but certainly the costigan Report was one element. And then of course there were my own personal concerns, which are I think well known.

A: *You were re-elected on 1 December 1984. The first meeting of the relevant ministers was held in March 1985, a meeting which was preceded by a meeting of officers and the drug summit itself was held on 2 April 1985. You moved with great alacrity to give expression to this campaign promise.*
RJH: Yes I did, but then we would expect to do so in relation to most campaign promises. We were also aware that this was a matter of some urgency.

A: *So you had measures dealing with interdiction, with surveillance, but as the communiqué issued at the meeting acknowledged, there was a recognition of the need also to address demand. And most importantly, the overall objective of the campaign was identified as harm minimization.*
RJH: Yes, politicians of course tend to lean towards policies favouring penalties and police action, both of which are obviously important in this matter, but which needed to be complemented by policies which addressed the need for treatment and demand.

A: *Australia's adoption of harm minimization as the objective contrasted markedly with the*

American policy of 'zero tolerance'. Was there pressure from the US to adopt policies consistent with theirs?
RJH: Well, as people who know me well would acknowledge, any pressure from the US of that kind was likely to be strenuously resisted. No, there was no pressure on me from the US and had there been it may well have been counterproductive. There may have been pressure at a lower level, at the level of officials, but I wasn't aware of it.

A: *The second meeting of the Ministerial Council was held in October 1985, in Brisbane, just months after the Drug Summit itself. Many of the arguments at this meeting related to whether or not all drugs should be included – is that right?*
RJH: Yes, there was considerable discussion in Cabinet as to what the emphasis should be. On the one hand dependence on illicit drugs was obviously a matter of some considerable importance, but then so were problems associated with alcohol and tobacco. The campaign would have lacked the necessary rigour had it concentrated only on illicit drugs and clearly it would not have been a credible campaign.

A: *The alcohol and tobacco industries were concerned that dependence on these drugs would be included in the campaign. Were you aware of pressure from either industry?*
RJH: Yes, they were concerned. The alcohol industry saw that restrictions were being placed on the tobacco industry, and they were understandably concerned that similar restrictions would be placed on them. But no, I personally was not approached by either industry, which is not to say they didn't make approaches at other levels.

A: *The alcohol policy aspect of the campaign was formally endorsed roughly three years after it was initially drafted at a meeting of the Ministerial Council held in Burnie, Tasmania, at which Dr Blewett himself acknowledged it was a somewhat watered-down version. In particular, it didn't tackle the tax issue whereby the tax paid on the alcohol in beer is higher than that paid on the alcohol in wine.*

RJH: Yes, I'm aware that that disparity exists and wasn't addressed in that policy document.

A: *How much as Prime Minister were you involved in the detailed administration of the Campaign having yourself personally initiated it?*
RJH: Not much, but then that wasn't unusual. I saw it as my role as Prime Minister to initiate a number of policies which I then handed over to competent ministers. All of my ministers were intelligent, albeit of varying intelligence, and of course I trusted them to implement the policy while holding myself available for discussion on specific points should they wish.

A: *In preparing for this interview I read your political biography and was surprised to note there was not a single mention of the Campaign. There was an acknowledgement of the problems involving your daughter, but no mention of the campaign.*
RJH: No, there wasn't.

A: *Those of us who work in the field accord exaggerated importance to policies that affect us and I can understand this was for you just one of a number of policies. Did you perhaps avoid mentioning it for reasons of the problems which you yourself were personally experiencing?*
RJH: No.

A: *It seemed to me that the policy was always a bipartisan policy.*
RJH: Yes, I think that was the case. Politicians are not anxious to take responsibility for such campaigns, fraught as they are.

A: *Mr Howard, the Prime Minister as of 1998, has personally intervened to stop the proposed heroin trial contrary to the advice given him by his own Ministerial Council and by most expert advisers.*
RJH: Yes, that is the case. I don't think I would have come to the same position as Howard, but it is, however, a very difficult issue.

A: *Are you aware that the Campaign which you initiated went on to enjoy very considerable international recognition?*

RJH: Yes, I was advised of this by various sources.

A: *For example, the Canadians emulated it almost precisely, although the Americans are critical of it, believing it to be too liberal.*
RJH: Well of course the Americans aren't right in everything and clearly given our coastline, the difficulty of interdiction, the fact that where there is demand there will always be supply makes any notion of ridding society of all drugs totally unrealistic. I perhaps didn't give too much emphasis to the Campaign or even what I knew to be the high regard in which the Campaign was held in my own biography, feeling that I shouldn't be blowing my own trumpet. I was after all already being criticized by the press as claiming credit for too much. Nor did I want it to appear that the Campaign owed its origin to my personal concerns rather than be a response to what I knew to be a national problem.

A: *Then there was the advent of AIDS which materially changed the situation and placed the emphasis back on heroin and on drugs which could be injected intravenously.*
RJH: Yes, that was the case.

A: *And of course attacks on Dr Blewett from as notable a source as the then President of the Australian Medical Association.*
RJH: Yes, and legal writs flying between them.

A: *Whatever the criticisms, Australia's policy in relation to AIDS is widely admired. While there has been a significant incidence of AIDS among the homosexual population, that among the intravenous drug-using population has been by international standards very low.*
RJH: Yes, I understand this to be the case.

A: *What would your own evaluation of the Campaign be, 12 years on?*
RJH: Well, I wouldn't pretend to have paid close attention to its detailed working, although I am briefed on government matters. But it seems to me it was always an appropriate response, a real-istic response, one geared to the nature of the problem.

A: *I wonder whether you would like to comment on a recent issue. There is now a parliamentary group for drug law reform which I don't think was in existence when you were Prime Minister.*
RJH: No it wasn't, and I tend to be somewhat sceptical of what is claimed for law reform. Take the case of marijuana: while there may be some grounds for revising the penalties associated with it, my understanding is that when used in association with alcohol it is very often implicated in road traffic accidents and that there is also evidence that those who use marijuana are more likely to graduate to other drugs. So making it legally available is I think too sweeping a reform. On the heroin trial, I would be in favour of allowing such a trial, given that it would be supported by reputable sources and those with expert knowledge.

The fact that where there is demand there will always be supply makes any notion of ridding society of all drugs totally unrealistic

---

A: *There has been, as there often is when a problem doesn't go away, renewed calls for tougher penalties. As you yourself acknowledged, politicians are prone to call for such when problems tend to be more longstanding than was initially anticipated.*
RJH: Yes, but then I wouldn't be in favour of reducing the resources committed to addressing supply. It seems to me that one must address both supply and demand. We have to do something to reduce the availability of drugs, so I wouldn't be in favour of removing resources for customs and for police, while at the same time I wouldn't want resources to be taken from those available for treatment and education.

A: *Have your international travels and contacts with people abroad persuaded you that anyone else does it better?*

RJH: No, I wouldn't say anyone does it better. I think our approach was appropriate, while acknowledging of course that the problems are still with us. I have continuing and frequent contact with the Chinese who are now starting to express concerns about the problem in their country, in particular the infiltration of opiates from the Golden Triangle.

A: *If you were still Prime Minister what would you be doing now in relation to this problem? Are there any new initiatives that you would take?*

RJH: No, I don't think so. I think that I would be asking my ministers and officials whether there is evidence that our programme is working and I would be asking them to consider whether from their international perspective there are countries whose policies we should be emulating. But no, it is perhaps a matter of holding the line, persisting with the present combination of policies.

Les Drew

Leslie Raymond Hill Drew was born in Australia on 23 April 1933. He was educated at Melbourne University and gained his BM and BS in 1955, his BSc in 1959, and a Diploma of Psychological Medicine in 1961. He was a Foundation Member of the Royal Australian & New Zealand College of Psychiatrists and was elected a Fellow in 1985. He was made a Member of the Order of Australia in 1986; and won the Rolleston Award in 1992. He is a Life Member of the Australian Professional Society on Alcohol and Other Drugs. Posts held include Teaching Fellow in Psychiatry, Harvard Medical School, 1962–63; Psychiatrist Superintendent, Sunbury Mental Hospital, 1965–69; Honorary Consultant Psychiatrist, The Alfred Hospital, Victoria, 1969–74; Senior Medical Adviser on Drugs and Alcohol and also Mental Health for the Commonwealth Department of Health, Canberra, 1975–88; Secretary, Mental Health Committee, National Health & Research Council, Canberra, 1978–88; Consultant, World Health Organisation, 1978–88; Director of Mental Health Services, South East Region, New South Wales, 1989–94; Senior Lecturer in Psychiatry, University of New South Wales, 1992–94; Senior Staff Specialist in Psychiatry, The Canberra Hospital and Senior Lecturer in Psychiatry, University of Sydney, 1994 to the present.

A Salvationist background

Addiction: *How did you first get interested in the alcohol and drug field?*

Les Drew: My parents and grandparents were Salvation Army officers. When I grew up, towards the end of the depression, there always seemed to be somebody at home with a problem being ministered to by my family and the church. I had initially intended to enter the ministry of the Salvation Army. But I then decided to study medicine. While I was a medical student, I came across patients with alcohol problems. Because of my long-standing involvement in the Salvation Army, my further involvement in this career seemed inevitable.

A: *Presumably as a Salvation Army member you do not consume alcohol.*

LD: That's right.

A: *Is it difficult for you to have compassion for people who mess up their lives and their families' lives because they drink too much alcohol?*

LD: No, that has never presented a problem for me. Their need has always been the issue for me,

rather than their behaviour. Again, this comes back to the Salvation Army and to William Booth, its founder. The whole emphasis of Booth was on helping the person rather than worrying about where they came from.

A: *Have you since remained with the Army, the starting point of your career?*

LD: Unfortunately not. I have always remained related to a stream within the Salvation Army. This involves a group of people who remain within the Army and have a vision of accepting or walking with people in contrast to the more authoritarian, fundamentalist approach. Unfortunately I was unable to influence the officials of the Salvation Army and how they decide their policies in this area.

A: *Religion has been an influence on you in terms of your personal and spiritual life and professionally too.*

LD: I was brought up in the Salvation Army, which was a way of life. All of my family were there. It was something to hold on to. It was a fundamentalist religion and also a joyful religion with roots in social philosophy and social programs. I always found it hard to come to terms with a fundamentalist religious approach and when I graduated in psychiatry I went into a seminary in York to try and get a balance between psychiatry and religion. There I was exposed to group psychology and eastern psychology. I came to value the eastern psychology I had never appreciated before. This was a non-rational approach to the world and so I have tried since then to try and find a balance of these two. For example, I think it is very important not to go overboard on double blind crossover trials as being the way to answer all questions. I pursued this approach all the way through and have constantly queried concepts and issues. This skepticism led me to challenge the notion that alcoholism is irreversible.

A: *Many people are intrigued by the fact that you do not consume any mood-altering drugs and yet as a public health official, making the best arrangements for society, you proceed on the presumption that many people are going to use mood-altering drugs come what may.*
LD: I do not see any contradiction in that. If I go back to Jesus, He did not cast people out, He tried to help them. William Booth, the founder of the Salvation Army offered prostitutes a refuge. He did not demand that they give up their profession before they entered.

The general philosophy I developed followed William Booth. He was the most important influence on my thinking. What he said and did seemed to me to be pretty sensible

---

Training in psychiatry

A: *Why did you choose to specialise in psychiatry?*
LD: Psychiatry seemed to me to be a logical discipline because of my interest in religion, in thinking and working with people. I did not feel I had the temperament to be a surgeon. I was also quite interested in paediatrics and obstetrics but I settled on psychiatry in my fifth year of medicine.

A: *When did you first begin to become seriously interested in alcohol and drugs as a sub-specialty within psychiatry?*
LD: I thought about this even before I graduated in medicine. There was an alcoholism unit in the hospital where I did my first year of training in psychiatry. A quite senior doctor, who was a recovering alcoholic, gave me many helpful insights. He ultimately died of his alcoholism. Also, Dr John Cade, who had discovered lithium treatment for bipolar disorder, was an important influence on my career. He had a great interest in alcohol and further stimulated my interest.

A: *Other early influences in psychiatry?*
LD: I was very fortunate when I started psychiatry to have strong support from Eric Cunningham Dax, the Director of Mental Health Services in Victoria, Allan Stoller, a world figure in mental health research, and Gerry Krupinski, the local doyen of research in Victoria. They took me under their wing and imparted the need to have a balance between clinical work, research and administration. I have kept on trying to do clinical work, research and administration ever since.

A: *Did you have any specific training in alcohol and drugs or did you pick this up on your own?*
LD: In those days you had to pick up any training on your own. I did get involved in an organization called the Alcohol Foundation of Victoria. About three years after I graduated, I went to work in Pentridge Jail. Alcoholism was also a major issue there. That is where I published my first paper on alcoholism.[1]

A: *Who or what were the major influences on the approach you developed in the alcohol and drug field?*
LD: The general philosophy I developed followed William Booth. He was the most important influence on my thinking. What he said and did seemed to me to be pretty sensible.

A: *While you are personally abstinent, you seem to have no wish to inflict your own beliefs on to others in the community.*

LD: I always thought that we have to avoid imposing our views on others. This is a general principle which goes well beyond alcohol. The middle road is a desirable road where people are enjoying themselves and not hurting themselves and are avoiding the excesses. Later, when I came to take an interest in alcohol policy, I saw that attempts to enforce prohibition, to make the whole community abstinent, got nowhere.

A: *After you qualified as a psychiatrist and now had a pronounced interest in the alcohol and drug field, you then developed a private psychiatric clinic with a strong focus on alcohol?*
LD: I worked with other doctors and social workers. I was a consultant to the Salvation Army regarding their alcoholism programmes and homeless people. In Australia at that time, doctors could admit any patient to a private hospital. We had Skid Row patients in hospital at the same time as we had people from business and industry. I sometimes used to park my fairly ordinary car in the car park next to a Rolls Royce. Yet inside the hospital I had patients who were homeless. That was an excellent time.

A: *How long did you keep that up for?*
LD: I worked in the clinic for five years.

A: *Was there at that time – apart from scattered individuals like yourself – any alcohol and drug field in Australia?*
LD: We had by the early 1970s established the Australian Foundation in Alcohol and Drug Dependence. This brought together people from all over the country, was multi-disciplinary and linked to a Foundation in each state. For ten years or more, it brought together people from diverse areas, including at that stage the liquor industry. The Foundations were pretty upset at the beginning when people started extending the work to include drugs other than alcohol. Clinicians such as myself were also concerned about this. We saw the other drugs taking the place of alcohol and thought alcohol was really the major drug. We had not yet come to the point of seeing tobacco as a major drug. The political hype about the other drugs had already risen to a level where the Foun-

dation had to include the other drugs if it was going to stay relevant.

Thirteen years in Canberra

A: *What was your next move?*
LD: I then moved from the clinic to Canberra and a ministerial advisory position called the Senior Medical Advisor on Drug Dependence and Alcohol. I stayed in that position for 13 years, from 1975 to 1988. I was also responsible for mental health matters.

A: *Why did you decide to take on this advisory position?*
LD: I had become increasingly concerned about the growing emphasis on prohibition of drugs that was developing in Australia at that time. Some people were pursuing this very aggressively. I saw the need for more emphasis on alcohol. I did not know who would take the job if I didn't. So I applied.

A: *What were your responsibilities?*
LD: The first responsibility was to make sure the job included alcohol because it was originally supposed to be only an advisory position on drugs of dependence. My responsibilities were really very limited. They were simply to attend meetings of two or three committees. I was supposed to write responses to ministerial inquiries and write speeches for the Minister or Director General of Health. That was about it. The rest of the time was up to me.

A: *How many Health Ministers did you serve?*
LD: About six.

A: *Did you have direct access to the Minister?*
LD: I had to go through the Department of Health.

A: *This seemed an extraordinarily productive period of your life.*
LD: Yes, it was. I had few specific responsibilities. The rest was up to me. It was a marvellous chance to do things I thought needed to be done.

The first achievement was to get a national meeting of drug and alcohol officials who were working with the state governments. We then met regularly over the 13 years. This gave us a chance to sort out problems.

A: *Had the state government officials never met each other before then?*
LD: They had met as underlings at Ministerial meetings on drug dependence which involved legal people and health officials. The drug officials had a very minor role at these meetings. The new meetings that I started allowed an opportunity for us to get together to talk about services and policies and improve coordination.

A: *When did that group of people first start meeting regularly?*
LD: The second day of our first meeting was in Perth on the eleventh day of the eleventh month of 1975. This was day that the Whitlam government was dismissed. When this news reached our meeting, we all retreated home at a great rate. This meeting of government officials became very important in 1985 when the (then) Prime Minister, Bob Hawke, established the National Campaign Against Drug Abuse. This Campaign began because the nation had come to learn that the Prime Minister's daughter was using heroin. That news had a dramatic impact and unleashed enormous demand for government action in response to drugs. At that stage, our group had been meeting for many years. We knew each other well. That campaign gave me the chance – actually I knew this was on the wing – to come up with a blueprint as to what ought to happen. I circulated this to all the states. They all came back with their suggestions and this plan could then be decided, almost as a fait accompli. The plan was then circulated throughout the Commonwealth Department of Health where it was approved and implemented. All of this happened between a statement by the Prime Minister in December 1984 and a meeting of the Prime Minister, all six Premiers and both Chief Ministers on 2 April 1985. This meeting was the so-called Drug Summit.

Establishing harm reduction as Australia's official policy

A: *How did it come about at that meeting that the Prime Minister, Premiers and Chief Ministers declared that harm minimisation was Australia's official national drug policy?*
LD: Because I pushed it within our department. At that time there had been no policy on illicit drugs in our department and no reason to 'fight drugs'. I kept asking my colleagues why we now had to 'fight drugs'. Nobody wanted to answer. I thought that the only reason we needed to be concerned with drug use was because we wanted to minimize the harms associated with drugs. To me that was an irrefutable position once it was clearly set out. We were able to influence Hawke and everyone else to focus on the harms from drug use rather than drug use *per se*. The group of government officials proved to be critical. We were able to influence all of the states and the commonwealth to agree that we could not have a war on drugs without also including alcohol and tobacco. But Hawke and his people did not want that. We argued that once we got all drugs included, then we could look at the harms caused by all mood-altering substances and be serious about harm minimization. This was the key to our concerns. All harms had to be measured so it was very important that we already had a system for measuring health costs that had been running for some time.

A: *The tangible accomplishments?*
LD: Two important accomplishments came out of this work. One was the focus on reducing harm rather than reducing drug use *per se* and the second one was the generic view that all drugs are drugs.

A: *Was it difficult to get harm minimization accepted?*
LD: Once it was through the Commonwealth Health Department there was no problem. I had a lot of support from within the department. In those days the hierarchy was medical and public health medical so this was a message they could

accept quite easily. It was politically not very palatable but to the senior people in the Health Department, this was clearly the policy that we needed.

A: *Did the Minister at the time, Dr Neal Blewett, sympathise with harm minimisation?*
LD: Oh yes, Neal was a very forward-looking person. He was, of course, constrained by being a Minister and the policies he wanted were not necessarily those that he actually got.

A: *Did you realise at the time that the adoption of harm minimization as the nation's official drug policy was going to be a momentous step?*
LD: I realized that it was extremely important to have harm minimization as our drug policy, because this enabled us to apply a single judgment against all measures – would the measure be likely to reduce harm? It also allowed us to set priorities and to determine resource allocation. However, I saw it as important – not momentous.

A: *What other achievements did you have after that?*
LD: One of the achievements I was very pleased with involved Joh Bjelke-Peterson, the Premier of Queensland. He was very outspoken and very conservative. Bjelke-Peterson had said that he was going to get the murderers who were promoting cannabis. We managed to persuade him to retract this statement in parliament because at that stage there had been no recorded deaths attributed to cannabis. We also obtained significantly more money for research and education. This was some achievement as the emphasis was originally supposed to be on law enforcement.

A: *Were concerns about HIV infection among injecting drug users already a major consideration when Australia accepted harm minimisation as the official national drug policy?*
LD: Perhaps HIV among drug users should have been a concern before harm minimisation was adopted, but it wasn't. One of the difficulties we had was developing a pragmatic response to HIV control among injecting drug users when the rhetoric was about waging a drug war – the 'drug offensive'. I could not get those words changed.

People wanted the policy to be hard on drugs and hard on drug users. It was seen as a war mentality then, and I am afraid it still is.

A: *Later on you had some major differences with the Minister. What did this involve?*
LD: All along my approach has always been one of temperance. It is critical to distinguish temperance from abstinence and prohibition. I always thought that prohibition would produce more problems and more division than it would ever solve.

I realized that it was extremely important to have harm minimization as our drug policy, because this enabled us to apply a single judgment against all measures – would the measure be likely to reduce harm?

A: *Around 1986, needle and syringe programmes became a big issue in terms of HIV prevention for injecting drug users. Did you help to nurse that policy through the system?*
LD: That was a bit fortuitous. I was being excluded from everything because of my position on prohibition and the department wanted a different policy. A new key official in the AIDS program, Elizabeth Reid, asked me to write something about drugs and AIDS. I was able to spend about three to six months with a project officer preparing a paper called 'The Second AIDS Epidemic'. This was a projection of the number of deaths, HIV infections and economic cost of an uncontrolled epidemic. It included not only what was going to happen to drug users but also what was going to happen to the general community – which was what the general community was really interested in. I have always believed that no one really cares about drug users. But they did care about HIV infection starting among drug users spreading within the whole community. The paper[2] had a limited distribution and was only available through the Commonwealth Department of Health.

A: *Do you think that paper was responsible for gaining the acceptance of the Needle and Syringe Programmes?*

LD: It helped no end because it became part of the AIDS policy for the whole department. Lots of things got me into trouble at that stage. I said things on television. I had a very clear view that prohibition had to be repealed. We had to come up with better alternatives.

A: *One of your other major achievements in that period would surely have been the development of the now national network of drug and alcohol research centres. When did you first get the idea of developing these research centres?*

LD: I have always been research orientated. I also saw the drug war as being an opportunity to get things we would never get otherwise. In order to get support for the drug and alcohol research centres, we had to talk about centres of excellence. The major resistance was not against spending the money but whether any researchers were worthy. Then there was also the politics of whether it would go from one state to another.

I am sure we have got more information and we have got more academic standing. I am not sure that we have actually made an impact on policy development through these centres

---

A: *The first centre was established in 1987 and there are now half a dozen around the country. Do you think that these national centres has actually made a difference?*

LD: I am sure we have got more information and we have got more academic standing. I am not sure that we have actually made an impact on policy development through these centres.

A: *Drug overdose deaths in Australia have increased from only six in 1964 to almost a thousand deaths in 1999. There has also been an equally spectacular explosion in the numbers of people using drugs. What is your view about these developments?*

LD: The increase in the number of deaths indicates the lack of interest in the community in drug users and in altruism. I wrote an article in about 1982[3] pointing out that of the people who had died in Canberra of a drug overdose that year, in almost every case the death occurred at the person's home. No one was concerned enough or aware enough of the need for vigilance when people are intoxicated. I may as well have never written the article. There was no response in terms of any educational program. There was just no interest. That has been the case whenever the view is put up of protecting drug users. We have not even got to the point yet of reporting back to drug users about the concentration of drugs circulating in the community.

A: *Does the community approach alcohol related harms differently?*

LD: The approach we adopted for alcohol was moderation. This involved educating people and trying to limit harm. I worked with Senator Peter Baume on a policy of low alcohol beer. I got our Department to support a policy emphasising how much alcohol people consumed rather than how much beer they drank. The next step was to get the brewers interested in low alcohol beer. There was a lot of resistance initially, but eventually they were persuaded. But a similar approach is not possible with illegal drugs. We cannot say 'we do not care how much opium or how much morphine you use as long as you do not cause any trouble to yourself or anybody else'. We are not allowed to say that. So I am not surprised we now have got even worse problems than we used to have. Also, drug use – including alcohol consumption – is an indicator of what is happening in society. At present, we have a pretty unstable and unhappy society. Under these conditions, it is little surprise that alcohol consumption is increasing. Alcohol misuse often indicates a level of discomfort people have with themselves, similar to suicide levels, which are also increasing among young people. It is not the only factor. In a stable society where everyone knew where they stood and were confident they could get support, I would not expect so many people to use drugs.

A: *Are you suggesting that one of the reasons that illicit drug use is increasing rapidly among young Australians at present is because, among other factors, they are going through very tough times?*

LD: Yes. We cannot attack the drug problem in isolation from everything else.

A: *Another area of interest was thiamine fortification. How do you see that issue now, looking back over the time since thiamine fortification of alcohol was first recommended in Australia in the 1950s?*

LD: I was involved in this issue all that time. I did not succeed in getting what I wanted, which was to get thiamine fortification in beer, and this was only because the nutritionists opposed it. They argued that if beer was fortified with thiamine, we would be promoting it as a nutritious product. But we did finally get thiamine fortification in flour. As far as I can see, alcoholic brain damage in the form of Korsakoff's psychosis has been reduced considerably. I have only seen or heard of one case in Canberra in the last three or four years. It had been a major problem prior to that. This has been a really major achievement. Unfortunately we did not get the follow-up public health study to measure the outcome.

A: *Do you see a parallel between thiamine fortification and needle syringe programmes?*

LD: They are the same thing. Making the world a safer place for intoxicated people and needle syringe programs are essentially the same philosophy. I was very impressed by the reduction in the road crash death rate in Sweden through random road side blood alcohol testing. Twenty years later we introduced the same policy in Australia. People now complain when ten people per thousand are detected with a positive blood alcohol level at these random roadside tests. When we started, about two to three per cent were over the limit. If you want to reduce problems, you have to attack them.

A: *Where does methadone fit in?*

LD: Methadone is a useful drug, in that it gets people more involved in a regular lifestyle and encourages them to move out of an illegal area. It helps to get them back on track and have a life.

A: *What were the other highlights in that 13-year period that pleased you?*

LD: The founding of the Australian Medical and Professional Society on Alcohol and Drugs, now called the Australian Professional Society on Alcohol and Drugs, and the establishment of the Drug and Alcohol Review, were very important to me. I have always been interested in historical aspects of this field. In the late nineteenth century and early twentieth century there was a very large alcohol problem in Australia. There was a very good institutional response and a good professional response. When the depression occurred in Australia during the late 1920s, alcohol consumption decreased and alcohol problems also declined. Most of the treatment institutions closed and the specialists disappeared.

If you want to reduce problems, you have to attack them

A: *And when you came on the scene?*

LD: By the early 1950s, when I came on the scene, there were very few people with any interest or expertise in this area. It took another 10 or 15 years to get any kind of response to alcohol problems. My view was that institutions last forever. I thought that if I could get an institutional response to alcohol problems in the form of a professional society and a scientific journal then that would be some guard against the danger of another professional vacuum developing. I think that we have got the alcohol problems down significantly in the last few decades in Australia. And we have established a professional society and a professional journal.

A: *Do you feel that the report of the 1977 Senate Select Committee on Social Welfare ('Drug problems in Australia – an intoxicated society?') had a major impact on the way Australia responded to alcohol and other drugs in the last quarter century?*

LD: It was an extremely useful document and a very constructive process. It definitely had an impact. The brewers, for instance, were very opposed to low alcohol beer and said that they could not possibly produce a low alcohol beer.

Two years later they suddenly did. There had also been a useful enquiry in South Australia a few years earlier by Professor Ronald Sackville. For most of the official inquiries, the right person was picked, given the answers and then told to find out the questions so that they would not rock the boat.

Leaving the Public Service

A: *You left the Public Service and the drug and alcohol field in 1988?*

LD: I left the alcohol and drug field in April 1988 when I left the Department of Health. I decided to make a clean break, so far as I could, although it took me about two years to extricate myself from committees and societies to which I belonged. On leaving the Department I became a community psychiatrist at Queanbeyan, a NSW town adjoining Canberra, and after a year I became the Director of Mental Health Services for the South East Region of New South Wales which covers about 40 000 square miles with about 200 000 population. In conjunction with that appointment I became Senior Lecturer in Psychiatry at the University of New South Wales. I left that position in July 1994 to become a community psychiatrist in Canberra, with a major focus on psychosis, and with an appointment as Senior Lecturer in Psychiatry at the University of Sydney.

A: *Do you think that in the 13 years since you left the Department of Health that your views have been vindicated?*

LD: My views are certainly more widely shared. But I'm afraid they have not shown much fruit as yet. I hope that they will one day. I was told in those days by my immediate superior that I was five years ahead of my time. I thought he was a fairly astute judge of the situation. That was 13 years ago.

A: *Why did you decide to leave the public service?*

LD: I had been doing a lot of travelling, I had neglected my family, my income was half that of other psychiatrists. I thought we had got everything going we could have got going in those

three or four years and I thought it was time to relax and enjoy life a bit more than I had been doing.

A: *Did you feel the job ahead of you, had you stayed in that position, was going to be impossibly difficult?*

LD: I did not think we were going to make it.

A: *Why did the Department of Health choose not to replace you?*

LD: It was part of the policy in the Department at that time to reduce the medical and specialty involvement of the whole department. I do not think there was anything special about me or about my position on drugs.

Balancing the population and person perspectives

A: *What has the contribution of psychiatry been to the alcohol and drug field in Australia?*

LD: One of my disappointments has been the withdrawal of psychiatry from the drug and alcohol field in Australia. I was very involved in the establishment of a section of alcohol and drugs in the Royal Australia and New Zealand College of Psychiatry. That section is still surviving, but not thriving. Most psychiatrists these days do not see themselves needing any special training in this field, I see in my current work in general psychiatry, the importance of alcohol and drugs in schizophrenia for example. People with dual diagnoses are very important as they are often most refractory to treatment.

A: *Your approach to alcohol and drugs seems quite unusual for a psychiatrist in that you have a population health perspective while most psychiatrists have a predominantly individual case perspective.*

LD: Yes, but I always look at the fields both from an individual case perspective as well as the population approach. That is really accepting the person and where they are from and not imposing my values on them. I think I had always realized that one had to look at the casualties as well as the community and sometimes it is easier to consider the community and forget about the provision of treatment for the casualties.

A: *Scandinavia seems to have been an important influence on your thinking and approach to alcohol and drugs?*

LD: I went there as the guest of an insurance company which supported abstinence from alcohol. They sent me there specifically so that they would have somebody in attendance who knew what was going on and could come back and be used in the Australian scene. I was a bit surprised that they thought that they could still get their money's worth out of me even though I have never been a rabid prohibitionist. I went for six weeks and I feel that this enabled me to make what was probably my most important contribution to the field. While I was there I was able to examine all their records. I was struck by the fact that there was nobody much over 50 years old in their data collection. I wondered why this was so. When I attended an international conference in Norway, I had the temerity to stand up and say that we knew very little of the natural history of people with problems due to alcohol. I suggested that it was just as possible that these patients were getting better in spite of rather than because of their treatment. That went down like a lead balloon. I went back to my seat with my tail between my legs, came home and wrote a paper. This paper took me three years to get published because nobody wanted an upstart colonial to tell the rest of the world that they had been misled for a long time. Eventually the paper was published in the *Quarterly Journal of Alcoholism* with the title 'Alcohol as a self-limiting disease'.[4]

A: *Do you think it is?*
LD: Yes, certainly.

A: *That paper has been cited often.*
LD: Previously the leading figures in the field had said that alcoholism was an irreversible and progressive disease. Of course later on I argued that alcoholism was not even a disease but initially my response to this work was to emphasise the need for harm minimization for alcoholism. If

alcoholism is a self-limiting disease, it seemed to me that health professionals should try above all else to not perpetuate the condition by what we do. Our paramount aim, it seemed to me, was to protect people while they are getting over their illness.

A: *That was an idea that you had several decades before harm reduction became associated with illicit drug use?*
LD: These thoughts all originated from my work on alcoholism in Scandinavia.

A: *What other things did you learn in Scandinavia?*
LD: I thought that they were dealing with a legal substance, alcohol, in a way that was not promoting it. This was particularly true in Sweden while I was there. If someone wanted a drink they could get one provided they were prepared to look around hard enough.

If alcoholism is a self-limiting disease, it seemed to me that health professionals should try above all else to not perpetuate the condition by what we do

---

A: *Do you think in those days that the Swedish people supported harm reduction?*
LD: They did, but they have not retained that stance.

A: *Did you also work with the World Health Organization?*
LD: I attended many committees meetings and workshops. There were two experiences I particularly savor. I had a good couple of weeks in Mexico City with David Hawks and Robin Room. That was very stimulating. I also had a week in the Philippines. I was not aware that the Regional Director of Health could hear all that went on in the committee room with his own private line. However he singled me out and accused me of being a socialist. I took this as a compliment because I had been opposing the

party line all the way through the meeting. Another happy memory was a meeting in Washington DC in 1977–78 where we developed the concept of alcohol dependence as a provisional syndrome.[5]

Moving on

A: *After 30 years working as a general psychiatrist in alcohol and drugs, was it difficult to leave the field behind?*

LD: After I made a decision that I would leave the alcohol and drug field, I extricated myself over about two years because I just felt so dejected. I was disappointed that I had not been able to achieve more change. Rather than keep on bashing my head against a brick wall, I though that I would be better off to get out and do something constructive somewhere else. I think I have been able to do that as a general psychiatrist.

A: *What are your views of the problem of so-called 'co-morbidity', people who have both alcohol and drug dependence and psychiatric problems? How do you feel about the way that communities respond to these individuals?*

LD: I have been working for some years in an inner city area with a number of people with schizophrenia including a high proportion of drug use. We need to be more assertive in outreach for people with drug and alcohol problems in the same way that we now are for psychiatric problems. We see it as our responsibility as a service if someone has a psychiatric problem to make sure that they get the best treatment available, whether they want it or not. The first point is to train the mental health staff in assertive outreach. This has to be based on mutual respect and the knowledge that sometimes staff have got to impose things on people, including sometimes in relation to their alcohol and drug use. We need to have an assertive approach but also have mutual respect. There has to be a long-term view and this has to be based on trying to help people to gradually improve their lives and to appreciate that their previous drug use is not going to be a part of their future and that any abuse of drugs is likely to impede their improvement.

A: *During the period that you have been very active and influential in the alcohol and drug field in Australia, the toll of mood-altering substances among indigenous Australians has unfortunately gone from bad to worse.*

LD: It comes back to the same principle that drug use is so often an indicator of general problems within a community. This is particularly true in the indigenous people of Australia at present. At one stage I went around Australia looking at alcohol and drug problems in the community, including among aboriginal communities. I was also personally interested in the response to these problems. I concluded that every community should be provided with a recreation officer to give the young people something to do. Aboriginal Australians love sport and are very good at it. But this suggestion was not taken up because it was not what was wanted. But there have been some major developments. In the 1970s there were no aboriginal professional people, no aboriginal medical students. But there are still some grave problems and I do not know what the solutions are.

A: *One of the recommendations the Baume enquiry made was to reduce per capita alcohol consumption. Do you support that view in general terms?*

LD: Perhaps in general, but one needs to look at the distribution. Per capita alcohol consumption can increase if all the abstainers start to drink a little bit, and this might be to their benefit. But concentrating on per capita consumption by itself is not enough. One needs to look at the distribution of alcohol consumption and minimize the dangerous drinkers. I was involved in an alcohol committee of the NHMRC committee where David Hawks and Rene Pols developed definitions of hazardous and harmful drinking.[6] This was a very important educational achievement.

A: *What about tobacco? We have been struck in Australia with little change in smoking prevalence and hardly any decline in tobacco-related deaths.*

LD: The Swedish alcohol system appeals to me for tobacco. That means creating a government monopoly managed by a commission whose job it is to minimize the harm associated with tobacco use. Again, I do not think we are ever going to get rid of tobacco.

A: *Do you see a reduction of tobacco consumption as a worthwhile policy?*

LD: Yes, most worthwhile.

A: *Why do you support reducing tobacco consumption as a goal in itself when you are opposed to the reduction of heroin consumption or cannabis consumption?*

LD: I am not opposed to attempts to reduce drug consumption. The problems I have are with the strategies adopted, particularly when a reduction in drug use becomes an end in itself. And I do not support reducing the per capita alcohol consumption as the primary goal but I do support efforts to try to change the distribution of consumption. There is a level of alcohol consumption where the benefits outweigh the risks. In contrast, there is no level of tobacco use that benefits health. We should be aiming for policies which minimize the use of tobacco both in terms of the numbers of smokers and the amount of tobacco smoked.

Free-rein choices

A: *If you were given free range to do anything you liked without political constraints, what would you do about illicit drugs?*

LD: The paramount principle for all drug policy is to minimize the health, social and economic costs of drug use to society. This must be the guiding principle. We have got to accept that as prohibition is only achievable for a few drugs, we have to come up with more pragmatic answers most of the time. That is why I support a government commission whose primary goal is to minimize the problems associated with drug use and the cost of drug use to society. It should be possible to set up the terms of reference so that these institutions would have to report to parliament annually with the Auditor General required to monitor them. The enabling legislation would require that the primary objective was reducing drug problems, not making money.

A: *Have you seen any examples where prohibition has worked?*

LD: The prohibition of 'Bex', a popular sedative in Australia, was effective. Prohibition can be effective with some drugs, but that is fairly rare. We almost achieved prohibition with amphetamine for 20 years.

A: *What would you do about cannabis?*

LD: We should have made cannabis a national industry 20–30 years ago and we should still do that now. It should be taxed and regulated like alcohol and tobacco. But it should not be promoted. There should be a commission responsible for cannabis.

A: *What advantages do you see in a taxed and regulated cannabis industry?*

LD: Firstly, in the long term, cannabis consumption would probably decrease. Secondly, we would have a regulated industry with income generated for the community rather than the present arrangement where the cannabis industry is outside the tax system. Thirdly, we would get rid of all the corruption. We could end up with fewer people in jail and fewer people traumatized by a cannabis conviction, fewer people caught up in the criminal justice system.

We have got to accept that as prohibition is only achievable for a few drugs, we have to come up with more pragmatic answers most of the time

---

A: *As a psychiatrist you presumably have seen a lot of young Australians with severe mental health problems exacerbated by cannabis. The contention is that if there was a taxed and regulated system for cannabis, the lives of these unfortunate people would be made even worse by cannabis. How do you see that?*

LD: I am not sure whether they are worse off with cannabis than without. They are pretty distressed people. Much of their cannabis use is symptomatic relief or an escape from the banality and lack of meaning of their lives. Perhaps if the community generated tax revenue from cannabis, some of that could be diverted into rehabilitation programs for these people and perhaps their need for cannabis could be reduced considerably.

A: *Do you see drugs like heroin, cocaine and amphetamines ever being taxed, regulated and sold?*
LD: I think that ultimately is the least-worst option. It will not be easy or quick, nor should anyone expect that drug problems would immediately disappear. These problems are not going to disappear. Unless there were similar changes in other countries, America would probably object strongly. I believe America objected very strongly more than 20 years ago when Australia was looking at more liberal approaches. I believe that in about 1985 when Bob Hawke went to America as Prime Minister, he was told Australia's beef imports would be stopped if we did not come into line.

A: *What do you feel about heroin prescription on a research basis?*
LD: It would be a small step forward. It would be very helpful to at least demonstrate that it would not produce increased problems. But the outcome would depend on whether the staff were really committed to reducing problems among the people receiving the heroin.

Problems with illicit drugs have got inexorably worse. It is very unlikely that prohibition is going to work in the future. There must be better ways of managing this problem

---

A: *Do you see cocaine as a drug that could potentially be prescribed or at least be evaluated for prescription.*
LD: I do not see it as being prescribed. I do see it as being legalized and made uncomfortable to get, expensive to get, yet less expensive than the illegal option. We just have to accept that some people are always going to use drugs. Prohibition has only worked on rare occasions and we have tried it now for 40 or 50 years. Problems with illicit drugs have got inexorably worse. It is very unlikely that prohibition is going to work in the future. There must be better ways of managing this problem.

A: *In the 45 years that you have been involved in this field, do you think that Australia has made progress or have we just been running on the spot?*
LD: We have made major moves forward with alcohol and tobacco but we have not done at all well with illicit drugs. We have not really stopped the progression towards worse and worse outcomes including overdoses, drug use, crime and corruption. It has all gone steadily backwards. Society has changed a lot in that time too. It is not all a matter of policy. It may also be that some of these changes would have occurred anyhow.

A: *How do you think Australia's approach compares with that of other countries?*
LD: Australia has much to learn from the rest of the world but also has some things to teach. I do not think we have to hide very much of what Australia has done. We have done a lot better than many other countries.

A: *The Salvation Army in Australia in the last three years has been very conspicuous in the public eye in promoting a zero tolerance perspective. How do you feel about the religion that you were nurtured in and have remained close to throughout your whole life playing a formative role in the entrenchment of prohibition in Australia?*
LD: I have always been concerned about institutional religion although I do not think that the Salvation Army is very institutionalized. I think the founder of the Salvation Army would be appalled to see where we have gone. In the same way, I think the founder of Christianity would be appalled to see where Christianity has gone. Institutionalization takes away the real message, the real meaning of religion.

A: *How did Chaos Theory come to interest you?*
LD: I got involved with Chaos Theory in about 1989 when someone gave me a book to read on a long plane flight. It was just what I had been looking for. On the basis of that I went on to write an article about chance as a major factor in the causation of mental illness.[7]

A: *Four months ago you were a passenger in the front seat of a car traveling at high speed on a highway. Unfortunately, you were involved in a head-on collision which resulted in the death of the driver of the other car and serious injury to yourself and the driver of your car. What did you learn from that experience?*

LD: I have learned how fragile we all are. I have learned to question in a new way the whole meaning of life. It has really strengthened the feeling I was coming to over the last few years that the meaning of life is about enjoyment, our own enjoyment and the enjoyment of others. I think of our identity with the whole of our environment. I even go out of my way not to stand on a slater [woodlouse]. They have as much right to life as we have, and are as much a part of the enjoyment of the universe as we are.

The meaning of life is about enjoyment, our own enjoyment and the enjoyment of others

A: *Do you think people have a right to enjoy drugs?*

LD: I think that they do have a right. But they also have to respect other people who are concerned about them exercising whatever benevolent influence they can exert. We should not stand in judgment on other people. One of the things I learned in those 13 years as Ministerial Adviser in Canberra was to be able to have violent intellectual disagreement with other people who had an opposite opinion to me and yet remain friends.

A: *You have a skeptical nature along with an open mind?*

LD: I have always been skeptical and have tried to balance this by a willingness to accept criticism. I try to appraise concepts and I have been seen as being opposed to a lot of orthodox people. Being critical of other people, I have always welcomed critical people into my own team. When I was a superintendent at a mental hospital, I recruited a young social worker who was a rabid socialist. He constantly challenged me, asking me why I sat so defensively behind my desk when I had staff meetings. So I had to move around to the other side of the desk. In 1990, when I established an academic unit in a mental hospital, my first appointment was a social anthropologist whose job it was to criticize what we were all doing. It has always been important for me to have people who have questioned me as well as me questioning other people. I think that is a balance one needs to keep.

References

1. DREW, L. R. H. (1961) Alcoholic offenders in a Victorian Prison, *Medical Journal of Australia*, **2**, 575–578.
2. DREW, L. R. H. & TAYLOR, V. K. (1998) *The Second AIDS Epidemic: spread via needle-sharing within the general community* (Canberra, Department of Community Services and Health).
3. DREW, L. R. H. (1982) Avoidable deaths from drug intoxication, *Medical Journal of Australia*, **2**, 215.
4. DREW, L. R. H. (1968) Alcoholism as a self-limiting disease, *Quarterly Journal of Studies on Alcohol*, **29**, 956–967.
5. EDWARDS, G., ARIF, A. & HODGSON, R. (1981) Nomenclature and classification of drug- and alcohol-related problems: a WHO memorandum. *Bulletin of the World Health Organisation*, **59**, 225–242.
6. POLS, R. G. & HAWKS, D. (1992) *Is there a safe level of alcohol consumption for men and women? 2ⁿᵈ edn*, (Canberra, National Health and Medical Research Council).
7. DREW, L. R. H. (1992) Chance: a major factor in the causation of mental illness, *Australian and New Zealand Journal of Psychiatry*, **26**, 284–286.

James Rankin

James G. Rankin FRACP FAFHPM FRCPC *was born in 1930 in Chatswood, NSW, Australia. He obtained his MB and BS at the University of Sydney, 1954. He is Emeritus Professor, Department of Public Health Sciences, University of Toronto, Clinical Professor of Medicine, University of Sydney, and Senior Staff Specialist, Drug and Alcohol Services, NSW Northern Rivers Area Health Service. He has worked in the drug and alcohol field since 1964 in both Australia and Canada as a researcher, educator, clinician and administrator. Senior positions include: Foundation Director of the Addiction Research Foundation Clinical Institute, Toronto; Director, Division of Drug and Alcohol Services, Health Commission of NSW; Director, Canadian Liver Foundation Epidemiology Unit; Director, University of Toronto, Division of Drug and Alcohol Studies; Chairman, Central Sydney Area Health Service Drug and Alcohol Services; Acting Director, Drug and Alcohol Directorate, NSW Health Department. He was foundation President of the Australian Medical Society on Alcohol and Drugs (now APSAD) and the Canadian Society of Addiction Medicine. He has been a special adviser to the WHO. Since 1994 he has concentrated on promoting and supporting the development of drug and alcohol programs in NSW Area Health Services.*

Addiction: *How did you first get into the field of alcohol and other drugs?*

Jim Rankin: It was serendipity. In 1963 I returned to Sydney with my wife and four children, after two years' research on hepatic physiology and disease in New York at Columbia University College of Physicians and Surgeons. At the time there were no suitable academic positions available in Sydney. By chance, I heard about one at St Vincent's Hospital, Melbourne in the University of Melbourne Department of Medicine, and was the successful applicant. The Sisters of Charity owned St Vincent's Hospital and were keen to have a clinic started for patients with alcohol problems. The hospital was located in an area that probably had the highest concentration in Australia of homeless people and people with alcohol problems. Carl de Gruchy, the Professor of Medicine at St Vincent's at that time, asked me to establish an outpatient clinic for people with alcohol problems.[1]

A: *Was this one of the first general hospital-based alcohol clinics either in Australia or elsewhere?*

JR: Yes. At about the same time, Dr Rod Milton established a rehabilitation unit at the Royal Brisbane and Dr John Moon established an outpatient clinic at the Alfred Hospital, Melbourne. Our clinic was intended to provide an outpatient and inpatient service, primarily for the community served by St Vincent's Hospital. The alcohol field in Australia then was almost a professional vacuum. Most treatment programmes had a 12-step orientation. The alcohol field was an unpopular area medically and professionally. However, the Phillips Royal Commission, then inquiring into the liquor laws of the state of Victoria, drew a lot of attention to problems related to alcohol.[2] Over a six-year period, substantial clinical services and a research and educational programme were established. The University of Melbourne Summer School of Alcohol Studies was held for the first time in 1966. The school provided many opportunities for people to learn more about the field and helped to develop an informal network of interested people across Australia. Problems of alcohol use were formally introduced into undergraduate medical education in Australia for the first time at the University of Melbourne. There were many research opportunities but no recognized funding source. Still, at St Vincent's we established a research programme that had a mainly epidemiological orientation.[3,4]

Off to Ontario

A: *After a few years in Melbourne, you moved to Canada. Why?*

JR: In late 1969, I was offered a joint appointment as Physician-in-Chief of the Clinical Institute of the Addiction Research Foundation of Ontario and Associate Professor, Department of Medicine, University of Toronto. Choosing between staying in Melbourne or moving to Toronto was very difficult. There was also the question of whether I should continue in the alcohol field or move into the much broader field of community health, then in its infancy in Australia. Probably what tipped the balance in favour of Canada was a comment by my colleague, the late Professor Albert Baikie, who said in his broad Scottish accent, 'Jim, you'd be mad if you didn't take the opportunity'.

A: *What did you find when you got to Canada?*

JR: The first thing I found was how incredibly cold Toronto could be. On the other hand, the people were incredibly warm. The Clinical Institute was a year away from completion. It was to be a 100-bed clinical research and training centre operated by the Addiction Research Foundation and also a teaching hospital of the University of Toronto. The expectation was that the centre would be fully operational by early 1971, a daunting challenge. The drug and alcohol field in Canada presented additional challenges. Provincial governments in Canada dominated the field through their various agencies of which the Addiction Research Foundation was the best-known example. It had flourished from the time it was established by the Ontario Government in 1949 and become an internationally renowned organization. But there was not much else going on in the drug and alcohol field professionally in Ontario and Canada outside these government agencies. By contrast, at that time in Australia it was the initiatives of individuals and non-government organizations that were providing the leadership in the drug and alcohol field.

A: *Why did you leave the world's then largest alcohol and drug clinical research unit to return to Australia in 1978?*

JR: After some pretty rocky problems at the beginning, things turned out exceptionally well in Canada. The Clinical Institute developed a full range of clinical services for the management of alcohol- and drug-related health, behavioural and social problems. These included emergency, outpatient and residential services. A research programme was developed[5] which included biomedical studies in epidemiology (Dr Mary Jane Ashley), clinical pharmacology (Drs Edward M. Sellers, Richard Frecker, Claudio Naranjo and Stuart McLeod), neurology (Dr Peter Carlen) and hepatology (Dr Hector Orrego). The focus was alcohol- and drug-related medical problems, their prevention, diagnosis and treatment. The other major area of research, developed by Dr Frederick Glaser, concerned treatment systems and methods. This programme introduced the 'core-shell' concept of treatment and treatment evaluation and also developed the matching hypothesis.[6] So many well-trained, imaginative, energetic individuals joined the Institute at that time. By 1978, I felt that I had fulfilled the major responsibilities of my appointment and wondered whether it was time to explore other opportunities.

> **The first thing I found was how incredibly cold Toronto could be. On the other hand, the people were incredibly warm**

Back to New South Wales

A: *So by 1978 you began thinking about coming back to Australia?*

JR: In 1978, I was asked to consider coming back to NSW to head up a new Drug and Alcohol Division within the NSW Health Commission. The reasons for the establishment of the Division were fairly obvious. There was a great deal of community concern about drugs. The problems of illicit drugs were perceived as rapidly getting much worse. Coverage by the media helped to fuel concern. Drug and alcohol services were much criticized and considered inadequate.

A: *What was the position you went to when you arrived back in Australia in September 1978?*
JR: I became Director of the Drug and Alcohol Division within the NSW Health Commission. My responsibility was to advise the Commission on alcohol and drug issues, develop new services and improve existing services. Despite many difficulties over the next three years, it was possible to bring together a group to plan and develop treatment and prevention programmes, related research and education. But, of great concern to me, there were no new resources available to increase services. We developed a wish-list while also trying to obtain the support and commitment of key people and organizations for any future developments.

Teaching hospitals have an enormous influence on the training and professional behaviour of physicians, nurses and other health professional staff

A: *What were the major achievements of this three-year period in Sydney?*
JR: A major opportunity to implement the ideas that had been developed came in late 1980. The NSW Government planned to decriminalize public drunkenness and support the new policy with a grant programme. It was intended mainly to fund non-government organizations concerned with public drunkenness and homelessness but funding Health Commission drug and alcohol services was not excluded. This was a once in a lifetime opportunity to fund new programmes along the lines that we had planned.[7] The grant to the Health Commission was not large – just A\$1.4 million. However, it was given with the understanding that the Commission would cover the continuing costs of programmes. At the time of the grant, Health

Commission drug and alcohol services were extremely limited. There were some services in psychiatric hospitals, community-based drug and alcohol counsellors and an embryonic methadone programme. Particularly lacking were programmes in mainstream health and medical settings including general hospitals. Teaching hospitals have an enormous influence on the training and professional behaviour of physicians, nurses and other health professional staff. One of my main objectives was to create nuclear drug and alcohol programmes within at least the major teaching hospitals and, if possible, beyond that in major hospitals across the state. We proposed appointments of a medical specialist and senior nurse at the level of Assistant Director of Nursing at each hospital with some additional support staff, such as residents and clerical staff. The major responsibility of these hospital-based staff was to develop a willingness and capacity of the hospital as a whole to respond to problems of drug and alcohol use among their patients.

A: *Was there any international model for this hospital-based network of alcohol and drug services?*
JR: No. This grant made it possible to establish drug and alcohol services in four metropolitan teaching hospitals and one rural hospital. The first staff specialists appointed to these services went on to play important policy, clinical, educational and research roles in the drug and alcohol field. The grant also supported the establishment of two 'non-medical' detoxification units based on the Ontario model. Another unique development was the establishment of a 24-hour hospital-based drug and alcohol telephone information service. The grant also funded research and development programmes concerned with the diagnosis of drug intoxication and overdose, alcohol-related brain damage and medical education. I particularly wanted to promote a very active and important role for the medical practitioner in the drug and alcohol field, something I believed in then and still believe in very strongly. The concept was to take the teaching hospital model and then hope to attract a group of people who would present clini-

cal, academic and professional role models. I well remember when, in 1979, I was asked to give a lecture on drugs and alcohol to Sydney University final year medical students. I was given an hour in the last term of the six-year programme. I resolved that I would never fall into that trap again. I decided that in future I would only support approaches to medical education that were more strategic.

A: *Were there any other important achievements during this period?*
JR: The other important one was contributing to the establishment of the Australian Medical Society on Alcohol and Other Drugs, that has evolved into the Australian Professional Society on Alcohol and Drugs, and serving as its first president.[8]

There is no evidence that drug prohibition has been successful and the costs have been enormous

Legal controls of drugs

A: *Looking back now two decades later, do you see echoes of the debate about alcohol intoxication in public then and the debate about illicit drugs now?*
JR: There was very little debate about the decriminalization of public drunkenness at that time. Over a long period, many people came to realise that public drunkenness could not be dealt with effectively by the criminal justice system. Most of the inmates serving sentences for alcohol-related offences then are very similar to the prisoners with drug problems now except the ones today are younger. In both groups Aboriginality, poor parenting, other forms of childhood deprivation, abuse and poor education are common. Both groups are fundamentally victims of their inheritance and environment. More people these days are starting to think about how to minimize the impact of the criminal justice system on drug users.

A: *And your own views on this matter?*
JR: If we look at the legal framework developed in response to alcohol and other drugs towards the end of the 19th and early part of the 20th century, the major emphasis was limiting alcohol and drug availability. We had Prohibition in the United States and at about the same time we had the evolution of efforts to control availability of other substances, initially opiates, then cocaine and marijuana. In the United States during Prohibition, the majority of the population broke a law they did not agree with. After a while, this situation became intolerable. Although Prohibition reduced alcohol consumption and diseases related to alcohol, there was an unacceptably high social cost because of the crimes associated with the illegal production, distribution and sale of alcohol, and the acquisition of wealth and its investment by criminal groups. Ultimately America had had enough of alcohol prohibition and repealed it, but prohibition of other substances has unfortunately continued even though it has proved to be no more effective than alcohol prohibition. The negative effects have been far worse than occurred with alcohol prohibition. As I look back, I am very cynical about the role of politicians, bureaucrats and politics in the development and imposition of drug controls. The evidence used to justify the introduction of prohibition had no credible scientific basis. There is no evidence that drug prohibition has been successful and the costs have been enormous. There are still many people who feel that the only approach is to maintain prohibitions on illicit substances despite more and more evidence that law enforcement has not worked. It is clear that public health approaches are far more effective. Repealing prohibition took the exorbitant profits out of alcohol. There is still some profit in the legal production and sale of alcohol but nothing like the lucrative profits at the time of prohibition. So if we ultimately move to a different framework with currently illicit substances there might be some way that these substances might be sold without the vast profits that drive the current system.

A: *Looking at all the new services that you developed between 1978 and 1981 in NSW, most have survived and been expanded apart from services for people with alcohol-related brain damage. How do you feel about that?*

JR: I was particularly interested in subclinical levels of brain damage that may be much more common in a drinking community than the few people with extreme impairment. This seemed to be a promising area and the idea was to try to see if we could get some funding, attract research and researchers and some resources. It did not progress the way I hoped. When the appointments were made, the attachment to the drug and alcohol field was rather peripheral and the attachment to neurology central.

So, although Canada did develop a National Drug Strategy it compared poorly with that developed in Australia

---

Another stay in Canada

A: *Why did you decide to move back to Canada?*
JR: It was a pragmatic family-based decision based on our needs and the comparative opportunities in Australia and Canada at the time. I felt quite depressed at the thought of having to leave what I saw as an area of expanding development, very much preferring to remain part of the developments in Australia. It is strange how things turned out. Soon after I returned from an interview in Toronto for a new position, I had an unexpected meeting with the then NSW Minister for Health, Laurie Brereton. He said, 'I am going to eliminate all the special directorates including yours because I do not think we need them'. The government had also decided to abolish the Health Commission. In fact, all the Commissioners of Health and many senior staff went. The new Health Department of NSW was left with was one adviser who was responsible for the fledgling methadone programme. Our very productive group in the Health Commission was reduced to almost nothing overnight.

A: *And the job in Canada?*
JR: I took up a position as Director of the Canadian Liver Foundation Epidemiology Unit at the University of Toronto in the Department of Preventive Medicine and Biostatistics. The Head of the Department at the time was Dr Mary Jane Ashley, with whom I had previously worked on the epidemiology of alcohol-related disorders when I first went to Toronto in the early 1970s. I was asked when I went back to Toronto whether I would take on the responsibility of coordinating the drug and alcohol education programme for medical students at the University of Toronto. That academic responsibility became an important part of my work and linked into my other activities in Canada in the medical education area. In the mid-1980s, the position of Physician-in-Chief at the Addiction Research Foundation became vacant and I was once more asked by the Foundation to take on that role.

A: *What was happening in Canada in the alcohol and drug field that struck you as either a major strength or major weakness?*
JR: One of the dominant features of the drug and alcohol field in Canada in the 1970s was the Le Dain Royal Commission into the Non-medical Use of Drugs.[9] This grew out of a major concern about drug use. Many of the issues that are currently being discussed were topical then. The Prime Minister was Pierre Trudeau. His Liberal government appointed Gerald Le Dain, a very respected jurist who became a Judge in the Supreme Court of Canada. He took a most scholarly approach. The Le Dain Royal Commission was well funded. The commissioners consulted widely and commissioned a number of key reviews. Month after month new reports appeared that contributed to public discussion. Issues such as decriminalization of marijuana were very much on the agenda. It felt as if the reports and recommendations of the Commission would have significant, positive outcomes.

A: *And in the event?*
JR: When the Royal Commission was over and Pierre Trudeau was no longer Prime Minister, all these efforts showed little tangible results other than the reports that are now largely lost and forgotten. So, although Canada did develop a National Drug Strategy it compared poorly with that developed in Australia. Going back to Canada

in the 1980s and 1990s, I did not see any major improvements. Intermittent media events created political crises and excited political responses but, from my perspective, there was no planned organized tangible movement forward at either the provincial or the federal level. Once a crisis was over, the issues vanished from the public mind and any initiative with them. The Canadian Centre on Substance Abuse was established. Again, that looked like a very promising initiative in terms of the calibre of people in leadership, research and education roles.

A: *And that Centre and the ARF, did they operate very differently?*
JR: The Centre took a very different tack to the Addiction Research Foundation. It was intentionally small and largely interactive in how it developed its initiatives collaboratively with other groups and people in the community. I saw that as a very positive move. I was aware of the decreasing importance and relevance of the Addiction Research Foundation as an organization. The original executive director, David Archibald, had the status of a Deputy Minister and reported to the Minister for Health. This is the most senior level in the Ontario Civil Service. By the 1980s David Archibald's successors reported to administrators at the Assistant Deputy Minister or lower. The reporting relationship of the Foundation was downgraded further and further. It was conceptualized as belonging and remaining within mental health. This was a time when, in government departments, 'content-free' general managers began to take over from people with expertise in the area they were managing. Today, the Addiction Research Foundation is no longer a separate government agency, having been incorporated into the new Centre for Addiction and Mental Health in 1996 as part of the reorganization of health services by the Ontario Government.

Positioning drugs and alcohol

A: *Where do you think the area should fit?*
JR: The drug and alcohol field does not fit into any single professional area: it is truly interdis-

ciplinary, and therein lies both its professional strength and its political weakness. If you look at the field from the broadest perspective of trying to resolve the problems resulting from alcohol and drug use, a public health perspective is critical. Primary prevention fits very neatly into this area. Secondary intervention with people at risk presents a major opportunity for general medical practitioners to contribute. The specialist physician is very important for people with serious complications of alcohol and drug use. There is an important role for psychiatrists and other mental health workers, particularly with regard to dual diagnoses. If you look broadly at medical practice in terms of the greatest opportunities for effective intervention, it lies in the area of primary health care and general practice. Such a professional perspective does not necessarily translate into how politicians and health administrators view the drug and alcohol field. For example, they may approach it as a separate administrative entity or fit it into an existing public health or mental health framework, each with its own potential benefits and costs. Personally, I consider that the field fits best within a public health framework, but only if the administrative environment within which this is done is supportive and well-integrated in its activities with other parts of health, and beyond to other jurisdictions.

The case for a heroin maintenance trial

A: *One of the recommendations of the Le Dain Royal Commission in the 1970s was that Canada should evaluate the costs and benefits of heroin prescription. That was your first recommendation in a report you prepared for the Premier of NSW in 1981.*
JR: In NSW in the late 1970s and early 1980s, there was a lot of concern about heroin and the increasing number of users. There was the constant confrontation with evidence of increased heroin use and uncertainty and controversy about what should and could be done to reduce the impact on criminal activity and health. The question was raised within the NSW Government of whether heroin itself should be used as a form of

maintenance therapy. As a result The New South Wales Committee of Inquiry into the Legal Provision of Heroin and Other Possible Methods of Diminishing Crime Associated with the Supply and Use of Heroin was appointed by the Minister for Health, the Honourable Kevin Stewart, on a request from the Premier of NSW, the Honourable Neville Wran. The committee was a diverse group, most of whom had no background in the drug and alcohol field. We travelled to the United Kingdom, the United States and Canada. We talked to experts about their views on the treatment of opiate dependence. I could not help but be incredibly depressed by what I saw of methadone maintenance and the alcohol and drug treatment system generally in the United Kingdom at that time. The attitude seemed to be one of out-of-sight, out-of-mind. Methadone programmes were hidden away, poorly resourced and run by people who seemed pretty uninterested. The impression was that methadone was a valuable form of treatment that had not been effectively translated into clinical practice. The committee considered that heroin maintenance treatment had been proved to be feasible but it was probably time for a clinical trial of its effectiveness. Our first recommendation was for a trial of the potential value of heroin maintenance in heroin addicted people where every other form of treatment had failed.[10] Many of the other recommendations were concerned with trying to improve methadone programmes through improved funding and training. We also made recommendations about the need for trials of substances other than heroin in treatment and we specifically mentioned buprenorphine, naltrexone and leva alpha acetyl methadol, the long-acting methadone.

A: *What happened to your recommendations? Were they officially accepted, rejected or just ignored?*
JR: These recommendations were made in 1981. It took another 18 years before these other drugs, particularly naltrexone, suddenly exploded in the media, seeking instant cures for heroin addiction. Why was the 1981 report not officially considered by the NSW Government? Why did it get lost? I think partly because the Health Commission was

dissolved. There was no advocacy for the recommendations concerning heroin maintenance and the introduction of new drugs. Methadone was available and the concerns that lead to the inquiry were no longer important. I think that we should recognize that although there are some exceptions, governments largely see committees of inquiry as a means of defusing a difficult situation without necessarily needing to respond to eventual reports and recommendations. Certainly, the present NSW Government was completely ignorant of the 1981 committee and its recommendations as it prepared for its 1999 NSW Drug Summit.

Our first recommendation was for a trial of the potential value of heroin maintenance in heroin addicted people where every other form of treatment had failed

A: *What were the circumstances of your rejoining the Addiction Research Foundation in 1985?*
JR: I proposed that the focus of my Foundation work should be largely outside the organization as the responsibilities of Physician-in-Chief were mostly administrative. The question became: how do we contribute to this outside world? One example was my involvement in the establishment of the Canadian Medical Society on Alcohol and Other Drugs, that is now known as the Canadian Society of Addiction Medicine, and serving as its first president. In the early 1990s yet another review of the Foundation was carried out. It was decided that research into the medical consequences of alcohol and drug use should cease and that the Institute should concentrate its research efforts on treatment research. Most of the academic medical activities within the Institute ceased, with the exception of those concerned with mental health. The President then put forward a proposal that the Foundation would support an Interdepartmental Division of Drug and Alcohol Studies in the University of Toronto as a new initiative with special funding. So starting in 1990 I began to pursue an expansion of my earlier education involvement.

A Chair in Sydney

A: *You returned to Australia again in 1994. Why was this?*

JR: In 1994 I came back to Australia as Chair of the Central Sydney Area Drug and Alcohol Service and a Clinical Professor at the University of Sydney. I completed this work in 1999. I am now working as a senior staff specialist in the Northern Rivers Area Health Service where I am assisting in the further development of its drug and alcohol services. In particular, I am working on a project whose aims are to promote and support the interest and ability of general practitioners to respond to patients with drug and alcohol problems.

A: *You have worked in Australia and Canada: what are the strengths and weaknesses of approaches in the two countries?*

JR: Australia is now rich in the number, variety and quality of professional people working in the drug and alcohol field. Relative to populations, there are far more people involved academically in Australia than in Canada. Although patchy, there is an increasing acceptance of the significance of the drug and alcohol field in the community in Australia and that is also increasingly true in Australia among professional people such as the Royal Colleges or groups of that nature. Also, the National Health and Medical Research Council in Australia has, over time, come to recognize the professionalism of people who work in this field and fund activities in this area. The drug and alcohol field has certainly come of age in Australia over the last quarter century. The breadth of services available in some parts of the country is unique. It is also true that standards vary considerably. Largely lacking in Australia are dedicated, organized, vocal, strong, credible, professional leadership and advocacy. This contrasts with the HIV area where dedicated individuals have done a tremendous job because of their credibility and their efforts to keep things on track. Australia does not have the professional organizational bases from which these activities can be sustained. Individuals are important but organizations are also critical. There is little registration or accreditation of treatment programmes. The three national Australian centres have been the source of important informed comment but they are fundamentally research and training centres.

A: *Western countries have responded to alcohol and drug issues in many different ways: what lessons can be drawn? How do we advance evidence-based policies and practices?*

JR: Since the early 1990s I have been interested in the development and operations of treatment systems, particularly at a regional level, that might provide for a population of 100000–250000. How can they best function? How should they be funded? What sort of staff should they have? My main interest now is trying to promote greater provision of services by mainstream health care and other relevant professionals. My approach now is based on a broad, population-based, community-orientated, public health view of alcohol and drugs and trying to promote approaches that will achieve significant change. That is a very different approach to that currently in the United States and Canada.

The drug and alcohol field has certainly come of age in Australia over the last quarter century. The breadth of services available in some parts of the country is unique

---

A: *You also became interested in the idea of folly as an important concept in understanding the gaps between evidence and policy.*

JR: I developed an interest in the politics of the drug and alcohol field in the early 1970s not long after I arrived in Canada. My interest arose out of an invitation to give the 1974 Leonard Ball Oration, held annually in Melbourne. I chose for my topic the politics of alcohol and drug use.[11] Many years later a Canadian friend recommended that I read Barbara Tuchman's *March of Folly*.[12] We had been discussing the inexplicable decisions of politicians who, when developing and applying policies, often ignore abundant evidence, informed advice and all that is going on around them. I had been thinking particularly about the response to illicit drugs in the United States at the time. I found Tuchman's approach to the problem of understanding obviously counterproductive decision making by government very enlightening. Tuchman considered several historical debacles including the American involvement in Vietnam and Britain's loss of her colony in North America. Why did the Trojans open the gates of Troy to the Greek horse? The characteristics of all of these follies are that the authorities are clearly unable to achieve their objectives but are determined to continue their policy to the bitter end, whatever the consequences. Illicit drug policies relying almost entirely on law enforcement are a perfect example of folly. Once the folly has become embedded in the system, does it remain like that forever or does some event change policy? Many people in the community now recognize that the drug policy we have pursued for decades has failed. But most politicians in positions of power are not prepared to even consider alternative options.

Illicit drug policies relying almost entirely on law enforcement are a perfect example of folly

Looking into the future

A: *Looking into on your crystal ball, what do you think is going to happen?*
JR: There are several possibilities. Shifts in policy of this nature are largely influenced by public opinion. There is mounting evidence that the traditional prohibitionist approach is simply not working. More and more people know that it is not working. The internet and e-mail are breaking down a lot of communication barriers and provide easy access to information that was previously inaccessible or unavailable though the mainstream media. The changes in drug policy that have occurred in Switzerland in recent years are very important. Despite being a conservative country, some radical changes in drug policy, including the legal provision of heroin, have been implemented. These changes occurred with the clear support and

understanding of the community, and with the involvement of the community in the decision-making process. Various reforms in the Netherlands happened in a similar way. The Swiss and the Dutch are following a different path to the United States, where the war on drugs continues. There have been pressures on these reforming countries to change their ways. A lot of misinformation has been disseminated about the results of their efforts. But given the more open information system available these days, the misinformation can now be countered fairly effectively. Some people liken this process to that which led to the fall of the Berlin Wall. Whether it is about heroin trials or supervised injecting rooms, the challenge of these alternative options to the conventional approach cannot be ignored. The environment, however, is increasingly favouring reform.

A: *In July 1997, a 6:3 majority of Australian Health and Police Ministers approved the next stage of a heroin trial (which had been under careful consideration for five or more years) but they were overruled by Federal Cabinet three weeks later. What are the lessons of that experience for Australia and other countries?*
JR: In the words of the common expression, 'it's not over 'til the fat lady sings'. On that occasion the fat lady was the Prime Minister, the Honourable John Howard. As Prime Minister he was able to veto the agreed-to trials despite support for them from many influential and thoughtful people. The Prime Minister, for reasons that are not really clear, considered that this was an inappropriate project for the country to pursue. That it would give the wrong message. Presumably he either did not have access to or ignored advice supporting the trial. I have been very interested in and influenced by the writings of the distinguished Canadian writer and thinker, John Ralston Saul. The thesis of his Massey Lecture, published as *The Unconscious Civilization*,[13] is that democracies are largely controlled by a combination of bureaucrats, politicians and powerful business and political groups. In reality, the only time that democracy is really evident is during elections. Beyond that period politicians largely do what they want to do. To a large extent the community

is unconscious and uninterested in what is going on around it and does not take any remedial action. Saul argues that it does not have to be that way. If the community was more conscious of what was going on, then it could prevent things happening which should not happen and it could get things to happen that should. If we take as an example the heroin trial, there was no community understanding or support. It was relatively unconscious. When asked during a radio interview for a practical suggestion for people who want to improve their community he said something like 'Every day when I wake up I ask myself which politician or bureaucrat can I irritate today?'

A: *You have long been interested in alcohol prevention emphasising the importance of a political economy perspective. Alcohol prevention has been crowded out of the agenda in the last 15 years by HIV and illicit drugs. Yet in most Western countries, alcohol consumption has declined and outcomes have improved. Does that mean that we are better off if public health advocates avoid entering the debate about alcohol prevention policy? Is there a natural tide in the way things happen anyway?*

JR: There is no simple answer to this question. Alcohol consumption in most industrialised nations has been falling for quite some time. Most of that decline is probably related to economic factors such as the cost of alcohol, the amount of money people have got to spend and what the spending options are other than alcohol. In terms of chronic effects of alcohol use, we have seen the benefits of that change. Drinking and driving became a major public health issue in Australia some years ago. The message got through, the public has learned, the politicians understand and the initiatives in Australia have been tremendous and they have worked. Awareness of similar issues involving alcohol and other safety concerns have increased. Research and policy focus seem to have shifted in recent discussions from the chronic effects, which are often related to per capita consumption, to the acute effects of alcohol which are not related to per capita consumption but are more influenced by patterns and circumstances of drinking. We need to do better at explaining to the community what these risks are and how they can be avoided.

A: *What is the most important achievement in your life in the alcohol and drug field?*
JR: It has been to play a direct or indirect role in providing the opportunities to a number of very intelligent, interested, thoughtful and committed people to work in the field, most of whom had not previously worked in it. They then have attracted many additional people now working in the drug and alcohol field in NSW, other parts of Australia or overseas. I recall the people who gave me similar opportunities, particularly Professor Ruthven Blackburn in Sydney and the late Professor Carl de Gruchy in Melbourne, and of their major, positive impact on me. They gave me the opportunity to contribute to the lives of many colleagues. I can see a train of events over generations that link people, principles, ideas and movements as we move into the future.

When asked during a radio interview for a practical suggestion for people who want to improve their community he said something like 'Every day when I wake up I ask myself which politician or bureaucrat can I irritate today?'

Acknowledgements

I wish to acknowledge the invaluable support, assistance and contributions of my many colleagues. However, in particular, I wish to acknowledge my wife, Patricia Rankin, without whose understanding, support and involvement the events described in this interview would never have occurred. JR

References
1.   RANKIN, J. G., SANTAMARIA, J. N., O'DAY, D. M. & DOYLE, M. C. (1967) Studies in alcoholism: a general hospital medical clinic

for the treatment of alcoholism, *Medical Journal of Australia*, **2**, 157–162.

2. Report of the Royal Commission into the Sale, Supply, Disposal or Consumption of Liquor in the State of Victoria (1965) (Melbourne, Government Printer).

3. WILKINSON, P., SANTAMARIA, J. N., RANKIN, J. G. & MARTIN, D. (1969) Epidemiology of alcoholism: social data and drinking patterns of a sample of Australian alcoholics, *Medical Journal of Australia*, **1**, 1020–1025.

4. WILKINSON, P., KORNACZEWSKI, A., RANKIN, J. G. & SANTAMARIA, J. N. (1971) Physical disease in alcoholism: initial survey of 1000 patients, *Medical Journal of Australia*, **2**, 1217–1223.

5. RANKIN, J. G. (1976) Alcoholism and Drug Addiction Research Foundation of Ontario: research goals and plans, *Annals of the New York Academy of Science*, **273**, 87–97.

6. GLASER, F. B., ANNIS, H. M., PEARLMAN, S., SEGAL, R. L. & SKINNER, H. A. (1985) The differential therapy of alcoholism: a systems approach, in: BRATTER, T. E. & FORREST, G. G. (Eds) *Alcoholism and Substance Abuse: strategies for clinical intervention*, 431–450 (New York, Free Press).

7. MOREY, S., BUTLER, D. & BATEY, R. (1983) Hospital-based drug and alcohol services, *Australian Alcohol/Drug Review*, **2**, 38–40.

8. RANKIN, J. G. (1991) The Australian Medical and Professional Society on Alcohol and Other Drugs: the first 10 years and beyond. The first James Rankin Oration, *Drug and Alcohol Review*, **10**, 339–349.

9. THE COMMISSION OF INQUIRY INTO THE NON-MEDICAL USE OF DRUGS (1973) *Final Report of the Commission of Inquiry into the Non-medical Use of Drugs* (Ottawa, Information Canada).

10. NEW SOUTH WALES COMMITTEE OF INQUIRY INTO THE LEGAL PROVISION OF HEROIN AND OTHER POSSIBLE METHODS OF DIMINISHING CRIME ASSOCIATED WITH THE SUPPLY AND USE OF HEROIN (1981) *Report of the New South Wales Committee of Inquiry into the Legal Provision of Heroin and Other Possible Methods of Diminishing Crime Associated with the Supply and Use of Heroin* (Sydney, Health Commission of New South Wales).

11. RANKIN, J. G. (1974) *The Politics of Alcohol and Drug Use*, 7th Leonard Ball Oration, pp. 1–23 (Melbourne, Victorian Foundation on Alcoholism and Drug Dependence).

12. TUCHMAN, B. W. (1984) *The March of Folly* (New York, Alfred A. Knopf).

13. SAUL, J. S. (1997) *The Unconscious Civilization*, CBC Massey Lecture Series (Toronto, Penguin Books).

David Hawks

David Hawks was born in 1938 in Perth, Western Australia. He obtained his PhD in 1967. From 1987–95 he was Director of the National Centre for Research into the Prevention of Drug Abuse, Perth, Western Australia (subsequently the National Drug Research Institute). Previously he worked in Canada, and in the UK as Deputy Director of the Addiction Research Unit, University of London, 1972–73. For a time he was a staff member of WHO Geneva. He played a role in advising on Australian responses to alcohol and other drug problems, chairing the committee which drafted his country's first national health policy in relation to alcohol; co-authoring Australia's first guidelines on responsible alcohol consumption, and establishing the first advocacy body devoted exclusively to the promotion of public health policies in relation to alcohol. Between 1983 and 1987 he was Director of the Western Australian Alcohol and Drug Authority. His was the first professorial appointment in Addiction Studies in Australia (Curtin University of Technology, 1987–97). In 1997 he received the Order of Australia.

Home town: Perth in Western Australia

Addiction: *Your home town is Perth in Western Australia. What sort of town was it when you were growing up there?*
David Hawks: It was and still is exceedingly isolated, but the sort of town where if you went with your mother shopping, you would almost invariably meet other people you knew in the main street. We had at the time one very small university which was fed by a limited number of schools.

A: *What sort of school did you attend?*
DH: I grew up in a working class area. My mother had gone to a scholarship school. If she had academic aspirations for me they were never stated, although she was very keen that I should accept the High School scholarship which took me to the same academic school she had attended.

A: *Tell us about your university career, what did you do?*
DH: I remember being asked at my primary school what it was that I wanted to be, and I said quite confidently that I wanted to be a cabinet maker. I went from primary school to the first of my secondary schools with that intention. It was usual then in one's final year to be visited by the voca-tional guidance officer and we were given a series of tests. I was persuaded that I should at least aspire to teach woodwork. I would, of course, have to matriculate and at that point the only opportunity I had to fund that was to accept a bond from the education authority that I then work as a teacher for a number of years. It was only when I had got myself to the teachers' training college that it was suggested I might go to university. I had had no expectation of going to university at all. No one in my family, either maternal or paternal, had ever gone to university. I didn't know anyone who had, and I had no notion of what I would even do at university. Preparing as I was for a teaching career I was told 'of course, you should do education', so I enrolled in the faculty of education, which then pre-scribed almost precisely what it was that one had to do. Among those first-year subjects was psychol-ogy. The first-year lectures were given then by the head of department, which was very unusual. He obviously captured my interest, but it was also a matter of pursuing what you succeeded in, and I obviously did well. So I persisted that year in the faculty of education, but when I came to register my units in the second year, I said, I really don't want to continue in education, and with some difficulty I transferred to Arts which allowed me to do a lot more psychology.

A: *By 1960 a lad who did not know anyone who had been to university, had majored in psychology with a first class honours degree in that subject. So that must have been quite an exciting and surprising moment?*

DH: I obviously enjoyed psychology and moreover did well. I still had the need to go back to Teacher Training College because I was under bond as a trainee teacher. But I applied for a Commonwealth Scholarship. I had to nominate where I would go and I have difficulty understanding even now how I lit upon the idea of going to the Maudsley. I guess I had at this stage become acquainted with behavioural treatments. I was aware of the changes that were taking place in the whole practice of clinical psychology and that the Maudsley was a significant centre. I had got out the University of London's handbook and wrote off to the Maudsley. I got a letter back from an S.E. Hague whom I assumed was a male, but who turned out to be female, informing me Yes, if I got a scholarship they would allow me to enrol for a Postgraduate Diploma in Abnormal Psychology.

We were asked out to supper and in Australia supper is something you have just before you go to bed, a cup of cocoa and the odd biscuit . . . we had an evening meal before arriving and then found that we were expected to eat a five-course meal

---

To the Maudsley on a British Council scholarship

A: *When did you arrive at the Maudsley?*
DH: It would have been in October 1961.

A: *Was that your first visit out of Australia?*
DH: Yes. I came as a British Council scholar and that was enormously advantageous. The Council then looked after its scholars. I came by ship and therefore had time to prepare for this monumental change in my life. For months previous I had watched ships come across the horizon. The British Council had appointed someone who arranged accommodation for us, and I remember that it had to be within one or two bus stops of the Maudsley. My scholarship provided for a single man; I had at that point married, but there was no concession made for that fact. We had to live exceedingly frugally and we found a flat just off Peckham Rye. I walked to the Maudsley. The British Council were frequently in touch and said they would arrange for me to go to the theatre, sit in on a debate at the House of Commons and other such attractions; they were enormously welcoming. We were asked out to supper and in Australia supper is something you have just before you go to bed, a cup of cocoa and the odd biscuit . . . we had an evening meal before arriving and then found that we were expected to eat a five-course meal.

A: *What was the academic course like when you got to the Maudsley and Institute of Psychiatry?*
DH: Well, it was then called the Postgraduate Diploma in Abnormal Psychology: a 13-month continuous course in which they tried to put 2 years into 13 calendar months. There were about 14 of us attending. Curiously the people whom I identified with at the Maudsley had all moved off and most of them had gone to Canada. When I arrived it was to find Monty Shapiro had charge of the course. I had the feeling somewhat that the revolution had happened and I had arrived too late. Eysenck taught, but he was not in charge of the clinical teaching although he was very much in evidence. Monty's lectures were the most memorable because he seemed not to have thought through the lecture in advance of giving it, there was a sense of his thinking aloud. He sort of took you into his confidence with all of the uncertainties that he may have had. It was almost a tutorial, but it was a tutorial conducted with a class, albeit a small class. It was a clinical training, but the Maudsley believed that clinical psychologists should be clinical scientists.

A: *Did you talk about alcohol or drugs at all during that course?*
DH: Not at all as I remember.

A: *So, you graduated from that course with the expected Distinction?*

DH: I don't know if it was expected!

Doctoral research in Canada

A: *The next move?*

DH: For my thesis I had got it into my head that I would follow up people who had been given the so-called simple tests of over-inclusive thinking to see to what extent they actually had diagnostic and prognostic significance and found that contrary to what was being claimed about them, they had no such clinical significance. Its principal author was Bob Payne who, while he did his original work at the Maudsley, had gone back to Canada (he was a native of Canada). I had been in correspondence with him in the course of doing my thesis and as a result was invited by him to Canada to become his research associate in 1962. Of course, in accepting this post I was going outside the requirements of the scholarship which had brought me to England which required that I return to Australia. Bob Payne advised me that he would pay me enough to enable me to get back to Australia even though I had forfeited my scholarship. I was a little over 2 years in Canada pursuing my doctoral thesis. At that point I was functioning as a research psychologist, working with schizophrenic patients.

A: *So you got to know another country – Canada, Ontario?*

DH: I did. I hadn't intended to go beyond England. I certainly hadn't anticipated going to Ontario, and as I said I actually broke the terms of the scholarship, but it seemed too good an opportunity to miss. Here was someone saying 'Look, I'd like you to come and work with me; we'll pay you. And if you then want to return to Australia you'll have sufficient funds to do so'. I was also, of course, going to work with Professor Payne whose work I had already given some attention, albeit rather critical attention. At that stage we were expecting our first child. In the event it proved to be a very awkward bit of my career.

Return to Australia

A: *Two years in Canada, and then in 1965 back to base after quite a few years out of Australia.*

DH: Yes, much longer than my mother had anticipated!

A: *And you were in Australia from 1965–67, for 2 years. Were you teaching there?*

DH: I left Canada having collected all the data that I required for my doctoral thesis and had written the first draft. At that point Bob Payne who was my supervisor himself moved to Temple University and the completion of my thesis became very difficult and protracted as a consequence, and the university was quite some time deciding who it would appoint as another supervisor. I could see this going on for a very long time and so decided since we were, at that stage, expecting our second child, that I would complete my thesis from Australia. I was still, believe it or not, under bond. When I got back from Canada it was to be told I was to report to such and such a school and to teach English and History. Fortunately, the education department allowed that as I had acquired a postgraduate qualification in clinical psychology I should be permitted to serve off my bond in the employ of the psychiatric services. And this I did for some little while, while completing the writing up of my doctoral thesis. I had to return to Canada to defend my thesis as the University absolutely insisted that one appeared in person. I had occasion to come back to England on my return journey to Australia.

A: *So by 1967 you had not only got your BA, you had obtained the Postgraduate Diploma in Abnormal Psychology from the University of London; you had been awarded your PhD and you had got a considerable research training, and you had worked and lived in England and Canada. Quite a lot had been achieved in a few years?*

DH: And I even visited mainland Europe which, for an Australian, was a monumental occasion! At the very end of my Maudsley training we had our first European holiday in Austria. This was real foreign country! They spoke a different language, they ate different things, their bedding looked different, they hung their mattresses out of their windows, it was absolutely seductive.

A: *Well, up to this point still no interest in alcohol or drugs?*

DH: No, that's not quite true. When I went back to Australia to work in the psychiatric services, I was the first psychologist to have the responsibility for developing a research programme within the State psychiatric services. In that capacity I established a psychiatric register which, among other things, recorded in great detail the discharge status of all patients. In the course of doing so I was asked to carry out surveys of both prison and psychiatric populations and that in part meant surveying drinking problems.

I had come to the conclusion that so far as I was concerned, prevention was going to be the way to go. At that time, as I recall there were no centres devoted to prevention. It was virgin country

---

To the Addiction Research Unit in London

A: *In 1968 a significant event happens. You were appointed to a staff position at the newly established Addiction Research Unit at the Institute of Psychiatry. What were the circumstances of that appointment?*

DH: The circumstances could hardly have been anticipated. I was returning from Canada having defended my thesis and having flown one way around the world decided that I would come back the other; I called into London and the Maudsley with a view to just chatting to people who had previously been my teachers, not with the intention of seeking employment, that was the last thing in my mind. But then I was told by Monty Shapiro that the Addiction Research Unit was seeking to recruit people, and was I perhaps interested. I was in a high euphoric mood as one would expect having completed my thesis and now being on

holiday. I was persuaded to meet two of the people who had been recently appointed: Celia Hensman and Jim Orford. I was told that there was a director, but the director wasn't accessible. I had a meeting with Celia and Jim. One couldn't construe it as an appointment interview – nothing formal. When I got back to Australia, as I did just days later, I found a telegram offering me a position which I hadn't sought and which came out of the blue and which required some very urgent deliberation.

A: *Did you have any problems in accepting that invitation?*

DH: No, I mean I was highly flattered to be offered such an appointment, all the more so because I hadn't really been formally interviewed for it! I think that when they agreed that we would be allowed to come back to England first class, that helped. I remember my wife saying I'm not travelling in steerage again, as we had obviously done when we had first come to England. At that stage the Suez Canal had been closed and we went round the Cape.

A: *So you arrived at the Addiction Research Unit in 1968 . . .*

DH: . . . in deepest, darkest Winter . . .

A: *It is my belief that soon after you arrived at the Unit you suggested that it might take as its identity a prevention research unit.*

DH: That idea certainly came fairly soon. I think I had come to the conclusion that although treatment is necessary, it is never going to be enough. I was persuaded of that, and I had persuaded myself by working out how many patients I could reasonably see in a year and making certain assumptions about the effectiveness of the treatments then available. The thing which interested me about alcohol and drug problems was their obvious external determinants – there are environment inducements that one can identify which actively promoted these problems. I had come to the conclusion that so far as I was concerned, prevention was going to be the way to go. At that time, as I recall there were no centres devoted to prevention. It was virgin country.

A: *You were at that time in a fairly lonely intellectual position?*

DH: In retrospect I can see that to have been the case.

A: *Here's a man who's trained in individual psychology, the behavioural analysis of the individual, and he starts to think 'populations'. What led you in that direction? Presumably none of your teachers invited you to go in that direction.*

DH: I can remember quite acrimonious discussions with Monty on this issue. I remember him getting quite cross with me for pursuing these ideas.

A: *He believed famously in the single case study?*

DH: Absolutely. I can remember Monty being quite irritated by me, because it looked as if I was not only abandoning my teaching, but even questioning the appropriateness of individual treatment. I think that's something I've had to contend with most of my professional life – the assumption that because I'm arguing the *necessity* of prevention, I'm therefore denigrating treatment. So it was a lonely thing. I think I was probably influenced by some of the writing that was then coming out of America by George Albee, for example, who had essentially come to the same conclusion, and may have come to it well before I did, and I remember reading with great excitement what he had written. My academic training had not prepared me for this task, and if I arrived at that conclusion it would, I guess, have been by reason of logic, an exercise in arithmetic.

A: *You arrived in 1968 and you spent 5 years at the Addiction Research Unit (ARU), becoming Deputy Director with yourself carrying out research in a number of epidemiological areas, so you had moved to population-based studies. What happened?*

DH: Suddenly I found myself in a research team and directing a section which was specifically concerned with drug problems. Drugs at that time were not a particular problem in Australia. I don't think I had met anyone in Australia who was drug-dependent. Suddenly I was in London having to interview drug-takers whose needs I barely understood, and whose problems and life experience were totally foreign to me. There were times when I came out into the night air and wondered what was I doing secreting myself in dark English basements. But it was hugely stimulating, and the great advantage of being at the ARU was that interest in the way the British were then addressing the problem meant that everybody who was anybody came to look. I just sat and waited and they all came through that door. And so there I was, still fairly youthful, discharging responsibilities greatly in excess of my previous experience, receiving delegations from this and that country, dealing with television and with invitations to consult with the World Health Organization in Geneva and Copenhagen. It was a demanding time.

A: *And you were learning about the management of research?*

DH: Yes, and that too was for me a very new experience. I had not previously had that sort of managerial responsibility for research projects. In Australia I had been running a so-called Research Unit, but it was essentially one-and-a-half people. Now I had to face the question, how does one manage or organize research in a way which is attentive to other people, acknowledges their different disciplines, their creativity, but at the same time with them and oneself remaining accountable. And that has continued to be a puzzle to be solved.

A: *And you also had a peer group of other young researchers working with you. It was a youngish group.*

DH: It was. It was a youngish field and this was a very new endeavour. I think most of us coming to that centre at that time were naive. I was among the most naive. Certainly I think most of us were interested in the area, but we could hardly claim expertise.

A: *Was the peer group important?*

DH: It wasn't a large centre at that time. The drug section was even smaller. We were constantly in conversation. There were a number of set occasions on which people presented their work and there were many opportunities for sharing ideas over coffee or lunch. We shared our disciplines and I certainly benefited.

A: *So after 5 years you left the ARU with by then quite significant experience in the drug and alcohol field.*

DH: Yes, and with an interest not only in research but also in policy. My stance was that one had a responsibility to do the research and to consider its policy implications. I pressed very energetically for exploration of those implications.

Meeting President Kaunda in Zambia stands out in my memory. . . . He had previously been imprisoned by the British and now he was President and occupying the very mansion that had previously been the home of the colonial governor

---

A: *During these years you got to know quite well, and so I think did your wife, Dr D.L. Davies, who had been Dean of the Institute of Psychiatry and a prominent figure in the alcohol world – he had published in 1962 that famous paper on "Normal drinking among recovered alcohol addicts". What are your memories of him?*

DH: Well, I remember him very well because my wife became his personal assistant, and secretary for the first Summer Schools. We lived not very far from one another in Dulwich. I remember him being somewhat unnerved by the prospect of having to work with an Australian woman, having previously only met Australian nurses in the army and seeing them as formidable, and he expected my wife to be similarly formidable. I think he was quite taken with her and theirs was a very good and friendly relationship. He did say to me something which I've never forgotten, that is when I decided to go to Wales. In his English clipped accent he asked, "Are there other psychologists in Wales?" The inference being that having enjoyed the enormous privilege of a Maudsley education, and moreover a Maudsley appointment, I was committing professional suicide in considering the possibility of going to Wales.

A: *Did you during your time at the ARU meet Kettil Bruun?*

DH: I remember where I first met Kettil, which was at the first overseas conference that I attended. It was a very significant experience.

Cardiff and secondment to WHO

A: *Your next career move was to a senior post in Cardiff, but while you were there, you were seconded to WHO Geneva.*

DH: Yes, to work on the Community Response Project, which was a multi-national project initially with links in Zambia and Mexico and Scotland. My responsibilities included oversight of the project and identifying within those countries principal investigators, recruiting teams around them, designing the instruments that were going to be used to assess the extent of alcohol-related problems in those communities, analysing the data and assisting with the writing of the report. In the event I didn't see the project out. My employers in Wales became very impatient with my secondment and despite the pleadings of the World Health Organization, they insisted on my return and the project was eventually completed by Irv Rootman, who followed me.

A: *Tell us a bit about the scenes and the people relating to the project.*

DH: Meeting President Kaunda in Zambia stands out in my memory. . . . He had previously been imprisoned by the British and now he was President and occupying the very mansion that had previously been the home of the colonial governor. We were ushered into his dining room and our photographs were duly taken and I found myself sat next to him. I have a prized photograph which shows him directing me to my chair and it being pulled out in expectation of my sitting down. He had just come back from a period of what I think he called religious retreat. He had been re-reading some of the scriptures. I think on reflection having to meet presidents or prime ministers, having to go to countries which were totally foreign to me, gave me nerve. I suspect one of the advantages is that I no longer frighten easily; I don't crumble under criticism; don't find it totally unnerving to be told that I have to go up to

Parliament House to brief whomever. I can be thankful, I think, that the experience that I gained in dealing with those countries and obviously dealing with the authorities in those countries conferred on me an ability to deal with people at a political level.

A: *So WHO was partly administrative responsibility, partly enormous opportunity to travel. But what about the in-house culture of WHO as a place to work in? Tell us about the corridors of Geneva.*

DH: WHO itself was both an exciting place to be and a disappointing place. WHO is essentially a bureaucracy and most essentially a political bureaucracy. It is not like a university. You are not rewarded for thinking. It doesn't have a collegiate life. You are recruited to persuade people to assist WHO, attend meetings, work as a consultant. You're not essentially recruited in your own right. So on the one hand it was immensely exciting to have oversight of projects, it was very interesting to attend meetings of the World Health Assembly, to prepare papers for their consideration, to deal with questions that were raised by any of its members. On the other hand, in a curious way I discharged less responsibility in that role than I did as Deputy Director of the ARU, or as I had as the head of a clinical department in Wales.

A: *Give us an example.*

DH: When the Director General visits another country, there is a memo put around the organisation inviting anyone who has business in that country to raise this issue with him if it still needs to be negotiated. I had been dealing with Zambia and there was something that I was wanting if at all possible to have finalized, and so I wrote to the Director General saying if there was an opportunity perhaps he would pursue this discussion, which he duly did. And to good effect. It was slightly mischievous, but I decided I would thank the Director General, so I wrote a brief memo in which I thanked him for having raised this matter and for having brought it to fruition. Several months later my memo came back and it had been counter-signed by, I think, six or seven people in different inks, and it epitomised for me an organ-

isation which was so bureaucratic as to have to censor even so innocuous a communication, as if I had committed an offence. I remember Norman Sartorious, with whom I had a good and easy relationship, being a little upset that I had done this rather presumptuous thing; I had chosen to communicate directly with the Director General, who himself I think was a very accessible and inspirational person, but I had committed an offence. Norman was given to doing things 'properly' and with a correctness to which perhaps we Australians are less suited.

A: *But the Australian habit of plain dealing was by this stage coupled with the capacity to deal with presidents.*

DH: Yes it was. When I reflect on how the schoolboy who would have had great difficulty speaking in public and who was never a member of any debating organization, could, with some equanimity, now deal with senior figures and address parliamentary groups, I would have to allow that my experience in WHO contributed to that process.

A: *What were some of the other things with which you were involved during your time at WHO?*

DH: I did a number of things apart from supervise the Community Response Project. I was a member of the Secretariat and so if expert committees were held on alcohol-related problems I attended them. That means that when all the consultants go home you are left with the report to finalize, and one can of course influence that to some extent. But most notably, Griffith Edwards was invited while I was there to prepare a paper for the Executive Board, the governing body of the Assembly or the Executive that is left behind after the Assembly has met. I don't remember the exact terms of the commission, but it certainly allowed us to argue, as the *Purple Book* had before, that alcohol-related problems were not going to be addressed only by the establishment of a treatment response. They would need to be addressed by taking a much more preventive orientation by looking at trade and at the activities of the industry. We'd written very plainly that WHO needed to concern itself with trade in alcohol if it was ever going to address the problems of developing countries. I remember a memorable phrase which said that the economic progress and development of some countries was being prejudiced, disadvantaged by the increase in consumption of alcohol in those countries and the harm which it was wreaking on them. These were fairly strong phrases for WHO, which is not used to sentiments of this kind. And I remember having enormous difficulty persuading Norman Sartorius to accept the plainness of our language. He kept giving me back the draft. I think we got up to something like 11 drafts, making tiny changes to them. I wasn't looking to pursue a career in Geneva, I really had nothing to lose, and in the end I said to him I'm not going to change another dot. If you want to change it, you change it, but I'm not going to do it. And I don't think he did beyond that. I remember Dr Cohen, who was then the Director General's personal assistant and who had oversight of all the papers that were submitted to the Executive Board, calling me up and telling me that this was really quite a dangerous document. It was much too forceful, much too plain. But I still think it was a very important document.

I remember a memorable phrase which said that the economic progress and development of some countries was being prejudiced, disadvantaged by the increase in consumption of alcohol in those countries and the harm which it was wreaking on them

---

A: *Was there any follow-through?*
DH: It allowed WHO some years later to initiate a project which looked at the impact of the alcohol industry on developing economies and which produced a number of case studies describing that impact. At that point I was no longer in the employ of WHO although I did attend some meetings. A report of that work was eventually made and somewhat curtailed in its distribution because of the plainness of its language and of its implications. Its essential message was that there's

no point in agonizing about the lack of treatment in these countries and the need for people to be trained in treatment, if at the same time no attempt is being made to address the greatly increasing consumption in these countries, consequent upon the activities of the alcohol industry in cultivating markets. Addressing that latter question had to be, and uniquely was, a responsibility of an organization like WHO.

A: *Were you in contact with WHO at a time when they decided not to publish the report on the activities of the multi-national drinks industry?*
DH: I was, and I was exceedingly disappointed that they had taken that stance. I remember going up in the lift with a very senior member of WHO and him saying to me, Look it's not that the Director General is unsympathetic with what you're saying (and I had no reason to disbelieve that), but he is fighting on so many fronts, the Nestlé front, the pharmaceutical front and so on. If he is to be re-elected as he wants to be, he cannot open up another front. You're just going to have to concede this. And indeed that was what happened. He was re-elected, but this particular issue was dropped from the agenda and while subsequently the book was published by Croom Helm, it didn't contain the foreword which WHO had specifically commissioned. It wasn't as widely circulated as it would have been as a WHO publication and didn't have the influence which it ought to have had. WHO subsequently sought to repair that situation to some extent by commissioning another study of the implications of international trade which said some of the same things, but said them in much less forceful language. Sadly an initiative was lost which WHO was uniquely able to address if only it had had the courage to do so.

Taking on administrative responsibilities in Australia

A: *After 2 years further experience and many new horizons both bureaucratic and geographical, you came back for a few years to Wales and then you went in 1982 home to Australia?*
DH: Yes, even while in Geneva I had been approached by the then director of the Western

Australian Alcohol and Drug Authority – the statutory authority in Western Australia having responsibility for provision of treatment, and also policy responsibilities. I'd been approached by him in relation to the possibility of going back home. At the time I hadn't realized that Thomas Bewley had been invited out to Western Australia to advise in relation to service provision. In the course of that consultation he had also presumably been asked by them whether there was anyone abroad they should be looking to recruit to a senior position, and presumably they would have preferred someone who was Australian. He must have identified me because quite out of the blue I was visited by Dick Porter, the then Director, and asked whether I would consider coming back. At the time I was not only under an obligation to WHO to assist with the completion of the community response project, but also to the South Glamorgan Area Health Authority which had allowed me to work with WHO on secondment, so there was no way in which I could accept then. Some time later I was invited back as Deputy Director. I think there was probably an expectation that the Director would retire at some time and that I would succeed him. Very sadly, Dick had a major heart attack and I was precipitated into the role of Director within about 6 months of returning.

A: *So you worked in that governmental position from 1982 to 1987, effectively responsible for running the treatment services, looking after prevention, with policy responsibility for alcohol and drugs for Western Australia, and with an academic position on the side. What did you achieve in those 5 years?*
DH: I could hardly have imagined at the time just how fortunate the timing would be, because not only did I assume responsibility for this organization earlier than I had expected, but almost coincidentally with my doing so it was announced that Australia would have a national campaign against drug abuse. This campaign gave the whole area a profile that it hadn't had previously. It was an immensely satisfying time because one of the delightful things about being head of a statutory authority enjoying even greater autonomy than a government department was that I suddenly inher-

ited an establishment of, I think, about 250 people – psychiatrists, physicians, nurses. There was some concern as to whether a psychologist could discharge this responsibility. It was suggested to me partly in jest but also I think partly seriously, that perhaps I ought not to be paid the advertised salary because it had been assumed that the position would be filled by a medical doctor. The Act provided me with career public servants who wanted someone to say in what direction this organization should go.

A: *What direction did you take it in?*
DH: I decided that an authority which was only providing treatment to people who were in the terminal stages of illness was completely misconceived and with hospitals which accepted patients for 10 or 12 months, was wrongly deploying its resources. They had no notion that detoxification could be undertaken on a domiciliary basis, the whole orientation was to address the most damaged rather than the least damaged people, it was not the policy to try and ensure that general hospitals and general practitioners identified the problems and intervened. Part of the budget received by the Alcohol and Drug Authority enabled it to support non-government agencies that were themselves providing services, so essentially what I said was that we would use that money to support those non-government bodies in the care of such people, acknowledging of course that they deserved and needed care. We established with the Salvation Army and a variety of other bodies that we would continue to support them in the provision of hostel-type accommodation for those who were needing that sort of care, while we employed our doctors and nurses in developing services in the mainstream medical and welfare sectors. We established clinics in the major teaching hospitals, gave over our own clinics and hospitals to the briefer or more domiciliary provision of care. We decided that this or that hospital would be decommissioned and the staff would be re-deployed, and of course there were the usual difficulties, but it happened.

A: *So you were working not only on treatment, but on treatment systems. What about your commitment to prevention?*

DH: That too was an aspect of the excitement. The Act allowed one to do such things. Coinciding at this time with the initiation of the national campaign, I suddenly found myself having to attend meetings as the minister's principal adviser and finding allies such as Alex Wodak, Les Drew, Bob Batey and Ian Webster – people who were also running systems, but had never been brought together. Suddenly we found ourselves established as a standing committee to advise the Commonwealth health minister in Canberra. We attended meetings of the Ministerial Council, albeit as advisers, not as speakers, and we were left behind as the executive group. It was a period of enormous momentum. The number of people and treatment places involved was increased hugely as was support for the non-government sector. There were two research centres established, there were 24-hour information services, there were legal initiatives, extradition treaties, consideration given to changes in penalties. There were enormous changes going on, many of which found expression in what we were doing in WA.

If anything has impressed me about the policy life it is the need to be there

How alcohol and tobacco came to be included in the Australian national campaign on drugs

A: Was there any intentional response on the prevention of alcohol problems?
DH: Indeed. Interestingly, when the national campaign was first announced in 1986, Bob Hawke (the Prime Minister) had stated prior to a federal election that if re-elected his government would give attention to this problem.

A: This problem being drugs so far as he was concerned?
DH: Well, his personal concern was a problem with drugs within his family. Interestingly, he didn't in his pronouncement confine the initiative to drugs, but certainly it was widely interpreted as

pertaining only to drugs and there were enormous pressures brought on him and on Neal Blewett, who was then Minister of Health, to confine his attention to illicit drugs. The tobacco and alcohol industries lobbied very strenuously to avoid the inclusion of legal drugs. Fortunately, one of the non-government agencies had called a meeting to address the problem and had invited Neal Blewett to attend this meeting and to give a keynote address. He acknowledged that if we were to have a national campaign it had to be a campaign which addressed the drugs of principal significance, and they were then alcohol and tobacco. An initiative which pretended to be a national campaign addressing drug use which did not address the problems associated with alcohol and tobacco was a fraud. He said this and his words were written down. In the event it proved very difficult to persuade the politicians to accept that definition of the initiative. There was one meeting I remember attending when Blewett was sitting between the Deputy Prime Minister and the chief number-cruncher for the Labour Party at the federal level. Meetings of the Ministerial Council moved around the States. They were usually chaired by the Minister of Health of that state and were attended by all the other Health Ministers. This particular meeting was held in Queensland. It was clear to us that other Commonwealth ministers were trying to keep Blewett on the straight and narrow. The straight and narrow was defined as not giving attention to alcohol and tobacco.

A: So what happened at that meeting?
DH: If anything has impressed me about the policy life it is the need to be there. As the chairman went around the table (and remember, this is a meeting of ministers at which advisers can't speak) there was a lot of indecision as to whether we should be including these other, legal, drugs. When the chairman got to my minister with whom I had established a very good relationship, I whispered to him that he might like to note that Dr Blewett in a previous forum made this statement, and I'd highlighted it for him. He very trustingly took it and said to the chairman, I would like to remind the meeting of what Dr Blewett has said quite recently. My minister then read out Blewett's

previous statement on this point there and then. So annoyed was Blewett with this statement being read out that he came across in the lunch break and remonstrated with my minister quite noisily. As we got out of the plane at Adelaide, which was Blewett's home, there was a monumental downpour. They were running umbrellas out to us to shelter us. As we came down the steps to be handed our umbrellas, I turned to Dr Blewett and said 'I'm sure we can look to you for hospitality if we can't get out tonight'. And he said 'Just go home, you bloody sandhoppers, go home'. Western Australians are known as sandhoppers. He, of course, was not disputing the rightness of what we were arguing. He had after all argued it himself and has done so subsequently, but he was clearly under enormous pressure not to give currency in that ministerial setting to that view.

A: *But that view prevailed?*
DH: That view prevailed. But one wonders whether it would have prevailed if people had not had the foresight to invite Blewett to speak beforehand. And if I had not attended that earlier meeting and had a copy of the talk. I had a relationship with a minister which allowed me to say Minister, literally as he was going to speak, you might like to make reference to this. If I've been persuaded of anything in my dealings with policy, it is that sometimes there is no alternative but to be there physically.

A: *You had trained as a researcher but now you were in a world of trying to influence policy. Is it dangerous to move from one to another?*
DH: Some people think it dangerous, certainly Bob Popham at the ARF had thought it dangerous. His experience was a very potent one for me; here was someone who'd moved from research to presuming to give advice as to what the implications of that research were, and who had then abandoned that attempt. But I have always felt as a researcher that without presuming to dictate to others I wanted to pursue the implications of research, I wanted to see that it did influence things. So I have throughout my career moved between periods of reflection and of residence within academia where one has the opportunity to read and to do research

and to think through things, to a period where one has the opportunity to give expression to that thinking. I find that an exciting thing to do, not that one always wins the arguments, but I would always want to be part of the argument. I would always want to be at the table at which the arguments were occurring. I don't think I have the patience for merely doing research which may accumulate in journals which does not get tested, does not get expression in policy.

Director of the National Centre for Research into the Prevention of Drug Abuse

A: *So then in 1987, 5 years on, another exciting opportunity developed and you become the first director of the National Centre for Research into the Prevention of Drug Abuse in Perth, funded by federal Australian funds. Can you tell us about that development? You talked about your commitment to prevention, now you found yourself actually running a prevention unit. What did that feel like?*
DH: It was very exciting, but again it wasn't something that I contrived – it almost happened incidentally. Those who were in a position to advise the Ministerial Council said clearly that there needs to be at least one national research centre. But as often happens in Australia with its federated system, the states are extremely jealous as to which of them will be the site for a new centre. So in this instance a number of the states put out prospectuses. We in WA never imagined that we would be competitive, given our distance from the eastern states and our distance from Canberra, and never even put out a proposal believing at the time there would only be one centre. When I was tipped off that they were giving consideration to there being more than one, I decided, along with other colleagues in WA, that there was no reason why one shouldn't be in WA. So with Ian Smith I wrote a prospectus which argued that WA was particularly well placed to undertake research which bore on prevention, because of the centralization of records, the fact that it had a very stable population – the fact that

its borders were so far away from any other state that what it did was not immediately contaminated by what was done alongside it; that the autonomy which was invested in the state parliament allowed it to innovate. So we put up this proposal and lo and behold it was decided that there should be two centres. There would be one located in NSW, which would have the brief to investigate the most effective means of treatment and to disseminate those findings. And there would be one located in WA, which would have a prevention orientation. The decision to locate it at Curtin University was taken, I suspect, for political reasons and with a view to favouring Curtin in its development as a university. In the event it proved to be a very happy choice.

Rules for success? Well, always to appoint the brightest people you can find and to appoint people who can write – the ability to write is a very important attribute

A: *But to an extent, your bluff had been called. You had been talking for a long time about the importance of prevention, and now suddenly there was a well-supported prevention research centre which was being set up in your own state. Did you apply for the directorship?*
DH: I was invited by the Vice Chancellor of Curtin University to apply and I was appointed after an extensive search, and then of course had to resign as director of the Alcohol and Drug Authority. There was nothing but a promise at that time of about A$660,000 a year. There were no people; I had to find people who would bend their minds to this task. What I did was to fill the posts with the brightest people I could find. Within 11 months we were reviewed, which was a hopelessly precipitant act. We were established as a 'centre of excellence'. This denoted the naivety of Australia in dealing with such things – to say 'this is a centre of excellence' from the beginning is really ludicrous and I avoided the description. Much of our early work was of a survey and descriptive kind, but of necessity that was the nature of the art at

that point in time. It was difficult to find anyone who had any background in the area at all, let alone a geographer or an economist who had an interest in the area, so I ended up largely appointing psychologists. The appointment of Tim Stockwell as Deputy was of great consequence, because here was someone who had worked in the field, albeit largely in the treatment context, but who was starting to be interested in both the policy implications and in prevention. I remember very clearly where I met Tim – it was in the back garden of Jim and Judith Orford's home, where I had gone with a view to persuading Jim to come to Australia.

A: *What in your view are the likely rules for success when setting up a new research centre?*
DH: Rules for success? Well, always to appoint the brightest people you can find and to appoint people who can write – the ability to write is a very important attribute. There is nothing more galling as a director of a centre than to have to review every thing that people write five times to get it readable. It's also important, of course, to keep a light rein and not to presume to ride roughshod over people's interests. You must give creativity its chance. I've also learnt that the best way to advance your own career is to advance the reputation of the unit that you direct, because in the end what falls into your lap falls there precisely because your centre or your unit is considered excellent.

Learning from the Australian experience

A: *Where do you think the excellence now lies – for what on the world stage would the Perth Centre rate?*
DH: Well, I think it rates for being able to show in a number of areas that it has undertaken the definitive research in Australia, which is not to claim that it has done so in the world, but its work has resulted in legislative and regulatory changes.

A: *Can you quote some of them?*
DH: Yes, one is the introduction of standard drink labels. A small gain – I wouldn't want for a moment to exaggerate its importance, but clearly

if people are to be encouraged to moderate their consumption in relation to advice they're being given, they need to know how much alcohol they are drinking. The introduction of truly random breath testing in WA is a thing which we can partly claim credit for – Ross Homel did the definitive work in this area when he was a Visiting Fellow to the Centre and undertook an analysis of the Western Australian data. And I think the whole discussion about fiscal policy is one which we initiated. The alcohol we in Australia drink in light alcohol beers actually costs more than the alcohol you drink in regular beers, and bulk wines are ludicrously cheap because there is no excise charge on them. We at least raised the necessary questions in the fiscal area.

A: *As well as running the unit in Perth, you continued at this time to be very involved in matters at federal level?*

DH: Yes, albeit in a different capacity. When I resigned as director of the Alcohol and Drug Authority, perhaps the most significant role I gave up was that of Principal Adviser to the State Health Minister. I was, however, as the director of a national centre still expecting to be heard on the national scene. I was also elected President of the Australian Medical and Professional Society on Alcohol and Other Drugs. I continued to write and lecture very widely.

A: *Well now, you've been back in Australia for 17 years and during the course of this interview we've mentioned the word Australia more than once. What should those of us who admire your country from a distance be willing to learn from the Australian response to substance problems?*

DH: The opportunity Australia has provided for people whose primary training was in research to have a place at the policy table is, I think, significant. It's only very recently that this advice is no longer being taken, and the reversal of the decision to go ahead with the planned heroin trial is significant. Experts having given approval for this trial, that approval was reversed for political reasons. Every country is different, and I would not imagine for a moment that what is being found to work in Australia will necessarily work else-

where. But when I travel and am asked to speak about the Australian experience, the surprise that people register is that someone like me, in charge of a research centre, has actually sat at the policy table, and passed a briefing note to the minister. While Australia is a vast country with a scarcity of people, the accessibility which we have enjoyed to the political process is probably much greater. Ministers have been accessible to us, we have had the opportunity to speak to them in the backs of taxis and look over their shoulders when we've attended ministerial meetings. While there is an unwillingness to be dictated to by experts in Australia, it's extraordinarily easy to persuade politicians of the rightness of a logical case. We have adopted truly random breath testing; we have stopped smoking in enclosed spaces. Australia has shown an enormous willingness to accept the implications of good research and to give it expression. I can expect to be stopped when driving five or six times a year and be asked to demonstrate that I've not been drinking.

Life scripts

A: *You've done many different things in the professional sphere – worked within many different roles, worked in different countries. Is there any strong thread of continuity which you see in your life? Is there one script or many scripts?*

DH: Well, there are several. One has been a fascination with 'abroad'. I think many Australians have that because we all have grown up in such isolated circumstances. We're also born into a culture which has its origins far away and there is a sense in which we all need to go home, if it's only to agree that it is no longer home and that home is back under the Southern Cross. For reasons which I find very difficult to identify I needed to go abroad and if my career has given me anything it is that opportunity, and I'm immensely grateful. I think another strand, as I've already identified, is an alternation between periods of reflective reading and of contemplation and of discussion, and then a growing impatience with the continuation, as such, the impotence of merely reading and of thinking and debating. The need then to

Yes, it matters that the individual person gets better, these things hurt, but that individual person will be replaced by another and another and another, until somehow or other we can reduce the flow from the tap

move into a sphere which enables one to give expression to some of that. But then equally as Bob Popham observed to me a long time ago, there is a danger in being caught up in the argument, in being overtaken by the need to decide everything in unequivocal terms, and then one comes to realize that it is dangerous to continue in that role; that one is really no different from people of a less scientific or reflective bent, and so I repair from that by going back into a more contemplative environment.

A: *Are you a child of a Protestant ethic – is that in any way the central thread?*
DH: I'm not the child in the sense that this was the religious persuasion of my parents. It was a persuasion which I found for myself. I think that it is significant, but I don't exaggerate my importance in the scheme of things. When a variety of opportunities have presented themselves I've always chosen the one that moves me on a little bit further. And it's moved me on in the direction of having the maximum influence, because I remain persuaded of my very early arithmetic that, yes, it matters that the individual person gets better, these things hurt, but that individual person will be replaced by another and another and another, until somehow or other we can reduce the flow from the tap. And I guess I've always been wanting to get my hand on the tap and to the extent that it's possible, I have wanted to reduce the flow.

David Penington

David Penington was born in 1930 in Melbourne, Australia. After schooling and initial university education in Australia, he continued his studies at the University of Oxford, qualifying in medicine in 1955. From 1963–67 he was a consultant physician at the London Hospital, and then returned to Australia initially as a first assistant in Medicine at the University of Melbourne (1968–70) and then as Professor of Medicine (1970–87). From 1978–85 he was Dean of Medicine at Melbourne, and from 1988–95 he was Vice Chancellor of the University of Melbourne. He has served his country through chairmanship of numerous state and national committees. He holds the qualifications of FRCP (London) and FRACP (Australia). In 1988 he was appointed a Companion of the Order of Australia for services to the community in the fields of health and medical education. In 1995 he was awarded an honorary LLD from Melbourne, and in 1996 an honorary DSc from Ballarat.

Setting the scene

In Australia since the early 1970s public concern about illicit drug use among young people has presented a problem for the State governments that have responsibility within the Australian Federal system of government for drug policy. In the middle 1990s, the drug policy debate focused on how to respond to a sharply rising heroin overdose death rate. Governments found if it difficult to formulate policy because the public and expert opinions that were presented in the popular media were polarised between proponents of harm minimisation policies who advocated trials of heroin prescription and injecting rooms and proponents of abstinence-oriented treatment approaches who advocated tougher law enforcement and 'zero tolerance' school-based drug prevention. The response to drug policy debates in the 1970s and 1980s was to appoint Committees of inquiry, usually headed by a Judge, to advise government on drug policy. These took time to report and produced recommendations that challenged existing policy. The 1990s saw a different response. The intensity of public concern expressed through the media gave an urgency to a government response that was not well addressed by referring the matter to a deliberate and considered judicial inquiry. In Victoria the Government responded by appointing an eminent person from outside the drugs field

who was asked to advise the government on how to proceed within a very short time frame. This was how Professor David Penington came to be asked to advise the Victorian government on drug policy in 1995 when the Victorian Premier Mr Jeff Kennett asked him to chair the Premier's Drug Advisory Council (PDAC) on Drugs.

The 1950s and Britain as a land of medical academic opportunity

A: *Why did you choose a career in medicine?*
DP: My father was a specialist internist so I grew up with great admiration for the role of the medical profession. As I grew older through my schooling I became fascinated by science. I also wanted to have a career that involved me with people and medicine offered those two intertwined, challenging intellectual things based on science and the fulfilment of being able to help people.

A: *You began your medical training at the University of Melbourne and then moved to Oxford on a scholarship.*
DP: I enjoyed my first few years of medicine in Melbourne but I found it all very didactic. I felt that I didn't know enough science so I was not able to make my own judgements. I did not want to go on

into clinical medicine being swamped with 'facts' that I had to learn without being able to question and understand them. So when given the chance of the scholarship to Oxford I jumped at the opportunity to spend two more years in science, in an environment where I knew people were challenged to think and to explore ideas. Indeed it offered all of that. It was a wonderful experience.

A: *What was it like being an Australian at Oxford in the 1950s?*
DP: England was just recovering from the effects of the World War II. It still had a very tightly structured social system, which I found extraordinary and amusing. Coming from what were then termed the 'colonies' I was outside the structure and accepted at any level in British society in a way that they wouldn't accept their own, unless they came from the right background. That amused me. But Oxford was intellectually a very challenging environment in which one was accepted for what one was and one could pursue ideas in great depth. I spent a lot of time in discussion, in libraries and things of that kind. There was far less didactic teaching; in fact, almost no didactic teaching compared to the endless lecturing that we'd had in Melbourne. I found that very stimulating. It influenced my whole approach to education, even when I finally came back to Australia.

A: *You married in Britain and had a family and practised in London for some considerable period after your graduation. Was that a choice or had opportunities presented themselves?*
DP: I think I always hoped that I'd come back to Australia but at every point there were better opportunities in Britain at that time to pursue research, clinical practice and teaching, the three areas in which I wanted to commit my career. I was given many opportunities to move up the ladder and to have my own laboratory with good funding from the Medical Research Council. At that time, had I come back to Australia which had a relatively poorly developed academic clinical medicine, I would have had to go into private practice rather than pursue a career in research and teaching as well as clinical practice that I was able to do in England.

In time I found clinical practice was very demanding so that it was difficult to fit in time in my position at the teaching hospital in London and my research laboratory both of which were part-time. Private practice was very remunerative but it wasn't what I wanted to do with my life. I was keen to get back to an academic position so when I was offered one back in Melbourne, even at a position less senior than I had in London, I jumped at the chance. In 1967 I brought my family back to Melbourne and I've never regretted for one moment having time in the laboratory to pursue research and to keep up to date in medicine, rather than just delivering services.

Returning home

A: *Had things changed much since you left Australia in 1950?*
DP: The whole country had changed enormously. It was a much more international country and more diverse culturally. Although the teaching hospitals had clinical academic departments they still didn't have the standing that they had in London as the leaders of the profession. There was still a preoccupation with what was then called the Honorary Visiting Staff who ran the hospitals and had control over most of the decision making. I found myself in an environment that was a little anachronistic. I was nonetheless well-placed with an academic position in a hospital that needed to develop medical specialties, and to develop full-time specialist staff in many disciplines. I found it an interesting challenge to facilitate that development in Melbourne.

A: *Over the next few decades you became very much involved in academic medicine as Professor and subsequently as Dean. Was that a conscious choice?*
DP: As Professor of Medicine, I wanted to change the hospital system to develop specialties, to support young academics. I wanted young people who had been trained overseas to come back and practise in their specialty instead of being told by the visiting staff to go out and earn a living outside as many of them did. And I found myself in

fairly vigorous battles as to how the hospital was to develop. I needed to be an agent of change and to be involved in developing hospital policy and academic medical policy. I also saw the need to change the whole approach to medical education, to teach people to think and to work out problems rather than to be taught in the very didactic way that had been my experience in the late 1940s and early 1950s. I wanted to reform the medical school, to improve the pattern of education. Becoming Dean was a way of achieving that change and a way to get more resources for training people in research. Supporting research was something that motivated me to become Dean of the Faculty.

A: *You went on seeing patients?*
DP: Throughout that period I still looked after patients, still had my own research laboratory, and my own research students. I did other things in addition to pursuing the career that I really came back to. Later on, having reformed the medical school and improved its approach to education and the quality of support for research, I was faced with the challenge as to whether those changes needed to be made across the University. When an opportunity came to bring about change in the direction I thought was needed, I took it. Administration, as such, never attracted me; it was a means to an end.

A: *In addition to your senior administrative, clinical and research roles you were also involved in developing the Melbourne University School of Social Work, chairing the National Blood Transfusion Committee of the Australian Red Cross and National AIDS Task Force and the Museum of Melbourne. How do you find the time for all of these interests?*
DP: I always found it a little difficult to say no when I saw something needing to be done and where I felt I had clear ideas on how it could best be achieved. It was always a matter of using every minute of the day to the best, working with teams of people who could share the burden. Recruiting people to help in all of those tasks was a key part. I guess having an idea as to what was needed, having a clear picture in one's mind was a key part of producing change, as was selling that picture to

other people so it became their picture. They would then support implementation of change. I've always had an interest in social issues. That came from my childhood. My mother was very committed in social development activities and free kindergartens and an aunt was concerned with public housing throughout her career. That's probably partly why I was always interested in looking at the social aspects of education and health care. It probably motivated me to become involved first with the issues of AIDS and more recently with illicit drugs.

Administration, as such, never attracted me; it was a means to an end

The Victoria Government Committee on AIDS policy, 1983–1987

A: *How did you come to chair the Premier's Advisory Committee on Drugs?*
DP: I was just stepping down from eight years as Vice-Chancellor of the University during which time I'd had a fairly high profile in higher education. Before that, after many years as a Professor of Medicine and Haematologist, I'd chaired the National Blood Transfusion Committee of the Australian Red Cross Society for seven years. At the meeting at which I announced my intention to stand down, the news broke of the transmission of AIDS by blood transfusion in the US. The National Health and Medical Research Council of Australia (NH&MRC), of which I was a member, gave me the task of putting together a working group to find out what needed to be done to contain AIDS as a public health threat. I put together a group to advise the NH&MRC and Government and spent the next four years between 1983 and 1987 struggling with the public health issues, public perceptions and the policy debate about AIDS.

A: *What at that time was the level of public awareness?*
DP: I sought to give the public a better understanding of the issues so that they could deal with

them as a public health problem, looking at evidence, rather than reacting emotionally through fear or prejudice. We had very good connections around the world through members of our working group, with the NH in the US, with the Pasteur Institute in Paris, and elsewhere. We kept closely in touch with CDC at Atlanta as weekly and even daily reports came out. During those four years we were able to significantly influence public opinion so that AIDS was no longer handled, as it had been initially, in an almost hysterical way by the media. We dealt with the antipathy towards the gay community and we worked with the gay community in the development of sensible educational guidelines for containment of spread. We made many policy recommendations to the public, to the NH&MRC, and to the minister on measures that were required to diminish the risk of spread of the disease in different situations. These included infection control in hospitals, in schools and kindergartens, in policing, ambulance and first aid situations, for surf life savers, tattooists, barbers, swimming pool owners and many others. I used to spend a huge amount of time handling interviews with television. The telephone would ring almost every morning at 6.30 with the latest story a journalist had picked up from somewhere around the world.

Australia was the first country in the world to have every single blood transfusion unit tested for HIV because we had a good organisation, good research and international contacts and good political support

---

A: *How did you fit those demands into the rest of life?*
DP: After three very busy years dealing with AIDS I stepped down from my position as Dean of Medicine because I was just too busy but I continued on as Professor of Medicine at St Vincent's. A year or so later, I felt I'd made all the contribution that I could in AIDS. There was controversy with the political wing of the gay community

who wanted to control everything, including our research activities. This was becoming a major issue, interfering with our work; nonetheless, we did well. Australia was the first country in the world to have every single blood transfusion unit tested for HIV because we had a good organisation, good research and international contacts and good political support. By 1987, I felt I'd done my bit and needed to stand down. I'd been already selected to head the University of Melbourne and I stepped right out of the AIDS controversy.

Ten torrid weeks: chairing the Premier's Drug Advisory Council, 1995

A: *But rather than resting you then stepped right into the heroin problem?*
DP: It was my AIDS interests that led the Premier to ask me to look at the problem of heroin, just as I was leaving the university. We had been responsible for introducing syringe and needle exchanges back in 1987 to help control the spread of AIDS but I'd had little interaction with the problems of intravenous drug use at that time. Nonetheless, it seemed to me that public antipathy to drug users was in some ways similar to the antipathy to gay men that we'd faced back in 1983 over AIDS so that my background there might be of value.

A: *Did you have any hesitation in accepting the invitation?*
DP: Yes I did. I didn't see myself as having expertise in the drug field. The Premier said he wanted a quick inquiry with an answer in eight weeks (later extended to ten). We could travel overseas if we wished but nonetheless he wanted an answer in eight weeks, after we'd considered public submissions, and after we'd held public meetings around Melbourne and regional Victoria!

A: *It must have been a very torrid ten weeks.*
DP: It was a very steep learning curve. The Premier had already selected several members of that Drug Advisory Council who he felt were 'politically safe' and would 'do the right thing'. I

got agreement for the appointment of others with special expertise. They all made great contributions. We learned from each other through the process, coming as we did from a very wide range of differing backgrounds. At the start we made a commitment not to try to make decisions until we had looked at all the evidence. Several members of that Council would say that they ended up with views very different from those with which they started as we worked through the issues.

A: *Were the public meetings valuable?*
DP: We held a series of meetings in metropolitan Melbourne and in regional Victoria. All were fairly lively, with large attendances and many vigorous questions. Controversial presentations were made, but nonetheless it was a process by which we got fairly wide understanding of the issues we were tackling. We dealt not only with heroin but illicit drugs broadly. The media gave a great deal of coverage, so that there was quite considerable community awareness of the whole process.

A: *And the wider consultations?*
DP: We consulted the literature on illicit drugs extensively (with which I was not familiar at that time). We had wide consultations with people expert in the field around Australia by telephone and also a number came in to visit us. We had a number of international teleconferences with experts in Washington, England and Scotland, and Holland. Commander Vischer in Amsterdam, had a good discussion with us, which was very helpful. A number of other experts contributed their views. All of this was packed into a very compressed program. It was not until some six weeks into the process that we even began to think as to what the recommendations might look like. We then had extensive discussions within the Council. The evidence really led us to one single set of over 70 recommendations, every single one of which was unanimous.[1]

A: *That was an extraordinary outcome.*
DP: It was where the evidence led us. Once we'd tested the evidence there was really no doubt where we had to go. We were aware that we were going to come forward with recommendations that were considerably more radical than the Premier had expected, but we gave him a briefing on them and explained the reasons. Initially we thought the Premier would back all our recommendations but conservative voices within the government parties were appalled at the thought of decriminalising possession of use and small amounts of cannabis.

A: *So what fell by the way?*
DP: There was intense lobbying from conservative groups, with threats to some parliamentarians that they would lose pre-selection if they voted for the change in legislation. The Premier told me that he considered that he would not have the votes in the Upper House so he did not accept the critical recommendations in respect of cannabis. He also did not accept the need to mobilise local communities because he felt that the government itself could achieve the necessary coordination of services. Those were the two areas that should have been tackled differently. Much else was done which was worth doing. There was, I think, far better understanding of the issues in the community at the end of the debate. In particular we got agreement from a conservative government to support the heroin trial which had been proposed from the ACT. This was an important step, against conservative opposition. I believe we would probably get bipartisan support on this issue even now in Victoria, although it has been blocked by the Commonwealth.

A: *Did you end up feeling frustrated?*
DP: I felt frustrated, needless to say, that what I thought were key changes that were needed to make a real impact on education, in changing the culture amongst young people, and for mounting a realistic 'health-based' campaign against cannabis abuse, were not adopted. I believe it is very important to acknowledge that cannabis abuse does cause problems in its own right. For experimentation with cannabis to be labelled as a criminal act means we don't have a basis on which to talk with the key young people. That was a major disappointment.

A: *Do you think that the public view on drugs meshes with the true complexities or will people always want simple solutions?*

DP: The reality becomes clear in the surveys we did during our more recent inquiry. There was widespread lack of knowledge in the community as to what it is all about and widespread feeling that drugs were 'bad' because they were associated with crime. For many, that must mean that drugs are immoral'. If they're immoral, then the answer is that they should be suppressed. A lot of people feel that's the only way to think about drugs. For many people with relatively little education, if there's a problem 'A', then there must be an answer 'B' that ought to be imposed. Many have great difficulty in understanding complex issues for which there must inevitably be complex solutions.

Two years after our recommendations . . . Victoria police introduced a cautioning program for possession and use of moderate amounts of cannabis and that program has now become the basis of a national diversion program

---

The proposal to decriminalise cannabis

A: *So the 1995/96 inquiry's most controversial recommendation was the proposal to decriminalise the possession and use of cannabis?*

DP: Yes, it was opposed by the tabloid media. It was opposed by the Secretary of the Police Association, who went on the television day after day saying that the whole of the community in Victoria would be 'stoned' and everybody would be affected by cannabis! He warned of 'carnage on the roads'. Quite extravagant claims were made. It is interesting that three years later, that same individual said publicly that he'd been wrong and the police shouldn't be involved in dealing with cannabis at all, that it ought to be handled as a health issue. The police were very opposed to change in 1996, even though the majority of police arrests in the illicit drug field were for possession

and use of small amounts of cannabis – a manifest waste of resources. Two years after our recommendations, however, Victoria police introduced a cautioning program for possession and use of moderate amounts of cannabis and that program has now become the basis of a national diversion program.

A: *The Council's recommendation on legislative change didn't succeed but the spirit of its recommendation on cannabis was acted on.*

DP: That's true.

A: *One of the unique aspects of your inquiry was that you were invited to address a joint sitting of the two houses of the Victorian Parliament.*

DP: It was the first time ever that it had happened in Victorian Parliamentary history. I was given a good hearing. There was absolute silence as I spoke, no interjections and there were questions and comments after I'd finished. There was a good discussion of many of the issues. After that however, some parliamentarians made statements that were clearly made for their constituents. They wanted to have it on the record that they were 'not going soft on drugs'. It was an event that gave the whole issue a high community profile. I think the fact that it was taken so seriously by government influenced the attitude of quite a lot of people. The arguments were on the public record as to why we needed change and what the consequences would be of continuing without change. I made the point that if cannabis was not taken out of the criminal arena, and if there was no health-based campaign against cannabis abuse, young people who used cannabis would be increasingly offered heroin which was becoming so cheap. We would then see a big increase in use of heroin by young people. That's exactly what has happened over the last five years, with a large number of young people embarking on heroin use.

A: *Why your emphasis on community mobilisation?*

DP: We believed that it was very important to mobilise local communities to tackle the issue so that they would feel that it was their problem and they were part of the solution. The local organisations we hoped to include were not only local government but education authorities, health authorities, police and community organisations, service clubs and the like. In our view that was an important part of the whole process. The government, however, felt that it could do it through its own officers. The role of local government became a very important one in our more recent inquiry. We saw local government as key players in mobilising the community broadly, parents and young people's organisations, schools and the lot.

A: *You addressed some of these issues when advising the Lord Mayors of the capital cities of Sydney, Melbourne, Adelaide and Brisbane on drug issues.*

DP: Yes. I was first invited by the Lord Mayor of the city of Melbourne. He was chairing the Australian Lord Mayors Organisation. I was asked to convene a group to advise all the capital city Lord Mayors of Australia on drug issues. That group met over a couple of years during which we looked carefully at evidence on what was happening elsewhere in the world. We were particularly interested in what was happening in Europe following the Frankfurt Resolution of 1991 and in the evidence of improvement in open street drug use that followed in Frankfurt, Zurich and Berne, and other European cities. We were particularly interested in the efforts made to get the drug problem off the streets, to get drug users into interaction with professional staff, and in the role played in this by supervised injecting facilities. We got agreement from all the Australian capital city Lord Mayors, regardless of their political persuasion, to support a resolution that this approach be explored in Australia as a way to ameliorate the problem. There were many other aspects to our recommendations that also touched on prevention and treatment.

A: *Returning to the Premier's Drug Advisory Council, some frustrations aside, how did the outcome of that process measure up to your expectations?*

DP: Well, firstly I had not really been in the area of illicit drug policy prior to chairing the Council

and I had no real basis for understanding what could be achieved. Of course I was disappointed that we didn't get the full set of recommendations adopted but the vast majority were, and I felt that that was well worth while. I also felt that the high level of community debate meant that there was a greater understanding of the issues than before we embarked on our exercise. That, in itself, was worthwhile. I also believe that the public debate we've had over the last five years has built on that starting point. I've always been of the view that one only gets policy decisions in controversial areas out of politicians if there is a significant community understanding and support for change. The public debate was an important part of achieving that.

I've always been of the view that one only gets policy decisions in controversial areas out of politicians if there is a significant community understanding and support for change

1999 and controversy around off-street facilities for injection

A: *Then in 1999 there was an unexpected change of government in Victoria and you were invited by the new Premier to chair a committee of experts to advise him on issues related to drugs. Did you have any hesitation in that time around?*

DP: I suppose I had hesitation in that I didn't want to be involved again in a lot more controversy, in a personal sense. I had also retired and had other commitments. Nonetheless, the Labour Party had gone into the election with a policies that were based, almost to a word, on those that I had publicly advocated during the Lord Mayors' inquiry. This included a commitment to trial of safe injecting facilities in a number of areas where there was open drug use in Melbourne; a commitment to re-examine the cannabis issue and a commitment to involve local communities through local government. They'd gone into an election with a controversial policy package. That was politically not an expedient thing to do, but they had nonetheless won government. I felt an obligation to support them in every way I could.

A: *The questions you were asked to address?*
DP: We were asked to look first at the question of drug strategies for local government and specifically at the possibility of a trial of supervised injecting facilities in the five areas where there was open street injecting. We were asked to report on that commitment within four months. We had the opportunity again to look at all of the evidence. Two of us visited Europe, where we were able to look at the operation of injecting facilities in Holland and in Hamburg and Frankfurt. We also talked with the German authorities who were, at that time, heavily involved in planning the proposed German heroin trial. We had a good opportunity to inform ourselves about the evidence in support of such a trial. We recommended that the trial of injecting facilities should proceed.[2]

A: *Was the opposition on-side?*
DP: I sought again and again to consult with the opposition parties on the issue but I was put off repeatedly. Even after we had reported to the government, the opposition parties, having unexpectedly lost government, were, I think, just looking for any issue on which they could gain public support by attacking the government. We had made a decision, after consultation with police and others, that we could only proceed with an injecting facility trial if there was appropriate legislative cover for the police. The opposition had no intention of evaluating the evidence thoroughly, and as they controlled the Upper House, they were able to block any legislation. Our recommendations were thus defeated, although passed by the Lower House.

Controversy may be better than bland lack of interest

A: *The expert committee has recently completed a further report, this time on issues including prevention.[3] There was an interesting contrast in the amount of controversy produced by the two reports.*
DP: Yes. In the process leading up to the first report on the supervised injecting facilities we had a series of public hearings in each of the local government areas concerned. These were very noisy affairs and there was very deliberate and organised opposition that sought to control the microphones and so on. Of course these attracted a lot of media interest and the media covered the issue of injecting rooms in great detail, with the tabloid media thoroughly opposed to legislative reform. But when it came to looking at the broader, more important issue of what can be done to reduce the use of drugs, the media showed absolutely no interest.

A: *An echoing silence?*
DP: Yes. We had a conference in which we had Dr Robin Room, currently from Stockholm, contributing to our discussions about the role of education and other strategies for prevention. We produced a discussion document on how to curb the use of drugs that was released at the end of August. We held a press conference which only two journalists attended. One of the journalists asked, after I had talked, amongst other things, about the importance of the atmosphere in the home in influencing young people's attitudes, 'Are you blaming parents for the increased use of drugs?' I said, 'No, that's not what I said' and explained again our balanced approach recognising the many factors. The journalist left and there was no coverage of the issue. Nonetheless, the document did go to every school in Victoria, every state politician and local government in Victoria, and to every parent organisation in Victoria that we could identify. Some 4500 copies of that document were distributed.

A: *What do you see as the importance of that document?*
DP: I think it's a very important document that gives a better understanding of factors that lead to the involvement, particularly heavy involvement, with illicit drugs. It sought to increase understanding of the social context, the family context, even the genetic factors that contribute and the difficulties in influencing peer attitudes and peer

behaviour. All of those issues need to be better understood if we are to have any chance of reducing the still growing use of illicit drugs in our community. We also covered a very wide range of other issues. These included the treatment and rehabilitation options and the need for complete re-integration into the community, with employment of people who've gone through detoxification and rehabilitation. We emphasised their need for support over an extended period. All of these issues have been discussed with local government organisations. They have been very supportive of our recommendations. They are in fact making many significant changes, such as working constructively across the state with adolescents and young people who've left school early, and so on. This was an important contribution that I felt we were able to make, quite apart from the formal recommendations to the state government on a wide range of other issues.

A: *I understand that the recommendations on prevention have an impact on the design of school-based programs for young people, particularly around cannabis. What type of approach did you recommend?*

DP: School-based programs had been implemented as a result of the previous inquiry. These had taken time to be fully implemented, with training of school teachers across the state. All government and Catholic schools and the great majority of the independent schools have adopted this program and worked constructively with it. We were therefore able to build on what had already been established. We wanted to particularly concentrate on the problem of cannabis abuse, something that was left over from the last inquiry. There's no doubt at all that heavy use of cannabis weekly and more than weekly use carries with it a significant association with social dysfunction, drop out from employment or education and the like, and for some people, sadly, the development of psychiatric disturbance and psychosis. We don't know, of course, in all cases which is the cart and which is the horse once a young person becomes very unhappy as a result of developing a psychosis. Nonetheless, heavy use of cannabis is common amongst these young people so we wanted there to be a very clear message on the

health dangers of frequent and regular use of cannabis in a way that young people are likely to listen to. Whilst they're being lectured at that it's criminal to experiment with cannabis they are likely to ignore messages about health risks, given that around 50% of young people have tried cannabis by the time they have left school. We are getting messages about the health effects developed and we've got young people developing the presentation of the message within schools. I've seen plays written and acted in by young people in schools that are then being presented in the community and to other schools. These are very useful mechanisms for getting the message across in a language young people are likely to listen to.

Whilst they're being lectured at that it's criminal to experiment with cannabis they are likely to ignore messages about health risks, given that around 50% of young people have tried cannabis by the time they have left school

---

A: *What in essence do you think are the particular contributions that the inquiries you have chaired have made to the drug policy debate in Australia?*

DP: What I've always brought to the table is a commitment to look at the evidence and to discuss the issues dispassionately rather than emotionally. Those who regard drug use as simple immorality usually tackle the issues in an emotive manner. The contrast has to be one of looking at the evidence and seeing what needs to be done. In no other field that I know of, in either health or law enforcement, would the community be willing to accept a mounting death toll, a mounting crime rate associated with illicit drugs, and increasing prison populations without there being a call for alternative approaches to be tried. Rather than pronouncing what the answers are, we suggested at every stage let us try a new approach and evaluate it to see whether it works and to see whether we can then move ahead in a more effective way. I think that message does get through eventually.

Rationality, public support and the role of the media

A: *And have you won support for such rationality?*
DP: During the recent drug inquiry we have had very strong public support from a large number of professional bodies which we didn't have five years ago. The local branch of the Australian Medical Association, the local Nurses Federation, the Ambulance Employees Association, the Pharmacy Society of Victoria, the Law Society of Victoria, and the Bar Council for Victoria all publicly supported our recommendations. The Institution of Engineers of Australia, Victorian Branch became a very strong public supporter. They organised public meetings at which our views were supported. So people who deal with the problem recognised that the drug problem isn't solved simply by labelling it as a moral and law enforcement issue. They were willing to look at alternatives.

Many people are attracted out of hope or desperation to simple solutions, such as that it can all be fixed by tougher law enforcement

A: *How has the media affected discussion of drug policy in Victoria?*
DP: I'm a little more objective in my assessment of the media now than I was five years ago. It is clear that the tabloid media and most of the talk-back radio appeal primarily to an audience with relatively low levels of education. They see their audience as wanting the simple black and white answers, and responding to dramatised pictures of drug users and to crime related to drugs. Those sections of the media that have audiences more interested in complexities and the understanding of broader issues have, in fact, been very supportive. The *Melbourne Age* was supportive throughout both inquiries and gave us good coverage whereas the tabloid media and the talkback radio generally were dramatic and sought the emotional responses that go with the law enforcement and moralistic approaches. That's something that we

just have to understand. That's what sells their newspapers or sustains their ratings and they're likely to continue to behave that way until we can shame them into taking a more objective approach or until we get broader understanding of the issues in the community.

A: *How would you compare your experiences in drug policy with your earlier experiences in the HIV/AIDS area?*
DP: That's an interesting question that I've thought a lot about . When I went into the inquiry in 1995 I saw many similarities and felt that perhaps as we'd done well with AIDS in Australia maybe we ought to be able to do just as well with illicit drugs. But there were differences. Back in 1983, the media in Australia were talking about a new Black Death sweeping the world and saying that everybody was at risk. In Australia we had initially a government-sponsored advertising campaign based on the Grim Reaper, showing everybody being bowled over by AIDS. I regarded that as unethical because it was simply untrue that all were at equal risk of spread of the disease, and I said so. We were able to deal with the AIDS issue in a much more objective way as a health issue. We were able to get the public to understand those facts, to understand what needed to be done to contain spread of the virus. People came to understand that AIDS wasn't something that was threatening everybody. It threatened particular groups and those groups needed to be worked with. We had a very positive response from the male homosexual community in educational terms early on and, I think, we got the community to understand that there was a role for compassion and good treatment of those unfortunate enough to be infected, rather than dealing with AIDS, as some tried to do initially, as a 'moral' issue.

A: *But it wasn't to be that way with drugs?*
DP: We found it more difficult when we came to the illicit drugs. I think that is for a number of reasons. One is that illicit drug use, and its consequences, is a problem right across the community. Although it is true that people from backgrounds of poverty or disadvantaged parental situations are at greater risk, nonetheless illicit drug abuse

does occur in all sections of the community. There are people in every section of the community that have suffered as a result of drug-related crime. I think for those reasons it is something that is closer to hearts and fears of the whole community. That also means that many people are attracted out of hope or desperation to simple solutions, such as that it can all be fixed by tougher law enforcement.

What makes a problem into a moral issue?

A: *You had some resistance from some of the churches to the message that illicit drug use is not simply a moral problem.*

DP: It is hard to generalise. We had strong support from the United Church, from sections of the Anglican Church, and strong support this time around from the President of the Baptist Union of Australia. These were all important. The Roman Catholic Church in Victoria, however, is led by a conservative figure who wished to see the whole thing as a moral issue. In his view nothing should be done which would facilitate or support immoral behaviour such as injecting of drugs. However, the Roman Catholic Church is not monolithic and we had very strong support from the Jesuit Social Services. The local Archbishop was strongly opposed and, after spending time with the Congregation for the Doctrine of the Faith in Rome, the successor to the Inquisition, he ruled that no Catholic Organisation must be associated with the trial of injecting facilities. The Sisters of Charity in Sydney were instructed that they should not be involved in staffing of the injecting facility in Sydney. This was all quite sad.

But given the Inquisition's record on Galileo, that puts us in good company!

A: *Did you ever discover what is meant by a 'moral issue'?*

DP: I found that when one discusses this issue with senior clerics it's very difficult to find out really what they mean by 'a moral issue'. They don't regard the use of alcohol as immoral but the use of certain other drugs that alter the mind is seen as immoral. It is not just injecting drug use because cannabis use is also seen as immoral. On the other hand, whilst widespread use of prescription drugs such as Valium or sedatives to relieve unhappiness may be agreed to be unwise, it is not seen as immoral. If the association with crime is the hallmark of immorality, it has to be acknowledged that this association is the consequence of the current prohibition arrangements. It is difficult to follow the logic behind this position.

Change will come as the problems continue to get worse. Those communities willing to change, such as Switzerland and some cities in Germany may shame us, in time, into a more rational approach.

References

1. PREMIER'S DRUG ADVISORY COUNCIL (1996) *Drugs and Our Community* (Melbourne, Premier's Drug Advisory Council).
2. VICTORIA: DRUG POLICY EXPERT COMMITTEE (2000). *Drugs: Engaging the Community* (April, Melbourne).
3. VICTORIA: DRUG POLICY EXPERT COMMITTEE (2000) *Drugs: Meeting the Challenge. Stage Two Report* (November, Melbourne).

Commentary
Practitioner Policymakers

Wayne Hall

Modern Australia is an English speaking, predominantly European nation of 19 000 000 people, located in the Asia-Pacific region, occupying an island continent the size of the continental United States. Two-thirds of its population live in the eight capital cities of its six states and two territories; and the largest cities, Sydney and Melbourne, contain a third of its population.

Australia began as a British penal colony in 1788. After a century of immigration and population growth it remains a largely European nation, with a small but increasing Asian population and an indigenous minority of 1.5%. It is a federation (established in 1901) with a parliamentary system of government in each of its states and in the Commonwealth. The head of state is a constitutional monarch, Queen Elizabeth II, also Queen of England. Under the constitution, state governments are legally responsible for alcohol and drug policies but the federal government influences policy because it levies the taxes that fund state government activities.

Australia has produced a high per capita number of policy makers in the alcohol and drug field. Social concern about alcohol began with the country's penal origins and continued throughout our early colonial history when heavy drinking was widespread and alcohol was a form of currency. Alcohol consumption had halved by the end of the nineteenth century under the influence of immigration and urbanisation. It declined throughout the early 1900s, reaching a nadir in the 1930s. Alcohol use increased after World War II until the late 1970s before beginning a slow decline.[1]

In the 1950s alcohol became a concern to health professionals such as Les Drew, David Hawks and Jim Rankin who dealt with the medical casualties of heavy drinking. Jim Rankin developed an interest in alcohol while working as a physician in inner city Melbourne in the late 1950s. His interest took him to a senior position at the Addiction Research Foundation in Toronto, Ontario before returning to Australia. David Hawks, worked as a psychologist in London before moving into alcohol policy at WHO. Les Drew's Salvationist upbringing exposed him to alcohol problems from an early age and prompted him to specialize in psychiatry.

These thinkers all came to advocate what would later be called 'public health' alcohol policies. Drew and Hawks did so as senior advisers in the Commonwealth and state governments where they argued for the need to reduce alcohol availability, increase its price and reduce its promotion. Their efforts culminated in a National Health Policy on Alcohol in 1989, although its final content was substantially weakened through the efforts of the alcohol industry.

Cannabis, heroin and amphetamines were first used by young Australians in Sydney and Melbourne in the mid to late 1960s,[2] although all Australian state laws had prohibited their use decades before. The political response throughout the 1970s was to increase funding for law enforcement and raise penalties for drug use and selling. Australia did not, however, follow the US in pursuing a 'war on drugs' during the 1980s. Instead, in 1985 it adopted 'harm minimisation' as the goal of its national drug policy as part of the National Campaign Against Drug Abuse (NCADA).

NCADA grew out of the personal experiences of the then Prime Minister, Bob Hawke, whose daughter had problems with heroin use. A 'drug war' was the response initially preferred by the media and political leaders, and the outcome many expected when Mr Hawk convened a special premiers' conference. Thanks to the advocacy of Les Drew, David Hawks, Peter Baume, Ian Webster, and many others, the outcome was bipartisan support for a national drug strategy that included alcohol and tobacco along with illicit drugs and had harm minimization as its goal.[3]

Bipartisan support for 'harm minimisation' provided the policy space for the introduction of needle and syringe programs (1986), the expansion of methadone treatment (1985), the partial decriminalisation of cannabis in South Australia (1987), and a feasibility study for the controlled availability of opiates.[4] The adoption of these measures owed much to the then Federal Health Minister, Neal Blewett and his advisers' receptivity to the advocacy of our interviewees and others.[5]

NCADA also produced a substantial body of research on alcohol and drug issues. Two national research centres were established, national household surveys of drug use began, and a large number of innovative epidemiological studies, evaluations of drug treatment and economic studies were commissioned on the contribution that alcohol and other drug use made to the burden of disease. This investment created a critical mass of researchers that has enabled Australian research to make such an international mark over the past decade.

Bipartisan support for harm minimisation wavered in 1996 with the election of a Conservative federal government. In 1997 the new Prime Minister, John Howard, vetoed a trial of heroin prescribing that had been approved by state health and law enforcement ministers. Ensuing public debate about the best way to respond to rising heroin overdose deaths prompted the Prime Minister to review national drug policy. The result was a National Illicit Drug Strategy (NIDS) and a new slogan 'Tough on Drugs'. 'Harm minimisation' survived, but as a goal on an equal footing with supply and demand reduction. Funding was increased for abstinence-oriented treatment and the diversion of drug users into treatment.

The weakening of bipartisan consensus on drug policy in the mid 1990s made it difficult for governments to act. The public health policies advocated within the field were at odds with the simple solutions advocated in the tabloids and popular media. A distrust of 'experts' (not confined to the addictions field) prompted governments to look outside the field for policy advice. This was how David Penington became involved in drug policy after a long and distinguished career as a physician, researcher, medical educator, university administrator and policy adviser on AIDS. His standing and reputation and his post-retirement independence made him the Victorian premier's choice to chair an Advisory Committee on drug policy. The Committee worked under a very tight time line to examine the evidence and consult widely before producing a unanimous report that made some controversial recommendations. David Penington has achieved considerable success, by the standards of the addictions field, in persuading politicians to accept many of his committee's recommendations.

The interviewees' careers exemplify the ways in which practitioner policymakers have persuaded Australians of the need to respond to the problems caused by alcohol and other drug use. Their contributions to the policy debate have displayed the directness and a robustness of expression of dissident opinion for which Australians are well known in Britain. They have made effective use of research and evidence in challenging accepted wisdom and have, in their turn, stimulated an appetite among Australian policy makers for evidence on patterns of drug use, drug-related harm and the effectiveness of interventions. Their advocacy, steady funding for research over the past two decades, and an increased political recognition of the importance of drug and alcohol issues, have attracted into the field a new generation of practitioners and policymakers who are building upon the work done by the Australians interviewed here. That is a legacy of which they can be justifiably proud.

References

1. LEWIS, M. (1992) *A Rum State: Alcohol and State Policy in Australia* (Australian Government Publishing Service, Canberra).
2. MANDERSON, D. (1993) *From Mr Sin to Mr*

Big: A History of Australian Drug Laws (Oxford University Press, Melbourne).

3. HAWKS, D. & LENTON, S. (1995) Harm reduction in Australia: has it worked? A review, *Drug and Alcohol Review*, **14**, 291–304.

4. BAMMER, G. (1995) *Report and recommendations of stage 2 feasibility research into the controlled availability of opioids* (National Centre for Epidemiology and Population Health and Australian Institute of Criminology, Canberra).

5. ALLSOP, S. (1995) Harnessing harm reduction in Australia: an interview with the Hon. Neal Blewett, *Drug and Alcohol Review*, **14**, 273–281.

Part IV
Tobacco Researchers

Richard Doll

Sir Richard Doll was born in 1912 in Hampton, Middlesex, UK. He qualified in medicine at St Thomas's Hospital Medical School, University of London in 1937. He obtained his MD (London) in 1945; DSc (London) 1958; and DM (Oxford) 1969. From 1948 to 1969 he worked in the Medical Research Council's Statistical Research Unit, at first under Sir Austin Bradford Hill and then as the Unit's Director. In 1969 he became Regius Professor of Medicine in Oxford, and in 1979 the first Warden of Green College, Oxford. Since his retirement in 1983 he has continued to work as an honorary member of the Clinical Trial Service Unit and Epidemiological Studies Unit. He was elected FRCP in 1957, and FRS in 1966. He was knighted in 1971, and made a Companion of Honour in 1996. He received the United Nations Award for Cancer Research in 1962, the British Medical Association's Gold Medal in 1983, and the Royal Society's Royal Medal in 1986.

Medical training

Addiction: *I want to establish the antecedents for your later research contributions. You qualifed in medicine in 1937 at the age of 24?*

Sir Richard Doll: Yes, I qualified through the Conjoint examination early in 1937 then took the London MB BS exam in June. I had gone straight from Westminster School to St Thomas's Hospital, but I had decided to do medicine only very late. The thing that gave me real pleasure at school was mathematics. I took A levels, Higher Certificate as it was in those days, in mathematics. I wanted to go to Cambridge to read mathematics, because I was told it was the best place for the subject and I tried to get an open scholarship. I sat the scholarship exam and did well on the first papers, but very badly on the last one. The tutor for admissions rang my father and said they couldn't give me the scholarship because of my last paper, but would I take an exhibition. I was so annoyed with myself – the reason I did so badly on the last paper was, in fact, because I had drunk too much of the strong Trinity College ale the night before – that I told my father that I wouldn't go to Cambridge to read mathematics but would do what he had always wanted me to do, which was to study medicine. It was essentially an emotional reaction, but I have often thought that the ale which I drank on my last night in Cambridge was the best drink I

ever had! I then had to study biology quickly. But I really didn't mind what I did as long as it was something scientific. I had always respected my father's work as a GP and was, in consequence, happy to do medicine. I got into St Thomas's the next year and have enjoyed every minute ever since.

A: *At St Thomas's was there in those days any opportunity for a medical student to engage in research?*

RD: No, there wasn't. But we had, as most medical schools had, a journal that was produced periodically – the St Thomas's Medical School Gazette – and I wrote an article on statistics in medicine, whilst a student, which recommended the use of Chi Square tests in medicine,[1] which was certainly the first time that this had been recommended at St Thomas's. What stimulated me to write this piece was that one of the surgeons was treating undescended testes with pituitary extracts as he had read a paper which reported that this treatment increased the proportion of children in whom descent of the testes would occur. The claim was that the treatment produced descent in about 70% of cases against the previous rate of about 63%, but numbers of cases were small. I was sceptical of the conclusion as I had maintained my interest in mathematics and been reading Fisher's book on *Statistical Methods for Research*

Workers which taught how to do a Chi Square test, and application of the test showed that similar or more extreme differences could have turned up by chance about 6 times in 10. That was in 1936 I think. But we had no opportunities for doing research. My clinical interest then was neurology and I got very interested in electro-encephalograms. I went and saw them being recorded by Grey Walter at the Maida Vale Hospital, and wrote an article on their use in medicine in 1937.[2]

A: *Is it apocryphal, I seem to remember Dennis Hill telling me, that as a medical student you pointed out that when it came to a measure such as haemoglobin, the mean wasn't enough and one had to think also of a standard deviation?*
RD: It is quite likely although I don't actually recall it.

I had always wanted to do research but in those days you really couldn't do research unless you had a private income

A: *When you qualified in 1937 did you think, 'Now for a research career', or were you considering neurology? Obviously the war was imminent.*
RD: I had always wanted to do research but in those days you really couldn't do research unless you had a private income. The grants were very few, and very small when you did get them. What you had to do was to become a Consultant Physician, get on the staff of one of the teaching hospitals, and then you could make enough money and have the facilities to do some research. That was really what I was hoping to do.

A: *How did you spend those two years before the war started?*
RD: I got my London degree in July 1937 and then applied for a House job at St Thomas's. I was fortunate enough to get one for a year: 6 months as Casualty Officer and Anaesthetist and 6 months as House Physician – so that took me through to

1938. I then tried to get a job at the Royal Post-graduate Medical School at Hammersmith, which was just beginning to get recognized as an outstanding centre for research. I went to see Fraser, the Professor of Medicine. His House job had been advertised but he said he couldn't offer it to me because he had promised it to someone else. However, if I were to do 6 months voluntary research at Hammersmith, I could be his House Physician when it next became vacant. This attracted me greatly, not least because it would pay me £100 a year. (At St Thomas' one had only free beer and free laundry.) In the meantime, however, I had to look for some way to earn a living, whilst I did the 'voluntary' research. Fortunately, a friend of mine suggested that I might share with him the job of Resident Medical Officer at the London Clinic. The reason they wanted a resident doctor at the clinic was that it advertised that there was always a doctor on the premises; but the last thing that any of the Consultants wanted you to do whilst you were there was actually to see any of their patients. They had, however, to have someone available the whole time. What was usually arranged was to have two resident doctors, one of whom was on call at night, and one who was on call during the day. This suited me very well. My friend was on call all day, while I worked at the Hammersmith, and then I was on call all night. This seldom interfered with my sleep (I was called only about 3 times the whole 6 months I was there) and it enabled me to earn sufficient money to keep myself while doing research at Hammersmith, under the cardiologist Paul Wood. My project was to develop a technique for measuring vitamin B1 in the urine as Wood had the idea that rather more heart failure might be due to alcoholism than was generally recognized and that B1 deficiency might be an indication of excessive alcohol consumption. The technique proved too difficult for me. I had to grow a fungus on blood, the amount grown being dependent on the amount of B1 in the substrate, but I could never get reproducible results and nothing came of the work. The only other interesting thing that I did at the time was to look for a factor in blood responsible for hypertension. In those days hypertension was thought to be a unitary disease. I took blood from a patient who was having a nephrectomy because of hypertension due to renal disease and gave it to another patient to see if his blood pressure would go up, but the blood clotted and the experiment was not a success.

Medical service during World War II

A: *So then the war came?*
RD: It came very soon after I started the House job. I started with Fraser at the beginning of August (or rather with Stuart Harris who was acting for Fraser during his holiday) and was called up on 1 September. This was because I had joined the Supplementary Reserve after Munich, when it became obvious that there was going to be a war.

A: *You were in the army all the way through from 1939 to 1945?*
RD: Not quite to the end of the war. I got renal tuberculosis in the middle of 1944 and was discharged early in 1945 after a nephrectomy. The tuberculosis fortunately turned out to be unilateral.

A: *I've read your recent BMJ articles. Tell us about your adventures around the time of Dunkirk. What happened to you after that? Did you remain on Regimental duties or were you in any research position?*
RD: I stayed with the Battalion for a few months and then, presumably because I had obtained the MRCP in the summer of 1939, I was posted to a hospital in Shaftesbury, where I worked for 3 months before being posted to the Middle East, as a member of a group of medical reinforcements. Before leaving I had a fortnight's course in tropical medicine in Liverpool, during which time it was blitzed fairly heavily, and I left for the Middle East in January 1941. I first worked there as a Captain in charge of the medical side of a small hospital in Cyprus. I was there for a year and after the fall of Crete it was quite an interesting place to be. At the time, there was no animosity between Greeks and Turks. The Greeks, who wanted union with the mainland, were content to discuss it in a civilized way over a cup of coffee or a glass of ouzo. Then I went back to Egypt, to the 63rd General Hospital at Helmieh, where I was eventually promoted to medical specialist and took charge of the ward for serious infectious diseases – diptheria, typhoid, typhus, poliomyelitis, and small-pox being the most important. I was there for 18 months before being posted to a hospital ship which spent its time sailing up and down the Mediterranean. We took part in the invasion of Sicily and the invasion of Italy, taking troops off the beachhead at Salerno, but much of the time we were sailing empty or transferring sick men from one port to another. Altogether it was one of the most enjoyable years of my life.

The only time we were in any danger was when we were in harbour or backing up the landings, and then we were part of a fair target

A: *You weren't being bombed or shot at?*
RD: The Germans were scrupulous in respecting the Red Cross on hospital ships in the Mediterranean. The ship I was on had been refitted in Alexandria after being hit by a torpedo from a submarine before I was attached to it. When the British protested Rommel asked if we could reasonably expect anything else when our hospital ships sailed without lights immediately behind a convoy. He assured us that if we sailed with our lights on and broadcasted our position we would be alright. So all that year we did. Many German planes came down and had a look at us and went away. The only time we were in any danger was when we were in harbour or backing up the landings, and then we were part of a fair target.
But Rommel was quite scrupulous in his adherence to international rules on the open sea.

Back to a difficult London

A: *So you came out in 1945 because of your kidney. By that time you were 32. Were you still thinking of a consultant job with a bit of research? Or had the war influenced your career choice at all?*

RD: I wasn't discharged from the army until early 1945, but I had already worked for 6 months during convalescence. I had been advised to take things easily so I convalesced at Roffey Park, a rehabilitation centre, but as a doctor, not as a patient. There I decided that psychiatry was certainly not the subject for me. It was too difficult. I felt that one was putting oneself in the position of God and I wasn't very good at it. I then got a job at St Thomas's as a Junior Medical Assistant to the Professorial Unit. I worked there for the whole of 1945. I didn't get on very well with the young people who held senior positions to me in the hospital. They assumed that, having spent 5 years in the army, I knew nothing about medicine. Indeed, it was true that I wasn't as up-to-date as they were, but I did have rather more clinical experience. Later many doctors began to be released from the army and I found the atmosphere rather unpleasant. Everyone was trying to become friendly with the senior staff in the hope of being given one of the very few hospital appointments that were available at that time.

A: *Did you succeed in doing any research at St Thomas's?*
RD: Yes, a bit. Professor McSwiney, the Professor of Physiology, tried to get me interested in respiratory physiology and its application to clinical medicine, but the subject didn't attract me. I did, however, complete one piece of research to test the idea that one could relieve severe asthma by administering a mixture of helium and oxygen. The hypothesis was that the helium molecules, having less mass than nitrogen and oxygen molecules, would make a mixture of oxygen and helium easier to get into the lungs than either pure oxygen or oxygen and air. It ignored, however, the complexities of streamline and turbulent flow and the independent diffusion of different gases, but it was claimed to be supported by empirical observations. However, when I sat by the side of patients switching from one mixture to another, some actually got worse on the helium mixture.[3] I also tried to do some research on the effects of labour on women with heart disease, although I never wrote this up. At that time advice was being given as to whether or not a woman should

become pregnant if she had heart disease, in what I thought was a very unscientific way. The obstetricians were also very unhappy about it. So I used to follow all pregnant women who had any form of heart disease (mostly rheumatic in those days), and again make detailed observations on how they got through their labour, with a view to being able to give better clinical advice as to whether or not a woman could have a baby.

The lung cancer question

A: *So you were clearly making a start on a research career but you say that you were unhappy with the competitive atmosphere prevailing at St Thomas's. How did you find a way out?*
RD: A young friend of mine, to whom I was subsequently married, was Dr Joan Faulkner. She was working at the Medical Research Council's headquarters and when I told her of my desire to find a research job she said that the MRC were wanting to support some research by Dr Avery Jones at the Central Middlesex Hospital, but that they couldn't find a suitable person to work with him. I went to see Avery and we immediately got on well. I started to work with him on a grant which he was given to study occupational factors in the aetiology of gastric and duodenal ulcers. From then on everything went very easily. We designed a survey of the prevalence of peptic ulcers in men employed in different industries in the neighbourhood of the Central Middlesex, with which Avery had already developed contact. We appointed a social worker as an assistant, who interviewed all the workers and obtained an indication of whether they had ever suffered from indigestion by the use of a standard questionnaire. I then saw all the workers with any suggestive evidence of indigestion plus a 10% sample of those with none to ensure that the screening procedure was satisfactory. We managed to interview 98.4% of a total of some 5000 workers. The work was reported to a committee under the supervision of Professor Ryle, with Bradford Hill as one of its members. Bradford Hill was very impressed with our having obtained a 98.4% response rate, because a number of studies in occupational medicine in those days

had been content with a 60 or 70% response and, after I had taken the course in medical statistics at the School of Hygiene, during the time I was working on Avery's project, Bradford Hill asked me if I would like to work with him on a study to try to find out the causes for the increase in lung cancer. This was to begin in January 1948, when Avery Jones's grant expired.

A: *What is your sense of the climate of medical ideas on the relationship between smoking and lung cancer at that time?*

RD: The starting point of our study was the increase in the number of deaths that were attributed to lung cancer. It was Percy Stocks, the Chief Medical Statistician at the Registrar General's office, who drew the MRC's attention to the dramatic increase in the number of these deaths. As a result the MRC held a conference in 1947 to consider whether the increase was real and if so whether anything could be done to find its cause. Following this, a small committee, consisting of Kennaway, Stocks and Bradford Hill, was set up to design a study to look into the reasons for this increase. While it could not be proved that this increase was real, there was much to suggest that at least part of it was, and in any case, it would have been very unwise to assume the increase was wholly artificial, in case some real increase had actually occurred. Plans were, therefore, drawn up by Bradford Hill, Kennaway, and Stocks for a study to be carried out by Bradford Hill with a research assistant, which I was fortunate enough to become. What we did was to list all the possibly relevant factors that we thought people could have been exposed to and which could have become more prevalent over the previous 50 years. There weren't very many and one of them was smoking and particularly the smoking of cigarettes. Kennaway was particularly interested in the possibility of smoking being a factor, but I don't think anybody else was. Bradford Hill certainly wasn't particularly keen on smoking as a cause, nor was I, while Stocks was particularly keen on the effect of general urban atmospheric pollution. I must admit that I thought that the latter was likely to be the principal cause, though not pollution from coal smoke which was terrible in those days but which had been prevalent for many decades and hadn't really increased. In fact coal consumption had already begun to diminish. Motor cars, however, were a new factor and if I had had to put money on anything at the time, I should have put it on motor exhausts or possibly on the tarring of roads. Because of course the whole road system in the country had changed with the advent of the motor car and we knew from Kennaway's work that the tar that was put on the roads contained many carcinogens. Various industrial developments were another possibility. We also thought of arsenic, which had been increasingly used in the treatment of syphilis, as a possible factor, although we weren't able to test this idea very effectively. But cigarette smoking was such a normal thing and had been for such a long time that it was difficult to think that it could be associated with any disease. Indeed in the medical textbooks of the time the only effects of smoking that were described were tobacco amblyopia – which is a disease that opthalmologists now tell me doesn't occur, but which could have been produced by heavy pipe smoking in the presence of dietary deficiency – and tobacco angina: that is, angina precipitated by smoking which was so rare that individual cases were written up.

But cigarette smoking was such a normal thing and had been for such a long time that it was difficult to think that it could be associated with any disease

---

A: *Was there no interest in the possibility of pipe smoking and cancer of the lip?*

RD: Yes, that association and the association with cancer of the tongue were really pretty firm. They were, however, more often thought to be due to the heat from the pipe stem than to the tobacco. Indeed, I remember asking our senior surgeon when I was a student, when we saw a case of cancer of the tongue in out-patients, whether he thought pipe smoking or syphilis was the cause (cancer of the tongue being commonly observed in association with syphilitic leukoplakia). Mr Maybury replied that he didn't know whether either was the cause of the disease, but he did know that the wise man avoided the combination of the two. These risks were fairly generally accepted, but not to the extent that people were advised not to smoke pipes.

A: *You then took your research forward and interviewed quite a large sample.*
RD: We actually ended up interviewing 3500 patients, including some 500 in rural hospitals because we wanted to get estimates of smoking habits in different parts of the country. But the main study was based on some 2900 patients in London and four other large cities.

The non-smokers in the lung cancer group just melted away when we came to check the diagnoses

A: *The technique was to go along with a questionnaire to hospitalized patients who had not got lung cancer and ask them about possible antecedents and compare their answers with those from patients who had got lung cancer?*
RD: That's right. Sir Harold Himsworth, the Secretary of the Medical Research Council, or rather Dr Green, his number two, wrote to 20 London hospitals and asked if they would collaborate by allowing us to see patients in their wards. We set out to see patients not only with cancer of the lung, but also others with cancer of the stomach or large bowel and a control series of patients with other diseases. One reason that we included patients with two other types of cancer was because it was hoped that the interviewer would not know which type of cancer the patient had, so that we could avoid bias due to knowledge of the nature of the patient's disease. The second reason was that we wanted to see if any factor that was associated with cancer of the lung was associated with cancer generally, or was specific to cancer of the lung. We employed four medical social workers, or Almoners as they were then

called, to interview the patients, as only Almoners were acceptable to the medical profession. Nurses in those days didn't interview patients. The four Almoners visited the hospitals weekly and went to the wards asking if any patients with these diseases had been admitted. We also had a system by which hospitals notified us of the admission of the sort of patient in whom we were interested. But by and large we found that the best thing was just to visit frequently the wards where we knew the relevant patients might be.

A: *Your role was the organization of this study. You weren't having to do the interviewing.*
RD: No, I didn't do any of the interviewing. It was of course my job with Professor Bradford Hill to design the questionnaire, to check the results of the interviews as they came in, and to see that we were getting the right number of controls matched appropriately with these cases. Then of course I had to check the diagnoses. We interviewed patients who were admitted with a diagnosis of 'query lung cancer, stomach cancer or large bowel cancer'. So every diagnosis had to be checked after the patient left hospital. This was important, not only to check the diagnosis but also to obtain information about the histology and the part of the lung in which the tumour originated. We soon found that many of the patients interviewed in the belief that they had lung cancer turned out not to have it. These constituted an excellent second control group, for they would be subject to the same bias, if any existed, as affected the results of the interviews with the patients who actually had lung cancer. As I went through and checked the diagnoses I saw that patient after patient in the 'lung cancer' group who was regarded as a non-smoker turned out not to have lung cancer; whereas, in those who were heavy smokers the diagnoses seldom had to be changed. The non-smokers in the lung cancer group just melted away when we came to check the diagnoses – they might have anything from fibrosarcoma of the chest wall to bronchiectasis, but they didn't have lung cancer. This was a striking finding and quickly drew our attention to the importance of smoking.

A: *What was the statistical technology, how were you handling this really very considerable mass of data in the days still of hand-driven calculators?*

RD: I didn't even use a calculating machine: I just listed the results in a book. Our questionnaire was relatively short as it was always part of Bradford Hill's teaching to keep questionnaires brief, and I've always tried to ensure that interviews should take less than half an hour. I have unfortunately failed in recent years, but for that first study we succeeded. I then extracted personally, from each form, the information that looked as if it might be of interest, entered it in columns in a record book, and added up the numbers in the columns. The whole thing was done with a nineteenth century clerical technique.

A: *You were getting some idea as to the excitement of the work from finding that the false diagnoses related to the non-smokers. But the real excitement must have been when you added up those columns and figures and did the first Chi Square. Back to your beloved Chi Square?*

RD: Well no, we didn't really need to do a Chi Square, the answer was so clear (but we did, of course, do one for publication). We started interviewing in 1948 and by the beginning of 1949 Bradford Hill and I were quite convinced that there was a strong association between lung cancer and cigarette smoking and not much of an association with any of the other factors we were interested in. When we had data on some 650 male patients with lung cancer we wrote up the results. We came to the conclusion, for the reasons which we set out in the paper, that we had found an association that we believed indicated cause and effect.[4] We reached that conclusion in 1949; but we took that paper to show Sir Harold Himsworth before submitting it for publication, because we realized that the conclusion was dramatic and Bradford Hill and I both had the greatest respect for his opinion. Himsworth said that the finding was so important that he didn't think we should publish it until we had found it again in a second series. He pointed out that the study had been entirely limited to patients in London hospitals and he wondered if there could be something speical about London that produced the result. He wanted to see results from elsewhere in the country as well. So we didn't publish, but arranged instead to interview patients in Bristol, Cambridge, Leeds, and Newcastle. We continued the study and we expanded it to cover over 1400 lung cancer patients.[5] Whilst we were still collecting the second set of data and it had become obvious that the results in these other towns were going to be the same, Wynder and Graham published their paper in the *Journal of the American Medical Association*.[6] That of course had the same effect as our check on patients in other towns. We went to Hugh Clegg, the Editor of the *British Medical Journal*, with whom Bradford Hill was on very good terms, and asked him if he could publish our paper quickly. He said that he would get it out in a matter of weeks and he did.[4]

A: *Did you know the Americans were on your tail?*

RD: No.

A: *It must have been rather a nasty moment, wasn't it?*

RD: It was disappointing, yes. We'd had this result for at least 9 months and had been sitting on it. But I don't regret having done so, because I think that the principle was right. It was a principle that I have tried to adhere to ever since: namely, that if you find something that is unexpected and which is going to be of social significance you have a responsibility to be sure that you're right before you publicize your results to the world. This does at least require repeating some of the observations.

A: *Firstly with Avery Jones and then with Bradford Hill you had come into contact with outstandingly able scientists. Had you been looking for a distinguished senior person to work with or was this just good fortune?*

RD: It was just good fortune. I knew as a young man wanting to make a career in research that one would have to work with someone who could set you on the right lines. I was happy to have gone to Avery Jones to work in the field of gastroenterology. He was a marvellous person to work with and I continued working with him for 20 years after I joined Bradford Hill. During all this time I continued with clinical research for 2 days a week at the Central Middlesex Hospital. So I wasn't actively looking for someone else to work with. I had quite anticipated that I could go on doing research with Avery Jones. But this offer from Bradford Hill was very exciting. Bradford Hill was by then established as a leading figure in medical science in this country from whom one could learn a great deal, while Avery Jones still had to make his name. The opportunity of working more in the statistical field and of being able to play with numbers a bit more was also very attractive, so I was just delighted by the opportunity.

If you once started saying what ought to be done with your own results you might get emotionally attached to them, whereas, as a research worker, you always ought to try to disprove your own findings

---

Stopping short of advocacy

A: *So that crucial paper came out in the BMJ in August or September 1950?*
RD: I think it was September.

A: *That work was published in 1950 and I think it was 1957 before any Minister of Health stood up and took it seriously. Were you disappointed, furious, or did you feel that it was not a research worker's job to do other than produce the research and let other people fight over its complications?*
RD: I was fortunate again in being associated with Bradford Hill at this time because I think he had the right attitude, and I have subsequently tried to model mine on his. His attitude was that the research worker's job is to obtain the results, to report them, and to comment on them if he is asked to, but to leave it to other people to act on them. The reason Bradford Hill gave for having this view was that if you once started saying what ought to be done with your own results you might get emotionally attached to them, whereas, as a research worker, you always ought to try to disprove your own findings. That indeed was what

we set out to do. Having said then that in our view cigarette smoking was a cause of carcinoma of the lung, we tried to think how the conclusion could be disproved. Bradford Hill had the idea of asking doctors what their smoking habits were, then following them up and seeing whether we could predict which of them had the greater risk of developing cancer of the lung. If our original findings had been wrong we should not be able to do so. We therefore started our second major project which was a cohort study of some 40 000 doctors from whom we had obtained details of their smoking habits. The American Cancer Society's similar cohort study was started by Hammond shortly afterwards with the specific intention of disproving the conclusion of our case-control study, which he told me he did not believe. He started the American Cancer Society's study[7,8] to show that we were wrong. We started our cohort study, not to show that we were wrong, but to see if we were wrong.[9-11]

Follow-up of doctors

A: *So in 1951 the first cohort was interviewed?*
RD: Yes. We decided to do this in the summer or spring of 1951. We wrote first of all to a random sample of doctors. It wasn't, in fact, truly random: we just took the first name at the top of each left-hand page of the medical directory until we got 200 names. It so happened that Sir Harold Himsworth's name was one of them. When we sent him the questionnaire he refused to believe that he was part of a random sample! The idea of the pilot study was to see whether doctors would respond. As they responded well, we decided to launch a major study. The British Medical Association agreed to help us. They provided the addresses of all the doctors in this country and sent out the letter and questionnaire that we had prepared.

A: *The reasons for choosing doctors?*
RD: We chose doctors for very good reasons. First, we hoped they would be more interested than the general public and would respond more readily. Secondly, we hoped that having had some

scientific training they would be more accurate in their replies. But thirdly, and most importantly, we thought that they would be easier to followup. Doctors kept their names permanently on the Medical Register so that you could know where they were and could keep tabs on them more easily than on a sample of the general population. As a result we found that even after 20 years we could trace 99%. So for all those reasons the choice was a good one. In fact, it turned out to be an even better choice than we realized because doctors were, I suspect, convinced by the results obtained from their own colleagues more easily than they would have been if the subjects of the study had been any other group. At any rate the British medical profession accepted the results and acted on them long before the medical profession did in any other country.

A: *You mailed them in 1951 and then carried out a number of waves of follow-up?*
RD: Yes. We mailed them at the end of October and regarded the study as starting on 1 November. We have, in fact, sent them further questionnaires about six times. Our published results are based on records obtained in 1951, 1957, 1962 or 1963, and 1971, but we also wrote to them again primarily for another purpose in 1978 and 1979, and to a recent sample. Getting new information has proved to be very important because there has been such a big change in habits.

A: *Can you recapitulate in essence what you think the findings have been from the doctors study?*
RD: Before answering that I should like to make just one comment on our case-control study, which is I think of some interest. It illustrates how very little attention was paid to smoking as a possible cause of disease in the late 1940s. When we chose our control patients, we obviously wanted to exclude patients whose disease might be due to smoking. Yet, the only patients we excluded were patients with cancers of the lip and tongue, which you referred to earlier; and patients with cancers of the mouth, pharynx, oesophagus, and larynx, as there was a little evidence relating pipe smoking to cancers of parts of the upper respiratory and digestive tracts. So we excluded those patients but we included patients with coronary thrombosis and even patients with chronic bronchitis. There was no suggestion among chest physicians in the late 1940s that chronic bronchitis could be due to smoking, although they of course recognized the existence of 'smoker's cough'. Today that's almost impossible to believe. We fortunately didn't have such a high proportion of patients with these diseases in the control group as to invalidate the study. But when we broke down our controls into groups with different categories of disease, we did find that those with respiratory disease smoked a little more than the rest of the population. We didn't, however, have any inkling that coronary thrombosis might be linked to smoking until we had the early results of the cohort study of doctors, the very first results of which indicated that such an association might exist.[9]

We didn't, however, have any inkling that coronary thrombosis might be linked to smoking until we had the early results of the cohort study of doctors

A: *That's very interesting. Going back then to the nub of the findings of the cohort study . . .*
RD: We published some results very early on, I think it was after 29 months of follow-up.[9] This was as soon as we got a statistically significant excess of lung cancer in cigarette smokers. We thought we should publish that straightaway to show that the case-control results were confirmed. Then we had more solid results in 1956, by which time we had some 50 months of observation. By this time too we had also found an association with chronic bronchitis and the association with coronary thrombosis was clear.[10] Of course by then the American Cancer Society had also shown the relationship with coronary thrombosis which they had concluded was causal.[7] The other outstanding finding in the cohort study was that the quantitative relationship with smoking was almost exactly the same as we had found in the case-control study. This showed that you could get not

only qualitative but also quantiative estimates of risk from a case-control study. As we got more data, so the dose–response relationship became firmly established and we found it to be practically identical with that deduced from the case-control study.

A: *But what you could get out of your cohort study which you could never get out of a case control was the impact of stopping smoking?*

RD: That's not entirely true. The case-control study has shown that ex-smokers were less at risk and were relatively less at risk the longer they had stopped. But what one couldn't get out of that study was the precise temporal relationship between the change in risk and the abandonment of the habit. Indeed now, after all these years, I still find that there are scientists who do not appreciate what the temporal relationship actually is. This is because many publications have shown only the relative risk in comparison with that in non-smokers and how this changes with the passage of time. If you present a graph showing the relative risk in current smokers and the trend in the relative risk in ex-smokers with the passage of time after stopping, all compared with the risk in non-smokers, you see a progressive reduction in ex-smokers with the relative risk gradually approaching unity. But this doesn't mean that the risk actually falls. What you are showing is a fall relative to that in non-smokers. Lung cancer, however, becomes more common in non-smokers as people age and if you plot the risk, not as relative to that in non-smokers but as an absolute risk, what you find is that the risk when you stop smoking first ceases to increase, staying more or less constant, and then slowly increases; because, after all, the ex-smoker is exposed to the same factors that cause lung cancer in non-smokers. What happens is that the curve approaches the curve for non-smokers asymptotically, which means that the risk increases in much the same way as the risk to non-smokers. So it is quite untrue to say that the risk falls when you stop. It is conceivable that there is a small drop for a few years after smoking is stopped, but the data are not enough to be sure whether there is a small drop or whether the risk remains more or less constant until the factors that cause lung cancer in

non-smokers begin to cause an increase in the ex-smokers. That is not to say, that it is not worth stopping. It is immensely worth stopping at any age. For if you continue the absolute risk increases dramatically with the passage of time and the ex-smoker is at much less risk than if he had continued, within only a few years.

We looked all around the world to see if we could find any evidence of a population who did not smoke but had a high incidence of lung cancer; there wasn't one

---

A: *Your major research thus employed just two functionally linked strategies?*

RD: In a sense, yes. But there is a point that is sometimes overlooked; our results were interpreted in the light of all the other available epidemiological information. We would never have said, on the case-control study alone, that cigarette smoking was a cause of carcinoma of the lung. We were as aware as many of our critics have been that an association doesn't necessarily imply causation and that the association we observed might have been due to an association between smoking and exposure to some other agent or to some other type of behaviour that was actually causing lung cancer, or even, as Fisher suggested, to an association between the tendency to smoke and a general susceptibility to the disease, although I must say that the last never seemed to me at all likely. We concluded that the association was causal only when we saw that it made sense in the light of all the other information that was available. For example, it made sense in the light of our knowledge of the sex ratio of the disease at different ages. It made sense of the fact that the disease was extremely rare in Iceland and very rare in Norway, when we found out that cigarette smoking had not been introduced into Iceland until the 1930s and that it had been uncommon in Norway. Then we found that the disease was particularly common in Finland and Austria, two countries which we knew had introduced cigarette smoking early on. We looked all around the world to see if we could find any evidence of a population who did not smoke but had a high incidence of lung cancer; there wasn't one. Similarly we looked to see if there was any area where smoking had been common for a long time and where there was a low incidence of lung cancer; again there wasn't one. I would prefer, therefore, to say that we also used a third ecological strategy. In sum, a causal relationship made biological sense in that there was a lower risk in lighter smokers than in heavy, a lower risk in ex-smokers, a lower risk in people who started to smoke later in life, a lower risk in women than in men, and a lower risk in communities in which cigarette smoking was rare. All this evidence enabled us to conclude that cigarette smoking was actually a cause of the disease. We said that in our first paper,[4] and the only credit I would claim for us is that we did pluck up our courage and state this openly. We believed that it was the sensible scientific conclusion.

A: *When it came to the Royal College of Physicians's report in 1962, the Secretary was Charles Fletcher and the Chairman was Platt. You were not on that Committee. Did you refuse to join it?*
RD: No. I wasn't asked to join it.

A: *Wasn't that extraordinary?*
RD: No. It was, I think, done intentionally, because it was thought that the conclusion of the Committee would be stronger if it was independent of Hill and myself.

A: *But you must have been talking to Charles Fletcher and the others at the time.*
RD: Yes, but we didn't discuss that initial report. With subsequent reports I have been involved more, but that first report was prepared quite independently and I am very glad that it was. To go back a moment, if I may, about our conclusion on causality. We were entirely supported in this by Sir Harold Himsworth, whom I mentioned earlier and whose scientific ability I greatly admired. He refused to organize any further research on the question from long before 1957, which you mentioned as the time when the Ministry of Health first took the conclusion seriously. Himsworth had been repeatedly asked by the Department of Health to do more studies on the relationship between smoking and lung cancer, at the request

of the Cancer Advisory Committee to the Ministry of Health, which didn't accept our conclusion. Himsworth, I think, as early as 1951[12] replied to the Department of Health and said that he wouldn't waste money on the subject as the matter had been proved. His backing from the day of our first publication was very valuable. Later, of course, in 1957, he got the Medical Research Council to state its support for our conclusion formally.[13]

A: *Did Horace Joules come and talk to you at the Central Middlesex?*
RD: Yes, of course. I talked to Horace frequently during my time at the Central Middlesex Hospital, where he was the Medical Director. He became, as you know, a powerful advocate of public education about the effects of smoking. He battled on the Central Medical Advisory Committee of the Department of Health from 1951 on. Every time the Committee had a meeting he asked it to make some statement about the effects of cigarette smoking but it always refused to do so. It wasn't until 1957, after the Government had formally asked the Medical Research Council for its opinion, that the Department accepted the conclusion.

A: *He was also a member of the Cancer and Radiotherapy Standing Committee.*
RD: Yes, and he certainly pressed it hard there.

Attitudes of the tobacco industry

A: *Are there any of the things you have mentioned which you would like to enlarge on?*
RD: There is the question of the attitude of the tobacco industry. This has been quite interesting. Soon after our publication the Chairman of the Imperial Tobacco Company, which was the leading manufacturing company in this country at the time, asked to come and see us. He had brought with him a statistician by the name of Geoffrey Todd, and they challenged us over the correlation between lung cancer mortality and cigarette consumption in different countries. The correlation coefficient, they said, was only 0.5 and therefore we must be wrong. Bradford Hill replied that this sort of crude ecological correlation was

very unreliable and that in his experience a correlation coefficient of 0.5 should be regarded as strengthening our conclusions. That rather set them back. They then said that smoking histories are too unreliable for us to have been able to draw any conclusion from them. That was easy, as any unreliability would merely weaken the real relationship. Finally, they said that the increase in mortality was more likely to have been due to the increase in atmospheric pollution. We didn't believe that there had been such an increase and, moreover, we had been unable to find much of a relationship with pollution in individual patients. When they left they initiated some research of their own. Five years later, Todd had found that people's smoking histories were recorded surprisingly accurately, and that habits were surprisingly constant and he was unable to make an association with atmospheric pollution stick. Todd then told the industry that we had convinced him that cigarettes were the principal cause of the disease. He told the Imperial Tobacco Company and the Research Council that the industry had set up, to which he was responsible, that unless they accepted the conclusion that smoking caused lung cancer, he couldn't work for them any longer. So they said thank you and goodbye. He took Joan and me out to dinner that day before he left telling us that it was the last expenses account dinner he would get out of the tobacco industry. Six weeks later he rang me and said that the industry had taken him back on his conditions. From that day on, for some years, we had a very good relationship with the tobacco industry in Britain. They agreed that they would not say anything to imply that smoking did not cause lung cancer or some other diseases, but they would continue to take the view that as people enjoyed smoking, they would continue to provide them with tobacco. So our relationship with the tobacco industry in Britain was initially good and

> So our relationship with the tobacco industry in Britain was initially good and all our contacts were both serious and polite.... I wouldn't take the same view now

all our contacts were both serious and polite. This, of course, ceased to be true when the power structure in the tobacco industry in this country changed and other influences came to determine its attitude. I wouldn't take the same view now.

A: *That's a very temperate statement to say that you wouldn't take the same view now. Would you take the opposite view?*
RD: I think that the tobacco industry in some other countries has behaved absolutely abominably. In this country BAT has behaved in a quite unacceptable way in some of the statements they have made. The situation now is quite different from what it was initially.

Passive smoking

A: *What is your view on the current evidence on passive smoking. How convincing do you find the statistical evidence?*
RD: I have found this difficult to assess. Basically I agree with the conclusions of the working party on tobacco which I chaired for the International Agency for Research on Cancer.[14] Their conclusion was that environmental tobacco smoke contained many chemicals that were known to be carcinogenic to animals and that smoke was known to be carcinogenic to humans if breathed in actively, so that it must be assumed that environmental tobacco smoke caused some lung cancers. But they would not commit themselves to an estimate of the amount. I thought that this was appropriate at the time and it was my view too. Three years ago there were a dozen studies of the subject – most of which showed a greater riks of lung cancer in non-smoking men and women if their spouses smoked than in non-smoking men and women whose spouses didn't smoke. The results varied substantially but this was only to be expected with the numbers of patients. They showed, however, no statistically significant heterogeneity. But it seemed to me that there was a possibility that a woman who was a non-smoker, if married to a smoker, might have smoked a bit more in the past than a non-smoking woman who was married to a non-smoker. I thought that there must be a bias of that sort and, that being so, it was difficult to say that

the two lots of non-smokers were at exactly the same risk and could be expected to have the same lung cancer rates apart from their exposure to environmental smoke. Therefore I didn't think that you could put a figure on the size of the risk. Since then Professor Nicholas Wald, who worked with me for many years and is now Professor of Epidemiology at St Bartholomew's, has made some careful analyses of the extent to which non-smokers married to smokers would have to have given incorrect reports of their smoking histories in order to create the quantitative differences that have been observed. He showed conclusively that it is very unlikely that biases of the sort I have referred to could account for the results that have been obtained. They might perhaps account for a quarter of the excess, something like that. But this is more than compensated for by the fact that the non-smoker is also exposed to smoke from outside his or her home. When you take that into account as well, the quantitative estimate of the effect of passive smoking that has been made is probably an underestimate rather than an overestimate. So I have now come round to the conclusion that you can put a figure on the number of cases of lung cancer produced by environmental tobacco smoke with some confidence. But it must be less certain than the figure for the effect of active smoking.

Advice to young researchers

A: *Besides your research career, did you continue to be involved personally in clinical practice?*
RD: I continued as a clinician with Avery Jones until 1969. All that time Bradford Hill encouraged me to continue to work with Avery Jones because he thought that it was invaluable for an epidemiologist to have some direct knowledge of clinical medicine. I had four beds in Avery's wards all the time until 1969, and treated patients with peptic ulcer and gastric cancer, doing clinical research on their causation and on different forms of treatment. Indeed, I have always thought that one of the more important pieces of research I have ever done was to demonstrate that a bland diet was of no value in the treatment of gastric ulcer. That contributed to saving millions of people from

having the miserable diets that used to be imposed on them. But I had beds only for research purposes and held only special research clinics. I never carried responsibility for routine admissions of acute patients.

A: *Today if a young man or young woman came to you and said – Professor I've got an interest in mathematics and have qualified in medicine, have written a bit for the College Journal, have got my membership and I am now thinking of a career in research – what would you advise them to do so as truly to acquire the skills of a research worker? Become apprenticed to a senior scientists? Go to America for a couple of years? Do a PhD? Take a degree in mathematics? What would you say?*
RD: I don't think it is necessary for a medical person to do a PhD. It is essential in many subjects because it is the certificate of qualification to do research. There are many fields in which you really can't get a research job until you've got a PhD. But medical training is already so long that the acquirement of a PhD is an unreasonable burden. My advice is to get into a good research unit as soon as possible and get on with doing research. I did incidentally want to do a PhD myself. I got my London MD by examination and was sorry that I had never written a thesis. I therefore registered at London University to do a PhD on the aetiology of cancer of the cervix; but before I had completed it Bradford Hill got the university to give me a DSc instead. A PhD really isn't essential for a successful career. My colleague Richard Peto was elected to the Royal Society a few years ago without ever having acquired a PhD because he got into research straight from his MSc and produced such excellent work. My advice to someone going into medical research is that if you can get into a good research group and produce good work, you don't need to worry about degrees. But that I know is not generally true for someone who qualifies in biochemistry or statistics. Peto was quite exceptional.

A: *Do you have any worries in your area of science about the continuing strength of the British research base?*
RD: I would rather not express an opinion on what's happened in the last 10 years because,

although I have been continuing to do research, I have not been involved in the day to day work of universities; and I am really not *au fait* with the problems facing young people and research departments. I have also been particularly fortunate in being associated with the Imperial Cancer Research Fund. Working for them has been like working for the Medical Research Council, as it used to be in the 1950s. That's to say if you have a good idea you ring them up and they say (or have said until recently), 'Get on with it, how much do you want?' So I am really not in a position to comment. There is a lot of first-class research going on, but I know that my senior colleagues are having to devote more and more time to writing out long research applications, something that has restricted the production of American research for the last 20 years. This requirement is spreading in England and I think it is very unfortunate. I still believe that some major sponsors of research should be willing to back individuals and to give them relatively free hands and not to make the financial solvency of research units dependent on preparing long and complicated research applications. It should rather depend on the productivity of their past work.

I can't say that I have been disappointed by the public's reaction to our work. It never struck me that the reaction would be quick

---

The government response to research

A: *Another question. There was a paper published 40 years ago by yourself and Bradford Hill telling us that smoking causes lung cancer. There are still in this country about 100 000 deaths a year related to smoking. But what do you think now about that story, the impact of your paper, the 40 year gap, the continuing mortality? Would you still take the line that the scientist must keep away from over involvement? Or do you feel a need to make that work have its public health bite.*
RD: Well, so far as my own position is concerned I am now much more prepared to take an active part. Indeed I have done so in a number of international organizations and in broadcasts. The danger of such activity biasing my future work is by now quite small. So I have changed my views with the passage of time. But that isn't to say that I would advise a young person to become an activist when he first obtains some socially interesting results. I can't say that I have been disappointed by the public's reaction to our work. It never struck me that the reaction would be quick. Smoking was so ingrained in the population. Until the press and the radio and television became convinced of the relationship there really wasn't much hope of getting the message through to the general population. You could get through to scientists and to doctors with your publications, but not to the general public, if every time you had published a report that cigarette smoking caused disease X, the media reported that the issue was controversial and that somebody else believed that the disease was caused by something else. That continued to be the position for at least 15 years after 1950. So how could you expect the ordinary person to take the matter seriously? 'These scientists', they would say, 'They can't agree amongst themselves.' So, I never thought the public would take the matter seriously until we had a change of heart by the leading figures in the press and broadcasting. This occurred in the early 1970s and was quickly followed by a big change in the attitude of the public.

A: *And conviction at governmental level?*
RD: Until the government was sufficiently convinced of the need to do something effective and particularly to increase taxation, I didn't expect to see any big change. I wrote to Dennis Healey, when he was Chancellor of the Exchequer, on the first occasion that a Chancellor announced in the House that he had increased taxation on tobacco on health grounds, and congratulated him for doing so. I got a personal reply from him, saying that he didn't receive many letters congratulating him on increasing taxation, and he was pleased to get mine. But I have been disappointed by the Government's failure to increase taxation recently and by their failure to ban advertisements. At present young people can reasonably say, 'Oh well,

smoking can't be all that bad or the Government would never allow tobacco to be advertised in the way it is'. So I have been disappointed in those two ways. I have never been disappointed at the failure to persuade children not to take up smoking. My reaction to this was formed early on, in about 1953, when I gave a lecture on smoking and lung cancer at the London School of Hygiene. In the subsequent discussion a man got up at the back of the hall and said that our conclusion was very important and that it obviously meant that we had got to try to get at children to stop them starting to smoke. It was, he said, no good aiming propaganda at adults because they were addicted and you couldn't get them to change. So, he said, we have just got to stop children from taking up the habit. I didn't recognize the man and he turned out to be a representative of the tobacco industry. It was quite clear to me from then on that the industry knew that as long as young adults were smoking, and providing role models for children, it didn't matter how much you tried to educate children not to smoke, because they would not take any notice. I have taken the view ever since then that while education about the harmful effects of smoking should be a part of general biological education in schools, it shouldn't be a specific and separate subject. What you had to do was to get young adults to stop smoking, particularly sportsmen, TV stars and anyone else that children look up to, including doctors, teachers and even parents. I have not been disappointed by children smoking, but I have been by the slowness of the Government's reaction. Much of what has happened in this country in the last 20 years has been encouraging. We have seen a big change in the incidence of lung cancer – and that I find really exciting. Some of the reduction in incidence is due to the introduction of low-tar cigarettes. They are not the whole answer to lung cancer and they don't reduce the risk of most of the other smoking-related diseases, but they do reduce the risk of lung cancer. We now see in this country that the mortality from lung cancer in men under 35 years of age has gone down by 80% from its maximum just after the war and the reduction has gradually spread to older and older people until we now have a situation in which the mortality is coming down in men at all ages under 85. Epidemiological evidence tells us that if you want to predict what is going to happen to cancer mortality in the future you have to examine the trend in young people. We saw the epidemic first appear in young people and it is now fading in them almost as quickly as it came. I am, in consequence, optimistic about the future trend of smoking-related diseases.

A: *So the scientific insights in the long run haven't just remained on the shelf?*
RD: They certainly haven't. The worrying thing now of course is the spread of smoking to the developing countries where one can see that the increase in mortality from these smoking-related diseases more than compensates for the decrease in the few countries that have already taken the smoking problem seriously.

A: *If you have someone lighting up a cigarette in front of you in a restaurant do you find that is just a cross to be borne, or do you move away, expostulate, send for the head waiter . . . ?*
RD: No, I ignore it. I decided on Bradford Hill's advice not to get involved in public education and to try not to be emotional about the subject. I don't mind in the least if someone in the room lights up a cigarette – it's their decision and their life, not mine. In the last few years, however, as smoking has become less common, I have come greatly to prefer a smoke-free atmosphere. And I am now beginning to get irritated if someone smokes in a restaurant, because I find it rather unpleasant.

A: *It would be a bold smoker knowingly to light up in front of Richard Doll.*

References

1   DOLL, R. (1936) Medical statistics, *St Thomas's Hospital Gazette*, 294–297.
2   DOLL, R. (1937) Notes on the Berger rhythm and the electroencephalogram, *St Thomas's Hospital Gazette*, 157–159.
3   DOLL, R. (1946) Helium in the treatment of asthma, *Thorax*, **1**, 30–38.

4   DOLL, R. & HILL, A. B. (1950) Smoking and carcinoma of the lung, *British Medical Journal*, **2**, 739.

5   DOLL, R. & HILL, A. B. (1952) A study of the aetiology of carcinoma of the lung, *British Medical Journal*, **2**, 1271–1286.

6   WYNDER, E. L. & GRAHAM, E. A. (1950) Tobacco smoking as a possible etiologic factor in bronchogenic carcinoma, *Journal of the American Medical Association*, **143**, 329–336.

7   HAMMOND, E. C. & HORN, D. (1954) The relationship between human smoking habits and death rates: a follow-up study of 187 766 men, *Journal of the American Medical Association*, **154**, 1316–1328.

8   HAMMOND, E. C. & HORN, D. (1958) Smoking and death rates: report on forty-four months of follow-up of 187 783 men, *Journal of the American Medical Association*, **166**, 1159 and 1294–1308.

9   DOLL, R. & HILL, A. B. (1954) The mortality of doctors in relation to their smoking habits. A preliminary report, *British Medical Journal*, **1**, 1451–1455.

10 DOLL, R. & HILL, A. B. (1956) Lung cancer and other causes of death in relation to smoking, *British Medical Journal*, **2**, 1071–1076.

11 DOLL, R. & HILL, A. B. (1964) Mortality in relation to smoking: ten years' observations of British doctors, *British Medical Journal*, **1**, 1399–1410 and 1460–1467.

12 WEBSTER, C. (1984) Tobacco smoking addiction: a challenge to the National Health Service, *British Journal of Addiction*, **79**, 7–16.

13 MEDICAL RESEARCH COUNCIL (1957) Tobacco smoking and cancer of the lung, *British Medical Journal*, **1**, 523.

14 INTERNATIONAL AGENCY FOR RESEARCH ON CANCER (1986) *IARC Monographs on the Evaluation of the Carcinogenic Risk of Chemicals to Humans: Tobacco Smoking*, Vol. 38 (Lyon, International Agency for Research on Cancer).

Charles Fletcher

Charles Fletcher 1911–95, was born in Cambridge, England. He was educated at Eton, Trinity College Cambridge and St Bartholomew's Hospital Medical School. He specialised as a chest physician with a research interest in the epidemiology of respiratory disease. He was Director of the MRC pneumoconiosis unit and later held a Chair at the Royal Postgraduate Medical School. He was a Fellow of the Royal College of Physicians, served as Secretary to its Committee on Smoking and Health and was a founder member of Action on Smoking and Health. He was a pioneer in bringing medical issues to the public via television.

Professional training

Addiction: *Could you start by briefly taking us through your medical education.*
Sir Charles Fletcher: I went to Cambridge in 1930. My father, by the way, was an eminent medical scientist, the first secretary of the Medical Research Council, and when I was 17 he asked me what I wanted to do. I said that I might want to be a doctor, so I took my first MB before I went to Trinity College, Cambridge. My father gave me two bits of advice. He said if you think you are going to do medicine, then while you are at Cambridge don't spend your time with medical students, because you will spend the rest of your life with doctors. Widen your education by talking to other students. The other excellent advice was to enjoy Cambridge – leave your evenings free during the terms and do the hard work during the vacations. I failed to get an entrance scholarship to Trinity College, but I managed to get a first class in my first year exams, and in my second year finals I managed to get a first again in Physiology, Zoology and Chemistry. I was then offered a senior scholarship at Trinity.

A: *And in your third year at Cambridge?*
CF: In my third year I was spending a lot of time rowing because I was in the Cambridge crew. At the end of that year I was in the position to attempt my second MB which I passed. But I was then rather fascinated by the idea of doing physiological research, so I did the second part of my degree course in physiology and got a first in that in 1934.

A: *You delayed your clinical training to do some more research?*
CF: Yes, I settled down to do some research in physiology having got a research studentship at Trinity. I worked on the action potential of the unstriated muscle of the edible mussel, which had various properties which were rather interesting. I worked next door to Alan Hodgkin, who was in his fourth year, two years behind me. I put in a fellowship thesis on this work, but Alan Hodgkin did something nobody had ever done before and put in a fellowship thesis in his fourth year. Professor A. V. Hill was the referee for both our theses, and he told me many years later that mine would have been awarded a fellowship if it hadn't been that Alan's was so superb. So I was beaten to a fellowship by a future Nobel Prize winner. I was offered a fellowship at Peterhouse, to supervise their medical students. But by that time I had decided that I wanted to practise medicine, so I left Cambridge and went to Barts [St Bartholomew's Hospital, London], where I was given a free education in memory of my father, who had qualified in medicine there.

A: *You went to Barts when?*
CF: My period at Cambridge was 1930–1936. Then I went to Barts and managed to get the final

year clinical prize, the Brackenbury scholarship. Nobody had previously managed to get it in medicine and surgery. It was rather a curious thing but one had to choose which to take, and I took the medical one of course, so there's no record of this double.

A: *When did you finally qualify in medicine?*
CF: In 1939 when I was 28, which was very late.

A: *And then you became a house physician at St Bartholomew's Hospital. And then?*
CF: My first job coincided with the outbreak of the war. Barts was evacuated to mental hospitals in St Albans and New Southgate where I mostly worked. Acute admissions to Barts were transferred there and patients from the waiting list, so I had little training in acute medicine. I wanted more experience in academic medicine, so I wrote to Leslie Witts, formerly Professor of Medicine at Barts and then Nuffield Professor in Oxford, and he offered me a job as his house physician at the Radcliffe Infirmary. After that he took me on as a Nuffield Research Fellow (equivalent to a junior lecturer). While there I developed acute diabetes, and also passed the exam for membership of the Royal College of Physicians. My uncle, who was a senior fellow of the college, told me I got easily the best marks of any candidate in that exam. My success in exams was not because I was a great scholar, which I have never been, but was due to good technique. For example, I discovered in vivas that if I couldn't answer a question, and just waited patiently and looked at the examiner, he would give you a useful hint. I was also very good at guessing likely questions in written exams. My exam performance was always above the level of my professional performance.

A: *You were the first person to give an injection of penicillin to a patient?*
CF: Yes. Professor Florey and his team, having shown that penicillin was very effective in mice, managed to produce enough for a clinical trial. Florey came over to Leslie Witts, and asked if he had someone who could do the clinical trials. I happened to walk into Witts's room at that moment and he asked me if I would take this on. Florey first

asked me to find a patient who had a fatal disease and was going to die soon, so that if for any reason penicillin was fatal, this would not matter. There were no ethical committees in those days. I found a woman who had disseminated breast cancer and she agreed to have this injection. I told her that it wouldn't do her any good but that it could one day help a lot of other people. So with Florey and Witts standing by I gave an intravenous injection of penicillin to the patient. It gave her a brief fever but nothing more. I next explored if you could give it by rectum, by mouth, or whatever. I then treated seven patients by intravenous drip and showed that it could cure gross staphylococcal infections for which there was then no effective treatment. The first patient we tried it on therapeutically was a 43 year old policeman who had combined staphylococcal and streptococcal septicaemia. He had terrible abscesses on his face and orbits, discharging sinuses, abscesses in his lungs. He was desperately ill and we knew he had everything to gain and nothing to lose from treatment. Five days after treatment began the improvement was incredible, but in the end the penicillin ran out and he deteriorated again and died a month later.[1] I returned to Barts in November 1942, soon after my wedding, as a young registrar, but since most consultants were away at the war, my job was effectively that of a consultant, only three years after I had qualified.

Pneumoconiosis research

A: *Would you, in the normal course of events, have hoped to have got an appointment at Barts?*
CF: Do you mean a staff appointment? I had to make a decision in 1945. I had got rather fed up with the routine clinical work at Barts and I wanted to get into more academic research oriented work. So I went to see a friend of my father's, Professor Francis Fraser, who had moved from the chair at Barts to that at the Postgraduate Medical School at Hammersmith. During the war he had been seconded to the Department of Health to run the wartime emergency medical service. He suggested I should go to see John McMichael, who was acting professor at Hammersmith. I found McMichael pioneering cardiac catheterisation. He

was short of a lecturer, who had just developed tuberculosis. He took me on and I worked under him for nearly a year. With his help I published my only cardiac paper. I used to drive to work with him because we lived close together just outside London. One day in early 1945 he told me he had a letter from Sir Edward Mellanby, secretary of the Medical Research Council, saying that they were looking for someone to run a pneumoconiosis research unit in south Wales. He didn't suggest me, but Leslie Witts and Ronald Christie did. I then had to face a terrible problem. I wanted to go on in clinical medicine but most of my contemporaries had done military service, which I had avoided because of my diabetes. I didn't want to go into pneumoconiosis because I was interested in gastroenterology, but I went to Cardiff to do this job because I thought that this was a way that I could serve the country, so to speak.

A: *You went from Barts to Hammersmith to do research?*
CF: Yes, I did some rather elementary research there but it was cut short by this invitation to go and run the Pneumoconiosis Research Unit in Wales in 1945. But I did my MD thesis in gastroenterology, on diagnosis by gastroscope. With the help of some insurance money on the family silver, which had been stolen, I bought a gastroscope and I used to go regularly from North London to Avery Jones at the Central Middlesex Hospital to learn how to use it.

A: *So in spite of your obvious interest in research you really wanted to be a clinician?*
CF: I did want to be a clinician. But I had a sort of vain hope that I might be a professor of medicine. I wanted to be an academic physician. Because I strongly disliked the idea of private practice. I didn't only want to treat patients who could afford it. I wanted to do medicine unfettered, so I joined the Socialist Medical Association and vigorously supported the NHS.

A: *At that time was that a radical thing for a doctor to do?*
CF: Yes, I was in a minority at Barts. On one day I was called a communist by a medical student and

a bloody Conservative by a member of the communist party. I was extremely keen on the Health Service and delighted when it came about. Medical students in those days were a tremendously conservative lot. They were mostly sons or daughters of doctors who were mostly Conservatives. Whilst at Barts some of us thought that it would be nice if we had some say in the way that we were educated. So we held a meeting and agreed that we ought to approach the staff to ask for some influence on the way they taught us. At the meeting one of the students got up and said that when he was at school he didn't criticise his masters and so why should he start now?

With the help of some insurance money on the family silver, which had been stolen, I bought a gastroscope

A: *You went to Eton, Cambridge and then to London. You had a very traditional education. Where did you develop these rather radical ideas?*
CF: My family were Liberals. The tragedy in my life was that my father died when I was only 21, during my third year at Cambridge, so I no longer had his influence. But I continued to feel it within me very much. In one way this made life rather difficult. He was a great scientist and a Blue, a Fellow of Trinity, and an FRS. He was very disappointed when I didn't get a scholarship to Trinity, Cambridge and when I eventually did get a scholarship I had a feeling that I had joined his class. I think I was keen on research but had no real originality. I think that because of my father's influence I thought I ought to do it.

A: *So when you were invited to become director of the first pneumoconiosis research unit in South Wales was that a difficult decision?*
CF: Very difficult. I hesitated a long time and eventually consulted my brother-in-law who was a parson. He made me see that this was a question of perhaps doing what I ought to do rather than what I wanted to do.

A: *How would you summarize the contribution that research unit made, and your own contribution?*

CF: Well, by the time I left the unit in 1952 we had shown how pneumoconiosis could be prevented. The National Coal Board acted on our proposals and coal miners' pneumoconiosis has now disappeared from British mines. My own contribution was to devise a quantitive method of x-ray diagnosis. When we started, the classification of chest x-rays of miners was purely descriptive. There were obviously two types of disease: a simple one where dust in the lung produced a speckling effect, and a complicated one in which you got huge fibrosing masses growing and causing severe breathlessness. This could be quantified by the size of the masses.

To quantify the simple form I got 100 films of the condition, ranging from normal to very marked, and asked 10 different doctors to classify them all into 5 grades. To my great surprise there were enormous differences between them. There were 30 films in this series which one doctor on one occasion said were quite normal, and another doctor on another occasion said were certifiable pneumoconiosis. I went up to London and asked Peter Kerly, who was then the top radiologist in the country, why there were these differences in diagnosis. He said it was because none of the doctors were radiologists. I got him and another radiologist at the Brompton Hospital to read all these films twice and the same thing happened: there were 30 films which one of them said were normal and the other said was certifiable pneumoconiosis. He was absolutely shattered and thought this was impossible. This was the beginning of my lasting interest in medical observer error. What we did was to develop standard films, based on many doctors' readings, which the reader would refer to and compare to each x-ray. We achieved reproducible readings and ultimately found, from the films of men who died, that the readings agreed closely with the amount of dust in their lungs. This method is now used internationally.

A: *So you really developed a scientific approach to diagnosis.*

CF: There had been few studies of that kind then, but after that it became a major interest, especially in the unit at Cardiff. Subsequently, observer error has been found to affect virtually every diagnostic test, and steps have been taken to reduce it. The other thing I did at Cardiff was recruit an extremely competent team. This was mostly good fortune. Many scientists had been doing operational research in the armed forces and were seeking the sort of work which our unit was doing. Sir Henry Dale, a great friend of my father's, was then President of the Royal Society. He knew what I was doing and he asked me if I would like to come to London to a symposium they were holding on war time research. I went around at the symposium telling the bright young people there about the pneumoconiosis problem and four of them said that they would like to join in. Philip Hugh Jones joined us, then John Gilson, who said that this was just the sort of research he wanted to do. Later, when I was looking for an epidemiologist, it happened that Archie Cochrane had just returned from the USA and Jerry Morris told me he was in London. He wanted to research into tuberculosis and since we then thought the complicated stage of pneumoconiosis was a form of tuberculosis, we persuaded him to join us.

A: *Then in 1952, when you were 41, you were invited back to the Royal Postgraduate Medical School at Hammersmith in London by John McMichael. How did that come about?*

CF: John Crofton, who was lecturer on chest diseases at the Hammersmith, left to become Professor of Tuberculosis in Edinburgh. John McMichael asked me to take his place. I had always had a hankering to get back to academic clinical medicine and I continued to have a low opinion of myself as a pure scientist, and wanted to help patients – so I went back to Hammersmith. It was an appalling shock at first because having been out of clinical medicine for seven years I found it hard to catch up with new clinical knowledge. I was precipitated into a severe depression and I was referred first to a Jungian psychiatrist. This didn't help me at all. He was always asking me about my dreams and one effect of the depression was that I had none. Eventually

I told him that I had decided to commit suicide and he referred me to William Sargant's department at St Thomas's Hospital where I had two ECTs. The effects were dramatic. Till then I had been able to think of nothing other than how I had wrecked my life, but after the shocks I began to think positively.

A: *Why did you think you had wrecked your life?*
CF: Because I had been a world expert on pneumoconiosis but never trained as a chest physician. I was a gastroenterologist by inclination. I had never been to the Brompton Hospital and learned all the tricks of the trade. I came back to find that my registrars knew much more about chest medicine than I did.

A: *Why then did you accept the invitation to go back to the Hammersmith?*
CF: Because I thought that it would be a delightful chance to get back to clinical medicine.

A: *What was the post at Hammersmith?*
CF: Clinical lecturer in respiratory diseases.

During my six months off work for tuberculosis I read all about chest diseases. When I came back to my clinical work at least I knew something about them

Research on chronic bronchitis

A: *So you went back to Hammersmith. What happened next?*
CF: I also developed tuberculosis. I had an idea of investigating ciliary action in the bronchi by getting people to inhale fine barium dust and then watching by x-ray how it was cleared from the lungs. My colleague at the Pneumoconiosis Research Unit, Martin Wright, who developed the Wright Peak Flow meter, had invented a machine for getting animals to breathe in dust. So I breathed in some fine barium dust from his machine and had an x-ray taken. There was an

obvious tuberculosis lesion visible on the x-ray. So I had 6 months off which was really valuable. I was asked to write a section on chest diseases for a medical text book which meant that during my six months off work for tuberculosis I read all about chest diseases. When I came back to my clinical work at least I knew something about them.

A: *When was that?*
CF: The second half of 1953.

A: *You recovered from depression. Was that when you became interested in bronchitis?*
CF: Before the war chest disease had been almost synonymous with tuberculosis. When this came under antibiotic control chest physicians started looking around, and it was obvious that there was an enormous amount of bronchitis and emphysema around. As the biggest problem in chest diseases it was the obvious thing to work on. I started a bronchitis clinic and was handicapped by not being expert at pulmonary physiology. I knew from my experience at Cardiff that you could only unravel the early stages of a disease by surveys outside the hospital. Encouraged by Professor Donald Reid at the London School of Hygiene, who had done epidemiological studies among postmen, I designed a study of diagnostic methods among post office workers. It involved using a questionnaire on respiratory symptoms which we had developed at Cardiff. My first task was to see how observer error could be reduced. We had three doctors and three nurses doing duplicate interviews on each subject, all recorded on tape. We found that if interviewers stuck to the questions strictly you got reproducible results, but if they added words of their own there were serious disagreements. For example, one of the nurses would ask about phlegm by starting 'it is not a very nice subject but I produce some so don't be shy'. She got about twice the incidence of phlegm that other interviewers got. From this work came the MRC standard questionnaire on respiratory symptoms, used all over the world.

Another important event was the great London smog of December 1952, which arrived in London just after I had come back from Cardiff. Our beds were flooded with bronchitic men dying from suffocation. The government set up various anti-smog committees which led to smoke control legislation. The MRC set up a Bronchitis Research Committee with Professor Ronald Christie as chairman. I was asked to be secretary of that committee. So I suppose it was the impact of the fog and the air pollution problems that led me to work on bronchitis.

A: *What did this committee do?*
CF: Well it sponsored my research in the Post Office. After that research we had formed a hypothesis on the natural history of bronchitis – that the irritants of tobacco and smog caused hyper-secretion of mucus, causing expectoration. This increased liability to infection which in turn caused emphysema. To test the idea I asked the MRC to finance a prospective trial over five years of men working on London Transport buses and trains, and at the Post Office savings bank – a large population with a small turnover.

A: *Your interest in a scientific approach to diagnosis had a very practical effect in the bronchitis field didn't it?*
CF: That's right. At that time there was chaos in the terminology of bronchitis and related disorders. The words bronchitis, asthma and emphysema were used without any agreed definition of their meaning. On a lecture tour in the USA in 1957 I found that these words were used in different ways in different centres and usually differently from their use in the UK. When I got home I suggested to Kenneth Donald and John Gilson that we should arrange an international conference to seek agreement. They suggested that we ought to get agreement within Britain first, so I asked the CIBA foundation to arrange a symposium. For three days a meeting of clinicians, physiologists, pathologists, and epidemiologists, which I chaired, defined these terms. The 400 copies of the report were used within a few months and it led to a general international acceptance of the meaning of these words which greatly reduced confusion.

A: *If I could go back historically. During the time you were in Cardiff were you aware of the work Doll was doing on smoking and lung cancer in the 1940s?*

CF: I was only aware of it when their first paper was published.[2] I knew Richard Doll well and asked him to come as epidemiologist to Cardiff. Although he was keen, for a variety of reasons he didn't come. When their paper was published, of course I asked myself why aren't we looking at the effects of smoking?

A: *Doll and Hill's paper was published in 1950, when you were still in Cardiff. Did that change your work?*
CF: We started asking about smoking habits and found that smoking and bronchitic symptoms were closely related.

A: *Am I right in thinking that at the beginning of the 1950s when you went back to Hammersmith, Doll did not think there was a connection between smoking and bronchitis?*
CF: I went back in 1952. Their paper showed a close relationship between smoking and lung cancer, and also with bronchitis as a subsidiary finding. The history of this is interesting because when they decided to study lung cancer they thought of air pollution, traffic and various things, but only as an afterthought did somebody say 'what about smoking?' To their astonishment they found that it was closely related.

A: *Can you summarize the development of your interest in the relation between smoking and bronchitis.*
CF: The Post Office study showed a very close relationship between bronchitic symptoms and smoking. This was published in 1959. It was from that study that the hypothesis was developed that smoking caused hyper-secretion which made the lung susceptible to infection, which could cause emphysema. There was also a lot of evidence from pathologists suggesting that infection might be causing emphysema. I realized that one couldn't really test this hypothesis by cross-sectional research. A prospective study was essential to see how the disease developed.

A: *When did you start the prospective study?*
CF: In 1961 intending it to run for five years, but we saw that we needed a bit longer and carried on until 1968. That was by far the most important

study I ever did. But it was muddied a bit at first by the fact that Richard Doll had asked Bradford Hill's son, David Hill, to do the statistics. He was interested in mathematics but uninterested in the problem. This became frustrating so I told Richard that this arrangement wasn't working very well. He agreed and suggested that we might try a young mathematical scholar who had just joined his unit from Cambridge – Richard Peto. He transformed our study which disproved the hypothesis we had started with. It showed that infection played no part in causing emphysema which was a direct effect of smoking. We completed the study in 1968. Richard Peto had a lot of other things on his plate, including the 20 year study of doctors smoking, so our study wasn't published until 1976, as a monograph with a summary in the *British Medical Journal* the same year.

A: *So what you had established in that work was that smoking was the true or major cause of chronic bronchitis?*
CF: Yes. It was the direct effect of smoking. This also caused hyper-secretion and infection but there was no causal relationship between the infection and the obstruction. At the beginning of that time I was appointed a reader in epidemiology but I didn't get the chair until later on. I think that was because John McMichael didn't really think epidemiology was a scientific discipline.

A: *You became a reader when you were 51 and got a chair when you were 62. That is late isn't it?*
CF: It was very late. I know that some of my friends had been writing to John McMichael suggesting that I ought to have a chair. The absolute blindness of clinicians to the fact that in the wards they see only the late stages of diseases – so that you had to study early onset in the general 'healthy' public – always surprised me. Of course at that time English medicine was remarkable at developing a plethora of people interested in epidemiology: Jerry Morris, Donald Reid, Richard Doll.

A: *You're talking about the 1940s/50s?*
CF: Yes. We led the world, but epidemiology was really not regarded as part of medicine.

A: *Let's move on to another aspect of your work. Between 1961 and 1972 you were medical advisor to BBC television. How did you get into that?*
CF: Shortly after I came back to London a BBC producer, Andrew Miller-Jones, had been given the job of producing a series of five programmes on medical subjects, called 'Medical Matters'. That was in 1952. He was assisted in designing these programmes by Dr John Agate, who had done industrial medicine at the London Hospital and eventually became one of the first leading geriatricians. He had helped Miller-Jones with the medical aspects of these programmes. They wanted an anchor man and John Agate suggested me. We met the producer, who seemed to think I was alright and so that was the first series which I presented on television.

A: *How long did that series last?*
CF: It was only five programmes at fortnightly intervals I think. It was broadcast early in 1953. The BBC had broadcast one or two isolated programmes before, but I was the first person to run a series. They did one on pain and one on dust. Andrew Miller-Jones was impressed with the way I coped. The shows were all done live. When we were doing the one on dust, I left out something, they prompted me, and I was able to take the prompt without breaking my flow at all.

The absolute blindness of clinicians to the fact that in the wards they see only the late stages of diseases – so that you had to study early onset in the general 'healthy' public – always surprised me

A: *Why were you so good at it?*
CF: I don't really know. I've always enjoyed acting and even flirted with the idea of going on the stage. I did a lot of amateur dramatics at Cambridge and at Barts. I think another reason I find it easy to talk to a camera is that I have a habit, when puzzling over a question, of talking to myself about it. I think that when I was talking to the camera I was really talking to myself. There was a gap after the Miller-Jones series and then a series called 'The Hurt Mind', for which

Christopher Mayhew stayed two nights in a mental hospital and described his experience. This was a series of five programmes whose purpose was to get the public to realize that mental disease was a disease like any other and not a 'madness'. They did a study of public opinion before and after the series and found a considerable shift in attitudes. This was about 1955.

A: *You presented this?*
CF: I shared it with Mayhew. He presented the first two and I presented the last three. Then in 1958, Mary Adams, who was in charge of scientific programmes at the BBC, asked me if I would introduce a series on medicine and surgery in hospitals called 'Your life in their hands'. The BBC had done a programme at St Mary's Hospital which had received a tremendous public response, and one of the regional offices of the BBC asked why they concentrated on London. So they allocated two programmes to each of the five regions of the BBC, ten programmes altogether. They were done live and I introduced them. These were such a success, attracting large audiences, that they did three more series of programmes over the next few years.

A: *How did the medical profession react to these programmes?*
CF: Many of them were bitterly opposed.

A: *Why?*
CF: I think it was a feeling, dating from Victorian days, in middle classes that the inside of the body should be treated with disgust.

A: *They just didn't think that the body should be talked about?*
CF: In the polite classes it wasn't. My mother told me that in the early part of the century, a guest at her home mentioned the word appendicitis at lunch. There was a ghastly hush and the subject was quickly changed by my grandmother.

A: *Surely that wasn't the only reason?*
CF: Another was that when medicine was ineffective the only weapon doctors had was magic. Here was somebody breaching the secret code

which doctors thought was their own. The BMJ published five leading articles in successive weeks called 'Disease education by the BBC', or something like that, attacking the television series.[3] There was even a debate in the House of Commons on the impropriety of talking about this sort of thing in public.

A: *Did this reaction bother you?*
CF: It bothered me a lot. My chief, John McMichael, asked me to see him after the second programme which showed a heart operation. He told me I must withdraw from the series and assured me that if I did not I would not be promoted in the distinction awards system, and that I would lose the confidence of my colleagues. That was fairly tough. But I felt I couldn't leave it in mid-stream. I thought its benefits were going to be greater than any harm it might do.

A: *Did it damage your career?*
CF: Well it didn't, because that year I was elected to the Council of the Royal College of Physicians and I was promoted from a C to a B merit award. So the warnings he gave me were disproved within a year.

A: *Was he warning you or threatening you?*
CF: Warning me. In a friendly way he was saying 'Look I don't think it is in your interests to do this'. The Professor of Surgery at the Hammersmith on the other hand, Ian Aird, was a tremendous support to me. There was extensive correspondence in the BMJ about the programme, some favourable but most unfavourable.

A: *Things have changed haven't they?*
CF: Well, I have never really thought I was a revolutionary but shortly before he died Theodore Fox, who was the editor of the *Lancet*, said to me that it must be wonderful to have brought about a revolution in medicine. It happened so gradually I never thought of it as a revolution.

A: *The radical idea was doctors talking openly and publicly about medicine, destroying the magic?*

CF: Yes, although they didn't say that of course. They said it was improper, it would cause hypochondria and frighten people.

A: *So the prevailing attitude seemed to be that medicine and health care were the province of the professionals, not of the people that needed protection?*
CF: Yes, but preventive medicine was alright – it was alright to tell people how to keep well, but not to tell them how to get well once they'd become ill.

A: *Its very relevant to what we are going to discuss about smoking isn't it, because once the causes of smoking-related diseases had been discovered, there was not all that much to do except prevent them.*
CF: Yes. You see I had been nurtured in preventive medicine in Cardiff. Pneumoconiosis was untreatable so our role was to discover the cause and see how it could be avoided. The critical thing was that dust could be suppressed in the mines but to what level? We showed that by a combination of mass x-rays of the miners and dust measurement you could determine a safe level.

A: *So you went on from your successful television work to write on the importance of communication.*
CF: Well that was much later. The Nuffield Provincial Hospital's Trust awarded me a Rock Carling Fellowship in 1972. This meant that you had to study a subject for a year, write a monograph and deliver a lecture summarizing the monograph. I was given the subject 'communication in medicine'.[4] In preparing that, I asked a recently retired medical librarian to look out some references for me. Practically all these references were about the way that patients didn't understand their doctors, work of which I had not been aware. So I wrote the first chapter on communicating with patients and left the section on communicating with the public to the second half of the book. I was genuinely unaware that my patients had any difficulty in understanding what I said to them. I was probably better than most doctors, but even so I didn't take deliberate steps

to check that they had understood and accepted what I had said. The idea of patient non-compliance had only recently been recognised by doctors, when they found that tuberculosis patients weren't taking antibiotics as instructed. This was thought to be wilful disobedience by the patients and no blame in those early papers was placed on the doctor.

A: *Can we go back for a moment? What was the reaction, professional or public, to the 1950 Doll and Hill paper?*
CF: Disbelief. It can't really be true.

A: *Did you have close connections with the MRC in the 1960s?*
CF: Yes, they were supporting the research I was doing.

A: *Did they accept the Doll and Hill conclusion?*
CF: First of all the Ministry of Health published a report saying that they accepted the findings. But it was hardly referred to in the press. The MRC said they agreed that this study had shown that smoking was the main cause of lung cancer, and they published an official report in 1954, also with little response.

A: *What made you start thinking that you should do something like getting the Royal College of Physicians to publish a report?*
CF: My research was concerned with bronchitis. It became very obvious that smoking was the cause of bronchitis and also, of course, I was seeing patients with lung cancer in increasing numbers. At the same time we were concerned about air pollution after the 1952 London smog. Patrick Lawther was appointed director of an air pollution research unit in Barts. We were collaborating with him on studies on masks to protect patients with bronchitis and also to protect them in the ward. A doctor from the Ministry of Health called Max Wilson came to see what we were doing. As he was leaving I asked him 'when is your Ministry going to justify its title and do something about smoking?' He reported this to George Godber, Deputy Chief Medical Officer, who invited me to lunch. He said that he wanted to talk about what we could do about smoking. He made it clear to

me that his chief, Sir John Charles (the Chief Medical Officer), was dead against the Ministry being involved in any action on smoking because he thought it would cause trouble. I asked him if he thought it would help if we asked the Royal College of Physicians to produce a report on smoking, sort of side-stepping John Charles.

A: *At this stage what was your position in the College?*
CF: I was just a fairly junior fellow. Robert Platt had just become president, and he said that if any fellow at the college had a problem which they thought he should know about he would be glad to hear from them. Based on that encouragement I rang him, although I didn't know him particularly well, and asked to see him. 'What for?' he asked. I told him that I thought the College should produce a report on smoking. He immediately said 'Of course we should. Who should we have on the committee?' Later Avery Jones told me that he had made the same suggestion to his predecessor, Russell Brain, who had replied in a letter that smoking was no concern of the College.

A: *The Royal College of Physicians did not have a tradition as a campaigning body, did it? Why was Robert Platt interested in taking on such a controversial subject?*
CF: I think, possibly, because he had been a chain smoker and had managed to stop shortly before he became president. He realized that this was important and he just had a wider vision for the college. He didn't only do this. He started postgraduate lecturing in the college – previously there had just been about five formal lectures a year and otherwise the college was only an examining body. The last time the college had acted on a public health problem was in the 18th century when it petitioned the government to take action against cheap gin. Robert Platt was a remarkable man to change the college as he did.

A: *So he formed a committee?*
CF: I suggested that he should invite Avery Jones, Guy Scadding, and Bodley Scott, who had written an article on the effects of smoking in the BMJ some years previously (in which he hadn't mentioned lung cancer). I had suggested him because he was an eminent physician interested in smoking. They sug-

gested other members and the college approved, but asked the committee to include air pollution in its remit. When we met we decided that air pollution was so obviously unimportant compared with smoking we took no notice of this.

A: *You were largely responsible for the drafting of that first report[5] weren't you? How was the work of writing the report handled?*
CF: I think that I have got a slight talent at writing simple English. I really had in mind the average Member of Parliament as the audience for this report. Each member of the committee wrote a chapter which I then re-drafted into a consistent style. Well, Professor Crew, who had been Professor of Public Health in Edinburgh, described the House of Commons as the 'pharmacy of preventive medicine'. That phrase had stuck in my mind.

A: *So from the beginning you realized that the voice of doctors, expressed through the report, must influence the politicians?*
CF: That's right. We were really quite sure about that. They were the ones who had to act.

A: *So you had a press conference to advertise the report and there was tremendous coverage of it.*
CF: This was because of two fortunate things. Firstly, there was no other important headline in the newspapers that day. Secondly, we were a group of practising doctors saying smoking was dangerous. I think that was the thing that the media recognized as being new, compared with official statements by the Medical Research Council and the Ministry of Health.

A: *Do you remember how many copies Pitmans published?*
CF: I remember we bargained with them. They said they thought that it wouldn't be worthwhile printing more than 5000 and we asked for 10000. They agreed but said that we would have to pay for any losses. The 10000 went in the first two days and they did a second printing within a week. The American Cancer Society also ordered 5000 copies to distribute to their members.

A: *What was the response of the politicians?*
CF: Neglect. Enoch Powell was Minister of Health and he agreed that the Ministry of Infor-

mation should produce some posters, but he said that any action on this must be taken by local authorities through their health education money.

A: *He accepted the conclusions of the report?*
CF: Yes.

A: *What was the response of the tobacco industry?*
CF: That brings in Geoffrey Todd, who had been dismissed from his post as public relations officer with the tobacco manufacturers when he told them he accepted that smoking caused lung cancer. But they missed his administrative skills so much that they re-appointed him. He wrote to me before the report was published and said that he would like 20 copies to distribute to the main manufacturers because he wanted to insist that they took the issue seriously. Later the manufacturers set up a research division directed by Todd, which financed some of my work at Hammersmith. John Partridge, chairman of Imperial Tobacco, accepted the evidence but was sure their scientists would be able to find a way of removing the cancer producing substance from the smoke. There's an interesting side issue here. His son was appointed a chaplain at St Martins in the Fields, which alerted me to the fact that he was a keen Anglican. So I wrote and asked how he reconciled his Christian beliefs with killing people through smoking? He asked me to meet him and some of his staff. At this meeting the head of the Wills Division in Bristol asked me 'Do you think you are justified in trying to destroy our industry?' John Partridge said he was sure they could overcome this temporary problem.

A: *What was behind the American Cancer Society's great interest in the report?*
CF: They were quite different from any cancer organization in this country, in that they were involved in health education and persuading people that cancer could be prevented or cured. Here was a report indicating the cause of cancer and so they circulated it to their members. President Kennedy got to know about it and told Luther Terry, his Surgeon General, that he had to produce a better report and so they produced the first[6] in the marvellous series of reports which have gone on ever since.

A: *In Britain you were disappointed with the lack of response to the report. What happened then?*
CF: Well about 1970 it seemed obvious it hadn't had the effect we hoped so we thought another report might rectify this. Sir Max Rosenheim was then president of the Royal College of Physicians. He agreed so we set up a new committee and produced the second (1971) report.[7]

A: *Why did you think that if the first report had not produced real change that another report might?*
CF: Basically because if you fail once, you try again.

A: *Had there been any change in public or political opinion during the 1960s after the first report?*
CF: Temporarily but it wore off pretty quickly, as was shown by the recovery of cigarette sales. We were rather more forceful in our introduction to the second report; I put in more colourful words. I said that the word holocaust could describe it and that it was like the worst of the epidemics of the past. Keith Joseph, the then Secretary of State for Health, said that that was the sort of lobby he couldn't refuse.

A: *So the Royal College of Physicians published a second report in 1971, which you also drafted?*
CF: Yes. At the same time we approached the college about setting up an anti-smoking organization.

A: *What exactly did you propose?*
CF: That we should have a council which should incorporate all the main medical societies and should act as a channel for communication about the effects of smoking.

A: *What was Max Rosenheim's reaction?*
CF: He agreed and called a committee to see how it should be set up. The name we first proposed was the Council for Action on Smoking and Health, until we realised that it would be abbreviated to CASH. So we took off the C and called it Action on Smoking and Health. The American ASH was fairly different from ours and was set up by a lawyer.

A: *When you first suggested that the Royal College of Physicians should set up an advocacy body were you surprised that they agreed?*

CF: No. Max Rosenheim had been chairman of the committee for the second report and was keen for action to follow.

A: Was this an implicit acknowledgement that the information which you had successfully communicated through the report wasn't enough?
CF: That's right. Dr John Dunwoody was the first (part-time) director of ASH, but he soon wanted to go back into general practice.

A: So you advertised for a new director of ASH. Did you get many applications?
CF: Just three – an elderly man, an elderly woman, and Mike Daube. He was so eager and confident we were clear that he was our man. He turned us from rather an inactive information facility into a real campaigning body.

A: In its first year or so ASH's function was to disseminate information and to try and change public opinion?
CF: Well not so much the latter. We wanted to, but at first it simply acted as an information centre. We were given £125 000 to help get started by Keith Joseph, who said that we weren't going to get any more. Mike Daube changed ASH fundamentally. For example, he took all the tobacco trade papers, got to know of new cigarette brands that were coming along and succeeded in stopping some. He insisted that we must, if we were going to have any real effect, be a campaigning organization. He set up an inter-party group on smoking and health in the House of Commons, and he got us into the position where the Department of Health found us helpful and has funded us ever since.

A: So the council of ASH was happy with the direction Mike Daube wanted to take?
CF: Yes. He made the tobacco companies really angry with us. They said that we couldn't be a charity and campaign politically. Lord Goodman's committee on charities found that many other charities were doing political work, such as Shelter, and felt that this was perfectly legitimate. Our original terms of reference were to encourage research and the dissemination of information. After that we were able to change to take an operative role.

A: Can you remember whose idea it was to create ASH?
CF: I think it was myself and Keith Ball. He said that he and Avery Jones had already been to see Rosenheim before I did. I hadn't known that. I was impressed by the much greater activity in the USA by the American Cancer Society and other medical societies.

A: What are your hopes for the development of tobacco control advocacy during the next decade?
CF: I think that the most effective weapon is price, but that this is difficult for politicians because of its effect on the retail price index. I think banning advertising is also very important, and that cigarettes should be sold in plain brown packets with large health warnings covering most of the surface.

A: Is there a danger at all that if you have a campaining body like ASH, the professionals might feel that they don't have to go on speaking out?
CF: I don't think so. The BMA are actively commited now and we get tremendous backing from them. Nicotine is a very addictive substance and we won't ever achieve complete non-smoking. Even a small number of doctors still smoke.

Cigarettes should be sold in plain brown packets with large health warnings covering most of the surface

A: You mentioned getting diabetes when you were at Oxford. Has this been a handicap during your career?
CF: It hasn't because I've managed it without getting any of the serious complications from which many diabetics suffer.[8] It is a nuisance, mainly because of the inevitability of recurrent hypoglycaemia caused by my careful avoidance of

hyperglycaemia. Fortunately my wife and many colleagues, especially secretaries, housemen and registrars, have tactfully reminded me to take glucose when they notice me acting strangely, to avoid awkward consequences.

A: *Several decades after you first started to emphasise the importance of communication for doctors, we are in a position for doctors to speak out and play a very active role. Would you agree with that?*

CF: Yes. But I think it's absolutely crucial that they continue to do so. They really do have a powerful voice, and it's a voice that politicians cannot lightly ignore.

References

1. FLETCHER, C. (1984) First clinical use of penicillin, *British Medical Journal*, **289**, 1721–1723.
2. DOLL, R. & HILL, A. B. (1950) Smoking and carcinoma of the lung, *British Medical Journal*, **2**, 739–745.
3. BRITISH MEDICAL JOURNAL (1958) Disease education by the BBC, *British Medical Journal*, **1**, 388, 449, 510, 569.
4. FLETCHER, C. M. (1973) *Communication in medicine* (London, The Nuffield Provincial Hospitals Trust).
5. ROYAL COLLEGE OF PHYSICIANS (1962) *Smoking and health* (London, Pitman Medical).
6. US SURGEON GENERAL'S ADVISORY COMMITTEE ON SMOKING AND HEALTH (1964) *Smoking and Health* (Washington, US Public Health Service).
7. ROYAL COLLEGE OF PHYSICIANS (1971) *Smoking and health now* (London, Pitman Medical).
8. FLETCHER, C. M. (1982) Avoiding diabetic disabilities without loss of freedom, *Journal of the Royal College of Physicians of London*, **16**, 78–79.

Ove Fernö

Ove Fernö was born in 1961 in Göteborg, Sweden. He studied at the Royal Institute of Technology, Stockholm from 1936–1940, qualifying as a chemical engineer, and worked for the pharmaceutical company Aktiebolaget Leo of Helsingborg from 1941–1981. He was Director of Research and Development from 1946–1961, Vice President of Research and Development from 1961–1973, and Executive Vice President from 1973 until his retirement in 1981. In 1987 he was awarded the Polhem Prize for the development of nicotine chewing gum for smoking cessation.

Training in chemistry

Addiction: *Could you start by telling me what you studied at University?*

Ove Fernö: I finished school in 1934 in Helsingborg in southern Sweden and I intended to study biology at the University of Lund. But I started with chemistry because I thought it goes well with biology. I was at the lab practically 10 to 12 hours a day for two terms. I became more and more interested in chemistry and thought then that maybe a future studying biology would not be so interesting – that I would be a teacher or something like that. I was more interested in research so I decided to continue with chemistry and go to the Royal Institute of Technology in Stockholm.

> When I finished school, in 1934, I cycled with a friend to Barcelona. It took about 2 months to get there and back

A: *So you went to Lund to do a chemistry degree?*

OF: I did not take a degree. To take a degree would take another year. At Lund I did a one year laboratory training and it proved very useful for my further studies.

A: *So you finished that in 1935?*

OF: When I was 19 yes, then the next year I did a course in physics and mathematics which was

necessary to enter the Royal Institute of Technology and I also worked six months or so in a chemical company. In 1936 I got into the Royal Institute of Technology to study Chemistry and Chemical Technology. I finished my studies there in 1940, qualifying as a chemical engineer, and in the same year got married to the daughter of one of my teachers in Helsingborg. I had got to know her by giving her lessons in mathematics.

A: *Before you went to university you were something of a cyclist weren't you?*

OF: Yes, when I finished school, in 1934, I cycled with a friend to Barcelona. It took about 2 months to get there and back, for which we had 300 Swedish crowns each. I remember I collected a lot of flowers and beetles. It was a wonderful trip.

Joining the Leo Pharmaceutical Company

A: *Were you a smoker in those days?*

OF: Yes, I took up smoking during my military service in the war and smoked 20–30 a day for more than 20 years.

A: *How did the opportunity arise to get a job in Helsingborg with the Leo Pharmaceutical Company?*

OF: One Saturday in January 1941 I was on the way to the library. Because I was smoking I was standing at the place reserved for smokers in the tramway, when I saw my old professor of organic chemistry, Bror Holmberg, smoking his pipe. He told me that he had had a telephone call from the Leo Pharmaceutical company in Helsingborg saying that there was a situation open for an organic chemist and he asked me if I was interested. I started there on the 1st March 1941. I was lucky that the head of the Leo research laboratories, Adam Deutsch, was a very good organic chemist and was also interested in biochemistry. So I had a good training there for about the next five years. When he left for a position at Lund University, I became the research director, in 1946.

A: *Could you say briefly what research you were doing?*
OF: The first thing I did was to synthesize some of the new anti-histaminic compounds which were being studied at the University of Lund. Then due to the war there was a shortage of pharmaceuticals and I got the job to synthesize a lot of organic compounds. Among other things Adam Deutsch and I developed and patented a new method to produce neostigmin.

A: *Tell me about your work at Leo before you developed nicotine gum.*
OF: Well during the 1940s the laboratory expanded so that it included organic chemistry, biochemistry, pharmacology and pharmaceutical research. As an example of our work in 1948 we produced a polymer, polyphloretin phosphate, which was the starting point of several new drugs, polyestradiol phosphate, for example.[1] We also got products under licence from pharmaceutical companies abroad including Rhone Poulenc, Janssen, Smith Kline & French. So the company was growing steadily and in good financial health when the nicotine gum project started in 1968.

The nicotine gum project

A: *How did the nicotine gum project start?*
OF: It started when on 12th December 1967, I got a personal letter from a friend of mine, Dr Claes Lundgren at the Department of Aviation Medicine at the Physiological Institute of Lund University. He and his colleague Stefan Lichtneckert suggested a tobacco substitute for oral use in such a way that suitable doses of nicotine could be administered, which would prevent the user from being exposed to the many harmful constituents of tobacco smoke.

A: *Did he have any idea what kind of product it would be?*
OF: No. But he had noticed that submariners, because they were not allowed to smoke, could switch to chewing tobacco in the boat without too much difficulty.

A: *Why was he interested in submariners?*
OF: He was in the aviation medicine and respiratory field. His main interest was in aviation and then in submarines also, in respiratory physiology at different pressures.

> He had noticed that submariners, because they were not allowed to smoke, could switch to chewing tobacco in the boat without too much difficulty

A: *So the story began with an observation that submariners who smoked needed to continue using tobacco?*
OF: More that they needed to continue with nicotine. He told me on one occasion that some years earlier he himself had tried chewing tobacco and that quite of a sudden, he observed that for a few hours he had not smoked a cigarette. Then he realized that it was due to the nicotine in chewing tobacco. So then the idea was in the back of his mind so to say. He was quite an innovator.

A: *What was your reaction to his letter?*
OF: I became immediately very interested. I was also primed, because I had had an experience with nicotine free tobacco. During the 1939–45 war I became a heavy smoker. Tobacco was rationed and on one occasion I was running out and so bought a tobacco substitute (I remember the head of an American Indian on the label). I realized very

soon the absence of nicotine and threw it away, so I was convinced that nicotine was the substance I needed. So when I received Claes Lundgren's letter I did not have the slightest doubt that nicotine was the main element in the smoking habit. And I realized that a tobacco substitute could help many smokers like myself who could not stop. Then I realized also that such a product would be important for the Leo company. At the time, pharmaceutical research reported to me and so now I was in a position to do something.

A: *How did you start?*
OF: Before meeting Lundgren and Lichtneckert I started some preliminary trials with an extremely clever pharmacist, Bengt Ohlsson, and his assistant Kerstin Andersson. Our first idea was to use an aerosol containing nicotine.

A: *The aerosol was to be inhaled?*
OF: Yes.

A: *What happened to it?*
OF: Well it tasted terrible but we also realized that it was too complicated – it was not very handy to use, so we abandoned it. This happened around the end of 1967. After that we focused our attention on oral administration.

A: *How did you get the idea to put nicotine in chewing gum?*
OF: I think it was a logical idea. We reasoned like this – with an orally administered product, nicotine must be absorbed in the buccal cavity, like chewing tobacco and oral snuff. If swallowed, nicotine will pass the acidic milieu in the stomach before it is absorbed in the intestine. If you were to swallow large quantities of nicotine it could be dangerous. If you produced nicotine in a lozenge or tablet and several of them were swallowed there was the risk of accidental poisoning, particularly for small children.

A: *Could you absorb enough nicotine through the gut to kill yourself?*
OF: If you swallow enough nicotine, yes.

A: *Wouldn't it be metabolized?*

OF: A small amount is metabolized to cotinine in the liver but a large amount would get through. Nicotine is very toxic if given orally. It is one of the most toxic substances known.

A: *So you were looking for a way of administering nicotine orally that was safe.*
OF: Yes, so that if you swallow a large amount of this product it would not be absorbed quickly. Then you had to protect it from being released too quickly, and then the idea of using chewing gum as a vehicle for nicotine presented itself. From chewing tobacco to chewing gum is not a large step.

A: *That strikes me as a rather modest view. What was the next step?*
OF: We prepared some rather primitive chewing gums in the laboratory, each containing 5 mg of nicotine, and then we chewed them for a various amounts of time – 1, 2, 5, and 10 and more minutes – and analysed how much nicotine was left. The release was much too quick and the taste was terrible. The gums were emptied in a very short time and then practically all of the nicotine was swallowed and not absorbed.

A: *So the problem was that you needed to slow down the release of nicotine?*
OF: Yes.

A: *What was your idea to do that?*
OF: A few years before I had been interested in ion exchange resins as carriers of certain orally administered drugs, in order to get a prolonged absorption, but I did not come across a good idea to apply this possibility.

A: *Is it possible to explain in simple terms what an ion exchange resin is?*
OF: A practical example would be hard water – water with too much calcium in it. You use an ion exchanger loaded with sodium to take away the calcium.

A: *How does that work?*
OF: An ion exchanger could be a natural product, some kind of mineral or clay material. It

could also be an organic polymer of high molecular weight, in other words an immensely large molecule.

A: *Why is the size of the molecule important?*
OF: Because it must be insoluble and absolutely inert. Then such a molecule should contain, in the case of nicotine, acidic groups as acids. If you add nicotine, it will combine with this acid forming a nicotine salt of this very big molecule, which is completely insoluble. This is what you put into the gum. Then if you chew, the cations in the saliva – like sodium – would enter the chewing gum and exchange with the nicotine so that the nicotine comes out as nicotinium ions and the sodium ions are fixed to the carboxylic groups.

A: *Let me see if I understand the basic principle. You attach the nicotine to an ion exchanger, you put it into the gum, then when the gum is chewed the saliva goes into the gum and releases the nicotine from the gum into the mouth. Is that basically correct?*
OF: Yes, you have to chew in order to release the nicotine.

A: *And the importance of that is that you can control the rate of release of nicotine?*
OF: By varying the intensity of chewing yes. If you chew intensely the nicotine is released in 20 to 30 minutes. But also safety. If you swallow the gum the nicotine is not released because it is attached to an insoluble inert molecule.

A: *So you had chewing gum with nicotine in it bound to ion exchange resin. Can we get the dates clear? Did you do this in 1968?*
OF: Yes. Then we had the technical problem of producing the gum. We got into contact with a German manufacturer of machinery for making chewing gum and they helped us to produce our first chewing gum. We gave them the ingredients to put into the gum. Later, around 1971, we contacted a small Danish chewing gum manufacturer, which later on was incorporated into the Leo company.

A: *How long did it take to solve the ion exchange problem?*

OF: We tested many different ion exchangers – there are hundreds of them. We had to have an ion exchanger where the acidic strength matched the basic strength of nicotine. But we found a suitable product on the market rather quickly around the beginning of 1969.

A: *Where did you get the nicotine from?*
OF: That you can buy although you have to make a distillation in order to get a pure product. The clinical trials started and we worked to develop the taste of the chewing gum. It took some time. This was quite a new field for us, of course. We also realized that we must have a method of analysing nicotine in the blood of smokers, so we started in 1969 to develop such a method.

A: *Did you start the clinical trials as soon as the gum was ready in early 1969?*
OF: No, not before the end of 1969. In 1969 and 1970 I started to chew the gum myself, then some other people, and then some patients, until we were a little more confident. The first trials were presented at the London conference, the Second World Conference on Smoking and Health in 1971.

For many years I had wanted to stop smoking but couldn't. That was one of the reasons why I was interested to start working with gum

A: *Is this when you stopped smoking?*
OF: Yes, in 1969 after using the nicotine gum, and I stopped chewing after one year or so.

A: *Had you wanted to stop for a long time?*
OF: Yes. For many years I had wanted to stop smoking but couldn't. That was one of the reasons why I was interested to start working with gum.

A: *How did you decide what strength to make the gum?*
OF: We reasoned like this. An ordinary cigarette weighs about one gram and contains 1–2% of

nicotine, that is about 10 to 20 mg, with the inhaled smoke containing about 1–2 mg of nicotine. We made a guess that the chewing gum should contain 5 mg. Later, when we decided to produce three different strengths, we arrived at 4, 2 and 1 mg, and eventually decided to market 2 and 4 mg gum.[2]

Clinical trials

A: *Can you tell me about the first clinical trials?*
OF: We were very lucky that Dr Håkan Westling became interested. He was Professor of Clinical Physiology at the University of Lund, a city 30 miles from Helsingborg. He was at the time a habitual pipe smoker but eventually he stopped with the help of the nicotine gum. He and Claes Lundgren knew each other and were in contact. There had been a smoking clinic at the hospital from 1966–1967 and there was a list of patients who had not succeeded in stopping smoking. So at the beginning of 1970 some preliminary trials started with these patients. As soon as a better version of the gum was available a double blind controlled study was made of one week's duration, during which the subjects were allowed to smoke. A significant decrease in tobacco consumption was found in the group receiving nicotine gum. As a result the smoking cessation clinic was re-opened and over the following years it treated a large number of smokers. These first results were presented at the second world conference in 1971. Uncontrolled trials were continued, achieving success rates of about 40%, falling to about 30% when abstinence was checked with carboxy-haemoglobin measurement. Other Swedish clinics started to use the gum and some were even started because of it.

A: *I take it you were encouraged by these early trials?*[3,4]
OF: Very. There is one thing that one forgets a little when trying to objectify the research with the chewing gum. In all these trials there were very dramatic individual experiences with chewing gum. Some people stopped immediately without difficulty with the chewing gum, like small pieces of

sunshine in rather cloudy weather. It was stimulating and showed that there was something there really. The press were interested and in one interview in January 1972 Westling told reporters that there were more than 300 people on the waiting list, and that because of limited capacity only people with smoking related disease could be treated. These first trials in Lund were important. They gave us confidence in the product but we also started to realize that the gum needed improving. This led us eventually to the buffered gum. Much later when we were trying to get the gum registered in the first countries, especially Britain and Sweden, it was important to be able to refer to the long-term experiences in Lund.

Some people stopped immediately without difficulty with the chewing gum, like small pieces of sunshine in rather cloudy weather

---

Improving the gum

A: *Why you say the gum needed improving?*
OF: We thought that the results should be better.

A: *But you have already mentioned success rates of around 30%.*
OF: Yes but we expected a greater difference between placebo and nicotine gum. Just chewing a gum supposed to contain nicotine could have a strong psychological effect, and it was important to demonstrate that the gum had a real effect due to nicotine. The establishment were mostly dubious about the effect of nicotine and over-emphasized the psychological part of the smoking habit.

A: *Or perhaps under-emphasized the pharmacological part of smoking. How did you go about improving the gum?*
OF: Well, we wanted to find out if enough nicotine was being absorbed from chewing, so the first thing was to develop a method to measure nicotine levels in the blood. We wanted to compare the absorption of nicotine from cigarettes with the

absorption from the gum. It was very very important to do that in order to know what you are doing. Without that you are absolutely in the dark.

A: *So you started looking for a method to measure blood nicotine?*
OF: Yes. Our analytical laboratory developed a gas chromatographic method about the same time as Michael Russell and Colin Feyerabend. They did this in order to get scientifically based knowledge of the pharmacology of smoking, a prerequisite also for clinical studies in smoking cessation.

A: *When did you start this work?*
OF: In 1969. The method was ready in 1972 but was not published until 1975, somewhat later than Feyerabend and Michael Russell's study.[5,6]

A: *Did you know that Mike Russell was developing a method for measuring blood nicotine at the same time?*
OF: No we didn't.

A: *Did you then start measuring blood nicotine levels in people chewing the gum?*
OF: Yes, we made the first measurements in 1972 in people using gum, cigarettes and snuff, and discovered that the absorption of nicotine was poor when compared with the absorption from cigarettes and snuff.

A: *So are we now at the next stage of development, the third major technical challenge – to improve absorption of nicotine from the gum?*
OF: Yes. The problem is that normal saliva is neutral or very slightly acid with a pH of about 7.0. At this pH only about 10% of nicotine occurs as a lipid soluble base. About 90% occurs as positively loaded nicotinium ions and these are insoluble in lipids. Only the lipid soluble nicotine base can be absorbed in the buccal cavity. So not much nicotine was available to be absorbed across the buccal membrane. So you need to increase the proportion of lipid soluble nicotine base by increasing the pH of saliva – making it more alkaline – by adding a buffering agent. We tested many buffering agents. Since my pulse rate is very sensitive to nicotine I started chewing nicotine

gum again to test different buffers and within two months I was addicted to nicotine again. After many trials we found that adding small amounts of sodium bicarbonate to the 2 mg gum and sodium carbonate to the 4 mg increased the pH of saliva to about 8.5. At a pH of 8.5 about 50% of the nicotine is in lipid soluble form and the absorption is increased by well over 100%. We found that increasing the pH further did not markedly increase nicotine absorption further.

A: *So by the 3rd World Conference on Tobacco and Health in New York in 1975, you had the gum ready in more or less its final form.[7]*
OF: Yes.

A: *You said earlier that it took some time to develop the taste of the gum.*
OF: One of the first flavours was a mocha taste. The taste is important because nicotine has a very strong taste and it has to be masked in some way.

A: *So could we say that the fourth technical problem was masking the flavour of nicotine to make the taste of the gum acceptable?*
OF: Yes, that was very important and it took until about 1975 until we really had succeeded.

A: *All of that time you were trying to find a flavour?*
OF: Not all the time. We were satisfied with the first trials for some time. But flavour is an important area and we co-operated with two big companies, one in Switzerland and one in France, to find the best flavour. By combining one flavour from each company we got the flavour of the 1975 version of the buffered gum.

A: *Was there patent protection of this flavour?*
OF: No, flavour companies do not patent their flavours.

The importance of patents

A: *Can we talk about the importance of patents? If all you had needed to do was put nicotine into chewing gum and sell it, that would not have been very helpful would it?*

OF: Well, if it had been that simple, there would have been nothing to patent. Then anyone could have copied it and sold the gum cheaper since they would not have had the research and development costs. But of course it was not that simple, and there was a long period of research and development, with technical problems to solve, which we just discussed. We did need a patent and to get a patent we needed an invention. Putting nicotine into chewing gum is not an invention. Fixing the nicotine to an ion exchange resin and putting that in a chewing gum to enable the chewer to control the rate of release – that is an invention.

A: *So to make a living as an inventor it is not enough to have a good idea? It has to be a good idea that can be patented?*
OF: Yes, an idea that no-one has had, or more correctly, that no-one has patented before.

A: *So the first invention that you were able to get a patent on was the ion exchanger?*
OF: Yes, and the second one was the buffer. By the way, it is interesting that in 1907 an American inventor, Carleton Ellis, patented nicotine containing products that could be used by tobacco chewers.[8]

A: *But most of the patented inventions were never developed?*
OF: No, none of them were put into practice, they were all desk inventions.

A: *Is the problem that the people patented these ideas for nicotine substitutes but were unable to find a manufacturer who was interested?*
OF: I don't think so, I think it was rather that nobody thought the thing through. When we were working on our own patents we saw a lot of patents in the literature for using nicotine in a similar way but it appears no-one put any of them into practice. The patent literature is worth studying. I think that if Carleton Ellis had been born in this century he might have invented the gum.

A: *Did you have a good patent lawyer?*
OF: Yes. When I first met him in 1954 I realized that he was a very good and innovative patent lawyer.

A: *What makes a good patent lawyer?*
OF: He must be able to write an application so that examiner is convinced that this is a good invention. And then the formulation, how to put the idea so to speak, must be good – it needs to be innovative. In the case of the buffering agent, for instance, he did not say that we increased the pH in order to get better absorption, because the improved absorption could be considered a logical consequence of increasing the pH of the saliva. It may not have been considered a new invention. Instead he said that by increasing the pH the taste was more acceptable; that was not in the literature. In fact the taste was much improved by the buffering agent. Like the ion exchange resin the buffer solved two problems.[9]

A: *So a good patent lawyer is a creative thinker?*
OF: And a good writer.

A: *Was the same lawyer involved in writing the patent on the ion exchanger?*
OF: Yes.

A: *How did you meet him?*
OF: I met him – his name was Gordon Hueschen – in 1954, the first time I was in the States. At the time he was running the patent and legal department of the Upjohn Company in Kalamazoo, Michigan. Soon after that he started his own company and became our consultant in patent and legal matters.

A: *We are talking about 8 years of development up to the point where you had the product ready for serious clinical trials?*
OF: Yes, and then it took quite a few more years to get it registered and of course we couldn't sell it until it was registered.

A: *We are jumping ahead a little bit here but in fact the first placebo controlled double blind trial with one year follow-up, which established that the gum works, was in 1982, seven more years after the final 1975 version of the gum was ready.*
OF: Yes, 14 years after we started the project.

This trial was very important in gaining acceptance in the US.

A: *Chewing gum is an unusual product for a pharmaceutical company isn't it? To what extent did your company, Leo, support your research to develop this product?*
OF: As Director of Research and Development for pharmaceutical research and for the medical department I did not need anybody's permission. It was my decision to start the project but when we continued it was important that Håkan Westling at the University Hospital of Lund was interested to do clinical trials, very important.

A: *His interest suggested to the company that it was a worthwhile line of enquiry?*
OF: Yes, although at this stage the company's investment was rather small. The only people working on nicotine gum were myself, Bengt Ohlsson at the pharmaceutical lab, and he had to do other things as well, and one assistant to him. So it was not a dramatic investment. Then things moved on and I got the analytical laboratory interested to help me. But the problem was that chewing gum is not a typical product for a pharmaceutical company. Most people in the company did not realize the potential in this idea at all. But during the development the people working with the project have been very enthusiastic.

The company's attitude

A: *So the company didn't understand the potential of the product and wasn't supportive, but it didn't stop you working on it?*
OF: That's right. As an example of this you could quote the Swedish Pharmaceutical Journal of September 1975, where all the leading Swedish companies presented the research they were conducting. The Leo report makes no mention at all of Nicorette even though I had given them details of the work.

A: *Do you think it was omitted deliberately?*
OF: I think they must have thought that the image of the company's research might have been diminished because it was chewing gum, because it was not a traditional pharmaceutical product. It is remarkable because by then the product was so far advanced. The company president at the time was actually very negative about the gum, but he was due to retire soon. His successor, Per Eric Schyberg, became positive about the nicotine gum project.

A: *What was the attitude of the company's research foundation?*
OF: They were a scientific advisory committee consisting of clinicians and scientists in the medical field and included several university professors. They warned that nicotine gum could be looked upon as unethical by the medical profession, and thus might negatively influence the company's reputation. Otherwise during the development of the gum, the press was neutral or positive, ordinary doctors neutral or positive, some members of NTS (our equivalent of the UK organization ASH) including the manager positive but others were negative. They over emphasized the risk of non-smokers, including children, becoming addicted to nicotine from the gum.

> But the problem was that chewing gum is not a typical product for a pharmaceutical company. Most people in the company did not realize the potential in this idea at all

Michael Russell's involvement

A: *Why did the scientific advisory committee consider the gum might be thought unethical?*
OF: They were worried because of the nicotine, and they had a general concern because it was such an unusual product. But all this changed during the late 1970s, particularly after the publications from Michael Russell and his group.

A: *During the seven years it took you to develop the product into its final form, from 1968 to 1975, did you ever have any doubts about the eventual success of the idea?*

OF: I never had any doubt about the pro-duct but sometimes I doubted if the timing was right.

A: *What do you mean?*
OF: That it might be too early for such a product. Most doctors were not ready to accept it, but I changed my mind after the first results with the buffered nicotine gum.

A: *In 1971 you presented the initial results achieved with the unbuffered gum at the 2nd Second World Conference on Tobacco and Health in London. Were you able to interest anyone in the gum?*
OF: Yes it was the first time nicotine gum was mentioned internationally and there were a few people who were interested. I met some people from ASH (UK) and over the next two years we were contacted by Francis Avery Jones who had been told about the gum by Charles Fletcher. He mentioned that Keith Ball was interested and in 1973 we were also contacted by Walter Fee. Charles Fletcher was quoted in the Sunday Times on 21 January 1973 as saying: 'Nicotine gum is worth looking into but the trouble is that anti-smoking clinics are getting absolutely no help and encouragement from the Department of Health'. I think that Michael Russell tasted the gum then for the first time and then started to do some inve-stigations with it. But he was not particularly im-pressed by the results and it was not until after the 3rd World Conference in New York in 1975 that he really started work with the gum. That was one of the most important things that happened with Nicorette, that Michael Russell and his group started to work with it.

A: *What happened at the 3rd World Conference?*
OF: The chewing gum was ready in its final form. It was the buffered gum with the better absorption, we had succeeded in getting a good taste, so now the product was right for the final development stage – to get registration as a drug. I was invited by Murray Jarvik, together with my colleague Anders Axelsson, to his session on smoking cessation and during the conference Michael Russell developed a definite interest in the product. There were also some other people inter-ested from the United States. So this was really an important meeting for nicotine gum.

A: *In 1975 then, when the buffered gum was ready, did that result in new collaboration with Mike Russell?*
OF: Oh yes. That still continues. The importance of his role in the nicotine gum story as well as in the general field of smoking and smoking cessa-tion cannot be over-emphasized.

A: *Could it be said then that in 1975 you had completed the most important research and devel-opment and had to hand over to the scientists to do the clinical research?*
OF: Yes that is right.

'I believe that your chewing gum represents a major break-through for the treatment of heavy smokers'

A: *Why was Mike Russell's involvement so important?*
OF: Because of his genuine interest in the subject and, I think, the fact that he had the resources – a group of researchers in an addiction research unit – working on smoking cessation. Also, amongst all the researchers it was only Michael Russell and his group – I would like to mention here Colin Feyer-abend, Martin Jarvis and Martin Raw – who had access to blood nicotine determinations. We could do it at the Leo laboratories but did not have such a great capacity. Michael Russell started extensive studies of the absorption of nicotine from the gum and already in 1976 he wrote to me saying: 'I believe that your chewing gum represents a major break-through for the treatment of heavy smokers'. Many important publications came during the following years from the London group but the landmark study was the 1982 publication of a randomized double blind placebo controlled study with long term follow-up and biochemical validation of outcome, the first in the world.[10] Abstinence was 47% in the nicotine gum group compared with 21% in the placebo, which was

gum containing 1 mg of unbuffered nicotine, so it was a fairly stringent test. Important studies were also done by Karl-Olov Fagerström and Agneta Hjaimarsson in Sweden.[11,12] These and some other studies made it possible to register the gum as a drug, including Westling's work. Over the years he treated several thousand smokers at Lund and the results showed that the gum was safe, which was very important in getting registration in different countries. It was registered first in Switzerland in 1978, then in Canada (1979), Great Britain (1980), Sweden (1981), and the USA (1984). By 1993 Nicorette was registered in 56 countries.

A: *Why did it take so long to get the gum registered in Sweden?*

OF: Well the legal situation was rather complicated. Sometimes I even feared that our management, together with Leo's Scientific Advisory Board, which consisted of a number of leading university people as well as clinicians, would stop the project. In 1974 the Swedish Drug Authorities decided that agents acting against the desire to smoke were not drugs. The consequence of this decision was that a chewing gum containing nicotine was classified as a foodstuff, as chewing tobacco and snuff had been for a long time. However if such agents could be proved to cure a disease caused by smoking they could be considered drugs. We regarded that possibility as theoretical only. Next we looked at the possibility of selling the gum to pharmacies or directly to doctors and smoking cessation clinics. In 1975 together with Lars Ramström (the Director of NTS, the equivalent of the British ASH) we organized a meeting of leading figures in the anti-smoking field. The participants emphasized strongly that nicotine gum must be controlled as a prescription drug. In 1977 the Swedish food authorities ruled that nicotine chewing gum should not be regarded as a food.

A: *So now it wasn't a drug or a foodstuff?*

OF: That's right. It was an impossible situation and for us, quite a serious problem. For years we had provided millions of pieces of the gum free to doctors and smoking clinics and as I said earlier, some of these clinics had opened because of the gum. We had to stop giving the gum to these clinics. Then the Tobacco Committee of the Ministry of Social Affairs held a meeting at the Parliament, at which Anders Axelsson and I presented Leo's case. Håkan Westling also wrote to the committee describing his experience with the gum since 1970 with literally thousands of patients and other clinics also sent evidence. This led in 1978 to the gum being classified as a drug. We reapplied for registration and this was granted in 1981.

A: *Is there anything important that needs to be said about clinical trials after 1982?*

OF: Well after that I had more or less left the scene. I retired in 1981 when I was 65 and acted as a consultant for the next two years, working on the nicotine nasal solution.

A: *Did your involvement then finish completely?*

OF: No I still have some contact.

A: *Was NNS – the nasal solution – your idea?*

OF: Yes. It started in 1979 when Michael Russell and I met in Toronto. We discussed the possibility of nicotine absorption through the nose. I did some development work on the idea we published together in 1983.[13]

A: *Is it licensed anywhere yet?*

OF: So far a nicotine nasal spray has been licensed in Iceland, Denmark, Sweden and Britain. By the way, the Leo company is now part of the large Swedish company Pharmacia.

A: *I suppose after 1982 the next stage for the nicotine gum for Leo was getting the product licensed around the world and marketing?*

OF: And the development of other products, yes.

A: *How did the gum come to be called 'Nicorette'?*

OF: The name was suggested by Claes Lundgren. It means roughly, nicotine (Nico) delivered in the right (rette) way.

A: *Who first thought of transdermal nicotine absorption?*

OF: I don't remember exactly but recently I

talked about it to Leo's former head of organic chemistry, Hans Fex (we are good friends and play chess every fortnight). He remembers an evening with Gordon Hueschen (our patent attorney) in 1981 when I asked if a patch with nicotine could be patented. As a matter of fact Claes Lundgren and I had discussed this possibility. But at that time Leo was not interested. If they had been we would have had the first patent on a nicotine patch.

A: *Do you know why?*
OF: I think they thought they had enough to do with the nicotine gum. They were really not interested in the NNS either at that time. I had to fight to make sure it was patented.

A: *Nicotine absorption with the NNS is much quicker than with the gum isn't it, so that it is more like smoking in that respect. Is it possible more people will become addicted to it?*
OF: Perhaps, but there are indications that NNS is particularly helpful for heavy smokers.[14] If they did then have difficulty giving up NNS they could perhaps switch to the gum or the patch for a while. Don't forget that the pharmacokinetics of nicotine absorption are very different from smoking and chewing gum, much slower with the gum. I'm sure this is why it is very easy for most people on the gum to give it up. I think NNS will be licensed in many countries.

I suppose I think of myself as the parent and the gum as a child

A: *In the early years of developing Nicorette did you contact companies around the world to try to interest them in making and selling it in their countries?*
OF: Yes and to get their co-operation with the development, so that they could start trials in their country, increase the information available and speed up the registration procedure.

A: *And were many companies interested?*
OF: We contacted many companies in Europe and the United States but no-one was interested. If someone in a company was interested the management often said no. I remember one executive in a US company saying that stopping smoking was just a question of willpower. We had a long-standing relationship with a large US company called Warner Lambert, who owned one of the world's largest manufacturer of chewing gum, American Chicle. But after a few years on the gum project they lost interest. I think they may have felt that selling a chewing gum containing a poison might have had an adverse effect on their ordinary market. On the whole you could say that interest from pharmaceutical companies was negligible – until, that is, the product was registered in Sweden and the UK.

Looking back

A: *You said that you never doubted the product. Were you convinced in 1970 that nicotine chewing gum would be a global product?*
OF: Yes I was.

A: *And that the gum would work?*
OF: I think that Håkan Westling's early trials were crucial. He never promised smokers it would be a panacea. In the trials there were people who did not do especially well with the gum, but there were also some extraordinary results. By the way, Westling himself was a heavy smoker who was sceptical about his chances of stopping smoking, but stopped smoking with the gum.

A: *Looking back to 12 December 1967, when you got that letter from Claes Lundgren, almost 30 years ago, does anything give you especial satisfaction?*
OF: It has been great fun all the time and very rewarding and interesting. If I had to mention one thing especially it would be the friendship and collaboration with Michael Russell. I think also that one should give credit to the nicotine gum itself.

A: *But it was your idea.*
OF: I suppose I think of myself as the parent and the gum as a child. But I am thinking also of the fact that the nicotine gum has been used in more basic research, so it has been helpful in establishing that nicotine is an addictive drug.

A: *Well, however much credit the gum deserves, you have clearly fought hard at times to keep the work going, often in the face of considerable scepticism. Are you a fighter?*

OF: I like to fight with problems not with people.

A: *You had an idea, struggled to persuade people of its value, saw that proved, and have seen it become a global product which has undoubtedly saved many lives. That must be a very satisfying achievement.*

OF: Yes it is. But in some way I still feel that it is the gum which is, so to speak, a strong child.

A: *You mean that the idea was so strong that once it was articulated it didn't really need much support?*

OF: Something like that.

A: *But you admitted that chewing gum is an unconventional pharmaceutical product. Isn't it more of a classic invention story? A good idea which most people couldn't see at the time?*

OF: Perhaps it was important that I and my colleagues at Leo did not push the idea too hard. We allowed the gum to do its job, so to speak, all the time of course trying to improve it. Also people in the smoking field have slowly but gradually accepted the idea. I think that in some sense the time was right. Psychological methods had been tried for years with only limited success so that the time was right for something new. I think that was borne out by the fact that at about the same time we started to develop nicotine gum, quite independently Michael Russell started his work on nicotine, both following the same line of thinking until, as you know, we met.

A: *Was Nicorette the most important thing you did in your professional life?*

OF: Looking back, yes, think it was.

References

1   FERNÖ, O., FEX, H., HÖGBERG, B., LINDEROT, T., VEIGE, S. & DICZFALUSY, E. (1958) High molecular weight enzyme inhibitors. III. Polyestradiol phosphate, a long-acting estrogen, *Acta Chemica Scandinavica*, **12**, 1675–1689.

2   FERNÖ, O., LICHTNECKERT, S. I. A. & LUNDGREN, C. E. G. (1973) A substitute for tobacco smoking, *Psychopharmacologia*, **31**, 201–204.

3   OHLIN, P. & WESTLING, H. (1971) Nicotine containing chewing gum as a substitute for smoking, in: RICHARDSON, R. D. (Ed.) *The Second World Conference on Smoking and Health* (London, Pitman Medical).

4   BRANTMARK, B., OHUN, P. & WESTLING, H. (1973) Nicotine containing chewing gum as an anti-smoking aid, *Psychopharmacologia*, **31**, 191–200.

5   FEYERABEND, C., LEVITT, T. & RUSSELL, M. A. H. (1975) A rapid gas–liquid chromatographic estimation of nicotine in biological fluids, *Journal of Pharmacy and Pharmacology*, **27**, 434–436.

6   FALKMAN, S. E., BURROWS, I. E., LUNDGREN, R. A. & PAGE, B. F. S. (1975) A modified procedure for the determination of nicotine in blood, *Analyst*, **100**, 100–104.

7   FERNÖ, O. (1977) The development of a chewing gum containing nicotine and some comments on the role played by nicotine in the smoking habit, in: STEINFELD, J., GRIFFITHS, W., BALL, K. & TAYLOR, R. M. (Eds) *Smoking and Health II. Health Consequences, Education, Cessation Activities, and Governmental Action* (US DHEW Publication No. (NIH) 77–1413) pp. 569–573.

8   ELLIS, C. (1907) Masticable Tobacco Preparation. US Patent No. 865,026.

9   FERNÖ, O. & OHLSSON, B. (1974) *Buffered Smoking Substitute Compositions*. US Patent No. 3,845,217, 29 October 1974.

10 JARVIS, M. J., RAW, M., RUSSELL, M. A. H. & FEYERABEND, C. (1982) A randomised controlled trial of nicotine chewing gum, *BMJ*, **285**, 537–540.

11 FAGERSTRÖM, K.-O. (1981) A comparison of psychological and pharmacological treatment in smoking cessation, *Journal of Behavioural Medicine*, **5**, 343–351.

12 HJALMARSSON, A. I. M. (1985) Effects of nicotine chewing gum on smoking cessation

in routine clinical use, *British Journal of Addiction*, **80**, 321–324.

13 RUSSELL, M. A. H., JARVIS, M. I., FEYERABEND, C. & FERNÖ, O. (1983) Nicotine nasal solution: a potential aid to giving up smoking? *BMJ*, **286**, 683–684.

14 SUTHERLAND, G., RUSSELL, M. A. H., STAPLETON, J., FEYERABEND, C. & FERNÖ, O. (1992) Nasal nicotine spray: rapid nicotine delivery system, *Psychopharmacology*, **108**, 512–518.

Commentary
Pillars of Smoke

Robert West

Of the two main schools of thought on history, the 'history is bunk' school and the school that argues that those who fail to learn from the mistakes of history are doomed to repeat them, I tend to follow the latter. Yet even I have to force myself sometimes to look back into the dark recesses of the pre-Medline literature to glean a perspective on where we stand today in my chosen field – smoking. The three interviews in this volume with the three great pillars of the smoking (or more accurately anti-smoking) field are ideal for me in offering a wonderfully incisive short-cut into that perspective without the physical effort of visiting my medical school library.

I have heard Richard Doll speak on a number of occasions and have always found his talks engaging and stimulating, but this interview provides for the reader now and in generations to come a fascinating insight into the life, values and ideas of this great man. Professor Doll is perhaps best known for the discovery with his colleagues of the link between smoking and lung cancer. However, given that Wynder published a similar study at the same time, one might argue that this work was not in itself world-changing. Important, certainly, influential, undoubtedly, but world-changing, possibly not. For my money, it was the next step that made Professor Doll the giant that he has become: the initiation by him and Bradford Hill of the British doctors study. There was so much that was right in the choice of the study and the way that it was carried out. Not least of these, I believe, was the decision, largely for pragmatic reasons to carry it out on doctors. It has been argued that choosing doctors may well have helped to bring about the decline in smoking prevalence in this group and as a result ultimately

in the UK population as a whole. Leaving that aside, however, the study continues to provide vital information about the epidemic of smoking-related diseases and to shape the thinking of everyone working in the field. I have no doubt that it will continue to do so for many decades to come.

Then we have the interview with Charles Fletcher. Professor Fletcher may be best known as the doctor who first injected penicillin into a patient, but, like Professor Doll with the first case-control study on smoking and lung cancer, in some ways that reflected more a case of being the right person in the right place at the right time. The story behind that is fascinating, and equally fascinating to me as someone who spends some time educating medical students is his story about the huge variability that existed in reading chest x-rays of miners looking for signs of pneumoconiosis and how he and his colleagues developed a simple systematic procedure that dramatically improved this area of clinical practice. But if I had to choose one legacy of Professor Fletcher that stands out above all the others, it is his pivotal role in founding the organisation Action on Smoking and Health (ASH). Because of the way this organisation was founded, with its strong foundation in science and clinical practice, to this day it is held in the highest respect by policymakers, clinicians and academics alike. It has been and continues to be truly influential and the present director, Clive Bates, deserves special mention in the way he has carried the organisation forward.

Finally, there is the interview with Ove Fernö. Ove Fernö invented nicotine chewing gum and is the founding father of modern pharmacotherapy for smoking. When one considers the many millions of smokers who have used nicotine products and, more recently, Zyban, to help them stop smoking, surely this makes Ove Fernö one of the most influential figures, not just in the field of smoking, but in public health – not bad for the director of research of a pharmaceutical company. Like the other two interviews, this one is replete with interesting insights. It is fortunate that I was reading this interview alone because any companion would have been regaled every few minutes with a 'did you know . . . ?' Here is one for the afficionado: most of us thought that the reason why it was decided to use chewing gum as a delivery system was because of the poor bioavailability of swallowed nicotine – poor absorption in the gut and most of the absorbed nicotine being metabolised by the liver before it could reach the brain. Not so apparently. It was because of concerns about the toxicity of nicotine and the need for a slow release form which would not be poisonous if swallowed accidentally. In fact nicotine gum was not a big success at first and it was only with some perseverance that a palatable formulation with reasonable nicotine delivery could be found. The work was being undertaken with relatively little interest from the company and it is gratifying to read that Ove Fernö gives credit to the importance of my erstwhile boss, Professor Michael Russell, for giving the project the impetus it needed to make it the success story that it has become. Michael saw the potential of nicotine replacement therapy as a treatment for cigarette dependence and the rest is, as they say, history.

So in these three interviews we see the three main pillars of the smoking cessation field as it is today: Richard Doll provided convincing evidence of the horrific death toll that cigarettes produce and the work that he began will continue to bear fruit for decades to come. Charles Fletcher was pivotal in establishing an organisation that has won the respect of all sections of the policy, clinical and research community and has no doubt hugely influenced the way that the smoking epidemic has been handled. Finally, Ove Fernö founded modern pharmacotherapy for cigarette dependence which has given hope to millions of smokers who have decided to choose a life free of cigarettes over an untimely, miserable death. There are many great men who are great because they have shaped the world not necessarily for the better. If one measures greatness in terms of lives that have been saved and suffering alleviated, it seems to me uncontentious to assert that the three subjects of these interviews have achieved it in full measure.

Part V
British Drug Researchers

Joy Mott

Joy Mott was born in 1933 in Cape Town, South Africa. She gained an MA in psychology from the University of Natal in 1956. She was a Research Officer, Home Office Research Unit (now Research Development and Statistics Directorate), London, 1962–65 and Principal Research Officer from 1966–94. Her professional interests include the links between opiate use and crime, the epidemiology of drug misuse, and the relationship between science and policy in the drugs arena.

Addiction: *Why did you leave South Africa and come to London?*
Joy Mott: I left in 1957 intending to stay in Britain for a year or two, get a research job, broaden my experience, and to do some travelling. My first jobs here included 18 months as a research assistant to a psychiatrist working on depressives' sleeping patterns and then a year as a clinical psychologist at a neurological hospital.

A: *What was your training?*
JM: I did an Arts degree at the University of Natal in Pietermaritzburg and then went on to do a Masters in Psychology. This involved writing a thesis on the effects of different types of rearing environment on rat learning behaviour.

A: *When did you join the Home Office Research Unit?*
JM: I joined in January 1962. The unit had started in 1957 and most of the research was concerned with crime and evaluations of the effectiveness of different types of court sentences. I worked on several studies of juvenile offenders before taking on drugs research. I worked on a study of the operation of the juvenile court in Crawley and, providentially, was working on it at the same time that the heroin outbreak occurred there. I landed the drugs desk in 1967. That was after the Brain Committee (the Interdepartmental Committee on Drug Addiction) had published its second report in November 1965[1] and made recommendations for major changes to the British system for treating heroin and cocaine addicts. My

experience as a clinical psychologist meant that I knew something about drugs – in the late 1950s and early 1960s amphetamines were often prescribed for the treatment of minor depressions.

Getting into drugs research

A: *What was your first drugs project?*
JM: The first drugs project I worked on was a description of drug offenders appearing before the London juvenile courts between 1965 and 1968. The magistrates were concerned about the increasing numbers of drug offenders appearing before them and wanted research to help them in their sentencing decisions. The study found, in terms of three-year reconviction rates, that fines were most effective for first offenders (this was in the days before the police began to use cautioning), and probation for those with previous convictions.

A: *And what then?*
JM: What was then called the Drugs Branch (the department in the Home Office responsible for drug policy) wanted some research on heroin addiction and crime. American research, which was just about all that was available at the time, suggested that crime would increase as the number of heroin users increased. In about 1970 Dr Peter Chapple, one of the few general practitioners who had been willing to treat addicts and who was not one of the over-prescribers identified by the Brain Committee, agreed to cooperate and made his clinical records available. The Research Unit gave him

a grant to employ Marilyn Taylor to extract and analyse the descriptive and clinical material on the patients as well as their criminal records, and between us we wrote the report which was published in the Home Office Research Studies series in 1974.[2] Our main finding was that addict and criminal histories tended to run in parallel. Those who had been criminal before they became addicted continued to be but with the addition of drug offences, while those who started offending only after they became addicted tended to be convicted only of drug offences usually involving heroin.

Some civil servants took quite a long time to see the value of research. Some of them had a bit of difficulty when the answers weren't quite what they expected

---

Bing Spear – a famous Chief Inspector

A: *What was your role at the Home Office?*
JM: A large part of the job was advising the administrative division. You kept them up to date with current research, and answered questions. That developed over the years and to some extent it depended on personal relationships, for example who was there and if they were sympathetic to research. Some civil servants took quite a long time to see the value of research. Some of them had a bit of difficulty when the answers weren't quite what they expected. There was always this balance one had to keep. But for all the time I worked with the Home Office Drugs Branch I found that they were interested, receptive, had ideas, and wanted research done. I always worked very closely with the administrators in the administrative division and obviously with the inspectorate, particularly with Bing Spear who became the Chief Inspector in 1977.

A: *What was your working relationship with Bing Spear?*
JM: We got on well together, we liked each other. He soon got me enthusiastic and interested in the drugs scene. I will always regret not taking up his invitations to join him in his midnight walks around Piccadilly Circus seeing what was going on there in the mid- and late 1960s. Until I came along he had been the only person in the Home Office doing research on drugs, although most of it was in the form of internal reports. He knew more about the British drug scene in the 1960s and 1970s than anyone else and was in touch with many of the London addicts of the time. A while after he retired we collaborated on a paper describing the history of the control of cocaine use in the UK. I successfully nagged him into writing a book on the events of the 1960s and after. We also talked about doing a joint project, after I retired, on the life histories of the surviving 1960s addicts he was still in contact with. He did not finish the book before he died in July 1995 and left me his papers and the draft of the book. There was a dreadful time when the parcel his son sent me containing the computer disks got lost in the post but fortunately he found another set six months later.

A: *You were both in your posts for a long time. That doesn't really happen any more does it?*
JM: The administrators tend to stay in a division for three or four years and they expect to move on. Every three or four years you've got to establish relationships with new administrators and some take a little longer than others to be convinced of the advantages of research. New people, new relationships. Which seems perfectly reasonable. But the Chief Inspector of the Drugs Branch does tend to stay in post for much longer so you have a good relationship with one part of the drugs branch.

The Home Office index as a research tool

A: *Who decided what you would spend your time researching?*
JM: How did it happen? Clearly the high time for new policy development was the 1968 Dangerous Drugs Act which introduced the notification of addicts and licensing of doctors to prescribe heroin and cocaine, and of course the 1971

Misuse of Drugs Act. Those 3–4 years at the end of the 1960s were really very important for policy development. After notification was introduced in 1967, we had the advantage of access to what you might call a relatively unbiased sample. The advent of notification and the Addicts Index gave one the opportunity to draw nationally representative samples. We did a large study to see if addicts who were first notified by hospital Drug Dependence Units were different in any way from those who were first notified by prison medical officers – the difference between what might be called 'criminal addicts' and other sorts of addicts.

A: *And was there?*
JM: There was but not quite what we expected. We drew representative samples of male addicts from the Addicts Index in 1969 and followed them up through the Index. The most noticeable thing was that only 25 per cent of the prison medical officer notifications reappeared in the Addicts Index, compared with 92 per cent from the Drug Dependency Unit sample. I didn't really think we could argue that being in custody at that time in the early 1970s – which provided a period of abstinence from drugs – helped cure people as a result of that experience, so one could only really conclude that prison medical officers and hospital doctors were using different criteria to notify. It looked as though prison medical officers were notifying rather too many cases. You could argue that the setting that prison medical officers work in is not really conducive to diagnosing addiction.

A: *What did you do next?*
JM: After that there was a curious fallow period after the implementation of the Misuse of Drugs Act 1971. I didn't do any drugs research for several years and went back to working on juvenile offending. In the 1970s there was what can only be described as a period of apathy about drugs in the Home Office, to quote Bing Spear. There was the new legislation, the treatment centres had been set up, the view was 'let's see how they work' so we don't really need to do any research. I used to spend quite a lot of time talking to senior members of the Drugs Branch more or less imploring them to let me set up projects, for example, to have another

look at the crime figures. But they didn't see the need for research at that time.

The Hartnoll–Mitcheson study

A: *What other research was going on at the time?*
JM: The most important piece of research that was initiated in the 1970s was the random allocation trial which Richard Hartnoll and Martin Mitcheson did comparing oral methadone with injectable heroin.[3] This was an important question. The drug treatment centres were rapidly ceasing to prescribe heroin. Cocaine prescribing had disappeared much earlier. Doctors were prescribing methadone without seeming to know a great deal about it and they certainly weren't prescribing it in the way you would expect them to, as Vincent Dole was recommending in terms of maintenance. It was a very important study which took a rather long time to be published although it was long known in the field. The findings were also misrepresented – but that's not quite fair – people took from them that which they wanted.

A: *What conclusions did you draw from the study?*
JM: 'You pays your money and you takes your choice.' There was no definite superiority of one form of treatment over another. In terms of treatment of addiction, the study influenced prescribing policy with a move to shorter-term methadone, and with a new interest in treatment contracts. I don't think the idea of contracts derived from that particular study, but it supported that kind of treatment approach. From the Home Office's point of view our concern was about the effect on criminal behaviour. In terms of reducing drug-related crime, at the time heroin was a better bet.

New heroin problems emerge

A: *Around 1979 and 1980 the new heroin problem emerged on the Wirral area in the North West of England. How did you first hear about it in the Home Office?*

JM: The Addicts Index statistics showed that something was happening. But it was in fact the local authority that got in touch with the Home Office, roughly speaking saying 'help us, do something'. They didn't want money for research, and had found a very good researcher in Howard Parker. They wanted support and advice. The Wirral was the first new heroin outbreak that we knew about, Edinburgh was a little bit later. The Wirral outbreak was interesting especially in contrast to the earlier outbreak in Crawley in the mid-1960s. Crawley then was a comfortable new town, with full employment, good schools, good housing and all of a sudden out of the blue a rather large number of mostly boys aged between 14 and 21 were found to be injecting heroin. The heroin epidemic of Crawley had happened in an economic period when people had 'never had it so good'. The boys were living at home, with loving parents and all the rest, and the outbreak should not have happened, so to speak. It seemed to be the least fertile ground for a heroin epidemic, and yet it happened. Fortunately there were two very good researchers there who described this epidemic in considerable detail – Raj Rathod and Richard de Alarcon. This was a landmark study which has stood the test of time.[4] The important thing they did was they looked for the initiators of heroin use, the first users and then followed friendship lines. I happened to be doing research for the Juvenile Court in Crawley at the time on sentencing practice, and so I was able to help. We looked at the young heroin users and at first offenders, and we also had a control group of children attending local schools of the same age and gender. We looked quite hard to see if there was anything different between these three groups. Well, we simply didn't find anything. There was very little difference in terms of adverse social factors or signs of maladjustment between the three groups. Certainly we found no evidence whatever to support the notion that initiators of a new epidemic would be the most maladjusted. If you were asking where was the 'infection' coming from, it was 'carried' from your mates, who were buying heroin in Brighton, which was one of the main sources. But your susceptibility was not because of anything peculiar to do with you. It was

because you went to school with the lad or you were his next door neighbour or you drank with him in the pub.

A: *How did the Wirral compare with Crawley?*
JM: The comparison between Crawley and the Wirral is absolutely fascinating. In the Wirral heroin also followed along friendship networks, but the differences were in the social circumstances: in the Wirral the highest levels of heroin use were found in the most seriously deprived areas. This was a complete contrast socially and economically from what happened in Crawley 15 years earlier.

The heroin epidemic of Crawley had happened in an economic period when people had 'never had it so good'. The boys were living at home, with loving parents and all the rest, and the outbreak should not have happened, so to speak. It seemed to be the least fertile ground for a heroin epidemic, and yet it happened

---

A: *Was this the first time in England that there was a marked link between drug use and deprivation?*
JM: Well it would be, in modern times. The Wirral outbreak was among the same sort of age group as in Crawley, but it was occurring in very adverse social circumstances, that was the big contrast. Similar to Crawley, heroin use was passing along friendship networks. The way I can explain it is to describe it as a sort of 'companionable' use of heroin. There was also the importance of availability. Why did it become available? I think it's merely a matter of chance. Somebody visited, tried it, and said 'it's lovely'.

A: *You could say it's a matter of chance which network heroin gets into. But would you suggest that in the case of more deprived populations in many cities in the UK, something else may be going on?*

JM: Yes indeed – but I'm not terribly sure what. Geoffrey Pearson suggested that using heroin was one way of spending the long workless days. That thieving, scoring and using heroin gave people something to do. But Geoffrey Pearson also pointed out that in the early 1980s there was heroin use on the Wirral/Liverpool side of the Pennines but not so much the Newcastle/ Sunderland side. So there was a geography to it. What was also important was that drugs research was now being done outside London: the problem was outside London and provincial universities were able to meet the challenge.

A: *Did you nurture good researchers?*

JM: Oh yes. At first the Research Unit tended to be reactive to external researchers, to some extent because the current policy issues were fairly obvious. People would telephone and say 'don't you want some research done on X?'. For example, the Home Office was responsible for Approved Schools until the late 1970s and there was always interest in what was happening in them. An important study in the mid-1960s at Kingswood School, in Bristol, compared therapeutic community treatment, which was very fashionable at the time, with the conventional approved school regime. The psychologists, including Ron Clarke, working there had been able to get random allocation between the houses running the different regimes and the Research Unit funded a research worker for the project which I kept an eye on. Over the years the Research Unit became more proactive. After the Rothschild Report was published in 1971 – which recommended that government-funded research should be on a customer–contractor basis – we began to commission projects. So you went out and looked for researchers rather than waiting for them to come to you. If there was somebody who had interesting ideas at the right place and the right time, then yes indeed you nurtured them. I used to worry that we weren't nurturing enough new people because you could only commission someone who had already done some research in the field.

A developing research agenda

A: *What were the issues at the end of the 1980s?*
JM: In 1988 the licensing laws in England and Wales were changed to allow pubs to be open continuously for 12 hours a day on weekdays. For a short time there was a Ministerial Group on Alcohol for which I provided the Home Office research input. The group lasted for, I think, two or three years, published two reports and then faded away. One of my jobs was to write a review of the literature on alcohol and crime, with particular reference to violent crime. There were several research studies that showed that most alcohol-related violent incidents in England and Wales occurred on Friday and Saturday nights after the pubs closed when there would be a crush of young drunken men on the streets outside.

A: *And what else?*
JM: In the latter part of the 1980s there was an interest in community safety and safer cities. This involved setting up demonstration projects within a community using particular policing strategies to see if this would reduce particular kinds of crime – household burglaries, for example. In the drugs field this meant mobilizing local authority departments and voluntary bodies – all of whom had a small piece of the field. The question was whether it would be possible to produce a prevention strategy without spending any new money, just by getting better coordination. The Home Office funded a project by the National Association for the Care and Resettlement of Offenders – which was supervised by Roger Howard for a time – in Bristol and in Birmingham. They tried to get every voluntary or statutory organization which had any involvement with drugs to develop a coordinated strategy depending on local needs. This was a fore-runner of the Drug Prevention Initiative. The main lesson from that is that with all the good will in the world, at a time of cuts in local authority budgets, you simply needed money. There was no way of persuading hardpressed social workers to do anything more than their job description required unless you employed some more people. Valiant efforts were made and some very interesting things were done on a shoestring. One of the

interesting things that people did in Birmingham was to print drug prevention leaflets in several Asian languages: that hadn't been done before. Other things included ways of getting young people off the street to do things that they were interested in doing, such as music workshops and dancing. But in order to do that, you had to find somewhere to do it, you had to find the equipment, you had to find someone to help them and that was voluntary effort, you couldn't really pay for it. So this project provided a blueprint and highlighted the problems in getting all the local agencies to coordinate and work together and the whole notion of partnership.

A: *When did the Drug Prevention Initiative start and did it incorporate evaluation?*
JM: It started in 1989 and was quite separate from the Research Unit. It had a pretty large research budget and its own research manager. The DPI took off in a big way because there was political will and enough money.

A: *Was that the first Home Office drugs project to incorporate evaluation?*
JM: No. You always had problems about evaluative research with new projects; do you allow them settling-in time, always describing the problems of settling in, that is also a part of research and evaluation. The workers sometimes get a bit unhappy about that. But we have to point out that was important for other people to learn the difficulties.

A: *And after that?*
JM: Then in the 1990s it was back to looking at drugs and crime particularly trying to estimate the amount of crime that heroin users might be responsible for. And, of course, there was cocaine. The Research Unit funded a large study to look at the prevalence and pattern of cocaine and crack use and a study in Nottingham comparing cocaine users in 1989/90 and 1991/92. Also, I wrote a chapter on the history of notification of addicts for the book on the British system edited by John Strang and Michael Gossop which is now of historical interest.[5]

What place for national surveys?

A: *What is your view on national surveys of drug use?*
JM: There was a long debate about national surveys of self reported drug use, which I was opposed to for good reasons. I have always stressed the importance of local studies. There is such variation in terms of patterns of drug use, drugs used, and attitudes to drug use which you lose no matter how big your sample is if you do a national survey. Not that a national survey isn't useful as a benchmark of course. But you can't have just one or the other, you need both. A question on cannabis use was put in to the first British Crime Survey which was carried out in 1982. And then there was a question in the 1984 British Crime Survey, and then not again until the 1992 British Crime Survey. During this period the surveys were getting more and more sophisticated and the size of the samples was increasing. Now British Crime Surveys are conducted every two years. There were lots of earlier surveys of different populations, which I reviewed in the *Bulletin on Narcotics* in 1976.

A: *I was surprised in that paper to see the levels of drug use reported among university students: 50% of first-year social science students reported having used cannabis.*
JM: Don't forget that's late 1960s sociology departments.

A: *Are you now an avid supporter of national population surveys?*
JM: Well, not an avid supporter, I simply think you need both. If I had to make the choice, I would spend money on a series of local surveys using the same methodology. In fact the first project which was commissioned by the Central Drugs Prevention Unit was just such a study, the Four Cities Survey.

A: *Surveys count drug users, but are rarely sensitive enough to identify drug problems. Does that distort political thinking?*
JM: Well, political thinking is always seized by

the number-crunching, about the question 'how many are there?' There is also the notion that changes in prevalence are a measure of the effectiveness of policy. There was a long debate about national surveys of self-reported drug use, which I was opposed to for good reasons. I have always stressed the importance of local studies.

> There was a long debate about national surveys of self-reported drug use, which I was opposed to for good reasons. I have always stressed the importance of local studies

---

Britain's national drug strategy

A: *How did policy develop in your time?*
JM: *Tackling Drug Misuse* was the first strategy document. It was produced in 1985 by the Ministerial Group on Drug Misuse which was set up by David Mellor. It focused on reducing supplies, improving enforcement, improving treatment, and prevention.

A: *Was the ministerial group important?*
JM: Well, yes, because there are so many different government departments involved. The Home Office is the lead department because of the Misuse of Drugs Act; then there is the Department of Health, the Department of Education, the Department of Employment, the Foreign and Commonwealth Office, the Department of Transport for drugs and driving – to name but six. Rather fewer than are involved in alcohol problems. Its always much easier to coordinate policy when everyone's sitting around a table at regular meetings. So that was the first national strategy. I remember being at a meeting of the Advisory Council on the Misuse of Drugs (ACMD), and the view being put that ACMD had been sidelined. Others felt that we should be grateful that someone was doing something – or words to that effect.

A: *You were very familiar with the workings of ACMD?*

JM: My role there was, so to speak, the Home Office research handmaiden, in the sense of informing Council of current social research and doing literature reviews if required.

A: *How effective was ACMD?*
JM: Dear oh dear, you can't expect me to answer questions like that. I think it took a long time in the 1970s to feel its way and to become influential in the field. Certainly the report on Treatment and Rehabilitation published in 1982 was extremely important, as was the report on Prevention. The three reports on AIDS were enormously influential. I think there's always a regret at the Advisory Council that it didn't have its own research budget. It could only advise on research and every report always had its chapter on further research. But nobody was going to give it the funds to commission research, which I'm sure successive chairman would have liked to have done. Until 1979 there was a tradition in the Home Office of having advisory bodies; there was an advisory council on the penal system, which meant getting an academic input into policy development. During the 18 years of Tory government these committees disappeared but the ACMD didn't. It is a statutory body, part of the Misuse of Drugs Act, so they couldn't abolish it without changing the legislation. They would have if they could, I have no doubt about that, but they couldn't. It always, in my experience, had pretty good people on it, some very long-serving, which is good evidence of lack of political interference in the appointments. Where does it go from now? Well I don't see any prospect of changing the legislation, so it must still exist. And there are surely enough issues to look at in this thoughtful way. It's a very English thing in that it is advisory, with its authority coming from the carefulness of its work rather than coming from money or political patronage. There's frequent talk about wanting to set up a Royal Commission into drugs, but part of the answer is that you've got an advisory council.

A: *Part of 'new policy' was the abolition in 1997 of that great British institution, the Addicts Index. What did you make of that?*

JM: I was sorry it went, not least because a version of it had been running since 1934. The practice for entering someone in the Index changed over the years, with the major change in 1968 when doctors had a statutory duty to notify their addict patients. The statistics produced from the Index were criticized because not all doctors notified all the patients they should have, and because they were only required to notify people addicted to one or other of 14 drugs including heroin and cocaine, the drugs that caused the most concern. Measures of treatment demand are obviously needed for developing services and the addict statistics were not able to totally fulfil that role because they related only to a small portion of the drug-using population. That was the reason the Department of Health set up the Drug Misuse Databases.

A: *Does the way the Index was closed exemplify some of the problems that existed of trying to organize information across government departments?*
JM: Well, I suppose in practical terms you had two very similar systems running at the same time, although one is more comprehensive. So why not save some money by closing one. It is a pity that it's disappeared because I'm not convinced that the Regional Drug Misuse Databases can totally take its place. I'm not entirely sure that all the agencies report and do so properly. It seems to me that a lot more work needs to be done in ensuring comparability of the data collected. And as for the issue of anonymity, I understand the arguments for this being not to frighten clients, but it does restrict their usefulness for research. You cannot use the databases for follow-up studies, because you can't link names. Also the statistics produced are difficult to understand. You've not got double counting within agencies but you've got double counting between agencies. That is a measure of treatment demand, I agree, but it makes for difficulties of interpretation. It seems to me that an extremely important source of information has been lost. The Addicts Index was limited to a number of drugs, but nevertheless it was an extremely useful research resource. Anybody who was doing a follow-up study of patients or epidemiology went to the Index.

The funding of research

A: *What is your view on drugs research funding policy in the UK? Has there ever been a strategic plan for drugs research?*
JM: Numerous plans have been drawn up, but the problem was one of implementation. The last attempt that I know of was in 1990, after the world drug summit on cocaine. There was also a United Nations special session, and there was almost a requirement that all member states should set up research programmes, not specifically with reference to cocaine but that was the stir. So I and Liza Catan at the Department of Health produced a drugs research agenda, but this ran into the ground. One of the problems – which I hope has now been solved – is that it was really easier *not* to get a big research programme off the ground because of the question of which departments are going to pay. That response was used to avoid doing anything. The different departments approached their research agendas rather differently. The Home Office had its in-house research unit which used resources which the Home Office had, such as the Addicts Index because we had direct access to that, and of course the statistics on drug offences and criminal statistics generally. So it seemed sensible for the Home Office Research Unit at the time (in effect me – there was never more than me and a research assistant from time to time) to use the resources that were on the doorstep and only to fund projects which we couldn't do.

A: *Demarcation disputes?*
JM: There were demarcation disputes between government departments. Obviously the Home Office could not fund research into treatment. I was anxious to do something on treatment, because I wanted to know what effect being in treatment had on addicts' criminal behaviours. I argued that as crime was the major emphasis that would not upset the Department of Health. Then there is the question of epidemiology: that seemed to belong to the Department of Health but it ended up with the Home Office putting questions on drug misuse into the British Crime Survey, because that seemed to be the only way one was going to

be able to get that sort of study off the ground. We lacked a US-style National Institute on Drug Abuse, or some organization whose exclusive job was to organize government-funded drug research.

A: *Do we need a drugs research strategy in the UK and do we need a single funded stream for research?*

JM: Yes, if having a strategy means that there are funds pay for it. The new UK Anti-Drugs Coordinator has a research programme and has the funds to pay for it. In that sense centralization is no bad thing, the key is to have funds. But I am also a great believer in spreading the research effort widely through as many universities and research organizations around the country as possible. I am sure that the research should not be too highly centralized in London. The drugs problems are different in different parts of the country and I think it's very important to have local researchers working in local areas on local problems. That is one thing I'm absolutely certain of.

A: *What have you been doing since you retired: have you continued working on drugs?*

JM: Yes, and on alcohol as well. I was the researcher and report writer for a Mental Health Foundation expert working group on persistent street drinkers, which published its report as *Too Many For The Road* in 1996. Then, in 1997, the Police Foundation set up an independent inquiry into the Misuse of Drugs Act 1971 under the chairmanship of Ruth Runciman and I was offered the job as research secretary. The inquiry looked at the effectiveness of the law and its implementation, and assessing options for change.

A: *Based on your experience, what do you think drives a department's drug research agenda?*

JM: The political and social issues of the day drive the research agenda. After the flurry of demand for research in the late 1960s, there was not much interest again until the early 1980s in spite of some valiant attempts by the ESRC to stimulate it. It took AIDS and the evidence of the amount of crime committed by the increasing number of heroin users to put drugs back on the political agenda.

We lacked a US-style National Institute on Drug Abuse, or some organization whose exclusive job was to organize government-funded drug research

---

References

1.   MINISTRY OF HEALTH AND SCOTTISH HOME AND HEALTH DEPARTMENT (1965) *Drug Addiction. The second report of the Interdepartmental Committee* (London, HMSO).
2.   MOTT, J. & TAYLOR, M. (1974) *Delinquency Amongst Opiate Users*, Home Office Research Study No. 23 (London, HMSO).
3.   HARTNOLL, R., MITCHESON, M., BATTERSBY, A., BROWN, G., ELLIS, M., FLEMING, P. & HEDLEY, N. (1980) Evaluation of heroin maintenance in controlled trial, *Archives of General Psychiatry*, **37**, 877–884.
4.   RATHOD, N. H. (1972) The use of heroin and methadone by injection in a New Town, *British Journal of Addiction*, **67**, 113–121.
5.   MOTT, J. (1994) Notification and the Home Office, in: STRANG, J. & GOSSOP, M. (Eds) *Heroin Addiction and Drug Policy: the British System*, pp. 270–291 (Oxford, Oxford University Press).

Thomas Bewley

Thomas Bewley MA MD MD (Hon) FRCP FRCPsych FRCPsych (Hon) was educated at St Columba's and Trinity Colleges, Dublin. He was a Consultant Adviser on Drug Dependence to the Department of Health, London, from 1972–81, a Member of the Standing Advisory Committee on Drug Dependence and Advisory Council on Misuse of Drugs, 1966–84, President, the Royal College of Psychiatrists, 1984–87 (and Dean from 1977–82), a Member of the General Medical Council (Screener for Health) from 1989–96 and a Consultant Psychiatrist at St Thomas, St George's and Tooting Bec Hospitals, London, from 1961–88. His professional interests are in alcohol, tobacco and other drugs.

An Irish Quaker background

Addiction: *You came from an Irish Quaker background with a strong medical tradition?*
Thomas Bewley: Yes. My grandfather and my father were both physicians and they both looked after a small Quaker mental hospital. My grandfather, when he was 78, wrote a paper called, if I remember correctly, 'The cardiazol treatment of dementia praecox'.[1] I had a large number of relatives who were doctors, and I knew that if I didn't think of anything else I would end up as a doctor.

A: *Is there a strong Quaker presence in Ireland?*
THB: There are a few Quakers, not very many, but they have had an impact beyond their number. They have been there for a long time. There are now about a couple of thousand altogether. They are all interrelated and no Quaker is much further than a second cousin from any other. They were in such things as banking, making biscuits and milling. My family set up the well known Bewley cafes in the last century. Although the Quakers have become wealthy they have always been well thought of. They are seen as a concerned group who want to do their best for other people. They gave much practical help at the time of the Famine.

Professional training

A: *Where did you receive your medical education?*

THB: At Trinity College in Dublin. It was a very pleasant time. I was there from 1944 to 1950. At that time the University and Medical School were small and students were involved with all disciplines. One's general education was the better for that, and at that time we all had to take an Arts degree as well. I studied English, French, Mechanics, Logic and Ethics. The medical education was essentially a training to be a general practitioner. There was no research, and the teaching was didactic. One went to lectures and passed the necessary exams, and then at the clinical stage one learnt most of one's medicine. Medical students lived in the hospital during the two clinical years, and those students were doing what would be done by pre-registration house staff (interns) today. I enjoyed those years very much. I made two films, and had been the university's chess champion, and did not overdo my medical studies until I qualified.

A: *You qualified in 1950 at the age of 23–24. What next?*
THB: At the end of my time in house jobs in surgery and medicine I went to see Norman Moore for advice about possibly taking up psychiatry. He said to go over to England, take the London Membership (the equivalent of Boards in Medicine), and then come back and see him. If I had done this I might have been a dermatologist today. Chance is very important in medical careers, including mine, since three weeks later I received a letter from him saying 'you have been appointed a Senior House Officer (SHO) in Psychiatry at St

Patrick's, can you start on such and such a date?'. I was then at St Patrick's in Dublin for 2 years where I had my basic psychiatric training.

A: *Can you tell me something about St Patrick's?*
THB: It was Swift's hospital, founded over 200 years earlier. It had changed markedly over time from being a hospital for the poor to becoming a quiet private mental hospital with few patients, mostly the aristocracy. It then became a very active unit after Norman Moore came back to Dublin at the end of the war. It was the teaching hospital for Trinity. It was also a referral centre to which people came from all around Ireland, mostly private patients at first, but there were many other patients at the hospital later who were the equivalent of NHS patients. In the 1950s it was *the* place in Ireland in psychiatry. Norman Moore himself had taken up psychiatry following tuberculosis. He trained at the Crichton Royal where he worked with Meyer Gross and Erwin Stengel. Then he became the Director at St Patrick's, and passed his approach to psychiatry on to me. (This was the school of Adolph Meyer, who had guided Meyer Gross.)

A: *Was that a good place to learn psychiatry?*
THB: Yes. I learnt much which has stood me in good stead. First of all to be thorough and work briskly, secondly always to take a proper history, including a history from others as well as the patient. Thirdly always to do a physical examination, remembering that psychiatry is a branch of medicine. I learnt good habits and the basic drills. After 2 years I realized I might begin to drift, so I thought I had better get further and different experience, and that was when I came to England.

A: *To the Maida Vale hospital in North London?*
THB: Yes, that's right. I did a neurology course for 3 months as I had learned little in Ireland, and then looked again for jobs in psychiatry but failed to get into the Maudsley at that time, so went to Claybury and then to St Clements, and then reapplied successfully for a post at the Maudsley.

A: *What are your recollections of the Maudsley at that period? Was it, as some may say, a great*

training school and an immensely inspiring experience, or was it as others suggest, a work camp dominated by the evil influence of intellectualism?
THB: It was a mixture of both. It was good for status in the sense that everyone liked to have been to the Maudsley, but I went on to the States after being there for a year because I thought one year there or five would not make a huge amount of difference. I did not know whether I would end up in the United States, in England, or back in Dublin. I had put together a rotational training programme for myself. St Patrick's was an acute unit, then at Claybury I worked on the back wards, as I had no experience of chronic psychiatric illness, then at the Maudsley (acute psychiatry again) and finally I went to a psychoanalytically orientated unit in the United States for a year in Cincinnati. But I had learnt a lot at the Maudsley. When you arrived you were given a note which said 'you will discover that many people say diametrically opposed things here, but you are old enough now to be able to make up your own mind about who is talking sense', or words to that effect.

I learnt much which has stood me in good stead. First of all to be thorough and work briskly

A: *One of the senior people there when you arrived was presumably D. L. Davies?*
THB: Yes, though I got to know him rather better later, not at that time. The same with Aubrey Lewis, whom I saw infrequently, until much later. I worked with Felix Post, and at St Francis.

A: *Did your self-designed rotational training offer anything to do with alcohol and drugs?*
THB: At St Patrick's there was an active programme for treating alcoholics, and Richard P. who was the first member of AA in the British Isles worked there at that time. The treatments were modelled on an AA approach but with everyone getting disulfiram. That was a time when most doctors didn't want to have anything to do with alcohol problems, so I think I am probably the

only person alive in this country who was treating alcoholics before Max Glatt.

A: *You arrived at Tooting Bec Hospital in 1960. Could you, for those who don't know that hospital, give us a sketch of what images the phrase 'Tooting Bec' is likely to conjure up?*

THB: Tooting Bec was indeed a very odd hospital. I became a consultant there by accident in the sense that I had unsuccessfully applied for jobs at Warlingham, Springfield and Claybury before finally getting a post at Tooting Bec. I knew a bit about this hospital because when I had worked at St Clement's and St Francis I discovered that they had a unit for acutely disturbed patients. When it was impossible to find a bed for a patient anywhere else, one always rang up Dr Lloyd at Tooting, and he said 'send him round tomorrow'. It was the old LCC (London County Council) senile dementia hospital. In 1960 there were 2100 patients, nearly all elderly or with very chronic illnesses. In order to maintain a nursing school they had to admit some acute patients as well. In the time I was there the numbers went down from 2100 to a few hundred, and the hospital finally closed this year (mid-1995). It was a totally atypical hospital in that it had no catchment area. It had, as Physician-Superintendent, the only psychiatrist I have ever met who was as intelligent as Aubrey Lewis. Before the age of 35 he had his MD, his MRCP, his DPM and was also a barrister. Before the war he had been the youngest Superintendent ever of an LCC hospital. I reckoned that he earned more money for less work than anyone I have ever met. I learnt practical things from him such as 'when you are writing to the Regional Board, if there are two points you want to make, always write two letters. If you send two points in one letter they will respond to the easy one and ignore the other'.

A: *That Medical Superintendent was J.E.S. Lloyd?*

THB: He was J.E.S. Lloyd, John Lloyd, and a strange man. When I arrived he gave me the flavour of the hospital. 'Bewley,' he said, 'I am glad to see you are a proper doctor. The only other proper doctors here are Dr Cooper (the Chaplain),

myself and Dr Zed, who is a patient.' 'The rest' he added, 'mere courtesy titles.' He also told me that 'any wood on the Estate' was one of the doctors' perks. This sounded odd to someone becoming a consultant at a psychiatric unit in the middle of London.

A: *We need to pause at this point and to try to understand what would have been the interim judgement if one had looked at your career at this juncture. One might have said, here is a young man who has shown considerable initiative in exposing himself to different types of psychiatry. To have gone off and worked in America in an analytically orientated hospital would certainly have seemed bold in those days. You had grown up and gone to university in Ireland, you had made a ready transition to the British medical system, you had got your doctorate by thesis. But then people might also have said, well, what a very curious thing to do, he is not building on this experience and going to some great clinical or research centre, he is not going to somewhere which will obviously stretch his mind, he has taken a post in a hospital which is kindly and generously caring for highly disadvantaged people, but it sounds as if this young man's career has in a careerist sense taken a wrong turning.*

THB: I didn't see it that way. If a position had come up in Dublin at that time I might have returned to Ireland and remained there for the rest of my life. If I had been able to get a post at a London teaching hospital I would have preferred that, but such posts were very few. I hadn't been at the Maudsley long enough to look there. At that time I was uncertain about my career, but had many options between the United States, London or Dublin. I also had a view that once you became a consultant you could more or less arrange your work any way you liked, which at that time was true. In those days I was not obviously academic.

The birth of the British heroin problem

A: *Having arrived at Tooting in 1960 and become a consultant there in 1961, from that base you wrote a letter to the* Lancet *in 1964 entitled*

'Opiate addiction'[2] *followed by an article recommending changes in treatment policies.*[3] *Within a few years you had published the first of several papers on the development of a small drug epidemic,*[4] *which was at the start a shadow no bigger than a man's hand. You seem to have had a research opportunity, and seized it.*

THB: It was partly accidental. Tooting Bec was the most central mental hospital which accepted patients from anywhere in London. In the 1960s I used to admit alcoholics of no fixed abode, and we had an alcoholism programme. One of my registrars described it as patients coming in for their 1000 gallon check-up. Patients were admitted with multiple problems. We detoxified them, saw to their physical health, gave them disulfiram, introduced them to AA, and encouraged them to go out to work from the hospital. A small number of heroin addicts were also admitted as no one else wanted to have much to do with them at that time. When I first wrote to the Lancet I think I had seen about 20. I don't think any one else in the country had seen more than two then. This was how I became an 'expert'. I knew little, but everyone else knew less. I was interested and thought about it, and that was why I continued to write.[5]

A: *Who were these 20 heroin addicts?*
THB: Most of them were people who had been getting prescriptions for heroin and cocaine from Lady Frankau (a private practitioner in Harley Street). Others got their drugs from Lady Frankau's patients. A mixture of people. Some were Canadians who had come over to London after hearing about Lady Frankau who went on a lecture tour in North America.[6,7] There were probably about 3 to 1, men to women, they were all young, and were all non-therapeutic addicts. The group were different from the standard, traditional doctor or pharmacist addict, or those treated for chronic pain who had then become dependent on an opiate. In retrospect it is an obvious point, but I was the first person to make it. Subsequently I was asked to give evidence to the second Brain Committee. In order to make my viewpoints clear I decided to write a short memorandum, which I published as an article in the Lancet.[3] When the Committee brought out their

report[8] the recommendations were those in my article.

A: *What were those recommendations?*
THB: That there should be notification; that there should be controls on prescribing; that there should be specialized treatment centres; and that there should be an Advisory Committee to keep drug addiction under review. The first Brain report[9] had totally misunderstood the problem as was pointed out immediately by a retail pharmacist.[10] (This may have been why Lord Brain insisted on very narrow terms of reference for the second Report[8].)

A small number of heroin addicts were also admitted as no one else wanted to have much to do with them at that time. When I first wrote to the *Lancet* I think I had seen about 20. I don't think any one else in the country had seen more than two

---

A: *So these early addicts you were seeing were using heroin . . . ?*
THB: Nearly all of them were using large amounts of both heroin and cocaine, on prescription, or from their friends. Some were on huge doses. There was one man who was on 1000 milligrams of pure heroin a day. I wondered if he was using it all, so I asked him to inject himself intravenously with 250 mg and he didn't bat an eyelid, he had a high tolerance.

A: *Was smoking heroin known at all?*
THB: I hadn't heard of it at all in the 1960s.

A: *So you saw a small number of addicts and you immediately gave evidence to the Brain Committee, your recommendations seem to have been the planks of the new British policy.*
THB: Yes. What happened next was that Sir George Godber, the Chief Medical Officer at the Ministry of Health, asked the teaching hospitals to

take on the treatment of heroin addiction. They all said 'We can't do that, we know nothing about it'. His reply was that since they were so much more clever than other psychiatrists, they must be the best group to do it. They could hardly disagree with this, so they said 'We haven't got the money'. He then gave them the money. At that stage they found they had been hoist with their own petards and had to open units. I was then asked by the South West Thames Regional Hospital Board to take a couple of consultant sessions at St George's, St Thomas's, the Westminster and Tooting Bee Hospitals. This was not feasible and I agreed to St George's and St Thomas's with an inpatient unit at Tooting Bec. I was given a completely refurbished ward to be used for addicts. I still continued in part to be a general psychiatrist, but was now in charge of a drug dependence service.

A: *What year?*
THB: The first planning meetings with psychiatrists were held in 1966, but there were many delays and the plans were only implemented in 1968. At the same time the Regional Hospital Board decided they would not have a proposed alcoholism unit at Tooting but would develop one at West Park instead, so that Tooting Bec could concentrate on drug dependence. It was the largest inpatient unit for drug dependence the country.

I prescribed both heroin and cocaine at first

A: *How many patients had you got there?*
THB: I had 30 beds, 15 for men and 15 for women. It was a big double ward with plenty of space. The women's beds were never full, so we usually had about 20 patients.

Prescribing heroin and cocaine

A: *How did you treat these patients? Was it modelled on your ideas on how to treat people with drinking problems?*
THB: Yes, in one way it was. I considered that addiction was a chronic relapsing disorder and

that, as in treating alcoholism, much would be symptomatic, dealing with complications and providing care for those who failed to recover. There was a tendency at that time to hope that you would get everybody better and the problems would all go away. I took the view that initially what we would be doing would be sympathy, detoxification and encouraging patients to get back to work again. The Department of Health's policy was that from a certain day all private practitioners would cease to be able to prescribe, not having been given licences to prescribe heroin to addicts. Licences were only issued to consultants at NHS hospitals or doctors working with them. On the appointed day (notification regulations came into force on 22 February 1968 and prescribing regulations on 16 April 1968) one wrote a prescription for what a person said he was getting. We took over all those having heroin and cocaine prescribed. Later there was a move to using methadone.

A: *You were involved in prescribing heroin?*
THB: Yes. I prescribed both heroin and cocaine at first. I took the view that one would have to find out what was best. About this time I had been given a WHO Fellowship to visit the United States and Canada. In six weeks I visited 10 cities and 40 centres. I wrote an account of that trip for WHO, who told me it was one of the best they had from a Fellow and could they publish it, which they did.[11] That report reviewed the range of available approaches: detoxification, religious exhortation, the methadone programme, the use of narcotic antagonists, community programmes and so on. I thought we should change over to methadone by a process of gradual evolution. Vincent Dole was the most intelligent and rational person I had met on my trip and I thought he had shown clearly the value of a long-acting opiate. Jerome Jaffe worked with him at that time.

A: *When you first got into treating heroin users in a big way, you were prescribing heroin and cocaine and acting in the tradition of British doctors as had evolved from the 1920s, rather than at that moment going in the American direction of methadone?*

THB: Yes, but we didn't go on prescribing cocaine for any length of time. We had taken over a lot of addict patients from private and other general practitioners, and the first thing to do was take a history and find out what it was all about, and then try and tidy up the prescribing. I would not have been happy to continue prescribing without thinking about what was the most rational way to do it.

A: *Can you tell us what safeguards you had in place so that half the heroin you gave would not be sold down the road?*
THB: At first there were no safeguards. The situation was chaotic, and almost certainly everyone was selling about one-third of the drugs that were prescribed for them. There was no source of heroin for new addicts at that time except for pharmaceutical heroin prescribed for other addicts. It seemed common sense to reduce the amounts prescribed, but there was no way of knowing what was the 'needed dose', apart from seeing how much tolerance the person had. That is why some were asked to inject themselves in order to find out their degree of tolerance.

A: *They picked up the heroin from a community pharmacist?*
THB: They picked it up from a retail chemist. We changed the dispensing arrangements so that everybody had to pick up a daily supply rather than for a month, which introduced a further degree of control.

A: *But a dose of 100 mg, 200 mg or 300 mg of pure heroin would not be an exception?*
THB: That would be on the high side as a single dose. The highest dose I came across was something around 1000 mg daily. Vincent Dole considered that 120 mg of methadone a day was a reasonable dose. If someone was on more heroin than that I would be tending to bring the dose down and also gradually change from heroin to methadone milligram for milligram. Initially I prescribed injectable methadone and only later moved to oral methadone in liquid form (methadone mixture 1 mg/1 ml).

A: *You describe the situation as chaos at that time. Was it the right first aid policy, or do you think that Britain walked into unnecessary chaos?*
THB: No, I don't think it could have come out very differently. The only alternative would have been to have done nothing as there was no one with any experience of these problems. It was probably better to get on with it and learn by trial and error.

A: *The purpose of this policy was to benefit the patient, or was it seen as a way of undercutting the black market? Was policy being influenced by fear of the Mafia?*
THB: Both considerations were there. There was a belief that if you gave addicts large amounts of heroin on demand the problem would go away. There was also a fear that if controls were too stringent it might lead to the development of an illicit traffic.[8] There was much heat, but not much light. I considered that one purpose of specialized units was to try to make the use of drugs rather more boring, the response being more clinically orientated with doctors quietly getting on with treatment as they would with any other condition.

There was a belief that if you gave addicts large amounts of heroin on demand the problem would go away

A: *Was it possible in these circumstances to get to know the young drug addicts that came your way?*
THB: Oh yes, they were all well known. Unless somebody came solely to be detoxified you would see people regularly. One of the things I discovered, which hadn't been thought out before, was that the doctor–patient relationship was totally different from any other variation of the relationship that I had ever come across. A patient would want to get a lot of drugs in order to feel different, and possibly to sell some. This is not the usual reason for seeing a doctor. Each doctor had to be careful and think out exactly what the relationship was going to be. It would be easy to get it wrong; either to be totally soft-headed by giving the patient everything they wanted (as was done by

some early private practitioners), or to go the other way and take a punitive approach by rapidly reducing the amounts to nothing. The idea that simply to write a prescription constitutes 'treatment', is a limited view anyway.

A: *What was 'treatment'?*
THB: Treatment was seeing in what way a patient was not functioning and then trying to help them function better, avoid overdoses, avoid getting abscesses and, when appropriate, come off all drugs. Another aspect of treatment was giving syringes to people and educating them in how to inject safely. I had done a small study with a registrar[5] by asking 50 people 'How do you inject yourself?' We found that none injected in a clean manner. All shared dirty equipment. Harm reduction was part of what we were doing.

A: *And that was so in those early days?*
THB: From the very early days. From the 1960s.

A: *How long would you spend with a patient?*
THB: I always took the view as a psychiatrist that when you saw somebody for the first time it was impossible to assess them without having at least a couple of hours. Two hours was set aside to assess new patients. If they turned up late we would give them another appointment with adequate time to assess them.

A: *And you had a social worker in the clinic?*
THB: Yes: we worked as a team with a social worker and a nurse in the unit who advised patients about such things as self-injection.

The decision to stop prescribing heroin

A: *Did anyone come off drugs?*
THB: Oh, yes. A certain number of people came off. If, for example, a woman was pregnant she generally would want to stop, although many restarted after their baby was born. Others would want to get off, would come off and stay off.

A: *Was it a pleasant or unpleasant situation for a doctor trained in the usual traditions of medi-*

cine and psychiatry to find himself giving out heroin and cocaine, knowing that one-third of the dosage was sold down the road, responding to a political imperative and operating in conditions of chaos?
THB: What was interesting was that it was something new. There is no doubt that getting involved in problems of drug dependence gave me a lot to think about. I was younger then. I was much involved with planning, travel, meeting experts, and it was all great fun in a way. It led to work for the WHO and to becoming Consultant Adviser on Drug Dependence to the Department of Health and Social Security.

A: *When did you stop prescribing heroin? Did that peter out, or was there a sudden decision?*
THB: It was gradual. I started changing people on to methadone. In phase one I got everyone fairly rapidly off stimulants, because I could see no rationale for that. I then changed patients over to injectable methadone (and later to oral methadone) and gradually reduced the dosage. I did not take any patient off if they did not wish me to.

A: *So by 1980 would you have been prescribing any injectable drugs?*
THB: By 1980 almost certainly not.

A: *Why did you give up prescribing injectable drugs?*
THB: It was partly because my colleagues in other units were doing so. It would have been quite difficult for one consultant to prescribe in a markedly different way to the other units. A trial was needed comparing methadone with heroin which was carried out by Martin Mitcheson and Richard Hartnoll.[12]Some policies evolved through regular meetings of consultants treating addicts. They met once every month or two, to exchange ideas, initially at the Department of Health and later at the Home Office.

A: *A group of London consultants?*
THB: Yes, initially this was a London problem and was not a major problem elsewhere. Between us we decided we would move in a certain direc-

tion. There was also some pressure from Dr Alex Baker of the Department of Health, who appeared to believe that rapid total abstinence should be the only goal.

A: *Was it that oral methadone was such better technology for treatment so that everyone in time began to use it?*
THB: Injectable heroin could give a high and a withdrawal three times a day. With oral methadone, the patient was neither high nor getting withdrawal symptoms, and those were important differences.

A: *Some people believe that once upon a time there was a national treasure called the British System deriving from the Rolleston Committee, where British doctors prescribed injectable heroin and all was well. Then this sensible policy was wiped out by political interference. The call is that the golden age needs to be rediscovered and we should once more use injectable drugs more widely. In your view is that analysis correct, was the golden age destroyed by heavy-handedness, and would you like to see a movement in that direction again?*
THB: No, I wouldn't. The analysis you outline is a misunderstanding of history. There never was a 'British System'. It wasn't British and it wasn't a system. Before the 1950s there were absolutely no non-therapeutic addicts. When we began to encounter non-therapeutic as opposed to therapeutic addicts, the situation was quite different.[13] I don't think there was an earlier Golden Age during which we successfully handled a street drug problem by liberally prescribing drugs. Those who were receiving large amounts of injectable drugs weren't necessarily doing very well, and there was quite a mortality among them, mostly from overdoses. It wasn't that with injectable heroin one lived happily ever afterwards.

The Wootton Report

A: *Let's move on to some of your other policy involvements. You were in the early stages a member of the Advisory Committee which pre-ceded the Advisory Council on the Misuse of Drugs (ACMD), and you were involved in Lady Wootton's report on cannabis?*[14]
THB: Yes. Lady Wootton was a very, very nice person and was immensely able. There are few people I ever met that I have considered to be in a league above me in terms of intelligence. She certainly was highly intelligent and at the same time a very humane person. She chaired the cannabis subgroup and she co-opted Aubrey Lewis to review the literature. He finally came back one day having completed this task and she was agog, as we all were, waiting for the answer. She asked Sir Aubrey, 'What did you find?' and he said in effect 'It was terrible, there was hardly a decent paper among the lot, with the exception of the 1894 Indian Hemp Report.'[15] Someone suggested 'We might just re-issue the Indian Hemp Report in paperback and not bother to write anything further.' It was an interesting committee because those on it constituted a wide cross-section, ranging from Peter Brodie, a hard-nosed Assistant Commissioner (Crime) from the Metropolitan Police at one end of the scale to Nick Malleson, a Student Health doctor, at the liberal end. We produced a very good and short report.[13] I remember when we finally got it all completed, Barbara Wootton asked us 'Would you like me to go through it and tidy up the language?' She did this, which was why it was also very clearly written. All the subsequent reports on cannabis came out in large, or several, volumes at immense expense, and all came to the same conclusions as the Wootton Committee.

A: *What in fact did that report say?*
THB: It said that the dangers of cannabis had been much exaggerated, but that we should not encourage people to use it and it would be a mistake to do so. We considered that the penalties were way out of line, and that it was a historical accident that it had been classified with heroin. At a later stage I chaired a working party which reviewed the possible alternatives to the present system of control as well as their consequences.[16]

A: *And then you were again involved in policy issues, when from 1972 to 1984 you were a* member of the Advisory Council on the Misuse of Drugs, a group which has responsibility in the United Kingdom for advising Ministers. Can you give some idea of what the ACMD does?

THB: What they did was take specific topics and write reports and give advice. The original Standing Advisory Committee was more exciting because it was breaking new ground. By the time the Advisory Council came into being the task was more that of keeping the system working rather than looking forward and preparing new policies.

Progress and barriers to progress

A: And now, has Britain simply adopted American policy, or is there still a radically different, homegrown policy?

THB: I think there has been a coming together. The totally free prescribing of anything anybody wanted, which has been seen as the old 'British System', has disappeared here, and the 'No prescribing at any price' has gone in the United States. Some of the differences between the two countries were not so much that the views about drugs were opposed, but that the way medical services were delivered were very different.

One thing that has been unfortunate is that some doctors can have a very clear-cut view of how problems should be seen and solved, with all other views ignored

---

A: Do you have any views on the role of the private practitioner in the treatment of addicts?

THB: I don't see any objection in principle to the private practice treatment of addicts. It can be difficult for a single-handed private practitioner. They can get themselves into difficulties because they are isolated and have not got an NHS team to support them, and they may not have colleagues. There are fewer difficulties for those working from a private hospital. It is the single-handed practitioners in Harley Street who have run into trouble. In that sense there can be problems for private practitioners.

A: Another aspect of your professional life is that you arrive here as a young Irishman, and eventually you become President of the British Royal College of Psychiatrists. You envisage life as frequently a matter of accident and luck. What accident led you to be President of the Royal College?

THB: I was not much in favour of the foundation of the college, as I would have preferred an Academy of Medicine, something modelled on the old Glasgow Faculty of Physicians and Surgeons. This might have come about if the London Royal Colleges of Physicians and Surgeons had joined together in the 1920s. The Royal Medico-Psychological Association (RMPA), the precursor of the College, sent me a letter about the setting up of the College and its proposed elections and committees in 1970. I put my name forward for the Council, and was elected. I was then elected a Sub-Dean, later Dean, and finally President.

A: Was it your impression that your psychiatric peers in general saw drug and alcohol problems as rating lower in the hierarchy of this new college's concerns than the more traditional sections of psychiatry?

THB: Initially people were not very enthusiastic about dependence problems. This was partly because few psychiatrists had been trained in this area. I don't think anyone believed that those who were dealing with the problems of drugs and alcohol were better or worse than other psychiatrists. I encouraged the setting up of a group within the college which later became the section dealing with substance misuse.

A: Looking broadly at, say, the last 25 years, can you discern any special barriers to progress, anything that you would warn against?

THB: One thing that has been unfortunate is that some doctors can have a very clear-cut view of how problems should be seen and solved, with all other views ignored. To a certain extent the disease concept of 'alcoholism' provides an example. When you consider this issue carefully it is not as straightforward as some people believe. A simplistic approach can hold things up. Another misguided approach to the treatment of alcohol problems led to the setting up of peculiar little units where people would go for 3 months' psychotherapy. That formula had practically nothing to offer for the sum total of needs of the very large number of people with alcohol problems. Those Ministry guidelines[17] held up what was really required, which was to make sure that general practitioners would deal with most alcohol problems and only refer for specialist advice when there were added difficulties.[18] There is also the danger of an over-simplified view of drugs that this is mostly a criminal matter and something the police should deal with. The biggest difficulty is that society does not wish to accept that these problems are long term, damaging, relapsing, chronic disorders. Some people start off with much less in the way of advantages than others, and having drifted into misusing drugs and alcohol, have the greatest problems and are understandably the hardest to treat, but need the most support.

A: *So much for blocks. Who are your heroes?*
THB: On this side of the Atlantic probably D.L. Davies, because if you look at what he did and the various people who worked with him, he was the person who had most influence in bringing about a re-evaluation of alcohol problems and how we should respond to them. On the other side of the Atlantic I could see Vincent Dole in that role. He started to do something that no-one else except himself could have done, and in a very humane way. He also measured what he did, stating 'Here are my results'. They were the two people who most changed our views on the way we should try to deal with these problems.

A: *Would your advice to government today be 'steady as she goes', or do you see any need for radical change in the way in which we are responding to drugs?*
THB: I wouldn't see any need for radical change in policy. I would rather take a pragmatic view. Where government can go wrong is when they want to do something active and hasty rather than do research first, and then do something more sensible later. Politicians are clearly always keen to do something rapidly – 'fight against drugs' or something similar. They often don't know what they are doing, and can rather easily talk rubbish. The Pompidou initiative provides one example. Many of the things that are done are not going to have

much effect, but it makes the person doing it feel better, which is why there have been so many useless Health Education campaigns.

My ethical view of life is that of the Society of Friends (Quakers). They don't proselytize, but nevertheless they think there is a difference between right and wrong, and we should try and do the former. That would be my background, where I come from

---

A: *Much of what you said emphasizes pragmatism. No great belief in master strokes, respect for science and forgiveness of the human condition. Not muddling through, but neither expecting too much nor too little. Not expecting too much from the State. Where does this view come from?*
THB: That sounds like a Quaker view. Let me say I'm a rather atypical Quaker in the sense that as far as I know I am the only Irish Atheist Quaker. My ethical view of life is that of the Society of Friends (Quakers). They don't proselytize, but nevertheless they think there is a difference between right and wrong, and we should try and do the former. That would be my background, where I come from.

References
1.   Bewley, H. (1938) The cardiazol treatment of dementia praecox, *Irish Journal of Medical Science*, VI, **156**, 762–765.
2.   Bewley, T. (1964) Opiate addiction (Letter), *Lancet*, i, 938–939.
3.   Bewley, T. (1965) Heroin and cocaine addiction, *Lancet*, i, 808–810.
4.   Bewley, T. (1965) Heroin addiction in the United Kingdom (1954–1964), *British Medical Journal*, **2**, 1284–1286.
5.   Bewley, T., Ben Arie, O., James, I. P. & Marks, V. (1968) Morbidity and mortality from heroin dependence, *British Medical Journal*, i, 725–732.

6. FRANKAU, I. M. & STANWELL, P. M. (1960) The treatment of drug addiction, *Lancet*, **ii**, 1377–1379.

7. FRANKAU, I. M. (1964) Treatment in England of Canadian patients addicted to narcotic drugs, *Canadian Medical Association Journal*, **8**, 421–424.

8. HMSO (1965) Second Report, *UK Interdepartmental Committee on Drug Addiction (Second Brain Report)* (London, HMSO).

9. HMSO (1961) Report, *UK Interdepartmental Committee on Drug Addiction (First Brain Report)* (London, HMSO).

10. REPORT OF THE INTERDEPARTMENTAL COMMITTEE ON DRUG ADDICTION (MEETING OF SOCIETY FOR THE STUDY OF ADDICTION), *British Journal of Addiction*, **57**, 81–103.

11. BEWLEY, T. (1969) Drug dependence in the U.S.A., *Bulletin on Narcotics*, **21/2**, 13–20.

12. HARTNOLL, R. L., MITCHESON, M. C., BATTERSBY, C. B., ELLIS, M., FLEMING, P. & HEDLEY N. (1980) Evaluation of heroin maintenance in controlled trial, *Archives of General Psychiatry*, **37**, 877–884.

13. SPEAR H. B. (1969) The growth of heroin addiction in the United Kingdom, *British Journal of Addiction*, **64**, 245–255.

14. HMSO (1968) *Cannabis, Report by the Advisory Committee on Drug Dependence* (London, HMSO).

15. INDIAN HEMP DRUGS COMMISSION REPORT (1894) Simla, 1894, 7 volumes.

16. LOGAN, F. (Ed.) (1979) *Cannabis: Options for Control* (London, Quartermaine).

17. STANDING MEDICAL ADVISORY COMMITTEE (1973) *Alcoholism* (London, DHSS).

18. STANDING MEDICAL ADVISORY COMMITTEE (1989) *Drinking Problems: a Challenge for Every Doctor* (London, DHSS).

Raj Rathod

Raj Rathod was born in Pune, India, in 1919. In 1942 he obtained the LCPS from B. J. Medical School, and in 1948, after a short service with the Indian Army Ordnance Corp, obtained the MMBS from Grant Medical College, Bombay. He came to the UK in 1952, obtaining a DPM from the University of London in 1955, and was later elected FRCP and FRCPsych. He became a Consultant at Graylingwell Hospital and had responsibility for the Crawley and Horsham areas until his retirement in 1981. He has worked with the World Health Organization and was Secretary to the Society for the Study of Addiction from 1972–80, and Consultant to the Home Office from 1972–78. He was a member of the EEC planning group on medico-social risk for alcohol consumption from 1977–79 and a tutor/lecturer with the International Council on Alcoholism and Addiction from 1975–85. His main interests have included developing psychiatric services in the community, especially for people harmed by substances within general psychiatric services.

Heroin in Crawley New Town

Addiction: *In 1966 you became aware when working in Crawley New Town that there were a number of heroin takers in your local area. That was, at the time, enormously surprising and disturbing news – until then everyone believed that heroin use was entirely a London problem. How did you make that discovery?*

Raj Rathod: It was the patients who told us when we doctors had failed to make the diagnosis. I remember two or three such patients who had several admissions to hospital and we still didn't pick up what was going on. Then I had to go and see a chap in Brixton Prison who was a heroin addict and I asked him to teach me something about heroin. That's one thing about these people, they are very good at sharing their knowledge. Our paper on signs of heroin use was based on what we learned from our patients.[1]

A: *And this man you saw in Brixton Prison?*
RR: He came from Crawley and he was on remand for possession of heroin and some other drugs; he was only 18 or 19. Brixton is a London remand prison. I asked him to tell me if he knew any more heroin users in Crawley, and he said, of course there were. I said, how can I find out? He told me that he knew the names but he was not going to give them to me. He suggested some bargaining to which I didn't agree. Anyway, I got his confidence and I scribbled something and said that this would definitely be confidential and I showed him that what I had written was in Hindi. I said this is how I am going to write down anything you tell me so that nobody but myself will be able to read it. He immediately gave me 18 or so names.

> I scribbled something and said that this would definitely be confidential and I showed him that what I had written was in Hindi. I said this is how I am going to write down anything you tell me so that nobody but myself will be able to read it. He immediately gave me 18 or so names

---

A: *Eighteen names of heroin users in Crawley New Town?*
RR: Yes, in Crawley New Town. And we thought at first that this was perhaps a fantasy. Richard d'Alarcon was working with me and we

decided we ought to do something about this news. We got really excited and said, let's find out if there are more. And we then tried to use the same system: I recorded the names in Hindi and transcribed them into what I called a 'diary', and that proved to be a very useful record; chronological information about everybody we knew who was connected with drugs. Over the 6 months period and through many cross-checked sources we found that these people were telling the truth and the original Brixton informant had certainly been truthful. The subjects who came afterwards gave us more names but many of the old names recurred. We then became interested in the mode of transmission of the habit from person to person and the sources. The sources were mostly friends who were buying drugs on the illicit markets.

A: *Where did they go to get the drugs?*
RR: Piccadilly, the London scene. The Piccadilly chap might come to Gatwick, and a contact would pick it up there and then distribute it amongst his friends. There was an inner circle and an outer circle: friends and acquaintances. Friends were relied upon and entrusted with money and they would rarely break that trust, and they handled the business. Acquaintances just received the distribution.

A: *To begin with all the available heroin was NHS overspill from prescribing?*
RR: Yes. And then came the black market, the so-called Chinese heroin.

A: *What kind of dose level were these subjects using?*
RR: No more than say 10–20 mg per day. Tablets of heroin were dissolved and injected. I cannot recall anybody taking more than three or four 10 mg tablets a day. It was always by injection. They used matches and candles because they had to dissolve their tablets. Other drugs were supplementary – amphetamines and barbiturates more than anything else.

A: *And then users would introduce friends to heroin use?*
RR: That's right. That was the mode of trans-

mission. New people were encouraged by example, that's the account we were given. There was an aura – you sat and somebody was injecting – it was a status thing. The person using the heroin sang its praises. Somebody watching would be attracted to the same experience and this is how it was sold – 'If you really want it, I will show you how to fix.' We only found four people who had a very bad name – they would do anything just to get money. It was not only money for sustaining their habit but money for other purposes. This was a minority group who were really what I would call traders as well as users. We cross checked information on initiation between the initiator and the initiatee and built a chart on transmission. Richard d'Alarcon published a paper on this after he left the Crawley area.[2]

A: *You were then continuing to check the information you got against other multiple sources?*
RR: Yes. All our data was of this sort: we had no lab tests. The patients, their relatives, the probation office and the police were our sources; the other main strength was continued cross-checking and updating of information. We had a few GPs telling us that jaundice was occurring as a new problem among young people, so we did a survey of that. And we also looked at Accident and Emergency departments. Our first paper on epidemiology was based on these data.[3] I was interested in trends of prevalence – as indicators of the shifts in what was happening. I did one trend study.[4] I regret I could not repeat this.

A: *What sort of people in general were these young heroin users?*
RR: Ordinary working-class teenagers. Many of them I wouldn't call delinquently inclined although a proportion would be. Their lives were chaotic and at school they hadn't achieved particularly well. They were often in fights and things like that. They had often been school truants. They were mostly male. There was money about in Crawley so it's my assumption that money was not a great problem for these young people. They were getting money from parents and then some of them were real experts at stealing from shops. These people were more likely to be exposed to

severe parental discord or substance abuse.[5] We also found that delinquency was not a predictor of use of heroin.[6]

A: *What was Crawley like as a place to live in?*
RR: It was a New Town which afforded very good opportunities for work, especially if you were a semi-skilled or skilled worker. It had good housing facilities and it had a large central shopping centre. What it did lack was a sense of neighbourhood and whether that contributed to the use of heroin is an open question. About 80% of the houses in Crawley were state owned. If you took Horsham, which is 8 miles away, it was the reverse: a long-established community with far better social opportunities. Horsham had far more telephones pro rata than Crawley. Horsham, strangely enough, didn't have a drug problem although it was just 8 miles, 15 minutes drive from Crawley. We used to call the inhabitants of Crawley immigrants or economic refugees. They had to go somewhere out of London to find houses and work after the war and that explained the population make-up of the New Town. Horsham, on the other hand, was a place where people went by choice. Living there was associated with status and people could buy their own homes. It was a quiet community. Also the journey from Horsham to London was a little bit tedious while from Crawley it was very easy to get to London and Gatwick.

A: *Addicts came to see you because you were offering them treatment?*
RR: We had publicized ourselves and that was how our clientele increased. I was, with Richard's help, in charge of psychiatric services for Crawley and Horsham. So we had a very clear field, we could do what we liked by way of service provision. We offered firstly refuge and secondly we offered inpatient detoxification by symptomatic treatment. We offered inpatient treatment to many people at that time and I was lucky because I was in charge of the newly established Alcoholic Unit at Graylingwell, which was our base hospital until 1968. So I had a ward where I could put alcoholics for detoxification and I used to put heroin users there for detoxification as well. I used the same

kinds of drugs for both classes of patients: mostly symptomatic treatment. Occupational Therapy was also very important. That was all we did do. Some patients we kept up to 8 or 10 weeks. We rarely discharged a patient; the patient would say thank you very much when he thought it was time to go, or absconded. We never have practiced opiate maintenance, neither with heroin nor methadone.

A: *At that time all Drug Dependence Units in London were giving injectable heroin but you stood out against that practice?*
RR: I didn't see the logic in it. I had worked for about 10 years with alcoholics before this period which we are talking about and if the processes of habituation, tolerance and dependency, as I understood them, were similar, why should the treatment strategies be different? And I was also being old-fashioned: I thought it's a doctor's job, as a doctor, not to take on the burdens of the whole society. So if for alcoholics I did not give any drug substitutes (and alcoholics tried their own substitutes which didn't work) why shouldn't that strategy work for heroin users? That was one philosophical issue in my mind which I possibly rationalized on a scientific basis. The second thing was that there were reports – if not reports at least anecdotes – to suggest that maintained addicts were still using other supplementary drugs. I said if they are going on using, what is the sense in colluding? I would only be increasing their ability to take more and more drugs. And the third consideration was that although we believed in total abstinence (whenever the patient could make it) we never forced abstinence on anybody except when inpatients. We would take people in many times for detoxification if necessary. I used to hear horrific tales of the aggressive things addicts used to do to doctors when the news got around that under pressure that doctor would give drugs and I thought that was a ridiculous situation. If I accommodate a special 5% and give them substitute narcotics, I don't know when the 5% will become 50%.

A: *Were you put under pressure from colleagues to start prescribing?*

RR: People are very polite in this country. They don't say that kind of thing in open terms. I certainly got the feeling that I and Richard were oddballs – standing out against prescribing. But we used to refer people to other clinics if they wanted to have maintenance, we never objected to that. Most of them, however, came back disillusioned.

A: When you started to publish reports on your research and experience, what sort of professional response did you get?
RR: Let me put it this way, I didn't get any opposition. People in this country have two ambiguous phrases: one is 'Interesting' and the other is 'How very nice'. 'Interesting' means nothing or can mean a lot. And not being an Englishman I didn't know how to diagnose the nuances. 'Very nice' may mean 'I don't want to be impolite to you'. Nobody opposed me in my work except temporarily at Roffey Park Hospital which I joined in 1969 but I don't think I got active encouragement from anybody despite the fact that a complimentary report on our work was submitted by the Addiction Research Unit to the Department of Health. After that I saw quite a few people and institutions who could have helped but nothing came of it. I felt hurt that there we were, we had done some exciting work, somebody said we had found a research goldmine, pity we did not mine any gold. But if you meet adversity you just have to stand up to it. It is possible that few others were as excited about our work as we were.

A: Had you always been waiting for a wonderful research opportunity to blow through the window? Were you waiting for this to happen?
RR: I don't think I was because I did not expect it. I secretly hoped for some tangible encouragement. But as they say in India, 'Hope is like a passing cloud'.

A: Were you surprised that addicts would trust you and talk to you? There were plenty of people around who could read Hindi.
RR: Perhaps the addicts could detect an underdog in my own approach. Yes, I must say that I was blessed in that I haven't encountered many patients who haven't trusted me. Without the trust from my patients I would have learned or con-

tributed very little. So I am fortunate that on the whole I found heroin users very, very helpful to me and they were often clever. I think I respected them for that. I certainly felt that I had something to contribute and, if you like, it was inverted arrogance on my part – why should I bother what people were thinking as long as I believed in my work? The reasons why this work did not win wider recognition were probably several. I was in the periphery, that's one thing. Then I was pursuing clinical practices which were quite at variance with the perceived wisdom: for instance I tried conditioned aversion[7] instead of maintenance, and treated alcoholics and addicts together. And the third factor, maybe, was my ethnicity. I don't know, I think the last one might be just a sour grape thing. I really cannot explain why this work did not have more influence.

A: Where did you obtain your medical training?
RR: Ah, well I am perhaps one of the few dinosaurs that are surviving. There used to be an LCPS Diploma in India.

People in this country have two ambiguous phrases: one is 'Interesting' and the other is 'How very nice'. 'Interesting means nothing or can mean a lot

---

From India to England

A: LCPS?
RR: Licentiate of the College of Physicians and Surgeons. This was for people who could not afford to do M.B., B.S. (or M.D., as they would call it in the USA). So I did that. I went to the B.J. Medical School in Poona. It is now a medical college. I was determined that, if because of lack of money, I could not do my M.B., B.S., I would find another way. So I joined the Government service – in an ordinance factory. Which was the last thing I wanted to do – those were the days of the 'Quit India' movement – after getting the LCPS, but I did it because they would let me work for the M.B., B.S. and subsidise it. I was very

fortunate that, although my pay was only £4 a month and I had to cycle about 10 miles each way every day, the workers contributed to my salary each month. I was very proud and touched. I was working in general medicine.

A: *General medicine – so you qualified in what year?*
RR: I qualified in 1940–41 and I left Government service in 1946. Then I got a 2-year research scholarship in India from the Indian Council of Medical Research. I was happy and I was going along nicely. My research was on liver function tests and chronic diarrhoea. I found a lot of people dying with chronic diarrhoea and I didn't understand it at all. Then I did a Registrar job in the Grant Medical College, Bombay. And then I came to England by accident. I used to attend the psychotherapy clinic although what went on sounded like mumbo-jumbo. I was interested in the psychological problems of people with chronic diarrhoea, they taught me how painful life can be. So I said, well let's do something. At that time some friends of mine had returned from America, and as we were sitting around chatting they said, 'We challenge you to go to England and do some study'. I said, 'You're on, get me the money', because I didn't have the money. And to my surprise within about a month they had raised the money – I was so moved.

A: *How did they do that?*
RR: Well some friends were rich, some friends borrowed money, some friends got it from a trust – they thought of all these things. Then they said, 'Right, there is your money'. Then I said, 'Well I don't know where to go'. And Dr Masani (the Director of the Psychiatric Clinic) said, 'If you are really interested in psychiatry you should go to the Maudsley'. I had never heard of the place. He wrote a letter to Dr D. L. Davies who was the Dean then, and who later played an influential part in my life. And he was very quick in sending a letter back saying he had given me a place. So I came here as a Clinical Assistant, a postgraduate clinical student without pay, and worked 6 months on that basis. I did not enjoy being a clinical assistant and by this time funds were drying up and I had achieved nothing. So I

just had to say to Dr Davies, 'Either you tell me I am no good as a psychiatrist and I'll pack my bags and go back, or I should be given a job'. There were some Clinical Assistants who were given paid jobs but I wasn't asked to apply so I hadn't applied. Dr Davies said, 'Well you didn't apply'. Next day I approached Miss Arnold his secretary, she was marvellous to me, a very kindly lady, she said, 'Well, don't worry, come and see me the day after tomorrow', and she gave me a lot of hope. Then she said that she thought a letter was in the post and they had appointed me. So that's how I got the job of Registrar (Resident, in American terminology) at the Maudsley.

> At that time some friends of mine had returned from America, and as we were sitting around chatting they said, 'We challenge you to go to England and do some study'. I said, 'You're on, get me the money', because I didn't have the money. And to my surprise within about a month they had raised the money – I was so moved

A: To *what extent does coming in as an outsider confer advantages or disadvantages to the psychiatrist?*
RR: I can only tell you from my viewpoint. The great advantage I had, and which I still believe in, has to do with coming from a culture which confronts you with poverty and deprivation. If you are not well off in that culture you see the rough end of life. Secondly, I think this research with diarrhoea really disturbed me quite a lot: that human beings were dying and I was achieving nothing except doing the tests and presenting a published paper. So all these things must have combined and I do feel that I can identify much more easily with the underdog. To me, psychiatric patients, and especially those abusing substances, are treated as underdogs, and often denied understanding and sympathy. I found this much more here than in India. Many of these people find themselves at the

bottom of the 'snake pit' and many of them make it back to 'normality'. Those of us who have been spared either of these experiences cannot begin to understand the suffering and the effort involved. This way of looking at patients may have given me a head start. Another major advantage that a person from another culture has is the freedom from prevailing prejudices in the host country. The disadvantages are more cultural and social rather than professional ones. I have also been fortunate in my patients and colleagues and having known a few individuals who have been very generous to me.

A: *Do you see anything specially arbitrary or limiting in a Christian way of seeing the nature of existence?*
RR: The question is too complex but I will try to answer. I feel that Christianity gives two fundamentally conflicting messages. On the one hand everything is ordained by God, and on the other hand Man has freedom of choice. Freedom of choice is a moral concept about good and evil and its role is overemphasized. Moral values are learned and not inborn and all learning is limited and relative in application. Freedom of choice therefore is limited and relative. My experience tells me that ordinary people have very limited freedom of choice. Early influences and experiences and prevailing circumstances often dictate human behaviour. Looking at my life, something within me must have impelled me to come to London, or circumstances just happened. That way I did not make much of a free choice. And the patients I have seen, they often had very little freedom of choice. They drifted into situations which made free choice difficult.

A: *This fatalism, is this part of the Hindu religion?*
RR: As I understand it, suffering is integral to existence in Hindu philosophy; it being the consequence of deeds in past existence. Man should, and does, try to do his best in the given circumstances to reduce suffering in lives to come. There is no absolution. There is no 'right way', each has his own way. There are situations where I can exercise my desire or sense of duty and make a choice, such as whether I talk with you or not. But if I was caught up in a thunderstorm, which is not of my choosing, I have to adapt myself to cope with it. Being unaware of the storm or its consequence has little to do with freedom of choice.

Follow-up research

A: *Let's return to the story of your research. Did it stop there or did you carry on with follow-up studies?*
RR: Well I carried it on until November 1988 when I retired completely. We did follow-up studies and we did look at the delinquency of patients who had continued with or stopped heroin. I produced a report on a 6–7 year follow-up[8] and I very much intend to extend it further. Although being retired from the service may pose some difficulties, the 67–68 cohort would provide a good sample for a 20 year follow-up specially because we have much information in the diaries.

A: *At 7 years what had happened?*
RR: Nearly 25–30% were abstinent. That's the same as alcohol users. And strangely enough we found that 30% do go up and down: relapse and remit. And for 30% we proved quite useless and many of them died of overdoses as would be expected.

A: *And what today is the heroin situation in Crawley?*
RR: It is endemic. I think there must be many users, not necessarily addicts, but we lack precise figures. But people are not risking so much, we don't see so many overdoses or infections now. Deaths don't happen that often so somehow users themselves are learning how to practice harm reduction. The smoking of heroin was becoming more prevalent in parts of Sussex. There are now a few heroin users in Horsham. What worries me is the increasing abuse of alcohol amongst those who abuse illicit drugs.

A: *What do you think the relevance is to present policies of all you have been able show and tell us with your research and many years of clinical experience? What is the central message in that life work for those who are grappling with drug problems today?*

RR: I can only tell you what I have learned. I don't mistrust patients that easily. Patients often tell the truth: they may not tell the whole truth but still the truth. Secondly, the essence of any good clinical research, 'good' means effective clinical research which will really benefit people and add to our knowledge, is consistent long-term monitoring, and monitoring does not mean a five minute appointment in out-patients saying, 'How are you?' And what I am more and more convinced of is that I don't think I have helped patients as much, or damaged patients as much, as life events have. Psychiatry underestimates the influence of life events in the process of human distress. The need for long-term consistent follow-up and a child-like enquiring mind would be my message. I stress the word childlike. A child is always inquisitive, 'What am I going to find?', it hasn't got preconceived ideas. That doesn't mean our minds should be chaotic but that inquisitiveness and an open mind should always remain an attribute, irrespective of rewards. Patients are reservoirs of rich data which they are willing to share – it is for the clinician to learn from them.

A: *What message does your experience give to current policy debates on perhaps more generous prescribing policies, or starting to prescribe injectable heroin again?*

RR: I can tell you about that from another angle. I have been to African countries quite a lot through ICAA, participating in training programmes for professionals and volunteers. I must have visited 10 or 12 countries and have stayed in each of them about 15 days or so. There are very few of them using substitute opiate prescribing, and they are doing no worse than we are. We could learn from them. We are sometimes arrogant enough to tell people what is right. In the countries I'm talking about the habit is more that of smoking opiates than injecting – let's keep it like that. The policy should be aimed at non-injectable consumption if at all possible and very

restrained narcotic substitution prescribing. And I also believe firmly that everyone has a vested interest in their lives. Even the most intoxicated addict has that investment. So I really would say try to inform people, educate people, change their attitudes but don't give drugs. It is this vested interest which will help change attitudes and nothing is so potent a promoter or deterrent as entrenched attitudes.

A: *How did you share out the work with your co-investigators?*

RR: Richard d'Alarcon and I joined the Maudsley on the same day. We were both foreigners, he was Spanish. We left the Maudsley, more or less, at the same time. We had a good rapport with each other. He was a much better-read person than I was and we got along together fine. Once I got excited Richard joined me and he too was also very enthusiastic. Ian Thompson was a bit more stoic but he was a very good lieutenant and he never dampened our enthusiasm. We agreed that we would rotate each person as the principal author. That agreement somehow didn't work out and that was a big disappointment to me but while we were all together, about 3 years, we worked as a team and we were very complementary to each other. We worked together many a long night and at weekends – it was fun. It was a pity that with administrative changes I was left working alone in Crawley from Roffey Park and Richard and Ian remained with Graylingwell – the team broke up. This was early in 1969.

> And what I am more and more convinced of is that I don't think I have helped patients as much, or damaged patients as much, as life events have

D. L. Davies and the Maudsley

A: *You have mentioned D. L. Davies as an important influence?*

RR: D. L. Davies – had it not been for him I wouldn't have got a job, and I believe that I was the first coloured person employed in a junior position at the Maudsley. That may not be historically correct but I believe that this is so. Secondly, Davies helped me after I had left the Maudsley and I was associated with him through the Society for the Study of Addiction. He gave me that first start and he always afterwards used to ask how I was. We had one thing in common – D. L. Davies was based in Poona during the war and I was born and brought up in Poona. He was, I gather, actually engaged to his wife in Poona. So Poona had a lot of affinity for both of us. I lost track of D. L. Davies for a time after I left the Maudsley and then met up with him again through the Society for the Study of Addiction, and I became Secretary of the Society. It was in terrible doldrums during the late or middle 70s. I carried on for 4 or 5 years. I worked with Philip Connell who was the President. I, in consultation with others, it always sticks in my mind as a matter of joy, asked D. L. Davies if he would become President. I thought that we needed a shake-up and I had always been impressed by D. L.'s ability to administer, organize and get the right people together. Philip Connell was saying that he'd had enough and I think it was a disheartening job. So when Davies became President I came to know him more and more in that setting and to admire his shrewdness. At the same time he was a very loyal man if he liked you. I always called him Dr Davies and I remember, talking of these English attitudes, he said, 'We have known each other for how many years?', and I said, 'Sir, so many years'. Then he said, 'I tell you what, I will call you Raj. Would you mind calling me David?' I thought it was an honour because in India you wouldn't dare do this and Davies was one of my gurus, so how would I ever call him by his first name? He invited me then to help with his famous Summer School and I continued with this for some years. I felt in his own way he cared a lot for me – he must have cared for lots of other people too, but he was like a father to me. Without him I don't know where I would be. I used the ideas of the Summer School in my local work. In the 80s, I and my three colleagues at the Crawley Addictions Team organised many study days and residential workshops in substance abuse. We published a booklet for lay people.[9]

A: *What was the Maudsley like in your days?*
RR: I don't know if we still believe that there is a camera hidden in the walls. There was a sense that every move was watched. It was an atmosphere that I had never experienced before. I was brought up to believe that what the teachers said was always true. Here for the first time I came across Registrars who questioned the teacher in a challenging way, not just as an exposition or enquiry but as a challenge.

It was really hard work and my first appointment was under Dr Kraupl Taylor which was dramatic. You can't forget being at the Maudsley. It taught me how to think and be independent.

A: *Did you ever again think of settling back in India?*
RR: Yes, but the scene was changing. India was changing and I certainly, as an Indian, had stood still – India was changing fast. I got the invitation to go back and take a Chair about two years after I had bought a house here and had settled into a job. Again they wanted me to come within a fortnight. But, I have often wondered about going to live in India. I did try to make contacts with lots of people. At this time I was acting as Consultant to the WHO but I felt I was not cut out to be a diplomat.

I was brought up to believe that what the teachers said was always true. Here for the first time I came across Registrars who questioned the teacher in a challenging way, not just as an exposition or enquiry but as a challenge

---

A: *What do you think of the argument that people from the developing world should serve their own countries rather than settle in the West? That's not a personal criticism, but what do you think of the general argument?*
RR: I will always live with that guilt because I believe that although it's nice to be wanted here and I am grateful to this country, I am not needed here. There are many people which Britain

produces who can do a job in England better than I can. India did need me and I think that if I were making a policy in India I would give very handsome bursaries to people to come to Britain to train, but then expect them to go back – a loan which they would have to pay back by serving the Indian community for at least so many years in India. So the criticism is in a way justified, we may be professional but we are also human. Life is a bit better here. What's wrong with being an economic refugee? But it doesn't do one's own country much good. I'm also convinced, though, that the West could do with a dose of humility about its achievements. No one should impose – people should evolve their own strategies. I would still like to go back to India but it's too late now. I have lectured in India a few times and I enjoyed it. But if I went back to India and if there were any research of a social or a cultural nature I honestly believe that I could not do it objectively on my own. Nor can a British person or any other Western person do it objectively either. We all carry the hang-ups of our own culture. So the answer is yes, I have that feeling of guilt, but I don't think I have brought India any shame. Nor I hope have I misused the hospitality of Great Britain.

References

1. RATHOD, N. H., DE ALARCON, R. & THOMPSON, I. (1967) Signs of heroin usage detected by drugs users and their parents, *Lancet*, 1411–1414.
2. DE ALARCON, R. (1969) The spread of heroin abuse in a community, *UN Bulletin on Narcotics*, **21**(3), 17–22.
3. DE ALARCON, R. & RATHOD, N. H. (1968) Prevalence and early detection of heroin abuse, *British Medical Journal*, **2**, 549–553.
4. RATHOD, N. H. (1972) The use of heroin and methadone by injection in a new town – a follow up, *British Journal of Addiction*, **67**, 113–121.
5. RATHOD, N. H. (1970) Early experiences in the life of a narcotic user, in: *The Proceedings of the International Institute, International Council on Alcohol and Addiction* (Lausanne), pp. 277–279.
6. MOTT, J. & RATHOD, N. H. (1976) Heroin misuse and delinquency, *British Journal of Psychiatry*, **128**, 428–435.
7. RATHOD, N. H. & THOMSON, I. (1968) Aversion therapy for heroin dependence, *Lancet*, 382–384.
8. RATHOD, N. H. (1977) Follow up study of injectors in a provincial town, *Drug and Alcohol Dependence*, **2**, 1–21.
9. RATHOD, N. H., ROSENBACH, A. F., ADDENBROOKE, W. M. & GEORGE, M. (1987) *Information sheets on substance abuse: Substance abuse project* (Crawley Hospital, Crawley, Sussex).

Commentary

Nascent Heroin Problems and the Unfolding British Response

Gerry Stimson

In the 1960s the UK woke up to new heroin problems. All three interviewees in this section pitched into research at this time. Their subsequent careers span a much longer period, but much of their later work and influence was shaped by the early research experiences documented in these interviews.

There were few addicts in the 1960s. Politicians were not interested in drug problems; there was little research expertise, few specialist treatment services, and little treatment experience. Few knew what was going on, and there were few experts. In 1964 Thomas Bewley wrote in *The Lancet* about 20 addicts he had seen, and that is how he became an 'expert' – 'I knew little, but everyone else knew less'.

What sticks out is that all three could spot that something interesting was happening. Thomas Bewley discovered a new type of heroin addict. Not the traditional English addict – a doctor, pharmacist or iatrogenic addict – but young men who started using heroin for pleasure, along with some Canadians who migrated here when they heard that London doctors could prescribe heroin. He found the London black market in heroin was fed by diversion from legitimate prescriptions. Raj Rathod (and his colleague Richard d'Alarcon) first described the spread of heroin use outside of London. They became aware of heroin users in Crawley New Town in 1966. Rathod asked an addict to teach him about heroin. 'Patients' as he says 'are reservoirs of rich data which they're willing to share – it is for the clinician to learn from them.' Joy Mott was also in Crawley, studying young offenders. One wonders how much their

ability to observe these new trends was helped by their being outsiders themselves – an Irish atheist Quaker psychiatrist, a Hindu doctor from Poona, India, and a clinical psychologist from South Africa.

The three biographies point to the serendipity of professional careers – the importance of being in the right place at the right time and seizing the opportunities presented. They did not embark with clear intentions to work in the addictions field. Thomas Bewley was working at Tooting Bec Hospital which admitted large numbers of alcoholics and some heroin addicts, mostly because few others wanted anything to do with them. Joy Mott joined the Home Office Research Unit in 1962 and was working on a study of juvenile courts in Crawley just at the time the heroin outbreak occurred. There is an ironic parallel with the careers of the heroin addicts. Raj Rathod compares himself to his patients. 'I did not make much of a free choice and the patients I have seen, they very often had little freedom of choice. They drifted into situations which made free choice difficult.' The Crawley heroin addicts were relatively ordinary working class teenagers, slightly more delinquent than their peers but otherwise unexceptional. Joy Mott found it hard to distinguish between the heroin addicts in Crawley, young offenders and children attending local schools of the same age and gender. It was more a matter of being in the wrong place, knowing the wrong people at the wrong time – 'it was because you went to school with the lad or you were his next door neighbour or you drank with him in the pub'.

What also comes through is the close link between people working in the field and their influence on policy. Bewley's observations fed directly into the emerging policy response – the ban on general medical practitioners from prescribing heroin or cocaine except under licence, and the establishment of the specialist drug dependency clinics in 1968. The downgrading of general practice and the 'psychiatrisation' of the problem is something we still live with. It was a time of consensual policy making, before drug policy became dominated by the interests and aims of politicians. It was a time when 'experts' had more influence than ministers.

Finally, all three are modest about what can be achieved. Bewley indicates that there are no great masterstrokes and that whilst governments want to be seen to be doing things, it is better to be cautious and pragmatic. Joy Mott reminds us, in a later period, of the very English way that policy was developed. Discussing the role of the Advisory Council on the Misuse of Drugs she points out that its authority came from the care and thoroughness in its work rather than from the money invested or political patronage.

There is also modesty about what can be done for people with drug problems. Bewley believes that the clinician should avoid ambitious expectations. What is needed is symptomatic treatment, help for people to function better, to avoid overdoses, to avoid getting abscesses, and if appropriate, to come off drugs. The term was not then in use, but he clearly describes a harm reduction approach. Bewley prescribed opiates. Rathod and D'Alarcon decided not to. But still, too, there is a modesty of what can be achieved, and tolerance for patients. They provided opportunities for detoxification and did not press patients to be discharged – 'the patient would say thank you very much when he thought it was time to go, or absconded'. Rathod reminds us that it is often things outside treatment that both help and damage patients, and that psychiatry underestimates the effects of life events on human processes.

So what mark have they left? Rathod pioneered a local epidemiology that illustrated the social networks by which people came across heroin and became heroin users. The classic paper on *The spread of heroin use in a community* is envied by many researchers. Bewley contributed to the development of the clinic system that we still operate. Mott persisted in getting research on the agenda, nurturing research projects and researchers, and reminding Londoners that research needed to be conducted outside London.

The biographies also suggest missed opportunities. Why did Rathod remain an outsider? British governments and other researchers did not exploit the Crawley research potential – a history since repeated with other singlehanded researchers. Why was there no effective clinic database or investment in treatment research? There are many missed opportunities and unfinished work. The *Addiction* journal interviews are an important part of the historical record, but tantalising because we know that all three could tell us much more.

Part VI
High Policy in the USA

Harold Hughes

Senator Harold Everett Hughes 1922–1996, grew up in a small town in Iowa and achieved one year of college education. He served in the US infantry, seeing action in North Africa and Italy. By 1946 he had developed severe alcohol problems but in 1954 took his last drink. He was Governor of Iowa from 1962–68 and US Senator from 1969–74. He was instrumental in securing crucial legislation relating to alcohol and other drugs and devoted himself to voluntary work in the cause of addiction. In 1987 he was given the Distinguished Public Services Award.

Sadly, Senator Hughes died on 24 October 1996. Senator Edward Kennedy was shown a copy of this interview with Senator Hughes and provided the following comment for publication: 'This eloquent interview with Harold Hughes reminds me of how much he accomplished in his extraordinary life and how much we missed him when he left the Senate. He was a powerful force for compassion and justice. His vigorous pursuit of fair treatment for persons battling addiction is legendary. He had approached his own problem with honesty and frankness, at a time when the rest of America discussed alcohol abuse in whispered tones, behind closed doors. Harold Hughes changed all that, and brought hope and help to vast numbers of his fellow citizens. The country continues to reap the benefits of his work, including the establishment of the National Institute on Alcohol Abuse and Alcoholism at the National Institutes of Health. If we see farther today on these important issues, it is because we stand on the shoulders of giants like Harold Hughes.'

Dealing with a personal drink problem

Addiction: *Senator Hughes, your actions as a United States Senator in the early 1970s made you a towering figure – a hero – to researchers and clinicians who are familiar with the history of US government policy dealing with problems with alcohol and other drugs. Almost single-handedly, you introduced the legislation that created the National Institute on Alcohol Abuse and Alcoholism. You advocated tirelessly for more funds for research and treatment. Then you inserted into the Drug Abuse Office and Treatment Act of 1972 the language that ensured the creation of the National Institute on Drug Abuse. Over the years you have been a public advocate for treatment, always asserting the fundamental humanity of those dependent on drugs. Before we discuss your accomplishments as a member of the United States Senate, can we go back in time to help our readers understand what led up to those momentous*

years? Perhaps we can start with when you were Governor of Iowa?
Harold Hughes: I'll go back even before I was Governor of Iowa. I sobered up in the early 1950s after a pretty long and staggering trail of drinking heavily, including public drunkenness, and had been in jail in six different states, before I finally stopped. And I have to give credit for my sobriety to the fact that I took the old 'faith' trail of getting on my knees and asking God for deliverance to help me stay dry and stay sober one day at a time. And I would have to say that's the only way I hung on for those first couple of years; because there was no science in the way I got sober, there was no medicine, there was no drying out. I was, in fact, at the point where my first wife filed a legal action to have me committed to what we used to call an 'insane asylum' in the 1940s, where we alcoholics were usually placed in 'tie-down wards' because that's what happened to alcoholics in the 1930s and 1940s. After that I started working

with men and women who had been committed to mental institutions, attending meetings and doing those sorts of things through the 1950s. I committed my life in a spiritual way to try to restore my strength, my health, my faith, and whatever; I'd lost it all. So the 1950s was a growing period for me of faith. I also worked in the trucking industry. I had been a truck driver in the 1940s, and after that I worked for the Iowa Motor Truck Association. I then started one of my own, called the Iowa Better Trucking Bureau, which brought me into relationship with the whole political arena. I was a Republican then, and I went to Republican conventions. I went to a State Republican convention as a delegate.

The Governor appointed me, in 1959, to chair a Citizens' Commission on Alcoholism for the State of Iowa. We could have caucused in a telephone booth

A: *Weren't you later elected Governor of Iowa as a Democrat?*
HH: Yes. As president of the Iowa Better Trucking Bureau, I went to the Iowa governor, who was a Democrat, Herschel Loveless, and protested the actions of the State Commerce Commission, which regulated the state's trucking industry. And he said, 'You're the most knowledgeable man I've ever known in the transportation industry. Why don't you run for the Commission yourself?' I said, 'I don't know that I can.' And he said, 'Well, why not?' I said, 'Well, I'm a recovered alcoholic.' And he looked at me and said, 'Why should that stop you from running? If you're recovered from alcoholism, you're well. Why couldn't you run for office?' And I said, 'For a man in your position to make a statement like that is pretty uplifting to me, because most people look at you like you've just crawled out from under a rock when you say you're a recovered alcoholic.' And he said, 'By the way, I'm told you're a Republican. If you're going to run, I hope you'll change your political party. You should be a Democrat. I'm a Democrat, and I believe you should run. You don't sound like a

Republican. You ought to rethink your political philosophy.'

A: *And did you rethink your philosophy?*
HH: To be brief, I did, and I ran for the State Commerce Commission. I was advised by everyone that knew me that it was the wrong thing to do, that I'd wind up getting drunk. They said I should shut up, be a good boy, go home and forget this baloney. And I said, 'Why? If alcoholism is a disease, as you've all told me it is, then why is it any different from heart disease or any other disease? Why, then, can't I seek public office? Even though I may have had the disease of alcoholism, I've recovered from it.' They said, 'You're always recovering.' I said, 'No I'm not. I got well. The Big Book of AA even says 'recovered' – it doesn't say 'recovering'. If I didn't recover, what did I do? And is abstinence not recovery?' They said, 'Well, we don't know.' I said, 'Then we should find out the truth, shouldn't we? We ought to be looking for the truth. And that's what I'm out for, to look for the truth, and I think politics is one of the answers and that's where we have to go to find out and to help ourselves.'

A: *What was the outcome of your decision?*
HH: I won the nomination; I won the office. I was serving a four-year term on the State Commerce Commission as Chairman when the Governor appointed me, in 1959, to chair a Citizens' Commission on Alcoholism for the State of Iowa. We could have caucused in a telephone booth. You know, the numbers of us who really had any interest in the problem were few. Nobody cared, nobody wanted to do anything about it. They especially didn't want to do anything about the men and women in prisons or in mental institutions. Alcoholics still weren't out of the mental institutions. We were still locking people away for a life-time just because they were alcoholics. When their families gave up on them, they couldn't get out of the institution and that was it.

Governor of Iowa and developments in state alcohol policies

A: *Were you able to change some of those conditions?*

HH: Yes, we were. Along with the Governor, we worked on interviewing those people and we got some changes made. And when Governor Herschel Loveless ran for the United States Senate in 1960, I ran for Governor of Iowa. I was soundly defeated in 1960 in the Democratic Primary. I never even thought about drinking after the loss. In 1962 I won the Primary, then defeated the Republican incumbent for governor. I was the only elected Democratic state official in Iowa.

A: *What actions did you take as Governor to deal with the problems you had identified?*
HH: One of my first acts as Governor, when I took office in 1963, was to work to legalize sale of liquor by the drink in Iowa. We were a 'storebuying' state, liquor could only be sold by the bottle in state-owned stores. It could not be sold by the drink over the bar or in restaurants. Well, all the 'drys' attacked me openly: what was I trying to do legalizing a substance that had caused my downfall? In my own Methodist church there was a coordinated mission to defeat liquor by the drink. Much of the church leadership, including pastors, wrote me very unkind letters regarding my advocacy of liquor by the drink. I went to the bishop and I asked him to bring his cabinet – his district superintendents – to meet with me in the governor's mansion and to discuss the subject of alcohol and the church, which he did. I explained to them quite clearly that the decision was not whether we drink or don't drink; we made that decision with the repeal of the Volstead Act. Because Americans had decided we would drink, the only question is how will we drink – whether we're going to drink with sanity and sense, or whether we're going to drink with insanity, and bury it, hide it, and bootleg it.

A: *What did you do after the meeting?*
HH: I introduced the legislation to legalize liquor by the drink in the State of Iowa and to change our local liquor control systems and it passed. I requested the Iowa State Bar Association to work with the judicial committees of the Iowa House and Senate to change the criminal code of Iowa. The result was a change in our legal code to give the judges the opportunity to sentence men and women to treatment rather than prison, if in the determination of the Court the reason they committed a crime was the disease of alcoholism. This took two years to accomplish.

A: *Was Iowa one of the first states to do this?*
HH: I believe so. I called the White House and talked to a friend there from Iowa about getting a grant. I told him there was a direct relationship, in my opinion, between the men and women in our mental institutions and in our jails and glutting the courts – a direct correlation between that – and alcoholism and alcohol abuse. And he asked me if I had any way to prove it. And I said, 'No, but I know it's true.' And he said, 'Well, Governor, you know I have to have the evidence.' And I said, 'Will you give me a grant so I can get you the evidence? If you can get me help to get the evidence in Iowa – we're a rather small state population-wise, under 3 million, we don't have a complicated society, we don't have large minority imbalances, we have a rather open society – I think we can find the evidence for you in a rather short period of time.' He called me back the next day and said the President okayed me to proceed to look into this matter for a possible grant and I'm to have you call Sarge Shriver. I called Sarge Shriver who was the Director of the Office of Economic Opportunity (OEO) as well as Secretary of Health, Education and Welfare. Shriver said that the White House had called him and told him to listen to me carefully and give me whatever assistance I needed in writing this application. He said he was told that the White House said it was something the Administration would like to consider, because if it could be used as a demonstration or pilot showing that we can impact crime and criminality related to alcohol abuse, then it was something we should know as a nation. Shriver said he was willing to assign a person, and pay his salary, to come to Iowa for six months to assist my staff in gathering the information if I would assign someone to help him and give them office space. They were to draw together the facts and then make an application to Shriver, as Director of OEO, for funds to form the grant.

A: *Did you get any support?*

HH: Yes, we got the thing started. But of course the President was assassinated in November of 1963, and I thought it would get lost in the confusion, but it did not.

Anyway, the man Shriver promised to send came out to Iowa. We went ahead with the research. We put together the application. Actually, Shriver's man from the OEO wrote the application to make sure we got it right and it would be approved and couldn't be thrown out by the various committees on its way through the review process. So they hand-carried the thing through the review process all the way, and they gave Iowa a grant of $1 million. One million dollars in 1965 was a lot of money.

A: *How did Iowa use that money?*

HH: We set up the Iowa Council on Alcohol Project (ICAP). We got through that first year and got out a report, which I presented to the Director of OEO in Washington, DC. A part of the grant was used to start an addictions treatment program at the University of Iowa Medical School.

A: *Given the lack of interest in the problem at most medical schools at that time, that was quite an accomplishment. How did you do it?*

HH: I did it, literally, by coercion. The University of Iowa needed money; and if they needed money they needed to go through the Iowa Executive Council, which I chaired. The Iowa tuberculosis treatment center had magnificent physical facilities – lots of buildings, lots of things were available there – and they only had three active cases of tuberculosis in the state. The University wanted all those physical facilities to convert for research and other things. I proposed to them that I would support their projects with the Executive Council and the Legislature to achieve their goals for utilization of the tuberculosis center, if they supported my goals and established an alcoholism treatment and research center in conjunction with the University Medical School and hospital. We finally worked out a reasonable arrangement in achieving our goals which did what I wanted.

Harold Mulford, PhD, was appointed Director and did an excellent job of coordinating all of the activities. In the beginning we experienced a lot of difficulty and resistance from the academic and medical community. With time and patience on both sides and me as referee we worked out an excellent program and long-lasting relationship.

A: *That was quite a challenge.*

HH: We set it up, and we did by trial and error what we didn't know how to do.

A: *What year did that happen?*

HH: That was in 1965, I believe.

A: *It must have been one of the first centers in the US of its kind. Even Vincent Dole, at Rockefeller, didn't have anything at the time that could be called a specific 'center'. After New York closed Riverside Hospital, the only research centers for addictions that included clinical work were the Federal hospital at Lexington, Kentucky, and the small effort of the Yale Alcohol Studies Center.*

HH: I coupled this with a re-write of the criminal law. That way I could say to the judicial districts of Iowa, we have the research center at the University of Iowa Hospitals, we have the auspices and the authority of the State of Iowa behind it, we have the Medical School and the Medical College faculty, we've got the judicial system and we've got the General Assembly – and here we are coupled together to try and find some solutions – whatever the solutions are. And I showed them the statistics that we'd been able to gather in Iowa on the relationship of alcohol-related problems to crime and criminality in the State of Iowa, to our mental institutions, and to a lot of our social problems, including unwanted pregnancies and high school dropouts.

We started a high school dropout program as a peripheral program related to this, too. As a result, we set up a special human resources center in the Governor's office, and I appointed someone to run the center and to take on the problems of unemployment, high school dropouts, jails, mental institutions, and all the parts of our system related to addiction, and coordinate their activities, including rehabilitation in the prisons.

We developed all the systems and we started training counselors. We had the first counselor training program that I know of in America that amounted to anything. And we sent addiction counselors in the next five or six years all over America to start programs and to work in programs, and if they had come through the addiction training center at the University of Iowa, they were well received and well accepted wherever they went. I still run into some of them who are my age around the country, who went through that center for training.

A: *What happened to the program after you were no longer Governor?*
HH: The program gradually was changed and altered each year by the Legislature until as the years went by I had difficulty in identifying it as trying to achieve the goals we started out to accomplish.

The Governor goes public on his drinking problem

A: *They were certainly ahead of their time. But weren't you also ahead of your time in speaking openly about your own history of alcoholism?*
HH: Yes. The first major breakthrough in that area came in late 1963 during my first year as Governor, when the renowned author Fletcher Knebel, who co-authored *Seven Days in May*, called me and said he had been commissioned by Cowles Publications, Inc. to do a magazine story for *Look Magazine*, which at the time was one of the most popular magazines in the world. He asked if he could come and discuss it with me. I told him I did not want to discuss it and I didn't want an article done about my alcoholism. His response to me was 'Governor, I'm very familiar with the problem. It has affected my own family and this is not a question of whether you want it done or not. I will do the story with or without your cooperation and it will be a major story.' So, I agreed to the interview.

Over the course of the next several months he was my living shadow researching, riding with me,

hunting with me, sitting in my outer office, writing in my back office, visiting all my friends and enemies, scouring my background with a magnifying glass. The story was to be published in April I was told, but didn't run until October, 1964, 1 month before I ran for re-election for a second term. That issue hit the news stands in Iowa with a white banner on the cover stating in large letters: IOWA'S GOVERNOR IS AN ALCOHOLIC. That story was to haunt me for the rest of my life. In political campaigns, used by enemies, discussed at every level of society, but it also probably saved thousands of lives. My executive assistant put an advance copy on my desk and I opened it, read it, cancelled my appointments for the day, had my driver take me to the mansion for my family to see before the newspapers carried the worst parts and I said to all of them, 'You might as well start packing – I'll never win a second term when this hits the streets – it's all over. I pray to God that it's worth the pain it costs all of us.'

That issue hit the news stands in Iowa with a white banner on the cover stating in large letters: IOWA'S GOVERNOR IS AN ALCOHOLIC

I won't go into detail of the story, but that was the opening curtain of a new era in my life, private and public, on alcoholism. My life would never be the same again.

A: *What happened in your public life after the* Look Magazine *article?*
HH: My Republican opponent in the gubernatorial race was running about 25% behind me. He was the Attorney General of Iowa, Evan Hultman, and in the final debate before election day on statewide television he challenged me, saying I had lied in the *Look Magazine* story about when I had my last drink, stating I had been in jail in Kissimmee, Florida after I stated I had been sober. When it was my turn to speak I told the audience I had been arrested in Kissimmee in February 1954 for drunk driving and I had put up bond and left the state without trial, which is an admission of

guilt. I stated that I had also been in jail in five other states and that I regretted the pain and suffering I had inflicted on others, especially my own family, but that I had recovered from the disease of alcoholism and hadn't had a drink since 1954. Now if my opponent wants to spend the rest of his time finding out what states I spent time in jail, he's welcome. I say let's get on with the important issues facing this state, one of which is getting people well from the disease of alcoholism. I feared defeat in the election but was tremendously surprised and shocked by an overwhelming victory. I received the greatest plurality ever given a candidate for office in the state of Iowa.

The following years as Governor constantly included talks on alcoholism and my own alcoholism personally. In 1967 I accepted an invitation of the Greater Baltimore Area Council on Alcoholism to speak to their annual meeting and fundraising dinner, the first time I'm aware of that an elected official had ever spoken on this subject to a large general audience, and once again the wire services and news media carried the statement of my personal story of recovery on a nationwide basis.

Running for the Senate

A: *The press asked you if you were going to run for re-election or run for the Senate.*
HH: My response was I was tired. No one had ever held the Governor's office for more than three terms in the history of our state. I had no interest in running for the Senate and I had an abundance of job offers from private industry, so I was keeping my options open but probably wouldn't run again.

A: *But you didn't quit politics?*
HH: No. One of the reporters said to me privately, 'You've got to run for the Senate. Your state and your country need you there.' I told him I didn't feel personally adequate or qualified to be a US Senator. He said, 'You're dead wrong.' The following week I received a call from Senator Robert Kennedy saying that our mutual friend the

reporter had called him and said I was going to quit politics. He said, 'Governor, you can't quit. He tells me, and I believe him, that you can win the Senate seat. We need your voice and vote to end the war in Vietnam. You could also do the things you've always wanted to do on alcoholism and I'll help you. Governor, I wish you'd come to the Empire State dinner that we're having in early November in New York City and let's talk about it.' And I said, 'I'll tell you what, Senator, would you consider running for President?' He said, 'I thought about it, but that's not what this discussion is about.' I said, 'Maybe it should be. You want me to run for the Senate; we've got to have somebody run for the Presidency other than Lyndon Johnson.'

Well, he said he didn't want to think about it at that moment; and I said I didn't want to think about running for the Senate, but I'd come to the dinner if we could discuss both subjects. He agreed to that; and I said, 'I'm not talking about ten minutes, Senator. You want to give me two or three hours to sit down and have a discussion and convince me that I can run for the Senate, and I want time to convince you that you ought to run for the Presidency.' 'Well', he said, 'I can't give you that much time.' I said, 'Then I don't want to waste my time coming in.' So he agreed to give me most of the afternoon the day before the dinner, and I agreed to come to New York.

A: *When did this meeting take place?*
HH: This was 1967. Believe me, this is all related to the alcoholism field. I'm not just talking politics. So I went in and we spent the afternoon talking, and he did convince me that I should run for the Senate. A lot of people had tried, but Bob Kennedy is the one that finally convinced me. The Senate had sent a group out to Iowa to see me. Walter Mondale had come; Joe Tydings had come; a number of men had come that I liked dearly, of my own political persuasion. But I had stiff-armed them, and said 'There's no way I'm going to run for the Senate. I don't want to live in that place (Washington, DC). I don't want to be there. I don't want to commit six years of my life to it.' But when I listened to Bob Kennedy, he drew

something out in me that made me feel that I owed not myself, but America, God, everything else, you know; that whatever my voice could be in fighting against that war (Vietnam) and bringing it to an end, I should let it be heard; that whatever I could do in the area I wanted to serve so badly, which was alcoholism, I should do it. I had never even thought of it that way before.

So here's another Kennedy connection – getting me to Washington to do what eventually set up the National Institute on Alcohol Abuse and Alcoholism. I asked Bob Kennedy how I could get to have some influence in this area. He said if I was elected he'd help me get appointed to a particular committee where I could set up a new subcommittee. He said he'd talk to his brother, Ted, who was the chairman of the health sub-committee, and they'd get the thing put together. If Ted Kennedy hadn't had the interest or author-ity, I could never have set up the subcommittee. So it was a Kennedy network that actually got me even to run for the Senate, and got me in there and on that committee. I never said this before.

A: *You're answering a question that many people have wondered about: how did a freshman Senator manage to get so much done?*
HH: Well, that's a part of the tie-in. Now I said to Robert Kennedy, 'Well, I can't even raise the money to run for the Senate. Would you help me raise money?' He said, 'Yes, I'll commit myself to it right now. When do you want it?' 'Well', I said, 'I just happen to have a date that I want you in Iowa for, for a fundraiser if I decide to run.'

He called and let me know that night that he would do the fundraiser if I would run. I asked him what else he would do, and he promised to get anybody, bring anybody, send anybody that I wanted to Iowa to help me win the race and to make sure I could raise adequate funds.

He said, 'I commit myself to you, Governor, one thousand percent. You need to run for the Senate. You may make the difference.' 'Well', I said, 'I'm going home and will consider this very seriously and I'll call you back in a couple of days. I can't do this without talking to my family and a couple of other people.'

One of those people was Park Rinard, who was my respected adviser in Iowa. He had been my 'stabilizer', my mentor, my teacher in my political career, and was the best speech writer I ever had. I said, 'Park, I won't go to the Senate unless you go with me.' He didn't want to leave Iowa either; but I said, 'I need you with me, because nobody else knows me like you know me, nobody thinks like I do, like you do. You trained me; everything that I've done, from a truck driver to where I am, and if I'm going ahead you can't drop me, because if you do, I'm not going.' He said, 'I'll go.'

So he's the reason I went along with Bob Kennedy. I decided to run, and called Bob back and he said he would stay with his commitment to come out to Iowa to support me. I said, 'When you come out I'm going to invite governors from 12 states to come here and meet with you to con-vince you that you should run for President.' He said, 'I don't think that'll do it.' I said, 'Well, why don't you give me a chance to let these men talk to you?' He said, 'Alright, I'll guarantee you the chance – that's all I'll guarantee you.'

But when I listened to Bob Kennedy, he drew something out in me that made me feel that I owed not myself, but America, God, everything else, you know; that whatever my voice could be . . . I should let it be heard; that whatever I could do in the area I wanted to serve so badly, which was alcoholism, I should do it

---

A: *When did that conversation take place?*
HH: This was before the New Hampshire primary in January. Bob Kennedy made two appearances for me; one was in January. Anyway, I announced my candidacy a week later for the United States Senate. Part of that was due to his commitment to me that if I got to the Senate he would guarantee his help; he would assure my getting assignments to the appropriate commit-tees, and perhaps establish the subcommittee for which Ted Kennedy would have to release author-

ity from the health committee. That couldn't be done if Ted didn't do that.

I asked him again, 'Can you assure me that can be done?' He said, 'Governor, nobody knows what's going to happen in the Senate. I don't know who's going to get elected. I don't know if you're going to get elected. All I can assure you is that you have my word that I will do everything I can to help you do what you want to do to get a sub-committee on addictions in the United States Senate. And that includes working with my brother.' I said, 'OK. I know you may not be able to produce it but I know you'll try, so I'll take your word for it.'

It had been the first time that a public official in the capacity of one of the 50 governors of the United States, and a candidate for the United States Senate, stood up and said to the world, 'Yes, I am an alcoholic'

A: *But shortly thereafter Robert Kennedy was assassinated.*

HH: Yes, he was killed and that shattered my beliefs for the future – what he might have been as President.

Then Brinkley Smithers (Christopher Smithers Foundation, Mill Neck, NY) invited me to speak at the International Congress on Alcoholism, a conference of 62 nations, that was planned for Washington that August. If I went, I knew I would have to talk about my history of alcoholism, so there was some real political risk for me to speak before this group. About all I could say to myself in prayer was 'God, you know I've got myself in a hell of a mess. I didn't bring this decision to me and I don't know what to do.' And the thought that kept coming to me – well a bird in the hand is worth two in the bush – if I don't do this and I get beat in the election, which I probably will, then I don't have either platform.

I called my Senate campaign staff together, and everybody that I trusted, and told them about the speaking invitation; and they voted 100 per cent

that I shouldn't do it. They said, 'Don't do it. Don't leave Iowa. Worst thing you could ever do is leave Iowa, let alone talk about your past alcoholism. Who cares about who is in prison and what they're gonna do? Who cares?' I said, 'Well I care, and I'm the person that's got to deal with it the rest of my life. The odds of my winning are not very good right now anyway – they're 50/50 and may get worse.'

So I called Brink back and said I would be there at the old Shoreham Hotel. He had invited me to come to his suite for dinner that night, and we talked about the speech and the people that were there in the press conference. And I made the speech and a worldwide press conference. It was well attended, and the word went out all over the world. It had been the first time that a public official in the capacity of one of the 50 governors of the United States, and a candidate for the United States Senate, stood up and said to the world, 'Yes, I am an alcoholic.' 'I have recovered from the disease of alcoholism, I'm not ashamed of the disease of alcoholism, I'm not ashamed to talk about it. I'm as competent as I've ever been, probably more so, stronger now than I've ever been. And I believe that if everybody came out of the woods and discussed what they had then we wouldn't be having the problems we have. The cause of one of the major problems is that we're all scared to death of our shadow.'

I said, 'I'm not going to be afraid of it. The people of Iowa knew for three elections that I had been an alcoholic and they re-elected me every time. Now if they want to use this as a cause – at this point I don't think that they will – they're probably going to be upset that I left Iowa for three days to come out here and talk to you people in Washington and all over the world – but they're not going to be concerned really that I'm an alcoholic. We've been through that out there, and the people have affirmed and reaffirmed in election after election that that is no longer an issue in Iowa. So I want to say to every politician in the United States that alcoholism in your life should never be an issue in your political campaign if you've got guts enough to face it.' At a later date, when Congressman Wilbur Mills asked my advice about his own alcoholism, I said, 'Don't quit because you're an alcoholic. If you want to quit and never run again, that's fine; but for God's sake don't quit because you're an alcoholic. Let's go down there to Arkansas and beat it. I'll come down and give every hour to help you beat it and win reelection.' He said, 'All right, that won't be the reason I quit. If I don't run again, that will not be the reason.' And it wasn't. I really believed him. I wanted him to run because I figured the world would say he quit because he was an alcoholic. I didn't want that flag waving out there anymore; I never wanted it to wave again.

The move to Washington: setting up a subcommittee on alcoholism and other addictions

A: *How did the speech at the International Congress on Alcoholism in Washington influence your campaign for the Senate?*
HH: In November I was elected to the Senate by a very narrow margin, but I don't think my speech had anything to do with it. I moved to Washington, came into the Senate, and in the selection process I was appointed a majority whip, among other things. It was based on the legislative selection calendar, which meant I had a voice. I was one of five people in the Senate who selected the legislation that came up for consideration, debate and vote.

When it came to appointing committees I mostly got the assignments I wanted. I didn't get on the Foreign Relations Committee, and it turned out that it was in God's wisdom, too, that I didn't. I did get on the Health, Education and Welfare committee that I wanted. I went to Senator Ralph Yarbrough when I got the assignment, and said, 'Senator, I'd like for you to set up a new subcommittee on the subject of alcoholism and alcohol related problems and other addictions.' Yarbrough said there wasn't money for another subcommittee. I said, 'Senator, is that the only thing holding you back? Would you, as Chairman of the committee, set up a subcommittee without any money?' He said that had never been done. I said, 'I'll tell you what I'll do. You appoint the subcommittee – or you give the authority for the sub-

committee – and you go with me to talk to Senator (Ted) Kennedy to see if he will give us the authority to release from the Health subcommittee his jurisdiction over this subject matter alone for a period of one year. Then we'll renew it next year (if we agree that it should be renewed). I'll take the subcommittee and we'll work for a year with no money.' He said, 'How are you going to do that, Senator? You know nobody works around here without money.' I said, 'I'll do it with volunteers.' He said, 'Where are you going to get volunteers?' I said, 'They're all over the place. They're everywhere. I can get people to run the subcommittee and it won't cost you a dime.' He said, 'Are you sure you can do that?' I said, 'I'm absolutely 100 per cent sure.' (I wasn't, but I told him that.) He said, 'All right. Let's call Ted up and talk to him.' So we got Ted Kennedy on the telephone and we talked to him. And we had a remarkable subcommittee, including Jack [Jacob] Javits, from New York, and Pete Dominick, from Colorado, Walter Mondale, and Harrison Williams.

A: *So the subcommittee was established?*
HH: Yes, we got the subcommittee and no money. So I said to Ralph Yarbrough, 'What I didn't tell you was, I need some space. So he gave me a small office under a stairwell. 'Now where are you going to get somebody to staff it?' he said.

I had a meeting with my office manager and administrative assistant and they agreed to a part-time assignment from my own staff along with volunteers until we got some money. Their decision was to assign Wade Clark an attorney on our staff and Mary Ellen Miller, one of our best legislative assistants, to staff the committee. Mary Ellen was Acting Director because of her years of Capitol Hill [Congressional] and Washington experience. They were to recruit volunteers. One of the key people who volunteered was Nancy Olsen, who later became a full-time staff member of the committee. We asked other committee members to loan us staff help as needed. All in all it worked out quite well.

I explained to the members of the subcommittee that we had no money, but I said, 'What I'll do is, I'll direct all my honorarium money to fund the subcommittee to pay an extra staff member if we can do it.' And I went to Brink [Brinkley] Smithers and some other people and said, 'We've got no money. Can you set up some sort of a fund so we can pay some support to people who can work for the subcommittee?' So they did, and I don't even know who contributed to it, I couldn't tell you, but Brink was the key figure in getting it done. I directed most of my honorarium money – practically all of it that first year (probably $10 or $15 thousand), to supporting that subcommittee myself.

At the beginning of the second year we went back to the committee and the chairman and got them to agree to make a request to the Senate to formally establish the subcommittee and to fund it, which they did.

So that was the beginning of that subcommittee and how it got done, and how it all began even long before I ever got to the Senate or even thought about running for the Senate. The Kennedy brothers, the President, Senator Robert and Senator Edward, all played a major behind-the-scenes role in the development of addictions treatment and research in America.

The Kennedy brothers, the President, Senator Robert and Senator Edward, all played a major behind-the-scenes role in the development of addictions treatment and research in America

---

A: *Then the bulk of the subcommittee's work began after you were formally established and funded?*

HH: Yes. We set up the subcommittee and we went to work. We got more office space; we got funding; we got the support of both the Republicans and the Democrats. Jack Javits [Senator Jacob Javits, a Republican] and I worked together as a team. Jay Cutler was with Jack, Nancy Olsen was with me, and Mary Ellen Miller was the director of the subcommittee. They're the ones that did all the work, and people all over the country collaborated. And we introduced the legislation creating the National Institute on Alcoholism and Alcohol Abuse.

Working with the Republican administration

A: *Early in that term (1969), President Nixon introduced the legislation for the Controlled Substances Act, which emphasized law enforcement. Yet, around the same time, you were able to get the National Institute on Alcoholism and Alcohol Abuse established. Can you tell about some of the interchange between you and the White House and other influential members of the Executive Branch?*

HH: Roger Egberg (Assistant Secretary for Health, in the Department of Education, and Welfare) was very influential with the Nixon administration. He and I later became very good friends. He came to me at the first hearing we held and said, 'Senator, you're being very mean to me and I'm on your side.' I said, 'I don't want to be mean to you, but I've got to force you to answer some questions. And when you're answering for Richard Nixon and the administration, I know you've got to answer for the administration. But when I say to you, 'Now, Mr Secretary, what's your personal opinion on the matter as a doctor?', how are you going to answer me? Are you going to give me the President's answer, or are you morally going to give me your answer?' He said, 'I'm going to tell you the truth, what I think.'

He answered the questions honestly, and his answers were excellent. They were the answers I was looking for. They were very positive in support of us. So actually when he came in to submit a position for the administration it was in opposition to us. But as an individual he said that he believed what we were doing was right, but that it was not his decision to make, that money was not his to appropriate, and the organizational structure was not his to decide on. And I said, 'I understand all of that, doctor, Mr Secretary, but still it is important to the people of the United States on this issue to find the truth.' I said, 'I committed myself, as a recovered alcoholic, when I crawled out of a bathtub thirty-some years ago after almost blowing my brains out, to try to find the truth of whatever the hell put me in that bathtub. And I'm still looking for it. I don't know what the truth is. I don't have any preconceived ideas about it. I know that a lot of people have found abstinence from alcohol through Alcoholics Anonymous. I know that one of the co-founders of Alcoholics Anonymous testified before this sub-committee and he himself said that he hoped he lived to see the day when tens of thousands of recovered alcoholics would be walking the corridors of this nation's capitol advocating for the cause of sobriety and alcoholism.' I said to Dr Egberg, 'All I'm asking you, the Department of Health, Education and Welfare, for is the money, the appropriations, the people and the space to do the research. You pick the people. You do the research. You report to the Congress and the people of America – the truth. You won't be reporting to the Democrat Chair of a subcommittee – you'll be reporting to the people of America the truth of what scientists can find out about this disease.' Dr Egberg said, 'I can't disagree with that statement.'

And we're still seeking the truth to this very day; we don't know the answers yet. Maybe we never will. Maybe the answer is, we won't find it, and we're going to have to live with what we've got, the best we can, but we're narrowing it down.

The disease concept as political lever

HH: I said to Roger Egberg (he favored law enforcement), 'I don't want to do anything that in any way will let alcoholism be used as an excuse for committing crimes. I'm not saying to anyone that a person who commits a crime should not be held accountable for the commission of that crime. I'm saying that if they do commit a crime, and the reason is that they're a victim of a disease that we know is a disease, called alcoholism, then we should have the responsibility of treating the disease that caused them to commit the crime. And if they can then be healed of that disease, that should be considered by the legal structures in what the future of that person should be. That's all I'm saying.' Egberg said, 'Well, I can't disagree with that, either.'

So that's what we were working on – trying to work our way through the structure, the administration presenting the law and order position on it and me presenting the health picture on it. I didn't look at it as an us or them situation.

A: *When you first came to the Senate, the Federal Civil Commitment statute of 1966, which mandated compulsory treatment of drug addicts (even those who had not committed any crime), was still on the books. How did you feel about that?*

HH: Everybody in the Congress was proud about it, and I felt very bad about it. You know, we had a bunch of people even on the committee who were the prime people that had written it and structured it and been recognized for everything that they had done. My point was very simple. I wanted to get people to recognize the fact that I'm no different from anyone else. If I have heart disease, I'm no different. But for some reason if I have what they've already decided is a disease that they don't know what to do with, I am still different. To this very day I have tried to get the American Society of Addiction Medicine to tell me when someone is well from the disease of alcoholism. I can't get them to tell me. Now I say to them, if you go free from cancer for five years, you can actually certify more or less that that person is free from cancer.

I committed myself, as a recovered alcoholic, when I crawled out of a bathtub thirty-some years ago after almost blowing my brains out, to try to find the truth of whatever the hell put me in that bathtub

---

A: *The American Psychiatric Association has used the diagnostic concept of alcoholism or addiction* in remission. *Many people have asked if this will mean you get labelled for life. That is, are you always in remission? Are you never over it? Is it always put on your medical chart?*

HH: You see, I have to lie any time I do anything. To this day, forty-some years later, the questions are there: 'Have you ever been treated?' I was never treated for alcoholism. Hell, they didn't treat anybody. 'Did you ever attend 12-Step meetings?' I wouldn't tell them the truth. Why should I tell them the truth? I've been abstinent longer than I was drinking. I mean, there are millions of people out there lying every day and saying they're working a program of honesty. We are forced to work a program of dishonesty.

Why can't the American Society of Addiction Medicine say to me, we have scientifically made a decision that a person who has continued abstinence for this period of time, working and living a normal life, is in remission from the disease *and is well*. That's it.

A: *There are a number of factors that keep them from doing that; but the main concern seems to be that if you say you're cured, then there's no reason you shouldn't behave like a 'normal' person, including social use of alcohol.*
HH: We are normal people.

A: *Some people believe that if you were once alcoholic you are always one drink away from relapse. Their view of the disorder is that no matter how long you have not been actively drinking, you cannot drink socially. Would you like to comment on that point of view?*
HH: I really believe that people recover from the disease of alcoholism. This is a subject matter I hope we live long enough to discuss. I don't believe we're always one drink away from drunk.

Kids were thrown in the DC jail and raped 25 times overnight for no more than smoking a marijuana cigarette. You know it was just an absolute abomination

---

Views on cannabis

A: *Can we return for a moment to your role in moderating some of the provisions of the Controlled Substances Act? For example, although President Nixon wanted the Department of Justice to have the power to determine which drugs it is illegal to possess, under the provisions of that Act, the Senate made the decision to give most of that power to the Secretary of Health. Did you have something to do with that?*
HH: I was a negotiator at the Vienna Conference on Controlled Substances. I represented the Senate in the negotiations, in 1973 or 1974, I don't remember exactly when it was. I was also a Senate

member of the National Marijuana Commission under the chairmanship of Governor Shaefer. Senator Javits was on the commission with me. Once we had completed our studies (on marijuana and heroin), a lot of which was done by professional staff who visited the Middle East and England and brought information back to us, Jack Javits and I considered that what we were doing on marijuana was wrong. Primarily we were approaching the law enforcement angle wrong because we were putting kids in jail for using marijuana, and that was just absolutely nuts. So what we did was introduce legislation, he and I together, that the simple possession of a limited amount of marijuana for personal use was not a criminal act. A kid down in Virginia had been sent to prison for 20 years or something – picked up down at the airport in Virginia, at Dulles Airport – which was absolutely atrocious. Kids were thrown in the DC jail and raped 25 times overnight for no more than smoking a marijuana cigarette. You know it was just an absolute abomination to us, so we corrected that part of the law by making that a non-criminal violation.

A: *How did you deal with the controversy about the Marijuana Commission's position on the legal status of marijuana?*
HH: As far as legalizing marijuana, you know people go incendiary over it. You know they just go up in smoke, saying that it's the doorway drug to everything else. Well as far as I am concerned, the doorway drug to everything else is probably tobacco, and then alcohol, and then maybe marijuana comes in a faraway third – y'know, so far back you can't see it running. But we were not going to face the issues of tobacco and alcohol because of money. We're in big dollars, big bucks, big influence, big everything; and until we got some people in government who were willing to call a spade a spade about tobacco – hell, it's not alcohol that's killing me, it's tobacco that's killing me. Every breath I draw I pay a price for every cigarette I smoked. And I was not an idiot.

I was Governor of Iowa in 1965 when they brought that first report in saying cigarettes were harmful to your health, and I sat there and asked the reporters did anyone on that Commission smoke after they brought in that report? They said, 'Yes, two people did.' I said, 'What did they smoke?' George Knowles, the primary political reporter said, 'I don't know.' I said, 'Find out, I'd like to know.' He came back and said, 'The guy smokes Larks.' Well I changed to Larks and smoked them for another 15 years. That's what an addict is. We were addicted, and just this year I see those guys sitting up and testifying that tobacco isn't addictive. Addictive? It's the most addictive drug that I ever got my hands on in my life – cigarette tobacco, worse than alcohol. It's worse than all the rest of them and it's more deadly.

And then we're saying to our tobacco companies, 'Well, all right, we'll help you grow all the tobacco you want, but you ship it all to the third world countries. You send it to Russia, send it to South America, send it to Africa. You addict two-thirds of the world's population – kill them off.' Is that a moral issue or isn't it? If we were using some form of chemical gas to do it we would be condemned in the world court, but if we use cigarettes to do it, it's wonderful. We're making a big profit. It shows up on the balance of trade. Now, marijuana scares the hell out of people. We ought to be doing more research on marijuana.

Presidential influence

A: *Senator, were you surprised when the Nixon administration decided to put a lot of money into making treatment available to drug addicts, even, for a short time, funding treatment more generously than law enforcement?*
HH: I was, and I would have to say in retrospect I'm more surprised by it, because some of the people that followed him in office I thought would pick up on that and advance it. President Carter tried to. He set up the National Commission on Alcoholism and Alcohol Related Problems. The Congress passed it. Carter appointed me to chair that Commission in 1978, but they never got the thing established and workable, and it was up to the President to fund it. Carter lost the election and Reagan came in, and Reagan refused to fund the Commission and let it die on the vine. So even though we had set up the offices and hired the per-

sonnel and had the system in place, Reagan just pulled the plug. Nixon wouldn't have done that. Nixon would have let that thing flourish. But I think there was a powerful political influence in the Reagan administration which cut that funding off completely. And it was strictly in the White House, not in the Congress, at that time.

That was my last political hold on doing anything. Of course Carter was the last Democratic president we had that we could work with. We tried to get Commissions established in the Congress and we failed each time. All the leadership – the older people in the Congress my age in both the House and the Senate – were gone. We died off, or didn't seek re-election, or were defeated. And it just gradually petered out – that's what happened. Yes, I was surprised that Nixon did what he did. I didn't think he did enough, actually, but he was a hell of a lot better than anyone we've had since on this issue.

A: *You and others in Congress must have felt some misgivings allowing Nixon so much power for the Special Action Office of Drug Abuse Prevention and for the Drug Abuse Treatment Act. Can you comment on that?*
HH: I didn't think that he'd do much with it. I'm not against the Executive having power. I want the right to monitor the power. I think in some ways the chief executive can do a lot more than the Congress can. I did it as Governor, for example. If we had left it up to the Iowa General Assembly to do what I did, there would have been nothing done in Iowa, absolutely nothing. It wouldn't have happened. But you put a powerful chief executive in there who can go to the people, and who gets his strength from the people, and can appeal to the people and make that an issue and say, this is what we need to do, the power is handled OK. And then the people force the pressure on the members of Congress and the Congress has to go along and supply the resources and the funding for what needs to be done.

I don't see anything wrong with the President – and I don't mean the White House, but the President – being held accountable for people he appoints. And I'd look at it all carefully; I'd want to monitor it, hold some hearings to see what did you do and how is it being done?

A: *And is that what you did? Did you hold a lot of hearings to monitor what was going on?*

HH: That's right. I was concerned about what was happening over in Vietnam. I was concerned about the fact that there was an awful lot of heroin coming in that seemed to be coming with American authority, and some of it through one airline that was supposedly owned by the CIA and being flown into Vietnam – and that we had addicted probably a 100 000 young Americans in Vietnam and then sent them back to the United States by releasing them from the armed services. Then we released a flurry of addicted young men across the country, in all 50 states – on a country that was ill prepared to do anything about the problem. We had created an epidemic in a war in Southeast Asia and released it in America. If it had been venereal disease, we'd have shot somebody; but because it was addiction all we wanted to do was put the men in prison.

A: *What did you think about Nixon's decision to change the code of military justice so that military personnel who were addicted or using drugs could receive treatment and not be dishonorably discharged from service?*

HH: I was surprised. I had worked for years to penetrate the Pentagon and their systems of justice to try and do that.

I was known as 'Mr Addiction' in the Congress at that time. Anybody in the Senate or the House who had an alcohol or drug problem called me

---

'Mr Addiction'

A: *How generally, informally, did your colleagues in Washington react to your interest in addictions?*

HH: Oh, I was known as 'Mr Addiction' in the Congress at that time. Anybody in the Senate or the House who had an alcohol or drug problem called me. I was a walking symbol of recovery and a lot of the members who drank heavily said they used to hide behind a statue when I walked by

because the word was out that I could tell an alcoholic at 300 feet while walking down the hallway. But most of them did not have a problem. The fact is that the Congress is highly visible, that every member is highly visible; but there is no greater percentage of them that have a problem with alcohol than in any other group. Politics is an honorable profession. I get upset at people who want to pick out the Congress or the administration or executives in government and say – look, they're a bunch of damn drunks. They are *not* a bunch of damn drunks.

A: *Senator, another important change in treatment methodology took place during the time of your influence in the Senate, and that was the approval of methadone as a treatment for opioid addiction. Can you comment on that?*

HH: Well, I wasn't for it. I had heard an awful lot about methadone being on the street, and the danger of methadone on the street, and the fact that it was an addictive drug itself, and it would be sold and re-sold. What changed my mind was Senator Javits. Jack Javits and I went to New York and held some hearings up there. In the process of the hearings we went down to 'the Tombs' one morning to see the men who were dragged to jail the night before who were heroin addicts – watched them climbing the bars and sweating and cursing and trembling and shaking and no way to get any help or anything, there in the holding tanks that were just massive human terror pits, actually. I said to Senator Javits, who I admired a great deal, 'My God, can't we do something about this?' He said, 'Well, Senator Hughes, we've got to do something about it, but we probably won't be successful.'

Then we starting holding hearings and we got methadone approved as an agent that could be used. I'm still criticized for it. Methadone has been misused on the streets a lot of the time and there are a lot of doctors that have prescribed it wrongly – I mean they give people a month's supply to take home in some places.

A: *Senator, you retired from the Senate after a spectacularly successful single term. You have continued, however, to be extremely active in educat-*

ing the public about alcoholism and working to reduce the stigma associated with alcoholism and drug addiction. Can you tell us something about these later activities?

HH: I've been involved in a great many public service activities since I retired. Here are a few that come to mind. I worked for the Senate Judiciary Committee under Chairman James Eastland, of Mississippi, for two years. I was appointed by the Senate to chair a Commission on the Operation of the Senate, which I did for two years. I was president of the International Congress on Alcoholism for six years. I established Harold Hughes Centers, Inc., in 1984, and am still involved in that activity to the present. I founded the Society of Americans for Recovery, Inc. and SOAR Foundation, Inc., in 1990, and served as Chairman of the Board of both organizations for five years. And, of course, I have lectured publicly for the past 15 years on the subject of alcoholism and addictions.

Jerome H. Jaffe

Jerome H Jaffe was born 6 July 1933, in Philadelphia, USA. He gained degrees in psychology at Temple University and his MD in 1958. He trained at the US Public Health Service Hospitals, Staten Island and Lexington, Kentucky and at the Albert Einstein College of Medicine, New York. He was awarded Speciality Board Certifications in Psychiatry and Addiction Psychology and has held numerous academic and public appointments including: Director, SAODAP, 1971–1973; Director, Addiction Research Centre, Baltimore, 1984–1989; Acting Director NIDA, 1985–1986; and Director, Office of Evaluation, Scientific Analysis and Synthesis (ADAMHA), 1990–1997. He was awarded the Nathan B. Eddy Memorial Award (CPDD) in 1994 and was made an Honorary Fellow of the SSA in 1997 and an Honorary Fellow of the Royal College of Psychiatrists in 1999. He has contributed extensively to the scientific literature.

Early background

Addiction: *It is always interesting to know something about the educational background of people we interview in this series. Before we get onto your university training, could you go a bit further back and tell us something about your earlier school experience?*

Jerome Jaffe: I went to a neighbourhood elementary school and junior high school, and then to a remarkable place called Central High School in Philadelphia. This was an institution that was so steeped in history that it continued to have the authority from the state to award the Bachelor of Arts degree as well as a high school diploma. It had its own library endowed by its distinguished alumni, which was very unusual for a public school. Anybody could come from any place in the city provided they met certain criteria which I never fully understood, but obviously it was for an elite group and it had that reputation. It happened to be the high school closest to my house and my brother had gone there.

A: *So, this imbued an idea of scholarship, science?*

JJ: Actually, it did almost the opposite. I thought that I was not academically adequate once I got there. The quality of the other students was very high. My best friend was at that time Charles

Epstein who turned out to be first in the class – the Valedictorian, first in all things actually. That was the gauge by which I measured my own intellectual capacities. I first heard about Harvard University when Charlie applied and went to Harvard; I drove him up there. I did not consider comparing myself with him or that I should go to college.

A: *Did your family put academic expectations on you?*

JJ: My mother did, but I wasn't certain that her expectations were at all realistic. My brother had gone to college on the GI Bill; my sisters had not gone at all. I think that among immigrant families of my parents' generation it was considered an accomplishment to have a son become a doctor.

A: *So you went to Temple University to study psychology?*

JJ: I didn't really go there to study psychology. I applied to Temple because I had been turned down for a job as an auto mechanic.

A: *How did that tragedy happen?*

JJ: It turned out that the people who were hiring did not believe that anybody who had gone to Central High School was serious about becoming an auto mechanic. So I was forced to apply to a college, and Temple had very reasonable fees, a very reasonable timeframe and was very close by.

You didn't have to apply six months in advance, the application was inexpensive and you could just walk down and take the exam. I had no specific plan; I thought that rather than argue with my parents I would register for some kind of pre-med courses. I wasn't very serious about college at all. During the first year I didn't care much about it. Then I registered to major in psychology because of some unpleasant interaction with the department of biology. I would have had to walk up four flights to register for the biology major and the rules were such that it had to be at a certain time. I had just had an appendectomy and I didn't think I could make the four flights of stairs two days after the operation. I registered to major in psychology. That took the next $2\frac{1}{2}$ years.

A: *Was there a particular slant to the psychology?*
JJ: Yes. My professor, Hubert Hamilton, wonderful man with a big walrus moustache, taught about behaviour – mostly animal behaviour – his lectures everyone else found dry and somewhat boring, and I found them wonderful. His descriptions of how people studied bees, and Muenzinger's work with rats, and Skinner and Watson, these to me were fascinating, as was talking to him about any subject. He would pause and look off in the corner and you could almost see his mind going through index cards and he would tell you about something and exactly when it was published: the date and the page.

A: *We're talking about the early 1950s aren't we?*
JJ: Yes, I think it was 1952/53.

A: *Did America at that time give a strong image of who one was?*
JJ: I don't think so. You have to understand this was post-World War II America. It was a time of reinvigoration of the economy, the colleges were filled with men who had served in the military, they were more mature than those of us who hadn't served, they had clear-cut views of what they needed to accomplish and they had the discipline to do it. It was a college experience not at all typical of later generations – this mixture of ages. You had 30-year-old freshmen. It was also a time

before America had this tremendous expansion of the scientific enterprise; it was that transition time. The National Institute of Mental Health had only been established a few years before; the federal willingness to fund the scientific enterprise had not yet really blossomed so that academia was very different then from what it later became. It was very small.

A: *As regards the society around you, would it be right to say that it was not a time of self-doubt?*
JJ: No, I think for most people it was a time of relative optimism. In 1950/51 we entered the Korean war and people of my age group were subject to the draft, unless you were in college. On looking back now I suspect that perhaps had some influence on why I stayed in college, and I do remember that it was an issue among my contemporaries.

A: *So you graduated in '54, and top of your class?*
JJ: It was a small class.

A: *You then went on and did a Masters degree in six months in experimental psychology, while waiting to get into medical school?*
JJ: Well, I had nothing better to do. I had not planned to go to medical school.

A: *But you decided at that point to enrol.*
JJ: There were a number of factors pointing in that direction. By that time I had become interested in research in psychology. This was at the time of a breakthrough in understanding of brain reward mechanisms. The other thing that was happening was that chlorpromazine had been described, so it was an era of tremendous excitement about what could be done in psychopharmacology. When I discussed the possibility of graduate work in psychology with Dr Hamilton, he suggested that there were very few resources for research in psychology and that I might be better off going into psychiatry and then going on to research. There seemed to be much more resources available for people in the medical area than for psychology. But when I decided to go to medical school it was already too late to enter. You had to take the exam almost a year in advance. So I pro-

ceeded to take summer courses and was left with the six months gap.

A: *Then you graduated in medicine and got your MD. That must have been a heady day.*
JJ: June of '58 and yes, it was a sense of completion; it was a good time. More than one thing was happening as I graduated, because Faith and I got married almost, if not the next day, certainly within that same week. The next morning after the wedding I reported to my internship and began work as an intern immediately.

I thought the logical place to go would be to wherever Wikler was working, which was at Lexington

The Lexington experience

A: *You started work as an intern in the US Public Health Service?*
JJ: All of us had to either go into the military or the Public Health Service (PHS) because we were deferred from the draft for the Korean War. And I entered the PHS because I thought that it would make it easier to make contact with Abraham Wikler. I had read his book in '57, this incredible, comprehensive review of the relationship of pharmacology to psychiatry.[1] It was what I was looking for. Shifting from psychology to psychiatry in order to do research, by that time I had become interested in psychopharmacology and really I found some kind of identity in that book. So I thought the logical place to go would be to wherever Wikler was working, which was at Lexington.

A: *So by stealth you approached Lexington?*
JJ: Well, it wasn't just by stealth, I had to take an internship and I signed up for the PHS but I was too naive to understand the ramifications of the various divisions in the PHS. Wikler belonged to a research division and I had signed up for the clinical division and once I had done so, they were very reluctant to part with my body and allow me to move into the more privileged research organization where I could work directly with Wikler.

A: *But in '59 you arrived in Lexington.*
JJ: Yes, the clinical division of that hospital which was in charge of treating addicts was actually the same building in which Wikler was located. So there were Wikler and Isbell and Martin and their co-workers.

A: *How did you first meet Wikler, did you call on him or meet him in the corridor?*
JJ: First I'd already corresponded with him, but that hadn't done any good. The fact is that they ran a course on Saturdays, and as part of the academic training for the psychiatrists in the clinical division we got academic lectures from the researchers at the Addiction Research Center. Both Wikler and Isbell gave some of those lectures and they provided an excellent core curriculum in the sciences. So I thought the logical place to go would be to wherever Wikler was working, which was at Lexington

A: *What do you remember of Wikler as a person?*
JJ: A man of humour, a man of tremendous intellectual rigor. He was widely read. On one of his sabbaticals he had learnt to read Russian and had gone to study Pavlovian theory in Russia. When he first entered the Public Health Service he had gone off to Yale to study with some of the best electrophysiologists in the world at the time. He had studied remarkably widely, but he was at the same time warm and interesting and easily approachable.

A: *And Isbell?*
JJ: Isbell was again one of the most unpretentious gentlemen that I had the privilege of meeting. He was a giant in that field and yet in no way did he let his stature make you feel that you couldn't approach him or talk to him.

A: *Lexington was presumably the first place you met a narcotic addict?*
JJ: Let me think. I don't recall ever meeting an addict as a medical student and I'm not sure I met any as an intern, so it probably was the first time.

A: *Was that a shock to the system – presumably addicts were not people of high repute?*

JJ: I think they were remarkably like us. Somehow I'd never ingested this image of dangerous 'dope fiends'. The remarkable thing is how little psychopathology you saw, how easy it was to talk to addicts and how difficult it was to imagine them doing all the things they said they did sometimes. I found them rather likeable.

A: *You'd gone there partly because you were inspired by reading Wikler and you were interested in psychopharmacology, but presumably you suddenly found an ancillary interest which was addiction?*

JJ: I knew Wikler was working with addiction and I also recognized that you could learn something of psychopharmacology working with addicts. Meeting and dealing with addiction was not separate from psychopharmacology, it was a means to explore psychopharmacology. I did a lot of reading, what people from Lexington had written and they had written almost all that was available on addiction at the time.

A: *The start of your personal involvement in research?*

JJ: I had actually spent a summer fellowship doing pharmacological research before I left medical school. I don't recall doing any research at Lexington; there wasn't the opportunity.

A: *Let me ask you this. Wikler and Isbell, famous founding fathers to whom we should be grateful, did research on human subjects and it included their study on rum fits.[2] They gave alcohol in large quantities to federal prisoners – patients – then withdrew the alcohol and got them to have fits. They did rather the same with barbiturates.[3] Now one could say that it would be wrong to judge these people harshly in the light of today's expectations. Having said that, isn't it rather surprising that any doctor should have exposed human subjects to that sort of danger?*

JJ: You had to, I guess, have lived in those times. The notion that what was being done was unethical never arose. In the same sense their basic approach to learning which drugs were addictive was to administer opiate drugs to addicts who had volunteered for this work. They would stop the drug and give a placebo, and people would go through withdrawal. It did not seem at the time that if one obtained consent that this was a particularly unethical thing to do. I realise that now review groups and institutions might not permit it. Of course, at many institutions you wouldn't be permitted to give a narcotic to someone and there are places where you couldn't give a dose of alcohol to a former alcoholic. The interesting environment that pertained at Lexington was that these were prisoners who volunteered specifically to come from other places, to come to this place because they were treated far better and they had lots of time before their sentence was up. For some it was an opportunity to do something they thought was worthwhile, to contribute to knowledge instead of sitting in a cell. Others I think might have been motivated by the possibility of time off from their sentence, and still others might have argued that if they had to be in prison they might as well be getting high on drugs. The important thing about that situation was that you did not have the ethical concern that if somebody started on a drug, they would then leave abruptly and continue to use that drug illicitly: those of us who do any research of this kind now may actually pose a higher risk to patients than Wikler and Isbell did in the great majority of their experiments. The patients who were prisoner volunteers – not sure what's the best way to characterize them – often stayed at least another year after they had their last drug.

A: *Lexington, was it at the time a sense of being an extraordinary place, a crucible of addiction studies?*

JJ: I thought so, but I guess I had a peculiar view because for most of psychiatry addiction was a backwater in which they were not interested. If people had an interest in addiction and psychopharmacology, Lexington was a great place. This was research in its entire range of activities, from the animal studies of Martin and the others to the studies of Isbell and Fraser, to the sociological follow-up studies of Jack O'Donnell, all of those people we could touch and talk to and look at.

A: *So the people who were your contemporaries, a roll-call that included Frederick Glaser and George Vaillant?*

JJ: And others including Herbert Kleber, Everett Ellinwood, Marie Nyswander and Donald Klein.

A: *So it was an influential place, but yet something of an accident of nature that this prison hospital had a research centre attached to it which was to become a crucial base for the study of addiction?*

JJ: Well, as a matter of fact I think that things were conceived in that way. Not that it would do so well, but from the beginning I believe that it was part of the mission of those hospitals to do research from the time they opened in 1935. The money for it was first put up in the late 1920s. They were to conduct research on how best to treat addiction, how to deal with the problem, so it was one of government's better ideas. But they were lucky to get the kinds of scientists who came to work there.

Time at Albert Einstein

A: *You then went to Albert Einstein Medical College in New York where you were in a post-doctoral fellowship programme in pharmacology, but also continued with clinical psychiatry.*

JJ: At the time the psychiatry being taught was still dominated by the psychodynamic view. My interaction with Wikler and my reading, had led me to believe that I wanted a thorough grounding in pharmacology and basic science before I completed any further work in psychiatry. Maybe in a sense I was even unconsciously emulating Wikler, who did not complete all of his psychiatric training until he had gotten that kind of special grounding in the sciences of behaviour. I think it was Dr Sydney Ellis (one of my medical school professors) who suggested that I try Alfred Gilman's department. I considered one other place – there was an institute at the University of Michigan and when I went there to visit I met Sam Gershon and I very seriously considered Michigan. But then I went to Einstein and met Dr Gilman and Murray Jarvik and Seth Sharpless. There was something about the place, I just knew 'this is the place'. For the

first time in my life somebody said, 'You know I've looked over your CV and you seem to be fairly bright, why don't you tell us what you would like to do?' I didn't have much of an idea what I'd like to do, but the notion that somebody would say that – this was Al Gilman – and meeting Seth Sharpless and Murray Jarvik, they were so bright and so knowledgeable, I felt what a wonderful opportunity, what a privilege. So I said yes. It was the notion of supersensitivity as a potential mechanism that might account for tolerance and physical dependence, that Seth and I discussed and began to bat around, and that was what I started off looking at when I came to Einstein.

A: *The idea evolved out of conversation between you and Seth?*

JJ: Well, Seth had been working on supersensitivity issues in slabs of brain. He was interested in this phenomenon generally. He had never thought much about addiction or tolerance or physical dependence. We began this dialogue, had the experiments planned, and just about the time we got our first paper written Emmelin published a review in *Pharmacological Reviews* on supersensitivity in the central nervous system.[4] We then went on to explore whether some of the implications might hold true; we didn't have all the tools we wanted, but we worked with what we had.

A: *So you were again in an environment which you very much liked – and no accident because you had selected yourself in.*

JJ: It was wonderful and probably the most stimulating place I've ever worked.

A: *And you started to produce your first papers. Did you go on with clinical psychiatry?*

JJ: I'm not sure why now, but I did. The hospital was across the street and I asked whether as part of the psychopharmacological training, I could complete the residency and after some negotiation they agreed. I was concurrently a Fellow and a Resident and part of the teaching staff at Einstein. Let me say something about what happened in those four or five years at Einstein in addition to the training. Perhaps the most important thing was that there was a heroin epidemic in New York. There was the 'beat generation' and the controversy about marijuana, and people who knew me from Lexington kept 'phoning me and asking for help of various kinds. And the faculty continually asked my input on this because almost from the first year I arrived there, I was giving lectures to the medical students on addiction. So, what was previously an obscure area of concern was moving to the forefront and I found myself, although still a trainee in some respects, the resident expert for that institution. In '64 Martin talked for the first time about cyclazocine, a long-acting opiate antagonist. The system back then was such that within six months or so I was able to get supplies of it and get permission to conduct a study. I had found in various contacts with addicts who knew me, that some wanted to try something to get clean, and so we were able to study cyclazocine as a treatment.[5] I also was studying with a few patients who used intravenous opiates. I was using oxymorphone because I could distinguish that from heroin in urine tests. The hypothesis I was testing was whether or not on a constant dose of oxymorphone people would inevitably begin to supplement with heroin, or whether under the proper contingencies they could remain on a stable dose.

With multiple options, how do we know which treatment works best for whom? That became my interest

---

A: *Did you know what Vincent Dole was doing at the time?*
JJ: I did not at first. Certainly when I started research with cyclazocine I did not know what he was doing – he had not yet published – but I think we met early in 1965 and we had good relations from the beginning. One of my patients was actually sent to me by Marie Nyswander.

A: *So here you were with a training in psychology, in psychiatry, and in psychopharmacology, and with an interest in drug addiction. Suddenly you were standing in absolutely the right place.*
JJ: Yes, standing in the right place at the right time. It was clear to me that what one needed to

know – because of the existence of the Therapeutic Communities (I had visited Daytop Village) – was, well, how does a clinician decide whether to use the antagonist or methadone or Therapeutic Community or detoxification? With multiple options, how do we know which treatment works best for whom? That became my interest.

The move to Chicago

A: *You left Einstein in 1966 and went to Chicago. What were the reasons for that move?*
JJ: Well, I had available to me at Einstein all the papers written by the researchers at Lexington (they were kind enough to give me a set of their reprints), and what I found was a paper describing the actions of L-alpha-acetylmethadol which I later called LAAM. I was thinking, methadone has to be given every day if you want to avoid diversion issues, but this drug might only have to be given three times a week. I was able to find a supply of it. This was 1965. I wrote a grant application which I thought could win funding because there weren't too many people applying for grants in this area. But then I began negotiating for some space at Einstein and it was a very strange situation. All I was asking for was a place where we could dispense LAAM and I thought we could get away with a room about 5×10 ft, a small nursing station. Although they had an entire empty tuberculosis hospital, I could not convince anybody to give me any space where I could carry out this study. The patients who were getting opiates from me before were picking up their medicines at the local pharmacy and that was fine; but on this experimental drug I thought that we should directly observe it. Finally, I asked for a janitor's closet. It was a generous janitor's closet, 5×6 ft. But the janitors objected; they had many other closets, but they seemed to need this one particularly.

A: *What happened?*
JJ: So I said I would not put in for a grant and then find I have no way to execute it. The institution was not yet ready to invest what it takes to carry out this kind of research. I had met Danny Freedman when I invited him to a symposium on

drug abuse. He was then the world expert on LSD and hallucinogens. In '65 or '66 he was appointed Chairman of Psychiatry at the University of Chicago; he asked me if I would join his department and do research on drug abuse and I said I would, after I found this impasse in New York. Then some interesting things began to develop that changed my direction as a researcher a great deal. Danny was asked to help the Illinois Drug Abuse Advisory Council to develop a plan for treating addiction. This was a governor's council with distinguished people: judges, clinicians, lawyers. He asked me if I would be a consultant to that group and I said yes. They were thinking of civil commitment and therapeutic communities and a variety of things, and I said there just isn't enough knowledge to say where you should put all your money. This was 1966/67, when the federal government had just passed a national civil commitment. New York State, in 1965, had passed a massive major civil commitment programme and were building facilities to confine addicts for treatment. The City of New York had recently invested a tremendous amount, not in Dole and Nyswander's methadone programme, but in Dr Efren Ramirez's approach to the therapeutic community, the origin of Phoenix House.

A: *What did you do when you got to Chicago?*
JJ: Basically I tried to educate people of good will who wanted to learn some things. We talked about antagonists, methadone and therapeutic communities. I said the only thing a sensible state could do was set up some of these, see if they can scale them up, try to do a study that will compare them, and expand those that seem to be successful.

A: *You used Illinois as your research laboratory then?*
JJ: It became the laboratory. That was the proposal that the Advisory Council recommended to the state legislature, but on the day before they were ready to send it – I think it was Jim Moran (who later became a federal judge) – said, 'We've decided your advice is excellent. We will recommend this to the legislature of the State of Illinois. But there's one condition: we will recommend it only if you agree to run it.' The money involved

was small potatoes – only about US$1m, but at that time it was significant for someone like me.

A: *How did you respond?*
JJ: It was a shock because I had won a federal fellowship, a research career development award, built around the work I had done with Seth Sharpless on denervation supersensitivity. I was funded to build a laboratory to try to find out more about the nature of tolerance and physical dependence. I was pretty sure I couldn't do both that and run this new Illinois initiative. I had met a few drug addicts over this period of six months while going back and forth between New York and the Illinois advisory group, and these were good people. At the time there was not a single bed in all of Illinois where one could get detoxified. There were no outpatient programmes. If you wanted to get detoxified in the city of Chicago you pleaded guilty to a minor crime and then they would put you in the medical unit of the local jail, where a kindly nurse might give you some chlorpromazine. Through some of the musicians I had treated in New York, I met musicians in Chicago and I realised that this was a backward place in terms of providing any kind of humane, decent treatment. It was a moral dilemma. I had a research career and I wasn't sure how serious the State of Illinois was in saying that they would not make these funding recommendations unless I agreed to do the job. But it really seemed to be a decision to give up lab science and to move into clinical and administrative areas that I was not trained to handle. I guess what I said was yes, I'll do it, because it was an opportunity to create treatment where no treatment existed.

A: *Was Einstein very upset when you left?*
JJ: I don't really think that they were. It was an interesting situation that the department of psychiatry did not consider me a real psychiatrist because I had training in pharmacology, and the department of pharmacology really didn't think I was a real pharmacologist because I had this interest in psychiatry. These interdisciplinary appointments or trainings worked to a slight disadvantage in those early years. I maintained cordial relation-

ships because I came back each year for many years to give lectures in pharmacology.

A: *So was Chicago a good place to live in those years?*

JJ: Yes and no. We found a lovely house not far from the University, but within a year there were the assassinations of Martin Luther King and Robert Kennedy and the place became tense and there were riots. We lived on the south side and there was a community leader who said over the radio that white people who lived on the south side perhaps should consider leaving. There was a sense of 'You don't belong here'; it did not make for great comfort. The neighbourhood I was in was quite pleasant, but there was a feeling of not being entirely safe, although many prominent people and University of Chicago faculty – black and white – lived there.

A: *You were doing something so different from experiments in laboratory settings. Were there different feelings about yourself – what did it feel like?*

JJ: It was probably the most gratifying time of my life. I wasn't meeting addicts in an institution, I was meeting real people, I met their families. We probably broke all the rules for psychiatry as we had been taught it – that you maintain your distance, you don't form personal relationships. The passivity of analysis was not appropriate in the arena in which I found myself. We built some treatment and got it started and I saw such transformations in lives that if I had only done that much and never anything more, I would probably have still felt that I had made a contribution. My wife and I remember all of those people with great fondness; we had some wonderful parties for the entire programme. We were almost like a family and we had the parties in my house. One of the therapeutic communities was only a few blocks away and we would go over there and they would adopt our kids, or maybe we adopted their kids. But it was this sense of neighbours and sharing that gave you a sense that you were changing people's lives in a way that was impossible for the average psychiatrist to do when we treated one or even a few people at a time. The state always gave

us more money because we were the most efficient programme you could possibly imagine. We innovated, we did not see a sharp distinction between methadone and therapeutic communities and detoxification. So people who were on methadone could go to a therapeutic community and learn about group therapy. And there were some people in therapeutic communities who said to people about to leave, 'Well if you're gonna leave and be using heroin, maybe you should go to the methadone programme'. And people recycled through who couldn't make it in one situation, they would try another. The other thing I was able to do early on: I guess by 1969 I was able to recruit Bob Schuster, Patrick Hughes and David Deitch. My own feeling is that David had developed the first real therapeutic community that was not a cult. Synanon was an extension of Chuck Dederich, but Daytop Village was a describable methodology for changing behaviour. I had met David in 1965 or 1966, but by 1968 he had had a break with the Daytop Board of directors, and I was able to recruit him and five or six of his people and mix them in with people from Chicago. He brought this wealth of experience to bear and it was an absolutely wonderful time, although I sometimes felt tremendously stressed.

I saw such transformations in lives that if I had only done that much and never anything more, I would probably have still felt that I had made a contribution

Lead-up to the White House

A: *This happy period where you were doing such worthwhile things and enjoying the human experience was suddenly thrown in another direction when you had the invitation to go to Washington in 1971, and take on the role of drug czar. How did that happen?*

JJ: It probably began with Bob DuPont. Bob was given the task of building a drug treatment programme in Washington DC in 1968/69. Nixon had been elected in 1968 and was making a commitment to deal with crime, and Bob DuPont's programme in Washington had attracted the interest of people in the White House. Bob probably mentioned that they might want to look at our programme as well as that in Washington, and I think somewhere in the spring or summer of 1970, a junior White House staff person – Jeffrey Donfeld – came out to visit our programme. Bob had mostly methadone and Donfeld was surprised to see that we had therapeutic communities, we had detoxification, we had something for youth, as well as methadone and narcotic antagonists. Donfeld looked at what we were doing and apparently wrote some notes to his superiors – he was part of John Erlichman's domestic council staff. Later, Donfeld asked me to put together a group of experts to prepare a report on how they could deal with treatment and demand issues. He wanted it in six weeks, he wanted it to be absolutely secret, and he wanted it to represent the best thinking scientifically. The demands that he made I didn't think could be met, but at that time being rather young and naive and impressed with the name 'White House', I said I would give it a try. So I gathered together some colleagues, people like Jonathan Cole, Sydney Cohen, Jack Mendelson, Jack O'Donnell, people whose names are still well known. We sat down and tried to think, If we had $50 m or $75 m, which at that time was a huge amount of money relative to what was being invested in treatment through the standard federal channels, what would we do if we were going to expand treatment? We produced this report. I had worked with Griffith Edwards on a paper for the World Health Organization. That paper talked about the need for a national strategy, some coherent plan that recognized the way in which the various facets of the drug problem interacted, government policies, drug use issues, treatment, prevention. You needed not just to do things willy-nilly, but to have a coordinated plan. Griffith had been discussing that perspective two years before and had a whole conference on it that I didn't know about. But the idea that there ought to be a national strategy found its way into the report that I wrote in only slightly modified form for the White House staff. The major recommendations that we made were basically that

there are an awful lot of people waiting for treatment with methadone and you just can't keep pretending that methadone is a small research project. The evidence looks compelling, you ought to approve methadone and expand treatment. We said a few other things. We actually had a fairly non-committal stance on cannabis; we laid out all the options. Clearly we thought that the criminal penalties for cannabis were inappropriate and that something which reduced the penalties would be more appropriate given the relative place of this drug in the scheme of things.

A: *And what response did your report to the White House evoke?*

JJ: We heard nothing more about it although I got a thank-you note from the President about a month after I'd turned the report in, which was in December 1970 and in the meantime the Illinois Drug Abuse Program continued to expand and to do other things. We did test LAAM in 1968, we wrote it up and got several papers published.[6–8] But I heard nothing more from the White House until some time in April or May of 1971, and it wasn't about my report. There was no decision made; they just called me up and wanted me to consult on another issue. They asked my opinion on what they could do about the drug problem among US servicemen in Vietnam. Apparently there had been a report that came out mid-April that said that up to 15% of GIs were addicted to heroin (in some reports it was higher). They did not have a plan of what could be done. They tried things like giving amnesty to anybody who turned themselves in for treatment. But the major issue was that they had not been able to bring the heroin supply under control, and their attempts to bring the use under control with courts martial for people found in possession of heroin were not particularly effective. At that point I made suggestions which were built around notions of the spread of heroin among users which was derived in part from work that we had done in Chicago,[9] which was in turn derived from some work by De Alarcon and Rathod[10] on the spread of heroin in Crawley New Town (UK). The notion was that you don't need draconian penalties to change behaviour. You need smaller penalties, but with certainty that those small adverse consequences will take place. This was pure hypothesis. And what I suggested was that anybody who uses heroin can't come home until they've been detoxified. If you set up testing to take place as the servicemen were just about to go home, that would give people the message that they should probably quit using for at least a week or two before departure. Then you might begin to do some testing of people about two months before and tell them that this will delay their return home if they test positive. And at some point you really have a system. There won't be any time where you can use heroin without encountering some adverse consequences.

A: *Did the White House take this advice?*
JJ: They listened, and the next thing I recall was that I was called to come and talk to the people at the Pentagon. The notion that the plan might go through was sufficiently strong that I called up the people who were making a special machine that detects opiates in urine in a matter of a minute or two, at the time a major technological break-through. It was something that Avram Goldstein helped to invent and which he told me about when they only had the prototype machine available – in February 1970. This was a technology that had only existed for a couple of months and it was not known to the military. I put forward my plan knowing that we had the technology to do it, but not knowing all the logistics that would be involved.

A: *So was the Pentagon enthusiastic?*
JJ: I arrived in the meeting and the Secretary of the Army was there; the three-star generals could sit at the table, but the colonels and the one-stars had to stand. And we talked about this plan and they didn't jump at it very fast. They said well, maybe in a few months we might be able to do something like that. I said I had the feeling that the President wanted action a little sooner than that; I said I knew they were very busy fighting the war and I didn't want in any way to inconvenience them, but if they would bring me a telephone I would call some civilians and I think we could get this thing set up. And I said this with all sincerity.

They interpreted this as being a well-disguised threat; that if they couldn't do it, they would be replaced. Richard Nixon had a reputation for being very decisive. So, they got the message. It was an unusual meeting because they asked for a pause, and they all walked into the other room – at least the three-star generals and the Secretary of the Army did. They came back and said, 'We'll be able to do it in $2\frac{1}{2}$ weeks'. And I said, 'Well that seems fine'. They made a commitment and I found them the machines. I had one on order for my own programme in Illinois and there was one other that they could buy. When the White House said that they thought this probably would be the way to go I had called up the head of the company and, using the credit of the State of Illinois, had one produced by having people work round the clock. Within a week there were two machines, the only two of their kind that I knew of in the world at the time, available to send to Vietnam for this experiment. And it was an experiment. We had no idea what the consequences would be. The fact however is that it looked like a sensible option when there were no other sensible options. As the plan went up to the President it was not woolly minded; it was concrete on exactly what would be done and I guess for that reason he decided soon afterwards to sign up on a whole effort to develop a national strategy, to coordinate all the treatment demand, prevention and research activities and to put some money into it. So the Vietnam issue and everything else came together.

A: *How did your personal role then further develop?*
JJ: I had been talking to these people at the White House, I thought I was an adviser to them and I was very pleased to be an adviser. Then they began talking about this special entity which when we wrote the original report for the White House – this group that Donfeld had asked me to put together – we thought this entity would be down somewhere in our Health Department, perhaps within NIMH. Maybe it was the beginnings of the idea of a national institute on drug abuse, but whatever it was we had no notion that this would be some kind of entity in the Executive Office of the President. Apparently, that's what they decided.

Drug czar

A: *How were you informed – a phone call, a letter?*

JJ: No, it came in a strange way. I recall I thought I was being a consultant. Then the President asked me to come in to the Cabinet room and that was unusual; I had never been in the Cabinet room before. I was sitting there in the Cabinet room and there was the leadership of the Congress (the Senate and the House), and the President explained he was going to create this Special Action Office that was going to do all this stuff. Then he pointed at me and said Dr Jaffe is going to run this office. I was 37 and it would never occur to me to say, Mr President, who told you that? I just remained silent; I didn't say anything.

A: *How many days before you had to move in?*

JJ: The appointment was announced a few days later on 17 June (1971) and I took office on that same day. When Nixon made that announcement we had a press conference. I moved into an office, but I hadn't been planning to stay in Washington; I hadn't even brought any clothes with me. Somebody went out and bought a new shirt for me so I could go to the press conference.

A: *So what did they give you in terms of resources to allow you to get a national strategy in place?*

JJ: The resources available to the White House when the President makes a commitment to do something seem to be limitless. I have never seen things happen in quite that way before or since. Offices emerged, space materialized, people were assigned, people did things, desks appeared, things happened, and we're not talking about in a week but in a day. Yes, things happened.

A: *And there was power?*

JJ: Power that is hard to imagine. But you immediately knew that you could not use power without careful thought. It's like one of these telephone cards: it looks the same, you keep putting it into the machine but it keeps subtracting something. And what it subtracts is political capital.

There's no way to change a system without stepping on somebody's toes. Every time you want to make a change that seems rational, somebody is going to be discomforted and that's burning up political capital.

A: *You had direct access to the President?*

JJ: I did and I didn't. The way the White House works is that you report through the White House Chief of Staff, so Cabinet people do not necessarily see the President. They are the Cabinet, they run their agencies, but at least in that administration you did not see the President unless you asked to see him and then you might not see him. I asked only once or twice. But we did make reports from time to time. I remember being in the Oval Office several times.

A: *What do you think you achieved during those two years, what were the highest achievements?*

JJ: Well, first I think I continued to be protected and advantaged by an absolute naiveté about what was do-able and what was not do-able. We took on things that I believe in retrospect were absolutely impossible, couldn't have been done. Accomplishments? We said that we're reversing finally as federal policy the 40 previous years of saying that physicians could not prescribe an oral opiate to stabilise and main addicts. The second important move was that we established the framework for the National Institute on Drug Abuse, and funded basic and clinical research through the National Institute on Mental Health. That early funding put money into things that really had an amazing impact. For example, Solomon Snyder has said that funding his research allowed him to identify the opiate receptor. I think we accomplished something in really jump-starting the research activities in substance abuse and – not the least – we laid the foundations for the current treatment system.

A: *A huge legacy.*

JJ: But what we said from time to time about creating a national strategy, I think that is dubious. You can pay real attention to it, or you can make it a paper exercise – I'm not certain that over the last 25 years it hasn't become a paper exercise.

Another thing I think was important, is that we did reverse the code of military justice. There were thousands of people whose heroin use caused them to be dishonourably discharged from military service, and that was reversed and eventually their discharge status was reversed and they were given ordinary discharges. I think we showed another thing: that working with demand can sometimes be effective when working with controlling supply has proven a total failure. I think maybe that there was another important lesson – from time to time less is more, that a tiny aversive intervention can be far more powerful than a capricious and draconian response. I'm trying to think . . . things we did that had long-lasting benefits. There is a whole list of them. We did the basic work on LAAM that later was used to get it approved after a surprisingly long wait. Another thing. Immediately after I was appointed the President sent me to Vietnam to see how the programme I had suggested was coming along. When I came back I reported to him and he directed me to write a book. 'I want you to write a book', he said 'on what you found about this effort because sometimes out of war come major medical advances.' Those were his exact words. I was only a month older than I was when he appointed me, so I said 'Yes Sir'. And that was the root of the Vietnam follow-up study.[11,12]

A: . . . directed by Lee Robins?
JJ: Yes.

A: Did you also experience frustrations during those two years?
JJ: There were many. They differed between the first year and the second. In the second year it was already a period of declining power, declining influence. The crisis had simmered down, the Vietnam issue was largely in a lower key; treatment had begun. The frustrations were the kinds of criticisms that I guess all people get in public life, that the people want everything to be solved immediately. And this is amplified by the press.

A: So they'd shoot at you from all directions?
JJ: That's the job. Congressmen want to know things, Why didn't you do this, why didn't you do

that, what are you doing about unemployment? In other words if addicts were unemployed this was now the special responsibility of the Office. There were these kinds of problems, and there were problems in getting implementation by the agencies. Agencies in our government, which is huge and sprawling, do not like to be subject to any oversight. If you lay out a policy and you want them to follow it, they usually say, 'Oh sure', and go about doing their usual things. We happened to have enough staff at the time and enough commitment from the President that we would try to get agencies actually to meet commitments. They did not take kindly to that. They didn't take kindly to the idea that we did not expect them to take the money and make a joke of it and use it for their own purposes. We had responsibility for a budget, and I remember some run-ins with the Secretary of Defence, who wanted to spend all kinds of money for putting movie projectors on every ship of the line so he could show drug prevention films. This was what he was proposing to do with our money. I suggested that maybe that was a little excessive and he sent back a blistering letter to the President about who the hell was running the Department of Defence?

Nixon was very smart, and that is what you remember about him. He was very quick at studying a problem

---

A: What did you make of Nixon as a person?
JJ: Nixon was very smart, and that is what you remember about him. He was very quick at studying a problem. But he gave political talks in rhetorical terms about how we're going to deal with this scourge of addiction, and the notion that drugs tore at the fabric of society. We prepared speeches for him about the need to have a rational policy, the need to gather data, the need to look at the number of new cases. We used terms like 'incidence' and 'prevalence'. We talked about a rational plan and he mastered the concepts. I saw him give a talk to a group of important invited people in which he barely looked at his notes.

A: *Was he the sort of man to look for simplistic solutions?*

JJ: I think he was a man who knew that the public wanted simple statements and you would have to speak to them in that way. The rhetoric had to be simple; behind the rhetoric he knew the complexities of what had to be done.

A: *Was he empathetic as a person, or frightening?*

JJ: Not at all frightening; he was very considerate. To me he was kind. At a Bill signing ceremony at the White House he said that he sometimes looked out and saw the light burning in my office at night. He said to my wife I know how hard he has been working, what a sacrifice this has been to the family and I want you to know that I appreciate it. He said that in public and I was touched and impressed that he had noticed. Whether he did that for everybody I don't know, but we were indeed working exceedingly hard.

At the White House I would go back home having fought over a hundred million dollars or a major principle, and at the university I was fighting over a tiny office for a secretary . . . or you fought over who would get the new typewriter

---

A: *Other frustrations?*

JJ: I guess the other great frustration was that my views on cannabis were that we were still probably more punitive than we had to be. The press would have liked me to say something that would disagree with the President's position which was that while he was willing to erase any criminal penalty for the first offence, he was not going to take away criminal penalties altogether. It may have been the only position he felt was politically viable at the time, and he was probably right. The great frustration was that somebody would ask a question that I couldn't dodge and couldn't answer candidly because you knew that they would twist what was said. In those circumstances there's a sense of terror, maybe not quite terror but it was

tremendous angst, that I would say something that would be distorted or taken out of context by the press, read the next morning by the President's staff and interpreted as being disloyal or not adhering to policy.

A: *Did you feel that your professional peers understood what you were trying to do?*

JJ: Not always. I gave a talk at the ACNP [American College of Neuropsychopharmacology], where one of the people who was also invited to speak was Mathew Dumont. He gave a very passionate rhetorical speech about the silliness of methadone maintenance, that you might as well give out wrist protectors if you found that most of your people were slashing their wrists, or perhaps you would issue sterile razors. And the entire group that was listening, which was a considerable-sized group of psychiatrists and researchers, stood up and gave him enthusiastic applause. And this was a direct attack on the policies that we had been working on. It did hurt to see that the people you respected as thinking, sentient scientists could be swayed by that kind of rhetoric.

Leaving the White House

A: *Tell me, looking back, are you glad you took the drug czar job?*

JJ: Yes, I feel that I served my country and feel that we accomplished things. I think that the great difficulty was that I had achieved more by age 37 or 38 than I had ever hoped to achieve or could ever hope to achieve again. And what that meant was that you left to return to a university to do things that you couldn't help but think were trivial. At the White House I would go back home having fought over a hundred million dollars or a major principle, and at the university I was fighting over a tiny office for a secretary with some other professor who claimed the same secretarial office, or you fought over who would get the new typewriter. I found the contrast from one position to another to be in a sense demeaning, there's an after-shock. Now the after-shock was made far worse because during the summer that I left [1973] the Watergate hearings were heating up. The very people that I had worked with were now being hauled before Congress and interrogated. Some people that I thought were very decent human beings – I know them to have been decent human beings – eventually were prosecuted and two were imprisoned. Erlichman I didn't know that well, but I knew that in a way he was the administration liberal. And Bud Krogh. He was a very young lawyer in his early 30s when he was asked by Nixon and Kissinger to head up the team which was trying to find out who was leaking White House documents to the press. He admitted that he had played some role in the famous break-in of the psychiatrist's office, he didn't do it himself, but he knew about it.

A: *So there was a sadness that people you liked and contacts with whom you had valued were now being bust?*
JJ: It was more than sadness. It was the sense that I knew – that when the President said to Bud, 'You need to do this for the national security' and Bud said 'Yes', he was younger than I was and less experienced in some ways. People did not take that into account when they considered his case, and I kept thinking, there but for the grace of God go I. What would I have done had I been asked to do something I was told was necessary for national security when I knew men were fighting and dying in Vietnam every day. I'm not talking about the Watergate break-in, that was totally different.

A: *What did Danny Freedman think about your involvement with the White House?*
JJ: I think that in some way he perhaps felt that he should have been given more credit for his contributions to the development of the Illinois programme and his advice should have been sought more seriously. I think he was probably right, but again I can only plead youth. I did not quite know how one treats a chairman of a department and the tough role of the chairman in making things happen. I was probably like a running back who does not acknowledge the front defensive line that opens the holes.

A: *And after two years you packed your bags and left Washington and the Special Action Office behind you.*

JJ: I had planned to leave because I just could not do the things that I felt needed to be done. After the election the President asked for everybody's resignation; he wanted a clean slate. I said 'You want a clean slate, fine, I'll be happy to leave'. I did not want to prolong this; I thought I would go back and be what I had started out to be.

A: *Who took your place?*
JJ: Bob DuPont. But a break with the White House did come on the issue of minimum mandatory penalties, which I disagreed with. I wrote a letter to the staff – I think to Erlichman – saying I don't think that minimum mandatory penalties are the way you want to go. That was leaked, and that was considered disloyal. At that point I got the message that they could find other people. But it was an amiable parting.

A: *Did you go back to Chicago, was that job still open for you?*
JJ: No. The job was still open, but I think that Danny felt that he wanted to have greater control of it than I had allowed for previously. And I felt that maybe a fresh start would be appropriate.

Columbia and Connecticut

A: *So you went to Columbia. Was that an obvious choice?*
JJ: Yes I did, but it wasn't an obvious choice. It seemed like a good place with some reputation. Although people had asked me I did not want to be a chairperson, I didn't want to be a father figure to anybody at that point. It was a time of tremendous emotional turmoil. You have to keep in mind that as I was leaving, all you heard was Watergate and it was a time of confusion and some disillusionment as well. So I did not want a chairperson position. Lawrence Kolb was very nice, he was *the* Lawrence Kolb whose textbook I studied when I was a medical student, and he was the son of Lawrence Kolb whose papers on addiction I'd read, and so I went to Columbia. That was an interesting experience, but it did not turn out quite as I had hoped.

A: *But you must have realized at that point that it was going to be a very difficult transition, from the White House and those powers and then with news of the White House as you had known it crumbling around you.*

JJ: That was the difficult part. There were multiple issues. It was the White House falling apart, it was the change from power to being part of a bureaucracy, it was the change again into a new community and a new job. If I had just changed from one university to another it might have been a time of some stress, but this was really a remarkably stressful time. I left at the beginning of the deepest recession our country had known in about the last 20 years. This was the 73/74 recession; it was also the oil crisis and within three or four months I was sitting in an office that was cold because the state of New York was trying to conserve fuel.

A: *Did you rest a bit, have a crash landing, sit around with your family, or was it possible to do productive things?*

JJ: It seems strange now, but one of the reasons I decided to leave was because I was given a contract in '73 to turn in the chapter for Goodman and Gilman's textbook the next year. I knew you couldn't do that in the White House. So I went to back to academia and was able to get that finished. I was able to write another one of those chapters.

Tobacco research

A: *You started doing tobacco research in the 1960s?*

JJ: Yes. So I had that to keep me busy for the first six months or so, and then I tried to get into another area altogether. I was always berated when coming out with a national strategy with, Why don't you pay more attention to alcohol and tobacco, why are you focusing on heroin? And I thought that there was logic to that and felt that I should pay attention to tobacco. I made up my mind that I would take a look at the issue of tobacco dependence and get involved with that.

A: *So that's where your tobacco research starts.*

JJ: Yes, it was an expiation of the guilt, I felt that I was unable to do more than just mention it in the first national strategy.

A: *What were you looking at in your tobacco research?*

JJ: First I wanted to know something about it, I knew so little compared to what I knew about other drugs. The second issue was the advent of the so-called low tar, low nicotine cigarettes and I was asking the question as to whether or not there could be a harm reduction approach to smoking. I had not fully grasped the significance of what people do with compensatory smoking, the way in which people titrate. We did do some work on smoking cessation. I actually got some samples of the early Nicorette. I felt that people who were interested in the addictions should look across the addictions.

A: *You moved on from Columbia where you were for six years and up to Connecticut to the VA Hospital, where you were for another five years. What sort of work were you involved in there?*

JJ: I had hoped to do more with the smoking issue because I had been promised that I would have access to many of these large-scale insurance companies that would have an interest. I also wanted to work with Roger Meyer who is an old friend that I like very much, and in a perhaps less contentious atmosphere than Columbia had become. So I decided to try Connecticut. It was good in terms of relationships, but not very productive and I really can't think of anything important I got done there.

Back to public service

A: *You then made what was to be a very significant further career move, and in '84 you went back to Baltimore to be director of the Addiction Research Center which was located in that city and subsequently you were acting director of NIDA, and within the government system your final posting was as Director of the Office of*

Evaluation, Scientific Analysis and Synthesis of the Center for Substance Abuse Treatment. What led you once more in this direction of public service?
JJ: One doesn't usually determine to go back into government at a reasonable level, you almost have to be asked. Bill Pollin, who was then Director of NIDA, called me one day and asked if I would be interested in taking over the ARC and I suggested some other names. I really wasn't interested in making another move. Bill, I think, was somewhat appreciative of the fact that I had convinced him to invest in tobacco research. By the way, that's the one thing I managed to accomplish at Columbia – establishing that tobacco belonged in DSM-III.

A: *So you took over responsibility for the ARC.*
JJ: When Bill asked me to come I was reluctant, but finally when he told me he was unable to recruit people like Chuck O'Brien and others, I thought I had a responsibility to come and help – that was the place that began my career in a way. It was what attracted me to Lexington; ARC was Wikler's, Isbell's and Bill Martin's place. I came down there to try to give it a fresh start. It had just moved from Lexington to Baltimore a year or so previously. I continued to have good relationships with Roger Meyer and Tom Babor and others at Connecticut, but here was an opportunity to reshape an institution that had helped shape me.

A: *Did that prove possible?*
JJ: It turned out to be far more difficult that I anticipated, but we did make some changes. First of all I spoke to Avram Goldstein about what really ought to be the change; he talked about getting into molecular genetic issues, looking at the genes from the molecular angle. That was not something I knew how to do, but he told me where I needed to recruit and the kinds of people I needed. ARC had never stopped being what it traditionally was. It was interested in abuse potential testing and some pharmacokinetics. But those things seemed to have become pedestrian, they had become work-a-day things that could be done in any university. An institute that was a national institute ought to have some special activity. I recruited people like Mike Kuhar and a few other

people to work on issues at the molecular level, and I think that those people were successful. I also tried to get people interested in looking at cocaine again which they had avoided doing since Isbell's time. One of the reasons for locating away from Lexington was because there are real drug problems in Baltimore. We created an outpatient branch that could do clinical studies. I guess that the key developments during that time were findings having to do with the dopamine transporter mechanism as the site for cocaine's action. Another major thing we did was a pivotal study[13] which should lead to the approval of buprenorphine as an alternative opiate for the treatment of opiate dependence. That design that we developed turned out to be important because it was one more bit of evidence that showed the dose–response relationship in opioid maintenance treatment. You don't have to do a placebo study to prove pharmacological effectiveness if you can show dose–response relationships.

Here was an opportunity to reshape an institution that had helped shape me

A: *You stayed with the ARC for about five years?*
JJ: Yes.

A: *Briefly at NIDA?*
JJ: For about a year of that time I was also the acting director of NIDA. It was the beginning of the AIDS epidemic and we were trying to persuade the powers that be within government that addiction was a major vector in the transmission of AIDS. They were sceptical; they thought that this was another bureaucratic manoeuvre to get a piece of the AIDS money.

A: *How wrong they were.*
JJ: Yes. And when people finally isolated the virus and showed that bleach could kill it, they would not let us disseminate that information. They said that would be the wrong message, and I considered this felonious – to know that you could tell people that

with simple household bleach they could sterilize syringes, since in our country many people did not have access to sterile materials. We were in a position to tell them how to kill the virus, but we weren't allowed to tell them. So that was a time of frustration, but of some progress as well. There are probably a number of things that we accomplished during that brief year. I frankly found the ARC to be a frustrating experience because we had people doing clinical research on things I was supposed to review and approve, but ethically couldn't so there were lots of conflicts about studies that people wanted to do that I didn't want them to do. So there were internal staff conflicts and I didn't come out a winner on that.

Leaving government

A: *And so to your final job with OTI.*
JJ: It was called OTI for a while – Office of Treatment Improvement – and we designed some really good studies I thought. Then it metamorphosed into what it is now: the Center for Substance Abuse Treatment. I continued to design and fund studies, or at least try to evaluate studies that other people had produced. I think we got things done, but I felt that at some point I would like to be free of all bureaucracy. I just wanted to be able to say, I'm not going to ask anybody's permission, I'll say what I want to say and write what I want to write. And that's something you really can't do when you're in government.

A: *And that transition in your life is happening almost as of this moment?*
JJ: Yes, almost as we speak they are probably preparing the papers which will free me.

Reflections

A: *Looking back on an unusually varied and productive life, with much given to individual people and your country and the world more widely, what strikes me is your almost pathological lack of selfseekingness. We have not even mentioned the Nathan Eddy award. What gods have you served?*

JJ: It's strange. You asked me about where I began. I thought I would be an auto mechanic and I would be an honest auto mechanic. So my general principle is an honest day's work for an honest day's pay, and I just happened to be standing in some places where the name of the job was prestigious, but I tried to do the best with the tools I had to deliver what they asked me to do. I never expected any of these things to happen, but they all happened, mostly by chance. Maybe the only decision I made was to go to Einstein, but after that there was a lot of happenstance – some of it for the good, some of it not so good. I think it's happenstance that I grew up at a time where addiction was so interesting. I've been fortunate in the people I've met, people that I've had a chance to collaborate with. My wife has been tremendously supportive of this hobby I have of reading academic papers. I really love reading journals. The output of that, or at least the by-product of reading them, is that you occasionally remember what you've read and then if somebody asks you, you know something that would take them longer to find out about. I don't see that that makes you anything but a second-rate computer search, but it's been interesting and I've been fortunate and lucky. I never saw myself, at least once I took on that Illinois drug abuse programme, as having serious scientific aspirations. When you leave science for policy implementation you pay a price – you're going to lose the skills, lose the real knowledge of how to get important scientific things done. You can't walk back into it as easily, at least I haven't. I guess I tried to synthesize some things from time to time and maybe to make a contribution here and there to the general well-being of society and I'm appreciative of the opportunities that people give me to make that kind of contribution. I don't think I would have had it any other way. Some of the mistakes have been mistakes that I am glad to have made.

A: *What's the most important paper you wrote, the one you like best.*
JJ: There are two or three that stand out. One is the study on heroin use in Vietnam that I initiated and helped design, but which was actually carried out by Lee Robins.[11,12] I was concerned at the time

that it might not have as much credibility if a government official was a coauthor so my name is not on it (although Lee has always acknowledged my role in it).[14] Another is the chapter 'Drug Addiction and Drug Abuse' that I first wrote for Goodman and Gilman's text book of pharmacology in 1965[15] and then updated every five years until 1990.

A: *Tell me a bit about the American drug research community, because that was surely a tremendously important background to your working life. You almost didn't need to leave a small area on the East Coast of America and a few other patches, to talk continuously to the best people with the best ideas.*
JJ: I think you're right. Again, this is happenstance that America and addiction science are to some extent synonymous. We take that for granted, that we will see each other at these meetings so generously funded by NIDA and by NIAAA, and from time to time by the White House. The concentration of bright minds looking at this issue is probably unprecedented. And I've had a chance to meet them and, more than that, because of a period of high visibility, people know more about me than I know about them. There's a sense of access that I have, that people are willing to talk to me. I have a chance to talk informally to people who are critical and important thinkers; I don't know whether they get much from talking to me, but I certainly get a lot talking to them. It's been an unending education.

A: *What you seem also to have been committed to is rationality. You were attracted young to science. Later you told the President that he had to have a rational policy. You seem to have been attracted to rationality rather than to grand theories. Where does this belief in rationality come from, this philosophical position? And all this in a messy area.*
JJ: It is messy, but I think the interesting thing is that I've never questioned the pursuit of rationality, I've never considered an alternative. Rationality and justice are somehow intertwined – the notion of a just society, a decent place, has to be built on some notion of rationality. I don't think

that it has been a formal influence, but in a certain sense, well, the statements of the Prophets: justice – is that ever far from one's mind? In Hebrew the words for charity and righteousness come from the same root.

A: *I seem to remember a story about your family sharing a Christmas turkey which sounded like an early induction into ethical principles made tangible.*
JJ: Family myths, perhaps they carried some message for me. I was too young to remember, but my brothers and sisters tell me that my father once took our Thanksgiving turkey out of the oven and took it to an unemployed man and his family. He said they needed it more than we did. The other story of that kind is about the Chinese laundry man across the street from my father's store who was being evicted. My father went over and gave him the money for the rent, but my mother had already given him money without telling my father.

Rationality and justice are somehow intertwined – the notion of a just society, a decent place, has to be built on some notion of rationality

A: *Did you ever engage in private practice?*
JJ: I don't think I would have ever made any money in private practice. When I had private patients and I heard their sad stories, I often treated them for free because I felt they needed the money more than I did.

A: *Is there any person who more than others has particularly touched your life?*
JJ: I guess I should be grateful to the man who refused to hire me as a motor mechanic, but I owe so much to so many that I hesitate to rank them. They include many of those I mentioned as having influenced important choices along the odd path I've followed: Hubert Hamilton and Sydney Ellis, at Temple; Abe Wikler; Al Gilman and Seth Sharpless, at Einstein; Vincent Dole, who encouraged

me; Danny Freedman; Griffith Edwards, who shared a wider vision of the world of drugs; Jeffrey Donfeld and Richard Nixon, who gave me an opportunity to influence national policy. I should also mention my father and mother, who by example taught me the meaning of hard work, honesty, and caring for those who were unable to care for themselves.

References

1. WIKLER, A. (1957) *The Relation of Psychiatry to Pharmacology* (Baltimore, Williams & Wilkins).

2. ISBELL, H., FRASER, H. F., WIKLER, A. & EISENMAN, A. J. (1955) An experimental study of the etiology of 'Rum Fits' and delirium tremens, *Quarterly Journal of Studies on Alcohol*, **16**, 1–33.

3. ISBELL, H., ALTSCHUL, S., KORNETSKY, C. H., EISENMAN, A. J., FLANARY, H. F. & FRASER, H. F. (1955) Chronic barbiturate intoxication. An experimental study, *Archives of Neurology and Psychiatry*, **64**, 1–28.

4. EMMELIN, N. (1961) Supersensitivity following 'pharmacological denervation', *Pharmacological Reviews*, **13**, 17–37.

5. JAFFE, J. H. & BRILL, L. (1966) Cyclazocine, a long-acting narcotic antagonist: its voluntary acceptance as a treatment modality by ambulatory narcotics users, *International Journal of Addictions*, **1**, 99–123.

6. JAFFE, J. H., SCHUSTER, C. R., SMITH, B. & BLACHLY, P. (1970) A comparison of acetylmethadol and methadone in the treatment of chronic heroin users. A pilot study, *Journal of the American Medical Association*, **211**, 1834–1836.

7. JAFFE, J. H. & SENAY, E. C. (1971) Methadone and L-methadyl acetate, use in management of narcotics addicts, *Journal of the American Medical Association*, **216**, 1303–1305.

8. JAFFE, J. H., SENAY, E. C., SCHUSTER, C. R., RENAULT, P. F., SMITH, B. & DIMENZA, S. (1972) Methadyl acetate vs methadone: a double-blind study in heroin users, *Journal of the American Medical Association*, **222**, 437–442.

9. DE ALARCON, R. & RATHOD, N. H. (1968) Prevalence and early detection of heroin abuse, *British Medical Journal*, **2**, 549–553.

10. HUGHES, P. H., BARKER, N. W., CRAWFORD, G. A. & JAFFE, J. H. (1972) The natural history of a heroin epidemic, *American Journal of Public Health*, **62**, 995–1001.

11. ROBINS, L. N. (1973) *A Follow-up of Vietnam Drug Users*, Special Action Office Monograph Series A. no. 1 (Washington, DC, US Government Printing Office).

12. ROBINS, L. N. (1974) *The Vietnam Drug User Returns*, Special Action Office Monograph Series A, no. 2 (Washington, DC, US Government Printing Office).

13. JOHNSON, R. E., JAFFE, J. H. & FUDALA, P. J. (1992) A controlled trial of buprenorphine treatment for opioid dependence, *Journal of the American Medical Association*, **267**, 2750–2755.

14. ROBINS, L. N. (1993) Vietnam veterans' rapid recovery from heroin addiction: a fluke or normal expectation? *Addiction*, **88**, 1041–1054.

15. JAFFE, J. H. (1965) Drug addiction and drug abuse, in: GOODMAN, L. S. & GILMAN, A. (Eds) *The Pharmacological Basis of Therapeutics*, 3rd edn, pp. 285–311 (New York, Macmillan).

Commentary
Present at the Creation

Mark A. R. Kleiman

'Had I been present at the Creation, I could have given useful advice for the better ordering of the Universe.' Alfonso X

While American drug policy has undergone profound changes over the past generation – the effort has expanded hugely in scale, tilted more and more heavily toward law enforcement, and coarsened both in rhetoric and in politics – it retains the marks of its origins in the Johnson administration and (especially) the first Nixon administration. The basic statutes (the Controlled Substances Act and the Narcotics Addict Treatment Act), the key institutions (the Drug Enforcement Administration on the enforcement side and the National Institutes on Alcohol Abuse and Alcoholism and on Drug Abuse on the research side), and most of the major data collection efforts (the National Household Survey on Drug Abuse, the Monitoring the Future series, and the Drug Abuse Warning Network, counting emergency room and medical examiner incidents) all date from that brief and distant period.

Harold Hughes in the Senate and Jerome H. Jaffe in the Nixon White House had more to do with the events of those years than any two others one could name. For someone working in the drug policy field today, reading interviews with these two giants calls forth awe at the size of their accomplishments, regret about the absence of adequate successors to the roles they once filled and the gridlock that now prevents anyone from moving as far and as fast as they moved, and frustration about opportunities not taken then and not available today.

To a visitor from Mars, or perhaps even from England, looking at US addictions policy with fresh eyes, one feature of that policy would, I think, seem almost inexplicable: the obsession with the illicit drugs (and to some extent nicotine) and the relative neglect of the far larger problem of alcohol abuse and dependency. (The 'needs assessment' studies find clinically diagnosable alcohol abuse and dependency approximately seven times as frequently as abuse and dependency related to all the illicit drugs combined.)

This massive disproportion between problems and responses is both among the causes and among the effects of the dominance of enforcement and criminal legislation, but it extends even to the research effort. NIDA, partly due to its role as the drug war's Ministry of Truth, has a budget about two and a half times that of NIAAA, and the gap between them in attracting mass media coverage and political attention for the research they sponsor is even greater. (The fact that NIDA is allowed, and indeed expected, to be 'anti-drug', while NIAAA must at all costs avoid being perceived as 'anti-alcohol', accounts for some of the difference. A crusade is naturally more newsworthy than an exploration, especially an exploration designed to avoid dangerous territory.)

The very existence of two separate agencies, one on drug abuse and one on alcohol abuse and alcoholism, embodies the fallacy underlying much of what is wrong with American drugs policy: that alcohol is not a drug. The bad effects of this mistake on alcohol policy are transparent, but the damage it does to illicit drugs policy is perhaps even greater. For if alcohol is not a drug, then most Americans do not use drugs non-medically, and 'drug users' and the 'drug culture' can consequently be demonized without any restraint.

Combining research on all the abusable intoxicants in a single agency might have made a substantial difference both in relative research effort and in the balanced presentation of results. How much impact that might have had on public, mass media, and political understanding of the subject cannot be known, but that impact might not have been negligible.

From this perspective, it seems strange that neither Hughes nor Jaffe, each of them reflective and self-critical far beyond the norm, makes any comment about the division. NIAAA was established several years before NIDA; why couldn't its mission have been expanded, rather than creating a new agency?

Was the choice to have two agencies rather than one driven by the potency of the alcohol lobby? (This is known to have been the reason for the exclusion of alcohol from the charge of the 'drug czar's' office.) Or was the cause the reluctance of individuals suffering or recovering from alcohol abuse disorders, their families, and their organized representatives, to think of alcoholics as a species of drug abusers? Or were alcohol researchers unwilling to dirty their hands with 'drugs'? Perhaps the silence of Hughes and Jaffe on this point implies that, in political terms, there was no choice, that any attempt to combine illicit drugs research with alcohol research would have been entirely futile.

On one central issue, American alcohol policy matches policy toward the illicit intoxicants: the laxity in practice of the criminal justice system toward continued substance abuse by those who have committed drug-related crimes. The Hughes interview captures the spirit here: progress is understood in terms of allowing judges to 'sentence' alcoholic offenders to treatment in lieu of prison.

This remains the 'progressive' formula today, in the guise either of diversion programs or of drug courts. A less 'progressive' version is treatment in prison. But always the emphasis is on treatment; only in drug courts is actual desistance from drug use insisted on. And all of these are special, more or less voluntary programs; an offender not in such a program who is also a chronic abuser of alcohol or other drugs faces almost no scrutiny about continued alcohol use, and only sporadic scrutiny (albeit with occasionally drastic consequences) about continued use of other drugs.

To find a policy for offenders involved with drugs that is neither punitive nor therapeutic, but which takes seriously the task of combining services with sanctions toward the goal of reduced substance abuse, reduced crime, and reduced time behind bars, would require a daring policy imagination and detailed knowledge of the functioning of criminal justice institutions in the 50 states. To make that policy effective in the face of the bureaucratic and ideological interests and understandings that tend to frustrate it would require someone with enormous energy, enormous toughness, and enormous influence. In summary, the necessary changes require more than the current scene seems able to provide: another Hughes and another Jaffe.

Part VII
Figures from Post-War Europe

Wilhelm Feuerlein

Wilhelm Feuerlein was born in 1920 in Nürnberg, Germany. He gained his MD from the University of Erlangen in 1948. He has held numerous medical and advisory posts: Senior Physician at the Municipal Psychiatric Hospital, Nürenberg, from 1949–60; Psychiatric Consultant at the Municipal Hospital, Fürth, Bavaria, from 1960–64; Head of the Psychiatric Outpatient Department and Crisis Intervention Unit, Max Planck Institute for Psychiatry, Munich, 1964–85; Member of the Faculty of Medicine of the Ludgwig–Maximilian University, Munich, 1969–86; Member of the Working Group on Addiction of the Deutsche Bundestag, Bonn, 1971–75; Chairman of the Deutsche Gesellschaft für Suchtforschung und Suchtterapie (German Society for Addiction Research and Therapy), 1978–82; and Temporary Advisor to the World Health Organization, 1986–89. His research include the epidemiology, diagnosis and treatment of alcohol problems, suicidal behaviour and the prevention of suicide.

A hard road for a graduating MD

Addiction: *You are one of the pioneers of alcoholism research and treatment in Germany. You have published many books and more than 300 papers about the subject. Where did you obtain your medical training and at what age did you qualify in medicine?*
Wilhelm Feuerlein: I was born in 1920. I grew up in Coburg, a town in Northern Bavaria, which has historical links with the English Royal Family. My life was markedly influenced by World War II. I started my medical training at the University of Munich in 1939, a few months before the outbreak of war. For reasons of health I was not called up to military service at that time. I passed my first exams in the summer of 1940 and attended the university of Vienna until 1941. I joined the Medical Corps (as an orderly). I spent most of the war in Italy. In 1944 I resumed my medical training at the University of Würzburg. During the last months of the war I was in the eastern parts of Germany on the staff of a military hospital. By the end of April 1945, the hospital was destroyed by Russian aircraft and the staff were scattered. In the first days of May 1945 I managed to avoid the Russian army and succeeded in reaching British troops near Lübeck. So I found myself as a British prisoner of war.

When I and my German comrades were confronted with the victims of Nazi cruelty we were deeply shocked and ashamed

A: *What was the situation like?*
WF: In the early days of May 1945 the British discovered, in the northern part of Germany, some Nazi concentration camps that were in a very terrible state. They were overcrowded with prisoners who were suffering from starvation and various diseases. The British were in urgent need of medical and nursing personnel. Therefore they recruited them wherever they could find them, including German prisoners of war such as myself. So I was transferred to the area of the concentration camp of Belsen-Bergen. There the Royal Army Medical Corps (RAMC) found about 40 000 people in a situation that cannot be described in words. When I and my German comrades were confronted with the victims of Nazi cruelty we were deeply shocked and ashamed. The work was rather hard, particularly the emotional aspects. I experienced and admired the British way of managing. They made clear decisions, were exact and reliable, very effective. Their behaviour towards us can be characterized by fairness but no fraternization. We were

treated as quasi-coworkers, and our human rights were aways strictly observed, for example we got the same provisions as the British troops.

A: *You were discharged from the priconer-of-war camp in October 1945 at the age of 25. What did you do then?*

WF: As the town and the University of Würzburg had been completely destroyed during the last months of the war I could not continue my study there. Within weeks I managed to be admitted at the University of Erlangen, a small town near Nuremberg. At this university I qualified in medicine in 1948. The conditions of life for a student in Erlangen were rather hard. The town had not been destroyed, however it was overcrowded. Therefore it was very difficult to find any accommodation. Food and fuel were rare, also books. The shortage in many things also played a role in forming my thesis. Because I originally intended to become an internist, I had the idea it might be helpful to start with pathology. So I asked the pathologist for a subject for a thesis. He invited me to join a research project using rabbits for experiments. However there was no food for the animals. He asked me if I could provide food. Because I had no connections to farmers I could not help. So he suggested we wait for better times. But I did not want to wait such an indefinite time and gave up this plan.

A: *So the shortage of rabbit food at that time eventually turned out as a great luck for the development of the alcoholism research in Germany! What did you do then?*

WF: I decided to ask a psychiatrist for a subject for my doctoral thesis. His name was W. von Baeyer (later Professor of Psychiatry at the University of Heidelberg and Vice President of the World Psychiatric Association). In those days he was in charge of the Psychiatric and Neurologic Department of the hospital at Nuremberg. He suggested describing and analysing a rare case of schizophrenia-like psychosis after a circumscribed brain trauma.

After qualifying and completing my thesis von Baeyer asked me to join his team at the Nuremberg hospital. It was a helpful offer for me because

it was extremely difficult to find a postgraduate training post. Psychiatry was also a favourite field of medicine for me. During my first terms in Munich I had done some studies in psychology besides the medical training. Therefore I agreed at once. In 1949 I started in Nuremberg. During the following years I got the special qualification in psychiatry and neurology. Von Baeyer was an excellent psychiatrist with profound knowledge in psychology and philosophy. In Nuremberg he introduced some modern psychiatric methods. For example, he established a department for child psychiatry, half way houses for schizophrenics, child guidance clinics, and so on.

Starting to work on alcoholism

A: *The start of your clinical and research work in the field of alcoholism was much later than the beginning of your training in psychiatry. Could you tell us about your first piece of research in alcoholism?*

WF: Around 1957 I started my work in the field of alcoholism with an article that described the prognosis of delirium tremens. In 58 cases I found that the mortality of patients suffering from a delirium tremens 'complicated' by other diseases or traumata (impacting alcohol withdrawal) was lower than the mortality of patients suffering from an 'uncomplicated' delirium tremens (i.e. with continuous consumption of alcoholic beverages).[1] Although this article found some interest among German psychiatrists I never anticipated that it could be the first of a series of articles on this issue later on. As long as I have been occupied with clinical work at the large municipal hospital of Nuremberg I have had no possibility of doing intensive and sophisticated research.

A: *You finished your work in the psychiatric hospital in Nuremberg. What was the next step in your professional career?*

WF: In 1960 I had been offered a private practice (neurology, psychiatry, psychotherapy) at Fürth/Bay, the twin-town of Nuremberg. At the same time I worked as a psychiatric and neurological consultant at the Fürth general hospital.

The practice was a very time-consuming job that left me no time for scientific matters (which I missed).

A move to the Max Planck Institute

A: *Was this the main reason that you applied for a job at the Max Planck Institute for Psychiatry in Munich?*
WF: Yes. And I had the great luck to get the post of the head of the outpatient department of the Max Planck Institute. I started on April 1st, 1964. Here I found a rather ideal ambience for research. Backing by the director of the institute (Dr Ploog), a large scientific community to discuss research with, and a large library. As my major task was to do clinical work I decided that to choose subjects for research I should follow a dictum by M. Erickson – take what the patient is bringing you. The first problem was a neurological one of very practical impact: the easy and quick identification of space-occupying processes in brain. I used the new method of echoencephalography which I had been familiar with for a few years. After discussing some methodological problems, we tried to measure the width of the third ventricle in normal subjects of different ages and in alcoholics.[2] We found it significantly higher in 20–50 year old alcoholics than in the non-alcoholic control group.

As my major task was to do clinical work I decided that to choose subjects for research I should follow a dictum by M. Erickson – take what the patient is bringing you

---

Another focus of my scientific interest was also a problem of our daily clinical life – suicide and parasuicide, a term that I used independent from N. Kreitman who had introduced it almost at the same time. I demonstrated three different aims of suicidal actions (cry for help, pause, self-destruction).[3] Later on I tried to show the psy-chopathological links between suicidal and addictive behaviour.[4]

Wide research interests

A: *So it was the Max Planck Institute where you began your intense research work in the field of alcoholism?*
WF: My interest in alcoholism began because of the immense number of alcoholics who were being referred to our outpatient department nearly every day. The situation for us clinicians was unsatisfying in various ways. We did not know what to do with these patients who were not aware of their condition and not motivated to cope with their problems. In addition the definition of alcoholism was unclear, the identification of alcoholics ambiguous, the treatment of alcoholism and, in particular, of patients suffering from delirium tremens was rather ineffective. There were only a few persons in Germany who occupied themselves scientifically with alcoholism problems. I had the idea that delirium tremens might be a model of so-called exogenous psychoses. So I started some research (as the subject of my postdoctoral thesis) on the alcohol withdrawal syndrome and delirium tremens – the conditions of development and the clinical issues. A general syndrome and two sub-syndromes. No significant differences were found between those patients with delirium tremens following alcohol withdrawal and those with delirium tremens without prior withdrawal.[5] Additional analyses of the two groups of patients with and without delirium tremens, were carried out in Germany and in Chile during a fellowship at the University of Concepción, yielded some significant differences – among the patients without delirium tremens were more subjects with somatic damage in the early childhood, with retardation of psychomotor and verbal development, with a discontinuous drinking pattern and with more suicidal attempts in their history.[6,7]

A: *And your other research interests in this field?*
WF: I established a small working group for this task. The first member was H. Küfner, a psychologist with whom I have a very good collaboration

which lasts till now. In connection with the delirium tremens studies I did some epidemiological research on the prevalence of alcoholism in West Germany,[8] and in various hospitals.[9] Another study dealt with partners of female alcoholics.[10] The epidemiological studies brought me to the problem of the diagnosis of alcoholism. I started with a small questionnaire that had been used in several epidemiological studies. Later on we tried to develop a more sophisticated diagnostic instrument: the Munich Alcoholism Test (MALT)[11,12] that combines a self-rating questionnaire with clinical findings. The MALT has been administered in many countries. It has been translated into 9 languages.

The definition of alcoholism was another issue I had faced in the seventies. I had the opportunity to join a WHO working group (headed by G. Edwards and M. M. Gross) that suggested differentiation between alcohol abuse and alcohol dependence. A consequence of my preoccupation with definition problems were some essays on the so-called disease model of alcoholism, here I referred to publications of the American sociologist Parsons and the British philosopher Engel.[13]

A: *A great part of your research is dealing with outpatient treatment. Did it have a special reason?*
WF: Yes. Because it was not feasible to establish a separated inpatient treatment ward in the Max Planck Institute for Psychiatry we focused on outpatient treatment. We initiated information groups (run by ex-alcoholics) open to all alcoholics who dropped in or were referred to the outpatient department, and motivation groups using a more structured program.[14] In the early seventies we started a comparative study on different treatment approaches: behavioural therapy, psychoanalytic therapy and a broad spectrum therapy (integrative therapy). In a follow-up study we could not find any signficant differences between the three treatment procedures.[15]

A: *But you did do some research on inpatient treatment too?*
WF: Because it was not feasible to carry out inpatient treatment for alcoholics within the Max Planck Institute, we had to restrict ourselves to the evaluation of treatment units focusing on methods and outcome. In 1981 we started a large prospective multicentre study involving 21 treatment units and 1410 alcoholic inpatients. Follow-ups after 6, 18 and 48 months were done. The study (Munich Evaluation of Alcoholism Treatment = MEAT) was completed in the late eighties. The results were encouraging – 46% were found to be abstinent during the whole follow-up period of 48 months, 66% abstinent during the last six months prior the last follow-up. Only a very small number of patients succeeded in keeping to so-called controlled drinking over the period of 48 months.[16]

An important German textbook

A: *One of the highlights of your career was the publication of your book on alcoholism which has become a standard work in the German language. Could you tell us about that?*
WF: My textbook on 'Alkoholismus – Mißbrauch und Abhängigkeit (Alcoholism – Abuse and Dependence) appeared in 1975. I tried to give a comprehensive and clear overview of the various theoretical and practical aspects of issues ranging from the pharmacology to psychodynamic psychotherapy. It has been translated into Spanish and Japanese and it has run through many German editions.

A: *You are one of the founders of the German Society for Research and Therapy of Addiction (Deutsche Gesellschaft für Suchtforschung und Suchttherapie). What was your role in that development?*
WF: The Society was founded in 1978. I had the privilege to serve as its first president. The society consists of more than 300 professional members belonging to various disciplines who are working on the field of (mostly clinical) research and treatment. Most of them belong to German speaking countries (especially Germany, Austria, Switzerland). The society organizes scientific meetings every year and edits a journal (SUCHT).

Reflecting on the play

A: *Do you think that scientists should play a more active part in public health policy?*

WF: You are right. But we have to keep in mind that the influence of addiction experts seems to be rather limited, at least in Germany. We have to face old traditions of consumption and, on the other hand, the power of strong lobbies. Nevertheless I accepted the invitations to join national and regional boards, e.g. the Enquete-Committee of the German Bundestag on the situation of psychiatry in (West) Germany, the Scientific Board of the German National Council on Dependence Problems (Deutsche Hauptstelle gegen die Suchtgefahren), and to collaborate with television and other mass media.

As long as alcoholic beverages have the image of something admirable and desirable, of an indispensible part of our food and our daily life, alcoholism will keep its place as one of the major health risks for the public

A: *What are the central messages of your life work for those dealing with addiction problems today?*

WF: The trend to use and abuse addictive substances can only be stopped or attenuated if we make progress in the field of general prevention, in particular if we succeed in changing attitudes towards addictive drugs. The rather effective campaign against smoking may serve as a model. As long as alcoholic beverages have the image of something admirable and desirable, of an indispensible part of our food and our daily life, alcoholism will keep its place as one of the major health risks for the public. That does not mean a plea for prohibition but a suggestion that we learn to handle alcohol in a reasonable way while being aware that it is a substance of high risk. This will be a task for generations.

Even if mankind as a whole will succeed in handling this problem we have to face the fact that a certain number of persons will stick to abuse of and dependence on addictive drugs. The experts will have to optimize their strategies to help these people. I expect that further research on all fields

may open new ways of treatment, perhaps introduce new paradigms. In particular I hope that research will find some medicaments to fight the sequelae of alcohol abuse, perhaps the craving for addictive substances, to optimize the treatment of the alcohol withdrawal syndrome and delirium tremens, to motivate patients more effectively to undergo treatment and to cope with lapses and relapses.[18] I guess we are now still at the beginning of this work.

References

1. FEUERLEIN, W. (1959) Zur Prognose des Alkoholdelirs, *Nervenarzt*, **30**, 38.
2. FEUERLEIN, W. & HEYSE, H. (1970) Die Weite der 3. Hirnkammer bei Alkoholikern (Ergebnisse echoencephalographischer Messungen) *Archiv für Pschiatrie und Nervenkrankheiten*, **213**, 78–85.
3. FEUERLEIN, W. (1971) Selbstmordversuch oder parasuicidale Handlung? *Nervenarzt*, **42**, 127–130.
4. FEUERLEIN, W. (1982) Sucht und Suicid, in: REIMER, C. (Ed.) *Suicid* (Berlin-Heidelberg, Springer-Verlag), pp. 45–50.
5. FEUERLEIN, W. (1974) The acute alcohol withdrawal syndrome. Findings and problems, *British Journal of Addiction*, **69**, 141–148.
6. FEUERLEIN, W. (1967) Neuere Ergebnisse der Alkoholdelir-Forschung, *Nervenarzt*, **38**, 492–500.
7. FEUERLEIN, W. (1980) Alcohol withdrawal syndromes, in: SANDLER, M. (Ed.) *Psychopharmacology of Alcohol* (New York, Raven Press).
8. FEUERLEIN, W. & KÜFNER, H. (1977) Alkoholkonsum, Alkoholmißbrauch und subjektives Befinden. Ergebnis einer Repräsentativerhebung in der Bundesrepublik Deutschland *Archiv für Psciatrie und Nervenkrankheiten*, **224**, 89–106.
9. FEUERLEIN, W. & KUNSTMANN, G. (1973) Die Häufigkeit des Alkoholismus. Vergleich zwischen verschiedenen Krankenanstalten, *Münchener Medizinische Wochenschrift*, **115**, 1991–1996.

10. Busch, H., Körmendy, E. & Feuerlein, W. (1973) Partners of female alcoholics, *British Journal of Addiction*, **58**, 179–184.

11. Feuerlein, W., Ringer, C., Küfner, H. & Antons, K. (1977) Diagnose des Alkoholismus: Der Münchener Alkoholismustest (MALT), *Münchener Medizinische Wochenschrift*, **119**, 1275–1282.

12. Feuerlein, W., Ringer, C., Küfner, H. & Antons, K. (1980) Diagnosis of alcoholism – the Munich Alcoholism Test (MALT), in: Galanter, M. (Ed.) *Currents in Alcoholism. Vol. VII* (New York, Grune & Stratton).

13. Feuerlein, W. (1990) Alkoholismus: Definition, Diagnose, Krankheitsbegriff, Ablauf, Ergebnisse und Kosten der Behandlung, *Versicherungsmedizin*, **43**, 21–27.

14. Pfeiffer, W., Feuerlein, W. & Brenk-Schulte, E. (1991) The motivation of alcohol dependents to undergo treatment, *Drug and Alcohol Dependence*, **29**, 87–95.

15. Pfeiffer, W., Fahrner, E.M. & Feuerlein, W. (1987) Katamnestische Untersuchungen von ambulant behandelten Alkohol-Abhängigen, *Suchtgefahren*, **33**, 309–320.

16. Feuerlein, W. & Küfner, H. (1989) A prospective multicentre study of in-patient treatment for alcoholics: 18- and 48-month follow-up (Munich Evaluation for Alcoholism Treatment (MEAT), *European Archives of Psychiatry and Neurological Sciences*, **239**, 144–157.

17. Feuerlein, W. (1989) Alkoholismus – Mißbrauch und Abhängigkeit 4. ed. (Stuttgart-New York, Thieme-Verlag).

18. Feuerlein, W. (1990) Impact of research on designing strategies for preventing and treating dependence on drugs and alcohol, *Drug and Alcohol Dependence*, **25**, 199–202.

Further reading

Küfner, H. & Feuerlein, W. (1989) *In-patient treatment for alcoholism* (Berlin-Heidelberg-New York, Springer-Verlag).

Albert Tuyns

Albert Tuyns was born in 1922 in Belgium. He gained his MD from the University of Brussels in 1948, trained at the Mèdecin-Hygièniste in 1949 and was awarded an MPH from John Hopkins School of Public Health in 1962. Posts included: Médecinè-Inspecteur, Ministère de la Santè Publique, Belgium, 1948–59, in charge of health statistics; World Health Organization Advisor on medical statistics, Morocco, 1959–60; Medical Officer, Cancer Unit, WHO, 1960–67; and epidemiologist with the IARC (International Agency for Research on Cancer), 1967–82. He was a recipient of the Jellinek Award, 1982.

A professor who gave inspiration

Addiction: *You grew up in Belgium?*
Albert Tuyns: I grew up in that country and was there during the war years. It wasn't very nice. Many of us got involved in resistance activities. Some were very active; some disappeared and never came back. I didn't do much really, just went through those four years without much pleasure. I was 18 when it started and 22 or 23 when it finished, so good years had gone. But I was alive and young, there were good times left.

A: *And you went to Medical School?*
AT: I started medicine in Brussels during the war. The Germans closed the university in 1941. Some students went to Liège, some went to Louvain, which is where I enrolled. We were liberated in September 1944 and most of us then returned to the University of Brussels.

A: *What would the University of Brussels' tradition have been in medical training?*
AT: In those days we were still predominantly influenced by the French. The Walloons, the French-speaking, they tended to go on to France for their studies, but the Flemish who were good at languages learnt English and many more trained in England or the States.

A: *Your first language is French?*
AT: My first language is French, but I became a Civil Servant at the Ministry of Health so I had to know the other language as well. At that time I was fluent in Flemish.

A: *And in 1948 you qualified in medicine?*
AT: Yes, and then I took a 1-year specialization in the field of public health. That meant in those days hygiene, the problems of obtaining clean water, all those traditional things. But also we had a course in social medicine with a man who was absolutely remarkable, René Sand.[1] He was Professor of Social Medicine. He was speaking a language which was quite different from the other teachers. He was the first to get me to realise that a medical–social problem has to be measured.

But also we had a course in social medicine with a man who was absolutely remarkable, René Sand. He was Professor of Social Medicine

---

René Sand was an outstanding Public Health person. In March–April 1946 he was invited by the UN to chair a 'Preparatory Technical Commission' in charge of working out proposals for the establishment of an international health organization within the UN family. In a few weeks' time, the 16 experts of the Commission outlined what such an organization should do and how it should operate. Their proposals were then submitted to an international health conference which met in June 1946, in the US. They adopted the Constitution of a World Health Organization.[2]

Such an organization had to incorporate the already existing international agencies such as the UNRAA, what was left of the SDN, PAHO and the like. This was the job of a so called 'Interim Commission'. The 'World Health Organization' was finally and officially created in 1948, along the lines defined by the initial group. What is unbelievable is that all the work achieved by René Sand was ignored in Belgium and that he remained unknown in his own country. He was teaching Social Medicine in our University in Brussels but few students showed any interest in these matters; in our group of some one hundred students, we were two, my friend Jean Vermeylen and myself, who became deeply impressed and enthusiastic when we were introduced to subjects which were precisely those we expected the medical school to teach us. Those who were interested in statistics in those days, we were very few.

My grandfather had made himself a name by creating a muzzle for police dogs designed in such a way that the dog could bark and make a noise, but not bite. He sold these muzzles all over Europe

A: *Why did you become a doctor?*
AT: I started medicine with a sort of idealistic idea of being good to people, trying to get them out of their diseases and that kind of thing. And then during the first six years I learnt everything except facts. I became a reasonably good doctor, diagnosed and treated patients, but it was only at the very last minute, the last year, that I came across this course in social medicine which was what I had been waiting for, those 6 years. So it came just at the right time.

Public health as a vehicle for idealism

A: *And your first job?*
AT: I went to the Ministry of Health. There was a vacancy to do with national health statistics because nobody wanted to work on that topic, nobody was interested. When I arrived there was

a dearth of national information, but after a few years we had reasonably good data under a number of headings.

A: *What took you in this career direction? Were there for instance political interests which made you concerned with society, or was there perhaps a family background of science or mathematics?*
AT: It was my idealism at the beginning, and that could not express itself for the first six years of training. It was only when I reached the last year that I found what I had been waiting for, the atmosphere I needed. Public health, I discovered, was what I wanted to engage in. Now when I started in this direction I had no idea at all how things were to be done: At the beginning I had no idea that statistics would be part of the demand. As for family influences, my father was a craftsman who worked in copper – a *ciseleur sur cuivre*. I still have some of his work. Later when he married he helped my grandfather and worked in the shop. My grandfather had made himself a name by creating a muzzle for police dogs designed in such a way that the dog could bark and make a noise, but not bite. He sold these muzzles all over Europe.

A: *So you got this job at the Ministry of Health where you stayed from 1948 to 1959, looking at infectious diseases?*
AT: Infectious disease, and particularly tuberculosis, which was a great problem at that time. There was a survey underway on tuberculosis and these were the first data that I worked on, and I constructed a good picture of the tuberculosis problems in Belgium. And we were organizing TB detection campaigns, population detection campaigns. That is something that I learnt about in Denmark and we tried to do the same in my country. The method of work included preparation of the population to persuade them to participate. We had cars in the streets with loudspeakers, there were posters, all sorts of things going on. I then tried to evaluate each of these methods to see which were the most efficient in convincing people to come along and be examined. In fact the most effective technique was personal interview with one of the persons on the spot, who then went around to talk with other people and get them an appointment.

A: *You made an experiment of this?*
AT: It was very strange, because the loudspeakers made an incredible noise. But there were people who did not hear them. There were immense posters and banners across the streets, but there were people who didn't see them. But talking to people worked much better. This work won me a prize from the Red Cross. Later I won the 'Prix Derscheid' named after the founder of the Belgian anti-TB league; it was usually given to a clinician or surgeon who had invented a new diagnostic or therapeutic technique. I received it for a study dealing with tuberculin indices and with prevention – and this was a *première*. Hence my pride. One prize was a medal, the second one was cash, and with that I bought a nice old cupboard which is still with me.

A: *You did further postgraduate studies during this period at the Ministry?*
AT: In 1956 I would have liked to go to London to the School of Hygiene to take the course with Donald Reid. Donald had always been very friendly to me, and he would have arranged for me to go there for 1 year. But no, the Ministry did not consider that this was useful. But then they gave me a 2 or 3-months' Fellowship to travel to the States. That was in 1956 and at that point I met Carol Palmer. Aronson and Palmer were the first to demonstrate that BCG was protective against TB in a study on the Arapahos, an Indian tribe in the USA. Palmer had also been the Director of a 'Tuberculosis Research Organization' (TRO) set up in Copenhagen soon after the end of the war. I have come across so many people in my life who have been kind to me and became friends. I was telling Palmer about the work I was doing back home and he seemed to consider that it was interesting, and then right in the middle of our discussion he said 'Well, why did you come over here? Did you come to have a tour and see nice people like me, or did you come to learn something?' I said obviously I had come to learn something. He said: 'Well, if you want to learn something you have to go to school'. I said: 'Ah, yes, there is logic in that.' He said: 'Would you like to go to school?' and I said 'Yes'. So next morning I started at Johns Hopkins, and I stayed there for three months. So going to Johns Hopkins seemed to be just a matter of making a telephone call, and the door was open. It was only later that I found out that it is not that easy.

A: *And was the experience rewarding?*
AT: Yes, in a way. There were some things that they were teaching there that I would consider to have been not too well developed. All the social side in terms of social insurance, health insurance, all these things. Britain had a fairly developed system early on because of Beveridge, and these ideas had come over to France and Belgium. Many politicians of Western European countries who had fled to the UK during wartime were impressed by Lord Beveridge's work; this work inspired most of the Social Insurance schemes that were created about 1947 in several European countries. What they were doing in the States in those days was really childish. But statistics, that's where I learnt a great deal. When I came back I wanted to use my new knowledge, and I tried hard for about two years without any success.

A: *They didn't want to know?*
AT: They were not particularly interested.

A: *But your Ministry had paid for you to go to America?*
AT: They paid for the first three months and it was Carol who found a way to pay for the three further months.

Morocco: an epidemic of paralysis

A: *Then in 1959 you went off to Morocco. Can you tell us about that story?*
AT: Yes. As I said, I was a little disappointed that I could not apply my new knowledge. Nothing changed in my Ministry for two years in spite of my efforts. At that time the WHO Regional Office for Europe had tried to find a health statistician for Morocco and the conditions were to know something of health statistics, to speak French, but preferably not to be French. I don't think this last term was written down, but that was it. Well, reduced to those criteria there are not a great many

Europeans to compete, so I had a good chance to get the job, and I asked for the job and I got it and off I went to Morocco.

A: *So what was the problem when you got there?*
AT: The main health problems in Morocco at that time were indeed malaria, trachoma, venereal disease and TB. The 'Meknassitis' epidemic was an unexpected extra for the health authorities. An epidemic of paralysis of unknown origin. In certain respects it looked like a poisoning, but there were also elements suggesting a viral disease. Quite honestly, it was impossible to say which answer fitted the facts best. The virologists and toxicologists were fighting. At that stage I said, well, nobody knows what's happening, let's try to find out, let's make a survey. So we embarked on a study of the last three weeks in the person's life before the start of the paralysis, that seemed like the incubation time for a possible virus. And we were also looking at what people had eaten, and so on. That was a very elementary type of survey. We found ourselves soon with 250 completed questionnaires, and one thing came out clearly and was that only one type of food had been consumed by every one of those people who had the disease – cooking oil. The oil came straight from the local airport. It was not really cooking oil at all, but diverted engine oil. Casablanca was at the time a military airport. On this airfield the Americans accumulated tons of all sorts of material including rinsing oil for engines. So what did they do when they left and gave the airport back to the Moroccans? They put an advertisement in the newspaper selling this oil for a very low price.

A: *And people turned it into cooking oil?*
AT: Of course. When you did a thing like that in Morocco it was like pouring the oil into the cooking pan, and that is exactly what happened. I put the information on punchcards and there were a couple of sorting machines available. No-one in Morocco had ever done anything like this before, and this came to the ears of Prince Hassan who was told that this chap had found the answer playing with cards.

A: *This sounds like a classic piece of epidemiological investigation – a questionnaire, a relatively small sample, and the mystery falls into place.*
AT: I was lucky in the sense that the oil turned out to be the *only* common item.

A: *And then you were involved in the Agadir earthquake?*
AT: Agadir. That earthquake killed 10 000, perhaps 12 000 people. I was there only after 3 or 4 days, but it was a terrible experience. Everything had been destroyed. They had not cleaned the place, they could not have done so, there were thousands of bodies under the stones heating together in the Moroccan sun.

I put the information on punchcards and there were a couple of sorting machines available. No-one in Morocco had ever done anything like this before, and this came to the ears of Prince Hassan who was told that this chap had found the answer playing with cards

---

WHO and IARC

A: *In 1960 you went to Geneva rather than going back to Brussels. That must have been a big career break.*
AT: That was the time that WHO created a cardiovascular unit and a cancer unit. They were recruiting an epidemiologist for each of these teams. Now this was something new, because the epidemiologists in WHO were up to that point the people working on leprosy, and other infectious diseases, of course, that kind of thing. I applied for the job with cancer and they gave it to me. The director of my unit was a Russian. That was the time that in WHO when they were introducing Russians for the first time. And instead of recruiting Russians one by one depending upon their training and capacity, they came in groups of 20 or 30 together. Our director had in fact left the unit before I arrived. When I got there, there was nobody in the unit other than two secretaries.

A: *You were in that cancer unit for seven years. Was it an intellectually stimulating post? Could you do what you wanted to do?*

AT: Yes and no. What was stimulating was the fact that just by watching the cancer rates all over the world, you could learn a great deal. Dealing in facts was a forgotten job that I had been developing in my own country: that was very interesting. This was how I discovered that in Africa there were cancer problems that were different from those in Europe, in Europe different from India, and so on. And then I tried to investigate these things by creating what I hoped would be local teams of researchers. That was rewarding, but the administration was very heavy. During this time I spent a further period at Johns Hopkins and got my MPH.

A: *Then in 1967 a new opportunity seems to open. With all your background experience you were invited to go to IARC, which was just being set up.*

AT: Yes, the International Agency for Research on Cancer or in French that is 'Centre International de Recherche sur le Cancer', which reads CIRC. To begin with we had very few scientific staff. In June 1967 we were six or seven qualified professional staff and perhaps a dozen secretaries. Funding came in those days from five countries which were UK, France, Germany, Italy and the United States.

A: *And at this stage, with a wealth of professional experience behind you, you started on the work which has made your name known in the alcohol research world.*

AT: In 1967 I put together a working paper describing the distribution of colon cancer, breast and oesophageal cancer in Europe. I got in touch with a student in Paris who had been writing a thesis[3,4] on the distribution of oesophageal cancer, cirrhosis and alcoholism all over France. She had located certain black spots in Brittany and Normandy. So starting from her data I wrote a very simple paper which was the first one to show a similar distribution for mortality from the three disorders, alcoholism, cirrhosis and oesophageal cancer.[5] There were data to compare the mortality experiences of different *départements* of France.

A: *So it was basically an ecological, cross-sectional comparison?*

AT: That's right, at the beginning. And then since the correlation was good with alcoholism I said, well, perhaps it might be due to the specific drinks in the west that could cause cancer and alcoholism more than cirrhosis. I offered the hypothesis that the agent might be calvados.[5] This hypothesis was indeed attractive but turned out not to be correct.[6] It is the total load of alcohol, whatever the beverage, that increases the risk of cancer.

A: *It's the same model, but I have the feeling that we're moving on somewhat from cooking oil.*

AT: Yes. Calvados is a brandy made from apple cider. I went to see some of my friends in the School of Public Health in Rennes at the centre of Brittany. Now with them I set up some more refined analyses, looking at smaller communities and showing that the black spots were in fact even more concentrated than I had originally thought. I was wondering what scientifically I would do next when I met a man who was working in nutrition, who I knew because I had met him before in Africa. And he said, well, you must see Pequignot because he knows all about alcohol problems and he is interested in cirrhosis, you should do something together. So I went to see Georges, and we understood each other straight away.

A: *How did he impress you?*

AT: He was one of those enthusiasts. But obviously he knew lots of things in terms of measuring alcohol consumption, and much about nutrition too, of course, with which I was not familiar. But his knowledge of epidemiology was rather limited. For me it was just the other way around. I knew epidemiology fairly well, but had almost no idea of what measuring alcohol was about. So we began to work together.

A: *You started case-control studies*

AT: Yes. The recording of cases was not too difficult because we found them at the cancer centre of the general hospital. There was an ENT surgeon which was helpful, and a professor of pathology who was collaborative, and all these people helped in producing cases. I also had the death certificates. We all got together, I knew how many cases of oesophageal cancer had been treated, and all those I could catch would be interviewed. It was of course at the same time, with the same control group and within the same study, that Georges and I studied the risk of ascitic cirrhosis.[7]

Alcohol and cancer

A: *And what did you establish?*
AT: The risk of getting cancer of the oesophagus was going up steeply, with daily alcohol consumption.[8]

A: *And this was the first definitive illustration of the dose–response relationship between a cancer and alcohol? Would that be true?*
AT: Rothman had done something of the same kind for cancer of the mouth, but I discovered that only later.[9,10]

About that time I mapped cancer of the larynx and found a sort of straight line cutting Europe into two, with France, Italy and Spain having high rates, and the rest of Europe rates at about half that level

---

A: *You looked for confounders?*
AT: One obvious confounder was smoking. It was surprising that the effect of smoking did not seem to be all that important, because I expected that it would be a major factor even if not as important as alcohol. And with 200 cases I could sketch out this famous skyscraper histogram, showing the combined interaction effects for consumption of alcohol and tobacco. For any given level of tobacco consumption, the curve goes up with alcohol consumption.[8]

A: *What sort of notice did the work receive? Were letters and invitations coming through the postbox, were the big centres interested?*
AT: No, not particularly. I would say that the main and most important outcome was the interest shown by the NIAAA. So we organised the first

working group to discuss the results of this work and to plan further studies.

A: *But you extended your work to look at laryngeal cancer?*
AT: The larynx. I think it was more or less the same process as for the oesophagus except in the meantime we had developed these relationships between the cancer registries in Spain, Italy, France and Switzerland, and we had established a group that was called the Ascension Group. This rather funny name for a scientific group comes from 'Ascension', a Catholic festivity mainly celebrated in Latin Europe. It is an official holiday in these countries and it is always on a Thursday. Thus by taking leave for only one working day (the Friday), this always provides a long four-day leave, most useful for a meeting of this nature. Another advantage has been to avoid the usual arguments as to the dates for the next meeting. We were very few at the beginning, about 12 or 15 collaborators, perhaps, no more, and we decided to meet to discuss our problems. This group developed well, and nowadays they number about 200. We looked around to see the kind of problems that we might all have in common, and one problem that was of major significance in all these countries was cancer of the larynx. About that time I mapped cancer of the larynx and found a sort of straight line cutting Europe into two, with France, Italy and Spain having high rates, and the rest of Europe rates at about half that level.[11] And of course that was of great interest, because the explanation had always previously been related to smoking. But when you look at the map of laryngeal cancer you have this distinction, it is just the other way round from the map of lung cancer. So now the question was, OK, smoking causes lung cancer and laryngeal cancer, but why does somebody who smokes get lung cancer when he is British, and laryngeal cancer when he is French?

A: *An interaction with alcohol?*
AT: It is one of my favourite theses that the aetiology of cancer is probably multi-factorial; the association of alcohol and tobacco is – I believe – the clearest demonstration of this. I tried to express this in an editorial in the *British Journal of Cancer*.[12] We embarked upon a parallel study

of the same design in five centres, with teams in Italy, Spain and France.[13] The international agency was there to conceive, to help in the training of investigators, to advise, but not to give money away. If people are really interested in the project they must manage to find the funding to do their part of work.

A: *A lot of this work, then, came together in the IARC monograph, is that right?*
AT: Alcohol and cancer? In 1989.[14] A large group of workers produced that monograph, people coming from various parts of the world. From the epidemiological standpoint we had no major difficulties, and I remember that we described the correlation between cancer of the breast and drinking. We all agreed that this finding had to be taken into account, although it was premature to conclude that there was a definite causal connection. So I think from the epidemiological side there was a good consensus.

A: *And the conclusion reached was that alcohol is a carcinogen?*
AT: The group concluded that alcohol is carcinogenic to man, and that went through. That is the official position of the IARC. But if a carcinogen is a chemical that produces cancer in laboratory animals, then alcohol is not a carcinogen. Either you have to admit that when a chemical produces cancer in man it must be rated as carcinogenic, or you have to find a way to speak in circumlocutions such as 'ethanol is not a carcinogen, it is a substance which when absorbed by the human subject may produce cancer'. As we would say in French – that is ridiculous.

A: *What is your view now on the alcohol and breast cancer question?*
AT: I still don't know the final answer. It is true that a few people have found the same effect, but with the level of risks that they have described, which is about 1.8 or 2, I would be cautious. My personal attitude, a bias I know, is that I won't accept anything that fails to reach a relative risk of 3. The confounders, if they are not related to the agent producing the disease, are likely to operate at any level of consumption and to increase or decrease the baseline risk. Now, if the

confounder increases the risk by 20% and therefore the consumer in the high category would have relative risk of 10.2 instead of 10, it doesn't make any difference. But if you are at the lower level of the scale and you have a relative risk of 1, then 20% increase means a relative risk of 1.2. If there is a bias resulting from confounders it is more likely to operate at these low levels.

Embraced by the alcohol research world

A: *At a certain point, having established a track record as a cancer epidemiologist, you suddenly found yourself embraced by the alcohol research world. Was that a surprise?*
AT: I was a little surprised. How come? Why did the world wait for me to appear until I looked at the alcohol and cancer connection? But I think there is an explanation. Epidemiology had developed much earlier in Britain and in the States, and only much later in Latin countries. And when the British epidemiologists started looking at problems concerning the epidemiology of cancer they focused immediately on the epidemic of lung cancer and tobacco. So all the epidemiological forces, cancer forces, went into the field of tobacco. About the alcohol research world, I should have mentioned that I found myself 'at home' straight away with people in that world. For them, the sociological aspects and the problems of prevention were of major concern – and this was of course in line with my own personal interests (this was in sharp contrast with the 'cancer world' I was used to).

A: *Alcohol was not a problem for those epidemiologists?*
AT: Somehow alcohol was left out. But just imagine that things had started out the other way round, and that epidemiology had developed in France first and then later in Britain. It may well be that alcohol would have been top of the agenda. And then, well, I happened to be there and to look at these maps and so on. That is how it happened. And I was very surprised. Quite honestly the scientific world that I have come from, technically speaking, is something quite good, but quite classical. Epidemiology is an orderly kind of investigation.

A: *But the best epidemiology is classical, isn't it?*

AT: Perhaps. But there was nothing particularly outstanding in my research. The outstanding fact is that once this work was done, immediately there was an interest in it coming from the alcohol researchers, and from NIAAA.

I feel that I have been useful, that I have respected my contract, as we say in French

A: *You started off describing yourself as having an idealistic view of medicine and feeling that you suddenly met the right opportunity when your teacher introduced you to a public health perspective. Can you now rejoice and believe that you really have served humanity? Do you allow yourself that indulgence?*

AT: I think that it is probably pretentious to say 'yes'. That is the kind of question that you ask yourself when you have time, when you have retired. You look at your past life and you say I have been working for 20, 25, 30 years, what did I do really? What has come out of it, beneficial or not? I did my job to the best of my capacities, that's all. I am grateful to society, to my parents, professors, friends, who gave me a chance to produce good work; in return I contributed some valid pieces of knowledge and other work which was not so valuable. I feel that I have been useful, that I have respected my contract, as we say in French.

References

1.   SAND, R. (1948) *Vers la Médecine Sociale* [*Towards Social Medicine*] (Bruxelles, Acta Medica Belgica).

2.   ORGANISATION MONDIALE DE LA SANTE (OMS–WHO) (1958) *Les Dix Premières Années de l'OMS* [*The First Ten Years of WHO*] (Genève, OMS).

3.   LASSERRE, O. (1963) Etude de pathologie géographique sur la relation alcool–cancer [A study of geographic pathology on the relationship between alcohol and cancer] Thèse pour le Doctorat en Médecine. Faculté de Médecine de Paris.

4.   LASSERRE, O., FLAMANT, R., LELLOUCH, J. & SCHWARZ, D. (1967) Alcool et cancer (Etude de pathologie géographique portant sur les départements français) [Alcohol and cancer. A study of geographic pathology on the French Departments], *Bulletin de l'INSERM*, **22**, 53–60.

5.   TUYNS, A. J. (1970) Cancer of the oesophagus: further evidence of the relationship to drinking habits in France, *International Journal of Cancer*, **5**, 152–156.

6.   TUYNS, A. J., PEQUIGNOT, G. & ABBATUCCI, J. S. (1979) Oesophageal cancer and alcohol consumption: importance of type of beverage, *International Journal of Cancer*, **23**, 443–447.

7.   PEQUIGNOT, G., TUYNS, A. J. & BERTA, J. L. (1978) Ascitic cirrhosis in relation to alcohol consumption, *International Journal of Epidemiology*, 7, 113–120.

8.   TUYNS, A. J., PEQUIGNOT, G. & JENSEN, O. M. (1977) Le cancer de l'oesophage en Ille-et-Vilaine en fonction des niveaux de consommation d'alcool et de tabac. Des risques qui se multiplient [Cancer of the Oesophagus in Ille-et-Vilaine in relation to tobacco and alcohol consumption. Multiplicative risks], *Bulletin du Cancer*, **64**, 45–60.

9.   ROTHMAN, K. J. & KELLER, A. (1972) The effect of joint exposure to alcohol and tobacco on risk of cancer of the mouth and pharynx, *Journal of Chronic Diseases*, **25**, 711–716.

10.   ROTHMAN, K. J. (1978) The effect of alcohol consumption on risk of the head and neck cancers, *Laryngoscope*, **88** (suppl. 8), 125–129.

11.   TUYNS, A. J. (1982) Incidence trends of laryngeal cancer in relation to national alcohol and tobacco consumption, in: MAGNUS, K. (ed.) *Trends in Cancer Incidence. Causes and Practical Implications*, pp. 199–214 (Washington, Hemisphere).

12. TUYNS, A. J. (1991) Alcohol and cancer. An instructive association, *British Journal of Cancer*, **64**, pp. 415–416.

13. TUYNS, A. J., ESTEVE, J., RAYMOND, L., BERRINO, F., BENHAMOU, E., BLANCHET, F., BOFETTA, P., CROSIGNANI, P., DEL MORAL, A. & LEHMANN, W. (1988) Cancer of the larynx/hypopharynx, tobacco and alcohol, *International Journal of Cancer*, **41**, 483–491.

14. INTERNATIONAL AGENCY FOR RESEARCH ON CANCER (IARC) (1988) Alcohol drinking, *IARC Monographs on the Evaluation of the Carcinogenic Risks to Humans*, Vol. 44 (Lyon, France, IARC).

Hans Halbach

Hans Halbach was born in 1909 in Horde, Germany. He studied at the H. Fischer Institute where in 1935 he was awarded a doctorate. His MD was obtained from the University of Munich in 1939. From 1947 to 1954, Professor Halbach taught in the Department of Pharmacology at Munich University. He joined the staff of WHO in 1954 and contributed over many years to WHO's programme on drug misuse and the formation of international policies. He was Chief of the Unit of Addiction-Producing Drugs. In 1975 he launched the journal Drug and Alcohol Dependence and served as its Editor-in-Chief until 1992. In that same year he was awarded the J. Michael Morrison Award for exemplary service in drug abuse research. Hans Halbach died on 3 May 2000.

Early professional experience

Addiction: *Tell me a little about how you started in the addictions, your training and how you got interested in the whole area?*

Hans Halbach: I started in an area which in those days had hardly anything to do with psychology or behaviour, but I was in one of the best schools of chemistry in Europe, with Hans Fischer, Munich, Nobel Prize winner for the elucidation of the chemical structure of blood and leaf pigments. The work was tough but exciting. After a doctorate in chemistry I studied medicine. By the time I had passed the exams in medicine the war broke out. The better part of the war was spent in aviation medicine. The problems were how to survive in high altitudes, how much oxygen do you need, how high can you go up without or with oxygen. There were many theoretical aspects, too. An example: the Allied Airforces had dropped leaflets telling the German pilots that flying at very high altitudes in pressurized cabins could be quite dangerous because if the cabin is shot at, the sudden de-pressurization would have an effect such as the disintegration of a deep-sea fish brought up to the surface. A bit exaggerated. I tried to find out. There is a contraption where you can have yourself shot up in no time to simulated high altitudes. I did it up to 19 km and nothing happened except for the trouble through lack of oxygen. It is still a world record, I believe. After the war I joined the Institute of Pharmacology, University of Munich.

It had been severely bombed and had to be rebuilt from almost nothing. In the beginning experimental scientific work was hardly feasible, except for teaching. In the early 1950s I somehow got excited about the 'cocktail liytique', a French invention based on chlorpromazine (the first anti-psychotic), mixed with other substances to protect vital functions. That opened up an entirely new era of anaesthesiology, and I developed a collaboration with anaesthetists as a pharmacologist providing the theoretical basis for their techniques. When in 1954 the World Health Organization looked for a successor to the retiring chief of the Section on Addiction Producing Drugs, I accepted the job, *inter alia* because the salary of an assistant professor could hardly support a family with three children.

A move to WHO

A: *Tell me about how you began to enter WHO work at that stage?*

HH: In those days, WHO's business, as inherited from the League of Nations, was to advise the United Nation's Commission on Narcotic Drugs as to which drugs should be controlled under the various international treaties for 'narcotics control'. Soon new developments required a thorough overhaul of these treaties. In the course of redrafting, WHO was to point out that classification on the basis of chemical similarity is impossible, and that the salient criterion for control is the drug's impact on individual and social or public health – now an evident truth. It was in this context and in the 1959 Kelynak Lecture that I coined the phrase 'drug–individual–society' as a triangular model, now a platitude of course. Speaking of dangerousness: as a corollary of control, quite a few doctors, in order to avoid cumbersome prescription writing and because they are afraid of dependence development, appear to refrain from prescribing opiates when they are indicated. This is deplorable. So we tried to forestall that by bringing into the Psychotropics (Vienna) Convention, the notion of therapeutic usefulness versus dangerousness. The greater the relative usefulness the less strict the control. WHO also saw to it that in both the Single and Vienna Conventions, the requirements of prevention and treatment were not entirely forgotten. In all this I had invaluable assistance from Expert Committees with key figures such as Nathan Eddy and Dale Cameron of the Committee on Problems of Drug Dependence (US National Academy of Science), and Fraser, Isbell, Martin, Wikler, and others from the Addiction Research Center, Lexington.

In the 1959 Kelynak Lecture that I coined the phrase 'drug–individual–society' as a triangular model, now a platitude of course

A: I suppose there were also other issues besides control through international conventions?
HH: After those conventions had been adopted by the majority of countries the UN Fund for Drug Abuse Control (UNFDAC) was established. It helped countries to live up to their obligations under the treaties and also to reduce the production of illicit drugs, for instance by growing tea or vegetables instead of opium or coca, a project which, by the way, was not a great success. One realized that reducing the supply of drugs ought to be complemented by curtailing the demand, a formidable task involving the assessment of the circumstances of the demand. So WHO started epidemiological studies on drug use and abuse

and issued a series of documents with targets and methodology for further work. There is one aspect which I think has not been given enough attention, and that is in relation to control. That is the matter of acculturation of the use of a drug. There are some classic examples. When the Incas chewed coca leaves ritually nothing bad happened. When the tin mines came and the labourers were paid out with coca leaves, the trouble began. Immigrants to the Maghreb who had been using marihuana moderately in their southern home countries exaggerated their consumption, with consequent troubles under the new environmental pressures. Conversely, khat, a traditional stimulant in the Red Sea area, produced no problems when used in London or New York by immigrants from those areas who might thus even be protected from heroin. The prohibition of a more or less acculturated drug has sometimes created greater problems. No sooner had Iran and Thailand prohibited, under international pressure, the smoking and eating of opium, without preparing the people for such a drastic intervention, than heroin occupied the vacuum and created much greater problems.

A: Would you be able to differentiate the role of controls in the developing and developed world, or do you think that there should be international controls across the board?
HH: The international control provisions are binding upon the parties to these treaties; there is no distinction. Practically the whole world is now Party to the Single Convention. About 80% adhere to the Vienna Convention. Attitudes were, however, different. When the Single Convention was being prepared, countries who had been or still were producing opium, said that to reduce production of opium would mean economic loss. The new treaty, they argued, should specifically cover new synthetic drugs which were more dangerous than the opiates, more difficult to control and from which the developing world (the victims of the old treaties) wanted to be protected. This was in general the voice of the developing countries. To obviate this discrimination we demonstrated in a study with N. B. Eddy and O. Braenden that synthetic drugs with morphine-like

effects are as good and as bad, as a class, as the drugs of natural origin. It is, though, easier to control laboratories and factories than a whole agricultural region. Early in this century an American bishop was moved to pity by the poor people in the Philippines who were on opium. This triggered the first treaty, the Hague Convention. If in those days the opium-producing countries had been as concerned about alcohol as Western countries were concerned about opium, we might have had an international convention on alcohol.

Other international contacts

A: *Tell me something about setting up the journal,* Drug and Alcohol Dependence, *which you have edited for over 15 years.*
HH: It was launched in 1975. The director of the publishing company Elsevier–Sequoia in Lausanne was aware of the activities of the International Council on Alcohol and Addictions. We sat together with the Tongues and Mr Bergmans from Elsevier, and after an enquiry among the international circles concerned, I thought I might give it a try. But the journal should be scientific and international. That's what I hope it is today, at least to a large extent.

A: *Do you get a similar proportion of papers on drugs and alcohol?*
HH: It's half and half. The United States provide quite a proportion of the contributions.

A: *What are the reasons that the Americans are so productive?*
HH: There are probably several reasons. They were the first to have national control laws like the Harrison Act. Secondly, they were the first to have well-organized research: remember Eddy in the National Institute of Health. And then they had this unique setting in Lexington. Perhaps the Americans had a more pragmatic approach and were more interested in the mechanisms of dependence and tolerance.

A: *What do you see as the role of ICAA?*
HH: ICAA was established as a world-wide organization to help solve the problems of alco-

holism. It was only with the WHO Expert Committee report on Services for the Prevention and Treatment of Dependence on Alcohol and Other Drugs, 1967, which advocated the so-called combined approach, that ICAA resolved to deal with drug addiction too. That expert committee was a joint effort of my unit and the Mental Health Unit. As a pharmacologist I had always thought it was not reasonable to make this clear separation in view of the similarities, pharmacologically and otherwise, between alcohol and other drugs. Experience in the area of alcoholism might be applicable, *mutatis mutandis,* to drug abuse and dependence. After the extension of its programme ICAA entered into an official relationship with WHO as a non-governmental organization (NGO). In this capacity ICAA has been attending WHO meetings, expert committees, and scientific groups more or less regularly, but I do not think there has been much material input of information or research data. I feel that is not their strength. ICAA is an agency operating either by itself or helping governments or other bodies to organize conferences and courses of regional or international character on matters of alcoholism and drug abuse, and contributing to information, education and inspiration.

A: *Do you think people concerned about drugs at WHO were aware of Jellinek?*
HH: Yes, definitely. Between 1951 and 1954 there were four WHO expert committees on alcoholism, all with Jellinek's participation, and a seminar on alcohol in Beirut, arranged by my predecessor P. O. Wolff. In the third report of the expert committee the stages of alcoholism according to Jellinek were defined. So in those days within WHO there was an acute interest in alcoholism. However, when I joined WHO I was not encouraged to continue this line, possibly in order to avoid entanglement with lay organizations.

A: *But what about drugs and alcohol in WHO now?*
HH: To accommodate the international narcotics control organs of the UN, definitions of drug addiction and habituation had been devised by WHO. They were outdated and had to be replaced by up-to-date descriptions, since defini-

tions are strictly possible in the exact sciences only. Besides, the term 'addict' was emotionally loaded with untoward consequences for the individual concerned. Instead, the term 'dependence' was elected as the common criterion in describing groups (categories) of substances liable to be abused. Of course, alcohol was included.

A: *As I understand it, drugs and alcohol were part of the Mental Health Division in WHO?*
HH: After several years of abstention WHO revived its interest in alcoholism. Joy Moser of the Mental Health Division admirably collected information from wherever it was available and put it in some order. The resulting reports and WHO offset publications gave an insight into the problem on a global level.

A: *Do you think the Mental Health Division was the place for drugs and alcohol?*
HH: After I had retired from WHO the functions were separated administratively. Questions relating to international control were left in the unit of drug dependence within the Division of Prophylactic and Therapeutic Substances (previously the Division of Pharmacology and Toxicology which I headed) and whose terms were considered incompatible with WHO's orientation towards developing countries. Later on the control business was again transferred to a new Division of Drug Policy and Management. The clinical and social side was given to the Mental Health Division. This administrative separation between two entirely different divisions was frankly deplorable. If the control people are left to themselves they may not be aware of the effects of control on consumption, treatment or prevention. And there have, of course, been other organizational shifts.

Moving to Hoffman LaRoche

A: *Tell me, you left WHO in 1970 and then went on to . . . ?*
HH: . . . Hoffman LaRoche in Basle, as a consultant. One of their strong points was (and still

is) the development of psychoactive drugs including, of course, basic research into the mechanisms of action. The consultation concerned ways and means of ascertaining the efficacy and safety of drugs, not only psychoactives, touching in many respects on the programme in drug efficacy and safety which I had developed in WHO after Dale C. Cameron had taken over the responsibility for drug dependence and abuse.

A: *So really your career has been as an academic pharmacologist and physician?*
HH: Physician for a short time during the war because, as I said, I had just finished my medical training when the war broke out.

A: *Did you manage to do research of a pharmacological nature, or supervise research, while you were working for WHO?*
HH: All the WHO recommendations and decisions regarding narcotics and psychotropics control were based on results of scientific research. Already in 1958 I suggested that not only the dependence-producing drugs should be screened, but all kinds of untoward drug effects deserved attention and ways and means should be sought to get hold of information at the earliest possible stage, as was done in regard to dependence liability. It took 3 years for the thalidomide disaster to convince the administration of WHO, and governments, of the urgent need for action. As an immediate measure an international system was developed for the collection of early information on adverse drug reactions including data pertinent to drug abuse. As a corollary the principles and requirements of the preclinical and clinical study of safety and efficacy were laid down in a series of expert reports. These texts were well received, especially where governmental regulations hardly existed. The WHO unit of Drug Dependence became the Division of Pharmacology and Toxicology, with 'Drug Dependence' under Dale Cameron as one section among others. The new activities led also to contacts with the pharmaceutical industry.

A: *Do you think that with Europe attempting to unite in some way, that this will act scientifically and research-wise as a powerful force?*

HH: Quite broadly, not only in regard to our area of interest, the European competence in research is considerable. One might ask whether the unification of Europe will have an impact just on European research as such, or in regard to the rest of the world. There are many international links already. Roche, for example, has two excellent and completely independent research institutes, one in Switzerland and one in the USA, where they do basic research which has no immediate connection whatsover with the development of drugs. Three Nobel Prizes came from the Basle Institute. There are many research-oriented drug companies on both sides of the Atlantic.

A: *What about the WHO as an international research collaboration centre?*
HH: Traditionally WHO has entertained collaborative research programmes in almost every one of its activities. Nevertheless, in the mid-1960s Director-General Candau wanted to give the organization a solid scientific base. A WHO Medical Research Centre was envisaged. The British were very interested, and the Scots even more so; they wanted to have it in Edinburgh. In 1967 a Division of Research in Epidemiology and Communication Science was established at WHO Headquarters in Geneva. To begin with, a high-powered scientific staff developed mathematical models and refined statistical methods. I had hoped that with their help the drug monitoring project could become a truly epidemiological exercise. Alas, after initial enthusiasm this global research enterprise fell apart. Perhaps it was too sophisticated. Besides, WHO's basic orientation changed when the new Director-General introduced himself and his goal of doing away with the social injustice in the world.

The European competence in research is considerable. One might ask whether the unification of Europe will have an impact just on European research as such, or in regard to the rest of the world

---

Tune over again

A: *If you were choosing your career again?*
HH: I grew up in an area of heavy industries, coal and steel, and felt that science was the thing to do, and chose to begin with the fundamental discipline of chemistry. I told you how I got into medicine and how the circumstances brought me into the business of international administration, coupled with science. If I were to choose a career now I would probably wish to base it on a broad education in natural sciences.

A: *What sort of family did you come from?*
HH: A family of printers and book binders since 1832.

Commentary
Outstanding Scientists in Hard Conditions

Ulrich John

The three European scientists represented in this section of the book survived World War II as very young men and started to work in new fields after its termination. What they had in common was addiction as their research topic but their approaches were different. In Germany, where two of them lived, only a few scientists had stayed, and only very few resources had not been destroyed. With the tremendous sufferings of other European countries, the situation there was very difficult too. In such a context when a new economy was to be developed with the help of those who freed Germany from National Socialism, elementary medical care was needed. But at the same time, a huge demand with respect to the care of alcohol dependants became apparent. The AA idea was spread out by American soldiers in the 1950s in Germany. Several other self-help groups re-emerged, with a tradition dating from the end of the nineteenth century in Germany. Large numbers of patients exhibited alcohol-related disorders. This was one of the main motivations of Wilhelm Feuerlein to engage in research in this field. Albert Tuyns, through his perception of the demand for intervention also came to his famous research findings on the combined effect of alcohol drinking and tobacco smoking on cancer of pharynx mortality.

However, at least in Germany until the 1990s no addiction research developed on a large scale. Thus, the two researchers mentioned as well as Hans Halbach remained individual outstanding scientists who developed their passion for this particular field in part by the circumstances, in part by their view of the needs. None of these three scientists followed in the steps of a teacher in addiction research. They all came from different

backgrounds in education and experience. Looking back on those early years after World War II, all three personalities must be seen as main contributors to the origin of addiction research on the European continent.

Hans Halbach and Albert Tuyns did not act on a national scene. They were engaged in WHO on a more transnational level of dealing with the problems. Thus, they were European and cosmopolitan scientists. Their respective fields were drug control by transnational activities and epidemiology. An individual approach was followed by Wilhelm Feuerlein, although he believed that the problem of alcohol-related disorders could only be solved by effective preventive measures. This attitude regarding necessary public health measures constituted one common viewpoint of the three postwar Europeans, although these measures have not up to now been instituted rigorously in their own countries.

A first question therefore arises whether these three single early postwar scientists managed to stimulate major activities in research and practice of public health. They did, indeed. Topics raised by them during their major periods of productivity have been further developed and are still highly important to this day. The findings of Albert Tuyns regarding the combined effect of smoking and alcohol have had an overwhelming influence on international research. The findings stimulated research on the conjoint effects of tobacco smoking and the drinking of alcohol on mortality, and the public health implications based on those findings. National institutions such as the CDC (Centers for Disease Control and Prevention) in the USA very much act on this basis of attributable fractions. Hans Halbach had been engaged in international drug control activities that are now strongly institutionalized on a European level. Wilhelm Feuerlein has strongly sensitized physicians in Germany with respect to addictive problems among their patients.

In some European countries the public health approach to lowering alcohol-related problems in their societies had a huge impact, but not so much in other countries. In Scandinavia, there were longstanding traditions in public health activities based on the idea that social questions and quality of life were basic aspects of health. On the other hand there was the idea of individual freedom predominant in other countries, putting emphasis on the idea that everybody has her or his own responsibility for their health. This viewpoint was particularly strong in Germany and turned out to be a major obstacle against public health intervention in spite of the tremendous health problems caused by tobacco smoking and harmful alcohol drinking. Thus, it may be concluded that there was not a very powerful public health oriented political climate in every European country during the post-war years. The influence of the scientists is nevertheless active.

The second question to be raised is whether the three scientists stimulated further addiction research. They did. Albert Tuyns stimulated research particularly in the epidemiological field, Hans Halbach, among other things, edited the journal *Drug and Alcohol Dependence*. Since that time research and treatment in drug addiction has developed considerably. Wilhelm Feuerlein stimulated numerous research activities. Many of my generation active in the field of addiction admired these activities that were outstanding and which stimulated research on the treatment of addictions. Single psychiatrists laid further foundations to this research. But a continuing lack of addiction research in Germany was apparent despite the longstanding activities of research groups, particularly the one of Feuerlein in Munich which was mainly engaged in research on treatment for alcohol dependence. They carried out the largest German study on this topic using an in-patient cohort of alcohol dependants, followed up for four years. Feuerlein stimulated research in many other ways, for example he added significantly to the foundation of the German Society of Addiction Research and Treatment. By such means he fostered research and research-based treatment approaches, multidisciplinarity and open discussion. Thus, important parts of the development of research and treatment in Germany are to his credit. He added to the call for more research. Now, a situation in Germany of research activities growing into international collaboration has developed. Altogether, the three scientists identified here had an impact on public health and care as well as addiction research, in their home countries as well as on an international level.

Part VIII
Community Activists in the USA

David Deitch

David A. Deitch PhD was born in 1933 in the USA. He is a clinical and social psychologist and currently Clinical Professor of Psychiatry at the University of California, San Diego, and Director of the Pacific Southwest Addiction Technology Transfer Center. He has had 40 years experience in the development of drug abuse treatment systems for adolescents and adults, nationally and internationally. He was Co-Founder of Daytop Village, Inc., and also served as Senior Vice President and Chief Clinical Officer for Phoenix House's Foundation. Earlier appointments were at Temple University, the University of Chicago, and the University of California at San Francisco. He has consulted to a variety of Departments of Correction and Ministries of Justice and Health in Latin America, SE Asia and Europe, as well as serving the US government. He is Regional Director of the Executive Committee of the Association for Medical Education and Research in Substance Abuse.

Starting as an outsider

Addition: *David, there are probably few people with as intimate perspective as you on how the therapeutic community treatment approach evolved. Can you tell us how you came to play a role in that evolution?*
David Deitch: Well, it was a long and circuitous journey. To begin at the beginning, I was a drug user, a heroin user. I began by being first exposed to marijuana, liking the culture of drug use plus jazz, and then being introduced to heroin by a jazz musician I admired. It might be a little less awkward to refer to myself as a 'casualty', although it never occurred to me to think of myself that way until recently when others suggested that it might be a more palatable way to describe that time in my life. So, one could say that I became one of the first victims of the 1948 to 1951 heroin epidemic that made its way into the urban centers in the United States. In this instance, my urban center was Chicago. I very much fit the psychological profile of the drug user that I have often talked about; I felt marginalized, alienated, probably in a lot of intrapsychic pain, and very curious about drug effects.

A: *Why did you start on heroin?*
DD: At first, heroin use was primarily a way for me to belong to a group that was different, exotic

and outside, which very much matched the feelings I had about myself. I was known as 'Monk', a nickname given to me because I was always reading. I was different from the gang on the corner, but at the same time I was very different from the academically orientated kids. I was undisciplined, with no guidance and quite lost. Also, I was moving from place to place, never having a friendship group, without any history with people – no shared school, neighborhood, activities. I was an outsider. So for me the world of jazz musicians was a world which I made a personal projection onto, seeing them as sensitive souls struggling to be creative in a world that no one really understood. I even tried learning to play the saxophone, but I didn't have the natural talent, the discipline or the resources to take lessons.

A: *Did the heroin begin to kick in?*
DD: Yes, the heroin began to kick in. At first it was a way of having relationships with other outsiders, of being special; then it also felt good and could obscure what I didn't have – real friends, money, status or serious disciplined interest in anything (except reading). Using heroin led to needing money and I manipulated and stole from anybody and everybody. I always felt terrible about it. This of course led to more time away from school, to more theft, and finally arrests, overnight lockups,

court – the awe of it all! But on some level I was always wanting to be okay, to not hurt my real family, to be liked. Once when I was placed on probation I tried going to Lexington for treatment, but after going back on the streets I didn't know anyone except those I had met through heroin culture activities, so back to heroin was the only route I knew. There were more arrests, more times spent in custody. Always during those times I was immensely interested in understanding myself and I availed myself of group and individual therapies. I really felt I wanted to change, if only insight or expression of pain could change me, so that I wouldn't want heroin and could feel normal. Naturally therapy didn't give me that but it was incrementally useful, just not curative (the magic word). I tried to express my intellectual and creative aspects during a brief period writing poetry, editing, directing plays, doing art – all activities of emotional expression or attempts to create identity – but heroin always took the upper hand and led to crime (primarily shoplifting, but with a flair). So, at 28, in New York, afraid of going to jail again, still looking for magic, and exhausted, I heard of a 'Miracle on the Beach'.

So, at 28, in New York, afraid of going to jail again, still looking for magic, and exhausted, I heard of a 'Miracle on the Beach'

It sounded perfect. Addicts, who I still romanticized as being sensitive lost souls, ran the place – Synanon. It was in California and there, at last, addicts were saying 'I got better'. That, for me, was the beginning.

Synanon and expulsion

A: *What happened to you after you joined Synanon?*
DD: I started, as all people did, at the bottom – scrubbing pots and pans, sweeping floors. After about three months, while I was talking in a 'seminar' one day, Charles Dederich, the founder and primary innovator of Synanon, challenged me

to continue elaborating on a concept I was trying to develop. This led him to invite me into a quite heated 'game', or 'encounter group', where he and the leadership essentially 'fried and cooked' me over. At the end of this session I felt brutalized, but then he invited me to participate in a group he was starting called the 'young lions'. This was a group he wanted to develop personally for fast-track movement because he saw the organization expanding. There were six of us who were selected to live with him in his separate house. We were trained day and night through seminars, game/encounter groups, probes, and were constantly under review with ever-present reprimands and ego reduction experiences. As a result I was chosen for another six-man team to open an East Coast branch of Synanon in Westport, Connecticut. Shortly after I arrived there the director, Jack Hurst, became quite ill and I was encouraged to take over, with the presence of an old-timer standing by to keep me anchored. I continued to grow in leadership by being given the opportunity, the experience, and finally the rank. Within 18–24 months I had moved from worker through expediter, coordinator, assistant director, to director. With that came a lot of premature clinical obligations.

A: *After you had achieved a position of leadership you left Synanon to work with Daytop Lodge. How did this come about?*
DD: Daytop's research psychologist, Alex Bassin, and Joe Shelley, who was head of probation for the Second Judicial District of the New York Supreme Court, visited Synanon on a number of occasions, probably at Dr Daniel Casriel's suggestion. Alex Bassin then applied to the National Institute on Mental Health (NIMH) for a grant to study placing addicted felons on probation in residential treatment. Shelley and Bassin attempted to replicate what they saw at Synanon without being able to appreciate either the philosophy or the methodology. They thought that if they could provide the veneer and the artifacts – the structure, the bones without the organs or the flesh – they could achieve the same outcome. And right away they got into very serious trouble. Thinking that this was not a unique model and

that criminal heroin users could be considered the same as alcoholics they hired a 12-Step AA guy to run the place. Within a couple of months these criminal, heroin-using, felony-convicted probationers ran this AA guy through hoops and there were all kinds of drugs being used. He was followed by a few more failed leaders, so now Daytop was in crisis and they were desperate for stable leadership.

A: *How did you enter into the picture?*
DD: I was expelled from Synanon and Dan Casriel who had written a book about Synanon called *So Fair a House*, recommended me to Daytop Lodge.

A: *You were expelled from Synanon? How did that happen?*
DD: Up until that time, Synanon was a staged treatment activity with a goal of ultimately returning the person to the greater community. The stages were live-in/work-in treatment; the next stage was live in/work out; and the third stage was live out/work out with ongoing relationship to the Synanon facility. Then a couple of people going into third stage failed, and at that point Dederich began putting forth the view that society is sick, rather than examining what Synanon could do to improve the outcome. The easiest answer was, we are the better environment because in this environment people don't use drugs and they stay drug-free while living in positive and moral ways, but in such a sick society they relapsed – a circular argument. So he stopped permitting people to move from 2nd stage to 3rd stage and issued a directive that all 2nd-stagers be returned to first stage. I chose not to agree with that, but I also chose not to argue. I continued to support people in 2nd stage and to have some people move to 3rd stage. This created immense tension. I was called back to California and essentially I was 'busted down', much like you would do in the military. At that point I was Director of the Westport facility and an Associate Director of the Foundation. They took away my 'rank' and everything else and I was returned to mopping floors and things of that sort for a few short weeks. In the meantime they had very serious pressing needs back in Westport,

so I was returned to Connecticut to serve at the Foundation level on 'development'.

A: *And next?*
DD: After a while I said, well, I think it's time for my wife to join me because I'm planning to leave the organization. At that point Dederich let me know that there was no such thing as gradually leaving the organization and said, 'You're out'. Ted Dibble, the guy who was told to actually throw me, his leader, out of Synanon was so totally undone by that order that I had to help him do it. I had to make an appearance that morning on a radio talk show where I talked all about the positive merits of Synanon. When I went back that evening I packed up my gear and told him, 'All right, Ted, you've got to drive me to town, give me two dollars and say goodbye, because this is the way it's done'. So I left Synanon, took up residence in the community and returned to school in Connecticut. I also led therapy groups for Dan Casriel in New York City and for Henry Jarecki in Connecticut.

Daytop and a different kind of community

A: *So it was Dan Casriel, a psychiatrist, who was instrumental in bringing you into Daytop?*
DD: Correct. Daytop turned to Dan Casriel who suggested that they talk to me, and I agreed to help them out. So I moved into Daytop Lodge with 35 nutty convicted felons who had been manipulating the system and began the process of changing behavior with a 16-hour meeting, during which I essentially moved them to the point of volitional disclosures about all of the drug-taking and where all of the stashes were in the facility, and ultimately moved them also to some level of 'expiation'. The notion was, if you want to stay, then you've got to atone. Remember, at that time we believed in shaving heads, and I had them shave each other's heads as part of this atonement process. That was the beginning of my role at the Lodge.

A: *What was to be special about Daytop?*
DD: I'll tell you two stories that I think are important at this point. My one other colleague

and I recognized that we could not operate this facility just by ourselves. We needed stability – not psychology – stability, non-drug-taking stability. And the only resource I had, contrary to common practice in the world of mental health at that time, were the spouses of those guys. So I began to hold special meetings with the spouses and began to have them in the facility as much as 20 hours a day, just so I had the reliability of somebody who wasn't a drug-taker being there in the midst of these people. The reason I'm emphasizing this story has to do with the development of "therapeutic community" (TC). I then had spouses move into the facility and I began to use them as administrative and clinical support. I had them participate in groups because my thought was, I don't need just addicts confronting addicts; I need people who also are stable involved with this process because we're going to deal with the behavior more than the drug-taking. As we expanded I recruited three educators into the clinical operation of this idea. So if you talk about the true development of the model at that point it involved not just 'ex-users' or 'people in recovery', it also made use of people with no drug histories at all. So by the end of 1964 we were already proving that this model was not dependent only on people in recovery operating it. Did we need their zeal, their passion? Oh, of course! But in the meantime the core group that began to emerge were a mix of users and non-users, academics and so forth. So there's the beginning of Daytop. At that point, we did not refer to Daytop as a 'therapeutic community'. The descriptive language used then, and still used at Daytop in Connecticut, was 'humanizing community'.

A: *Did you have dealings at this time with Efren Ramirez?*
DD: Mayor John Lindsay recruited Efren Ramirez, a psychiatrist from Puerto Rico, to New York City to be its first 'addiction czar'. Ramirez began relying on me a lot as he tried to push the envelope shaping drug treatment for New York City. He was, if not a disciple, an admirer of Maxwell Jones and had some training with him and used some of Jones's concepts in his project in Rio Piedras, Puerto Rico. Ramirez used the language 'therapeutic community'. He encouraged me to adopt that term because he believed it would have more currency in the world of mental health. We adopted it, much to my regret at abandoning 'humanizing community'.

A: *It appears that unlike Dederich, who was opposed to helping others develop therapeutic communities, you were not concerned about such proprietary constraints when Dr Ramirez asked for your help.*
DD: No. It was very different. A couple of years ago when I was preparing remarks for a memorial for Chuck Dederich I wrote about when I was a 'child of Dederich at Synanon'. I used that language to describe the time when he moved the 'young lions' into his house and for six months we sat at his feet in everything he did.

But when I 'grew up' and wanted to leave the people at Synanon were unhappy about my leaving and for years I was considered by them a bad person and a traitor to their cause. On the contrary, at Daytop I was a staunch helper and supporter when Ramirez came to New York. And when Mitch Rosenthal came back from the Navy I urged Ramirez to hire him as one of his principal deputies. I worked closely with Ramirez and was co-director of rehabilitation for the City of New York while I was still running Daytop.

The therapeutic community movement expands

A: *What else was going on in the therapeutic community movement at that time? Was anyone else actively involved in developing or expanding it?*
DD: Yes, there were others. We were helping Mitch Rosenthal, who was working for Addiction Services Agency of New York City at that time. Then Dr Judianne Densen-Gerber became involved with us and also with Ramirez, and we were participating in doing marathons for her group at Flower and Fifth Avenue Hospitals. One outcome of that work was that Judianne launched Odyssey House. I vacated one of the Daytop facil-

ities in New York City, moved all the people up to Swan Lake for a major retreat, and gave Judianne some Daytop staff so she and her staff could spend the first two weeks shaping up their group. I also sent Daytop staff to Mitch Rosenthal when he was developing a Phoenix facility at Hart Island, in the Bronx.

A: *Would you say that Rosenthal and the Phoenix House organization were more directly descended from the Daytop system than from Synanon?*
DD: No, actually. Mitch had contact with Dederich and Synanon when he was serving as a psychiatrist at the US Naval Hospital in Oakland, California. He was very taken with the group process and the structure, which fit the military, and he used it to start a TC program at the hospital there. When he started to develop Phoenix House in New York, two of the Synanon staff came to give him support, along with some of the Daytop people. And then a young guy named Frank Vitale left Synanon and came to me seeking work. I was a real fan of his and I recommended him to Mitch as a deputy that he could benefit from having. Then Mitch, Frank and others built Phoenix and it really is theirs. So I would consider them as much more in a direct line down from Synanon, with my being supportive to that.

A: *Were there any teachers or innovators that you feel were directly 'descended' from Daytop who went off to establish other therapeutic communities?*
DD: A whole line. All over the United States.

A: *Can you name a few of them?*
DD: Very direct descendants are Topic House on Long Island in New York; then you've got Marathon activities in Rhode Island and elsewhere in New England started by James Germano; and Gaudenzia in Philadelphia, with John Ruocco and Ben Cuevas; and Walden House in California. Then you move out from there and you get Gateway in Chicago, with Carl Charnett and Michael Darcy; and out of that Chicago activity comes Abraxas in Pennsylvania. After

that there is a next generation which goes farther afield.

A: *While you were in New York in the mid-1960s, Marie Nyswander and Vincent Dole developed methadone maintenance treatment. Can you tell us about any early interactions that took place between proponents of methadone maintenance and the therapeutic communities of Daytop, Phoenix and Odyssey?*
DD: Yes. The early interactions were quite antagonistic, with therapeutic community people, including myself, feeling that methadone was a threat to the TC approach. So when Vince Dole would speak, I would be there representing another approach and would view this notion that he was going to give drugs to everybody as a way of handling addiction as a terrible assault. What was interesting is that the therapeutic community movement at that time was actually hand in hand with the Federal Department of Justice which was opposing the development of methadone. I look back now and think, isn't that intriguing? We were dancing with Justice, while in other circumstances you would have to say that those people (Justice) don't appreciate the nature of the struggle of treating addiction.

A: *Did you ever change your view of methadone maintenance treatment?*
DD: Well, yes. I encountered a dentist and a young mathematician at Daytop, both of whom were doing what I thought was great work in terms of their careers but kept relapsing to drug use. Contrary to the therapeutic community myth that you can't come back in once you leave, I kept trying to reach out to them. You have to remember, my early leadership was very much based on mixing cognition and affect. I was stretching cognition all the time. I had a need for cognitive leaders. I didn't want therapeutic community to become this visceral, one-hand-clapping activity, which eventually began to occur. When one of them went on methadone I brought him into the facility and had him live down the hail from me as a way of trying to pull this off. After that I brought in another person who was on methadone and tried to work with him while he was on maintenance.

A: *How did this arrangement work out?*

DD: I grudgingly accepted it, that methadone was useful for some people who could not get their act together any other way even though they tried. However, I could not introduce this idea to the therapeutic community. I really felt it could undermine a drug-free effort, especially in a therapeutic community setting.

A: *Daytop expanded quite dramatically during the mid- to late-1960s, establishing facilities in many places. Did this expansion affect the structure and work of the organization?*

DD: Yes, we did expand, in two ways. We expanded residential treatment, first to Swan Lake (in the Catskill mountains, not far from New York City); then to another site, on 14th Street, in New York City; and then we were looking at expanding into Florida. Our other project was to expand into communities with a high incidence of drug use by doing outreach, using a very concrete model, to try to bring people into treatment.

You know, the fact that you're no longer using drugs is not enough; you now need to say thank you to the world

---

Dubbed a 'radical militant'

A: *In the late 1960s, you and a number of your associates left Daytop en masse. What precipitated your departure?*

DD: The New York Times characterized it best – in the Sunday edition I was labelled a radical militant who was using 'drug treatment' to organize social militancy for radical change; and I had said, yes, that was true. I did have the notion – still do – that addiction is also a disease of the social fabric, that things that occur in the society contribute to the problem, and that one thing we needed to do as part of the re-entry process was to do something about the world we lived in – to atone. You know, the fact that you're no longer using drugs is not enough; you now need to say thank you to the world. What better way to say

thank you to the world for giving you the opportunity to get better than to do something for your community. And so the block by block organizing was not only a way to get our people exposed to the stimuli that could produce craving, but it was also a way to say thank you and do social good. I was able to convince them that if we were going to do anything useful, every one of us had to do something in the block we lived on, that we could not be happy saying, 'We treat addiction', or just coming to this work every day. And the way we could do that was to create a group in our house, our apartment building, or on our block, and people would want to come (and did) for 'therapy'. But when they wanted therapy, the payment was, 'What will you do for the neighborhood in return for this therapy?' So the way we bartered was, 'Yeah, we'll talk about your marital conflicts and your self-esteem issues, and the trouble you're having with your art or your work, but in turn you have to do something for the block.' Those activities, I still think, were very important as part of the notion of what we were up to – it was called 'social therapy'. A question that is still difficult to answer is whether you can successfully recover without a social role and its integrative aspects.

A: *How did this cause you to leave Daytop?*

DD: Well, the Board of Directors began to perceive some of these things as slightly radical. There were rumors that I had gone to Cuba. There was no truth to that, but I was talking a lot about Che Guevara and I had a poster of him in my office. But there was truth that I had encouraged people to participate in marches against the war in Vietnam; there was truth that I had a relationship with members of the Black Panthers. In fact, we had a relationship with a splinter group of the Panthers called the Honor Guard, in Harlem, and engaged with them in an activity of photographing 'connections'. We used our photo labs and made huge posters which we then put up around the neighborhood labelled 'Enemy of the People'. It is true that, as we expanded projects and talked about disease within the social fabric as well as the individual, we organized a lot of block clubs and engaged in social/political action. Then at the annual retreat at Swan Lake one of the young residents decided he was going to wear what became popular five years later – a shirt made out of an American flag. So the tension on the Board kept building up.

Another thing that was occurring is that I made a serious effort to move people of color into leadership roles within Daytop and some people felt they would be bypassed as I did that, and there may be some truth to that. Also, I was proselytizing that what Daytop did was confront things like racism and all of these things, and some of the members were saying they did not agree with the social items. So all of these things resulted in a Board blow-up and they tried to fire a group of us; and we said, 'No, you can't fire us, we quit', and that sort of thing, and ultimately we departed.

It was when I joined Jaffe that I got the benefit of some of the best mentoring that I've ever had

Chicago with Jerome Jaffe

A: *Where did you go from there? This was in 1968 or 1969?*
DD: The end of 1968. Well, I left and formed, with a small group, something called Concepts West. Then we were all recruited to do some work for Jerry Jaffe, at the Illinois Drug Abuse Programs (IDAP) in Chicago, and in spite of the fact that we (at least I) had this blacklisted reputation he was brave enough to say, 'Why don't you come and work here?' We dropped Concepts West, moved en masse to Chicago, and joined the Illinois Drug Abuse Programs. For the second time in my career I was offered a university appointment in addition to a job title. That was done primarily through Jaffe's advocacy, supported by Dr Daniel X. Freedman, who was Chairman of the Department of Psychiatry at the University of Chicago. My first university affiliation and title, which I held from 1967 to 1969, was as Instructor in Psychiatry at Temple University Medical School, in Philadelphia. That came about as a result of many of their

people having attended one of our intensive training institutes within Daytop. Anyway, back to Illinois: Jaffe gave me this wonderful opportunity in Chicago.

A: *What were your responsibilities in Chicago?*
DD: I was Director of Training and Education for the State of Illinois Drug Abuse Programs, and a research associate, assistant professor level, in the Department of Psychiatry at the University of Chicago. I also tried to serve as a 'whisperer' to leadership. I no longer wanted to be a leader but I was willing to be a whisperer. You know, I had been burnt – really bad – by the Daytop explosion. It took me a long time to recover.

A: *Did you find your work in Chicago very different from being the leader of a therapeutic community?*
DD: It was when I joined Jaffe that I got the benefit of some of the best mentoring that I've ever had. Not only was he an intellectual mentor, he was also a professional mentor. He helped me become more professional. I was invited to meetings where we were solving problems and I felt that I was making a real contribution to the goal of the mission, but it was clearly his vision – and a vision based on science as well as an aspiration to do something that had meaning. For me it then became a very important opportunity. I remember participating, with his coaching, in a conference at Rutgers University. I had done some writing before and viewed myself as a poet, but I had no idea about how to write a publication for a conference. Other than off-the-cuff speaking (we did lots of that at Daytop and I'd been considered a great speaker), I had no idea how to do a scientific presentation. I was given the opportunity, because of Jaffe, to do a presentation at Rutgers University at a conference on Communication in Drug Abuse for communications people. He and I conspired a 'multimedia' presentation (he coached the writing), for which I picked out all the films playing in New York City that weekend, pasted the ads on a board, circled all the ones that were showing drugs, and passed the board around while playing popular tunes which focused on drug taking. That was in 1969, 20 years before any of

these communications people admitted that maybe there is some suggestive potential in what is presented as art and entertainment. It was a wonderful gift for me to work in IDAP, to have the opportunity to sit in on the educational meetings, the opportunity to collaborate. We had the first true multi-modality treatment system, but we took it over the top.

A: *Few people know that multi-modality treatment – a synthesis of different treatments – was created a long time ago and was effective. Will you describe how you did that?*

DD: For one thing, we created multi-modality residential treatment at Tinley Park, a facility near Chicago. In one building we had detoxification, rituals that engaged newcomers into treatment (either drug-free or methadone). Those on methadone were typically the casualties – the ones who were getting into trouble with booze or whatever – who were given the opportunity to live and work together in a therapeutic community at Tinley Park, sometimes along with their children. Later we closed our hospital-based detox unit and created still another facility, Safari, moving the system 'multi-modal' within those two residential units that were being shaped along therapeutic community lines.

I wasn't going to be deterred and I went right into community meetings where they were threatening to kill me

A: *You mentioned earlier that you recognized the benefits of methadone while you were still at Daytop, but how did you feel about actively recruiting people into treatment with methadone? Was it hard to accommodate to that idea?*

DD: No, not at all. The proof was in the pudding. Here were all these folks who needed treatment and our notion was that we could improve TC for those that weren't making it by giving them a chance with methadone and improving the clinics where people were getting into trouble by incorporating more 'psychosocial' environmental activities. Jaffe took on the entire city;

and in the Illinois Drug Abuse Programs were the seeds of the system he took national. The national system was an outgrowth of what he built at IDAP and I won't ever let people forget that. There wouldn't be a drug abuse treatment system in this country if it weren't for Jaffe. From the system perspective the basis of it all begins with Jaffe and his vision in Illinois.

A: *Psychosocial meaning what?*

DD: Let me give you one of the strategies. On the near northwest side of Chicago we had a speed and hallucinogenic drug phenomenon; four blocks away we had a gang-based, Puerto Rican, heroin phenomenon. We set up 'Pflash' ('Pflash Tyre: blown-out minds retreaded'), a program for the speed and hallucinogen users; and we increased the availability of methadone treatment for the Puerto Rican gang heroin users. I used my radical stuff – the same things that we used earlier at Daytop trying to stop gang violence. Our people worked with the gangs and used them to help us access that whole heroin network, making methadone treatment easily available. It was a wonderful social engineering intervention using methadone and other resources. We've never documented or written about it but it was an amazing social strategy – looking at a problem, how do you intervene?

A: *Where did your restlessness take you after your time in Illinois?*

DD: I was recruited away from Jaffe by Dr Arnold Mandell, who was chairman of psychiatry at the University of California, San Diego. The first thing I did was change the inpatient detox. Secondly, we created methadone units all over San Diego, and using the experience of Pflash Tyre in Chicago, I took methadone into communities where there was heroin use and made it immediately available and began effecting change. Then we then ran into some very bad political opposition from a Chicano group in another part of San Diego. I wasn't going to be deterred and I went right into community meetings where they were threatening to kill me, and we moved through that and recruited a lot of gang people, got them involved and trained them, much like we did at Tinley Park in Chicago. And then, using Tinley Park as a model, I started a multi-modal therapeutic community at Deer Park. We also experimented with having a bar on the grounds as a way of watching how people handled alcohol – an observational group. We were observing and seeing where people were getting into trouble and doing an intervention about alcohol. It's debatable whether that was a smart idea.

A: *How long did you stay in San Diego?*
DD: Until 1973 – not quite three years.

A: *Why did you leave?*
DD: I left because they put a researcher, Dr Audrey Holliday, in as my boss and I think I had a real hard time with that. I ended up in Berkeley doing all kinds of things, including getting my PhD, and then I was recruited to the University of California, San Francisco, at the associate professor level, to run their methadone treatment and some drug-free stuff.

A: *That's quite a transformation – from establishing the first therapeutic community outside of Synanon to running a methadone program.*
DD: But we had been doing it in Illinois; we had been doing it in San Diego. I was running the system at that point. But when it got to San Francisco I needed to do a lot of innovative things with outpatient detox as well as with the maintenance operation. Then I wrote a major piece[1] on what was occurring in the Synanon movement at that point and I was invited back to the World Federation of Therapeutic Communities meeting by Msgr O'Brien. I'd also been communicating with Mitch Rosenthal and his people, and during that visit he asked me to come back and do a bunch of activities for him, especially in light of the paper I'd written on the decline of Synanon – (sank into craziness is a better term). I began to spend a week every month back in New York, slowly turning over the UCSF service to others. I joined Mitch as Chief Clinical Officer and Senior Vice President of the Phoenix House system. I was interested in the challenge and I was romantic about returning to New York.

A: *Had the TC world changed in the meantime?*
DD: When I stepped back into the TC world it was a bit of a shock – especially a New York TC that had been relatively insulated. All those New York systems had been insulated from the growth challenges that had happened for drug treatment and therapeutic communities elsewhere in the country, especially in California. At the end of 1984, I told them that I would prefer to return to California, while continuing to be involved with strategic planning, which they agreed to. I left the Phoenix organization a few years later. I didn't want to leave Phoenix and do drug treatment somewhere else. I didn't feel that would be fair to them, and I really did and still do admire Mitch Rosenthal and a few of the other people in the organization. So for a while I worked for Psychiatric Institutes of America in their rehabilitation hospitals branch, where I developed head and spine injury units based on a modification of therapeutic community methods. And I returned to being a freelance consultant and therapist. Then Daytop asked me to please assist them in program expansion, and that slowly built into doing more and more and then it became a full time job.

The world the scene

A: *Was that when you began setting up therapeutic communities throughout the world?*
DD: Yes. Daytop, following in the tradition that I am proud to say I established, was always willing to help others. They had already spent some time helping therapeutic communities in Italy and Sweden. Then I got a letter (which had taken two years to reach me) from a group in Greece asking me if I would please give them a hand. The Daytop executive committee said, OK, let's do it. I became very taken with the group in Greece and how hard they were trying to apply the principles of therapeutic community and social therapy. Daytop also asked me to do some work for a group in northern Italy. Well, because I was so taken with the group in Greece, I decided I would help them build a training institute. I wrote a proposal that laid out the generic principles of

therapeutic community. Daytop encouraged me to share the proposal for the training institute with our State Department. People at the State Department read the proposal and said it was exactly what they needed. We first focused the training on Italy and Asia (primarily Malaysia, Thailand, Sri Lanka), and then worked in some Indo-European countries that are involved with the Colombo plan. We began to develop a systematic way of teaching, over a 6-week course, the fundamentals of therapeutic community. Then we got to use the training course in Latin America. We also began to train corrections personnel in prisons. Some of the best staff I ever trained were in the Malaysia prison system. They now have four therapeutic communities in Malaysia in the prisons run entirely by uniformed personnel. Thailand has 54 prisons using therapeutic communities run entirely by people trained in their system. And then I began to do this work for a group in Sicily. Then, because I wanted to see them move forward, I took the idea and shaped it into a proposal for them to take to the World Health Organization. In the meantime, it made its way reshaped and reconstituted a third time (still based on the original idea), and it was accepted by the United Nations to be implemented for six East Central European countries where we've been building treatment systems, not just therapeutic communities. More important, what we are saying is you can't develop good treatment staff if you only train in one model. You've got to give them a full spectrum of treatment models because they need all options or it isn't going to substantially impact the epidemic.

A: *David, are you doing similar work here in the US?*
DD: While I was carrying out the international work, I was also developing residential components for multiple offender youth – general behavior disorders and drug abusing young offenders. Then I was recruited back to the Department of Psychiatry at UCSD by another important mentor in my life, Dr Lewis Judd. I was given the task of developing day hospital treatment utilizing a modified TC approach for patients with mixed psychoactive disorders, including geriatric patients.

In addition, I was charged with developing our Department's managed-care initiative – a complex and not very rewarding task. Then through state and national competition we were awarded an Addiction Training Center grant from the federal Center for Substance Abuse Treatment (CSAT). In California we set out not to increase the size of the treatment work force (counsellors, etc.), but rather (and in my opinion more importantly) to enhance the skills and educational level of the existing work force. While carrying out all these tasks we also developed a Criminal Justice Advisory Committee and worked with them toward the development of a curriculum we could use for both custody and ancillary prison staffs. These have become extremely useful as we have expanded our activities to include training prison and community personnel to work collaboratively with inmates.

A: *More recently?*
DD: During the past five years I also chaired a national curriculum development committee for an entity now known as the Addiction Technology Transfer Center. This committee has made an immense contribution toward professionalizing the addiction work force. We first developed and published a set of 'Competencies' for this work force, and subsequently published the knowledge, skills and attitudes (KSAs)[2] that make up these 120 Competencies. I successfully built bridges between the work of the committee and that of the major national groups in the United States that certify professionals working in the addictions. As a result they have endorsed our work as a curriculum standard for their groups and have collaborated to develop a best practices manual. Because of my continuing involvement in the international work, the Competencies have been translated into Czech, Hungarian, Greek, Italian, Spanish and other languages, and serve as a basis for the corrections counsellor development activities in the respective countries. Finally, I continue to develop therapeutic community curricula, a treatment model which due to the amazing outcome of its use in prisons, is in demand.

That is all for now.

References

1. DEITCH, D. & ZWEBEN, J. E. (1981) Synanon: a pioneering effort in the treatment of drug abuse and a signal for caution, in: RUIZ, P. & LOWINSON, J. (Eds) *Clinical Issues in Drug Abuse*, pp. 289–302 (Baltimore, Williams and Wilkins).
2. US DEPARTMENT OF HEALTH AND HUMAN SERVICES, SUBSTANCE ABUSE AND MENTAL HEALTH SERVICES ADMINISTRATION (1998) *Counseling Competencies: the knowledge, skills, and attitudes of professional practice*, Technical Assistance Publication Series 21, DHHS Publication Number (SMA) 98–3171 (Washington, DC, US Government Printing Office).

Ignatius McDermott

Monsignor Ignatius McDermott was born in 1909 in Chicago, USA. He studied at Quigley Preparatory Seminary and Mundelein's St Mary of the Lake Seminary. He was ordained in 1936. His was a staff member of Maryville Academy from 1936–41 and Assistant Pastor of Our Lady of Peace from 1941–46. From the 1940s onwards his work focused increasingly on helping the drinkers of Chicago's Skid Row and he gained a Masters degree in social work in 1970. Awards include the 2000 Humanitarian for the Millennium Award, and the 2001 John H. McDermott Award for Civic Leadership.

The Cardinal's charge

Addiction: *Tell me something about your personal background.*

Ignatius McDermott: I was fortunate in emanating from a family where my mother and father were very precious and wonderful people. My father had emigrated from Ireland and started a milk business, and there were six boys and two girls in our family. My mother was a school teacher; her grandparents came from Ireland. My oldest brother became a judge – he was in the political world in Chicago. I had another brother who owned a tavern. I was born and raised in Chicago and I went to a grammar school, graduating in 1924. I used to go into church, close by across the street, run in there and make a visit. I realized that the Lord resided in the tabernacle and He was my friend, and I would talk to him and I would ask Him to tell me what He wanted me to do, and give me the grace to do it. So when I left school I went to the seminary in Chicago known as Quigley Preparatory Seminary. I went there for five years, 1924–29. We started out with about five classes with 40 in each class. In 1929, 95 of us graduated and we went to the major seminary. We were to be ordained six years later, but it took me seven. I was injured playing football and lost too much time and had to repeat a year. I was ordained in 1936.

A: *And what was the next move after you were ordained?*

I'm saying to myself, Missionaries – Oh! I'm supposed to go to the pampas, supposed to go to some vile country and eat rice

IMcD: The way God draws blueprints is better than any person who is human. We had been ordained on 18 April 1936; we pursued our studies till 30 May and then we were given a month's vacation. My brother had a summer home on Long Beach, Indiana, and I figured I would go there rather than be homeless on the beach. I would be getting an appointment within a month; I had a couple of class-mates with me, and I was down on the beach and we were playing ball, and my sister-in-law said to me, 'I got a call from the Chicago archdiocese and you are to see the Cardinal tomorrow'. So I called the office of the seminary and I said to the rector, 'This is Ignatius McDermott, and my sister-in-law received a call that I'm supposed to see the Cardinal tomorrow'. He said, 'Well, Ignatius, you had better be there'. I knew it was for real. So next day I arrived at the seminary. A few minutes later we were ushered into the Cardinal's office. He was sitting behind a desk, and we went over and greeted him and sat down. He said, 'I'm gonna make you young priests missionaries'.

A: *Was that good news?*

IMcD: Oh! Missionaries! I'm saying to myself, Missionaries – Oh! I'm supposed to go to the pampas, supposed to go to some vile country and eat rice. What about the Chicago White Sox that I love so much, and I want to see them play on my day off. And what about my mother and father? Those things were cantering through my mind. The Cardinal then said 'Where I'm sending you as a missionary, you don't have to board an ocean liner or go across to Europe or distant territories. You don't have to get on an aeroplane and fly to some distant shores. You don't even have to get on a ferryboat! Life here is hard in our own archdiocese, it's mission territory. I have appointed Father O'Connor as the superintendent of Merryville, a children's home in a poor suburb about 25 miles north west of Chicago, and I want you to report there on 30 June.'

A: *That job sounds like a pretty big demand on a young man.*
IMcD: I'm sitting at Merryville, and I took it for granted that I had a wonderful mother and father who were still living, and I had brothers and sisters. I'm 25 years old. I see hundreds of boys and girls running around out there at the children's home, and I'm saying to myself, 'God, how come you shortchanged those people? How come they're out here?' I'm 25 years old, and for the first time in my life I realized that I had taken something for granted. Parents were a gift from God. Why did He take a father or a mother away out of some family? A TB sanatorium, a death perhaps. Why did a mother die? I said to myself, 'God, you short-changed those gifts'. And I was beginning to realize how blessed I was to be out there doing this work. I felt sorry for my classmates. They think, maybe I got the worst appointment! But I saw myself as having the best. I'm looking upon these kids as my brothers and sisters. How fortunate, so many brothers and sisters.

Early interest in drinking problems

A: *And how did your interest in drinking problems begin to emerge?*
IMcD: While I was in the seminary from 1924–29, I had a job at a racetrack during the

summer vacation and I would board the train in the Skid Row area. I'd walk along and I would see the men populating the streets. My first real exposure to the Skid Row area in Chicago was, however, at Merryville, when I came across children who were not receiving any visitors. On one occasion that sent me down to Skid Row to find a parent who wasn't visiting. And at that time I became aware of alcoholism as a family sickness. I saw some of the parents coming out on a Sunday and they were, as we would say, 98% proof under the influence and rude to their own child.

A: *How long were you at Merryville?*
IMcD: After five years I left Merryville and was assigned to a parish in the south shore area of Chicago. There was a school of about 700 boys and girls, 1st to 8th grade, and the nuns taught the children while I was the religion instructor. Often when a boy or girl would begin to manifest behavior problems, the sisters would say, 'Well, we should release this child and let him go to a public school'. Recalling my exposure to the children whose parents had been dependent upon alcohol in the orphanage, I would again do a home visit, and ring the doorbell and get up the stairs before they knew who I was, and often as not the door would open and I would find a mother dependent on alcohol. That too lasted for five years, and then I was sent in 1946 to the Catholic Charities, again a residential home for children, and the office was two blocks from Chicago's Skid Row, and right next door to our building was the police station.

Skid Row

A: *What exactly is the social, human, meaning of this term 'Skid Row'? You must be one of the world's experts on that question.*
IMcD: Well, as I said, I became acquainted with Skid Row early in 1931 when I was working at the racetrack. I would have to walk from the bus three blocks to a railroad station, and I would be walking through the heart of the Skid Row area. Skid Row had been there for a long time, but I had never heard the men ever refer to themselves as

being a resident of Skid Row. Skid Row to the men is not a piece of real estate; it's a state of mind (and there are more alcoholics in penthouses than in flophouses). The origins I suppose are something like this. In the wake of the American Civil War we had more than a few widows. In those days there wasn't any veterans' assistance. The women had to live, and they had children, so they resorted to using their skills as housekeepers and cooks and laundresses. They started some rooming facilities along West Madison Street, because that was close to the Union Railroad Station and to the North Western Railroad Station. The canal and the railway tracks were under construction so the men could reside in that area, and then they could get on the train and go out to the place where they were working and return at night. Breakfast and a lunch-pack, and dinner would be ready and their clothes laundered when they returned at night. Time marched on and other people saw that this could be a good way of earning a living, and this generated all the hotels along Chicago's West Madison Street. So you had a proliferation of Skid Row hotels, and the men were living in cages. And then another disastrous development took place along this street – pawn shops and blood banks. You would have the reputable hospitals in the city coming down and buying the blood, and the donors were getting $5 for a pint of blood while it was being sold for $35.

Skid Row to the men is not a piece of real estate; it's a state of mind

Then too people began to look toward Skid Row as a source of cheap, exploitable labour. 'Slave marts' – that's the people who are running those employment agencies. They were prostituting the men. Some business would call them and say that they wanted 10 or 20 men for a job that had to be done in a hurry and the agency would contract to get $1 an hour for the man who did the work, and they turned around and paid that man at 65 cents an hour. How otherwise did the men survive the Skid Row area? Some of them had part-time jobs: they would pass out handbills; they would set up pins in bowling alleys; wash the

lettuce and clean the tomatoes in a restaurant or act as dishwashers, and this with many of them suffering from TB. So I talked to people from the Chicago Health Department about bringing a truck to take chest x-rays of their lungs. But the ones that got a card and knew they were positive, they would disappear to another Skid Row and they would not want to be taken out of circulation.

A: *When you were first involved with Skid Row, what kind of help was available for the men who inhabited this 'state of mind'?*
IMcD: In those days when the public inebriate was apprehended by the police he would be brought to the police station, he would be thrown into a cell in the basement, and the cell would reek of urine and excrement and there would be a trough for them to relieve themselves. The next day they would appear before the judge who would probably say, 'Well, why don't you try to be better, we don't want you back here again'. If a man was making repeated appearances, the judge might send him to the city prison. Of course, an alcoholic thrives on resentment, sending a man to prison generates lots of resentment, and the man would be saying, 'If you thought I was drunk the last time, wait till you see me when I get out this time'. And he didn't know he was on the path of self-destruction. With the alcoholic it's either the Desert or the Jones Town Flood. It's either majoring in dryness or in wetness. I would look in on the cells and throw the men cigarettes and talk to them, and I would see religious students coming down and talking to a captive audience and telling them about the wages of sin. And these were sick people, and here they were being incarcerated for being sick.

A: *Were there at the time any state institutions which offered help as an alternative to imprisonment?*
IMcD: There were two state institutions at that time, about 30 miles from Chicago, which catered for the homeless alcoholic. I would motor there every week and take some of the men with me, and all they were getting was a clean bed. As they used to say on Skid Row, 'You're getting three hots

from the cop' – you're getting three hot meals from the police. They were breathing in fresh air but nothing was done in the rehabilitation line. We would stop at a restaurant about two miles before the state institution and they would buy a hamburger or cup of coffee, and I would buy each one of them a pack of cigarettes. Later I would bring them back, and they would play many return engagements.

The men on Skid Row

A: *And who were these men you would find on Skid Row?*

IMcD: Every kind. You had to identify with them and believe in them, and you had to give them the dignity of man. Why should I be up here and them down there? Every man came from dust and to dust he shall return. I was beginning to find more than a few professional men on the street. In fact, I met a doctor on the street after he found out I was for real. He'd be sober from time to time and I'd be going in and out of the flophouses, so when I found the doctor in sober moments, I would ask him to come with me. Of course, he himself was experiencing a tremendous loss of self-esteem. Here he was, an MD, and found on Madison Skid Row. In the meantime, I came across a man who was a graduate at Rutgers University, and this man had taken a geographical cure. He had been a professional football player, and had majored in sociology. He found sobriety as a desk clerk in a hotel. I ran into priests on Skid Row who left their dioceses and found their way down here. They would be from the West coast and residing on Skid Row trying to lose their identity. It was looked upon solely and exclusively as something that's sinful, and you should be able to say your prayers and be able to escape the dependency on alcohol. The Church didn't realize, of course, about the illness of alcoholism.

A secret problem

A: *What role did you see AA playing in helping people on Skid Row?*

IMcD: AA is for people who want it. You have to have the desire to embrace sobriety and serenity. It's a program of attraction and you see living, breathing, walking examples of it. I read an article in the *Reader's Digest* about Alcoholics Anonymous and I learned that there was a Big Book. I met a vice president of a bank in Chicago and I asked him about this book, and he came out to the rectory to see me a few nights later and he had a large bag under his arm. There were three offices in the rectory and he said, 'We're not going to sit in this office are we?' We went to the middle office . . . 'Is the door going to be closed?' We went to the third office and sat down. He gave me the book, telling me I could keep it as long as I wanted, but don't ever call him at the bank. In those days he could have lost his job because of the terrible feelings that people had about alcoholics. They always felt that in order to be an alcoholic you had to live on Skid Row.

Later, Clem Lane, the city editor of the *Chicago Daily News,* would come over every day and make a visit to our chapel, and I learned that he was a member of Alcoholics Anonymous. At that time I began to see him often. I talked to him about establishing an AA facility in West Madison Street. So I said they could meet in our office and we put a sign on the door 'If alcohol is your problem, why not come to an AA meeting on Monday or Friday night?' and, of course, quite a few people had to say, 'Well, it's a rainy night, and I could go in there and I could twist the priest's arm and may be he would give me a buck and I could buy another drink'.

A: *When you were starting your own work on Skid Row, how well informed were Church attitudes on drinking?*

IMcD: Clergymen make a retreat once a year. The retreat master, he was not equipped to talk about alcoholism. Yet one of the talks usually would be on alcoholism, and often times the retreat master would be saying, 'Well, if you don't drink before nightfall, you'll never get in trouble. If you drink it straight, you'll get in trouble. So the best thing to do is always cut your gin or scotch or bourbon or rum, mix it with soda water, or with water. Never drink alone; if you drink alone you're in trouble'. A priest talks about alcoholism and he doesn't know what he's talking about. There were, though, more than a few priests in Chicago who were dependent upon alcohol and were members of Alcoholics Anonymous, and they were staying dry. Austin Ripley opened this place in Wisconsin, and he welcomed alcoholic clergymen; in fact, he went looking for them. He would bring them back to his place; he would have them always in the house as a clergyman, their trousers had to be pressed, they had to have a clean shirt and collar, they had to be shaven, they had to be tonsorial, and have a hair cut. As some of these priests began to recover, the priests in the neighbourhood were infatuated and they'd come over – 'Hey, what is this place?' Well, Austin Ripley would talk to them and his wife would work with them.

A priest talks about alcoholism and he doesn't know what he's talking about

A: *And general public attitudes to alcohol dependence. Was it always a secret problem?*

IMcD: There was a drug store across the street from where I was working in Chicago, and some of the children would go over there and have their lunch at noon-time. I became close with one of the pharmacists: my children used to go there at noon and he would joke with them. One day a woman rang the doorbell at the rectory and said she'd like me to talk to me about her brother. I said that I didn't know her, so how could I know her brother. She said, 'You know him very well, he's the pharmacist and he's across the street. I am unmarried and he's unmarried. We live in our parents' house, they are both dead. He has a dependency on alcohol, and when he's missing for two or three days and you talk to him, he tells you that he was sick. He did not tell you his sickness was a dependency upon alcohol'.

A: *And meanwhile, I imagine, everyone had a good drink, and alcohol had nothing much to do with alcoholism in the public mind?*

IMcD: I was at a wedding reception one night and was in the company of a judge and his wife.

I don't know what the custom is in other countries at wedding receptions, but in Chicago people would arrive and the bride and groom would receive them, and they would all be imbibing cocktails. So there'd be a cocktail hour, and then when they sat down to attack the solids at the table, there would be bottles of white and rosé wine. After the meal was consumed, the Master of Ceremonies would announce that the band is here: 'We're going to have dancing; there'll be a sweet table later, and the bar is re-opened'. You see all these wonderful people, how well-dressed they are, how self-confident, you see the family roots. Now, these people on their way home, they don't know how much they have been drinking, and it hasn't cost them anything. On the way home they could maim or kill somebody, behind the wheel of a car. Now, you are the judge I said, would you like to send those people to the jail? It was probably the father who over-imbibed and he's thrown in that jail, do you think that he's going to get his job back when he returns? What's going to happen to the source of income for the wife and children, are they going on general assistance and be a drag to the taxpayer?

A: *Did you get interest in this work from the university community?*

IMcD: The professor of sociology at Rutgers, we had met somewhere, and he said, would you come over and be a guest lecturer twice a year and talk to the students. So I went there and talked with these students and they were all saying 'How can we help you? We want to come over and help you'. After a year or two conversing with them in the class, I said 'I don't believe any of you people at all. I have been coming over here for two years, you said you wanted to come to Chicago, there was only one person that I know ever came down here and he didn't come out of the university, he came out of Michigan, Kalamazoo, a young Calvinist'. He came as a postgraduate student to these boys, and we had him living with us.

Establishing a residential facility

A: *You had over the course of some years become very close to the men who were living on*

Skid Row in a personal, feeling, compassionate way. How did you make the first move toward establishing any kind of formal helping facility?

IMcD: I was on a commission which was funded by the Mayor and we'd meet once a month. The group was composed of businessmen and newspapermen. The idea was to try to better the lot of the Skid Row men. We started with a reading room, a sort of warm-up centre where men could go for a day and have a shave and a wash. Dr James West, he and I became fast friends and allies, were both on this commission. In 1973 or 1974, he said there's an article coming out of Toronto about non-medical detoxification. So we went to Toronto. Dr West and myself at our own expense. We returned around midnight, and we were all agog. Boy, we'd got something to talk about to our fellow commission members at the next meeting. And our words fell on deaf ears. So I said about to Dr West let's open a social setting detoxification centre. We opened this place on 31 December 1975, and they passed the law decriminalizing the public inebriate in July 1976. The building was owned by the Presbyterian Church who had moved to other quarters. The roof was leaking. And we found the same thing as in Toronto, that less than 4% of the people needed the services of a hospital or an MD. We were saving the County Hospital close to a $1 million tangibly, but intangibly we were saving the people so that their toes wouldn't be amputated for frostbite. The first law mandated that the person would have to be seen by a doctor, but they later amended the law so that a medical opinion was not needed. When we opened our non-medical detox centre in December 1975 it was the first in the Mid-West. It was pretty much a pioneer project. We stayed in that place until the building was condemned and then we went in quest of another site.

A: *Was it easy or difficult to find new accommodation?*

IMcD: Looking for a building is one thing, and looking for a building owned by a person who's understanding is another. We found a man who owned property in the neighbourhood, and he had a building with two empty floors. The first floor had been a tropical fish business; the second overshoes, but both of those enterprises had gone out of business, and this man rented his property to us for altruistic purposes at a very modest cost. The men stayed on the first floor for a while and then they moved to the second, where the objective was to create an atmosphere to keep them dry. When the gentleman who had rented us this accommodation died, his son owned the whole block of property and didn't want to sell us just part of it. We didn't have enough money to purchase that building, a little over $300 000, so we went in search of some persons who would help us. Before we could develop this strategy, the building was sold to a Jewish father and son who ran a restaurant supply business. We asked them about purchasing the building from them, and they said 'We'd love to, but our present building is condemned and we have to move out into this property'. But they were wonderful and noble people and they said we'll give you a year to see if you can find another building for your center. We looked all over the city and we encountered an obstacle course because of zoning difficulties. Zoning is where in certain neighbourhoods you cannot put things in that you want to put in.

A: *And what was the state of play at the end of that year?*

IMcD: A year marched on and we needed another year, so we petitioned the father and son who owned the restaurant supply business, and we found them favorably disposed. In this day and age it's awfully hard to find people like that. We were into our second year when we found a building practically across the street. We bought the building for $1 m, and all we had was a monumental faith in the divine providence of God. I signed the letters at the Bank, and I had only one-third of the down payment. So we purchased this building and we moved the facility into what we called Haymarket House, because it was the scene of the Haymarket riots of 1886. When we came into our area and bought this building for $1 million-odd, all the windows were broken, there weren't any elevators, you could put saddles on the rats running out of the building. And people were questioning me – 'What kind of people are you bringing in here? Are you going to bring this neighbourhood down?' But before long I was able to say 'Hey, why don't you put some windows in your building; why don't you paint the frame. You're making our building look bad. We're out to help humanity, you're out to make a buck. You should be giving us money, because we're making your neighbourhood look better and enhancing it'.

A: *And you've moved on again since?*
IMcD: We are now into our third Haymarket House. The building we are now in, we get about 16 000 people there annually; it's open 24 hours a day, 365 days a year. When we again moved on to a new building we began to remodel the facility, and we had to generate funds which now would be in the neighbourhood of perhaps $12–14 million. I always felt that the success rate would be better if the environment is pleasant, clean, and attractive.

Kindness is the only language in the world that the deaf can hear, that the blind can see, that the dumb can speak

The career choice

A: *What kind of a person do you look for to work with you?*
IMcD: I'm looking for somebody who is going to identify with the people we are privileged to serve. And I want some people who have experienced alcoholism in their own lives, or in their families. I'm not myself an alcoholic. We interview all the potential members of staff. I want them to realize that it is a *privilege* to work with these people. I remember when I was a kid going to

Quigley, and I'd go down State Street every day, where the big stores are. I was always magnetized by a sign in one of the clothing stores 'Our best ads are worn, they are not written'. The most powerful thing in the world is the power of example. And I want our staff to look upon the people we are privileged to serve as the nobility, and we are the servants. If you forget that, I don't want you around here. You don't look upon them as 'things'. This is a beautiful place and when I walk through here and I see a piece of paper, it's not beneath my dignity to pick it up. And I'll keep telling them the Master is kindness. Kindness is the only language in the world that the deaf can hear, that the blind can see, that the dumb can speak.

A: *Your future plans? I doubt whether you are resting.*
IMcD: My 50th anniversary in the priesthood was in 1986, and that's when I founded the McDermott Foundation. We have a facility for women who are in the last three months of pregnancy. In this institution it's costing in the neighbourhood of $90 a day for taking care of a woman, but if you bring a crack-saturated baby into the world, it costs minimally $1000–$2000 a day in our country. We have 200 women on our waiting list and we're expanding our facility.

A: *Would you have done so much if you hadn't been a priest?*
IMcD: I don't know. I often wonder. I had ideas . . . love sport so well I thought I might be a sports writer – I love baseball and football. Write for one of the papers or become a sports promoter, or something of that nature. I figure, well, the Lord put me in the best arena in the world. I may not be on the pitching mound, but I'm on the mount of Melchizedek – that's pretty good!

Commentary
Back to Becker

Jessica Warner

In 1963, Howard Becker, then a young American sociologist, published the first edition of *Outsiders: Studies in the Sociology of Deviance*.[1] The book was in many ways the culmination of his earlier research into how once abstinent individuals became habituated to using marijuana. Becker, much like David Deitch and Ignatius McDermott, began his career on the back streets of Chicago, but unlike either man he was content merely to describe what he saw. Deitch and McDermott, by contrast, were moved by what they saw, and wanted to change life as they found it; this makes them, in Becker's words, 'moral entrepreneurs', each bedeviled by 'some evil which profoundly disturbs him', convinced 'that nothing can be right in the world until rules are made to correct it'. The contrast, one that is all too familiar to the readers of these interviews, is that between researcher and activist.

The career of Deitch is by far the more complex and peripatetic of the two moral entrepreneurs, and raises the question of whether a movement in which self-abnegation figures prominently can tolerate the emergence of new leaders with new approaches. The answer, as far as Alcoholics Anonymous (AA) is concerned, is a categorical no,[2] and to the extent that the therapeutic community borrowed some of its key concepts from AA it was inevitable that Deitch would run into trouble when he became a 'young lion' in the full sense of the term. This was especially true of Synanon, where Deitch managed both to rehabilitate himself and to launch a career. In the beginning, as a recovering addict, Deitch was 'fried and cooked' in a ritual euphemistically known as 'the game'; just two years later, he was himself one of Synanon's directors, only to be 'busted down' once he deviated from the organization's rules and effectively challenged Charles Dederich's status as a charismatic leader. In Deitch's own words, 'when I "grew up" and wanted to separate and chose to leave, that provoked a force-out'.

In the meantime Synanon was rapidly degenerating into a cult, furnishing a local newspaper, the *Point Reyes Light*, with both a story and a Pulitzer Prize. Dederich even went so far as to plot the murder of a lawyer who had sued the organization. He also went after Deitch, who had wisely already jumped to Daytop. There Deitch continued to expand his contacts in both the treatment and academic communities. This, in the words of the sociologists, constituted effective 'resource mobilization', characterized by bringing together individuals with as wide a range of talents and contacts – whether professional or political – as possible.[3] Deitch's growing list of contacts and allies thus included Doctors Daniel Casriel, Efren Ramirez (who at the time worked for Mayor John Lindsay), Jerry Jaffe, who went on to head up Nixon's drug programs in the Special Action Office of Drug Abuse Prevention, and Arnold Mandell, then chairman of the Department of Psychiatry at the University of California at San Diego. This same period also marked Deitch's foray into other social movements, consistent with Becker's profile of a moral entrepreneur. Hence his involvement, among others, in the civil rights movement, and hence, too, his passionate assertion that 'addiction is also a disease of the social fabric, that things that occur in the society contribute to the problem, and that one thing we needed to do as part of the re-entry process was to do something about the world we lived in . . .'.

Like Deitch, Monsignor McDermott has managed to assemble an impressive array of allies and contacts over the course of a long career. They include, naturally enough, the Archbishop of Chicago, in addition to local politicians and Dr

James West, who went on to become the medical director of the Betty Ford Center. McDermott's career has in many ways paralleled that of Father Flanagan, who is best known as the founder of Boys' Town. Both priests chose to serve a population that was both urban and marginal, both started on shoestring budgets, and both parlayed their life's work into large, permanent institutions, each receiving millions of dollars every year in both private donations and public funding. With additional funding the Haymarket Center has branched out to offer services ancillary to its original mission, including an outreach program for homeless individuals at Chicago's O'Hare Airport, medical and psychiatric services, and treatment for pregnant women abusing either drugs or alcohol.

McDermott also benefited from having the blessing of a larger institution, in this case, the Catholic Church. This contrasts with Deitch's peripatetic and in many ways frenzied career, itself a testimony to the fact that the therapeutic community is an evolving and by no means settled model. Of particular interest is the extent to which McDermott has mastered the languages of several cultures, whether of the police, local politicians, his superiors in the Archdiocese, or of the men and women who come to the Haymarket Center. This point was brought home in a fictionalized account of McDermott's work, published in 1966 under the melodramatic title of *The Liquid Cross of Skid Row*.[4] In it he is described as using 'a voice that is a curious blend of toughness and compassion', the tone of which also comes through in this volume's interview. In another passage from *The Liquid Cross*, 'Father Mac' confronts two men who have stolen a watch from an incapacitated drunk: 'The man in the dark suit understands the language and he can speak it too. Coolly but ominously he said, "You guys ought to know better than to try to scare me. You might take me, but it would get nosed up and down this street in two minutes, and they'd find your bodies in a dustbin in the morning. Now give me that watch." '

Are Americans more receptive to treatment by individuals other than medical doctors? The question has acquired new and in many ways ominous urgency in light of President George W. Bush's initiative to increase federal and private support for faith-based charities. While the question cannot be satisfactorily answered, it does seem that America has perhaps produced more than its fair share of moral entrepreneurs, consistent with its strongly religious roots. This may, of course, be a self-fulfilling prophecy, as the sociology of social movements is also uniquely American. And so, too, are David Deitch and Monsignor Ignatius McDermott.

References

1. BECKER, H. S. (1966) *Outsiders: Studies in the Sociology of Deviance* (New York, Free Press).
2. BLOCKER, J. S. (1989) *American Temperance Movements. Cycles of Reform* (Boston, Twayne Publishers).
3. GLEASON, W. F. (1966) *The Liquid Cross of Skid Row* (Milwaukee, The Bruce Publishing Company).
4. MCCARTHY, J. D. & ZALD, M. N. (1973) *The Trend of Social Movements in America: Professionalism and Resource Mobilization* (Morristown, General Learning Press).

Part IX
Interplay of Research and Policy in Scandinavia

Klaus Mäkelä

Klaus Väinö Mäkelä was born in 1939 in Helsinki, Finland. He gained his MA in 1963 and his PhD in 1971. Posts have included: researcher at the Institute of Sociology, University of Jyväskylä, 1962–64; researcher at the Social Research Institute of Alcohol Studies, 1964–80 and from 1972–75 as its Director; Chairman, Board of the Institute of Criminology 1972–75; Editor of Alkoholipolitiikka (Journal of the Finnish Alcohol Monopoly), 1972–74; Editor of Oikeus (Journal of the Society for Legal and Social Research), 1975–76; President, Society for Legal and Social Research, 1977–79; Editor of Sosiologia (Journal of the Westermarck Society), 1982–84; Professor, Department of Sociology, University of Helsinki, 1988; President, Kettil Bruun Society for Social and Epidemiological Studies on Alcohol, 1989–91; Editor of Acta Sociologica, 1998–2000; and Research Director, Finnish Foundation for Alcohol Studies, 1981–2000. He has had significant involvement with the World Health Organization, including various advisory roles and membership of the 1979 Expert Committee on Problems Related to Alcohol Consumption and the Expert Advisory Panel on Drug Dependence and Alcohol Problems, 1979–present. He has also served on various Finnish state committees and advisory councils in the fields of alcohol, social legislation, marriage law, penal law and constitutional law between 1966 and 1991. In 1984 he was awarded the Jellinek Memorial Award and in 2000 became a Professor Honoris Causa. Research interests include determinants and consequences of alcohol control policies, patterns of drinking, consequences of drinking, and mutual help movements.

Background

Addiction: *You were born in Helsinki and grew up there. Did you go to university in Helsinki also?*
Klaus Mäkelä: Yes, I am a local boy.

A: *Were you always in sociology?*
KM: In a sense I was always in sociology. I had what was called Practical Philosophy as my other main study – Practical Philosophy in the Aristotelian sense.

A: *And what were your original interests in sociology?*
KM: Maybe in the sociology of deviance. The criminologists and alcohol sociologists worked closely together, and there was this institution called the Nordic Summer Academy which had democratic and open ways of working. There were study groups in the different university cities, and then a session in the summer where people of different ages would meet on egalitarian terms. They had for a number of years a group on deviance and social control. The Norwegians were important – Nils Christie, Johan Andenaes, and Thomas Mathiesen – and they in turn had read the American labelling school of deviance. So this, in addition to analytical philosophy, was the main intellectual impulse in my early years.

A: *And you were also politically active in student movements?*
KM: That was somewhat later, and in the 1960s I was a few years older than most. But I was quite active in the 1960s, mostly in 'single issue movements' – like the peace movement, and the gender equality movement, and movements related to all kinds of social control policies, related to all kinds of misfits and stupid and dishonest people. Our argument was that there could be more just and more effective control policies, and that the pain should be distributed in a fairer way than it used to be – that the deviant people had too much to carry of the total pain.

A: *That was related to your interest in criminology.*

KM: Yes, it was.

A: *So Kettil Bruun recruited you, and what year was that?*

KM: That was in 1964. Before that, I was two years at the University of Jyväsylä, in the middle of Finland. They had a new Department of Sociology, and I was the first assistant to the professor and a kind of administrator and lecturer, and also expected to do my own research. Because it was a new university, there were only a few students and they were all enthusiastic and bright – the university was drawing on the hidden intellectual resources in the countryside. So they were really bright people who probably could not have afforded to study further away from home. At that time we still had intellectual reserves in Finland.

Johan Galtungspent spent time in prison because he refused to do military service and used that time to write his doctoral dissertation on the prison

A: *So you enjoyed those two years?*

KM: Oh, that was really great. The university had been first a training college for primary school teachers, then it was turned into a pedagogical college, and then into a university. So it had all these teachers' college traditions. Sociology was something new and radical. So it was double fun, really, because there was a big change in the general climate of that institution. The professor, Paavo Seppänen, was also interested in redefining how we related to the student – in a less hierarchical way than what was around us.

Coming to alcohol studies

A: *So Kettil Bruun recruited you from there?*

KM: I had met Kettil in Helsinki on several occasions. Both before and after I was in Jyväskylä I had contacts with Kettil and the other criminologists and alcohol researchers through this Nordic Summer Academy.

A: *What was your original task in the field?*

KM: I think it was to compare half-way houses for alcoholics with different treatment ideologies. One was 12-step inspired, and one was based on modern case work. The problem was that there was absolutely no way of comparing them because one was in Helsinki with a lot of job opportunities and the other was in Oulu in the north, where the level of unemployment was high. So whatever effect the ideology might have had was certainly not visible in the everyday functioning of the clients.

A: *This was a period when Finnish research was looking at treatment. I think Kettil published a book before that with Markkanen?[1,2]*

KM: Our half-way house study was not so much on the effects of treatment. In the comparison Kettil and Touko Markkanen carried out on two ideologically and formally different treatment regimes, it turned out that in practice they were almost the same. What happened on the everyday level was not that different even though the ideologies were different. Because of that experience we collected a lot of data on how the system worked, and we did not really do a follow-up in any strict sense. We just wanted to describe the treatment systems as social institutions. This was also partly inspired by the criminological tradition of Johan Galtung's study of the prison as a social system. He spent time in prison because he refused to do military service and used that time to write his doctoral dissertation on the prison. Almost like Knut Pipping, who was sociology professor at Åbo Akademi, the Swedish university in Turku, and who wrote his doctoral dissertation on the platoon he was serving in during World War II.

The Finnish liberalisation of alcohol control

A: *But you soon moved to doing other kinds of studies as well, being involved in the tradition of surveys on drinking attitudes and drinking behaviours.*

KM: In 1968–69, when the Finnish alcohol legislation was rather dramatically changed, I was responsible for the survey that aimed at finding out what happened after the new legislation.[3,4] That was the first representative drinking practices survey in Finland, establishing a tradition that has continued at eight year intervals up to now.[5,6,7] Now we have a rather long series of comparable surveys.

A: *If you can think back to before the 1968 legislation, what were your expectations of the effects of the legislation?*

KM: In the middle of the 1960s we would have been part of the general culturalist liberal argument that strict control legislation would actually produce more problems. The first time I think I started to doubt the general line was in a talk I gave to the Finnish Society for Social Policy Research in November 1967, a year before the actual change, where I tried to predict what might happen. At the time, nobody could understand how dramatically the consumption would increase, because all economic and other predictions said that the increase would be rather limited. But in fact it was close to 50 percent in one year. The share of alcohol in total private expenditure grew exceptionally fast from 1965 (4.2 %) to 1972 (7.4%), with a sudden jump in 1969. Such dramatic changes in the structure of the household budget are extremely unusual. It all happened in a period when there was rapid economic growth, so people had new money that could be put to new commodities. At the same time alcohol availability increased dramatically. If the reform would have been carried out in a recession period it probably would not have had so dramatic an effect.

A: *So can you remember what you predicted before the change?*

KM: I predicted that the frequency of heavy drinking would increase somewhat, particularly among young people and in the countryside, but I was nowhere close to understanding the true magnitude of the change.

A: *How soon after the change was it apparent that things weren't working as expected?*

KM: In one sense quite quickly, because the increase in demand was so big that even the breweries were not prepared to meet it. In fact, they sold beer that had not been stored long enough. When you have an expanding market, each of the competing units hopes optimistically that they can increase their market share. So if collectively they could not respond to the increased demand, then it certainly must have been a big surprise, not only to alcohol researchers but also to market actors.

But everybody was enthusiastic about this new freedom. Arrest rates started to increase right away although the control system was also becoming more liberal, but few people paid any attention. Everybody was quite euphoric about it. Drunk and euphoric. . . . But in the early 1970s, problems continued to increase.

A: *How long did it take before there was a shift in direction in how researchers were viewing it? Was it three or four years?*

KM: Not quite that long. But it also is a value issue. I still would argue that whatever the dangers of alcohol, it was not a fair thing not to have any liquor stores in rural municipalities. So you would have arguments about equity. And also, yes, we could not say that problems would go down, but we could still feel that we were prepared to pay the cost of this. In one sense I am still willing to do that. You have more alcohol-related misery and unhappiness, but you also have more occasions of euphoria. But we could not anymore say that everything gets better. We were well aware of the price that had to be paid.

Working on international comparative studies

A: *When did Kettil Bruun and your group become involved with WHO-Euro and with what became the alcohol control policy book?[8]*

KM: I think we started in 1972. It was quite established by 1973, at least, because we had a good overview of the contents and the general argument of the book by then.

A: *So the book gets published in 1975. Then you spent some time in Toronto in 1977, and at that time, you came up with the plan for the International Study of Alcohol Control Experiences (ISACE).[9] Why do that project? What was the issue? Did it arise out of 'the purple book'?[8]*

KM: Well, changes in alcohol policy are determined by the same basic historical processes as drinking is. You cannot think in terms of a course of change that goes one way so that you are free to choose whatever you want to do in the field of policy. In order to understand what is feasible you also have to study the determinants of alcohol control policies, including cultural and ideological expectations and the political economy of alcoholic beverages as commodities. The economic interests determining the Finnish alcohol policy in the 1960s and 1970s were not corporate interests. They were things like the interest of local communities to attract tourists. The leisure industries were an important factor in opening up the legislation, because you cannot compete for tourists if you don't let them drink. The point here was that there were economic interests, but they were not big corporations or nasty people wanting to push liquor onto innocent people, but rather there were marginal economic interests all over the social fabric. For instance, every grocery store owner had an interest in adding medium beer to the store's assortment.

The cultural idiosyncrasies are extremely important in the field of drink, and in order to understand that you need comparative studies

A: *But why not just do the study in Finland? Why do it as a comparative study?*

KM: Because there are more culturally unique traits in alcohol than in most other things. The cultural idiosyncrasies are extremely important in the field of drink, and in order to understand that you need comparative studies. They cannot be abstract typologies or just putting cultures in holes. They have to be historical and concrete. Unique things

come up and are understood when there are comparisons.

A: *So you were looking at it both from the point of view of material factors, and also how they interplayed with these cultural factors?*

KM: Yes, because what the material factors are able to do is determined by legislation which is determined by cultural tradition. It is symptomatic that the alcohol producers were not a really important factor pushing for the liberalization in Finland. They did not dare to challenge the power of the monopoly at that time – and that was related to a cultural, legal and historical tradition. So there is a complex interplay between economic processes and political and cultural processes.

A: *Skipping forward quite a bit, the other major international study that you were involved with, actually that you led (from 1988) was the International Study of Alcoholics Anonymous.[10] How did you develop that interest? Where did it come from?*

KM: I think generally we in Finland had lost all interest in treatment and treatment systems research. Already when the AA project started, it was clear that the Finnish alcohol policy system would change, and that alcohol research should re-orient itself and once again (as in the beginning) take treatment systems more seriously. Obviously AA is an important international movement of a very special kind. Again, from a historical perspective it was not that interesting to try to analyse the effects of a dose of AA, but rather to understand it as a movement and a tradition of thinking and organizing. Most of us did not know in advance how unique an organization AA was. In the early formulations there was something I wrote about how 'AA had successfully carried out large-scale economic activities, such as the production and distribution of millions of pieces of literature, without bureaucratizing the internal structure of the movement'. But I did not have a clear picture of how it really functioned. I still think it is a fantastic historic innovation as a social organization and as a network.

A: *Out of your experiences with the AA project and ISACE and with other international projects, what would you say about how to go about organizing an international comparative project so that you get a good result – so that you get a good book out of it?*

KM: There are different types of international studies. I have been part of several studies where the aim has been maximum comparability – e.g., Nordic drinking surveys, where a lot of energy was put into technical comparability, including coding details. It was a tremendous effort. Even with countries with similar traditions and the same level of technologies, the quantitative research process contains so many conditions that to get comparable data is extremely difficult. Charles Osgood did his huge worldwide project on the semantic differential and tried to get standardized data from I don't know how many different cultures, translating back and forth from English to the native languages in order to ensure that the concepts were comparable. But that required that he had American money to pay for all of it, and a very centralized system. Usually the money isn't there, and centralization is not a good recipe for an international study, either.

A: *So you would avoid too much centralisation?*
KM: I think you should let national research groups handle their own countries. That's the basic philosophy – that people own their own national project. Then you have to produce the consensus by having open meetings and discussions. You need something to structure the discussion, such as guidelines for data collection, but you have to keep the discussion open.

A: *Are societies ever comparable units?*
KM: Usually you cannot think that societies are really comparable units. The AA project was not a study of eight societies, it was a study *in* eight societies. It is a sociological mistake to try to compare societies as totalities, because first you have to determine the cultural and social position of what you compare. AA is not in all countries in the same relation to the mother culture or to the overall social structure. You compare movements, not societies. And that supplies a further argument for letting participant groups own their countries. It's not always easy because people come with abstract systematic views and frames of interpre-

tation. For instance, in the beginning of one study we had this Swiss guy who was a Jungian psychologist, and he brought in a Jungian frame of interpretation. What was Jungian and what was Switzerland was difficult to determine. But it is also useful to include theoretically ambitious people in any project group. In the AA project I believe there was a fruitful tension between those who were more into basic sociology, like Irmgard Eisenbach-Stangl and Ilkka Arminen, who wanted to have more theoretical perspective and others, including me, who were not that theoretical.

You have to represent the group ... to translate their thoughts into less theoretically loaded terms – into mutual, everyday language, into a more ecumenical language

A: *If you look at other projects that are built around the idea that each participating group owns its own data, you might have produced just 'Volume II', a series of case studies, in both of those studies.*[11,12] *Both the ISACE and the AA study went beyond being a series of case studies cemented together by an introduction. So you must have had some other principle in mind also.*
KM: It is important to have a jointly authored collective report using the material written by many people. That is a long process, where you use contributions of a large number of people to write the group's book. You have to represent the group. It is not an easy task to take in everything different people have to say and to fairly represent them. And then you have to translate their thoughts into less theoretically loaded terms – into mutual, everyday language, into a more ecumenical language.

Twenty years as secretary of the Finnish Foundation for Alcohol Studies

A: *For about 20 years you were the secretary of the Finnish Foundation for Alcohol Studies. What did that job entail? What were your main responsibilities?*

KM: We gave out grants, and I prepared the materials for the Executive Committee of the Board (who represented different branches of research) so they could discuss the applications. Then I tried to get money available to cover those projects that had been felt to be sensible. I took some initiative on a number of projects. The Finnish Foundation covers the whole field from basic biological research to clinical medicine, and from epidemiology to social and historical research. The executive committee did not divide the money into 'this much goes to medical and this much goes to social', but all applications were discussed at the same time. The process was different compared to most places I know of, where research money is divided between different branches of science. This was in terms of projects and priorities.

A: How should nations set priorities for research in alcohol and drug studies? What would you say your 20 years taught you about that?

KM: The research program is not a deductive exercise where you have goals and means. You might have that type of program if you are deciding where to put the money of a medical company – like, here we have a disease that many people with sufficient buying power suffer from, and then in order to get the remedy we have to do this for the next 20 years. This is not the way research in general can be programmed, although some research bodies have a tendency to try to formulate what to do in this kind of deductive goal structure. Rather, you try to put together a scientific idea or technique and something you believe is or should be a social problem.

A: How much attention do you pay to who's available? Because you can't always find someone.

KM: You have to work with the people you know, and you need to learn to know new people. Our comparative studies were based on networks where people knew each other. Ignacy Wald was a Polish psychiatrist and Brendan Walsh was an Irish economist. Their professional backgrounds were different, but the projects built on personal

contacts. Here the epidemiology section of the International Council on Alcohol and Addictions and the Kettil Bruun Society were important because they produced the networks which we drew on. The projects in turn expanded the networks; they did not always represent all the countries that we would have liked, but it was a continuous process. That differs from the European Union logic where you go from up to down – this is from down to up. And it makes all the difference in how things work. You have to have the people before you have the topic, but the topic finds new people. It is a kind of iterative process.

A: An example?

KM: To give one example: the Finnish Foundation has had a series of studies of the verbal interaction in treatment and control encounters involving social workers and their clients, and medical doctors in the primary health care system and their patients. That was based on the general idea that a lot of what the state does with people is to talk to them; those who do the talking are the professionals, but that should not be looked at as some technique comparable to medical intervention, but as linguistic interaction. At the same time, there was an emerging tradition of conversation analysis available, and some good Finnish representatives. The Foundation was able to fund and strengthen that tradition in a series of projects involving sociologists and linguists. We had what we felt was really frontier research, in a basic scientific sense, serving a practical social need.

A: Do you favour multi-disciplinary research?

KM: Multi-disciplinary research – where scientists come and put their expertise together – usually is shallow, it doesn't work. It doesn't turn out to be an intellectual community, but a set of specialists negotiating with each other. But occasionally you can have fields where two branches of science can genuinely and theoretically collaborate and interact. In the conversation analysis projects of the Finnish Foundation, the researchers were all conversation analysts, but some had their background in sociology and some in linguistics.

They would all meet studying the discussion in AA meetings, or how questions related to alcohol are taken up between medical doctors and their patients, or how social workers deal with people's requests for money and how they control whether or not the money is spent on drinking.

A: *When you've done those studies, do they have a practical implication?*
KM: I don't think that good social research needs to have any practical value. But the researchers have practical value because they get more sense of what's going on in society. Research needs to be relevant but not necessarily useful. For instance, there has been a strong tradition where what happens in face-to-face encounters was interpreted in psychological terms, in terms of what happens in my personality and your personality. Then if the participants are alerted to the fact that something trivial, in one sense technical, like the linguistic structures by which people operate, is important, then it provides a new way of looking at the whole thing. You don't necessarily stop all cases of misunderstanding or of people talking past each other, but it is no longer automatically interpreted in psychological terms. This is a big change in people's orientation, because it is so natural to give a psychological interpretation.

A: *Some other examples of what you designate as 'relevance'?*
KM: That work has had a big impact when medical doctors have been shown that the way they ask questions about drinking has an important impact, and that it's not a kind of psychological skill. There are also purely linguistic, technical issues involved. This means that something that has been hidden becomes visible. But making it visible doesn't necessarily change things. That I have been interested in conversation analysis doesn't help me to quarrel better with people. Even if you study family sociology, it doesn't mean that you would become a better family member in any technical sense. Nevertheless it can be useful in a wider sense.

A: *In 1983 you recruited Anja Koski-Jännes to the field of treatment studies and helped her go to*

America to study cognitive-behavioural therapy. Was that an initiative to introduce something new to Finland?
KM: Yes, to some degree. But my initiative was mainly administrative, and Anja Koski-Jännes did the thinking. Her innovation was to combine the theoretical ideas of the 1920s Russian psychologist, Lev Vygotsky, with the pragmatic ideas of such contemporary cognitive behavioural psychologists as Martha Sanchez-Craig, Alan Marlatt, William Miller and others. Vygotsky was interested in the formation of conscious and voluntary control of behaviour through the use of signs (words, numbers, pictures, etc.) as tools of behaviour regulation. Cognitive behavioural psychologists in their turn were developing such tools (e.g. drinking diary, 'road maps' to relapse, self-instructions, analysing 'triggers' of drinking urges, etc.). In other words, both parties of this unorthodox marriage were interested in developing a psychology which can be used to help people to manage their lives and reach their goals more effectively. Anja's influence has been deep and important. It has changed the ideology of Finnish professional treatment from a kind of diluted psycho-dynamic approach to a cognitive – behavioural approach.

Research needs to be relevant but not necessarily useful

A: *What were social workers at the time actually doing?*
KM: This is something about which I have a deep conviction: it was a bad thing that social workers and more generally people representing the state in relation to stupid and unfit individuals took Freud as their role model. They should have taken a lawyer as their role model. In the 1950s you were a good social worker if you knew the tricks of the trade, like how to get your client some services in a treatment program or how to get accommodation. That was what your skills were measured by, and what you were proud of. Today, universities offer quite different professional role models for the students, but real social workers continue to give out money, to offer or to

deny services and to use involuntary interventions as their background resource. It's a different situation compared to a physician and his patient. Feminists have rightly pointed out that this is also a power relationship, but it is even more so in the case of the social worker. The social worker additionally all the time has to resolve conflicts between various members of the client's family. They cannot be at the same time on the side of the mother and the father and the son and the daughter.

I have no doubt that every falling leaf follows both Newton's and Einstein's rules, but they are of little use when I try to catch it

A: *Had you read about cognitive–behavioural therapy? How did you know about this tradition? How did you come to see that as relevant to practical modern social and therapeutic work?*

KM: My value commitments pushed me to the cognitive–behavioural tradition. In America they had this theoretically odd coalition of Freudian psychiatry and AA – odd because AA's basic attitude is that you should not explain what happened and not call to mind why it happened, just do what you have to do right now. Many articles in AA's magazines contain cognitive analyses of temptations and how they are overcome. AA's idea is that it doesn't help you to know why you have become this way. It is more appropriate to know what you can do in the situation where you are.

A: *Where do you stand on this looking for explanations question?*

KM: I think I learned to dislike psychological explanations when I was very young, before I was a student. They always seemed too abstract, too general to me, and also always to include power-manipulation. Even everyday explanations, 'You do this because . . .', tend to belittle the person. When you use psychological explanations of an individual's concrete behaviours, you always tend to take a manipulative power position with regard

to them. The underlying reason might have been that I saw the cognitive–behavioural approach as a corrective to that.

A: *So what do you tell people about causal theories?*

KM: I think causal theories are useless in concrete cases, but in general I am quite interested in causal modelling, for example, of social network processes. At this level, causal models are interesting, but they are uninteresting when you meet concrete situations. I have no doubt that every falling leaf follows both Newton's and Einstein's rules, but they are of little use when I try to catch it.

The Finnish tradition that encourages specialist researchers to retain a generalist foothold

A: *One of the Finnish traditions that is unusual, looking at it from the outside, is that the Finnish social alcohol researchers have other interests outside the field. How did that happen?*

KM: At first it happened on its own, and then we encouraged it. In the 1950s the Finnish state alcohol monopoly was one of the few sources of funding for research work in the quite new field of sociology. So almost all prominent sociologists of the first generation had some contact with alcohol studies. Then, also, Kettil Bruun was an ideal leader of a research group. He gave people space. It's amazing that the alcohol research group in the 1960s and 1970s, although it was tightly related to the huge bureaucracy of the monopoly, had so much intellectual autonomy, so that it could present a challenge to academic sociology in Finland. That was partly Kettil's personal accomplishment. Also, the monopoly directors were broad-minded and were themselves social researchers. Pekka Kuusi and later Heikki Koski had prominent positions in Finnish academia.

A: *This tradition of maintaining a broad, generalist base continues?*

KM: Later on, alcohol researchers have done their best to keep close contact with their mother sciences. In between his alcohol and drug studies, Juha Partanen carried out a large-scale macro-sociological study of the structural transformation of Finland. Pekka Sulkunen was recently appointed to the professor's chair in general sociology at the University of Helsinki. He has been able to write general sociology although he has been a professional alcohol researcher during his whole career. A few years ago the chairmen of both the Finnish Society for Social Policy Research and the Finnish sociological association were from the Alcohol Research Group. Pekka Sulkunen was chairman of the Westermarck Society and Jussi Simpura was for many years chairman of the Society for Social Policy Research. Many of us have been editors of *Sosiologia*, the journal of the Westermarck Society, and I edited *Acta Sociologica*, the Nordic general sociology review. Alcohol researchers have taught university courses not so much on alcohol, but on sociological theory, qualitative methods and other general topics. Because of these contacts with academic institutions we had possibilities to recruit bright young people at the earliest stage.

A: *Do you think it has been important for Finnish alcohol research that it keeps these strong connections?*
KM: In any narrow field such as alcohol studies, the first generation usually has been qualified in general sociology. When you get the second and third generations of people doing their doctoral dissertations, there often is a tendency to narrow and professionalize and try to push out people who do not have the same specialist expertise. That's not a good thing. We have been very much aware of this and have tried to fight against it.

Different national traditions of alcohol research

A: *How would you locate the Finnish or Scandinavian alcohol tradition in the context of alcohol studies generally?*
KM: I think when the second wave of modern alcohol research started in the 1960s there were three traditions that emerged: the French toxicological tradition, the North American psychiatric tradition, and the Scandinavian social behavioural tradition. The traditions corresponded to the nature and image of alcohol problems in each culture. In France somatic consequences of prolonged drinking were studied in a dose-response frame. When you asked in France how you recognize an alcoholic, the response was, 'He has a red nose'.[13] When Americans responded to the same question, the answer was that he would be nervous and emotionally immature. In the United States deviant drinking patterns and drinking problems were measured as interchangeable symptoms of an underlying disease. In Scandinavia the focus was on social conflicts related to single occasions of culturally accepted heavy drinking. The three traditions also represented the outlook of different branches of science.

> When you asked in France how you recognize an alcoholic, the response was, 'He has a red nose'. When Americans responded to the same question, the answer was that he would be nervous and emotionally immature

A: *Do these distinctions remain?*
KM: There were minority currents in each culture. During the last thirty years increased interaction between researchers representing different cultures and academic disciplines has brought about many refinements and new combinations, for example within the Kettil Bruun Society and within the WHO structure. But my argument would be that the basic traditions persist. If we look at each tradition in terms of money spent, North Americans still excel in sophisticated measurements of the prevalence of alcohol dependence. Scandinavians still insist on describing drinking patterns as an expression of population habits. Things may be changing again, since the Scandinavian alcohol policy system that has defined the general frame of reference is collapsing. It remains to be seen what impact this has

on the conceptualization of drinking and alcohol problems. But I would not doubt that these traditions will still be visible.

A: *So the emphasis in the Scandinavian tradition, if you look at the individual level, has always been more on the intoxication episode?*

KM: On the conflicts related to single occasions of drinking. That often would require at least a minimum amount of drinking. I remember in the 1960s, American formulations were that drinking to feel the effects was seen as clinically pathological, which of course would make no sense in Scandinavian countries – actually even in wine cultures people also drink to experience the effects. The odd thing about that formulation is, what sense would it make if you adopted that same way of looking at the effects of smoking cannabis – obviously you can smoke cannabis to feel the effects without being pathological or culturally deviant.

A: *How do you see research developing in Scandinavia? What directions do you see it going in? Or what do you think should happen?*

KM: I don't know what is going to happen. Alcohol research in Scandinavia has been closely connected with the alcohol control administration. The task of that administration was to control the availability of alcohol and to educate people, and therefore there was a relative lack of interest in the treatment system. The treatment and control systems have always been part of the moral economy of drinking and defining limits for acceptable drinking, be it the police or the treatment agencies. What is important is not the impact of individual treatment intervention, but the overall effect of the whole treatment and control system. The relative importance of this system has increased. But the danger is that because of the old division of administrative tasks and the researcher's role in that division of labour, alcohol researchers continue to be interested in what is left of that old system – which is now reduced to education and perhaps local pre-emptive initiatives – which I think have limited significance. Then the whole treatment and control apparatus perhaps doesn't get the attention it would need. There is

also a problem because of the division of labour between the different ministries in Finland, since the treatment system is under the Ministry of Health and Social Welfare and alcohol researchers are now there.

Left-over business

A: *In relation to research, have you any sense of unfinished business, something left over which you would like to have a go at?*

KM: This is something I never was able to go further on. In AA folklore, members speak of different types of problems with alcohol at different stages of their drinking career, and of the control problems being different. It's not just that they become worse and worse (which they do) but there are qualitative shifts. From another perspective we know that there is a tremendous number of different physiological functions and mechanisms that are involved in the control of drinking. That is one mechanism that obviously affects drinking. It doesn't determine it, but it affects it. As we know from a Japanese study,[14] some 20 years ago practically no Japanese alcoholic patients had the flushing response. But when the society became wetter even people who flushed started becoming alcoholics.

Then you have a number of other interindividual differences – there is a lot of variation in how quickly the liver metabolizes alcohol, and some people have had alcohol concentrations in their blood that would have killed other people. Some people stop eating when they are drinking, some people don't. Some people at some stages in their drinking career have difficulty going to sleep, others get sleepy when they drink. There is no limit to the number of physical systems potentially differentially affected by drinking, and the effects probably also differ at different stages of the drinking career.

A: *And the implications?*

KM: This is something that is not at all visible in the clinical treatment literature. One would expect that from a cognitive behavioural perspective it would be a different thing to control one's drinking depending on what physical mechanisms are involved. Therefore if you want to match your cognitive–behavioural therapy to the patient's need, you should remember that different bodies pose different problems to different persons. The whole idea, then, would be a collaboration between researchers taking seriously what heavy drinkers know of these things, biologists being involved in order to understand the underlying biological mechanisms, and clinical people trying to design ways for how to advise people with different kinds of control problems.

A: *Have you ever presented this idea publicly?*
KM: Once I presented this agenda to Finnish biological researchers. They were all specialists on a particular mechanism, and they all thought that their mechanism was the explanation of alcoholism. They were at first not at all interested when I tried to get them to guess how much interpersonal variation there would be in their special mechanism. I would hope that biologists would take the variations in their own mechanisms as seriously as we take our standard deviations of whatever distributions we study.

If you want to match your cognitive–behavioural therapy to the patient's need, you should remember that different bodies pose different problems to different persons

---

A: *You are talking about variation both across individuals and across the drinking career, with the emphasis on how this affects self-control?*
KM: It's not looking for a unitary series of symptoms in the Jellinek or AA tradition, but recognizing that there quite likely are different careers of problematic drinking, that might well be related to individual differences in a number of physiological mechanisms. One more thing which this would accomplish: it would counteract the tendency in psycho-dynamic psychology and therapy, but also to some degree in cognitive behavioural

therapy, in order to show their autonomy, to speak of drinking in a way that neglects its physiological basis, and that this physiological system changes within the drinking career and with aging and therefore should be taken seriously.

Estimating Kettil Bruun

A: *What made Kettil Bruun so exemplary?*
KM: I was thinking of Kettil Bruun and his tradition. He studied history – that was his first academic degree – and then he worked with the statistical office of the City of Helsinki doing concrete research. When he turned to sociology, he was interested in the general mechanisms of how the control system meets the individual; he was not interested in explaining the individual's behaviour or how people are, but rather in explaining the interaction between the system and individuals. But he did this from a historical perspective. In one sense I have always followed Kettil. I've always studied Finland, not social systems or anything of that kind. Yet in order to study one society you have to adopt a comparative perspective. That is a different strategy compared to sociological classifying. It's looking at one concrete society against a background of whatever societies there are. Kettil's combination of historical concreteness and sociological imagination are still exemplary.

References

1. BRUUN, K. & MARKKANEN, T. (1961) *Onko alkoholismi parannettavissa?* [Can alcoholism be cured?] (Helsinki, Finnish Foundation for Alcohol Studies).
2. BRUUN, K. (1963) Outcome of different types of treatment of alcoholics, *Quarterly Journal of Studies on Alcohol*, **24**, 280–288.
3. MÄKELÄ, K. (1970) Dryckesgångernas frekvens enligt de konsumerade dryckerna och mängden före och efter lagreformen, [Drinking frequency according to beverage type and amount before and after the law reform], *Alkoholpolitik*, **33**, 144–153.

4. MÄKELÄ, K. (1971) *Measuring the Consumption of Alcohol in the 1968–1969 Alcohol Consumption Study*, Publication No. 2 (Helsinki, Social Research Institute of Alcohol Studies).

5. SIMPURA, J. (Ed.) (1987) *Finnish Drinking Habits: Results from in Interview Surveys Held in 1968, 1976 and 1984*, Publication No. 35 (Helsinki, Finnish Foundation for Alcohol Studies).

6. SIMPURA, J., PAAKKANEN, P. & MUSTONEN, H. (1995) New beverages, new drinking contexts? Signs of modernization in Finnish drinking habits from 1984 to 1992, compared with trends in the European Community, *Addiction*, **90**, 673–683.

7. MUSTONE, H., MÄKELÄ, P., METSO, L. & SIMPURA, J. (2001) Muutokset suomalaisten juomatavoissa: toiveet ja todellisuus [changes in Finnish drinking habits: hopes and reality], *Yhteiskun tapolitiikka*, **66**, 265–276.

8. BRUUN, K., EDWARDS, G., LUMIO, M., MÄKELÄ, K., PAN, L., POPHAM, R. E., ROOM, R., SCHMIDT, W., SKOG, O.-J., SULKUNEN, P. & ÖSTERBERG, E. (1975) *Alcohol Control Policies in Public Health Perspective*, (Helsinki, Finnish Foundation for Alcohol Studies).

9. MÄKELÄ, K., ROOM, R., SINGLE, E., SULKUNEN, P. & WALSH, B., with 13 others (1981) *Alcohol, Society, and the State: 1. A Comparative History of Alcohol Control*, (Toronto, Addiction Research Foundation).

10. MÄKELÄ, K., ARMINEN, I., BLOOMFIELD, K., EISENBACH-STANGL, I., HELMERSSON BERGMARK, K., KURUBE, N., MARIOLINI, N., ÓLAFSDÓTTIR, H., PETERSON, J. H., PHILLIPS, M., REHM, J., ROOM, R., ROSENQVIST, P., ROSOVSKY, H., STENIUS, K., ŚWIATKIEWICZ, G., WORONOWICZ, B. & ZIELIŃSKI, A. (1996) *Alcoholics Anonymous as a Mutual-Help Movement: A Study in Eight Societies* (Madison, University of Wisconsin Press).

11. SINGLE, E., MORGAN, P. & DE LINT, J. (Eds) (1981) *Alcohol, Society, and the State: 2. The Social History of Control Policy in Seven Countries* (Toronto, Addiction Research Foundation).

12. EISENBACH-STANGL, I. & ROSENQVIST, P. (Eds) (1998) *Diversity in Unity: Studies on Alcoholics Anonymous in Eight Societies* (Helsinki, Nordic Council for Alcohol and Drug Research).

13. FRÉOUR, P., SERISE, M., COUDRAY, P. & BENIER, J. (1969) Que pensent de l'alcoolisme les habitants des grands ensembles urbains?, *La Revue de l'Alcoolisme*, **15**, 97–143.

14. HIGUCHI, S., MATSUSHITA, S., IMAZEKI, H, KINOSHITA, T., TAKAGI, S. & KONO, H. (1994) Aldehyde dehydrogenase genotypes in Japanese alcoholics, *The Lancet*, March 19, 741–742.

Further reading

ARMINEN, I. (1998) *Therapeutic Interaction: A Study of Mutual Help in the Meetings of Alcoholics Anonymous* (Helsinki, Finnish Foundation for Alcohol Studies).

KOSKI-JÄNNES, A. (1992) *Alcohol Addiction and Self-Regulation: A Controlled Trial of a Relapse Prevention Program for Finnish In-patient Alcoholics* (Helsinki, Finnish Foundation for Alcohol Studies).

Gabriel Romanus

Gabriel Romanus was born in 1939 in Helsingborg, Sweden. He holds a Masters in statistics, mathematics, economics and political science from Stockholm University. Following 13 years as an MP in the Swedish parliament, he served for 17 years as head of the Swedish alcohol monopoly. He was a member of the executive board of the International Council of Alcohol and Addictions from 1988–95 and is currently chairman of its alcohol policy section. He was Chairman of the Swedish Council for Social Research from 1993–2000 and is currently President of the Nordic Co-operation on Alcohol and Narcotics Policy. Professional interests include social policy in a broad sense, including family policy and gender equality. His main focus of interest over the past 20 years has been alcohol policy, and to some extent drug policy.

Background

Addiction: *You came from a medical family?*
Gabriel Romanus: Yes, my father was a professor of surgery and member of the Swedish Council for Medical Research.

A: *And your mother is a feminist and also a doctor?*
GR: Yes. She's 90 now, and she gave lectures on sex education at least until five years ago. She is a dermatologist by profession, and a feminist and sex educator.

A: *So your family had a background in public health before you came on the scene?*
GR: Yes, and I thought I was going to be a doctor when I was a boy, until I went to the United States and had some very good teachers in social sciences. I changed my mind and went into social sciences, and then into politics. I was a junior teacher of statistics at the University of Stockholm while I was studying.

A: *And then you worked in the newspaper world for a couple of years?*
GR: Yes. Since I was at the University I had a rather long summer holiday, so I filled in for the summer vacation, writing editorials at what was at the time the biggest newspaper in Sweden, a

Liberal newspaper. Then politics took more and more of my time, so I skipped the job at the University and finished my studies more or less and went into writing editorials for a living. After a few years I had one year as head of information of the Liberal Party's main office. Then I was a candidate for parliament and was elected in 1968, and started in parliament just when I turned 30.

Parliament

A: *How would you characterize the politics of the Liberal Party in Sweden in those days?*
GR: Well, it has quite close cooperation with the Liberal Party and the Liberal Democrats of Britain, so they are very close politically, I would say. If you compare it to parties in the United States, I think the type of Democrats such as Stevenson and Kennedy and Humphrey would be the closest. At the beginning of the century the Liberal group had as many as 150 of the 380 members of parliament. It was the biggest group then. Nowadays it's much smaller, between 5 and 10% in recent elections.

A: *So you were a Member of Parliament for 13 years, and the Minister of Social Affairs for some of that time?*

GR: Yes, I started in Parliament in 1969 and I left in 1982. I was Minister of Social Affairs in a minority government, from October 1978 to October 1979.

A: *Were alcohol and drug matters within your mandate there?*
GR: Yes.

A: *Was that your first contact with these issues?*
GR: No, I had been a member of the Committee on Social Affairs from 1971, when the new parliament was formed (we went from a two-chamber system to a single-chamber system). At that time alcohol policy matters were actually the responsibility of the Committee on Taxation. Some leading members of the Committee on Taxation were very interested in alcohol policy and came from the temperance movement. Also, alcohol taxes were an important source of revenue, and the monopoly was handled by the Ministry of Finance. The Committee on Social Affairs had just a secondary role – it gave its views on alcohol policy to the Committee on Taxation.

> # In 1977, there was a new alcohol policy formulated which indicated the formal adoption of the goal of reducing total consumption of alcohol or per capita consumption of alcohol – so that policy was not only focused on misuse and abuse

A: *So you were involved in alcohol policy before becoming a minister?*
GR: Yes. But this became more emphasized just before I became a minister. The responsibility for alcohol policy became more clearly the responsibility of the Ministry of Social Affairs. Responsibility for alcohol policy was transferred from the Board of Taxation to the Board of Health and Social Welfare. So that was a clear acknowledgement of the fact that alcohol policy was an important part of social policy.

A: *In the post-war period, most of the countries*

that had a temperance tradition gradually took away many alcohol controls. In fact researchers talked about it as a ratchet mechanism, going in only one direction. But Sweden has actually turned backwards a few times in terms of alcohol control.
GR: Yes. I think that's interesting, particularly because some of the moves have not been top-down initiated but rather from the grassroots, which was also the case with the rationing system when it was introduced at the end of the 19th century.[1] In 1955, the old rationing system was abolished and that was of course an act of liberalization. Local monopolies were merged into the national retailing monopoly and there was a gradual liberalization, you might say, to the middle of the 1970s. One remarkable counter-instance was after medium-strength beer, which is quite an intoxicating beverage (about 4.5%), was allowed to be sold in grocery stores in 1965. This led to quite a marked increase in youth drinking, and there was a grassroots reaction against this which eventually captured Parliament. So in opposition to what is the common procedure – where the government gives proposals to Parliament to which Parliament reacts – there was an initiative from Parliament demanding that medium-strength beer be taken out of the grocery stores and handed over to the monopoly. This was decided on and put in effect in 1977.

A: *And other examples of that kind of going back?*
GR: In 1977, there was a new alcohol policy formulated which indicated the formal adoption of the goal of reducing total consumption of alcohol or per capita consumption of alcohol – so that policy was not only focused on misuse and abuse. The idea for this also came from Parliament for the first time in 1975, inspired I think by the temperance movement or some temperance politicians, and then it was officially adopted in 1978. Then during the 1980s it was quantified as a goal to reduce total consumption by 25% during the period 1980–2000.

A: *Any other similar example?*
GR: A third example was the legislation against

advertising or marketing which was adopted in 1977 and came into effect in 1978.

A: *Were there quite a few temperance members of Parliament at that point?*
GR: Since it is a group with members in most of the parties, they are one of the many non-partisan or multi-party networks in Parliament.

A: *In 1982 you switched away from an active role in politics and became head of the Swedish retailing monopoly. Was that your choice?*
GR: There is no formal application process, but after coming back from the government into Parliament I was hit by the same syndrome as everyone else who makes this transition. If you have been a front-seat driver and go back to the back seat, for most people it is rather frustrating.

A: *You were still a relatively young man at that point.*
GR: I was 39 when I came into the government and 40 when I returned to the back benches. After two years my party had to appoint members of a government again, and I was bypassed. My interpretation was that being of the male sex and living in Stockholm I would never make it to the government again. So I started to look for some other job where there was more of an executive role. Also, having been in Parliament for more than 10 years I thought that maybe I should do something else. There was a discourse in Sweden about Parliament being an artificial aquarium where the fishes swim – they don't see real life out in the sea. So I thought that maybe I should try to learn something about real life.

Appointment to head of the Swedish alcohol monopoly

A: *And so you moved to the monopoly?*
GR: I had been very happy to be selected to be a minister; I enjoyed it very much. So I began to long for another leadership position, an executive position. Then when the head of the Monopoly resigned, I informally notified the leader of the

Liberal party, who was then in the government as Minister for Foreign Affairs, that I was interested in the job. During the interim period the deputy manager of the monopoly had been functioning as the manager, and began to enjoy the job. Also, the staff and some of the parties who were represented on the board were thinking that maybe we shouldn't have a politician as manager of the monopoly but rather a technical person. So there was a vote by the board between the deputy manager and me and I was elected, I think by the deciding vote of the chairman. The deputy manager then continued as my deputy for almost 10 years and was a wonderful, very loyal, cooperative colleague, and a very good friend of mine.

> There was a discourse in Sweden about Parliament being an artificial aquarium where the fishes swim – they don't see real life out in the sea. So I thought that maybe I should try to learn something about real life

A: *When you came to the monopoly, how did it define its role?*
GR: This has been going back and forth through the years. At first, the monopolies were local. The person who really dominated the scene in the beginning of the century was Ivan Bratt, who started out as a medical doctor. He became head of the Stockholm monopoly, which was the biggest and the most influential. He was one of the leaders of the campaign against prohibition; his alternative was the monopoly system, combined with a rationing system. When the local monopolies were merged into the national monopoly in 1954–55, he had left the scene. The head of the new national monopoly was the former head of cooperative retailing operations in one of the counties, a Social Democrat. He was also quite conscientious on alcohol policy. He was then succeeded in 1967 by a former minister of the Social Democrat government. When he left in 1981, he had also been standing up for alcohol policy. I think it is fair to say, though, that the alcohol policy role of the Monopoly was not so visible in the media and to

the public then as it has been during the last decade, particularly because of the debate on European integration and the possibility of keeping our monopoly after entering the European Union. The monopoly being under the Ministry of Finance meant that the ministers in charge of the monopoly weren't interested in alcohol policy very much – they were more concerned with the financial aspect. But nobody denied that the monopoly was part of alcohol policy.

A: *When you became director of the monopoly, you immediately started going to International Council on Alcohol and Addictions (ICAA) meetings and formed the alcohol policy section. Is that right?*
GR: Yes. I remember, I started in May 1982, and the first summer I got an invitation to the ICAA Congress in Tangier. I wrote a letter to the ICAA proposing that the ICAA should take up as one of its tasks to try to work for comparable international statistics on alcohol. David Archibald, who was at the time ICAA's president, talked to me during the Congress and said that he thought that my proposal was interesting; he said he would propose to the board to start an alcohol policy section, and asked if I would be willing to chair this section. From then on, I have been chairing it.

I have always believed in contact between policy makers and researchers. In the Swedish parliament, we have clubs for everything, and we also had a club called RIFO (riksdagsman och forskare), which means parliamentarians and researchers

---

A: *So immediately after you came into office in the Monopoly, you were looking to international connections on the policy front. Why were you doing that?*
GR: Very soon I was aware of the fact that if the Swedish alcohol policy was going to survive in the long term we had to have close cooperation with research. And research of course is

international. I have always believed in contact between policy makers and researchers. In the Swedish parliament, we have clubs for everything, and we also had a club called RIFO (riksdagsman och forskare), which means parliamentarians and researchers. I thus had a model to build on.

A: *Were these international contacts useful?*
GR: Yes. Just one example was the age limit issue in the United States; I met people like Alex Wagenaar and others, and discovered that they were doing research on this. Then we had the demonopolization issue that came later in Iowa and in other places. It did not take long before I saw that there is a lot of research going on which was very relevant to my work. The other aspect is that the Swedish monopoly has always had the ambition, since it was formed in the 1950s, to inform the customers about alcohol: not only to give information about what wine to use with steak, but also to give the other side of the picture. The more contact you have with researchers, the better the information you can offer. At that time nobody in Sweden realized how important this was going to be with the move toward European integration. When I came in, we still had the idea that alcohol policy is something we are going to decide in Sweden; we don't have to win over the whole of Europe to our model, it's fine as long as the Swedish people accept it.

Comparing different monopoly systems

A: *But if you look at the other Nordic monopolies, they haven't been as active as the Systembolaget, the Swedish monopoly, in facilitating discussions with researchers on alcohol policy. Even Alko (the Finnish monopoly), which after all used to have many of the researchers inside it as employees, didn't have quite as active a role.*
GR: Well, that's possible. Each national monopoly has its own story. Alko was established as the most comprehensive monopoly, having production, a chain of restaurants, regulations, inspections of restaurants and research – everything within their walls, as well as the retail monopoly. Also they had a very strong political

element in their leadership. In fact, the leading figures of all political parties competed to get onto the board of Alko and also to be a manager of Alko when they retired from politics. Alko's director general during most of my time, Heikki Koski, was a former Social Democrat politician. He is now county governor in one of the big regions. But as a person he has a lower profile, and also the Finnish tradition is more to work behind the scene than in a visible way. Then Koski was succeeded by the former leader of the Conservative Party, Ilkka Suominen. It came out after some time that Suominen did not believe in the Monopoly. Also the Norwegian monopoly has had a strong role in alcohol policy and strong leadership. Unfortunately at one period they selected a manager who came directly from business and who interpreted his role as running it in a businesslike way, and not taking the alcohol policy aspects too much into account. He eventually came into a collision with his board and had to leave. I think that one aspect of the difference between the monopolies in the 1970s and 1980s is that the Swedish monopoly has all the time been only a retail monopoly, while both the Finnish and the Norwegian monopolies for many years also included the production side, and particularly the Finnish monopoly became more interested in exports. If you have the production side inside the monopoly, it tends to weaken the awareness of the alcohol policy role.

As I read in the newspaper yesterday, in Sweden if you say that something is very un-Swedish, that's considered a compliment; while in Denmark if you say to a Dane that this was very un-Danish, then it is an insult

A: *So you think that the decision that was made a long time ago to have two monopolies in Sweden, one for retail shops and one for production and import, actually turned out wisely from the point of view of alcohol policy?*
GR: Very much.

A: *Would you say that the North American*

monopolies, in the Canadian provinces and in 18 American states, have a much weaker identification with alcohol policy?
GR: Yes. I came into contact with North American monopolies rather early, and I was very eager to inform the Swedish public about the existence of retail monopolies in North America. Because in these matters Sweden has very low self-confidence: we feel that we are awkward, we are apart, we have to apologize for being different. As I read in the newspaper yesterday, in Sweden if you say that something is very un-Swedish, that's considered a compliment; while in Denmark if you say to a Dane that this was very un-Danish, then it is an insult. When I came into contact with the North American monopolies, I discovered that gradually, over the years from the 1930s when they were created, they have become more and more commercialized and less and less aware of their historical role. What I have been trying to do, in the contacts we have had with our North American colleagues, is to remind them that if you don't stand up for your role in alcohol policy, you will pretty soon be privatized.

A: *Basically if we take the world as it looked for you as the head of the Swedish retail monopoly, in 1990, say, the monopoly was on a sure foundation. Was there any sign before the discussion seriously began with the European Union that the monopoly was threatened?*
GR: Not really. Of course, we have this discussion about alcohol policy all the time in Sweden, and we had it at the end of the 1980s. One argument was that Swedes are immature, cannot handle alcohol and that's why we have a separate alcohol policy. If you go abroad, you don't see so many drunken people in the streets, so maybe we should be more civilized, drink more wine, and not get so intoxicated. Maybe after a few years we will be mature, and we can get away from our old-fashioned alcohol policy. My strategy to change this picture which was being offered was to try to make people aware of the fact that Swedes are just as mature as other people, it is just that because of our alcohol policy we have fewer alcohol problems. If we want to be like the others, we will also have to face the fact that we will have more

alcohol problems. Then also, that indeed we have the old tradition of getting intoxicated, being a spirits country, but that we were moving away from that, and that this movement was not in spite of the alcohol policy but because of the alcohol policy, since our alcohol policy had two features. One was to favour the weaker beverages by differential taxation, and the other was that the monopoly tried to teach people to drink wine with food instead of spirits to intoxication. And this was a rather successful policy. Many times we had to try to get more realism into the Swedish debate.

I saw it as my role to try all the time both to defend the monopoly and to explain our role, both to the public and to the staff.

Our alcohol policy had two features. One was to favour the weaker beverages by differential taxation, and the other was that the monopoly tried to teach people to drink wine with food instead of spirits to intoxication. And this was a rather successful policy

---

A: *So when you first took over the running of the monopoly, Swedish alcohol policy looked like being securely a Swedish affair?*
GR: Yes, before the beginning of the 1990s, we didn't think that we were going to be forced to abolish the monopoly as a result of European integration. When we started reading the Rome treaty, articles 30 and 36 stated particularly that there should be no barriers to trade, but there was one exception for interventions into the market or barriers to trade that could be motivated by considerations of public health and some other things. So we thought that that would give us firm ground to stand on. When we got into the negotiations we learned otherwise, because then we became familiar with the principle of proportionality. In short, the principle is that if you have

an intervention into the market of a certain kind, and if it can be argued that you could achieve the same results with a less interventionist measure, then you would be obliged to use the lesser intervention.

A: *But as it turned out, it was very much in question whether the retail monopoly would survive?*
GR: Yes. When the negotiations started, they started not as a membership negotiation, but a negotiation of creating what was called the European Economic Area (EEA), or the European Economic Space. There were some six nations negotiating for a trade agreement with the European Union: Finland, Norway, Sweden, Austria, Switzerland and Iceland. All of those had alcohol monopolies, if you count the wholesale spirits monopolies in Switzerland and Austria. Some of us thought that the monopolies countries should have a formal acknowledgement by the EU that their monopolies were compatible with the trade agreement. At the time Sweden also had a production and wholesale monopoly, and we felt it should be declared compatible because it was founded on public health considerations.

A: *But it didn't go that way?*
GR: No. Why not is still a matter for historical research, but I think that the reason was that the Norwegian government didn't want to bring it up because they thought that it would alienate the Norwegian electorate if it wasn't accomplished – it would alienate the Christian Democrats in Norway and they would vote against accession to the agreement. So instead the Nordic countries made a unilateral statement, annexed to the protocol of the agreement, pointing out that all the Nordic monopolies were founded on considerations of public health. But as we learned later, it was only a unilateral declaration that had no real judicial value. Some law professors and others in Sweden pointed out that there were some court cases showing that the import monopoly is not compatible with the Rome treaty, so the import monopoly would have to go. And they also said that a retail monopoly might be seen as functioning like an import monopoly, because as long as

you can only sell to the monopoly then it's an import monopoly.

A: *Round two?*

GR: When the Swedish membership negotiation started in 1992 and 1993, the Commission stated that the monopolies had to go. They said that they were surprised that the Swedish government had taken no steps to abolish the monopolies, since we were now bound by the competition rules of the Rome treaty in the EEA agreement. So during 1993 this became a more and more burning issue. Our Executive Vice President and I went on a tour to European capitals in order to convince them that our monopoly was not there to protect Swedish products, but was there because of alcohol policy reasons. Then we did what I think was a more important move: the Minister of Social Affairs invited the director-general of DG4 of the Commission to come to Sweden to see how we operated. The officials from the Commission went out with us into the backwoods and saw our stores, saw how many foreign brands we had on the shelves. Then they were convinced that we were not there to protect the Swedish alcohol industry. In December 1993, there was an agreement between the Commission and the Swedish government where the commissioner responsible for the enlargement stated that if Sweden abolished the production monopoly on spirits and the wholesale monopoly on import of all alcohol beverages, and if the retail monopoly was carried out in a non-discriminatory manner, then the commission for its part saw no reason to act against the retail monopoly. The Swedish government accepted that formula.

A: *And the views of the European Court?*

GR: The Commission also noted – which was important for the future – that this agreement did not prejudge what the European court would do. This was pointing at the fact that the agreement could be challenged by someone, and that was indeed what happened. Immediately there was a grocer, Harry Franzen, who was not really too interested in running a grocery, but was very interested in selling wine. He started to sell wine from

his grocery and alerted the police and the media, so that he would be taken by the police as a widely advertised test case. We were unhappy at the time, but of course it gave us a chance to be approved by the court. After a lengthy procedure, on 23 October 1997 the court came down with its verdict, which was more clear than anyone had dared to hope, actually supporting the retail monopoly, saying that it was not a violation of the Rome treaty. There was an extra bonus; the court said that it noted that the monopoly was created for promoting a public interest, which was public health.

But it is a very important victory, of course, to have the court accept the monopoly

A: *How was the European Commission handled this issue?*

GR: Although the European Commission accepted the retail monopoly and even supported it during the court deliberations, they now have quite a few people working in the different directorates, maybe because of changes of personnel, who in their heart have never accepted the monopoly and are trying from all angles to tie it down, to make it more commercial and less alcohol policy orientated, and eventually to have it abolished. So the process is by no means terminated. But it is a very important victory, of course, to have the court accept the monopoly. Now it is not a matter of having a monopoly or not, it is more a matter of does the monopoly have to accept conditions that will eventually undermine the monopoly.[2]

A: *Do you think that Swedish alcohol policy will have to change in the coming years because of pressure, particularly on alcohol tax levels?*

GR: Yes, I think that it is very likely, but it is not going to be very fast and dramatic change. This year there are going to be negotiations on whether Sweden is going to be allowed to keep its more restrictive travellers' allowances. Then the big issue becomes, what happens to alcohol taxes in our neighbouring countries? Are they going to be increased? If so, then it is easier for Sweden to keep our high tax level. If they are decreased or kept at the present low level, then Sweden will have to reduce the taxes, step by step.

Swedish alcohol research to me seemed fragmented and unfocused as compared to the situation in Finland, Norway and North America, where there were special institutes or centres for alcohol research. So I had for a long time the idea that maybe we should have something similar

---

Sweden and the total consumption model

A: *Stepping back from the recent history, Sweden seems to be unique as a country in which what is called in Sweden the total consumption model became official policy. Do you have a theory of what's special about alcohol policy in Sweden? Among other factors, does the Swedish alcohol policy process take social research more seriously than is true, say, in North America?*

GR: I think that we have a tradition of close cooperation between research and policymakers. That is particularly true for our government commissions. Hardly anything is changed in Sweden without having a government commission. What is typical for commissions, if it is an important area, is that they cooperate with researchers. This is a typically Swedish tradition. The fact that Sweden had earlier adopted the total consumption model I think was a little coincidental. Certainly Sweden was following what was happening in the WHO, with the purple book[3] and all that; but also it was very much the work of one person who was head of the parliamentary Committee on Taxation. He was a very strong person in the Social Democratic party. He was also a member of the Temperance movement. In 1975, I think, he actually succeeded in inserting into a committee report to Parliament, which was accepted by the parlia-

mentary majority, an endorsement of the goal to reduce per capita consumption. When the European office of WHO put out its goals for Health for All 2000, they mentioned the figure of reducing per capita consumption by 25%. Then the Swedish government inserted this in some document which was not initially so much observed and debated, it was just adopted by parliament. By then, some of us who thought this was politically important started to mention it all the time and kind of cemented it in as the view of the government.

Research and the policy connection

A: *In the time that you have been head of the retail monopoly you made quite a lot of efforts to stimulate research in Sweden, including a research fund sponsored by the retail monopoly. Did you see that there were needs that were not met in the research environment in Sweden?*

GR: Yes. Of course I was partly inspired by Alko in Finland, which had always put a lot of resources into research. In the monopoly we had two types of needs for knowledge. One was to know what we were doing, to follow what happens if we open a new store: do alcohol problems in this community increase, what happens if we change opening hours or if we go to self-service?[4] So we had a need to have competent researchers who could help us to analyse how to operate in order to keep alcohol consumption and alcohol problems down. The other need was to get more relevant knowledge that we could use in our information activities. This was particularly true when this whole business of alcohol being good or bad for the heart came up.

A: *The adequacy of the Swedish alcohol research base?*

GK: Swedish alcohol research to me seemed fragmented and unfocused as compared to the situation in Finland, Norway and North America, where there were special institutes or centres for alcohol research. So I had for a long time the idea that maybe we should have something similar. Jakob Lindberg, who was then deputy director of the Public Health Institute, and I put forward a proposal that there should be a commission looking into Swedish alcohol research. This commission came back with a proposal to create a centre,[5] which finally came into operation in 1999. I also thought that there was a need for more openings for funding research projects through some separate channel, focused only on alcohol research. So we put some money into a research fund, and also some money into education of our staff and into our training centre. I am a little disappointed about the outcome of the monopoly's research fund, because I think it is too dominated by medical research. We also make agreements with researchers commissioning research on particular issues. The retail monopoly has also supported some alcohol research for a professorship in clinical alcohol research in Lund. Also, we have specific projects where the research corresponds to a need for us, such as the KALK project, looking into unregistered consumption.[6]

A: *This is a model where the policy is in fact held up until the experiment is finished, right?*
GR: That is the ideal. We have to see and accept the difference between the dreams and the reality.

ICAA

A: *Back to the ICAA for a minute. What would be your vision of an organization that would be useful internationally as a non-governmental organization in the alcohol field?*
GR: I think it would look very much like the ICAA with some changes. It was understandable that the scientific community separated out of the ICAA. First the international biomedical researchers and then the epidemiological and social researchers broke away. There is a need for professional scientific organizations with a high scientific level. But I also think that there is a need for an organization of the ICAA type, where you bring together policymakers, practitioners, scientists and others. Think about it from my point of view, the alcohol policy point of view, and also believing there is a need for more population-orientated policies in most countries of the world:

it is an uphill battle to introduce those kind of policies, and I think it is necessary to bring together people from countries who have such a tradition and countries who do not have it and try, not to have a unified monolithic opinion, but to influence each other. When we were in Rome in 1985 I met some Italian psychiatrists and others who had had a meeting of their own, and it seemed to me that they looked like the Christians in the catacombs who were really coming up into the air – seeing that there is a world where there is the possibility of also having general measures of alcohol policy. The ICAA has had weaknesses. One of them is that its economic weakness makes it susceptible to invasion attempts from commercial forces. It is very hard to create a democratic structure which cannot be criticized. How do you defend democracy where 6 million temperance people from all over the world have one vote, and at the same time a person representing the Swedish alcohol monopoly has one vote, and a person representing a treatment centre in upper Canada has one vote, etc.?

The ICAA has had weaknesses. One of them is that its economic weakness makes it susceptible to invasion attempts from commercial forces

A: *What about the role of beverage industry and beverage industry-financed groups in a forum like the ICAA? Are they participating in the Alcohol Policy Section discussions?*
GR: Oh yes, we have made a point of inviting them. I think a dialogue is useful and necessary, but I do not think they should have voting influence. I think the commercial alcohol industry is so strong and has so much money that it should be kept out of an organization such as ICAA as far as both money and voting influence are concerned; but they should be invited to take part as individuals and also be invited to be represented on discussion panels. We have done that, with very favourable outcomes. It is necessary to have this dialogue, but I do not think they should be given

a section or they should be given plenary sessions to arrange according to their own desires. I do not think we need to provide propaganda platforms for the alcohol industry, they have enough of that. It is also going to undermine the credibility of the organization. I also think that it is very important to remember the classic words of John D. Rockefeller, who said in the foreword of the report he commissioned on how to handle alcohol sales in the 1930s, only as the profit motive is eliminated is there any hope of controlling the liquor traffic in the interest of a decent society.[7]

I think that it's likely that you are a better president of a big company if you also have other interests. That could be sailing, going out in the woods looking for mushrooms, whatever

---

Outside the alcohol field

A: *You've participated or been chair of a number of different committees in a broad range of areas outside the alcohol area – such organizations as a committee against anti-semitism, a state committee for equality between men and women, and so on. If I went to other people in Sweden who had been in important executive posts like yours, would I find the same kind of picture with people who have wide experience of non-profit voluntary participation?*

GR: Not necessarily, because being an executive in a big corporation, particularly maybe in a competitive situation, is rather demanding. If they are not too old, they also have a family life, and so on. On the other hand, many of the things that you mention come out of the fact that I was a politician. Politicians are people who know a little of everything and they are supposed to have a wide variety of interests. But I also have had some things that I have taken on later, such as investigating dental insurance, and chairing the committee looking into how well Sweden lived up to the UN Convention on the Rights of the Child.[8,9,10] In undertaking such activities I was supported by the

chairman of the monopoly's board, who also had a political background. There were at times questions from our employees, and from the trade union – do you have time for this really, are you in the office enough? I argued that I was a better executive by having these other interests. Some of the people who are executives in commercial companies have the same view. I think that it's likely that you are a better president of a big company if you also have other interests. That could be sailing, going out in the woods looking for mushrooms, whatever.

A: *So now after 17 years you have retired as the director of the retailing monopoly. You still have important roles that you are carrying forward; you are the chair of the Swedish Council for Social Research.*

GR: That is actually the only formal role that I have right now. I have decided to say no to everything for a year at least in order to get my papers in order. Chairing the Council for Social Research (a government body that finances research in the social science field) is also something which is very close to my heart. To tell the truth, I also like to be chairman, I like to chair meetings: that is one of my hobbies.

My first task now is, however, to try to organize all the papers I have from the 17 years in the monopoly and draw some conclusions from that, writing something. I am also going to be part of a small group that is going to do something about alcohol policy for the future. Those two, and then I hope to be able to work internationally with the ICAA, without having the platform of the monopoly. If the ICAA does not approve, I hope there will be some other international organization that I can work with. Then as I grow more into real retirement, I will probably devote more time to voluntary organizations of the anti-semitism type.

A: *And your grandchildren?*

GR: And my grandchildren and maybe some research into the family history. I have quite a lot of papers lying around from my uncle and my father and some others. It can be for the benefit of the family to try to put some of the family history on paper. Of course alcohol policy is my first interest, but then it is very hard not to get into drug policy and now also into gambling policy. There is plenty to do. That is one of the advantages of having an early retirement age. I asked my father why he retired when he did – he had an option of one year more when he retired. He said it is better to leave when you are asked why you are leaving than to stay till they ask you why you are not leaving. I think that is a good principle.

References

1. FRANBERG, P. (1987) The Swedish snaps: a history of booze, bratt, and bureaucracy – a summary, *Contemporary Drug Problems*, **14**, 557–611.
2. HOLDER, H. D., KUHLHORN, E., NORDLUND, S., OSTERBERG, E., ROMELSJO, A. & UGLAND, T. (1998) *European Integration and Nordic Alcohol Policies: changes in alcohol controls and consequences in Finland, Norway and Sweden, 1980–1997* (Aldershot, Ashgate).
3. BRUUN, K., EDWARDS, G., LUMIO, M., MÄKELÄ, K., PAN, L., POPHAM, R. E., ROOM, R., SCHMIDT, W., SKOG, O. J., SULKUNEN, P. & OSTERBERG, E. (1975) *Alcohol Control Policies in Public Health Perspective* (Helsinki, Finnish Foundation for Alcohol Studies).
4. SKOG, O.-J. (2000) An experimental study of a change from over-the-counter to self-service sales of alcoholic beverages in monopoly outlets, *Journal of Studies on Alcohol*, **61**, 95–100.
5. Alkoholforskningsutredningen (1995) *Forskning om Alkohol for Individ och Samhalle* [Research on Alcohol for the Individual and Society] (Stockholm, Folkhalsoinstitutet).
6. KUHLHORN, E., HIBELL, B., LARSSON, S., RAMSTEDT, M. & ZETTERBERG, H. L. (1999) *Alkoholkonsumtionen i Sverige under 1990-talet* [Alcohol Consumption in Sweden During the 1990s] (Stockholm, Oberoende Alkoholsamarbetet).
7. ROCKEFELLER, J. D., Jr (1933) Foreword, in: FOSDICK, R. B. & SCOTT, A. L. *Toward Liquor Control*, pp. vii–xi (New York, Harper & Brothers).
8. SOU (1996) *Barnkonventionen och utlanningslagen* [The UN Convention on the Rights of the Child and the law of asylum], no. 115 (Stockholm, Fritzes).
9. SOU (1997) *Barnets basta i framsta rummet* [The best interest of the child as a primary consideration], no. 116 (Stockholm, Fritzes).
10. SOU (1997) *Barnets bastaen antologi* [The best interest of the child: an anthology], no. 116, bilaga [supplement] (Stockholm, Fritzes).

Commentary

Northern Lights: The Interplay of Research and Policies

Robin Room

Taken together, the Nordic countries – Finland, Sweden, Norway, Denmark and Iceland – have a total population of about 23 million; between the population sizes of Australia and Canada, and about 40% of Britain's population size. Their influence on the addictions field, and particularly on alcohol research, is out of all proportion to this population size.

A crucial background to this is that, in most of the Nordic countries (excepting Denmark), temperance movements at the beginning of the 1900s were very strong. It was not only that the movements were strong in their own right, but also that they intersected with and mutually supported the other leading social movements of the time – labour movements and women's movements, nation building in Finland, Norway and Iceland, and the 'free churches' in Sweden. The temperance movements gradually weakened in the second half of the 20th century,[1] but they cast their shadows forward in the strength and specific forms of treatment for, and research on, alcohol problems, and later also on problems with other drugs.

Except in Denmark, counselling and treatment for alcohol problems was originally a partially lay enterprise centred on municipal temperance boards.[2] Alcohol treatment became professionalized as part of the project of the welfare state – which became a national project in each of the Nordic countries. This meant and still means that treatment for 'alcohol and drug misuse', not 'addiction', is primarily the responsibility of the social welfare system and social workers, not of the health system and doctors, with the partial exception, again, of Denmark. Reflecting this, Kettil Bruun entitled his paper about the Finnish system *Finland – the non-medical case*.[3]

The modern tradition of alcohol research in the Nordic countries started with the establishment in 1950 by the Finnish state alcohol monopoly of the Finnish Foundation for Alcohol Studies (http://www.stakes.fi/hyvinvointi/ats/en/). While the Foundation also provides support for clinical and biological research, it is best known internationally for the strong tradition of social research,[4] initiated particularly by two sociologists: Pekka Kuusi, who became the director of the alcohol monopoly, and especially by Kettil Bruun, who became secretary of the Foundation in 1955.[5] Klaus Mäkelä (interviewed in this volume) succeeded Bruun as the Foundation's secretary.

In 1959, what is now the National Institute for Alcohol and Drug Research was founded in Norway (http://www.sirus.no/; http://www.nifu.no/instkat/enginst/inst41.html), with an emphasis on social and epidemiological research.[6] As Mäkelä makes clear in his interview, Norway's strong criminological tradition had an influence on alcohol studies, not only in Norway but also in other Nordic countries. In particular, the criminologists Nils Christie and Ragnar Hauge have both made important contributions to alcohol and drug studies.

The modern tradition of Swedish alcohol research also got under way at this time, but until the formation in 1999 of the Centre for Social Research on Alcohol and Drugs (http://www.sorad.su.se) was mostly a matter of individual scholars and projects, often commissioned by parliamentary commissions on alcohol or drug policy. As the interview with Gabriel Romanus in this volume makes clear, both alcohol and drug issues have remained quite high on the Swedish political agenda in recent decades.

Since 1991 there has been a Centre for Alcohol and Drug Research (http://www.au.dk/uk/sam/crf/) at Aarhus University in Denmark. Danish research tends to have been focussed more on drugs than on alcohol. This has reflected a lack of sustained funding for alcohol research, which in turn reflects a historically lower level of concern about alcohol in Danish society. In the small world of Nordic cooperation and rivalry, indeed, it has been common for Danish opinion leaders to consider the other Nordic countries over-concerned about alcohol. It was a Dane who, as a high official in the World Health Organization, was reported to have remarked in 1983 that alcohol was a concern only of 'two small groups of countries', by which he meant the other Nordic countries and the Moslem world.

Along with lively national traditions, a feature of the Nordic alcohol and drug research scene has been the tradition of Nordic cooperation, under the auspices of the Nordic Council. A Northern Committee for Alcohol Research was formed in 1959, and under its auspices the first in what has become a tradition of joint Nordic comparative studies in the field was carried out and published.[7] In 1978, the Nordic Council for Alcohol and Drug Research was constituted (http://www.kaapeli.fi/nad/), with board members from each of the Nordic countries, and a mandate to promote and encourage joint Nordic research efforts and scientific exchanges. Headed by Pia Rosenqvist as its Research Secretary for most of its history, NAD has organized two or three meetings a year, including both general seminars and thematic meetings, and has published a total of 39 monographs. Another organ of the research community at the Nordic level is Nordisk Alkohol och Narkotikatidskrift (NAT; http://www.stakes.fi/nat/), edited by Kerstin Stenius.

Traditionally, Nordic cooperation and interchange has been carried on in 'Scandinavian', counting on the assumption that Swedish, Norwegian and Danish are mutually intelligible, so that researchers from those countries could use their native tongue. Finnish researchers have all had some competence in Swedish, and Icelanders in Danish. Original research reports were often published in one of 'our secret Scandinavian languages', as Bruun once jokingly called them. Then, in a second stage, a more internationally oriented report would appear in an English language journal. Recently, there has been some drift towards original reports appearing in English: many recent NAD monographs are in English, and NAT publishes an English language issue each year. The accession of the Nordic countries to the European Union or European Economic Area has added new patterns of research cooperation with Europe more widely, but so far without weakening the strong tradition of Nordic cooperation.

Except in Denmark, illicit drug use among young people is still low in Nordic countries, although drug problems have been growing and drug overdose mortality is fairly high. Official policies north of the Baltic have been quite restrictive, and there was a time when Sweden could claim that its policy of compulsory treatment was a success. However, many Nordic social researchers have been rather critical of official drug policies.[8,9]

It is in the alcohol policy field that Nordic social research has had its greatest international influence. Indeed, the term 'alcohol policy' arguably came into English from Nordic thinking.[10] Social alcohol research in Finland was until 1995 organizationally part of the government alcohol control structure, and the research program included from the start a series of experimental studies of the effects of changes in alcohol controls.[11] When alcohol controls were liberalized in 1968 in Finland, the results were not at all as expected, as Mäkelä mentions in his interview. Out of that experience[5] came the international project which brought new Nordic thinking about alcohol control policies, and their relation to consumption levels and alcohol problems, to international notice,[12] often known as the 'purple book'.

In his career as a politician and manager, Gabriel Romanus played a substantial part in carrying this perspective, called in Sweden the 'total consumption model', through into official policy. More than in any other country, the model became established in Sweden as government policy, although the model has become more contested in the years since Sweden's accession to the EU.[1] As Chair of the Alcohol Policy section of the International Council on Alcohol and Addictions, Romanus also played an important role in raising the profile internationally of public health approaches to alcohol policy.

As a researcher, Klaus Mäkelä took a different path. After participating in the purple book, he proposed and coordinated a new international project, the International Study of Alcohol Control Experiences (ISACE).[13] The purple book had been oriented to practical public health, arguing that policies affect the alcohol consumption in a population, and thus the rates of health problems due to drinking. ISACE was oriented more to social history: why had one society after another nevertheless moved in the opposite direction in the years 1950–1975, with consumption rising in a period in which alcohol controls were being relaxed? The dual orientation that the purple book and ISACE represent, both to practical work with policy implications and to arm's length analysis with the aim of understanding how society works, can be seen as characteristic not only of Mäkelä's own work, but more generally of the approach of Nordic social science in the alcohol and drug field.

Many from their generation besides Romanus and Mäkelä have played important roles in the development of Nordic research and policy in the field. Yet what Romanus and Mäkelä has each contributed is exemplary of what Nordic traditions of thinking and action can contribute internationally. With Romanus at the helm, the Swedish alcohol retail monopoly committed itself to cooperating with and financing a series of researcher-led experiments in the effects of alcohol policy changes. In the most recent of these, a random half of Sweden had liquor stores open on Saturday, while they remained closed in the other half. This study is a good example of the Nordic commitment to practical social experimentation, even at the expense, at least temporarily, of differential convenience. With substantial impetus from Mäkelä, Finnish alcohol and drug research opened up new directions of thinking and work, bringing to bear on the field, as occasion arose, such diverse traditions as Russian psychology,

French sociological theory, and conversational analysis.

As is implied by the title of a recent book,[1] these are somewhat unsettled times for Nordic alcohol policy and research. After decades of stable organization, both the Finnish and the Norwegian institutes went through institutional changes in recent years, although their strength is so far intact. The opening to Europe has brought in its wake both fears of the erosion of the Nordic policy system as well as hopes that Nordic perspectives will have more influence in Europe. Both the hopes and the fears may be somewhat overblown. Still, during the Swedish presidency of the EU in the first half of 2001, modest steps were taken towards redefining alcohol as a public health as well as a trade and agricultural issue (http://www.eu2001.se/static/eng/issues/health.asp) The Nordic experience in the field, of research that is oriented both to knowledge and practice, and of practical international cooperation in collaborative projects, has much to offer both Europe and the world.

References

1. SULKUNEN, P., SUTTON, C., TIGERSTEDT, C. & WARPENIUS, K. (Eds) (2000) *Broken Spirits: Power and Ideas in Nordic Alcohol Control* NAD, Publication No. 39 (Helsinki, Nordic Council for Alcohol and Drug Research).
2. ROSENQVIST, P. & TAKALA, J. P. (1987) Two experiences with lay boards: the emergence of compulsory treatment of alcoholics in Sweden and Finland, *Contemporary Drug Problems*, 14, 15–38.
3. BRUUN, K. (1971) Finland: the non-medical approach, in: KILOH, L. G. & BELL, D. S. (Eds), *29th International Congress on Alcoholism and Drug Dependence*, pp. 545–559 (Australia, Butterworths).
4. MÄKELÄ, K. (1988) Reports from research centres: No. 9: The Finnish Foundation for Alcohol Studies and the Social Research Institute of Alcohol Studies, *British Journal of Addiction*, 83, 141–148.

5. BRUUN, K. (1991) Interview with Kettil Bruun, Finland, in: EDWARDS, G. (Ed.) *Addictions: Personal Influences and Scientific Movements*, pp. 365–375 (New Brunswick & London, Transaction Publishers).

6. SKOG, O. J. (1987) Reports from research centres: No. 3, Norway: National Institute for Alcohol Research, *British Journal of Addiction*, **82**, 1073–1079.

7. BRUUN, K. & HAUGE, R. (1963) *Drinking Habits among Northern Youth* (Helsinki, Finnish Foundation for Alcohol Studies).

8. CHRISTIE, N. & BRUUN, K. (1996) *Den gode fiende: Narkotikkapolitik i Norden* [Suitable enemies: drug policy in the Nordic countries], 2nd edition (Oslo, Universitetsforlaget).

9. THAM, H. (1995) Drug control as a national project: the case of Sweden, *Journal of Drug Issues*, **25**, 113–128.

10. ROOM, R. (1999) The idea of alcohol policy, *Nordic Studies on Alcohol and Drugs*, **16** (English supplement), 7–20.

11. BRUUN, K. (1961) Alcohol studies in Scandinavia, *Sociological Inquiry*, **31**, 78–92.

12. BRUUN, K., EDWARDS, G., LUMIO, M., MÄKELÄ, K., PAN, L., POPHAM, R. E., ROOM, R., SCHMIDT, W., SKOG, O. J., SULKUNEN, P. & ÖSTERBERG, E. (1975) *Alcohol Control Policies in Public Health Perspective*, vol. 25. (Helsinki, Finnish Foundation for Alcohol Studies).

13. MÄKELÄ, K., ROOM, R., SINGLE, E., SULKUNEN, P. & WALSH, D., with 13 others (1981) *Alcohol, Society, and the State: 1. A Comparative Study of Alcohol Control* (Toronto, Addiction Research Foundation).

Further reading
1. BRUUN, K. & ROSENQVIST, P. (1985) International review series: Alcohol and alcohol problems research: 3. Nordic countries, *British Journal of Addiction*, 80, 245–253.

Part X
The Specialist Field

In Their Own Words: Conversations about the Evolution of a Specialist Field

Thomas F. Babor

'In this occasional series we record the views and personal experience of people who have contributed to the evolution of ideas in the Journal's field of interest.'

So began the editor's preface to each of the 30 biographical interviews reprinted in this book, as they first appeared during the past decade in various issues of the international journal, *Addiction*. The modest tone of this perfunctory introduction belies the important personal and historical messages contained in these conversations. In the telling, these interviews present not only the career experiences of a unique group of influential people, they also describe from a very personal perspective the evolution of a specialist addiction field.

Despite the growing interest in building a cadre of specialists devoted to the study, management and prevention of addiction, there is still virtually no systematic information, much less an organized body of knowledge, about the individual and social factors that contribute to the evolution of a specialist field like addiction studies. Making sense of career trajectories in this field is complicated by its diversity. There are many different roles, responsibilities, and professional skills that comprise the field, ranging from basic science to policy implementation. This is clearly reflected in the people who are the subject of the *Addiction* interviews. Some participants are relatively invisible players in the addiction field. These are the addiction specialists who work in treatment settings and research centers, neither seeking nor finding public recognition for their accomplishments. Others are visible participants who are prominent in setting the agenda for research initiatives or health

services, determining which issues get attention, and building institutions that are needed to carry on the work. Still others are supporting actors on the periphery of a larger movement, helping to translate addiction science into clinical practice or social policy. How did they get started in their addiction careers? What kind of individual is attracted to a career in the field? What do their career trajectories look like? And what did they accomplish with their working lives? These are profoundly interesting questions that can only be partly answered by the rich source of qualitative data collected in these interviews.

Getting started

'My majoring in social relations had a permanent impact on my thinking.' – Howard Blane

'It was serendipity.' – Jim Rankin

'I had ideas . . . I love sport so well I thought I might be a sports writer.' – Ignatius McDermott

Becoming a member of the addiction field seems to involve a large element of chance. Most people could have chosen any of a number of different career paths. Like marriage, proximity at the right moment, convenience, and individual preferences can all be cited as reasons. A large number entered the addiction field through the study and practice of medicine. Others were attracted from the social sciences and clinical psychology. At the time that many of these individuals entered the field, there was little indication that they were in the process of abandoning their chosen profession for a new line of work. They were merely specializing further in their professional discipline, be it psychiatry, epidemiology, gastroenterology, sociology, social work or clinical psychology. But almost all of the addiction specialists seem to have entered the field during a critical period soon after the completion of their professional studies.

A major determinant for many individuals was the influence of a mentor. According to the ancient Greeks, a mentor is a wise and trusted counsellor, a person who takes a special interest in helping another person develop into a successful professional. Almost all of the addiction specialists interviewed in this book mention the influence of a trusted adviser at a critical point in their career who channelled their interests and enthusiasm in the direction of addiction. As noted by Reg Smart, 'Having mentors was very helpful to me in deciding to be in the field and to stay in it as my interests developed.' The power of persuasion was stated even more clearly by Jim Rankin, whose mentor said to him: 'Jim, you'd be mad if you didn't take the opportunity.'

Many of the influences that brought these people into the addiction field were derived from exposure to other countries and cultures. Gabriel Romanus thought he was going to be a doctor 'until I went to the United States and had some very good teachers in social sciences'. David Deitch was introduced to the field by his own problem with heroin. Raj Rathod, David Hawks and Joy Mott, for example, were introduced to addiction studies in the UK after emigrating from other countries. Some addiction specialists, like David Hawks, spent a significant part of their careers abroad before returning to their native countries to assume leadership positions. It is unclear whether future leaders were created by international training experiences, or whether an international outlook is merely the sign of a future leader.

One thing that is clear from the selection process that brought these people into the field is that it favoured the recruitment of men rather than women. This is what makes the biographies of the few women in the ranks worth noting, and the possible influence of gender bias in the disciplines from which addiction has built its workforce.

Martha Sanchez-Craig mentions the difficulty of overcoming gender bias, but she also suggests that talent and promise played a larger role than gender in her initiation into the field: 'I learned from my supervisor that they had 54 applicants (for a position at the Addiction Research Foundation in 1972), that I was the last to apply, and that I was the only female applicant. I found that interesting.' Avram Goldstein mentions how his very accomplished wife had to separate her career from his to avoid the implication that she was merely his lab assistant. Others, like LeClair Bissell, a medical doctor, and Joy Mott, a psychologist working almost single-handedly on drugs in the British Home Office research unit, never mention whether there were external or internal challenges associated with their gender. All of the women interviewed were clinicians or clinical researchers, and their early contributions to the field are likely to have contributed to the growing numbers of women who have followed after them.

A special kind of individual

'For reasons which I find very difficult to identify I needed to go abroad. . . .' – David Hawks

'I had always realized that one had to look at the casualties as well as the community . . .' – Les Drew

'. . . discovery fascinates me, the kind of discovery that jumps out at you from the data.' – Martha Sanchez-Craig

Despite the fortuitous nature of being initiated into addiction studies and service, there are some identifiable characteristics of the people who are likely to have a successful career in the field. Many give evidence of early academic achievement, personal ambition, an interest in science, and social consciousness.

The social consciousness of these individuals is often reflected in a stated interest in the practical applications of their research and a sensitivity to public policy. David Hawks expressed it almost as a moral imperative: 'My stance was that one had a responsibility to do the research and to consider its policy implications.' Vincent Dole, who pioneered the development of methadone maintenance treatment for opiate dependence, drew inspiration from his personal experience of working in New York City: 'Sometime in the early 1960s I began to feel that I was working in an oasis in Manhattan . . . but commuting to it from the suburbs through an epidemic of drugs and poverty in the inner city. It seemed to me that this was a problem that should be considered by the medical community.'

Another common characteristic of both scientists and clinicians in this group is the ability to listen to patients. Raj Rathod, a clinician who pioneered the development of epidemiological methods to describe heroin epidemics in the UK, expressed it in these words: 'Patients are reservoirs of rich data which they are willing to share – it is for the clinician to learn from them.' Avram Goldstein observed that 'there was no way to learn about heroin addicts . . . except to set up a treatment program.' Martha Sanchez-Craig developed a self-help approach for people who want to change their drinking on their own: over the years she based her intervention techniques on the experience she gained from patients who followed her advice about their drinking. And the Addiction Research Center in Lexington, Kentucky was a major training site for future clinical researchers because of its proximity to a unique patient population.

Taking all of these observations into account, what kind of individual succeeds in a career in the addiction field? Perhaps the characteristics epitomized in the interview with Richard Doll speak best to this question: persistence, modesty, scepticism, respect for science, and political acumen.

The effect of institutions

'You can't forget being at the Maudsley. It taught me how to think and be independent.' – Raj Rathod

'. . . there was no other place in the world which was primed to do the kinds of things that were

being dome at the Alcoholism Research Foundation.' – Reg Smart (on the ARF)

'There were excellent researchers at Lexington who had made seminal contributions to the field . . . and I had begun to learn from them and from the library. After I had been there for a while I began to think, this is such an interesting field, I don't want to get out of it.' – Fred Glaser

In addition to the personal characteristics of individual scientists, clinicians and policymakers, the stories in these interviews make it clear that institutions play a prominent role in the formation of scientists and practitioners. But in an emerging field such as addiction, there were not many institutions to choose from. Many of the people interviewed in this book mention the effect that institutional affiliations had on them, especially during the early part of their careers. The Maudsley Hospital in London, now famous for its influence on world psychiatry, was also a major training point for addiction psychiatry. Thomas Bewley, a pioneer in addiction treatment in the UK, gives a sense of the intellectual atmosphere at the Maudsley during the 1950s: 'When you arrived you were given a note which said "you will discover that many people say diametrically opposed things here, but you are old enough now to be able to make up your own mind about who is talking sense".'

Another influential training site for young addiction specialists was the Addiction Research Foundation, which was established in Toronto in 1948. Jim Rankin, speaking about the 1970s at the ARF, notes that 'So many well trained, imaginative, energetic individuals joined the Institute at that time.' His colleague, Martha Sanchez-Craig, observes that the ARF provided an ideal forum for 'talking, trading ideas, sharing thoughts, with colleagues in other disciplines'.

A further institution mentioned with some regularity in the interviews in this volume (e.g. Glaser, Ball, Jaffe) is the US Federal Narcotics Hospital at Lexington, with its Addiction Research Center. During the 1950s and 1960s, Lexington was a centre for most of the drug abuse research going on in the US, an ideal place for training and research. According to John Ball: 'We had a critical mass of scientists . . . It was an extraordinary research opportunity . . . We were given a completely free hand to develop a whole social science research program from the ground up . . .' And WHO is yet another institution which receives frequent mention in these pages – see, for instance, Hans Halbach's account of his work at Geneva.

The sociocultural context

'I would board the train in the Skid Row area. I would walk along and I would see the men populating the streets.' – Ignatius McDermott

'So, I introduced Frank to LSD, and Frank introduced Timothy Leary to LSD, and the rest is history.' – Avram Goldstein

'I grew up in an area of heavy industries, coal and steel, and felt science was the thing to do.' – Hans Halbach

The sociocultural world an individual lives in has meaning and consequences for career development. To understand these addiction careers, we must take into account the society in which these people found themselves during the latter part of the twentieth century. Lives like these may seem to be self-directed, but they were also modified by changes in the surrounding culture, in social movements, in the world political situation and the emerging drug culture. Charles Leiber, Albert Tuyns, Hans Halbach and others had their early lives profoundly influenced by the events of World War II. Others, like Reg Smart, found themselves beneficiaries of post-war investments in medical and scientific research: 'I came into the field when it was expanding rapidly and there always seemed to be more money for the kinds of things we wanted to do.' Still others were caught up in the social movements and the drug epidemics of the 1960s, which was a time in some countries when the demand for expertise was greater than the supply. As described by Jerome Jaffe, '. . . there was a heroin epidemic in New York [in 1964] . . . So, what was previously an obscure area of

concern was moving to the forefront and I found myself, although still a trainee in some respects, the resident expert for that institution.'

Career trajectories

'. . . in the course of 22 years work at ARF our research program evolved into four formats of early intervention that vary in complexity and duration. They are designed to meet the needs of different types of clients, and the needs of professionals working in different contexts.' – Martha Sanchez-Craig

'Yes, I have had a very satisfying life in pure scientific research and am happy I could also make a practical contribution to smoking cessation that might have saved a large number of lives.' – Murray Jarvik

While some people make fleeting appearances in and contributions to the field of addiction studies, most of the characters featured in these interviews devoted their careers to addiction science, policy, and clinical care. Professional training in a discipline related to addiction, the right mix of personal characteristics, and the guiding influence of a nurturing mentor or institution are ingredients that set the stage for a successful career in the addiction field. The career trajectories are sometimes linear, often unpredictable and always interesting. Clinicians like Jim Rankin moved from research to policy while maintaining their commitment to the welfare of the individual patient. Physicians like David Penington contributed to social policy by mobilizing their colleagues, the policymakers and the general public to take action. Politicians like Bob Hawke and Harold Hughes, who applied addiction science to treatment and prevention policy, were motivated in part by their personal experiences with addictive substances. Ove Fernö first conceived the idea of nicotine replacement as a smoking cessation strategy in 1967. It took 11 years of research to achieve the first product licence in 1978, and another decade of development and testing to bring the product to market.

Leadership is a common characteristic of these careers. One gets the sense that as many of these individuals matured into the middle adult years they found they had the knowledge, skills, confidence and resources to lead others in the right direction. According to David Penington, 'having a clear picture in one's mind was a key part of producing change, as was telling that picture to other people so it became their picture'. Following an epiphany of sorts, Avram Goldstein called his lab group together and said, 'We're going to switch all the research we're doing . . . to work on opiates. And there's no way we're going to find out anything about opiate addiction . . . unless we know where the opiate receptors are.'

Leadership, too, is indicated by an ability to seize the moment. Jerome Jaffe describes how his report to Richard Nixon contributed to the implementation of a far-reaching U.S. drug strategy in the early 1970s.

> 'As the plan went up to the President it was not woolly-minded; it was concrete on exactly what would be done and I guess for that reason he decided soon afterwards to sign up on a whole effort to develop a national strategy, to co-ordinate all the treatment demand, prevention and research activities and to put some money into it.'

Finally, leadership is also manifested in the creation of new organizations, journals and institutions, which many of these individuals established during their productive careers.

Evolution of the field: looking back, looking forward

> 'I can see a train of events over generations that link people, principles, ideas and movements as we move into the future.' – Jim Rankin

> 'Rather than dramatic turning points, I see a slow evolution of understanding. Despite mistakes at all levels of administration, there nonetheless has emerged a body of experience and wonderful, caring clinicians, counselors, nurses and brave patients.' – Vincent Dole

> 'Others will take up the good fight.' – Fred Glaser

Winston Churchill once said that history would judge him kindly because he intended to write it himself. While autobiographical interviews have a way of bringing out the best in the interlocutor, they can also reveal a great deal about the fascinating interplay between personality, culture and history. Are scientific and social movements the product of creative individuals? Or is individual creativity the product of innovative times? The interviews printed in this volume give evidence in support of both perspectives, suggesting that the evolution of a specialist field such as addiction studies is the result of dynamic individuals applying their creativity and other talents during a period of scientific ferment and public need.

Studying the lives and careers of these people, expressed in their own words, one gets a picture of how addiction studies emerged from relative obscurity during the last 50 years to develop a coherent identity and to revolutionize not only the scientific understanding of addiction, but also its management, prevention and societal views of its nature and meaning. What are the characteristics of this evolving field?

An essential component of a specialist field like addiction studies is its people. Far from being names attached to frequently cited books and journal articles, these interviews represent real people whose interests, influences, challenges, mistakes and triumphs are interwoven with their professional careers. Just as an individual's professional career is more than a collection of scientific papers, so a field is more than a collection of scientists. A field is a social network of interconnected people, organizations, institutions, and traditions that take on elements of a culture. Some are motivated by the intrinsic pleasures of playing the game of science, while others seem more motivated by a desire for achievement in the policy arena. Still others seem driven by a concern for those afflicted by addiction. These groups are not exclusive, but they are worth considering separately in terms of their differences and complementary contributions to the evolution of the field.

And there is a fourth group, who are not formally part of the addiction field, but who have played an important role as supporters, promoters, and implementers. Together, they constitute a scientific subculture, sometimes called an 'invisible college',[1,2] characterized by a formal selection process, subdisciplines involving smaller numbers of active participants, widespread networks of communication and collaboration, a common set of goals and values, a separate identity that sets them apart as a field of interest. Despite the wide diversity of disciplinary training, what they all have in common is a relatively high level of education, intelligence and commitment to scholarship and social service.

A second characteristic of the addiction field is its differentiation into disciplinary and functional subgroups that are complementary and interconnected. Professional disciplines include the basic and social sciences as well as people involved in the translation and application of addiction science, such as clinical practitioners, policymakers and administrators. According to Reg Smart, 'It was a multidisciplinary field, a field where the skills of all sorts of different people seemed to be important. There were many interesting research areas.' But the addiction field's diversity has also been considered a weakness by some. According to John Ball, 'we have had only limited success up to the present. First, there's no one academic or scientific discipline that provides direction and credibility in this field. The biomedical and social science knowledge is not integrated. There's no one lead discipline that is committed to the drug abuse problem comprehensively.'

A third characteristic of the addiction field is its wide-ranging communication network and the mobility of its members. Many of the professional careers described in these interviews give evidence of movements from one country to another, and from one type of job to another, suggesting the emergence of an international system of values and rules. According to Thomas Bewley, 'What was interesting was that it was something new. I was much involved with planning, travel, meeting experts, and it was all great fun in a way.'

A fourth characteristic of the addiction field is its tangible accomplishments. The pace of addic-

tion science has accelerated over time; since the mid-1970s there have been remarkable advances in scientific accomplishments, technological innovations, organizational growth, public recognition, political support, and number of initiates.[1,2] The development of methadone maintenance treatment is a good example. In the words of Thomas Bewley, who was profoundly influenced by Vincent Dole's work in New York, 'He started to do something that no-one else except himself could have done, and in a humane way. He also measured what he did, stating "Here are my results".' Similar things can be said about the clinical innovations emerging from the work of Ove Fernö, father of nicotine replacement therapy, and David Deitch, who led the therapeutic community movement in the early 1960s. Clinical innovation often followed significant breakthroughs in the basic sciences and epidemiological research. Charles Lieber's research unravelled the mystery of alcoholic liver disease. Albert Tuyns's studies established the link between alcohol consumption and oesophageal cancer, while Richard Doll and Charles Fletcher did the pioneering work on the connection between cigarette smoking and lung disease. Klaus Mäkelä was responsible for some of the first population surveys of alcohol use on a national basis, and contributed to the first international collaborative studies of alcohol treatment, Alcoholics Anonymous, and alcohol control policies.

A fifth characteristic of the field is its institutional base consisting of research centres, scientific journals, professional societies, and national institutes for addiction research and policy. According to Les Drew, '. . . institutions last forever. I thought that if I could get an institutional response to alcohol problems in the form of a professional society and a scientific journal then that would be some guard against the danger of another professional vacuum developing.' Charles Lieber, with 'a small group of like-minded friends', founded the Research Society on Alcoholism. According to Lieber, 'In 1976, those of us who started this society could fit around one table, whereas at the 2000 RSA banquet, there were 92 tables and RSA has now grown to over 1400 members.' The same developments were taking place in other countries, as noted by Feuerlein's establishment of the German Society for Research and Therapy of Addiction (1978) and the society's journal, SUCHT.

Once a field has a critical mass of people and infrastructure, it begins to develop a sense of its own history and identity. Howard Blane observed that 'It may be hard to imagine today how tiny the alcohol field, research and clinical, was during the 1950s . . . Once you were identified as an alcoholism specialist, demands for your services and expertise grew tremendously and the longer you stayed in the field, the more you became enmeshed in the beginnings of its organization.' Those of us who have entered the field after 'the beginnings of its organization' would do well to take advantage of the foresight of our predecessors and the hindsight of our historical position in the evolution of addiction studies. To paraphrase the words that

Senator Edward Kennedy used to describe Senator Harold Hughes: if we see farther today on these important issues, it is because we stand on the shoulders of giants like these men and women.

References

1. BABOR, T. F. (1993) Megatrends and dead ends: Alcohol research in global perspective, *Alcohol Health and Research World*, **17**, 177–186.
2. BABOR, T. F. (1993) Beyond the invisible college: a science policy analysis of alcohol and drug research, in: EDWARDS, G., STRANG, J., & JAFFE, J. H. (Eds) *Drugs, Alcohol and Tobacco: Making the science and policy connections*, pp. 48–69 (Oxford, Oxford University Press).

Interviewees and Interviewers

An alphabetical listing of the people who were the subject of the interviews and their interviewers.

Interviewee	Interviewer
John C. Ball	Jerome H. Jaffe
Thomas Bewley	Griffith Edwards
LeClair Bissell	Anne Geller
Howard T. Blane	Gerard Connors
David Deitch	Jerome H. Jaffe
Vincent Dole	John Ball
Richard Doll	Griffith Edwards
Les Drew	Alex Wodak
Ove Fernö	Martin Raw
Wilhelm Feuerlein	Rolfe Wille
Charles Fletcher	Martin Raw
Frederick B. Glaser	Barbara McCrady
Avram Goldsteim	Jerome H. Jaffe
Hans Halbach	Ilana Glass
David Hawks	Griffith Edwards
Harold Hughes	Jerome H. Jaffe
Jerome H. Jaffe	Griffith Edwards
Murray Jarvik	Jerome H. Jaffe
Charles S. Lieber	Steven Schenker
Klaus Mäkelä	Robin Room
Ignatius McDermott	Deborah Brooke
Joy Mott	Gerry Stimson
David Penington	Wayne Hall
James Rankin	Alex Wodak
Raj Rathod	Griffith Edwards
Robert J. Hawke	David Hawks
Gabriel Romanus	Robin Room
Martha Sanchez-Craig	Harold Kalant
Reginald G. Smart	Robert Mann
Albert Tuyns	Griffith Edwards

Name Index

Subject Index